BALANCHINE'S
FESTIVAL OF
BALLET

VOLUME ONE A-M

Dancing is an action, showing outwardly the spiritual movements which must agree with those measures and perfect accords of harmony which, through our hearing and with earthly joy, descend into one intellect, there to produce sweet movements which . . . endeavor to escape and reveal themselves in movement.

GUGLIELMO EBREO, "William the Jew of Pisaro,"
Italian Dancing Master of the Renaissance

Vainest endeavor, to try to document dance, the most ephemeral of the arts. Suppose that you find the bricks and boards, the levers and pulleys of a theatre intact, and that your lunatic friend who loves the archives helps locate sources from which the scenic decoration, musical orchestration and plot evolution of a famous, forgotten ballet could be reconstructed. Suppose further that you were extremely fortunate in your friend and his treasure hunt uncovered even a precise, pre-Laban notation that enabled one to teach each pas to contemporary dancers. Still . . . Reason . . . would tell you that the essential movement would be missing. The trappings would be there, but you would not see the "dance urge" Heine saw watching Carlotta Grisi, or recognize with Kleist dance mannerism as a dislocation of the soul from the central still point of movement to the trajectory. Remember how different La Sonnambula *seemed only a few years ago as* Night Shadow? *Today's dancers . . . attend that sort of party only in line of duty and then look obligingly uncomfortable. So you leave the past buried and go back to the new theatre to watch the business at hand, ballet as it is danced today—which is the living issue, not the death mask of ballet yesterday. You leave reluctantly; besides the ballet's immediate sensual beauty, and its brilliance in time and space as a medium of silent ideas, an urgent part of the reason you had worshiped it before all other arts was the simple wonder of seeing a human body moving in the same step for the same reason as did its predecessors a century or more ago.*

GEORGE JACKSON, "Notes Towards an Anti-History of Ballet in Vienna,"
in *Ballet Review,* 1967

Each fairy tale is a magic mirror which reflects some aspect of your inner world, and of the steps required by our evolution from immaturity to maturity.

BRUNO BETTELHEIM, The Meaning and Importance of Fairy Tales, 1976

BALANCHINE'S
FESTIVAL OF
BALLET

SCENE-BY-SCENE STORIES OF 404 CLASSICAL
∽ & CONTEMPORARY BALLETS ∽
GEORGE BALANCHINE & FRANCIS MASON

VOLUME ONE A-M

A COMET BOOK
Published by the Paperback Division of
W.H. ALLEN & Co. PLC

A Comet Book
Published in 1984
by the Paperback Division of
W.H. Allen & Co. PLC
44 Hill Street, London W1X 8LB

First published in Great Britain by
W.H. Allen & Co., 1978

Excerpt from 'Quicksilver' by Marie Rambert. Used by permission
of St Martin's Press, Inc. and Macmillan & Co., Ltd.

Printed and bound in Great Britain by
Mackays of Chatham Ltd, Kent

ISBN 0 86379 062 3

To the Subscribers,
those who come to the ballet today, know it
and like it so much they will come also tomorrow

PREFACE

This book attempts to tell the stories of ballets of lasting importance in the history of the art and to provide a record of significant new work performed in the past twenty-five years—ballets that are still a part of the contemporary repertory or ballets that made an enduring impression at the time.

Ballets of lasting importance—and by that we mean ambition fulfilled—ballets like *La Sylphide, Giselle,* and *Swan Lake,* have held the stage for more than a hundred years; *La Fille Mal Gardée* for almost two hundred. The new ballets that we see nowadays with increasing frequency all aspire to the same longevity. While few succeed, many remain in the active repertory longer than is imagined. A great number, like *Petrouchka,* come and go; others disappear entirely. (That has happened, naturally, to some of my own ballets; there is no point in insisting on keeping what doesn't work; there is also no point in reviving what cannot be properly recalled.)

The new pieces of the modern repertory, and now fortunately there are many of them every year produced by the growing number of ballet companies, are all candidates for lasting value and inclusion in the quasi-permanent repertory. Hopefully, many described in this book will last. Those that have not done so since *Balanchine's New Complete Stories of the Great Ballets* in 1968 have given place here to new ballets. We have tried to keep the stories of ballets likely to be revived one day, or ballets of interest from the point of view of music, choreography, design, or performance. In 1954, when the first edition of this book appeared, 131 ballets were described. In 1968, 241 were described in the second edition. Now, minus some 40 from the latter, there are 404.

The ballet audience has grown tremendously in recent years. In 1965 it was estimated that one million people attended dance performances in the United States. In 1975 that figure was fifteen million. It has been projected to reach twenty-five million in the near future. I believe it.

New audiences for ballet, of course, are not created by new dances that have just a passing interest. What makes an audience, what makes a newcomer committed is a dance that will cause him to ask, "When can I see that *again?*" Those are the ballets we are all looking for.

I have watched ballet grow wonderfully. When we began work on the first edition of this book, New York was lucky to see two months of ballet, domestic and foreign combined, all year. In a recent season, it was possible to see in a single year more than ten months of ballet performances by native and foreign ensembles. The result has been a marvelous proliferation of new work performed by an ever increasing number of gifted dancers.

When Lincoln Kirstein and I began to work together and started the School of American Ballet in 1934, we knew that our dancers would one day be admired throughout the world. This happened much more rapidly than we imagined. Now, many schools associated with ballet companies throughout the country are turning out talented young dancers.

The same thing has happened in England, where Ninette de Valois founded her school the same year; the Royal Ballet is the result. Now the Royal Ballet and the New York City Ballet dance next door to each other in Lincoln Center. Both of us sell out. There is no end to what trained talent can give.

Audiences cannot be trained, of course, only advised a little—most of all advised to go to the ballet and to keep on going. It is the closest the observer can come to the steady training required of the dancer in order to create the performance that will captivate him.

Years ago maybe it was possible to go to the ballet regularly and not experience a great evening on every occasion; today, there are many great evenings. This book is designed to help find them and to give some preparation to those who do not trust their eyes and ears in the theatre first. Much as reading about ballet may be useful after enjoying performances, it will scarcely substitute for the initial excitement of seeing and hearing performance in the theatre. But if it leads to the theatre, we are pleased. Francis Mason and I have enjoyed working toward that possibility.

We wish to thank Harold Kuebler and Debra Groisser for prolonged editorial assistance and patience. I have other jobs to do and it has not been easy to give this one priority.

We often wonder what Lawrence Sherman and Marion Patton, our first editors, must think of how the book we first planned with them has grown. It is maybe like the Christmas tree in *The Nutcracker*.

GEORGE BALANCHINE

ACKNOWLEDGMENTS

Many have helped in the making of this book. First, those who made it possible to see the ballets described here—the press representatives of the ballet companies whose repertories we have made an effort to record. Second, the critics and other writers on dance whose work is often quoted in the text. When the first edition of this book was prepared in the early 1950s, the dance critics in the daily press in the United States could be counted on the fingers of one hand; now, with ballet and dance companies established in many cities or touring throughout the country, newspapers and magazines of repute have realized that they must have competent persons to write about them. (For the first time, in 1976, a Pulitzer Prize was awarded to a dance critic—to Alan Kriegsman of the Washington *Post*.) There has been a happy increase, too, in the number of dance magazines. What writers on dance have to say, in acute and informative reviews, is valuable not only as history but in giving here a round character to flat recollection.

The Dance Collection of the New York Public Library at Lincoln Center is the master source in the world, as I hope everyone now knows, for those who seek history and knowledge of the dance. It is also the liveliest archive in the world as it succeeds in holding for the future the most ephemeral of the arts. The Dictionary Catalogue of the Dance Collection, the major bibliography of all materials relating to dance, has recently been published in twelve large volumes. It is very simply a monumental dance index—a guide to who danced what when, in whose design, to what music, what was written about it, what the dancer recalled, perhaps, and what it looked like in photographs of the time or on film. The dancers, choreographers and designers, the collectors, historians, critics, and lovers of dance who have given to the Dance Collection over the years must take considerable pride in this rare jewel in the crown of the New York Public Library. What Genevieve Oswald, the Curator of the Collection, and her colleagues have done is not only to pin down the butterfly, but in many cases to make it fly again. For in the written and spoken word, in film, photographs, drawings, prints, the Collection is becoming increasingly valuable. Those who read these words and cherish their own collections and files of dance materials are urged to remember the Dance Collection's concern to keep such things permanent in a perishable world. The Collection is situated in the New York Public Library's Museum and Library of the Performing Arts at Lincoln Center, 111 Amsterdam Avenue, New York 10023. Don't throw anything away!

We are deeply grateful to the critics and writers on dance whose work is quoted in this book: Jack Anderson of *Ballet Review, Dance Magazine,* and the *Dancing Times;* Barbara Archer of *The Record;* Robb Baker of *FM Guide;* Clive Barnes, dance and drama critic of the New York *Times;* Patricia Barnes of *Dance and Dancers;* Ann Barzell of *Dance News;* Byron Belt of the *Long Island Press;* Elena Bivona of *Ballet Review;* Alexander Bland of *The Observer;* Jane Boutwell of *The New Yorker;* Erik Bruhn for his essay "Beyond Technique" (*Dance Perspectives 36*); Richard Buckle of *The Sunday Times* (London), founder and editor of *Ballet;* Mary Clarke, editor of the *Dancing Times;* Selma Jeanne Cohen, founder and editor of *Dance Perspectives;* William Como, editor-in-chief of *Dance Magazine;* the filmmaker Gardner Compton in *Dance Magazine;* the art critic and collector Douglas Cooper in *Dance and Dancers;* the conductor and writer Robert Craft; Clement Crisp of the *Financial Times* (London); Arlene Croce, dance critic of *The New Yorker,* founder and editor of *Ballet Review,* correspondent of the *Dancing Times;* Edwin Denby, poet, critic (for the New York *Herald Tribune, Modern Music* and *Dance Magazine*), author of *Looking at the Dance* and *Dancers, Buildings and People in the Streets;* George Dorris of *Ballet Review;* John T. Elson of *Time* magazine; Janet Flanner of *The New Yorker,* author of *Paris Was Yesterday,* edited by Irving Drutman; Joseph Gale of the *Daily News;* Joseph Galeon of *Dance News;* Nancy Goldner, author of *The Stravinsky Festival of the New York City Ballet;* Robert Greskovic of *The Soho Weekly News* and *Ballet Review;* John Gruen in the New York *Times;* Henry Haslam in *Ballet Review;* Doris Hering of *Dance Magazine;* Frances Herridge, dance critic of the New York *Post;* Allen Hughes of the New York *Times;* Michael Iachetta of the *Daily News;* George Jackson of *Ballet Review* and *Dance News;* Robert Jacobson of *Cue;* Lydia Jaffe of *Dance Magazine;* Deborah Jowitt, dance critic of *The Village Voice* and author of *Dance Beat;* Oleg Kerensky of *The New Statesman,* author of *Pavlova* and *The World of Ballet;* Lincoln Kirstein for innumerable sources, most importantly *Movement and Metaphor: Four Centuries of Ballet, The New York City Ballet,* and *Nijinsky Dancing;* Anna Kisselgoff of the New York *Times;* Vera Krasovskaya, the Soviet critic; Alan M. Kriegsman of the *Washington Post;* Herbert Kupferberg of the *National Observer;* Jean Battey Lewis of the Washington *Post;* John Martin, the first dance critic of the New York *Times;* Jacqueline Maskey of *High Fidelity;* Nancy Mason of *Dance Magazine;* Olga Maynard of *Dance Magazine;* Don McDonagh of the New York *Times;* Bob Micklin of *Newsday;* James Monahan of the *Dancing Times* and *The Guardian;* Sam Norkin of the *Daily News;* Patrick O'Connor of the *Jersey Journal;* John Percival, dance critic of the *Times* (London) and *Dance and Dancers;* Richard Philp of *Dance Magazine;* Andrew Porter of *The New Yorker* and the *Financial Times* (London), author of *A Musical Season;* Dame Marie Rambert, author of her autobiography *Quicksilver;* Alan Rich, music critic of *New York* magazine; Peter Rosenwald of the *Wall Street Journal;* Hubert Saal of *Newsweek;* Winthrop Sargeant of *The New Yorker;* Robert Sealey in *Ballet Review;* Marcia B. Siegel, dance critic of *The Hudson Review,* the *Soho Weekly News,* the Boston *Herald Examiner* and author of a collection of criticisms, *At the Vanishing Point;* Anna Greta

Stahle of *Dance News;* Walter Terry, dean of American dance writers, dance critic for the New York *Herald Tribune* and *The Saturday Review;* Rose Anne Thom of *Dance Magazine;* Arthur Todd of *Dance Observer;* David Vaughan of *Ballet Review* and author of *Frederick Ashton and His Ballets* (1977); the late James Waring in *Ballet Review;* William Weaver of the *Herald Tribune;* Anne Marie Welsh of the Washington *Star;* Thomas Willis of the *Chicago Tribune;* and Peter Williams, founder and editor of *Dance and Dancers.*

For permission to quote from books, we wish to express thanks to George G. Harrap Co., Ltd., London, for an excerpt from *Frederick Ashton, a Choreographer and His Ballets* (1971); Horizon Press for *Dancers, Buildings and People in the Streets* by Edwin Denby (1965); Macmillan and Co., Ltd., for "The Bumboat Woman's Story," from *Bab Ballads* by Sir W. S. Gilbert; Pellegrini and Cudahy, Publishers, for *Looking at the Dance,* copyright 1949 by Edwin Denby; Random House, New York, and Faber and Faber, Ltd., for *The Age of Anxiety* by W. H. Auden; Saturday Review Press for *At the Vanishing Point: A Critic Looks at Dance* by Marcia B. Siegel, 1972; the late Igor Stravinsky for *Stravinsky: an Autobiography;* the late Carl Van Vechten for "The Russian Ballet and Nijinsky" from *Interpreters* by Carl Van Vechten.

The press and public relations representatives of ballet companies have responded generously to frequent requests. We are especially grateful to Charles France, Director of Publicity and Public Relations for American Ballet Theatre, Elena Gordon, Assistant to Charles France, and Joan Ehrlich-White, Virginia Hymes and Irene Shaw of that company; Tom Kerrigan of the Brooklyn Academy of Music; Isadora Bennett, Rima Corben and Robert Larkin of the City Center Joffrey Ballet; Dick Hendriks and Rima Corben of the Dutch National Ballet; Winnie Sampson of the Dance Theatre of Harlem; Judith Jedlicka of the Harkness Ballet; Sheila Porter, General Press Representative, Hurok Concerts and John Gingrich, Associate Press Representative; Virginia Donaldson, Press Representative of the New York City Ballet and her associates: Leslie Bailey, Linda Cioffoletti, Marie Gutscher, Clarence Hart and Larry Strichman; and Vivien Wallace of the Royal Opera House, Covent Garden, London.

We are deeply grateful to William Como, editor of *Dance Magazine,* for permission to reprint entire the long interview between Jerome Robbins and Edwin Denby on the subject of the ballet *Dances at a Gathering,* and the filmmaker Gardner Compton's article on Robert Joffrey's *Astarte.* Also valuable have been interviews by Jane Boutwell in *The New Yorker* with Maurice Béjart, Leonard Bernstein and Jerome Robbins, and Kenneth MacMillan; in *Show* magazine with Rudolf Nureyev; and in *Dance and Dancers* with Eliot Feld. The invaluable books of Igor Stravinsky and Robert Craft and Eric Walter White's *Stravinsky: the Composer and his Works* (1966) have been consulted frequently. David Vaughan kindly permitted us to read part of the manuscript of his book of *Frederick Ashton and His Ballets* (Alfred A. Knopf, New York, 1977).

We wish to thank, too, the publishers of *Ballet Review,* Marcel Dekker, Inc., for permission to quote so frequently from the pages of that magazine.

For helpfulness and interest we should like particularly to thank Jane Allison of the Indianapolis *Star;* Frank Darvas; Darryl Dodson of American Ballet Theatre; Harvey Lichtenstein of the Brooklyn Academy of Music; Cora Cahan of the Eliot Feld Ballet; Richard Philp of *Dance Magazine;* Karel Shook of the Dance Theatre of Harlem; Betty Cage, Barbara Horgan, Edward Bigelow, Robert Cornell, Carole Deschamps and Mary Porter of the New York City Ballet; Nathalie Molostwoff and Elise Reiman of the School of American Ballet; Robert Irving, Music Director of the New York City Ballet; and the staff of the Dance Collection of the New York Public Library at Lincoln Center, especially Genevieve Oswald, Curator, Reynaldo Alejandro, Natalie Bassein, Paul Le-Paglia, Lacy McDearmon, Winifred Messe, Madeleine Nichols, Andrew Wentink, and Henry Wisneski.

Henry Wisneski's counsel and advice on the photographs in this volume were invaluable and we are much indebted to him.

Words are insufficient for the thanks we owe the photographers whose work appears in this book. Unlike the dance writer and critic, whose work exists in print and does not perish, the dance photographer takes thousands of valuable photographs, many of which never see the light of day and all too few of which are published. The photographers are the unsung heroes and heroines of ballet, recording its history in frozen moments of performance we strive to recall in words that only approximate reality.

We wish also to thank most warmly for editorial assistance throughout the book Shields Remine. Harold Grabau has prepared the final text in exemplary fashion.

FRANCIS MASON

CONTENTS

ILLUSTRATIONS

Galina Ulanova in *Swan Lake*
Alicia Markova and André Eglevsky in *The Nutcracker*
Vyacheslav Gordeyev
Rudolf Nureyev in *Petrouchka*
Jerome Robbins in *Prodigal Son*
Nina Sorokina and Vladimir Vasiliev in *Spartacus*
Merle Park and David Wall in *Walk to the Paradise Garden*
Margot Fonteyn and Rudolf Nureyev in *La Bayadère*
Lynn Seymour and Anthony Dowell in *A Month in the Country*
Karin von Aroldingen in *A Midsummer Night's Dream*
Suzanne Farrell in *Union Jack*
Peter Martins in *Tchaikovsky Pas de Deux*
Paolo Bortoluzzi and Jörg Lanner in *Nijinsky, Clown of God*
Suzanne Farrell in *Nijinsky, Clown of God*
Starr Danias and Dennis Wayne in *Sacred Grove on Mount Tamalpais*
Martine van Hamel in *The Sleeping Beauty*

PART ONE
Stories of the Great Ballets

ABYSS

Music by Marga Richter. Choreography by Stuart Hodes. Costumes by André Delfau. First presented by the Harkness Ballet at the Casino, Cannes, France, February 21, 1956, with Lone Isaksen and Erik Bruhn in the principal roles.

Based on a story by Leonid Andreyev, *Abyss* shows what might happen when an innocent young couple encounter bestial forces. One of Russia's great writers whose work in many ways resembles that of Edgar Allan Poe, Andreyev relates in his story a disturbing incident that is presented here in dance terms. A young girl and boy, not yet old enough to be seriously in love but close since childhood and certain one day to marry, walk one day alone in the forest. There they are suddenly attacked by three menacing figures. The boy is powerless to protect the girl and she is carried off by two of the men. When the boy eventually finds her again, she is distraught and half out of her mind. He is about to leave her in horror at what the attackers have done. But he finds himself also curious and attracted. The abyss opens before him and he, too, seizes the girl.

ADAGIO HAMMERKLAVIER

Music by Beethoven. Choreography by Hans Van Manen. Set and costumes by Jean-Paul Vroom. Lighting by David K. H. Elliott. First presented by the Dutch National Ballet, October 4, 1973. First presented in the United States by the Pennsylvania Ballet.

Inspired by the choreographer's listening to a recording by Christoph Eschenbach of the Adagio from Beethoven's *Hammerklavier Sonata*, this is a dance ballet. Eschenbach's performance, especially slow in tempo, stretches the possibilities of playing pianissimo to its extreme. His recording is used to accompany *Adagio Hammerklavier*, a dance for a boy and a girl, accompanied by two other couples.

Writing of a performance by the Dutch National Ballet in Canada in 1975, the critic Rose Anne Thom said in *Dance Magazine* that a pas de deux by Alexandra Radius and Hans Ebbelaar "communicated a sense of balance and confidence that was reassuring not only technically, but emotionally . . . It was the quiet understatement that made *Adagio* work . . ."

AFTER CORINTH

Music by David Gagne. Choreography by Walter Raines. Scenery by Gary Fails. First presented by the Dance Theatre of Harlem at the Uris Theatre, New York, April 29, 1975, with Virginia Johnson, Melva Murray-White, M. Elena Carter, and Roman Brooks.

A new perspective on the story of Jason and Medea, *After Corinth* takes the view that Jason's new wife, Glauce, victimizes his first, Medea. It will be recalled that in the dominant classical version of this story in the Greek drama of Euripides, Medea, enraged at Jason's desertion of her, devises the murder of Glauce. Medea then murders her own children by Jason. The ballet imagines that, after death, Jason and Medea return to earth and that Glauce is then seen as the murderess.

AFTER EDEN

Music by Lee Hoiby. Choreography by John Butler. Scenery by Rouben Ter-Arutunian. First presented by the Harkness Ballet at the Broadway Theatre, New York, November 9, 1967, with Lone Isaksen and Lawrence Rhodes.

After Eden is a dramatic ballet about Adam and Eve after the Fall and the expulsion from the Garden of Eden. It shows in dance terms, with no narration, something of the agony, regret, defiance, and resignation of the two lovers as they face the fate they had not imagined. In the process, their dependence on each other varies and it is this that makes the drama of the piece: Will they, after what they have come through, be able to stay together? At the start of the dance they are united in their misery and therefore mutually dependent. Later, realizing their new, appalling freedom, it seems briefly possible for them to separate or to entertain that notion. But not for long, for they have survived much and cannot go their separate ways. They are like magnets, alternately attracting and repulsing as they turn in different directions. In the end, they are newly united and apparently resolved to encounter the future together.

After Eden was revived by the City Center Joffrey Ballet, March 21, 1972, with Starr Danias and Dennis Wayne. Writing of this revival in the New York *Times*, the critic Anna Kisselgoff said that "Mr. Butler's symbolic images are so strong and so psychologically apt that he succeeds almost beyond belief in taking a specific emotional situation and generalizing it into a commentary on the universal human condition . . . Mr. Wayne and Miss Danias give a very strong performance . . . Miss Danias' Eve is fragile; she is much closer to the state of innocence just left behind than her partner. Mr. Wayne's Adam reacts through instinct, logically stressing the irrationality with which man often reacts to a new situation."

THE AFTERNOON OF A FAUN

Choreographic tableau in one act. Music by Claude Debussy. Choreography by Vaslav Nijinsky. Scenery and costumes by Léon Bakst. First presented by Diaghilev's Ballets Russes at the Théâtre du Châtelet, Paris, May 29, 1912, with Vaslav Nijinsky as the Faun. First presented in the United States by Diaghilev's Ballets Russes at the Century Theatre, New York, January 17, 1916, with Leonide Massine as the Faun.

The music for this ballet was written by Debussy as a *Prélude* to a poem by Stéphane Mallarmé. Nijinsky's idea of portraying a languorous faun whose rest is disturbed by beautiful nymphs is thus related to Debussy's inspiration. Debussy wrote of his score: "The music of this prelude is a very free illustration to Stephane Mallarme's beautiful poem. It does not follow the poet's conception exactly, but describes the successive scenes among which the wishes and dreams of the Faun wander in the heat of the afternoon. Then, tired of pursuing the fearful flight of the nymphs and naiads, he abandons himself to a delightful sleep, full of visions finally realized, of full possession amid universal nature."

When the curtain rises on the ballet we see a faun idling away a hot summer afternoon. He lies on a hillock, playing the flute and eating grapes. It is apparent that his wants are simple and innocent. Dressed in light brown tights dotted with brown patches below the waist, he seems to be half boy, half animal.

A group of seven lovely nymphs on their way to bathe in a lake near by enter the faun's domain. They move in a line, forming a likeness to a Greek frieze, their bodies always turned to the audience, their faces always in profile. The faun has never seen such beautiful creatures before and climbs down from his hillock to observe the naiads with the golden hair and soft, gauze tunics more closely. The nymphs, in turn, are astonished by this creature who seems to be a handsome boy spotted like a goat with small horns growing from his forehead. What can he be? they wonder. Soon, as the playful faun leaps about them, the startled nymphs flee to the forest.

When they return, the faun tries to ingratiate himself with them. But still the naiads are frightened, and again they run away. All except one. This nymph is less embarrassed than her sisters and more anxious to discover the faun's secret. The faun is emboldened to make playful amorous gestures. The nymph allows him to touch her; she seems to respond to him, but then she eludes his grasp. She is frightened and rushes off to join the others. As she leaves, a silken scarf from her garment falls to the ground.

The faun, no longer playful, is sad at her departure. He picks up her scarf and holds it as if it were a treasure. He returns to the hillock, holds the scarf in his hands as if it were a woman's face, and touches it tenderly. Now he lays the scarf down softly and as he caresses it, imagines it to be the naiad he frightened away. With his possession of the scarf, the faun is content with his afternoon revery. It is as if the nymphs had never appeared, as if he had dreamed of their presence and in his dream possessed utterly the most beautiful of them all.

NOTES *The Afternoon of a Faun* was Vaslav Nijinsky's first ballet. In its choreography and in its dancing the work completely rejected traditional forms. It was not a ballet in the accepted sense; it was a "choreographic tableau," a moving frieze, a work to be seen only from the front, a two-dimensional ballet. In his imitation of Greek paintings, Nijinsky was faithful to the spirit and to the letter; the traditional movements of classical ballet were altogether rejected in favor of an angular rigidity that would make possible a new expressiveness for the dancer's body.

Since Nijinsky's first performances, many dancers have taken the leading role in *The Afternoon of a Faun,* among them Leonide Massine, Serge Lifar, David Lichine, Igor Youskevitch, Leon Danielian, and Jean Babilée. Dame Marie Rambert, who knew Nijinsky well, has written of his achievement in her autobiography *Quicksilver:* "One is often asked whether his jump was really as high as it is always described. To that I answer: 'I don't know how far from the ground it was, but I know it was near the stars.' Who would watch the floor when he danced? He transported you at once into higher spheres with the sheer ecstasy of his flight.

"The most absurd theories were put forward about his anatomy. People said that the bones in his feet were like a bird's—as though a bird flew because of its feet! But, in fact, he *did* have an exceptionally long Achilles' tendon which allowed him with his heels firmly on the ground and the back upright to bend the knees to the utmost before taking a spring, and he had powerful thighs. As to his famous posing in the air, he indeed created the illusion of it by the ecstasy of his expression at the apex of the leap, so that *this* unique moment penetrated into every spectator's consciousness, and seemed to last. His landing, from whatever height he jumped, was like a cat's. He had that unique touch of the foot on the ground which can only be compared to the pianist's touch of the fingers on the keys. It was as subtle and as varied.

"And then there was his unique interpretation. He wafted the perfume of the rose in *Spectre de la Rose;* he was the very spirit of Chopin in *Les Sylphides;* he looked like a Hamlet in *Giselle;* his Petrouchka broke your heart with his sorrow, and his Faune had the real breath of antiquity.

"As to his choreography, I would not hesitate to affirm that it was he, more than anyone else, who revolutionized the classical ballet and was fifty years ahead of his time. Fokine was a logical development of Petipa, but Nijinsky introduced completely new principles. He produced three ballets in all: *l'Après-midi d'un Faune, Jeux,* and *Sacre du Printemps.* For each of them he established a basic position strictly adhered to all through the ballet. For *Faune* he took his inspiration from Greek vases and bas-reliefs. The body was facing front while the head and feet were always seen in profile. The deportment had to be classical, yet the head had independent movements not connected with deportment in the classical vocabulary, and so had the arms. It was an orchestration of the body, with each part playing a totally different melody. There was nothing you could do automatically. The walking was all done on one line parallel to the footlights, the whole foot on the ground. It was an incredibly difficult position to achieve, let alone use in walking, or changing direction, or combining with highly stylized arm movements. He did not explain why he wanted them thus, but he showed again and again the way they had to be done until he obtained a perfect copy of his own movement. His method of creation was diametrically opposed to Fokine's. Fokine always took the dancers into his confidence and allowed them, even encouraged them, to participate in the creation of a character. Not so Nijinsky. When once I was extolling the virtues of *Petrouchka* to him, saying it was Fokine's masterpiece, he said that it *was* so, as far as the three main characters went, but the crowd was treated too loosely, and everybody did what they wanted within the space indicated to them. Nijinsky on the contrary did not allow the slightest freedom of movement or gesture and exacted only a perfect copy. No wonder it took some 120 rehearsals for *l'Après-midi d'un Faune,* lasting about ten minutes, to be achieved as he wished, since not a single movement could be done spontaneously, each limb having to be studied separately. He required a perfect ballet technique and then broke it down consciously to his own purpose—and then it proved a masterpiece. Each nymph looked a goddess. Although they were incapable of understanding Nijinsky's intentions, the mere fact of faithfully copying his unique movements gave them the requisite style. He told them: no expression in the face, you must just be as though asleep with your eyes open—like statues.

"Once when a new girl had to learn Nijinsky's sister's part, in which the Nymph suddenly sees the Faune, turns away and walks off—he said to her: 'Why do you look so frightened?'

"She said she thought she was meant to be. Thereupon, quite in a rage, he said that the movement he gave her was all that was required of her, he was not interested in her personal feelings. And how right Nijinsky was for his particular choreography! It acquired an impersonal, remote character—just like the paintings on Greek vases or bas-reliefs—not that he ever attempted to copy any particular poses from these, but created them by the profoundest penetration into their very spirit. The walking was done not strictly to the music, but rather loosely as though walking 'through' the music."

In 1936 Edwin Denby reviewed a performance by David Lichine:

"The *Faun* is an astonishing work. After twenty-three years it is as direct and moving as though it had been invented yesterday. It gathers momentum from the first gesture to the last like an ideal short story. From this point of view of a story, the way the veil is introduced and re-emphasized by the nymph is a marvel of rightness. From the point of view of visual rhythm the repetition of the nymph's gesture of dismay is the perfection of timing. It is, of course, because so few gesture motifs are used that one can recognize each so plainly, but there is no feeling of poverty in this simplification. The rhythmic pattern in relation to the stage and to the music is so subtly graded that instead of monotony we get a steady increase in suspense, an increase in the eyes' perceptiveness, and a feeling of heroic style at the climax.

"It is true that most of the gestures used have prototypes in Greek reliefs and vase paintings, but, in addition to that intellectual association with adolescence, the fact is that when the body imitates these poses, the kind of tension resulting expresses exactly the emotion Nijinsky wants to express. Both their actual tension and their apparent remoteness, both their plastic clarity and their emphasis by negation on the center of the body (it is always strained between the feet in profile and the shoulders *en face*)—all these qualities lead up to the complete realization of the faun's last gesture. The poignancy of this moment lies partly in the complete change in the direction of tension, in the satisfying relief that results; and the substitution of a new tension (the incredible backbend) gives the work its balance. But besides, the eye has been educated to see the plastic beauty of this last pose, and the rhythmic sense to appreciate its noble deliberateness. That it is so intensely human a gesture, coming after a long preparation of understatement, gives it, in its cumulative assurance, the force of an illumination. This force of direct human statement, this faith in all of us, is the astonishing thing about the *Faun*. It is as rare in dancing as in the other arts. These last moments of the *Faun* do not need any critical defense. But they have been so talked about that I am trying to point out for intellectuals that they are not a sensational tag, but that the whole piece builds up to them, and reaches in them an extraordinary beauty.

"The De Basil company danced the *Faun* beautifully. Lichine in the title role excelled. It is a part that demands exceptional imagination as well as great plastic sense. And Lichine had besides these a fine simplicity."

Music by Claude Debussy. Choreography by Jerome Robbins. Set and lighting by Jean Rosenthal. Costumes by Irene Sharaff. First presented by the New York City Ballet at the City Center, New York, May 14, 1953, with Tanaquil LeClercq and Francisco Moncion.

Mallarmé's poem that inspired Debussy's music *Prélude à l'après-midi d'un Faune* describes the reveries of a faun and his real or imagined encounter with nymphs. In 1912 Nijinsky presented his famous ballet, drawing his ideas from both the music and the poem, among other sources. This *pas de deux* is a contemporary variation on those themes.

The scene is a room with a mirror, very much like a modern ballet studio with one wall a mirror so that dancers can watch themselves. The mirror wall is the imaginary wall toward the audience, so that when the dancers stare out at us they are really looking at their own reflections. The setting, with walls and ceiling of transparent cloth against a blue sky, seems to float in space; it is as remote and silent as the sylvan scene of Nijinsky's work. On the floor of the room a boy, naked to the waist, lies asleep. At the call of the music, he stirs, rolls over, arches his back, stretches like a cat. He sits up and stares out at us with such interest and objectivity that we know he appraises himself in the mirror. He stands, watching himself, adjusts his belt, poses to the sensuous music, gestures, then slowly somersaults and lies on the floor again, languorous and satisfied with himself. He falls asleep. A girl in white practice dress approaches the room. She pauses at the door, prepares her ballet shoes for the work to come and looks at the mirror. From the door she is drawn toward her image—and does not notice the boy. She has eyes only for her own reflection. She poses at the mirror, then kneels. She then begins to exercise at the *barre*. The boy wakens like a startled faun and watches her. She observes herself closely. When she comes to an open pose the boy steps in and lifts her up and away from the *barre,* as if she were coming up for air. The boy holds her in poses that please her image, both always looking into the mirror and never directly at each other. She likes the way she looks as he supports her, misses his hand at her waist when he is not there. She luxuriates for a moment, then stands and looks at the floor. He comes to her, his hands touch her hair, but she rises immediately into a formal *attitude,* rejecting any contact except what will make her more lovely to herself.

The enchanted boy, now watching only her in the mirror, lifts her now to his shoulder; she descends, her loose hair falling about her face. They separate then to opposite sides of the room, watching each other in the mirror. Their cool concentration on the invisible reflections before them is so intense that we know when one of them is watching the other. They approach each other slowly, reaching out. They stand side by side for a moment. The boy makes a circle of his arms and the girl slips through them, held there full length, swimming in the air. Then her body collapses as if a spell had been broken. She kneels on the floor, the boy beside her. He now looks at her directly while she still watches in the mirror. He leans toward her, his face comes close, he kisses her cheek. Her hand slowly moves up to her cheek. She stands and still looking straight ahead in the mirror, walks backward out of the room, her hand still at her face. He watches her in the mirror. She is gone. The boy lies down on the floor, pushes himself up on his arms and descends slowly again into sleep.

NOTES   Since this ballet was first performed, it has been danced throughout the United States and many countries overseas by the New York City Ballet, by the Royal Ballet, and by Jerome Robbins' Ballets: U.S.A. The latter performed it at the White House, April 11, 1962, following a state dinner given by President and Mrs. Kennedy for the Shah and Queen of Iran.

Soon after the first performance of *Afternoon of a Faun,* Doris Hering wrote in *Dance Magazine:* "*Afternoon of a Faun* is a work of great awareness and wry insight and one that shimmers with atmosphere from beginning to end . . .

"There is a wonderful sense of theatrical rightness in Mr. Robbins' choice of the antiseptic studio atmosphere for history of nascent love vying with narcissism—not only because dancers live in a world of mirrors, but because this particular format allowed him to concentrate on the rich mood relationship between the music and his own choreography. And instead of making a dance' in the formal sense of the word, he allowed the movement to flow out of the materials of the classroom, which are often more beautiful than their embellished stage versions. And he found two exceedingly sensitive performers in Francisco Moncion and Tanaquil LeClercq."

THE AGE OF ANXIETY

Dramatic ballet in six scenes. Music by Leonard Bernstein. Choreography by Jerome Robbins. Scenery by Oliver Smith. Costumes by Irene Sharaff. Lighting by Jean Rosenthal. First presented by the New York City Ballet at the City Center, New York, February 26, 1950, with Tanaquil LeClercq, Francisco Moncion, Todd Bolender, and Jerome Robbins in the principal roles.

Inspired by Leonard Bernstein's Second Symphony, *The Age of Anxiety,* and the poem by W. H. Auden on which this music is based, this ballet concerns the attempt four people make to find themselves. The ballet follows the sectional development of the poem and music.

THE PROLOGUE   The curtain rises on a scene that might be a public place in any part of a large modern city. A man enters on the left and walks slowly to the center of the stage. A girl appears on the right and walks toward him. Two men join the couple. All are strangers. The four figures stand opposite each other to form a small square, as if they were standing about a table. They sit together, become acquainted, discover mutual interests and a common problem, and with quiet, implicit understanding agree to set out on a journey together.

It is clear that each of these four people has something to fear. Their gestures and smallest movements are timorous and tentative. Because they do not know each other well, they seem always to be seeking something in their relationship to make it seem less odd that four strangers should meet and instantly, instinctively, feel a need to share each other's thoughts. Strangers they certainly are, but in their immediate awareness of a common problem their relation assumes an interested tenderness, a feeling of relief that companionship is still possible. All are humble in the face of this unstated problem, which seems at first to be loneliness. The journey they take together is a metaphor, a figure in dance terms, of the long exploratory conversation they begin to have in order to learn more of themselves and their age. The dance mirrors their talk.

THE SEVEN AGES   The four characters show us the life of man from birth to death in a set of seven variations. In the first variation, one of the men learns to stand, to walk, to articulate. In the words of Auden's poem:

> Behold the infant, helpless in cradle and
> Righteous still, yet already there is
> Dread in his dreams at the deed of which
> He knows nothing but knows he can do,
> The gulf before him with guilt beyond,
> Whatever that is, whatever why

Forbids his bound; till that ban tempts him;
He jumps and is judged: he joins mankind . . .

The girl comes forward and dances the second age. Her movements are warm and open, joyously happy. The girl is not only conscious of herself, but conscious of life about her, and displays an eagerness to participate in that life: she sacrifices part of herself to the world.

In the third variation, the four strangers meet love—the inevitable consequence of knowing and discovering something outside the self. It is love on an elemental, physical level, the love of extreme youth that recalls Auden's lines:

Since the neighbors did,
With a multitude I made the long
Visitor's voyage to Venus Island . . .

The fourth age shows us the plight of social man, man thrust into the world of ambitions. Here he becomes aware for the first time of what he must do to climb the road to his ideal, how this road sometimes diverges and how he is perhaps deceived about his goal. Here he faces the problem of realizing a dream in an apparently dreamless world: which fork in the road shall he choose?

Now, in the fifth age, the dancers find material success and discover the price paid to achieve it. Here we imagine very easily a great modern city where nature is entirely absent, where everything moves on a fixed schedule, and where citizens are mere readers of timetables, conforming religiously to the demands of a huge machine that they have no power to control.

The sixth age shows us a reaction to this superhuman condition—disillusionment, a brief effort to rise above it, a danced argument as to which is better: to give in to the determinism of the city or to fight against it fearlessly. The four strangers split into two groups and take these differing points of view. At the end, one of the dancers tires. His fist moves to his mouth to stifle a yawn. He sits, curled up like a child.

In the final age, man has abandoned hope, abandoned his rage at human error, and ceased to have any reason to act. The dancer walks slowly, is ignored by passers-by. He reaches out, collapses, and is carried off. Slowly a figure moves across the stage, dragging behind him a long piece of crepe. The end has come. Man is dead and no longer a member of the minority.

THE SEVEN STAGES   The four figures come together again. They stand in a close line and move together awkwardly, reaching out in unison toward an invisible goal. They separate and look about, then start on a dream journey to find happiness.

Four figures dressed exactly like them, but with masks covering their faces, enter. Lines of masked creatures file in and dance between the four characters and their doubles, who imitate precisely the movements of the four.

One by one, and with different partners, the four strive for a goal where they will have no doubts and feel secure. They wander in a maze, lose their way, lose each other, then meet again safely. Nothing definite has been gained, but together they have had a harrowing common experience. They repudiate their doubles, pushing them aside. Now the four not only subconsciously know each other very well, but they are friends, too.

THE DIRGE   The four friends fall flat on their faces as the All-Powerful Father enters. This father symbol is depicted as a huge figure on stilts, a tin man of faith. He beckons to them with mechanical movements and stalks forward. They take courage and touch him. Other people enter and pay homage to the Father. It is interesting that he moves awkwardly, that he requires the assistance of his disciples. He is not so much a religious as a political figure: a representation of power that exists not through his own will alone. He sits on the shoulders of the crowd. The girl dances before him ecstatically, fascinated with the new-found rapid grace in movement his presence gives her. She reaches out to him supplicatingly. The Father responds to her plea by falling over, collapsing. The four regard him as the god that failed.

THE MASQUE   The exhausted girl falls against one of the boys. There is silence for a moment. Then carefree music blares out. The music simulates jazz, and the four characters cavort about the scene forgetting their problem in playful versions of jive. But soon their vigorous efforts to be cheerful begin to pall. One of them stops dancing and stomps in raging despair: it is the kind of protest of the half-intoxicated, the man who knew that drink would solve nothing at all. The girl curls up on the ground.

EPILOGUE   One of the men seems to die. The girl and another man go to him and help him. Now all four stand together as at the beginning of the ballet. They kneel together, then rise. The girl reaches out to the men, as if she wants to ask a final question the answer to which is very important to her. But they all have such questions. Gradually they turn and walk toward the four corners of the stage from which they came. Just before they exit, they turn and bow slightly to each other in gratitude for the faith they have given each other in the anxious age.

NOTES   W. H. Auden's *The Age of Anxiety: A Baroque Eclogue* was published in 1946. *The Age of Anxiety*, Leonard Bernstein's *Symphony No. 2 for Piano and Orchestra,* on which the ballet was also based, was first performed by the Boston Symphony Orchestra, Serge Koussevitzky conducting, on April 8, 1949. The composer was the piano soloist. At that time Bernstein offered a description of his work and its source, the poem by Auden. "The essential line of the poem (and of the music) is the record of our difficult and problematical search for faith. In the end, two of the characters enunciate the recognition of this faith—even a passive submission to it—at the same time revealing an inability to relate it personally in their daily lives, except through blind acceptance . . . If the charge of 'theatricality' in a symphonic work is a valid one, I am willing to plead guilty. I have a deep suspicion that every work I write, for whatever medium is really theatre music in some way . . ."[*]

[*] Program notes of the Philharmonic-Symphony Society of New York, 1949–50.

Jerome Robbins, who had collaborated with Bernstein on two ballets for Ballet Theatre, *Fancy Free* (1944) and *Facsimile* (1946), was inspired by the music to choreograph a new work, his second as Associate Artistic Director of the New York City Ballet. Robbins has pointed out, however, that his ballet is different from both the poem and the score: "It is a ritual in which four people exercise their illusions in their search for security. It is an attempt to see what life is about."

AGON

Music by Igor Stravinsky. Choreography by George Balanchine. Lighting by Nananne Porcher. First presented by the New York City Ballet at the City Center, New York, November 27, 1957, with Diana Adams, Melissa Hayden, Barbara Walczak, Barbara Millberg, Todd Bolender, Roy Tobias, Jonathan Watts, Arthur Mitchell, Roberta Lubell, Francia Russell, Dido Sayers, and Ruth Sobotka.

While the New York City Ballet has in its repertory many works by Igor Stravinsky, *Agon* is the third Stravinsky ballet composed especially for our company. Lincoln Kirstein and I had always wanted a new Stravinsky work to follow *Orpheus,* and at first it seemed possible that this might be based on another Greek myth. We looked into a number of possibilities, but none of them seemed to work out. We began nevertheless to discuss possibilities of a new ballet with the composer. It was Stravinsky who hit upon the idea of a suite of dances based on a seventeenth-century manual of French court dances— *sarabandes, gaillards, branles*—he had recently come across. We all liked the idea, especially as Kirstein and I recalled Stravinsky's other masterful treatment of polkas and other dance forms, including ragtime rhythms. The title of the ballet, *Agon,* the Greek word for *contest, protagonist,* as well as *agony* or struggle, was a happy inspiration of Stravinsky's. It was to be the only Greek thing about the ballet, just as the dancing manual, the point of departure, was to be the only French.

Stravinsky and I met to discuss details of the ballet. In addition to the court dances, we decided to include the traditional classic ballet centerpiece, the *pas de deux,* and other more familiar forms. Neither of us of course imagined that we would be transcribing or duplicating old dances in either musical or dance terms. History was only the takeoff point.

We discussed timing and decided that the whole ballet should last about twenty minutes. Stravinsky always breaks things down to essentials. We talked about how many minutes the first part should last, what to allow for the *pas de deux* and the other dances. We narrowed the plan as specifically as possible. To have all the time in the world means nothing to Stravinsky. "When I know how long a piece must take, then it excites me." His house in California is filled with beautiful clocks and watches, friends to his wish for precision, delicacy, refinement. We also discussed in general terms the character each dance might have and possible tempos.

When we received the score I was excited and pleased and set to work at once. Sounds like this had not been heard before. In his seventy-fifth year Stravinsky had given us another masterpiece. For me, it was another enviable chance to respond to the impulse his music gives so precisely and openly to dance.

Music like Stravinsky's cannot be illustrated; one must try to find a visual equivalent that is a complement rather than an illustration. And while the score of *Agon* was invented for dancing, it was not simple to devise dances of a comparable density, quality, metrical insistence, variety, formal mastery, or symmetrical asymmetry. Just as a cabinetmaker must select his woods for the particular job in hand—palisander, angelique, rosewood, briar, or pine—so a ballet carpenter must find dominant quality of gesture, a strain or palette of consistent movement, an active scale of flowing patterns which reveals to the eye what Stravinsky tells the sensitized ear.

I was fascinated by the music, just as I had been fascinated and taught by Stravinsky's *Apollo* in the 1920s. As always in his ballet scores, the dance element of most force was the pulse. Here again his pulse built up a powerful motor drive so that when the end is reached we know, as with Mozart, that subject has been completely stated. Stravinsky's strict beat is authority over time, and I have always felt that a choreographer should place unlimited confidence in this control. For me at any rate, Stravinsky's rhythmic invention gives the greatest stimulus. A choreographer cannot invent rhythms, he can only reflect them in movement. The body is his medium and, unaided, the body will improvise for a little while. But the organizing of rhythm on a large scale is a sustained process, a function of the musical mind. To speak of carpentry again, planning a rhythm is like planning a house; it needs a structural operation.

As an organizer of rhythms, Stravinsky, I have always thought, has been more subtle and various than any single creator in history. What holds me always is the vitality in the substance of each measure. Each measure has its complete, almost personal life; it is a living unit. There are no blind spots. A pause, an empty space, is never empty space between indicated sounds. It is not just nothing. It acts as a carrying agent from the last sound to the next one. Life goes on within each silence.

Agon was written during the time of Stravinsky's growing interest in the music of Anton Webern and in twelve-tone music. He has said: "Portions of *Agon* contain three times as much music for the same clock length as some other pieces of mine." The score begins in an earlier style and then develops. The piece contains twelve pieces of music. It is a ballet for twelve dancers. It is all precise, like a machine, but a machine that thinks.

Like the score, the ballet is in three parts, performed without interruption. The first part consists of a *pas de quatre* for four boys, a double *pas de quatre* for eight girls and a triple *pas de quatre* for all twelve dancers. The curtain goes up before the music begins. There is no setting, only a plain backdrop. Four boys in practice clothes stand facing the back. They turn toward us quickly; as they step forward, the music begins, with a bright trumpet fanfare. The boys soon give way to eight girls. To a faster rhythm they, too, seem to be warming up. Then the boys come back and as the music, now a variation and development of the previous section, becomes more familiar and Stravinsky gives short solo passages to some of the principal instruments, the dancers stand in a state of readiness. Supported by the full confidence of the orchestra, all twelve dance.

There is another fanfare and three of the dancers, two girls and a boy, face us. They dance a *pas de trois*. The boy then dances a *sarabande*. Stravinsky's scoring is for solo violin, xylophone, tenor and bass trombone. This seems an odd combination on paper, but it is lovely in fact, and the contrast between the instruments is very interesting to the ear. The music changes then and we have the two girls dancing a *gaillard* featuring three flutes, chimes, mandolin, harp, and the lower strings in marvelous combinations. This gay dance with leaping steps merges into a coda for all three, as the boy comes back. The coda is the first piece in twelve-tone style and, now that our ears have been tuned in, we are ready for its complexities.

After a fanfare and a brief orchestral interlude again, the first *pas de trois* is replaced by another and the second part of the ballet begins with three *branles*. Descriptions of many old *branles* are available in dance histories, but my dances of course are improvisations. The two boys show off the girl, lifting her, balancing her, then she leaves.

Robert Craft says in his notes to the recording of *Agon* that Stravinsky saw an engraving in the old French manual depicting two trumpeters blowing accompaniment to a *branle simple* and that suggested the brilliant combination of those instruments for the next part, which is canon form. The two boys each take the part of one of the trumpets.

The *branle gai* is a solo for the girl, dominated by the rhythmic sound of castanets and the sort of dance style they suggest. The full orchestra then intervenes and the boys rejoin the girl for a final *branle double*.

Next comes the *pas de deux*, again after the fanfare and a short interlude. The music of the adagio is scored for strings, with a concertante part for the solo violin. There are variations for the boy, the music of which recalls the second *branle*, and the girl, and a coda. A brief quartet for mandolin, harp, violin, and cello is especially memorable in the score.

Four horns then recall the opening fanfare. The music for the first movement of the ballet is repeated and the piece ends as it began, with four boys dancing alone. They face the backdrop as the curtain falls.

In his book *Movement and Metaphor: Four Centuries of Ballet* (1970), Lincoln Kirstein, who commissioned *Agon* from Stravinsky for the New York City Ballet, has written interestingly about the background of the first production and given his impressions of the ballet. He writes that "the innovation of *Agon* lay in its naked strength, bare authority, and self-discipline in constructs of stressed extreme movement. Behind its active physical presence there was inherent a philosophy; *Agon* was by no means 'pure' ballet 'about' dancing only. It was an existential metaphor for tension and anxiety . . ."

Edwin Denby, the poet and critic, in *Dancers, Buildings and People in the Streets* (1965), fortunately now available in paperback, has written at length of "The Three Sides of *Agon*."

ALBORADA DEL GRACIOSO

Music by Maurice Ravel. Choreography by Jacques d'Amboise. Costumes by John Braden. Lighting by Ronald Bates. First presented at the New York City Ballet's Hommage à Ravel at the New York State Theatre, Lincoln Center, May 22, 1975, with Suzanne Farrell and Jacques d'Amboise in leading roles. Dedicated to Richard Boehm. Conducted by Robert Irving.

Ravel composed this piece of music as "an experiment in writing music that would sound improvised." Written first for the piano, and later orchestrated, it was originally part of a suite called *Miroirs* which consisted of pieces dedicated to five friends of the avant-garde, the "Apaches."

An *alborada* is an instrumental early Spanish folk form translatable as "dawn song" or "morning serenade." A *gracioso* is a comic or grotesque lover, perhaps like Don Quixote. Later, the *alborada* developed into a kind of dance especially popular in the Spanish province of Galicia near the Basque country of Ravel's ancestry. This is the structure upon which Jacques d'Amboise based his ballet.

Writing after its premiere the critic Herbert Kupferberg reported to *The National Observer* that this ballet is "Jacques d'Amboise's most notable achievement."

ALLEGRO BRILLANTE

Classic ballet. Music by Tchaikovsky. Choreography by George Balanchine. Costumes by Karinska. Lighting by Jean Rosenthal. First presented by the New York City Ballet at the City Center, New York, March 1, 1956, with Maria Tallchief and Nicholas Magallanes; Carolyn George, Barbara Fallis, Barbara Millberg, Barbara Walczak, Arthur Mitchell, Richard Rapp, Jonathan Watts, and Roland Vasquez.

Tchaikovsky's first piano concerto is played so often that many forget his other compositions for piano and orchestra. If my ballet to his second piano concerto, *Ballet Imperial*, has made that work better known, I am delighted. The music of his unfinished third piano concerto, Opus 75 in E Flat, has also seemed to me most appropriate for dancing. This was in fact the last music Tchaikovsky composed; he died less than a month after finishing the orchestration of the first movement, *Allegro Brillante*, on October 15, 1893. The composer had originally projected this music for use in a symphony, but after dismissing that idea, he rewrote the first movement for piano and orchestra and discarded the rest. As its marking suggests, the score is brisk and declarative but it is also deeply contemplative, I think.

The ballet is arranged for two principals and an ensemble. I had no narrative idea for the work, only wishing to have the dancers complement the music as best I could. The leading dancer of the work follows the piano in the cadenza, but her cavalier also has his important part, as do the supporting dancers, in conveying what I hope is the spirit of the work.

L'AMOUR ET SON AMOUR (Cupid and His Love)

Ballet in two scenes. Choreography by Jean Babilée. Music by César Franck. Settings and costumes by Jean Cocteau. First presented by Les Ballets des Champs-Élysées, at the Théâtre des Champs-Élysées, Paris, December 13, 1948, with Jean Babilée and Nathalie Philippart in the title roles. First presented in the United States by Ballet Theatre at the Metropolitan Opera House, New York, April 17, 1951, with Jean Babilée and Nathalie Philippart as Cupid *and* Psyche.

The story is told in mythology of Psyche, the daughter of a great king, who was so beautiful that the goddess of love became jealous of her. Wrathful Venus thereupon sent to earth her son, Cupid, to excite the girl with a passion for a hideous and hateful man, as a penalty for thus emulating the most beautiful of all the goddesses. Cupid came to Psyche to fulfill Venus' designs, but was so enchanted by the girl's loveliness that he fell in love with her. Secretly he came to earth every night to visit Psyche, taking leave of her before the break of day to conceal his identity, lest Venus discover his treachery in love.

Psyche's sisters knew of these visits and in their jealousy instilled doubts within the girl's heart: why should a lover conceal himself in the dark? The next night Psyche vowed to see her lover. As he slept, she lighted a lamp and saw the handsome god. But a drop of oil from the lamp fell on Cupid's shoulder, and he awoke to see her watching him. The youthful god rose up, told Psyche that her lack of faith had spoiled their love, and vanished into the night.

The desperate girl waited night after night, but her lover never returned. She went in search of him, beseeching the help of all the gods and goddesses. At last she came to the temple of Venus and humbly invoked her aid. The goddess swore vengeance and devised for Psyche a series of tasks she must accomplish before she could find her love. Venus' instructions were so difficult to carry out that Psyche almost died in her efforts to fulfill them. But Cupid, observing her plight, encouraged and aided his love from afar.

Venus became reconciled to the girl's beauty and no longer despised her. Psyche joined Cupid in the heavens, and the two lived happily ever after. Psyche is the Greek word for soul, and the girl in this myth thus represents the human soul that strives and labors through insuperable difficulties to reach the supreme happiness of Olympus.

L'Amour et Son Amour does not recount the details of this story. Instead, the ballet strives to present the quality of the love that gave rise to the myth, to portray in movement the reunion of the god with the earth-bound girl and the attachment that made that reunion possible. The ballet carries a motto by

Jean Cocteau: "Love has no explanation—do not seek a meaning in love's gestures." The music is César Franck's *Psyché* Suite.

The subdued music begins slowly. A drop curtain, white against a misty violet, depicts the profile of a youth whose eyes are directed toward a small opening in the painted frame that contains his image. The music heightens slightly and subsides again as the violet of the curtain changes to green. The curtain rises. A bright backdrop, painted in the sunny colors of the Mediterranean, pictures an imaginary map; it is framed by a Greek design. The scene is earth.

Psyche enters on the right. A flesh-color, skintight bodice reveals the beauty of her body. About her waist she wears a dark net skirt. Her long dark hair reaches to her shoulders. She moves slowly, almost listlessly. The graceful poses she assumes become an impressionistic rendering of the flow of the music. She moves as in a dream.

A man enters on the left, then another. The two approach Psyche, kiss her hands, and pay tribute to her beauty. They lift her gently, and the girl moves in mid-air between them. They hold her as she poses ethereally, like a drifting cloud. She stands alone for a moment, enchanted by some distant reality the men know nothing of. They come close to her again, and the three dance. The girl's arms stiffen. Holding her hands, one of her partners lifts her to the other. Psyche leads the dance with soft gestures, as if to instruct her admirers in the realm of her imagination. Her arms gesture with tender voluptuousness.

The men leave her, and Psyche stands alone, her arms at her sides. The music whirs to announce the arrival of seven zephyrs, who enter breathlessly. Their misty green gowns float in the air behind them. They surround Psyche in a wide semicircle. She responds to them with a gesture of sudden awakening. The zephyrs kneel and bow their heads, and Psyche dances alone. The zephyrs rise, and she dances among them, taking their hands as they weave in and out into a close circle that encloses her. Their hands flutter over Psyche's head to the accompaniment of the harp. Psyche falls back in the arms of one of the zephyrs. Another comes and lifts her legs, and three zephyrs carry her off toward Olympus. The other zephyrs fly into the twilight. The drop curtain falls.

After a brief interlude, the scene changes. Now we are high in the heavens. It is night. White lines sketch in the outlines of great constellations made by twinkling stars. The sky is warm, midnight blue. Psyche enters on the left. She marvels at the spacious beauty of the scene, its limitless starry light. The zephyrs stand behind her as she dances with them. Psyche senses that her dream is about to come true. The zephyrs rush her off.

Cupid leaps in, seemingly sustained in the air by the white wings he wears. He circles the stage in bold and daring flight. He becomes thoughtful and kneels. He looks toward the left and beckons with a noble godlike gesture toward the light. He leaves the scene. Just as he steps off, Psyche enters with the zephyrs; she moves in retarded, slow motion. The glow of the sky darkens. Psyche lies down. The stars black out.

Cupid appears in a circle of soft white light that seems to emanate from his person. He moves his arms slowly, as if he were pulling effortlessly invisible wires. Psyche attempts to rise. Cupid goes to her. Now she stands, holding onto his shoulder for support. The young god puts his arm about the girl's waist in recognition, and the two dance, softly and slowly, backward and forward. The music mounts to a crescendo. The two lovers kneel together. Cupid rises, turns with tremendous speed. Psyche imitates his movement. He holds out his arms, and the girl rushes toward him. He catches her foot in his hands and carries her back swiftly as she hovers over him.

Psyche steps down and poses against Cupid's back. He kneels, and the girl walks around him as he holds her hand. The music gradually loses its intensity. The two dance together gently. The light dims. Cupid holds up his left hand. The girl circles the stage and disappears. The light fades. Cupid stands in his domain, governing the light of the stars with his hands. The stars lose their luster; the circle of light about the god narrows to a pin point.

ANASTASIA

> *Scenario and choreography by Kenneth MacMillan. First performed in a one-act version by the Ballet of the Deutsche Oper, Berlin, June 25, 1967, with Lynn Seymour in the title role. Music by Bronislav Martinu (Symphonic Fantasy). Introductory score by the Studio for Electronic Music of the Berlin Technical University. Designed by Barry Kay. Film scenes from the Aero Film production From Tsar to Stalin. Conducted by Ashley Lawrence. First given in three-act version by the Royal Ballet at the Royal Opera House, Covent Garden, London, July 22, 1971, with Lynn Seymour as Anastasia, Derek Rencher and Svetlana Beriosova as the Tsar and Tsarina, and Antoinette Sibley and Anthony Dowell as Kschessinska and her partner. Music for Acts One and Two by Peter Ilyich Tchaikovsky (Symphonies Nos. 1 and 3). Scenery and costumes by Barry Kay. First presented in the United States by the same ensemble with the same principals at the Metropolitan Opera House, New York, May 5, 1972.*

The nursery was the center of all Russia's troubles.
SIR BERNARD PARES

Anastasia tells the story of the royal Russian princess who survived, some believe, the Bolshevik Revolution to live on and recall her past. Robert Massie in his book about the last Russian Tsar and his wife, *Nicholas and Alexandra,* quotes an older relative of the real Anastasia, who knew the child well, the Tsar's sister, Grand Duchess Olga: "My telling the truth simply does not help in the least, because the public simply wants to believe the mystery." This three-act ballet relates the young Anastasia's early life in the Russian imperial family and concludes with a scene in a Berlin hospital in 1920 where A Woman Who Believes She Is Anastasia looks back on her story. The same dancer depicts both. Through Anastasia's personal history the Russian past and cataclysmic public events are telescoped and recaptured.

Tsar Nicholas II came to the Russian throne in 1894 at the age of twenty-six. His wife, Alexandra, bore him four daughters—Olga, Tatiana, Marie, Anastasia—and one son, his first heir, the Tsarevitch Alexei, a hemophiliac. The

Tsarina believed implicitly in the power of the Russian priest and mystic, Rasputin, to treat her son's bleeding.

The boy's tutor, the Swiss Pierre Gilliard, later wrote: "The illness of the Tsarevitch cast its shadow over the whole of the concluding period of Tsar Nicholas II's reign and alone can explain it. Without appearing to be, it was one of the main causes for his fall, for it made possible the phenomenon of Rasputin and resulted in the fatal isolation of the sovereigns who lived in a world apart, wholly absorbed in a tragic anxiety which had to be concealed from the world." And Alexander Kerensky, the Russian revolutionary leader removed by the Bolsheviks, declared: "Without Rasputin, there could have been no Lenin."

In March 1917 the Tsar abdicated as a result of the outbreak of revolutionary activity and, following the Bolshevik October Revolution that same year, the imperial family was imprisoned. On the night of July 16/17, 1918, the Tsar and his family were killed by Bolshevik forces at Ekaterinburg.

It was in 1920 that a woman patient in a Berlin hospital was recognized by some as one of the daughters of the Tsar. Since then this woman has endeavored to prove her identity as the Grand Duchess Anastasia.

ACT ONE: IN THE COUNTRYSIDE, AUGUST 1914   The imperial family is at a picnic in a birch grove by a lake with guests, who include the Tsarina's great friend Madame Vyrubova, Rasputin, and a group of naval officers. The party ends as the Tsar receives news of the outbreak of World War I.

The royal family is seen here to be a loving, close-knit group who have a congenial but necessarily distant relationship with the officers and courtiers who surround them. On this informal occasion, a picnic in the country, where the young can romp and play, where the Tsar can relax and take snapshots of his children, there is an illusion of tranquility broken only by the presence of young officers. Dominating the scene is the Tsarina's concern for her son and her faith in Rasputin's power to keep him from any dangerous accident. One of her relatives later recalled: "The Empress refused to surrender to fate. She talked incessantly of the ignorance of the physicians. She turned toward religion, and her prayers were tainted with a certain hysteria."

Anastasia, in a sailor blouse, enters on roller skates. She soon establishes a forthright, playful character, yet is considerate of others. She dances with three of the young officers who attend the family and, later, dances with her mother, who shows her the steps of an old Russian dance. When a telegram is brought to the Tsar and news of war breaks the calm, the soldiers and sailors in attendance begin to practice drills and maneuvers. The Tsar dances reassuringly with his wife, Rasputin leads them all in prayer, and there is a hope of victory. But one senses that it is a thin hope. The critic Peter Williams, remarking on the silver-birch setting of the scene, noted that some of the trees "have been cut down, with just their stumps showing, to suggest that the ballet opens where Chekhov's Cherry Orchard left off—a warning wind symbolic of the passing order."

ACT TWO: PETROGRAD, MARCH 1917   Despite rapidly growing unrest, the

Tsar is giving a ball to celebrate the coming out of his youngest daughter, Anastasia. He has invited his favorite ballerina—with whom he had a liaison before his marriage—to dance for his guests. Anastasia is puzzled by the outburst of revolutionary activity.

The setting of the ballroom, like the first act, is circular in form, with a circular staircase descending like a vortex just off-center. Before the ballroom, however, an outside scene, with slogans and discontent in the streets, reminds us of unrest among the Russian people.

In the ballroom itself, which contrasts vividly with the poverty we have just seen, there are ceremonial dances for the Tsar, the royal family, and their guests. Anastasia, who has come of age, looks lovely and has a new maturity. The ballerina Mathilda Kschessinka, one of the great Russian ballerinas, first dancer of the Maryinsky Theatre for more than twenty-five years, enters and with her partner performs a *pas de deux* to the second movement of Tchaikovsky's symphony. Favorite of the Tsar before his accession to the throne and later the wife of the Grand Duke Andrei, the real Kschessinkaya in fact left Russia to live in Europe, where she danced triumphantly and taught for many years. Margot Fonteyn, and numerous other dancers were among her students. She died in Paris, in 1971, at the age of 99.

Later, when the ballerina has changed from her costume to a ball gown and joined the party, there is a *pas de quatre* in which she appears with the Tsar, the Tsarina, and Rasputin. Kschessinkaya's partner later joins in that dance, where old and new relationships excite the participants. The young Anastasia watches her parents and their friends and is bewildered; coming of age is more complicated than she has imagined if life, and love, are like that. An officer who tries to involve Anastasia herself is repulsed.

Now the action shifts back to the unrest in the streets of St. Petersburg. Soon the populace and troops outside the palace interrupt the processions and formal dances of the ballroom. They invade the premises and the ball ends in disaster.

ACT THREE: SOME YEARS LATER For the woman who believes she is Anastasia, past and present intermingle. She relives incidents from the years since the massacre of the Tsar and his family; her rescue by two brothers; the birth of her child; her marriage; the death of her husband; the disappearance of the child; her attempted suicide; the confrontation over the years with relatives of the imperial family who deny her identity as the Grand Duchess Anastasia.

The scene here is a Berlin hospital, where Anastasia sits on a white iron bed. She has recovered from a long period of unconsciousness and, reliving the past, is trying to find out who she is. Is she a plain person named Anna Anderson who has suffered simply a series of personal tragedies, or is she the Grand Duchess Anastasia who, in addition to personal misfortune, symbolizes another world? Filmed flashbacks of the past aid her memory of historic events, shown in newsreels and still photos, while her personal history and relationships are danced and depicted on stage. We see her rescue, the man who becomes her lover, their child, their happiness. This, too, is destroyed by another firing squad, for her husband is shot. She escapes yet again with his brother. Intermingled with the recapitulation of history and personal tragedy are confrontations the girl endures with members of the imperial family who refuse to recognize her as Anastasia. She herself, however, has no doubt; transcending all of her prolonged personal misfortune is her vivid recollection of the lovely past, when families might picnic under the silver birches and a young girl in a sailor suit might be so beloved by her parents that she would surely have a happy life. The ballet ends as we see Anastasia poised high at the foot of her hospital bed. The bed begins to move, coming toward us like an open royal limousine, it progresses; Anastasia, still and triumphant, receives silently the homage of the world.

Reflecting on Kenneth MacMillan's achievement in the three-act ballet form, Arlene Croce wrote in *The New Yorker* in 1974: "Of the three full-evening ballets MacMillan has produced so far, *Anastasia* seems to me the best, not so much because of what it achieves as because of what it attempts. In *Romeo*, MacMillan had before him both Leonid Lavrovsky's version for the Bolshoi and Cranko's for the Stuttgart; in *Manon* he is working à la Cranko. But in *Anastasia* he produced a personal fantasy about a global cataclysm entirely from nothing. I don't think he was being pretentious, and the insults that were showered upon him for missing the mark themselves missed the mark. MacMillan's taste, musical instinct, and technical skill place him first among those British and European choreographers whose careers began in the fifties."

APOLLO (Apollon Musagète)

Ballet in two scenes. Music and book by Igor Stravinsky. Choreography by George Balanchine. Scenery and costumes by André Bauchant. First presented by Diaghilev's Ballets Russes at the Théâtre Sarah Bernhardt, Paris, June 12, 1928, with Serge Lifar as Apollo, Alice Nikitina as Terpsichore (Alexandra Danilova alternated with Nikitina in this role in the original production), Lubov Tchernicheva as Polyhymnia, and Felia Dubrovska as Calliope. First presented in the United States by the American Ballet at the Metropolitan Opera House, New York, April 27, 1937, with scenery and costumes by Stewart Chaney. Lew Christensen was Apollo; the three Muses were danced by Elise Reiman, Holly Howard, and Daphne Vane.

To the Greeks, the god Apollo was many things: he was the god of prophecy, the god who punished wrongdoers, the god who helped those in trouble, the god of vegetation and agriculture, and the god of song and music. Apollo received different epithets, different names, for each of his various powers. Because of his powers of song and music, he was also closely associated with the Muses, goddesses who represented the different arts and derived inspiration from Apollo's teaching. This ballet concerns itself with Apollo, leader of the Muses, the youthful god who has not yet attained the manifold powers for which he will afterward be renowned among men.

The three Muses of the ballet were selected for their appropriateness to the choreographic art. In the words of the composer, "Calliope personified poetry and its rhythm; Polyhymnia represents mime; Terpsichore, combining in herself both the rhythm and the eloquence of gesture, reveals dancing to the world and thus among the Muses takes the place of honor beside Apollo."*

The ballet begins with a brief prologue that depicts the birth of Apollo. Before the opening curtain, the string orchestra intimates the theme that will become identified with the god as the ballet progresses. This theme receives a rhythmic accompaniment from the lower strings, and the curtain rises.

The scene is Delos, an island in the Aegean Sea. It is night; stars twinkle in a dark blue sky. Back in the distance, in a shaft of light, Leto gives birth to the child whom the all-powerful Zeus has sired. She sits high on a barren rock and holds up her arms to the light. The music quickens, the woman buries her face in her hands, a hurried crescendo is cut off sharply, the strings are plucked, and Apollo is born. Leto disappears, and in the shaft of light at the base of the high rock stands the infant god, wrapped tightly in swaddling clothes. He hops forward stiffly to a swift, flowing melody.

Two handmaidens leap softly across the stage and come to Apollo. The newborn god falls back in their arms; his mouth moves in an inarticulate cry for help, and the two women begin to unwrap his swaddling clothes. They circle the god, unwinding the rich cloth, but before they can finish, Apollo spins suddenly and frees himself of the garment and looks about the dark world, not seeing clearly, not knowing how to move. After this burst of energy, he is frightened. His head is crowned with golden vine leaves and his body is endowed by nature with sinuous strength, but the young god is bewildered.

The two handmaidens bring to him a lute, sign of his future greatness in music. Apollo does not know how to hold the instrument. They place it in his hands and stand behind him, reaching out their hands to pluck the strings. Apollo follows their example and finds the first clue to his immortality. There is a blackout.

The musical statement that marked Apollo's birth is repeated sonorously. When the lights come on again, the scene is brilliant, as if a flash of lightning had been sustained and permanently illuminated the world. Apollo, dressed now in a short gold tunic, stands in the center of the stage. To the music of a solo violin, he plays upon the lute. He whirls his arms around and around in a large circle over the strings, seeming to draw music from the instrument with his youthful strength. Other strings now accompany the solo violin softly. Apollo places the lute on the ground and dances alone. He reaches out to the lute for inspiration and moves tentatively, carefully, but with a new-found ease. Now that he has proved his potential grace in movement, Apollo picks up the lute again. He turns slowly in attitude, holding the lute before him. The solo violin concludes the theme.

Three Muses appear to Apollo, walking slowly and respectfully toward him from three corners of the stage. With a godlike gesture, the god welcomes them. The young goddesses bow to him, then in unison bend in low arabesques

* From Igor Stravinsky, *An Autobiography*, Simon and Schuster, Inc., New York, 1936.

about the lute he holds high in his hands. They break this pose and stand together. The melody is strong yet moving, vigorous yet simple, like the youthful, inexperienced quality of the dance that now begins.

Apollo reaches out and, touching their hands gently, draws the Muses close to him. The three girls stand close together, one behind the other. Apollo takes their hands one by one. They pose in arabesque for an instant and move to the center of the stage. He motions two of the girls aside; Terpsichore, Muse of song and dance, falls back in his arms. He leaves her kneeling alone and, enclosing the other two girls in his arms, he lowers them slowly to the ground so that they also kneel.

Terpsichore rises and, dancing on point, slowly takes the hands of her sister Muses and encircles their kneeling figures. Now the three Muses stand again in a close line. The lower strings play the poignant theme with deep strength, and Apollo circles the stage in broad, free leaps as the girls move their arms in rhythm to the music.

The god returns to the Muses and supports each as she turns close to the ground. The girls form a line behind Apollo and move across the back of the stage, their bold, youthful figures imitating the dance of their leader. The girls pause and kneel, then rise at once. Apollo, arms outstretched, supports them as they hold hands and form a circular tableau.

When this tableau is broken, the Muses form a close line in front of Apollo. This line moves backward as one, the young god and goddesses shuffling awkwardly on their heels. The line comes to a rest. The three girls stand motionless; Apollo bends down and tenderly pushes them into motion with his shoulder. Led by Terpsichore, the Muses dance alone. The melody ends.

Apollo presents each of the Muses with the symbol appropriate to her art. To Calliope, Muse of poetry, he presents a tablet; to Polyhymnia, Muse of mime, a mask that symbolizes unearthly silence and the power of gesture; and to Terpsichore, Muse of dancing and song, he gives a lyre, the instrument that accompanies those arts. The Muses accept these gifts with delight and respect, form a line, and hop like pleased children to the side of the stage. Apollo commands the Muses to create and sits to watch what they will do.

Calliope comes forward with her tablet. She holds it out before her, then clutches it to her heart. Placing the tablet on the ground, she dances. The melody she moves to is based in form on the Alexandrine, the classical heroic measure of French poetry. Her dance is emotional, yet not weakly so; as she circles the stage before Apollo, her leg boldly sweeps the air before her. She is scribbling hastily on the palm of her hand when her dance nears its end, wondering if she has done well. She becomes a little sad, the music seems to cry out softly with her, and she goes to show Apollo what she has written. He does not approve.

Brilliant chords herald the dance of Polyhymnia, who soon puts her mask aside and dances rapidly to a sprightly, rhythmic melody. The girl holds her finger to her lips throughout the dance, as she tries to maintain the dignity of her mask, but her youthful enthusiasm gets the best of her: she forgets—as she responds to the happy, worldly music—and before she knows what has happened, her lips have moved and she has spoken. Terrified, she claps her hands over her mouth, punishing her own naughtiness, but Apollo sees what she has done and censures her.

Terpsichore comes forward and dances in profile with her lyre. She holds the instrument high above her head, her curved arms suggesting the shape of the lyre, and her feet pluck at the ground as if they played upon it. She moves adroitly and sharply, with assured grace; the gestures she makes—with her arms as she poses in a series of balanced arabesques show us that her whole body is coordinated to beauty. The music she dances to is similar in melody to Calliope's, but the rhythm is different; like her dance, it is more pointed, less romantic. Of all the Muses, she alone dances perfectly, and Apollo commends her.

Now the young god dances alone. Majestic chords announce the theme of his variation. He reaches his arms up toward Olympus, leaps grandly into the air, then kneels. To the quiet rhythms of the music, Apollo performs with ideal perfection, setting an example to the Muses and reminding us that he himself has acquired the skill he demands of them.

As his dance ends, Apollo sits on the ground in a graceful, godlike pose. Terpsichore appears before him and touches his outstretched hand. The young goddess steps over his arm and bends low in extended arabesque beside him. Now the girl rises and sits on Apollo's knees. He holds his arm up to her, she takes it, and both rise to dance a muted *pas de deux*. The melody is softly lyrical, but at the same time strong; it depicts in sound an awakening of Olympian power and strength, beauty and grace.

Apollo supports Terpsichore in extended arabesque, lifts her daringly high so that her body curves back over his shoulder, holds her as she extends her legs and sinks on the ground to rise on point in graceful extensions. She pirouettes swiftly and sharply in his arms then entwines herself around Apollo. The music brightens, they separate, dancing playfully, then meet again. Both kneel. Apollo puts his head in Terpsichore's open hands. Now, at the end, she falls across Apollo's back as the god bends down to give the Muse a short swimming lesson as a reward for her beautiful dancing. Her arms push the air aside as if they were moving in the water. When Apollo rises, Terpsichore's body is curved against him.

Calliope and Polyhymnia rush in and join Apollo and Terpsichore in a joyous coda in which the Muses surround Apollo with their new-found pleasure in movement. The young god, in their midst, holds out his arms; two of the girls grab hold, and he swings them through the air. The quick grace of the Muses is accompanied by lively, shifting rhythms in the music that rushes to a finish. Apollo takes them by the hand and drives all three across the stage in a swift chariot race. As the music ends, Apollo stands alone. The three girls walk toward him together and in unison clap their palms. Apollo leans down and places his head against their hands.

From on high, Zeus calls his son Apollo home with mighty crescendos of sound. Apollo stands motionless, as if under a spell, listening. The three Muses sit upon the ground. Apollo walks slowly around them. As he stands in back of them and reaches out over them, the three girls lift their feet to meet his hand. Apollo blesses them with a noble gesture. The Muses reach their arms up, and

Apollo lifts them up beside him. For a moment the arms of the four figures are entwined, then the three Muses pose in arabesque behind Apollo's profiled figure to form a tableau in which the goddesses are as one with him.

Now Apollo takes their hands and draws them like a chariot across the stage. He takes them to the foot of the high rock, then walks forward and begins to climb to the summit, pointing the way to Olympus. The Muses follow. The four figures are silhouetted against the sky, holding out their arms to the sun. Leto, Apollo's mother, falls back in the arms of his handmaidens as she reaches up to her son in farewell.

NOTES   *Apollo* is not the kind of ballet most people expect to see when they know its name. When the ballet was first performed, a French critic said that this was not Apollo at all, that the choreographer had cultivated the deliberately odd, that Apollo would never have done this, or this, or this, etc. When the critic was asked how he knew what Apollo would have done, he had no answer. He was thinking of some familiar statue of Apollo, the Apollo Belvedere perhaps, and imagined that a ballet about the god would personify sculptural representations. But *Apollon Musagète* is not Apollo Belvedere; he is the wild, half-human youth who acquires nobility through art.

Stravinsky's *Apollon Musagète* was originally commissioned by Elizabeth Sprague Coolidge and received its first performance at the Library of Congress in Washington on April 27, 1928, with choreography by Adolph Bolm, who danced the principal role. Ruth Page (Terpsichore), Elise Reiman (Calliope), and Berenice Holmes (Polyhymnia) were the three Muses. After this first performance, Stravinsky offered the score to Diaghilev, who assigned the ballet to me.

This was the second time I had worked closely with Stravinsky's music (*Le Rossignol* was a first attempt, an exercise set me by Diaghilev in 1925). *Apollo* was a collaboration. As I wrote in *Stravinsky in the Theatre*, "I look back upon the ballet as the turning point in my life. In its discipline and restraint, in its sustained oneness of tone and feeling, the score was a revelation. It seemed to tell me that I could, for the first time, dare not use all my ideas; that I, too, could eliminate. I began to see how I could clarify, by limiting, by reducing what seemed to be myriad possibilities to the one possibility that is inevitable.

"In studying the score, I first understood how gestures, like tones in music and shades in painting, have certain family relations. As groups they impose their own laws. The more conscious an artist is, the more he comes to understand these laws and to respond to them. Since working with Stravinsky on this ballet, I have developed my choreography inside the framework such relations suggest."

Stravinsky, in his 1936 *Autobiography*, notes that the invitation to compose a ballet for a contemporary music festival in Washington gave him an opportunity to carry out an idea that had long appealed to him, "to compose a ballet founded on moments or episodes in Greek mythology plastically interpreted by dancing of the so-called classical school . . . I had especially in my thoughts what is known as the 'white ballet,' in which to my mind the very essence of this art reveals itself in all its purity. I found that the absence of many-colored effects and of all superfluities produced a wonderful freshness. This inspired me to write of an analogous character. It seemed to me that diatonic composition was the most appropriate for this purpose, and the austerity of its style determined what my instrumental ensemble must be. I set aside the ordinary orchestra because of its heterogeneity . . . and chose strings.

"On June 12, 1928, I conducted the first production of *Apollo* . . . in Paris . . . George Balanchine, as ballet master, had arranged the dances exactly as I had wished—that is to say, in accordance with the classical school. From that point of view it was a complete success, and it was the first attempt to revive academic dancing in a work actually composed for the purpose. Balanchine . . . had designed for the choreography of *Apollo* groups, movements, and lines of great dignity and plastic elegance as inspired by the beauty of classical forms . . .

"As for the dancers, they were beyond all praise. The graceful Nikitina with her purity of line alternating with the enchanting Danilova in the role of Terpsichore; Tchernicheva and Dubrovska, those custodians of the best classical traditions; finally, Serge Lifar, then still quite young, conscientious, natural, spontaneous, and full of serious enthusiasm for his art—all these formed an unforgettable company."

The importance of *Apollo* to the history of ballet has been described by Lincoln Kirstein: "*Apollon Musagète* introduced to ballet in its time a spirit of traditional classicism absent since Petipa's last compositions almost thirty years before. It demonstrated that tradition is not merely an anchorage to which one returns after eccentric deviations but the very floor which supports the artist, enabling him securely to build upon it elements which may seem at first revolutionary, ugly, and new both to him and to his audience. *Apollon* has now lost for us the effects which offended, irritated, or merely amused an earlier public. We forget that much of the 'modernism' of adagio movement in our classic dance derives directly from *Apollon;* that many ways of lifting women, of turning close to the floor, of subtle syncopation in the use of *pointes,* of a single male dancer supporting three women, were unknown before *Apollon.* These innovations horrified many people at first, but they were so logical an extension of the pure line of Saint-Léon, Petipa, and Ivanov that they were almost immediately absorbed into the tradition of their craft.

"Glenway Wescott said that instead of *Apollo, Leader of the Muses,* the ballet should have been entitled *Apollo's Games with the Muses.* The mimed athletics, the strenuous atmosphere of violent physicality recall the nervousness of runners before a race. Each variation seems a training for the final translation to Olympus. In the chariot-race finale which evokes memories of the profiles on Roman coins and cameos and of the decathlon, visualized in the newly extended idiom of Russian ballet, a transformation of the Olympic games into contemporary dancing takes place. Of all Balanchine's works *Apollon* is the most significant historically, the most compact, the most influential . . ." (In "Balanchine Musagète," *Theatre Arts,* November 1947.)

North German Television in 1967 made a film of rehearsals and a performance of *Apollo.* A spoken commentary by John Drummond described the occasion, in which Stravinsky and I participated. The dancers were Jacques d'Amboise as Apollo, Suzanne Farrell as Terpsichore, Gloria Govrin as Calliope, and Patricia Neary as Polyhymnia.

APPARITIONS

Dramatic ballet in three scenes with prologue and epilogue. Music by Franz Liszt. Choreography by Frederick Ashton. Book by Constant Lambert. Scenery and costumes by Cecil Beaton. First presented by the Sadler's Wells Ballet at the Sadler's Wells Theatre, London, February 11, 1936, with Robert Helpmann as the Poet and Margot Fonteyn as the Woman in Ball Dress. First presented in the United States by the Sadler's Wells Ballet at the Metropolitan Opera House, New York, October 25, 1949, with the same principals.

The inspiration of a poet is the subject of this romantic ballet. Here the poet derives his work not from real life, or from anything connected with it, but from the realm of the fantastic imagination, from apparitions. The ballet thus depicts the poet as character rather than creator, as a victim of the apparitions he finds it necessary to invoke. The scenario of *Apparitions* was suggested by the synopsis Hector Berlioz wrote for his *Symphonie Fantastique*. The music, orchestrated by Gordon Jacob, was selected from the later works of Franz Liszt by Constant Lambert.

PROLOGUE   The curtain rises on a scene representing the poet's study. It is an immense, dark, high-ceilinged room with great leaded windows—the kind of room in which we think instantly of hidden shadows lurking in the corners. It is night. On the right, a lamp stands upon a desk. Seated at the desk is the poet. He is evidently engrossed in composition, for at first he does not look up. Soon, however, he rises and gestures impatiently. His poem is not progressing as he would wish; he seems to require a fresh stimulus to continue.

The poet is astonished as light appears outside the windows. He is amazed further when he observes in the window frames mysterious apparitions. There stands a beautiful young woman in a formal ball dress, there a handsome hussar, and there a monk. Immediately the poet is enamored of the woman, who smiles at him in recognition. He sees in her an idealized version of all women, a picture of the perfect romance, and for a few moments he imagines that he has the key to the end of the poem he has been writing. But the woman and the other figures disappear. He reaches out toward them, then turns and sits again at his desk. Now his inspiration is so intense that words will not come. His mind is preoccupied with the source of his inspiration rather than the lines she might assist him to create. His mind whirls with romance. He gives up in impatience, abandons the poem, and takes a potion to induce sleep. The curtain falls.

SCENE ONE: A BALLROOM   Now the scene shifts to the locale of the poet's dream. The curtain rises on a ballroom, where fashionable couples are dancing. The poet enters, observes the scene, and wishes to participate in the discreet gaiety, but the dancers look through him as if he were the empty air. At a pause in the dancing, the lovely woman in the ball dress enters the room. All the men—particularly a handsome, swashbuckling hussar—are deferential to her dark beauty and vie for her favor. The dancing recommences. In this new dance, the women change partners constantly, and suddenly the poet is holding in his arms the apparition that delights him. But she is unaware that she has seen him before and turns her head away to catch sight of the hussar. She leaves the scene when the hussar rejoins her, and soon the ballroom is empty. The poet, alone, despairs.

SCENE TWO: A SNOW-CLAD PLAIN The dream changes, and the poet finds himself in the lonely winter forest. He longs for the reappearance of the woman, but imagines that she will again reject him. He hears bells in the distance, wonders what they are for, and dancers who wear skirts shaped like bells move around and around him, giving vivid expression to his romantic hallucination.

A funeral procession enters. Cloaked figures carry the body of the deceased on a bier. The poet is startled to see that the procession is led by the monk who appeared in the window of his study. Now he has seen again all three: the girl, the hussar, and the monk. Is this the end? What will happen? Will his dream be resolved?

He is drawn to the bier. Before the monk can prevent it, he snatches away the burial cloth and discovers the face of his beloved. Again he despairs. The monk reprimands him. The procession moves on. The poet falls to the ground to weep and to pray.

SCENE THREE: A CAVERN The scene now is a dark, secluded cavern. Creatures in red costumes have gathered here to practice some secret, magical rite. The poet joins them, seems to be accepted among them, rejoices, then falls back aghast as he sees before him the creature of his imagination, her face defaced, grotesque, ugly. The poet disclaims responsibility for his dream and seeks to escape. The woman is now attracted to him and will not let him go. The poet faints. As he passes into deep unconsciousness, her face miraculously takes on its previous apparent beauty.

EPILOGUE The final curtain rises on the poet's study. He is still asleep. Gradually he wakens. He cannot shake off his dream, and as he pieces it together, he sees the dream as a telling, romantic poem on his own pursuit of romanticism—a perpetual destruction of the self in the seeking of the unattainable. He kills himself.

The woman of his imagination enters and grieves. She turns her face away as cloaked figures take up the poet's body.

ARENA

Music by Morton Subotnick. Choreography by Glen Tetley. Lighting by John B. Read, executed by Gilbert V. Hemsley, Jr. First presented by the Netherlands Dance Theatre at the Royal Theatre, The Hague, February 4, 1969. First presented in the United States by the Stuttgart Ballet at the Metropolitan Opera House, Lincoln Center, New York, June 4, 1975, with Richard Cragun, Egon Madsen, and Dieter Ammann in leading roles.

When *Arena* was first danced, the choreographer has recalled, critics tried to read into it the Cretan myth of the Minotaur—doubtless because the composer of its electronic score, Morton Subotnick, had given his work the title *The Wild Bull*. "But I did not consciously intend any such meaning," Tetley has said. "The relationships that I tried to portray arose solely from the kinds of movement that I wanted to use, and from tensions implicit in the music. However, for the sake of those who find it hard to get by without some kind of 'plot,' let me essay the following interpretation: The ballet seems to me rather like a set of variations on the theme of might, dominance, pure power. When people are forced into close proximity, the mutual tensions can lead to an explosion of violence, which may manifest itself on either a physical or spiritual plane. These were the thoughts that had been suggested to me by the music."

The action of *Arena*, which is danced by six men, takes place in an undefined space from which there is apparently no clear escape. A struggle develops between two of the men; jealousy and love in varied ways are displayed until one of the major participants, in understandable rage, begins to throw chairs around the stage.

The dancer and writer James Waring reported to *Ballet Review* in 1971, after the ballet's premiere: "*Arena* is about self-doubt, and self-confidence, and their oscillation. The six men are gladiators of some sort, in a circus of the mind. Three of them function mostly as decor. Of the other three, Frans Vervenne (sometimes, Harmen Tromp) sleeps on a pile of nesting chairs. Hans Knill is a final challenger who overcomes the principal figure, Jon Benoit. The ballet unfolds in a series of physical challenges, alternating with periods of retreat."

ASTARTE

Created and choreographed by Robert Joffrey. Music performed by Chamberlain, conducted by Hub Miller. Commissioned score composed by Crome Syrcus. Lighting design and set by Thomas Skelton. Costumes by Hugh Sherrer. Film created and photographed by Gardner Compton. Produced by Midge Mackenzie. First presented by the City Center Joffrey Ballet at the City Center, New York, September 20, 1967, with Trinette Singleton and Maximiliano Zomosa.

Astarte, moon goddess of love and fertility, borrowed from the Babylonian-Assyrian Ishtar by the Greeks, is the heroine of this multimedia work. Astarte gave herself to all men, but was owned by none. She has been called the patron goddess of Women's Liberation, lover and destroyer, bestower of both life and death. The ballet that celebrates her powers uses music (an acid-rock score specially commissioned) amplified dramatically, lights (incandescent and strobe), film, and dance in the first combination of these elements in the theater of ballet. Techniques and impressions familiar in the discothèque are here, melded with dance to produce a dramatic *pas de deux* unlike any seen before.

What happens in general is simple. As the music starts full volume, the darkened theater is suddenly filled with varied kinds of light. A steadily blinking strobe stares out from the front of the stage so that no one in the audience can see for a moment of necessary adjustment; the stage itself begins to have some light on it, and searching spotlights are aimed at the audience, trying to find we know not what.

We soon find out. The backcloth of the setting on stage is a tightly stretched white cloth pulled in at the center like a belly button, and, against a drop farther back, a frantic film is being projected, of frantic birds and a hypnotic girl —the goddess Astarte. The seeking spotlights find a boy seated on the aisle in the audience as the eye of the goddess winks. He rises, transfixed by her glance, and slowly makes his way down the center aisle of the theater as we all watch. He crosses then to the right, toward steps to the stage, meanwhile looking at the stage at the goddess who has materialized before us. He goes up on stage and, standing there, still staring alone at the eyes of the goddess, begins to take off his clothes—all of them, down to his briefs, as her image looms huge above him on the screen. Soon his image, too, is seen to merge with hers. The rock singer has begun to sing, and the boy puts his clothes tenderly on the ground under the watching eye of the mysterious girl. He now goes to her, holding out his hands and, reaching her, molding them to her body. She steps forward then, and he begins to hold her in a dance that is anticipated, gesture by gesture, by the film that wraps around them and shows through them. The dance is slow, cool, collected, as the music blasts, and the boy and the goddess who controls him are in a different world, out of all contact with those who watch. There is no appeal here for attention to the spectator; there is only attention to each other, and the spectators are beyond reality. The boy in his dance worships the girl as he maneuvers her, lifts her, touches her. He attempts in mounting frenzy for a moment to control and subdue her as an erection rises in the stretched jersey of backcloth, and to kiss her. Then the music quietens. In the film we see his body branded with the impress of the goddess's as his passion is spent. She lets down her hair, and the dance of engulfment continues relentlessly, he, as always, powerless to resist her beauty and powerless, too, completely to claim her. He falls back, and, in the film, we see him somersault in pain and fall forward so that she in triumph can cause him to writhe at her feet.

She hovers over him as the rapid pulse of the strobe illumines them. She raises her leg over him, and the boy crouches there below her. Then, holding her above him, he rises and, before we realize it, he is carrying her and displaying her curved body aloft, as the filmed image has already anticipated, her legs locked about his head, his hands clasping her ankles. It is a posture of glory for the remote goddess and proud submission for the boy. He kneels at last so that she can step down. Before he realizes it, she is gone. The backdrop dissolves, and the boy walks back, back, through the back wall of the stage, where huge, high doors open for him, through the storage of scenery and props, to the exit to the street. These doors, too, open for him and, still transfixed by the goddess and his joy in her, he moves out into the light and traffic, perhaps to rejoin the world.

NOTES   Gardner Compton, who created the films for *Astarte*, has had some interesting things to say about its composition. Writing in *Dance Magazine*, he said: "The discothèque is the temple of electricity with its light shows, audio-visual devices such as film (which, in essence, is merely the reproduction of light), and other visual effects. In these new temples, some dance to electronic music while others sit in small groups on the floor watching the God Electricity (Light) perform on the walls and ceilings. The milieu of *Astarte* was precisely this new house of worship.

"One of the elements of this new creed is the use of multimedia devices to obtain involvement. *Astarte* sought to bridge the gap between the loose, unrefined area of the happening and a legitimate art form—in this case, ballet. What Robert Joffrey and I tried to avoid was the looseness of form characteristic of the happening. Our concept was more classical in nature. The choreographer was using movement in a magnificent sustained counterpoint to the amplified acid-rock music. It was the dancers who were receiving the audio massage, a massage that tuned them *out* on the world of the audience. In so doing we hoped that the fantasy of the film media combined with the reality of the dancers would tune *in* the audience on the ritualistic milieu of the discothèque.

"But *Astarte* was merely a beginning, a primer for what is to come. It is only one of the first steps in the direction of a totally involved multi-media theatre experience. And I believe this will be a vital concept of the whole.

"In order for choreo-cinema to be successful, there must be a perfect blending of these concepts to form one unified artistic viewpoint. . . . I remember Martha Graham giving an image in class that made first position a reality to me. The essence of that image was as follows: Your arms are carried from the back as though you are standing in a shower and the water is like energy draining down the arm and off the middle fingers of the hands. A cameraman should film a dancer so that the last object to leave the frame is that portion of the body that moves the energy from space to space. The camera itself should also move the energy from one space to another, or it is not contributing. Timing and framing are the essential tools of a dance cameraman. One must frame on space and let the dancer move into it. Space is the dancer's canvas, whether on stage or on film. Both space and movement, too, may have to be modified or distorted to make the choreo-cinema effective to an audience.

"The camera is the eye of the audience, the establisher of the involvement, the point of view, the movement. Why should the joy of movement be limited to the dancers? The members of the audience, too, can enjoy it, but only if the camera works for them. Thus if someone were to ask me the difference between a *pas de deux* on stage and a *pas de deux* on film I would answer as follows: A *pas de deux* on stage is a dance for two people (usually a boy and a girl), whereas a *pas de deux* on film is a dance for a boy, a girl, *and* camera. If cinematographic movement techniques are used successfully with dance, a successful marriage can result. One must wed the movement of one art to the movement of the other in order to achieve a true choreographic end.

"In *Astarte*, Robert Joffrey choreographed for the stage. What I filmed was Joffrey's choreography (even the abstract images are derived from images of the dancers themselves). However, I selected and chose for my camera, making the film very different from what the dancers were doing on stage. Often to reach a total choreographic concept, I borrowed the fugue form from music. I repeated themes in such a way that the movement would start with the live dancers and then be repeated and built through film, although the dancers on stage were then doing something altogether different. At other times the film would initiate the theme and then the dancers would echo it and build it to climax which the film would again pick up. . . ."*

AS TIME GOES BY

Music by Franz Josef Haydn. Choreography by Twyla Tharp. Lighting by Jennifer Tipton. Costumes by Chester Weinberg. Assistant to Miss Tharp: Harry Berg. First presented by the City Center Joffrey Ballet at the City Center, New York, October 24, 1973. Conducted by Seymour Lipkin.

As Time Goes By is a dance ballet to wonderful music by Haydn—the third and fourth movements of the *Symphony No. 45 in F-Sharp Minor*. Mozart once said, I think, that Haydn's music had given him immense amusement and also the deepest reflections. Mozart, as usual, was right. The music here is the famous *"Farewell"* Symphony, where the players get up and leave the stage one by one. What the choreographer does with that situation, and with other plots and developments of the music, is her own special business. The critic Marcia B. Siegel described it for *Dance Magazine*: "Beatriz Rodriguez' opening solo in silence is allegro ballet laced with those odd dislocations of body parts, those big transformations with smooth, almost lazy recoveries that we've come to think of as Tharpian. As Haydn's minuet begins, five other dancers join her and they slip through a long chain of decorous attitudes and preparations that melt or click into surprise partnerships. Haydn leaves the music dangling on an unfinished cadence, and the dancers redeploy themselves to begin The Four Finales, a glorious rout in which you can just pick out elements of various overworked dance endings, exits, and climaxes, all overlapped and out of joint and meticulously mistimed. Finally, to Haydn's famous adagio, where the musicians leave one by one, Larry Grenier spins out an extraor-

* Reprinted by courtesy of *Dance Magazine*.

dinary solo in one long, sinuous, self-involved phrase of movement, while the stage fills with dancers and empties again. You can't remember where he came from and you can't imagine where he'll stop. The curtain goes down while he's still dancing.

"I'm not inclined to take the title of *As Time Goes By* too seriously—it might have come about by accident. A harried person from the Joffrey publicity department runs into the studio a week before the premiere and pleads: 'Twyla, time is going by. The papers are screaming. We've got to have a title for your ballet!' Without taking her eyes off the rehearsal, Tharp mutters: 'Okay, call it *As Time Goes By*. Now don't bother me.'

"However that was, the ballet seems more concerned with continuity than with time itself. It shows us the bridges between things, the awkward foldings that precede the beautiful unfoldings, the movements that connect rather than the poses that separate. The beginning is the end is the beginning. Amen."

Arlene Croce, dance critic of *The New Yorker*, has written of Twyla Tharp's work in the November 19, 1973, issue of that magazine:

"Twyla Tharp is the Nijinska of our time. *Deuce Coupe*, an unidealized portrait of American youth in the nineteen sixties, is her *Les Biches*, and *As Time Goes By*, an abstract fantasy about individuals against the blank canvas of a tribal society, is her *Les Noces*. Of course I'm generalizing, but not, I hope, idly. *As Time Goes By*, created this season for the Joffrey Ballet and employing an all-Joffrey cast and Haydn music, is a study of classical dancing. Its 'tribal' ethos is that of young, hard-working New York-American dancers, subspecies Joffrey, and its light-speckled fancies and serene inversions of classical principles are as far from the iron wit of *Les Noces* as the heterogeneous home-style social dances of *Deuce Coupe* are from the monolithic encounters of that Parisian salon in *Les Biches*. Nevertheless, the parallel persists between Twyla Tharp and ballet's greatest woman choreographer. I think that, like Nijinska's, Twyla Tharp's work exacts a primitive force of expression from its subject, which is classical ballet. It seems to seek out first principles and turn them over with curiosity, finding new excitement in what lies on the other side of orthodoxy. And it gains a secondary kind of raw power from what seem deliberate lapses from ballet decorum and refinement. Sometimes, a classical step is resolved with a new twist; it forms itself and then re-forms itself backward. But sometimes the step isn't all there; it seems truncated or only half-quoted; the effect is of a surgical cut, a slash at the fat body of unusable style. The negations and distortions of Nijinska's choreography cut away rhetorical flab. The turned-in toes and obsessive stiff pointwork of *Les Noces* were a radical distortion, necessary if women's feet and not simply their points were to become significant once more on the stage. In much the same way, Twyla Tharp is moving toward a new quality of plain speech in classical choreography. At times, she seems to be on the verge of creating a new style, a new humanity, for classical-ballet dancers. If she doesn't go all the way to a full enunciation of that style, that is probably because the ballet is not long enough. Time, in this ballet, goes by much too fast.

"*As Time Goes By* is in four sections, quasi-dramatic in their progression. Beginning with the Individual, it moves on to the Group, then to the Mass, and finally back to the Individual. (These designations are my own; I prefer them to the unevocative titles in the program.) The opening solo is danced by Beatriz Rodriguez in silence. It is a concise statement of the material that will be developed, a ball of string that will be unwound. We see semaphore arms, snake hips, pirouettes stopped in mid-whirl, a paroxysm of flexions in *relevé*. Rodriguez, who looked childlike in *Deuce Coupe,* is transformed again. She is monumental, like a Nijinska iron woman. Three boys and two girls join her (Adix Carman, Henry Berg, William Whitener, Eileen Brady, and Pamela Nearhoof) and the music begins—the Minuet and Trio of Haydn's *'Farewell' Symphony.* The dance that accompanies it is not one dance but six—one for each member of the sextet. All six dances go on at the same time, now linking up, now separating, and the whole moving from one tight cellular cluster to another. This sextet, which builds up the fascination and the deadpan humor of a clockwork toy, is a classical arrangement of the Tharpian group dance and typically democratic. The multifocal viewpoint makes a special event of the partnering (which keeps changing hands). It also eliminates the conventional hierarchy of the ballet ensemble. No one here is a ballerina; anyone may partner or be partnered. The sextet builds up pressure, too. The little hexagonal unit seems to become more and more confining, but the sweet musicianship of the choreography keeps the scene clear, its density unharrowing.

"The music breaks off, and one of the girls does a little walk-around in silence as new dancers enter. The Presto movement of the symphony starts. Suddenly, the stage seems to expand to unbelievable size. Dancers pour on and spread out. The broadened pattern has released us, but the tempo has stepped up the pressure, and we redouble our concentration. Now, against a complex background of moving dancers, solo variations occur; one, for Nearhoof, is galvanically funny, though at this breathless speed the laughs can't keep up with the jokes. Nor can we keep up with the ballet. There is no time to ponder the new logic of the steps—new in the way they combine close musical fit with a 'natural' loose look suited to each individual dancer; there's just time enough to enjoy it. One would like the key to that new logic; what makes it work at this tempo? Whatever it is, the result is a hyperkinesthesia that takes hold of the audience and doesn't let up until, once more, Haydn waves his wand and the dancers stroll nonchalantly away.

"The end of the piece is as Haydn would have wished it. To the Adagio finale of the *'Farewell'*—so called because the instrumentation thins out until only two violins are left—a dancer (Larry Grenier, whose attenuated lyrical style is itself a statement of slackening force) moves alone while others set about disappearing in a fashion that is unpredictable and sometimes chancy. A girl leaves, only to return a moment later. A boy lifts a girl off, turning her twice in the air, so another girl has to duck three times to avoid being hit. Ultimately, Grenier is *all* alone, having spun out the last thin skein of movement.

"*As Time Goes By* is not a pretentious enough ballet to make people feel that they have witnessed a heroic new undertaking in choreography. Its fifteen minutes are loaded with interest, but, like all of Twyla Tharp's work, the piece is peculiarly horizonless. Although each work she has made is self-contained and perfectly lucid in its own terms, each seems almost accidentally bound by the rise and fall of a curtain, and to be part of a larger continuity that exists out of time—out of the time, that is, of this ballet we have just seen. Somewhere, perhaps, there are unseen dancers unrolling the patterns and following up every implication, but we in the audience are spared their tortuous zeal. Twyla Tharp makes us feel that a ballet is nothing more than divisions of a choreographer's time. Although she understands cheap sensation and uses it well, there is no gloss, no appeal for attention, no careerism in her work. It's amusing to think of what a promoter like Diaghilev would have done with her. First, I think, he would retitle the sections of this ballet *Ariadne, Athens, The Labyrinth,* and *Theseus.* Cocteau would write the program notes and design the costumes. (The ones we have, by the Seventh Avenue designer Chester Weinberg, are examples of modest chic in shades of taupe.) Diaghilev would call the whole piece *The Minotaur,* because there's no Minotaur in it, and he would proclaim 'La Tharp' the herald of a new age. Which she is."°

AT MIDNIGHT

Music by Gustav Mahler. Choreography by Eliot Feld. Décor by Leonard Baskin. Costumes by Stanley Simmons. Lighting and scenic supervision by Jean Rosenthal. First presented by American Ballet Theatre at the New York State Theatre, Lincoln Center, December 1, 1967, with Bruce Marks, Christine Sarry, Terry Orr, Cynthia Gregory, and Eliot Feld in the principal roles. Sung by William Metcalf. Conducted by Kenneth Schermerhorn.

Danced to four of the "Five Rückert Songs" of Mahler, lyrics arranged by the composer to poems by Friedrich Rückert, *At Midnight* is named for the first of those songs. But the ballet is not based on what the songs say. They are rather an accompaniment to a danced narrative that reflects the motto of the ballet, a quotation from Thomas Hardy: "In the ill-judged execution of the well-judged plan of things, the call seldom produced the comer, the man to love rarely coincides with the hour for loving. Nature does not often say 'See!' to her poor creature when seeing can lead to a happy doing or answer 'Here!' to a body's cry of 'Where?' till the hide-and-seek has become an irksome, outworn game."

The curtain rises on a dark stage. Illumined in the back is a painting of a face in torment surrounded by two ravens. We make out on stage toward the left a crouching group of men. A half-naked boy climbs onto their bent backs, lying there for support in an hour of need in the middle of the night. He stretches out and rolls off onto the floor as the baritone begins the song "At Midnight." The men cluster around the boy, covering his face with their hands. He is lifted high and then let down to dance alone. At the end, he leaps back into the arms of the men, where he first curls up, then stretches, his arms reaching out in an agony that has not gone away.

The backdrop changes to a painting of a figure crouching in despair. To the song "Ich atmet' einen Lindenduft" (I breathed a fragrance soft and sweet), a

° "A Moment in Time," by Arlene Croce. Reprinted by permission; © 1973 The New Yorker Magazine, Inc.

boy and girl, she in flowing yellow, he in gray, move in an intense yet lyric dance. Two extraordinary catches at the end of this buoyant *pas de deux* yield to a high lift, and the boy carries the girl away as she rides on his shoulder.

A boy, lost and never a part of a group of other boys and girls who dance happily and unaware about him, laments his loneliness and tries to imitate them. The music is the song "Ich bin der Welt abhanded gekommen."

The second song is now repeated. To its music, a girl joins the couple of the second song. There is no real communication between them, however, as she dances along and the couple, preoccupied, stands and sits together. They remain after the girl leaves and seem to waken from their reverie. Four other couples join them now, as do the lone girl of the last song and the boy of the third. Here, too, each of the single figures is so engrossed in trouble and separation that they have no eyes for each other. Amidst all these persons there is no new personal contact. They remain on stage as the song ends, alone as we first saw them.

NOTES   Anna Kisselgoff of the New York *Times* has called *At Midnight* a "landmark ballet, poetic in its depth but accessible to everyone on its theatric level." Reviewing the ballet in the *Dancing Times*, the critic P. W. Manchester wrote that Eliot Feld's "first ballet, *Harbinger*, premièred in the 1967 spring season, indicated that a new talent had arrived. *At Midnight* more than confirmed the promise of *Harbinger*. Feld has set it to four of Gustav Mahler's songs. The first one provides the title for the ballet and is also the finest part of the work. It is a study in man's aloneness. The choreography, marvelously interpreted by Bruce Marks, aches with the doubts and loneliness of the fears that come only in sleeplessness. The second song . . . is a *pas de deux* for young lovers, done with exquisite, unsentimental sweetness by Christine Sarry and Terry Orr. . . . *At Midnight* is both moving and masterly. And . . . Feld is entering on his career as a choreographer while he is also just beginning his best years as a dancer. . . . His closeness to his company as colleague as well as choreographer may well be a major factor in what everyone is hoping will truly be a new era for American Ballet Theatre, one in which it will at long last have its own choreographer, creating for its particular talents, moulding its special and unique style."

Writing of the première in the *Jersey Journal*, the critic Patrick O'Connor said: "It is a unique privilege to be present at the first presentation of a great American work of art. But that's what happened to me last night at the American Ballet Theatre. In truth, there's no such thing as an American work of art. There are only works of art sometimes, too rarely, I'm afraid, composed, put together, by an American. Last night it was *At Midnight* by Eliot Feld. I won't say choreographed. It seemed much more than a dance composition. Feld is involved in what Doris Humphrey once called the art of making dances.

"Movement is, of course, the essential element but so is the painter's brush, the dynamics of stillness, the sacrifice of the mass, the crucifixion, the resurrection, the healing power of love. The whole piece was bathed in love and so was the audience; they knew it, felt it and were grateful.

"It seems almost profane to talk about the dancing. It wasn't dancing; it was another kind of activity—exalted movement. Cynthia Gregory in pentecostal lavender made one weep, and Christine Sarry in pentecostal yellow sustains stillness miraculously. She also danced brilliantly. Bruce Marks—as the Christ figure?—gave a shattering performance. Feld the dancer served Feld the choreographer like a ministering angel. A rare privilege, an historic occasion, something to tell my grandchildren."

Reviewing a 1975 performance by the Eliot Feld Ballet with Lawrence Rhodes, the English critic John Percival wrote in *Dance and Dancers:* "Rhodes, perhaps the greatest of American male dancers today, for some reason has never settled down with one of the major companies, and nowadays combines membership in Feld's company and the Pennsylvania Ballet. He has a slight, supple physique and the ability to make every movement eloquent. *The Consort* shows him to be capable of a show-off solo, but a role like the central figure of *At Midnight* suits him even better . . . He gives it great bitterness."

AUREOLE

Music by George Frederick Handel. Choreography by Paul Taylor. Lighting by Thomas Skelton. First presented by the Paul Taylor Dance Company at Connecticut College, New London, Connecticut, August 4, 1962.

A dance work that has happily entered the repertory of the Royal Danish Ballet and been seen in presentations by Paul Taylor's ensemble with Rudolf Nureyev, *Aureole* has proved itself a most distinguished work in the contemporary repertoire. Paul Taylor, regarded by Clive Barnes as "one of the most talented and innovative choreographers this country has ever produced," has danced it with his own company at home and abroad. It was my pleasure some years ago to work with Paul Taylor in the New York City Ballet's *Episodes.*

Aureole is a dance for five—two boys and three girls. Its content is a most original response to Handel's lyric and expressive score (the *Concerto Grosso in G* and the fourth movement of *Alexander's Feast*).

BACH SONATA

Music by Johann Sebastian Bach. Choreography by Maurice Béiart. First presented by the Ballet of the Twentieth Century, 1970, with Suzanne Farrell and Jorge Donn. First presented in the United States by the same ensemble at the Brooklyn Academy of Music, New York, January 29, 1971, with the same principals.

A *pas de deux* set to Bach's *Sonata No. 5 for Violin and Harpsichord,* and designed to show the artistry of the two principals, *Bach Sonata* is not the usual display piece for the ballerina and her partner. Instead, it poses the problem of how an infatuated boy can encircle and win a girl who appears to be indifferent to everything he does.

LE BAISER DE LA FÉE (The Fairy's Kiss)

Ballet-allegory in four scenes. Music and book by Igor Stravinsky. Choreography by George Balanchine. Scenery and costumes by Alicia Halicka. First presented by the American Ballet at the Metropolitan Opera House, New York, April 27, 1937, with Gisella Caccialanza as the Bride, William Dollar as the Bridegroom, and Kathryn Mullowney as the Fairy.

Stravinsky dedicated this ballet "to the memory of Peter Tchaikovsky . . . It was his Muse (like our Fairy heroine) whose fatal kiss, imprinted at birth, made itself felt in all the work of that great artist, and eventually led him to immortality. Thereby does our ballet (with a similar tale) become an allegory." The story of the ballet is derived from a tale by Hans Christian Andersen—"The Ice Maiden." Stravinsky selected elements from this long and beautiful fairy tale to compose his scenario. Here, the Ice Maiden comes down from the sky to claim for her own a hapless youth. When he is a child, abandoned in the snow, the fairy kisses the boy coldly with a fatal kiss that seals his eternal devotion to her. The babe becomes a man and, with no recollection of the fairy's power over him, is engaged to be married. The Ice Maiden returns to fulfill the prophecy of her kiss and to carry him away to the ends of the earth.

FIRST TABLEAU: PROLOGUE—THE SNOWSTORM The curtain rises soon after the orchestra has begun to play softly a lilting lullaby. The scene is deserted, barely lit. Snow begins to fall. A woman enters, carrying a child. She dances across the stage, her hood flowing behind her. She lifts the child in her arms lovingly and covers it with her cape. At first she does not appear to be alarmed at the snow, but the lullaby to which she dances changes to an ominous melody presaging a severe storm and the woman is frightened for her child. She covers it more carefully, holds it close to her breast, and continues on her way. Winds leap across the stage from right and left, passing close to her, then circling about her as if to enclose her with their freezing force. She cowers in terror. Myriad snowflakes enter behind her, hover over her, and leave her shivering on the ground. The piercing winds return, their frigid capes streaming from their shoulders; the snowflakes re-enter and surround the mother. She rises helplessly and attempts to flee, but the snowflakes divide into groups and block her escape. The music increases its ominous force. The snowflakes force her to the front and drown her with freezing snow. As the mother cowers beneath them, she thinks only of her child. She dies. The winds remove her body, and the child is abandoned to the snowflakes, who pass over the pathetic bundle as they vanish.

The winds pull in a swift white sleigh that brings onto the scene a beautiful fairy, the Ice Maiden. A spotlight catches her imposing figure. She stands in statuesque pose, holding high a wand of ice; her noble head is crowned with a star of white jewels; her dress is white, long, and full. She steps down from the sleigh, presents her wand to her escorts, and directs them away. Immediately she begins to dance. Each one of her open, flowing movements is imitated by a figure in black, who stands in the distance like a shadow to remind us that the beauty of the fairy is bewitching. The fairy dances close to the child. She stands over him; her flowing white dress seems to cover him as she turns brilliantly on point. She bends over the child, reaches out, draws him close to her face. She kisses him tenderly, yet coldly, and places the child on the ground. Now that she has sealed the fate of the helpless child, the fairy dances away slowly on point. Her shadow disappears with her.

The scene darkens. A peasant enters, carrying a lantern. He is followed by a group of mountain climbers, who help him as he seeks to recover the lost child. The music imitates their anxieties. At last one of the men sees the small bundle in the snow. The light is brought nearer, and the other men hold him as he reaches down and picks up the child while the orchestra sounds climactic chords of pathos. The scene blacks out as they hurry off.

SECOND TABLEAU: THE VILLAGE FESTIVAL   Twenty years have passed. Befriended by peasants, the child has grown up to become the most popular young man in the village. He is to be married soon to the miller's daughter.

After a brief orchestral interlude, the lights come up on a colorful mountain scene overhung with fir trees; snow-capped peaks are seen in the distance. Boys and girls of the village dressed in gay Swiss costumes stand in a wide circle dancing a folk measure to a rhythmic, holiday tune. A group of boys then move to the center, where they are surrounded by the smiling girls. They all gather behind the village bandsmen and parade around the stage.

A high-spirited boy carrying a gun runs into the crowd. This is the bridegroom. Everyone welcomes him, particularly the girls, and it is clear that he has the affections of them all. He dances forward with two of the girls to the light rhythm of the music, which soon becomes strong and robust. Everyone joins them in their youthful dance. When the dance is over, the young man calls one of his friends and directs him to shoot at a distant target. The boy aims and misses. Another boy tries and misses. The bridegroom seizes his gun, shoots, and hits the target, to the delight of the girls, who playfully congratulate him.

The bride enters, surrounded by six of her bridesmaids. She dances briefly before the company, and then the boy joins her for a happy duet that reflects their mutual joy. Several of the village girls start a yodeling contest, which is interrupted for a final festival dance by the bride, the bridegroom, and all their friends. The peasants encircle the bride and bridegroom and begin to leave the stage. The bride goes off with her friends. The boy seems to depart with the rest, but as the stage empties, we see that he has remained. He sits on the ground in quiet meditation. One of his friends tries to persuade him to continue with the celebration, but the boy refuses. He is alone.

On the right a beautiful gypsy enters. She is dressed in black and white. The boy does not notice her as he looks at the ground thoughtfully. The gypsy crosses the stage in a determined stride, her arms gripped at her sides. The jewel she wears on her forehead catches the light for an instant; her face is a frigid mask. It is the face of the Ice Maiden, who has disguised herself to discover the boy. She approaches him, circles him several times, as if to be sure of his identity, then sits down close beside him and looks up straight into his face. The orchestra sounds a sharp chord; she grips his wrist fiercely and examines his open palm to foretell the fate she herself has planned for him.

The boy is completely passive to the strange gypsy fortuneteller. His body falls back as she circles his hand before her savagely. She rises, throws his hand away from her in a gesture of triumphant recognition, and dances before him. The boy watches as she steps with fascinating, malevolent vigor, flinging her loose black hair over her face. He responds to her exotic dynamism and comes to her. He holds the gypsy obediently while she walks forward as if she were driving her points into the ground. Now they cross the stage to the right, the gypsy whirling rapidly, the boy following and falling at her feet as she extends her leg to lash the air above him. He rises to embrace her, but she shoves him away contemptuously, then seizes him violently and passionately. The boy is obedient to her every gesture as he realizes her power to fulfill his fortune. She turns him around, stands in back of him, points her arm forward over his shoulder, and pushes him in its direction. The boy does not resist; he walks in a dream as the gypsy directs him toward his destiny. Blackout.

THIRD TABLEAU: INSIDE THE MILL   A group of peasant girls are arranged in an open triangular tableau as the lights illuminate the interior of the bride's home. The rough wood walls are decorated with wreaths; candles hang low from the ceiling; there are two large windows at the back. The scene is framed with old Swiss lace. The day of the wedding is approaching, and all of the bride's friends have gathered to prepare for the occasion. The peasant girls dance gaily to a blithe melody, led by a girl in a bright yellow skirt, whose energy and enthusiasm are expressed in precise, rapid steps.

The bride enters and dances in front of the group. Dressed all in white, she wears a small wreath of white flowers in her hair. The girls in back of her imitate her movements. The bride walks back to welcome her friends; some of them form a circle around her. She bows, then bows to another group that surrounds her. She blows kisses to them all and exits.

The peasant girls dance again; the bride returns just before the music ends and she stands in the center of a beautifully posed group her friends form about her. The girls run off and leave the bride alone. The orchestra begins to play quietly a lovely, sweeping melody. The bride circles the room, goes to the window, looks out expectantly, but sees nothing. She is waiting for the bridegroom. She walks over to the other window, her back turned to the room. The bridegroom enters. The bride does not see him. He circles the room looking for her. She moves away from the window as if she felt his presence, but does not find him, for the boy has walked behind her. Both stand in the center of the room, their arms held out, seeking. Their backs almost touch and they move away in opposite directions to circle the room again. The boy kneels. The girl sees him, runs up behind him softly, and leans over his shoulder to welcome him playfully. He rises. Their *pas de deux* begins.

The couple cross the front of the stage together, extending their arms to the side in rhythm to the flow of the music. The bride falls back in the boy's arms. The music changes, as a clarinet states the theme of their adagio. The boy holds the girl about the waist as she dances quickly but softly, like a sylph. He lifts her as they move together, and her points continue their dance in the air. The bride kneels and watches the boy dance. Then both circle the stage. The girl beckons to him and whispers something. They stand together in the center of the stage. They bow low to each other. The boy holds out his hand and, as the orchestra states the climax of the theme, the girl takes his hand and poses in a low, deep arabesque. She rises and falls back against his arm. He raises her off the floor with low lifts in which the girl bends her knees softly. He holds her under her arms, and the girl sits on his knee, smiling happily, her legs extended before her.

The bridegroom stands aside and watches the girl dance alone to a fresh, piquant theme. She dances flirtatiously, flouncing her skirt high. She mimes her intense happiness, feigning intoxication from her joy. The black shadow of the Ice Maiden suddenly appears before her and points menacingly. The boy does not see the apparition, who disappears before the girl has rushed backward into his arms. The bride looks toward the vanished shadow and moves her hand in front of her face in innocent, unbelieving astonishment.

A pounding drum announces a sharp, accelerating dance melody. The peasant girls re-enter to take up its rhythm, and the bride and bridegroom leave the stage. The bridegroom returns to dance a short, brilliant variation. He is followed by the bride, who comes down the stage diagonally, dancing smartly on one point, extending her other leg straight out to the side with every step. She finishes her dance with a series of rapid turns that delight the whole company, then runs across the stage at full speed toward the bridegroom, who catches her daringly in midair.

The couple leave the stage to the dancing peasants for a moment, then return to join them in a final ensemble. At its conclusion one of the girls brings out the bride's veil and throws it playfully over her head. The girls gather about the bride and separate the two lovers. The bride leaves the stage with her playful friends. The bridegroom remains alone. The light dims.

The bridegroom turns rapidly; as he comes out of his spin, he sees on the right a girl dressed in white, her head and shoulders covered with a long white veil. As he recognizes his fiancée, he seems also to be remembering slowly and with effort that he must have known her like this always—tall, beautiful, and in white. He moves toward her, fascinated by his illusory recollection and the new loveliness she has for him. The girl does not move; she remains motionless, drawing the boy toward her with mysterious and bewitching magnetism. He stands in front of her, reaches around her strongly, and holds her tightly by the waist, his face buried in the frigid whiteness of her veil. Thus holding her, he lifts her feet off the floor; her body arches back, and he carries her walking slowly backward. Now the orchestra states fully but quietly the melody of Tchaikovsky's "None But the Lonely Heart," which was suggested softly at the beginning of the scene.

The boy lets the girl down gently and falls helpless against her. His limp body falls to the floor at her feet. The girl bows over him, opens her arms wide, takes his hand, and pulls him up as she circles about him. They move a short distance together; then the boy kneels. He stretches his arms back; the girl takes his hands. He crawls forward. The girl stands against his back, her body in arabesque, her face falling over against his. Her white veil envelops his face in a glacier of tenderness. The tragic melody, now at its height, accompanies them as they move across the stage.

The boy falls forward on the ground. The girl bends down and covers him with her veil. He rises under it, throws the veil back over her head, and stands transfixed as he beholds her face—the face of the Ice Maiden and gypsy in one. The Ice Maiden stands regally as we saw her in the first scene, her lovely, noble head crowned with a star of shimmering crystals. The boy backs away from her in terror at his recognition, then draws close to her again in helpless, passionate longing. He rests his head on her breast. The Ice Maiden stands rigid, head back, her arms stretched out behind her. Slowly she lifts her arms and touches the boy's head with a retarded and considered gesture that seems to freeze the gentleness of her touch and turn him to ice. Now she moves her hand down the boy's trembling arm, takes his hand, and leads him away. The scene blacks out.

FOURTH TABLEAU: EPILOGUE   The lights come up on the same scene. The bride enters the room, searching for her fiancé. She circles the stage, looks out of the windows from which she has so often seen him come to the mill. He is nowhere to be found. She waves her veil over her head sadly and begins to despair. Then suddenly, in the back, the wall of the room disappears and the bride beholds in the sky a scene that makes her tremble. High up, far away in the distance, the Ice Maiden sits in the cold blue winter sky holding out her arms to the bridegroom, who strives to reach her. He stretches out his arms to the magical fairy, who seems to enfold him. They rise together in the sky. The bride kneels and, weeping, waves her wedding veil in farewell.

NOTES   At the end of 1927, when he was finishing the music of *Apollo*, Igor Stravinsky was asked by Madame Ida Rubinstein to compose a ballet for her. Bronislava Nijinska was to be the choreographer, Alexandre Benois the designer. Stravinsky writes, in his autobiography: "The idea was that I should compose something inspired by the music of Tchaikovsky. My well-known fondness for this composer, and, still more, the fact that November, 1928, the time fixed for the performance, would mark the thirty-fifth anniversary of his death, induced me to accept the offer. It would give me an opportunity of paying my heartfelt homage to Tchaikovsky's wonderful talent.

"As I was free to choose both the subject and scenario of the ballet, I began to search for them, in view of the characteristic trend of Tchaikovsky's music, in the literature of the nineteenth century. With that aim, I turned to a great poet with a gentle, sensitive soul whose imaginative mind was wonderfully akin to that of the musician. I refer to Hans Christian Andersen, with whom in this respect Tchaikovsky had so much in common. To recall *The Sleeping Beauty, The Nutcracker, Swan Lake, Pique Dame,* and many pieces of his symphonic work is enough to show the extent of his fondness for the fantastic.

"In turning over the pages of Andersen, with which I was fairly familiar, I came across a story which I had completely forgotten that struck me as being the very thing for the idea which I wanted to express. It was the very beautiful story known to us as the 'Ice Maiden.' I chose that as my theme and worked out the story on the following lines. A fairy imprints her magic kiss on a child at birth and parts it from its mother. Twenty years later, when the youth has attained the very zenith of his good fortune, she repeats the fatal kiss and carries him off to live in supreme happiness with her ever afterwards. As my object was to commemorate the work of Tchaikovsky, this subject seemed to me to be particularly appropriate as an allegory, the Muse having similarly branded Tchaikovsky with her fatal kiss, and the magic imprint has made itself felt in all the musical creations of this great artist.

"Although I gave full liberty to painter and choreographer in the staging of my composition, my innermost desire was that it should be presented in classical form, after the manner of *Apollo*. I pictured all the fantastic roles as danced in white ballet-skirts, and the rustic scenes as taking place in a Swiss landscape . . ."

The ballet was performed for the first time November 27, 1928, at the Opera, Paris, with the composer conducting. It was performed in other European capitals and, in 1933, at the Colón Theatre in Buenos Aires. November 26, 1935, Frederick Ashton choreographed a new version of the ballet for the Sadler's Wells Ballet. This version, designed by Sophie Fedorovitch, featured Pearl Argyle, Harold Turner, and Margot Fonteyn—her first created role. Frederick Ashton, interestingly enough, had danced in the original Nijinska production. I staged the ballet in 1937 for the American Ballet's Stravinsky Festival in New York.

Certain parts of the story of the ballet are hard to make clear on the stage. At the beginning of the Second Tableau, for example, how is the audience to know that the bridegroom is the child of the Prologue? Believing that everything must be clear on the stage, I have tried to indicate this in a number of ways in different revivals of the ballet, as I have also endeavored to make it obvious that the gypsy is, in reality, the fairy disguised. The finale of the ballet also presents a mechanical difficulty. Ideally, the ending should have a magical effect: the fairy should appear to be suspended and the bridegroom, just below her, must seem to be swimming through space, as it were, to reach her. The Ice Maiden drags the boy down into the lake with her, and in recent revivals I have tried to indicate that the two figures are moving together in the water, but limited audience visibility of the back of the stage has prevented this plan from attaining real success. There is no question but that the final Tableau requires a stage high and deep for the achievement of full illusion.

The Fairy's Kiss has been revived twice by the Ballet Russe de Monte Carlo: on April 10, 1940, at the Metropolitan Opera House, with a cast headed by Alexandra Danilova as the bride, André Eglevsky as the bridegroom, and Mia Slavenska as the fairy; and on February 17, 1946, at the City Center, New York, with Alexandra Danilova, Frederic Franklin, and Maria Tallchief. It was staged for the Opéra, Paris, July 2, 1947, when Tamara

Toumanova, Alexandre Kaliujny, and Maria Tallchief took the principal roles. At its revival by the New York City Ballet November 28, 1950, the leading roles were danced by Tanaquil LeClercq, Nicholas Magallanes, and Maria Tallchief.

Although his version of the ballet is unfortunately unknown in the United States, Sir Frederick Ashton choreographed Le Baiser de la Fée for the Sadler's Wells Ballet at the Sadler's Wells Theatre, London, November 26, 1935. The production was designed by Sophie Fedorovitch and the leading dancers were Pearl Argyle, Margot Fonteyn, and Harold Turner. An excerpt from this ballet, a pas de deux, was performed at the Royal Opera House, Covent Garden, in July 1970, at the Gala Performance in Ashton's honor.

The Royal Ballet revived Le Baiser de la Fée in a new version by Kenneth MacMillan at the Royal Opera House, Covent Garden, April 12, 1960, with Svetlana Beriosova, Donald MacLeary, and Lynn Seymour in the principal roles. This production, designed by Kenneth Rowell, was introduced to the United States by the Royal Ballet at the Metropolitan Opera House, New York, September 27, 1960, with the same principals.

In 1972, for the New York City Ballet's Stravinsky Festival, our celebration of the composer's ninetieth birthday, I arranged new dances for music from this ballet under the title Divertimento from Le Baiser de la Fée. This was based on Stravinsky's symphonic suite from the ballet, which uses just under half the score and which he called Divertimento. The dances were new ones, though some remembered gestures and movements were retained as I wished. The piece was presented without a setting and without a story line, as a dance ballet, for the first time on June 21, 1972, at the New York State Theatre, with lighting by Ronald Bates. Robert Irving was the conductor and the leading roles were danced by Patricia McBride, Helgi Tomasson, Bettijane Sills and Carol Sumner.

Writing about the staging of the Divertimento for the Stravinsky Festival in The Nation, Nancy Goldner said: "One of my favorite moments was a sequence of jumps for Helgi Tomasson in the Divertimento from Le Baiser de la Fée. All the sequence amounted to was a variation on something very commonplace: a preparatory sliding step with a little spring in it, called a glissade, followed by a moving jump in which one leg is thrown forward and the other backward. Usually, after the glissade the weight is on the front foot. This gives the dancer the momentum to jump off the floor on the front foot, with the back one swinging forward and up into the jump. His back is straight and he faces the line of direction. But that is not what Balanchine had Tomasson do. Instead of springing naturally off the front foot, he jumps off the back foot. Instead of facing the line of direction, his whole body is almost at right angles to it. He does these jumps in a circle, leading with the 'wrong' foot and at the 'wrong' angle. The effect is that of a car skidding around a corner on its outside wheels. Tomasson was so skimming and elegant in this unnatural deployment of momentum and balance that he seemed like those flying saucers that reportedly can veer at a right angle without slowing down."

The critic Anna Kisselgoff, reviewing a performance in the New York Times in 1974, said: "In Helgi Tomasson, the New York City Ballet has one of the best classical male dancers in the world today. No wonder then that George Balanchine chose him as the dancer upon whom to create one of the most unusual and poetic male solos in the Balanchine repertory.

"Saturday night at the New York State Theater, Mr. Tomasson's special combination of elegance and virtuosity was evident again in that solo, in the short ballet entitled *Divertimento from 'Le Baiser de la Fée,'* choreographed by Mr. Balanchine for the 1972 Stravinsky Festival . . . Perhaps it might be wiser to forget the now-discarded story line for the first Balanchine version of *The Fairy's Kiss* (the ballet's English title), and to view the current divertissement as a plotless pure-dance excerpt. Yet the fact that Stravinsky's original scenario had a hero and not a heroine as the protagonist might help explain why the choreography for the male dancer tends to overshadow the ballerina's.

"In this bright, joyful and tender *pas de deux,* backed by an ensemble, Mr. Balanchine has reserved the most inventive sequences for Mr. Tomasson. The man's variation, with its unexpected changes of direction, suggestions of swoons and a series of jumps followed by falls to the knee, appears totally original. In the coda, the extraordinary way Mr. Tomasson seems to be off balance when he is not is a tribute to both the imagination of the choreographer and the rock-firm technique of the dancer. At the same time, Mr. Tomasson is one of dance's most finished classic stylists."

Music by Igor Stravinsky and Peter Ilyich Tchaikovsky. Choreography and book by John Neumeier. Costumes and sets by Jürgen Rose. Lighting by Jennifer Tipton. First presented by the Frankfurt Ballet in 1974. First presented in the United States by American Ballet Theatre at the New York State Theatre, Lincoln Center, in 1975.

The choreographer John Neumeier has devised a new libretto, with a flashback technique, for his ballet on this theme. In addition to Stravinsky's score he uses two short works of Tchaikovsky in his score: the "Feuillet d'Album," Op. 19, No. 3, and "None But the Lonely Heart," Op. 6, No. 6—a principal element, of course, in Stravinsky's.

The action of the ballet follows this libretto:

PROLOGUE: THE WEDDING CELEBRATION   The marriage of Rudi and Babette is being celebrated at a party with their friends. Among the guests is a stranger who sings a lovely, melancholy song, at the end of which she gives Rudi a kiss. Her song, and the kiss, awaken in him the memory of an old desire, as intangible but as haunting as perfume. With the memory, Rudi feels an inexpressible yearning, disturbing the happiness he hopes to find with Babette.

SCENE ONE: REMEMBRANCE (BALLET BLANC)   Rudi's *Sehnsucht* (his subconscious yearning self) takes him back to his childhood and the memory of an experience. In a clear, white world, Rudi, as the child he once was, is entranced by the vision of beautiful dancing creatures. One of these, the most dazzling of all, gives the boy a kiss, then disappears among the others. Rudi searches in vain for her, in an agony of love and longing that will haunt his life.

SCENE TWO: THE WEDDING CELEBRATION CONTINUES Rudi realizes that the mysterious singer is the same beautiful creature from the pure, white world of his childhood for whom he has searched his entire life. Rudi's longing once more takes him in search of her.

SCENE THREE: IN THE GARDEN Stealing away from the party, Babette finds Rudi in the garden, where she again expresses her love for him. They are interrupted by the departing guests, making their adieux. Together again, Rudi turns to Babette, feeling in her presence the strength of a love great enough to overcome his yearning for the unattainable. Reassured, Babette re-enters the house to prepare herself for their wedding night.

SCENE FOUR: TOWARD ETERNITY Alone in the garden, Rudi's *Sehnsucht* grows stronger and stronger, overpowering Rudi's will . . . It compels him to obey the unearthly summons of the Fairy. Rudi goes in quest of his glorious tormentress, leaving Babette to wait in vain for his return.

BALLADE

Dramatic ballet in one act. Music by Claude Debussy. Choreography by Jerome Robbins. Scenery and costumes by Boris Aronson. Costumes executed by Karinska. Lighting by Jean Rosenthal. First presented by the New York City Ballet at the City Center, New York, February 14, 1952, with Tanaquil LeClercq, Janet Reed, Nora Kaye, Roy Tobias, Robert Barnett, Louis Johnson, John Mandia, and Brooks Jackson.

This ballet's program note reminds us that a *ballade* (or *ballad*) is "a musical composition of poetic character . . . a dancing song, a poem of unknown authorship which recounts a legendary or traditional event and passes from one generation to another." The legendary or traditional event in the ballet is enacted by the legendary and traditional characters Harlequin, Columbine, and Pierrot, who find themselves in a band of other, more modern, theatrical characters. The music for *Ballade* is Debussy's flute solo *Syrinx* and the same composer's *Six Antique Epigraphs*, orchestrated by Ernest Ansermet.

Snow is falling on a quiet scene as the curtain rises. Seven people lie asleep in chairs that are grouped about the stage. In the back is a drop curtain that depicts the sun and moon surrounded by clouds of ice. The people take no notice of the snow; their bodies lie limply in the chairs, and they seem like so many rag dolls.

To the quiet music of a flute, a strolling musician enters, carrying balloons. The snow stops falling. Slowly he goes to each of the chairs and at each one he leaves a balloon. When he has distributed balloons to all seven, he watches as the hands that hold them are drawn mysteriously upward. Gradually all the figures waken and rise toward their balloons. They bow to the strolling player and look up at the balloons he has left them as he leaves the scene.

One of the girls steps out. She is dressed in Harlequin's traditional costume of varicolored diamond patches. Slowly she turns; the others move the chairs back and run about the stage with their balloons. Now they tie the balloons to the chairs and come forward to dance in a semicircle.

The rest of the group retire as three boys dance forward rapidly and, like clowns and tumbling artists, execute a rushing, circusy number. When they finish, the girl dressed as Harlequin comes forward. She reaches down, takes her foot in her hand, brings it around behind her back, and turns. Now she somersaults and her movements take on an angular quality. As the music becomes faster, she leaps wildly, circles the stage, revolves in bouncing turns, and goes back to her chair.

A girl in pink, her cheeks spotted with circles of bright red rouge, begins to dance. This is Columbine. A boy, also dressed in pink, kisses her hand. He kneels before her as she begins to dance to quick, subtle music. The girl is indifferent to the boy and wanders almost accidentally into his arms. He tries to get some reaction as he declares his love, but the girl, like a rag doll, looks at him stupidly. Finally he embraces her and kisses her throat. The girl reaches into her dress to find her heart and brings out a handful of sawdust. The astonished youth retires, and the girl sits on the floor at the left.

Now a girl representing Pierrot takes the center of the stage briefly. The melody sounds hauntingly. Pierrot collapses and dies. Two boys take up her loose, disjointed body and carry her. The others grieve. Pierrot is given a balloon and slowly she rises. She wonders at the balloon's magical force in bringing her to life again. The strange figures watch breathlessly as she ponders this mystery and makes a decision. The music stops. Pierrot stares up at the balloon, then deliberately allows it to slip through her fingers. In stunned silence her fellow actors imagine that she has sacrificed her life. Everyone watches as the balloon disappears overhead.

Forgetful of Pierrot's sacrifice, the whole troupe dances a happy ensemble. Suddenly the lights begin to go down. The strolling musician returns, and the players return to their chairs. As he takes their balloons away, each collapses and becomes lifeless again. The strolling musician stares at Pierrot, who stands alone without a balloon. Slowly he leaves the scene. Pierrot looks after him for a moment, then goes to each of the chairs, trying to waken their occupants. She cannot stir them. Snow begins to fall again, and the curtain descends as Pierrot, sad that she alone possesses a life outside the magic of the theatre, stares off into the distance.

BALLET IMPERIAL (TCHAIKOVSKY CONCERTO NO. 2)

Classic ballet in three movements. Music by Peter Ilyich Tchaikovsky. Choreography by George Balanchine. Setting and costumes by Mstislav Dobou-

jinsky. First presented by the American Ballet at the Hunter College Play-house, New York, May 27, 1941, with Marie-Jeanne, Gisella Caccialanza, and William Dollar in the principal roles. Revived by the Ballet Russe de Monte Carlo at the City Center, New York, February 20, 1945, with Mary Ellen Moylan, Maria Tallchief, and Nicholas Magallanes in the leading roles. Revived by the Sadler's Wells Ballet at the Royal Opera House, London, April 5, 1950, with scenery and costumes by Eugene Berman and a cast headed by Margot Fonteyn, Michael Somes, and Beryl Grey. Revived by the Ballet of La Scala, Milan, with scenery and costumes by Eugene Ber-man, March 25, 1952, with Olga Amati, Gilda Maiocchi, and Giulio Peru-gini in the principal roles.

Great ballets of the past are directly associated with great composers of the past. *The Sleeping Beauty,* the masterwork of the great nineteenth-century choreographer Marius Petipa, survives not only for its dancing, but also for its music. Petipa created more than sixty full-length ballets during a half century of work as ballet master at the Imperial Russian Theatre. Few of these works are performed today. This is not because the dancing in these ballets was not good; it is because their music was not good enough to inspire the dancing to new heights. Audiences have wished to forget the bad music and, conse-quently, the dances that went with it.

Since the death of Petipa, in 1910, much has happened to the classical dancing he developed into so high a form in his famous ballets. The basic vo-cabulary is the same, but we have added new words, new phrases; classical dancing today is much more difficult, more complex, more intricate, more de-manding. Oftentimes people are inclined to think that the great dancers of the past were incomparable and that dancers today are as nothing beside them. This is not true. The great dancers of the past were incomparable for what they did. Today we do something else.

Ballet Imperial is a contemporary tribute to Petipa, "the father of the classic ballet," and to Tchaikovsky, his greatest composer. The ballet is set to Tchai-kovsky's *Piano Concerto No. 2 in G.* It is a dance ballet and has no story.

FIRST MOVEMENT: ALLEGRO BRILLANTE   The orchestra and piano introduce the opening theme, a brilliant and noble melody. The piano develops this theme alone, and a quick rush on the strings signals the second theme. The curtain rises. Eight couples in classical costume stand in a diagonal, the boys facing the girls some distance apart. They begin to dance. The stage frame is draped with blue velvet trimmed with ermine. We are in the room of a palace. In contrast to this sumptuous warmth, in the distance there is a view of the snow-covered Fortress of Peter and Paul. The royal gates that direct our eyes to this view are embellished with the imperial eagle. The dancing is quick and formal, bright and dignified.

Eight girls join the eight couples, and after them comes a soloist, a beautiful young girl who prepares the stage for the ballerina. The ballerina enters, dances to a piano cadenza, and by her loveliness in performance convinces us that we are watching a queen among dancers. At first she dances alone, finishing her variation in open rapid turns that encircle the stage. The music is softer, has now a stately romantic quality, and the ballerina dances with a cavalier. Now the ballerina and the *corps de ballet* leave the stage and the soloist performs a *pas de trois* with two boys. The second theme has returned with the same signal from the strings, it has merged with the first, and the music gathers to a flourishing finish. The ballerina and the *corps de ballet* dance to this music with young, regal splendor, and the movement is over.

SECOND MOVEMENT: ANDANTE NON TROPPO   After a brief introduction, the piano plays alone the principal theme. This is music of sentiment, pathos, and high feeling—slow, almost retarded, in its romantic commitment. A solo violin plays the theme accompanied by the piano. The ballerina enters with her cavalier. Eight girls form a maze through which the ballerina and her partner move. Now she and her partner are lovers. They appear to be happy, but then the man pleads with her intently and we understand that their love is not perfect. But soon the ballerina responds to her lover's plea and dances with tender intimacy. The *corps de ballet* dance protectingly around the couple and lead them gently into the wings.

THIRD MOVEMENT: ALLEGRO CON FUOCO   The music is gay and assertive with a fiery brightness and crispness. The ballerina is carried in high on the shoulders of her partner. He sets her down softly, and she dances with ravishing quickness to the brilliant music. She and her partner leave the stage for a moment to the *corps de ballet,* but return again and again to lead the dancing. The ballerina's partner dances a variation, the soloist is seen briefly leading the crowded stage of dancers, and the ballerina comes back to finish with her court the final, electric flourish of ensemble movement.

NOTES   *Ballet Imperial* has been danced by a number of companies in recent years. The Royal Ballet mounted a new version, in a setting by Carl Toms, October 18, 1963, and the New York City Ballet on May 19, 1964, presented its own production, staged by Frederic Franklin. Its scenery by Rouben Ter-Arutunian and costumes by Karinska suggests the splendors of the Imperial capital in Russia, Peter the Great's "Window on the West," the city of canals and painted stucco that recalls the heroic grandeur of Italy. In the background, across the broad Neva River, framed by the rostral columns celebrating Russian naval supremacy, is the lancet spire of the Peter-Paul fortress. The azure draperies reflect the color of the Maryinsky Theatre of Opera and Ballet for which Tchaikovsky composed his great theatrical scores.

On January 12, 1973, with its name changed to *Tchaikovsky Concerto No. 2,* the ballet was presented in a new version by the New York City Ballet at the New York State Theatre, Lincoln Center. Patricia McBride, Peter Martins, and Colleen Neary were the principals. The setting was a plain cyclorama and the costumes much simplified. So also was the Second Movement, where the pantomime of the cavalier was eliminated. I made these changes because the times have changed since the ballet was first done. Our audiences these days don't require elaborate costumes and decoration in a ballet, and rightly so. We see dancing better than we used to and prefer to see it directly, unencumbered. The music and the dancing themselves are enough here, I hope, to form illusions that scenery and costumes only made specific.

BALLET SCHOOL

Music by Liadvov, Shostakovich, and Glazunov. Choreography by Asaf Messerer. First presented by the Bolshoi Ballet at the Metropolitan Opera House, New York, September 17, 1962.

This work originated from a collection of dances presented by pupils of the Bolshoi Ballet School upon their graduation. It shows in compressed form the years of training and work required to become a classical dancer. The ballet was made by the ballet master at the Bolshoi, Asaf Messerer, who has said of his work: "I endeavored to show to the audiences the richness of the Russian classical school and give some insight into the training of its dancers—from the initial steps of the child pupils to the mature masters of ballet. I tried to avoid brilliance of technique as an end in itself and did not wish to turn the performance into a mere display of the skill of the soloists. I aimed also at introducing to the public many of our promising and gifted dancers. Thus, not only such stars as Maya Plisetskaya and Fadeyechev dance in it, but some of the younger members of the company, among them Nina Sorokina, Natalia Bessmertnova, and Mikhail Lavrovsky."

Before the leaps and the pirouettes lie long hours of systematic practice at the *barre*. Before the child is given exercises in the center of the classroom, she must be taught the five basic positions at the *barre*. *Rond de jambe, arabesque, grands battements*, each *pas* is learned under the discerning and exacting eye of the ballet master. The children learn the small leaps, the *changement de pieds*, the *entrechats*. And finally in *adagios* and *pas de deux* they are able to demonstrate such taxing exercises as the *grande fouettée*. Groups of male dancers leap across the stage. To the familiar strains of Glazunov's music the *jetté* is displayed.

UNE BARQUE SUR L'OCÉAN

Music by Maurice Ravel. Choreography by Jerome Robbins. Costumes by Parmelee Welles. Lighting by Ronald Bates. First presented at the New York City Ballet's Hommage à Ravel at the New York State Theatre, Lincoln Center, May 29, 1975, with Victor Castelli, Daniel Duell, Laurence Matthews, Jay Jolley, and Noland T'Sani.

A dance for five boys dressed in white and blue who move against a vibrant sea color in the background, this ballet responds to the music without specific narrative. The boys move like waves and eddies or submarine currents, reacting to water and wind, the forces and whims of nature.

Reflecting the work of Impressionist painters, Ravel, like Debussy, was interested in water movement: its perpetual shifts and shimmering colors. By orchestrating *Une Barque*, as Lincoln Kirstein has written, Ravel enlarged his theme so that "as the music gathers resonance the arpeggios grow to sweeping splashes of harp and the whole orchestra seems to vibrate as much with color and with physical motion of the waves." Jerome Robbins, I have heard, calls his ballet *Sailing*.

BARTÓK NO. 3

Music by Béla Bartók. Choreography by John Clifford. Costumes by Ardith Haddow. Lighting by Ronald Bates. First presented by Los Angeles Ballet Theatre, March 27, 1974.

This is a dance ballet to Bartók's last work, the *Piano Concerto No. 3*. There are three movements, the first led by three girls with accompanying corps de ballet, the second a romantic *pas de deux* supported by six girls, the finale an ensemble for the entire group.

When *Bartók No. 3* was danced in New York, by the New York City Ballet (May 23, 1974), Bob Micklin of *Newsday* wrote that he liked Clifford's ballet "very much. It is the best work he's done to date."

LA BAYADÈRE

Ballet in four acts. Music by Ludwig Minkus. Book by S. N. Khudekov. Choreography by Marius Petipa. First presented at the Maryinsky Theatre, St. Petersburg, February 4, 1877. First presented (Act IV) in the United States by the Kirov Ballet at the Metropolitan Opera House, New York, September 14, 1961, with Kaleria Fedicheva as Nikiya, and Sergei Vikulov as Solor.

The libretto for this ballet, which is still active in the Soviet repertory, tells the story of a hapless Indian bayadère—a temple dancer—named Nikiya. The bayadère is loved but badly treated by Solor, a young warrior who breaks his pledge to her and marries another. Nikiya is poisoned by a confidante of her rival and dies. In the final act, the repentant Solor dreams that he seeks his beloved in the "Kingdom of the Shades." Though, like Orpheus and Albrecht, he finds her, she eludes him, despite his pledge that he will never forsake her again.

But the important thing about Act IV of *Bayadère* is not the story but the dancing. What happens is that the wraithlike inhabitants of the "Kingdom of the Shades" descend upon the stage down a long ramp at the back, parallel to the audience, all in profile in *arabesque penché* at each step. There are thirty-six Shades. These and their ensuing steps, while basically simple for dancers to perform, so direct the attention by their repetition that an otherworldliness results. Next there is a *pas de trois* for three of the Shades, followed by variations for each. Solor now dances a variation that reasserts his humanity in this atmosphere of immortals. The *pas de deux* between the two lovers ties them together as it were by a long diaphanous scarf. As Nikiya holds one end of the scarf with one hand, Solor at the other end supports her in a series of turns that is rivaled only by the lifts in the final act of *Giselle* for an expression of close spirituality.

NOTES Rudolf Nureyev's fine production of *La Bayadère* for the Royal Ballet has become well-known in the United States. Another production, by Natalia Makarova, was presented in July 1974 by American Ballet Theatre. Arlene Croce wrote in *The New Yorker:* "It is an astounding success—more evidence that self-exiled Russian stars have as much to give as to gain in the West. *La Bayadère* (short for *La Bayadère*, Act IV: The Kingdom of the Shades) is an old Petipa classic of which most Westerners were unaware until the Kirov Ballet toured it in 1961. When Rudolf Nureyev, who defected on that same tour, produced it two years later for the Royal Ballet, it seemed that a miracle of transposition had taken place. Makarova has wrought an even greater miracle. She's not only reproduced a masterpiece of choreography, she's taken Ballet Theatre's corps and recharged it from top to bottom.

"The process of transformation is as yet incomplete, but never in my experience had the company danced a classical piece in so strict a style, on so broad a scale, and with such clarity of rhythm. Without these qualities, *La Bayadère* wouldn't be fun—it wouldn't even be *La Bayadère*—and what's *most* fun about this production is that every girl on the stage seems to be aware of the sensational progress she's making. . . . What matters . . . is that the motor impulse is there, solidly pumping energy into the right channels.

"Makarova's direction has been faithful and revealing. That motor impulse is basic to Petipa's exposition of movement flowing clean from its source. It flows from the simple to the complex, but we are always aware of its source, deep in the dancer's back, and of its vibration as it carries in widening arcs around the auditorium. This is dancing to be felt as well as seen, and Petipa gives it a long time to creep under our skins. Like a patient drillmaster, he opens the piece with a single, two-phrase theme in adagio tempo (arabesque, cambré port de bras), repeated over and over until all the dancers have filed onto the stage. Then, at the same tempo, with the dancers facing us in columns, he produces a set of mild variations, expanding the profile of the opening image from two dimensions to three. Positions are developed naturally through the body's leverage—weight, counterweight. Diagonals are firmly expressed. Returning to profile, the columns divide and flutter one by one to the rear. The final pose is of two long columns facing the wings with annunciatory arms. Now, to a collection of beer-garden tunes (the composer is Ludwig Minkus), Petipa sets dances for five soloists—a ballerina, a danseur, and three principal Shades—while behind them the vast, tireless corps responds in echoes, diverges, vanishes, regathers into garlands, into gateways, tosses, and freezes. The choreography is considered to be the first expression of grand-scale symphonism in dance, predating by seventeen years Ivanov's masterly designs for the definitive *Swan Lake*. But our first reaction is not to how old it looks but to how modern. Actually, the only word for this old-new choreography is immemorial. *La Bayadère* (1877) looks like the first ballet ever made: like man's—or, rather, woman's—first imprint in space and time.

"The subject of 'The Kingdom of the Shades' is not really death, although everybody in it except the hero is dead. It's Elysian bliss, and its setting is eternity. The long, slow repeated-arabesque sequence creates the impression of a grand crescendo that seems to annihilate all time. No reason it could not go on forever. And in the adagio drill that follows, the steps are so few and their content is so exposed that we think we'll remember them always—just like dancers, who *have* remembered them for a hundred years and for who knows how long before Petipa commemorated them in this ballet. Ballets, passed down the generations like legends, acquire a patina of ritualism, but *La Bayadère is* a ritual, a poem about dancing and memory and time. Each dance seems to add something new to the previous one, like a language being learned. The ballet grows heavy with this knowledge, which at the beginning had been only a primordial utterance, and in the coda it fairly bursts with articulate splendor. My favorite moment comes in the final waltz, when the three principal Shades are doing relevé-passé, relevé-attitude cambré to a rocking rhythm, and the corps, seeing this, rush to join them in the repeat. They—the corps—remember those cambré positions from their big dance.

"It's the corps' ballet—a fact the management should recognize by allowing a company call after, as well as before, the soloists have taken their bows. But the soloists in the performance I saw—Cynthia Gregory, Ivan Nagy, Karena Brock, Deborah Dobson, and Martine van Hamel—deserved their applause. Gregory was at her greatest. She took her grand port de bras the way it was meant to be taken—straight up out of the floor and through the body. Van Hamel, who may be the most talented of the company's younger ballerinas, did her variation the hard way by not coming off point until she was well up and into arabesque, and the excessively slow tempo made it even harder. Nagy has a way of filling a role superlatively without actually doing the steps. In his variation, he gathered himself powerfully and unfurled something that started like double assemblés and ended halfway to double sauts de basque. In the *pas de deux* with the veil, he didn't parallel the ballerina's steps and poses— but this is one of the differences between Makarova's staging and Nureyev's. Another difference is that she doesn't stroke the upbeat, or break the path of a gesture in order to point it. The way these two have staged the piece corresponds to their styles as performers—hers, musically more fluid; his, more emphatic. Also, her arabesques are not penchées, the solos are arranged in a different order, and she ends the ballet with the corps stretched along the floor in a semicircle rather than backbent in a sunburst. I prefer the Royal Ballet's orchestration, with its drumrolls and its protracted climax that accompanies the sunburst, and I think I prefer the sunburst, but apart from those things there's little to choose between these productions. They're both marvellous. Marcos Paredes' costumes for Ballet Theatre are in the Victorian style traditional to this ballet, and I liked his headdresses for the women—beaded circlets à la Anna Pavlova."°

In *Baryshnikov at Work*, the dancer Mikhail Baryshnikov calls *La Bayadère* "one of the great, if not the greatest, classical works in the history of ballet. It is Petipa's idea of life in the beyond . . . Poetically, it is unmatched in the classical repertory."

LE BEAU DANUBE

Ballet in one act. Music by Johann Strauss. Choreography by Leonide Massine. Scenery and costumes by V. and E. Polunin, after Constantin Guys. Costumes by Comte Étienne de Beaumont. Book by Leonide Massine. First presented in a two-act version by Comte Étienne de Beaumont's Soirée de Paris, Paris, May 17, 1924, with Lydia Lopokova as the Street Dancer. First presented in the final one-act version by the Ballet Russe de Monte Carlo at the Théâtre de Monte Carlo, April 15, 1933, with Alexandra Danilova as the Street Dancer, Leonide Massine as the Hussar, Tatiana Riabouchinska as the Daughter, Irina Baronova as the First Hand, and David Lichine as the King of the Dandies. First presented in the United States by the Ballet Russe de Monte Carlo at the St. James Theatre, New York, December 22, 1933, with the same principals.

This famous character ballet takes place in a public park, the Prater, in old Vienna. Nowadays we are somewhat used to ballets that are set in parks— where policemen romance with governesses, where children rollick and get into mischief, and where the perennial gigolo tries to interest the young, innocent girl. These are all adaptations of *Le Beau Danube* (*The Beautiful Danube*) and a tribute to its popularity. Roger Désormière arranged and orchestrated the pieces by Johann Strauss that make up the ballet's score.

The curtain rises on a charming wooded park in Vienna. It is Sunday afternoon, about a hundred years ago. A gardener is tidying up the grounds, a young artist is painting at an easel; we hear the sound of a Strauss waltz and we believe the pretty picture we see on the stage. Strollers soon enter and enjoy the beauty of the scene: a family with two daughters, ladies of the town, seamstresses and dandies.

The artist is attracted to the first hand, the seamstress, and flirts with her as he sketches her portrait. The girl is pleased with the artist until the King of the Dandies rushes in and whisks her away from him.

Now a dashing hussar, in immaculate uniform, promenades with one of the daughters of the family. He is deferential to her family and is apparently formally engaged to her, for when he dances a mazurka with the girl their romance appears to be permanently happy. They leave the scene hand in hand.

° From "Makarova's Miracle" by Arlene Croce. Reprinted by permission; © 1974 The New Yorker Magazine, Inc.

A small band of street entertainers enter and set up to amuse the crowd that has gathered. The manager of the troupe points with pride to his principal artiste, a dancer, and the beautiful girl begins a lively solo that thrills the crowd. The manager and an athlete with bulging muscles join her; the dance becomes hilarious and everyone applauds them.

The hussar and his fiancée stroll back into the park at this point, and the hussar is embarrassed to see his past catch up with him. The street dancer instantly claims him as a former devoted lover and, to his fiancée's horror, pretends that the hussar has deserted her! The poor girl swoons during this scene of simulated jealousy and her family escort her out of the park, vowing vengeance on the ne'er-do-well hussar. The street dancer, not to be outdone by her rival, pretends to swoon also.

The hussar is distressed at what has happened, but he could hardly control the whims of the street dancer and there is nothing else for him but to take up with her again! The crowd wanders off and they are alone. The first familiar bars of the *Blue Danube* Waltz are heard. The hussar is moved to dance; quietly and slowly the music accompanies his recollection of his romance with the dancer, and he opens his arms to her. He waits, not moving. She too remembers. She feels false jealousy no longer, and they begin to dance, their initial restrained steps building gradually to an ebullient and joyful whirling with the persistent swell of the waltz.

But just as the former lovers seem to be reunited, the hussar's fiancée returns. She has run off from her raging family and insists on claiming the hussar: after all, she loves him. Why should she give him up so easily? The hussar, who has never seen such determination in a woman, is charmed by her completely and again forgets the street dancer. The *Blue Danube* has ended.

The young girl's family race in and try to separate their daughter from the fickle hussar, but the younger daughter steps in, cajoles and persuades, and tears turn to laughter. The hussar is properly deferential again to his fiancée's family; the father blesses the handsome couple; and the crowd in the park dance in celebration of the happy resolve. The street dancer, too, congratulates them with a final display of high-spirited dancing, and the charming park becomes a place where nothing unpleasant can ever happen.

BEAUTY AND THE BEAST

Dramatic ballet in two scenes. Music by Maurice Ravel. Choreography by John Cranko. Scenery and costumes by Margaret Kaye. First presented by the Sadler's Wells Theatre Ballet at the Sadler's Wells Theatre, London, December 20, 1949, with Patricia Miller as Beauty and David Poole as the Beast. First presented in the United States by the Sadler's Wells Theatre Ballet at the Denver Auditorium, Denver, Colorado, November 14, 1951, with the same cast.

Ravel's *Mother Goose* Suite is made up of five movements, each based on a famous fairy story. The familiar tale of "Beauty and the Beast" inspired the

fourth movement of the suite, but the English choreographer John Cranko
has been inspired to use this dramatic theme as an accompaniment to almost
all of Ravel's score.° The ballet is an intimate drama, actually a long *pas de
deux* for the two principal characters.

The curtain rises soon after the music has begun. The scene is the forest
where the beast is king. The light, almost transparent, cloth on which the trees
of the forest are painted is cut into strips, giving a jungle effect. The light is
dim. The beast reclines alone in the forest. He seems to be sleeping; he wakens
and rubs his eyes with his long, clawlike hands. Then we see that he is weeping. His whole body shakes with violent sobbing.

Behind him, a beautiful young girl enters the forest. The beast does not see
her, and the girl, unaware that she has happened upon a dangerous wood,
moves in and out among the trees. The beast rises, sensing a strange presence.
He wishes to welcome the girl, but knows he will frighten her. As her back is
turned, he reaches out to her plaintively. The girl moves off into the forest,
and the beast follows her. She begins to feel that she is not alone.

The ragged trees rise, and the scene changes to another part of the forest.
Here in the center of the jungle is a dark clearing. A little light penetrates the
darkness through an entrance formed by curving trees. Here the girl enters.
Now she is thoroughly lost and frightened and she does a little dance to allay
her fear—a kind of whistling-in-the-dark variation. Gradually she tires and sits
down to rest. Soon she falls to the ground and sleeps.

Light begins to fill the jungle through the grottolike entrance formed by the
trees. The girl wakens and looks about. She observes birds in the trees, dances
happily, gesturing lovingly to the surrounding forest. She approaches one of
the trees to pick fruit. As she takes the fruit, she sees that it is held in the
hairy paws of the beast, who has been observing her secretly.

The girl faints. The beast picks her up and holds her carefully. The girl sobs
in his arms and releases herself. She attempts to flee the forest, but at the entrance, branches of trees reach out to restrain her. The door of the cage has
been shut, and the girl looks at the beast in terror.

The beast tries to convince her that he means no harm. Gently he kneels before her and holds out a red flower. Again the girl wishes to escape. The beast
grovels on the ground, then crawls helplessly. He drops the flower and begins
to cry. The girl goes over to him, but she is still too frightened to indicate her
pity. She turns to run through the entrance, where the confining branches have
disappeared. She passes through, out into the light, but her hand still holds the
side of the entrance: she is uncertain and returns.

She dances back into the jungle. Now she is completely unafraid. She stands
over the beast and helps him rise. He lifts her high in his arms and holds her
so that she almost stands above him. The girl reaches down and holds his face
in her hands. The music rushes magically; the beast releases her; and we see
that his face is no longer the fierce mask of a ferocious beast, but the face of a
handsome young man. The girl caresses his face, and the two lovers dance a

° The section *"Laideronette, Impératrice des Pagodas"* is omitted in the ballet.

flowing *pas de deux* in which the changed beast holds the girl secure as her feet gently touch the ground. At the end, the lovers reach out to each other and the curtain falls.

BHAKTI

Based on a Hindu theme and musical setting. Choreography by Maurice Béjart. Costumes by Germinal Casado. First presented by the Ballet of the Twentieth Century in 1968. First presented in the United States by the same ensemble at the Brooklyn Academy of Music, New York, January 25, 1971.

A Hindu love poem in dance, *Bhakti* is a ballet in three parts. The themes of those parts have been described by their creator, Maurice Béjart: "It is through love that the worshiper identifies with the divinity; and each time he relives the legend of his god, who is himself only one of the faces of the supreme and nameless reality." The three parts of the work are *pas de deux* between certain girls and their heroes:

RAMA   an incarnation of Vishnu. His love affair with Sita, symbol of purity, is related in the celebrated Hindu epic *Ramayana*. This poem forms the basis of every classical dance or theatrical production in India.

KRISHNA   another incarnation of Vishnu. He is the God of Youth and Beauty, the divine Player of the Flute whose affairs with the shepherdesses and the lovely Radha are sung in the *Gita Govinda*. He is also the teacher par excellence, and it is he who speaks in the *Bhagavad-Gita*, one of the most important books of all.

SHIVA   the third person in the Hindu Trinity (*Trimurti*): Brahma, Vishnu, Shiva. As the "Destroyer," he kills illusion and personality. God of the Dance, his wife Shakti pursues the vital energy that flows from and returns to him, immobile, yet forever in motion.

Introduced by three young men, the ballet proceeds to representations of these gods and their ladies, each supported by appropriate ensembles.

LES BICHES

Ballet in one act. Music by Francis Poulenc. Choreography by Bronislava Nijinska. Scenery and costumes by Marie Laurencin. First presented by Diaghilev's Ballets Russes at the Théâtre de Monte Carlo, January 6, 1924, with a cast that included Vera Nemtchinova and Anatole Vilzak, Alexandra Danilova, Bronislava Nijinska, Felia Dubrovska, Ninette de Valois, Alice Nikitina, Lubov Tchernicheva, Nicholas Zverev, and Leon Woicikowski. First presented in the United States by the Marquis de Cuevas' Grand Ballet

*at the Century Theatre, New York, November 13, 1950, with a cast headed
by Marjorie Tallchief, George Skibine, and Olga Adabache.*

Two ballet companies have preferred to call this ballet *The House Party* and
The Gazelles.* It is certainly about a house party. There is a hostess, a woman
considerably older than her youthful guests; she seeks to form an attachment
with one of the young men at her party. The relations of some of her guests
are similarly romantic. The ballet thus has a romantic theme rather than a
specific plot; the characters are dancers. The ballet is in eight parts, corre-
sponding to the divisions of the score: "Rondo," "*Chanson dansée,*" "Adagietto," "*Jeux,*" "Rag Mazurka," "Andantino," "*Chanson dansée,*" "Finale."

Before the curtain rises, the orchestra plays a short introduction; slow at
first, the music becomes smartly quick and pulsating and reminds us of the vitality of youth. The curtain rises on an enormous room that bears the mark of
the fashionable interior decorator. Painted blue curtains at the back enclose a
window. A large blue couch stands at the rear. Twelve girls enter and dance
pertly to the rhythm of the music. Their long, cool pink dresses whirl about
them in innocent contrast to the sophistication of their steps. The girls kneel,
rise, circle on point, bend back seductively, and choose partners as the music
hastens to a brisk finish. They run off in gushing, schoolgirl fashion.

Three boys in bathing trunks enter to the strong, choppy beat of the *"Chanson dansée."* They dance in a line; their movements are assertive and angular.
They thrust out their chests and display their biceps in a dance that stylizes
athleticism. The two boys on the side imitate the turns of the dancer in the
center. They kneel. The twelve girls run in. The boys continue their dance for
the girls' benefit, while the girls try to attract them. They surround each of the
three boys, then stand in a semicircle behind them. The boys kneel before the
girls, but seem to be disinterested.

A girl dressed like a page boy in white tights, blue tunic, and white gloves
enters on the right and interrupts the scene. She crosses the stage on point,
holding her hand up stiffly, as if she were on some secret errand. She takes no
notice of the guests, but the boys are fascinated. The girl leaves and, abandon-
ing all hope of winning the boys, four of the girls flounce away and arrange
themselves decorously on the sofa. The others continue their flirtation with the
boys, who abandon them again when the girl enters as before. One of the
youths is attracted to her; she dances off, and the flighty girls take up with the
other two boys. The strange girl recrosses the room, but pauses this time to
dance briefly. Her hands are joined and she holds out her arms as she poses;
her movements are softly angular. Two of the boys have gone off with the girls
in pink, and one of the boys watches the girl in blue as she dances alone, apparently oblivious of his presence. He comes up behind her as she finishes her
variation, comes close and holds her arms; the two exit together.

The two boys return with the girls and begin a rollicking game. The boys

* Literally, *les biches* means *the hinds,* but colloquially it also means simply *girls,*
or *young ladies.*

slide the couch forward. They stand on it, lifting the girls over it; then the girls dance across the couch one by one and hop off the arm onto the floor. The boys walk off. The sofa is turned with its back to the front, and the girls hide behind it as the girl in blue re-enters with her partner. They dance briefly and exit when they see they are being watched. The boys come back to find the girls. They move the couch back near the window, and all leave the stage.

A woman in an elaborate yellow dress enters and crosses the stage with mannered steps. This is the hostess. She brandishes a long cigarette holder pointedly, as if she were posing for a stilted advertisement, and at the same time nervously belies her pose by playing with her long pearl necklace. Her hands are constantly in motion; she cannot remain still for an instant. Her dance is the dance of a woman who can never imagine herself alone; it is the perpetual and desperate performance of a woman who has to be seen to appreciate herself. No one interrupts her parody of a youthful dance, and she stops. She arranges herself languidly on the couch.

The two young men enter suddenly. They dance proudly, asserting their masculine strength. They approach the hostess, stomping their feet. She is delighted and joins them in a dance to the "Rag Mazurka." Vigorous at first, their *pas de trois* slows down. The hostess is enamored of both her partners. Both boys offer their arms. She doesn't know which to choose. She takes a chance and breaks free. Both boys follow her off.

The girl in blue meets her partner in the center of the stage for a *pas de deux* to the "Andantino." Their gestures and steps are strangely discontinuous; they move, pause, move again—formal, but intimate. Their dance ends as the boy holds the girl straight in his arms; then, with an intricate twist of both their bodies, the girl is poised high on his shoulder. They leave the stage.

To a sprightly tune two young girls enter and dance a lively duet in which each tries to outdo the other in expressing their attachment. Their dance becomes secretive when they imagine they are not alone. They blush and exit hurriedly.

In different groups that turn rapidly as they cross the stage, the entire ensemble gradually returns for the finale—first the girls, then the boys, followed by the hostess and the girl in blue. All romantic attachments seem to be forgotten as the ensemble joins together for a final fling.

NOTES   One of the popular ballets of the Diaghilev era, *Les Biches* is regarded by its choreographer as the modern equivalent of *Les Sylphides*. It has been revived since its first production by the Markova-Dolin Ballet, when Alicia Markova danced the part of the girl in blue and Anton Dolin danced her partner; and by the Grand Ballet of the Marquis de Cuevas, where the production met with critical and popular approval, both in Europe and New York.

The composer, Francis Poulenc, noted in the English magazine *Ballet* (Volume 2, No. 4) that *Les Biches* "is a ballet in which you may see nothing at all or into which you may read the worst . . . In this ballet, as in certain of Watteau's pictures, there is an atmosphere of wantonness which you sense if you are corrupted but which an innocent-minded girl would not be conscious of."

Nijinska revived *Les Biches* for the Royal Ballet December 2, 1964, with Svetlana Beriosova, Georgina Parkinson, David Blair, Keith Rosson, Robert Mead, Maryon Lane, and Merle Park in leading roles. This revival was first presented in the United States at the Metropolitan Opera House by the Royal Ballet the following spring.

THE BIG CITY

Music by Alexander Tansman. Book and choreography by Kurt Jooss. First presented by the Jooss Ballet at the Opera House, Cologne, November 21, 1932. Costumes and lighting by Hermann Markard. First presented in the United States by the City Center Joffrey Ballet at the City Center, New York, February 28, 1975. Staged by Anna Markard. Costumes and lighting by Hermann Markard, re-created by Ray Diffen and Jennifer Tipton. Pianists: Stanley Babin and Mary Roark. Conducted by Sung Kwak.

The Big City was originally presented just four months after Kurt Jooss' masterwork, *The Green Table*, had won first prize in an international dance competition. Although the ballet is often described as the first dance composition to deal with social criticism, Jooss maintains that this was not his intention. He has described the work as an "attempt to portray the loneliness of city people by means of dramatic dance." He was inspired by the "bustle of city life, backyard gloom and the glamour of dance halls." The Joffrey Ballet version, taken from the final 1935 version, was staged by Jooss' daughter, Anna Markard.

The action of the ballet is compressed into three graphic scenes accompanied by music (Tansman's *Sonatine Transatlantique*) that recalls the time of Europe's first appreciation of *le jazz hot*. The plot: "In the hurrying throng of a continental city are seen a young Girl and a young Workman, her sweetheart, homeward bound after the day's work. A Libertine, in search of new conquests, follows the young Girl to her home. Dazzled by the promise of adventure, she fares forth on his arm to the dance halls, where disillusion awaits her."

Writing of the American revival of *The Big City* in *The Village Voice*, the critic Deborah Jowitt said that "the life of this city is a bitter cartoon of what we can imagine life in a German city at the edge of World War II to have been like." . . . What makes the ballet absorbing and moving is not the sad little plot or the social message, but the delicate way Jooss was able to suggest characters, social backgrounds, occupations of people through the ways he made them move. What he gives you in many cases seem like rapid sketches of something he means to develop later—but what sketches!"

Interviewed in the New York *Times* by Anna Kisselgoff at the time of the Joffrey revival, Kurt Jooss said that *The Big City* "must be seen now as a period piece of the nineteen-twenties . . . I am not a social-protest choreographer . . . I consider myself a choreographer first."

BILLY THE KID

Ballet in one act. Music by Aaron Copland. Choreography by Eugene Lo-
ring. Book by Lincoln Kirstein. Scenery and costumes by Jared French. First
presented by Ballet Caravan at the Chicago Opera House, Chicago, October
16, 1938, with Eugene Loring as Billy, Marie-Jeanne as the Mother *and*
Sweetheart, *Lew Christensen as* Pat Garrett, *and Todd Bolender as Alias.*

The story of Billy the Kid is already a legend in America, a part of the larger
legend we know as the Opening of the West. The facts known about him—that
his real name was William H. Bonney; that he was born in New York City in
1859; was taken to Kansas when he was three; killed his first man in Silver
City, New Mexico, when he was twelve; and by the time he was hunted down
and shot, at the age of twenty-one, had killed a man for every year of his life—
these facts remind us of a gangster movie. But actually these facts do not tell
us the whole story of the Kid. They do not tell us that, although Billy the Kid
was regarded as the most dangerous desperado of his time, he was loved and
admired as much as he was feared, and that the Far West after the Civil War
was a place where these emotions could interchange and resolve—to make of
his life the heroic myth it has since become. This ballet is not, therefore, a simple biography of a wild West killer: it is the story of the life of Billy the Kid as
it became a part of the life of his time.

PROLOGUE   The first, slow notes of the music are subdued and eerie, like
sounds in the wilderness at night. The curtain rises. Across the front of the
stage a spotlight shines, making a path of brilliant orange light. The rest of the
stage is suffused in a semidark glow, as if bathed in the light of the golden
sun. An arid khaki-colored desert and tall, branching cacti are seen in the distance. From the right, a man dressed in a cowboy outfit steps boldly into the
path of light. Later we shall learn that this is Pat Garrett, the sometime friend
of Billy the Kid who becomes sheriff and kills him. But at the moment he is
simply any American pioneer, moving westward toward the blaze of the setting sun. He moves stiffly, with determination; for each step forward he will
take none back. Then his progress becomes a dance, the movements of which
remind us of the frontiersman's work: he circles his arm high over his head to
lasso invisible cattle; he pulls back roughly on invisible reins to halt a covered
wagon, then drives the horses on with a lash of a whip; he kneels motionless,
gun pointed, to catch the imaginary Indian. The music gains in strength with
his vigorous movements. It becomes stronger still, as Garrett is followed by another man and a woman. The man copies every one of his leader's gestures,
while the woman sets a dance pattern for the pioneer mother who rocks her
children to sleep even when danger surrounds her. Other couples enter, and
the orchestra builds gradually to sound a mighty processional as the pioneer
figures follow their leader in this formalized march to the West. Now Garrett
thrusts his arms forward, pushing back the frontier. He faces directly into the

light. He pirouettes rapidly, spine in the air, and repeats these movements as all the men in the caravan follow his lead. All the dancers catch the full vitality of the music, which itself pushes forward to a resistless, persistent climax. Then, at its fullest volume, the music is cut off sharply. There is a blackout.

STREET SCENE   When the lights come up again, the backdrop still depicts, as it will continue to do, the same arid desert, but before the curtain move a group of particular characters—not pioneers simply—who place this episode in the hot and sunny main street of an early Western town, just north of the border. Woodwinds play an old Western tune that the rest of the orchestra takes up gaily and playfully. A smiling, sinuous Mexican in a wide-brimmed hat struts about, pawing the street with his boots like a tame but unbridled stallion. Pioneer women, dressed for the town in close-fitting bonnets, pass him by, their arms crooked to carry invisible burdens. The Mexican ignores them. Cowboys ride across the scene, spurring on the imaginary horses they straddle. Three dancing girls enter, their hands on their tightly corseted hips in an impudent attitude. Two women look them up and down and, noting their high-buttoned gold shoes and garish red tights, turn up their noses in disapproval, sniff at the air, and walk away. Eight cowboys ride on, and there is a short rodeo. At the end three of them stop and take up with the dance-hall girls. A group of lovely Mexican girls come onto the scene, and now the street seethes with activity. The people stand about, some talking, some flirting, others going about their private business.

Then suddenly the music is quiet. An oboe sounds a theme, and on the left a small, attractive woman comes in. She is dressed in city clothes and is clearly a stranger to the community. A big, gangling boy, dressed only in overalls and a straw hat, hangs onto her skirts, and they move through the crowd. This is Billy the Kid. The boy looks about and appears to want to stop, but his mother walks on ahead and they exit. The Mexican and the four Mexican girls dance together briefly, and then the Kid and his mother return. This time the Kid shows off his strength by softly lifting his mother around for several measures. She pushes his cheek to tell him how silly he is, and he turns his face away, blushing, but he persists at the game and the two waltz off.

Meanwhile something has happened to the crowd. They stand closely packed together, watching an argument between the Mexican and a man in red. The argument becomes a fight. They hit each other in slow motion, neither falling. The music accompanies their blows with retarded rhythm that increases in volume and speed as the fight becomes serious. The people in the crowd begin to sense that they should stand back. Now, as a trumpet sounds the theme militantly, the Kid enters with his mother. Both of them are fascinated by the brawl and stand on the fringe of the crowd. Just as they join the group, the Mexican pulls a gun. The man in red turns quickly to defend himself and steps against the crowd, right next to Billy and his mother. The Mexican fires. He misses. Billy's mother doubles up in agony. She falls against her son, who stands transfixed, staring straight ahead, not comprehending. She grasps his arm, slides down slowly to the ground, and dies. The people are horrified, but they, too, are motionless. They remain still and shocked as the

Kid shakes off his dream, grabs a knife, and dashes over to the Mexican. Billy kills him with one quick stab in the back. He topples over. Everyone steps back, unbelieving. Billy looks about wildly, wondering where to go. Pat Garrett steps in to help him, but the Kid ignores him and runs off. Already he has chosen his way.

One of the men stoops to pick up the body of the Kid's mother, and the whole crowd leans over in unison, expressing the common grief. Another man kneels down beside the dead Mexican, throws him over his shoulder, and carries him off. But the Mexican will reappear. He becomes Alias, a character of many disguises who haunts the Kid constantly throughout his life and finally helps to kill him.

The crowd begins to disperse. Couples walk away, shaking their heads, still stunned by the two murders. But instead of leaving the stage, they mill about, circling slowly, and we see after a few minutes that perhaps they are not the same men and women who saw Billy the Kid's first crime. The men lift their women affectionately, just as Billy lifted his mother, but everyone is wary and suspicious. The people have changed. They have grown older and, as we have been watching them, years have passed in the street. Finally, one by one, the couples leave and the stage is empty.

THE DESERT   The Kid enters in the back. He is no longer a child. He is dressed in black and white striped riding breeches, boots, a wide-brimmed hat; there is a skull on his shirt pocket. He dances alone. In this dance we understand a little of how the Kid has grown up. The proud pose that begins and ends the dance is confidently self-assertive, and in between the Kid performs a series of difficult movements with ferocity rather than grace. He stomps loudly with his heavy boots, circles an imaginary foe with his gun ready to fire, spins swiftly in the air, lands, and kicks out at his victim. He is going through the only vocabulary he possesses, and we realize that all of his life, every waking moment, is a practiced preparation for the next time he will have to kill. His dance gesture for shooting is a quick aim at the target, then a spin in the air that matches the speed of a bullet, and finally a vicious kick. It is the gesture of a man who hates his dead foe and the whole world. And there follows inevitably the same pose of self-assertion. Never does this man doubt that he has done the right thing, never has he supposed himself guilty of a crime. Shooting happens to be his way of living: a murder is just like lighting a cigarette.

As the Kid nears the end of his soliloquy, he is interrupted by the arrival of a small posse. Three men canter across the stage in formation, circle, and try to close in on the Kid. He hides. Then he aims, spins, and kicks. The leader of the three men falls dead. The Kid prances slowly and softly, then draws himself up to his full height and stands triumphant. The scene blacks out.

A spotlight at the front of the stage comes on. Sitting close to the footlights, around a campfire, the Kid and Pat Garrett are playing cards. Garrett is now sheriff, but still a friend to the Kid. The light from the fire makes enormous silhouettes of their figures against the backdrop. The orchestra plays a quiet, wistful melody. The Kid shuffles the cards and deals. The two men draw their cards. A man and two cowgirls, all friends of Billy, approach the fire. The man stoops down to watch the card game. Garrett is distracted for an instant, but turns back to find the Kid cheating. He protests. The Kid is patient with him at first, denies cheating, and attempts to humor him. Pat continues to protest, but when he sees that the Kid will not accept his friendship, will not even admit to overt cheating, he rides off into the night. Billy's three friends gather about the fire and take up the cards while the Kid stands aside. His rage mounts. Pat has got the better of him. He stomps angrily, regretting that he did not kill his friend. The group at the fire turn and stare at him; they are frightened at what he may do. But the Kid does not have time to act. Shooting is heard in the distance, and before he can flee, the stage fills with people. The drums boom with gunfire as Pat Garrett leads a posse on in pursuit of the Kid. Billy moves to defend himself, shoots wildly as his friends gather about him and his attackers fall on their faces to protect themselves. A fierce gun battle ensues, during which the Kid continues to shoot out indiscriminately at all comers. He and his friends are hemmed in by two lines of gunfire. They are all killed except Billy. As he is about to fire another round, he trips over the body of one of his own men. Two men move in to hold him. One of them is Alias. The Kid kills Alias. The other is Pat Garrett. Pat is quick: he sticks a gun in the Kid's back and rides him off to jail. The Kid does not seem to care in the least.

The posse that has helped capture Billy—cowgirls and cowboys—now join together to celebrate and dance joyfully. In the midst of their frolic, the Kid's sweetheart, a beautiful Mexican girl, walks in and tries to find her lover. No one pays any attention to her. She leaves the scene disconsolate. The celebration is blacked out.

THE JAIL   Billy stands on one foot, shuffling cards. Naked above the waist, he wears a kerchief about his neck, arm bands, and black riding togs over white tights. His jailer, Alias, stands at his side, ready to receive his cards. Billy bides his time, shuffles the cards slowly, and shifts to the other leg. The jailer grows impatient and turns away for an instant. Billy moves openly to grab his gun, as if the jailer expected him to. The jailer, of course, sees the move but ignores it. He suggests that it is all part of the game and that Billy won't do anything wrong. He walks away. The Kid sneaks up on him softly and this time does grab his gun. The jailer turns back, expecting the Kid to hand it over. The Kid laughs. He kills the jailer and stands again triumphant. Blackout.

THE DESERT   The Kid gallops across the stage to his hide-out. He disappears. A posse follows, but they are unable to pick up the trail. Billy enters again, screened by two Mexican girls, who stand between him and the posse. Alias, now disguised as an Indian guide, leads him away. The Kid arrives at a quiet spot, and Alias leaves him. Pat Garrett and his riders pass by, but see nothing. Billy takes his hat off and undresses to go to sleep. He is so tired he seems to be asleep already. He crouches on the ground to the right and stacks his clothes automatically, as if in a dream. His sweetheart enters on the left, behind his back. She dances on point, formally. He does not turn and see her, but looks up, seeing her in his mind's eye. He looks back down at his clothes. The girl touches his shoulder and poses briefly. He stirs, first swings his right leg out and back from his crouching position—a movement in stylized keeping with the girl's remote intimacy. She stands close beside him, but he is never aware of her real presence. He rises, stretches; the girl holds onto him and poses again beautifully, and they begin a short *pas de deux* to a sensuous waltz. He lifts her gently and swings her body slowly, not looking at her at all; he might be dancing with any girl and she with any man. Almost immediately he abandons her and goes back to stretch out to sleep. The girl dances off as quietly as she came, with no protest. The dream is over.

Pat Garrett, led by Alias, comes in and watches Billy asleep. Billy has not heard them, but wakes up as if warned by something. He reaches for his gun, holds it ready. The night is black: he sees nothing. For an instant he is afraid. Garrett and Alias stand stock-still, holding their breath. Billy calls out "¿Quien es?" ("Who is it?"), his voice hoarse with fear. There is no answer. He waits. Still no sound. He laughs to himself, silently. To reassure himself, he laughs harder; his body shakes with laughter. He stops, takes out a cigarette, strikes a match, and illuminates his face for a flickering moment. Garrett fires. Billy falls. He is dead.

Long-robed Mexican women enter and stand over his body. They pass by slowly, mourning, to music of lamentation, and the light fades.

EPILOGUE   The setting sun shines across the stage, and Pat Garrett walks in boldly, as he did at the beginning of the ballet, leading a host of pioneers. All march facing west, then turn back east, then west again, as the music impels them forward.

BIOSFERA

Music by Marlos Nobre. Choreography by Arthur Mitchell. Scenery and costumes by Fred Barry. First presented by the Dance Theatre of Harlem at the ANTA Theatre, New York, March 10, 1971.

Biosfera is a dramatic *pas de deux*, not the usual display piece for two dancers but an opportunity for the two artists to become involved in a situation beyond themselves. The curtain rises on a dark stage where we gradually make out a girl and a boy, posed on platforms at opposite sides of the scene. The girl is dressed all in white, he in black. They leave their platforms to dance in a spotlight in the center. The music is lightly electronic, mysterious. The dance has a kind of detached romanticism about it. At the end, the girl and the boy return to the platforms at either side of the stage.

Reviewing *Biosfera* in the New York *Times* in March 1971, Clive Barnes said of the dancers: "Sheila Rohan is the girl, dancing with a crisp clarity, and the man is the distinguished and elegant Walter Raines, who at one point has to stand on his hands for what seems like two minutes . . . Mr. Mitchell has gotten himself the makings of a first-rate American classic ballet company."

BIRTHDAY OFFERING

Music by Alexander Glazunov. Choreography by Frederick Ashton. Costumes by André Levasseur. First presented at the Royal Opera House, Covent Garden, London, by the Sadler's Wells Ballet on May 5, 1956, with Margot Fonteyn, Beryl Grey, Violetta Elvin, Nadia Nerina, Rowena Jackson, Svetlana Beriosova, Elaine Fifield; Michael Somes, Alexander Grant, Brian Shaw, Philip Chatfield, David Blair, Desmond Doyle, and Bryan Ashbridge in the principal roles. First presented in the United States by the same company at the Metropolitan Opera House, New York, September 11, 1957.

Birthday Offering was the Sadler's Wells Ballet's danced celebration of its twenty-fifth anniversary. Set to music from Glazunov's *The Seasons, Ruses d'amour*, and other works, as arranged by Robert Irving, the ballet displayed the special gifts of the first dancers of the company and was a tribute to the tradition and practice that had made the ensemble famous. That *Birthday Offering* is more than a *pièce d'occasion* was suggested by a revival in 1960 when it was danced by young aspiring ballerinas. Mary Clarke wrote in *The Dancing Times:* "This quality of youth and freshness gave the ballet a different kind of charm. Choreographically, it is a wonder. Each of the solos is a small masterpiece and the flow and patterns of the ensemble work are marvelously smooth yet delicate. Ashton here, in a Maryinsky mood, proved himself to be the equal of Petipa."

The score was taken from the following compositions of Glazunov: Entrée: *Valse de Concert, No. 1;* Grand Adagio: *Scènes de Ballet;* Fifield's Variation: *Scènes de Ballet;* Jackson's Variation: Winter (*Les Saisons*); Beriosova's Variation: Winter (*Les Saisons*); Grey's Variation: Summer (*Les Saisons*); Fonteyn's Variation: *Ruses d'amour.*

BLUEBEARD

Comic ballet in two prologues, four scenes, and three interludes. Music by Jacques Offenbach. Choreography by Michel Fokine. Book by Michel Fokine. Scenery and costumes by Marcel Vertès. First presented by Ballet Theatre at the Palacio de Bellas Artes, Mexico City, Mexico, October 27, 1941, with a cast headed by Anton Dolin as Bluebeard, Alicia Markova as Hermilia, Irina Baronova as Boulotte, Ian Gibson as Prince Sapphire, Antony Tudor as King Bobiche, Lucia Chase as Queen Clementine, Miriam Golden, Jeannette Lauret, Nora Kaye, Rosella Hightower, and Maria Karnilova as Wives of Bluebeard, and Dimitri Romanov, Donald Saddler, Annabelle Lyon, Jerome Robbins, and Hugh Laing as the Queen's Lovers. First presented in the United States by Ballet Theatre at the Forty-fourth Street Theatre, New York, November 12, 1941, with the same principals.

Bluebeard is a comedy with a double plot. Its characters are everywhere at once, and if you don't have a clear idea of who they are and what they're up to, the ballet doesn't turn out to be as funny as it might be. The music, arranged and orchestrated by Antal Dorati, is taken from Offenbach's operetta *Barbe-Bleue* and other scores by that composer. The time is the beginning of the sixteenth century; the place is the mythical kingdom of King Bobiche.

FIRST PROLOGUE   There is a rousing, thumping overture. The curtain rises. King Bobiche, a tottering old man in purple robes and ruby crown, enters the scene carrying an infant. This is his daughter, Hermilia, who must be exiled because she is not a son. The old king doesn't know quite how to go about this, but he is determined that the child's birth shall be kept secret. Count Oscar, his chancellor, brings on a basket. The dejected monarch secures a necklace about the child's throat to identify her royal lineage; the two men place her carefully into the basket and sneak off to set her adrift in the river. Blackout.

SECOND PROLOGUE   Count Bluebeard sticks his head through the curtains and steps out quickly. He tweaks his beard, rolls his eyes, smacks his thigh, and appears to be a real devil of a fellow. He embraces a girl who comes along and kisses her so passionately that she collapses. This is his first wife. The same thing happens to two other maidens. A fourth girl is so overcome by the mere sight of Bluebeard that she falls in a trance before he can grab her. The fifth wife drinks with her husband. When she dies of the poison prepared by Bluebeard's henchman, Popoloni, Bluebeard stands over her body with an eager and how-was-that-for-killing-them-off leer.

ACT ONE: THE PALACE OF KING BOBICHE   The drop curtain rises on a medieval castle. Huge battlements rise up in the distance. It is night, some eighteen years after King Bobiche cast his daughter into the stream. On the right is a garden bench.

Queen Clementine dances in, followed by a page of the court. The page immediately begins to make love to the queen on the garden bench. The queen does not seem to care in the least. Bobiche interrupts them, parts the two lovers as if he'd spent his life dealing with his wife's infidelities, and then storms about with pretentious jealousy.

The queen pleads with him, but the king is adamant and orders that the page be hanged. When the poor lad is dragged off by the king's soldiers, the king chases his queen about the garden. They disappear for a moment. By the time the queen returns, two more suitors, dashing Spaniards with castanets and guitars, are ready to pay court to her. She is enchanted and watches with pleasure as the two men draw swords and fight for her affection. The two men readily see, however, that the queen is generous and can love them both. They put down their swords and alternately she kisses them as she joins them in a *pas de trois*.

Again the king interrupts and again we have tears, royal insistence, and an order for two more executions. This process goes on until five of the queen's many lovers have been caught in the act and sent off to be hanged. But still the king is not satisfied. He can certainly not expect his wife to love him and his mind goes back to the daughter he might have loved so much. He turns his back on the queen and weeps. He must get his daughter back, if by some miracle she is still alive!

The king orders his chancellor to search every corner of the kingdom for Hermilia and then condescendingly takes the hand of the queen. Members of the court kneel as the royal pair leave the garden. The drop curtain falls.

FIRST INTERLUDE: A CITY STREET   On his way to carry out the king's order, Count Oscar encounters the lovers of the queen, who are being led by their executioner to the gallows. He takes pity on them and inquires if they have any money. Luckily, they have. Good old Oscar empties their pockets and pardons them. The five men dance for joy while the chancellor counts his money.

ACT TWO: THE COUNTRYSIDE   With a roll of the drums, the curtain rises on a bright scene in the country. Scarecrows look out over the wheat fields in the distance, and the sun shines with an intense, glowing yellow. Peasant girls and boys dance together happily, circling and forming a chain, moving in vigorous, youthful harmony. One of the girls we notice right away because she is the prettiest of them all and because everyone seems to admire her. This is Floretta, in reality Hermilia, the daughter of King Bobiche. As if this weren't enough, the shepherd with whom she dances a romantic *pas de deux* is actually no shepherd at all but Prince Sapphire!

As Floretta sits on her shepherd's knee, a stunning blond girl comes in and berates the shepherd. She brags of her jealousy in a big emotional display, stamps her foot at Floretta, and the two lovers fly from her rage. Boulotte follows them.

Popoloni, the old alchemist who has helped Bluebeard kill off his wives, comes onto the scene. He tells the peasant girls that Bluebeard needs a new wife and that he will choose one of them for his bride. Bluebeard follows him almost immediately in an absurd chariot, and the girls quake at the sight of him. A few of the more courageous girls surround him, while others manage to form a line. Bluebeard looks the girls over one by one as if he were examining fresh meat. He doesn't like what he sees and pouts. As all the girls circle him, Boulotte re-enters. Bluebeard is just another man to her. She smacks him on the back, tweaks his beard, and treats him as if he were a rough and ready peasant. Ready Bluebeard obviously is: no woman has been so bold with him in years. He dances with her and soon proposes. Boulotte instantly consents, and Bluebeard carries her to his chariot. All wave as they exit.

Now the two plots of the ballet cross. Count Oscar, the chancellor, enters with one of the king's men. He is searching for the king's lost daughter. Popoloni engages Oscar in conversation, and as they talk, Floretta and her shepherd pass by. The shepherd bids the girl a hurried good-by as soon as he sees the count, who would expose his disguise. Count Oscar approaches her, asks politely to see her necklace, and Floretta is revealed as Princess Hermilia! Floretta fears that her shepherd might not love a Princess and wants to make sure of his affections. But, of course, Prince Sapphire is off sulking with similar thoughts. The drop curtain falls.

SECOND INTERLUDE   Bluebeard and Boulotte are racing across the stage to celebrate their marriage when their chariot passes Count Oscar and Hermilia. The fickle Bluebeard eyes the princess, and already he has had enough of the bouncing blonde. He must marry her, he decides, and vows to set a new plot in motion.

ACT THREE: A CELLAR IN BLUEBEARD'S CASTLE   The scene is dark as a dungeon. This is the laboratory of the alchemist Popoloni. On the left, at a table, chemicals burst into flame as he mixes them together. He chuckles to himself, delighted that his master has given him a new project. On the right are five vaults, each bearing the name of one of Bluebeard's dead wives! A sixth grave, as yet uncovered, is ready to receive another wife.

Bluebeard stalks in to give Popoloni his final orders: Boulotte must die! Boulotte enters and slaps him on the back. Bluebeard, out of all patience, tells Popoloni to be hasty. Boulotte takes one look at the five graves and clasps Bluebeard frantically in her arms. He pushes her off and Boulotte rolls about on the floor in despair. She rises and hangs on Bluebeard's neck, pleading with him to save her. "No!" he answers, and leaves her alone with her poisoner.

Boulotte goes over to Popoloni and tries to flirt with him. But the old man pushes her off his knee and tells her to leave off. He tells her that he has something for her and bids her drink from two goblets. Boulotte looks toward the open grave and refuses to drink. When Popoloni turns his back for a moment, she picks up a goblet from his table and drinks that one, instead. Poor girl, all the goblets are filled with the same poison! She falls to the floor.

Popoloni pretends grief; he is joined in his sorrow by Bluebeard, whose body shakes with sobs. He kneels beside his beloved and then, suddenly, he is up dancing as if he is absolutely delighted! He leaps over the body and dashes off in pursuit of the Princess Hermilia.

Old Popoloni's grief turns out to be genuine. He takes a feather, touches it to Boulotte's face, and she is alive again. Then, at a clap of his hands, all the graves open and we see that all the other wives have been similarly brought back to life by the alchemist. Bluebeard's first five wives surround Boulotte and pay tribute to the kindly Popoloni in a happy dance. The scene blacks out.

THIRD INTERLUDE   Bluebeard, too, has his qualms. The ghosts of his murdered wives circle around him as he recalls his crimes. For a moment, he is sorry.

ACT FOUR: THE COURT OF KING BOBICHE   King Bobiche leads his queen to their great, ermine-draped throne, and both prepare to welcome the Princess Hermilia to her true home. They embrace their daughter, who is strangely unhappy. They find out why when the king proposes that she marry a prince named Sapphire. Hermilia doesn't want a prince; she wants her shepherd. She storms about the court, refusing to consent to her father's wish. In despair, the king calls for Prince Sapphire, and when he appears, Hermilia cannot believe her eyes. Everyone rejoices.

But not for long. Bluebeard, no longer remorseful, is determined to wed Hermilia. He dashes in and flourishes his sword. The king is terrified and hides behind the throne. Prince Sapphire, the only fearless member of the court, suggests a duel. They begin to spar with their swords. Bluebeard tricks the prince and stabs him in the back. Bluebeard chuckles as his rival falls dead. Hermilia mourns her lover while the heartless Bluebeard wipes his sword and turns to her. Now, indeed, she must marry him!

Popoloni enters the court leading five masked women. Bluebeard is so busy sitting in Hermilia's lap that he doesn't pay much attention. Poor Hermilia can do nothing but cry. When Bluebeard looks up, the five women unmask: he sees all his dead wives! He leaps high into the air and runs for his life. The wives close in and beat him soundly. He frees himself and threatens Popoloni. But he observes that one of his former wives was really worth saving, after all. He drops the sword and goes to embrace her.

But King Bobiche has other ideas. The queen's five lovers have returned from the dead, too, and something must be done quickly: so he pairs them off with Bluebeard's wives. Old Popoloni recalls Prince Sapphire to life, and Hermilia is happy. The royal couple parade with Bluebeard and Boulotte, trumpets blare, Boulotte whirls around and around and around, and the colorful assembly of courtiers and peasantry rejoice.

BOURNONVILLE DIVERTISSEMENTS

Music by various composers indicated below. Choreography by Auguste Bournonville. Staged by Stanley Williams. Costumes by Ben Benson, after the original designs. Lighting by Ronald Bates. First presented by the New York City Ballet at the New York State Theatre, Lincoln Center, February 3, 1977, with Nichol Hlinka and Daniel Duell; Patricia McBride and Helgi Tomasson; Merrill Ashley, Robert Weiss and Kyra Nicholas; Suzanne Farrell and Peter Martins; Colleen Neary, Adam Luders, Victor Castelli, Muriel Aasen, Wilhelmina Frankfurt, Heather Watts and Bart Cook.

I hope that by this time everyone knows the Danish ballet is built on a technique established in the nineteenth century by the great August Bournonville (1805–79), himself a remarkable dancer and choreographer, creator of many lasting works in the repertory of the Royal Danish Ballet. Bournonville was a pupil of Auguste Vestris, the first universally renowned male dancer in Europe, and brought superb technique to Denmark which he afterward modified in his own way. We see the result of his teaching in every ballet the Danes dance and whenever Danes dance. I have known and respected Bournonville's work ever since I worked at the Royal Danish Theatre in 1929 as guest choreographer.

Stanley Williams of our School of American Ballet is a much respected authority on Bournonville and we thought it would be good for our dancers, and for our audiences, to come to know well some of Bournonville's finest dances. Stanley Williams then put together a most entertaining ballet.

The ballet is in five parts, the first the *Ballabile* from the first act of *Napoli*, 1842, Bournonville's masterwork, with music by Paulli. Next, the *Pas de Deux* from Act I of *Kermesse in Bruges*, 1851, with music by Paulli. The third dance is a *Pas de Trois* from *La Ventana*, 1854, with music by Lumbye. The two concluding pieces are the famous *Pas de Deux* from *Flower Festival in Genzano*, 1858, with music by Helsted, and the *Pas de Sept* from *A Folk Tale*, 1854.

As Svend Kragh-Jacobsen observed in our program at the New York City Ballet, these five pieces made up a well-varied program with which to present Denmark's grand old master to a new audience.

BOURRÉE FANTASQUE

Classical ballet in three parts. Music by Emmanuel Chabrier. Choreography by George Balanchine. Costumes by Karinska. Lighting by Jean Rosenthal. First presented by the New York City Ballet at the City Center, New York, December 1, 1949, with Tanaquil LeClercq and Jerome Robbins, Maria Tallchief and Nicholas Magallanes, Janet Reed and Herbert Bliss as the principals.

This dance spectacle in three movements has no story, but each of the three parts has its own special character and quality of motion to match the buoyant pieces by Chabrier that make up the ballet's score. Each movement of the ballet is danced by a different *premier danseur* as principals. The "Joyous March" that serves as the overture sets a festival pace for the proceedings: loud, cheerful chords, crashing cymbals, and themes so blatantly vivacious that our senses are prepared for the high-spirited geniality with which the ballet both begins and ends.

BOURRÉE FANTASQUE   The curtain rises just before the overture finishes its final crescendo. Transparent white gauze curtains are draped across a blue background, and from the ceiling of the stage hang three black chandeliers, each holding differently colored candles. To the extreme right, standing in a straight line at right angles to the footlights, are four couples waiting for their cue. They are dressed in smart, crisp black; the girls fan themselves with small black fans. The sprightly music begins. The couples join arms and dance across the stage with jaunty, playful steps. The boys encourage the girls, who turn rapidly as their movements become more complicated. Four girls enter at the back; the couples stand back on either side as the newcomers move downstage, dancing in unison a series of bright, high steps. All the dancers are manifestly enjoying themselves immensely as they execute the precise, sparkling routine, yet they all maintain a firm, dead-pan expression, which makes their dancing absurdly comic. The boys leave their partners and pull the girls into their line. Everyone bows low.

A tall girl and a boy much shorter run out onto the stage and dance together briskly. The girl wears flowers high in her hair and fans her face impatiently. They stop suddenly; the music hesitates. The girl turns her back on the boy and looks down at her fan, which clearly amuses her more than he does. The boy tries to make a graceful pose and grabs hold of the ballerina's waist for support. She looks down at him with bored contempt; apparently he will think anything funny. He puts out his leg and looks on incredulously as the ballerina steps across it with little, mincing steps. He smiles at her gratefully; every one of her gestures is marvelous to him. She collapses in his arms and dances frantically. She holds her leg high, and he obligingly supports it under the knee. He stoops down close to the floor to watch her feet closely. The ballerina is determined to exploit his patience at every opportunity and when the boy supports her in attitude, she throws her leg up behind him and kicks him in the back of the head. The boy continues, however, to fancy that she is perfection itself. He moves to sit down, but the ballerina jumps into his lap before he reaches the floor. He tries to engage her flirtatiously, but she will have none of it; he nods his head beseechingly, but she shakes her head insistently. They rise and exit with a flourish.

The eight girls and four boys dance briefly. Like the ballerina's partner, the boys crawl on the floor to admire the girls' dancing feet. Then they move between the two rows of girls and join them in witty steps to the staccato verve of the music.

The ballerina and her partner return and enliven the fun to a high pitch of merriment. The boy holds the ballerina about the waist and squats low behind her as she hops toward the back on one point. Then he joins the other four boys in a dance that becomes intensely brisk. The ballerina fans herself calmly. The girls come forward and rejoin the boys, and the ballerina's partner twirls her about. He catches her in a tight embrace, but she bends her body back, trying to escape. He attempts to put his arms around her neck, but she holds his hands; their arms tangle hopelessly. The two move close to the footlights and forget all classical pretensions as they turn swiftly around and around on one foot, like circus performers. They both stop this exhibition simultaneously and join the group in a final round of merriment that ends abruptly on a note of rampant gaiety.

PRELUDE The gauze curtains are pulled slightly higher over the empty stage. Eight girls enter from the wings and cross the stage fleetingly, softly, devising a fragile, romantic mood to the new sensuous melody. They arrange themselves in two striking poses about their leaders. A lovely girl walks out slowly from the back. She is looking for someone; she approaches like a sleep-walker and notices no one. A boy emerges from the opposite side. He, too, moves as if he were in a dream. The boy and the girl wander in different directions, weaving in and out among the other dancers as if caught in a labyrinth that will never lead them to each other. Each appears to sense the other's presence, but as they pass closely, their hands almost touching, their reverie does not allow them to see and after a pause they continue on their search.

At last the boy discovers the girl. Her back is turned to him. He places his hand on her shoulder; at his touch she poses gracefully. The boy takes his supporting hand away; the girl stands motionless on point for an instant until he has moved in front of her. She places her arms on his shoulders, and the boy assists her as she displays her comeliness in open turns that cause her black dress to flow about her. Their contact is intimate but also remote, warm yet formal; they recognize each other only in the perfection with which they dance together. She falls back in his arms.

The boy turns briefly to support two of the other girls, but returns to the ballerina. She pirouettes rapidly with her arms high over her head; the boy catches her still turning figure and circles with her. He lifts her tenderly. Momentarily, he is separated from the ballerina and the other girls group themselves around him. He kneels and they cover his head with their arms possessively so that he does not see his lover approach him. She moves away listlessly, returns, retires, then moves back toward him determinedly, in a running leap. The boy looks up and catches her falling body tenderly as the other girls back away. He lifts the ballerina high, and they move forward diagonally across the stage, two girls following along closely, their arms stretched up to clasp the ballerina's outstretched hands. The other girls move by in the opposite direction, passing under their arms swiftly and creating an impression of effortless speed. Now the boy moves backward with the ballerina and the group moves forward beneath her. He lifts her down and for an instant he loses her. The sumptuous music nears its fullest statement as he finds her again. He holds her hand, she rises on point and extends her leg slowly but firmly. Her extended point seems to pierce the richness of the melody.

With an elegant flourish, the ballerina bends low before the boy in a formal gesture of gratitude and acceptance. She rises to turn rapidly in attitude; the boy steps forward quickly and catches her about the waist as she turns full circle. The movement is repeated several times, after which the lovers stand close together, her head on his shoulder. They move apart; the girls glide in between them, forming the same intricate pattern that separated them at the beginning. They look about, seeking, wandering in and out; they pass, pause, but do not find. Both walk off as they came, preoccupied with their private dreams. The others dance slowly into the wings.

FÊTE POLONAISE   To the tune of a lively fanfare, a girl and a boy run out onto the stage. The boy kneels, takes the girl's hand, and holds her secure as she races around him. They are followed by three couples, who repeat this routine while the orchestra hurries its preface to the principal theme. Two other couples join the group. These two girls place their hands on their hips and look out into the audience with the gay impudence of chorines. A loud beat is sounded on the drum, and the exhilarating polonaise begins as the two girls are thrown high by their partners.

The other couples join the dance; the boys kneel around the girls in a circle and with a whipping motion encourage their cavorting. Directly all the dancers have caught the vivacity of the music, the ballerina enters to make the scene more animated still. Her grace and high good humor infect the dancing with fresh lightness. She seems astonishingly light as her partner swings her high about him. Finally, he catches her in a breath-taking leap and the two exit.

There are now eight couples on the stage, who dance together briefly before the ballerina and her partner return. This time the boy swings the ballerina about him on one arm; her legs beat together in midair. The girls circle them; the ballerina is turned rapidly by her partner as the girls dance around them; then she kneels. She leaves the stage, and the romantic ballerina of the prelude enters with her group of dancers. Soon all three ballerinas and their partners are assembled with the entire *corps de ballet*. The corps de ballet form concentric circles about the romantic ballerina, who is lifted high above them, and for a few moments the entire scene whirls with movement as each circle of dancers runs around and around.

All the boys dance a short routine with boundless energy, and the three ballerinas come to the front of the stage with their partners. Now it is almost like a competition between them. The ballerinas gather with their different groups. They take turns leading the groups of eight girls across the stage diagonally with broad, running jumps. The groups crisscross in midstage as the music nears a climax of jubilation. Then all the ensemble is reunited for the height of the festivity. Their ensembles are grouped behind the three ballerinas in a spectacular pose as the music ends and the curtain falls.

LA BOUTIQUE FANTASQUE (The Fantastic Toyshop)

Ballet in one act. Music by Gioacchino Rossini, arranged and orchestrated by Ottorino Respighi. Choreography by Leonide Massine. Scenery and costumes by André Derain. First presented by Diaghilev's Ballets Russes at the Alhambra Theatre, London, June 5, 1919, with Enrico Cecchetti as the Shopkeeper, Lydia Lopokova and Leonide Massine as the Cancan Dancers, and a cast that included Lydia Sokolova, Leon Woicikowski, Stanislas Idzikowski, Vera Nemtchinova, Lubov Tchernicheva, and Serge Grigoriev. First presented in the United States by the Ballet Russe de Monte Carlo at the Majestic Theatre, New York, March 20, 1935, with a cast that included Alexandra Danilova and Leonide Massine (Cancan Dancers), Eugenia Delarova, Tamara Grigorieva, Nina Verachinina, Yurek Shabelevsky, Roland Guérard, David Lichine, and Serge Grigoriev.

Like *Coppélia*, *La Boutique Fantasque* is based on the charm of the mechanical doll. Here, in a great fantastic toyshop in southern France, dolls from all over the world entertain customers from all over the world, who have come to see the detailed and charming workmanship of a master dollmaker. The time is the 1860s.

At the rise of the curtain, the sunny shop is empty. It has been closed for lunch. The shopkeeper and his helper return and open the doors for business. While they are busy preparing for their work, a dirty little boy comes in and attempts to steal gold lace from one of the shopkeeper's prize dolls. The thief is apprehended and, fleeing, bumps into two prospective customers, an English old maid and her companion.

The old maids want to see the best dolls and when the shopkeeper has shown them the mechanical peasant dolls on display, they ask to see more. New customers, an American family with two children, charge in. The family know the English ladies and after all the customers have exchanged greetings, the American turns to the shopkeeper and asks to see his dolls.

The shopkeeper obsequiously consents, and two tarantella dancers are wheeled in. When the customers have examined them, the two dolls, an Italian girl and her sweetheart, break into an animated tarantella to the lively accompaniment of rattling tambourines. Then, as if their mechanism had run down, the dancers collapse.

Next there is a mazurka, danced by dolls representing the Queen of Clubs, the Queen of Hearts, the King of Diamonds, and the King of Spades.

A Russian couple enter with their four children. The English ladies resent the intrusion of these foreigners and take their leave.

The next set of dolls displayed by the shopkeeper represent a snob and a melon hawker, a combination of the rich and the poor. The snob bustles about busily while the melon hawker slices a melon and presents it to him. Then the melon hawker shines the shoes of the snob, who trips over the hawker, only to rise again in a mechanical miracle.

The customers are now convinced that they are seeing a great and marvelous entertainment. Their mutual enthusiasm makes them all friendly and they watch with delight as more dolls perform.

Five Cossack dolls led by a chief perform a rapid dance next. Then the chief Cossack is joined by a Cossack girl doll, who kisses him while the soldiers snap to attention. The porters of the fantastic toyshop drill the Cossacks off.

Now two dancing poodles display their skill by walking on their hind legs. The female dog tries to attract the male dog by her cavortings and the male dog, in his enthusiasm for her dancing, rushes around and around her. The American couple are shocked at this amorous display and blindfold their children.

The shopkeeper now informs his prospective customers that they are about to see the most ingenious dolls of all: the cancan dancers. The couple who are wheeled in dance with such gusto that all the spectators are bound to agree. As the girl doll abandons herself in the cancan, her partner is so delighted that he performs marvelous gravity-defying tricks.

Now both families who have been watching the dolls want to buy the cancan dancers. The American children like the male doll best, the Russians the girl. Their fathers talk to the shopkeeper, agree to pay his price, and leave, saying that they will call for the dolls in the morning.

Night has fallen. The shopkeeper and his assistants lock up and leave.

Now that they are alone, all the dolls in the shop emerge from their boxes and become more animated than ever. They are very happy to be dancing so freely, but they are also sad. The cancan dancers are to be separated tomorrow. The two lovers dance together for what seems to be the last time, and the other dolls dance about them, celebrating their love. At the end of the revels there is a general cakewalk, danced by all the dolls.

When morning comes and the shop is reopened, all appears to be as it was the night before. But when the American and Russian families call to pick up the dolls they have engaged to buy, something is amiss: the cancan dancers have disappeared from their boxes! The children howl, the fathers berate the shopkeeper, and the mothers rage. The shopkeeper and his assistants are beaten, and the whole toyshop is attacked by the disappointed customers.

Just when it seems likely that the irate foreigners will destroy the shop completely, the toy dolls come to the rescue. The poodles attack the Russian mother; her husband and children are set upon by the card toys; and the Americans are routed by kicking ballet-dancer dolls. Finally the Cossacks drive the customers from the shop.

Unbelieving, the Americans and Russians stand outside and look back through the window. They see all the dolls in the shop dancing together a brilliant ensemble, a final happy dance. The shopkeeper and the cancan dancers shake hands. All the dolls rejoice that the two lovers are still together.

BRAHMS QUINTET

Music by Johannes Brahms. Choreography by Dennis Nahat. Costumes by Willa Kim. Lighting by Nananne Porcher. First presented by American Ballet Theatre at the Brooklyn Academy of Music, New York, December 1969, with Cynthia Gregory, Ivan Nagy, Mimi Paul, Gayle Young, Naomi Sorkin, Ian Horvath, Eleanor D'Antuono, and Terry Orr as principals.

This dance ballet to a masterpiece by Brahms uses the score for its narrative. The music critic Donald F. Tovey referred to the Brahms *Quintet in G Major, Op. 111*, as "an immensely powerful outburst of high spirits. . . . The first movement seems unlimited in its capacity for expansion. The adagio . . . is one of Brahms's tragic utterances. Its tempo is slower than that of any other piece of classical music since Beethoven's C Minor Concerto." Tovey found the third movement to be an "exquisite plaintive little scherzo and trio" and the finale "vigorous. . . . At the end its coda breaks away into a completely new dance tune, the phrases of which reel down in bacchanalian irregularity to explain themselves with impudent assurance as connected with the main theme by ties as intimate as a borrowed visiting card." (From *Cobbet's Cyclopedic Survey of Chamber Music*, 1963.)

Reviewing the ballet for the Washington *Post*, the critic Jean Battey Lewis said that "Nahat's *Brahms Quintet* is one of those flowing, floating dance works so appealing to us these days. It has a lovely, curving wind-swept quality and an abstraction that still celebrates the affection between the dancers."

BRAHMS-SCHOENBERG QUARTET

Music by Johannes Brahms, orchestrated by Arnold Schoenberg. Choreography by George Balanchine. Scenery by Peter Harvey. Costumes by Karinska. First presented by the New York City Ballet at the New York State Theatre April 19, 1966, with Melissa Hayden and André Prokovsky, Patricia McBride and Conrad Ludlow, Allegra Kent and Edward Villella, and Suzanne Farrell and Jacques d'Amboise in leading roles.

In talking about music that is good for dancing I have often said that most string quartets are not suitable—they are too long, they are full of repeats, and of course they are meant for smaller audiences. This quartet of Brahms, the *Piano Quartet in G minor, Opus 25,* I have always liked a great deal but it never occurred to me to use it for a ballet until Robert Craft told me about Schoenberg's orchestration.

This undertaking was of course most unusual for Schoenberg. But in a letter to Dr. Alfred Frankenstein, Schoenberg gave his reasons: "1. I love the piece. 2. It is seldom played. 3. It is always very badly played, as the better the pianist, the louder he plays and one hears nothing of the strings. I wanted for once to hear everything and this I have achieved."

I liked hearing everything too, and wanted to see the piece danced. The result is a dance ballet, with only a musical narrative. The movements are marked *Allegro, Allegro ma non troppo, Andante,* and *Rondo alla Zingarese: Presto.*

BROUILLARDS

Music by Claude Debussy. Choreography by John Cranko. First presented by the Württemberg State Ballet at the Opera House, Stuttgart, March 8, 1970. First presented in the United States by the same ensemble (the Stuttgart Ballet) at the Metropolitan Opera House, New York, April 30, 1971.

Nine piano preludes by Claude Debussy are the inspiration for *Brouillards* ("Mist"). The choreographer, John Cranko, said: "Mist, snow, heather and sails are the transient pictures in Debussy's music: the mist dissolves, the snow melts away, the heather fades, and the sails grow slack—leaving behind remembrance and regret only because of their beauty. Every day passes away—like all human relations." While thus a ballet without a narrative, *Brouillards* may be said to have a mood plot set to music.

The piano begins and the curtain rises on a dark scene where we gradually discern a chain of dancers in white. They swirl and gather in the center, undulate in the mist, separate, return and cluster. A girl and three boys, to the music of *La Puerta del Vino* ("The Gate of Wine"), perform a bright dance in which, first riding on the back of one, then dancing an adagio with another, and finally turning to respond to the third, the girl shows that she likes all three. The boys leave her, sulking, at the end.

To *Voiles* ("Sails"), a girl and boy dance, responding to the music with daring lifts, slides, and turns, he going in one direction with the wind, as it were, she in another. Next, a *Cakewalk*, a comic turn to quick, witty music for three boys. *Bruyères* ("Heather"), which follows, is a dance for a boy who is enamored of a sleeping beauty who lies nearby on a bench. He kneels at her feet, kisses her, dances for her, but she does not respond. When, finally, he shakes her in exasperation, she rises and coolly walks away.

Two girls dance to the music of *The Fairies Are Exquisite Dancers* and make of it a joyful competition of held poses and leaps. To *Dead Leaves* there is another *pas de deux*, a passionate adagio. *Homage to S. Pickwick, Esq.* is a tribute to John Bull, armed with bowler hat and umbrella, by six boys who kid him and rag him until he collapses. They cover him up, the bowler on the umbrella remaining as a kind of gravestone.

Footsteps in the Snow is for a girl and two boys, both of whom seem to follow in pursuit of the girl, and the *Finale*, again, is an ensemble piece, the group of dancers filling the surface of the stage with swirling mist.

BUGAKU

Music by Toshiro Mayuzumi. Choreography by George Balanchine. Scenery and lighting by David Hays. Costumes by Karinska. First presented by the New York City Ballet at the City Center, New York, March 30, 1963, with Allegra Kent and Edward Villella in the leading roles.

Over the years the New York City Ballet has had a happy association with Japan. The company danced there in 1958, and in 1959 the musicians and dancers maintained by the Imperial Household known as *Gagaku* came to the United States and appeared with great success on the regular programs of the New York City Ballet. The *Gagaku* is the oldest dance company in the world, with an uninterrupted tradition of repertory and performance extending almost a hundred years. Having heard the *Gagaku* and seen their fine dancers with so much pleasure, I asked the gifted young Japanese composer Toshiro Mayuzumi to write the music for a ballet. The work was commissioned by Mrs. Norman LaSalle. Our idea was that the piece would be in the style of Japanese court music (*Bugaku*), but for Western orchestration.

Mayuzumi's score I liked very much when we received it. Just as the composer had transposed the Japanese court music into a Western vocabulary, I attempted in the dances to transpose the classic Western academic ballet into a style suggested by the music.

The setting is a severely simple arena-like stage typical of formal Japanese presentations. The costumes are a free fantasy on traditional Japanese court dress. The dance is in three main parts. At the beginning, before any dancers appear, the ear takes in the strange sounds of the orchestral introduction. Five girls enter and dance with grave formality, following the lead of a girl in a rose-petal skirt. They are joined by five boys, who file on to the vigorous sound of drums. Later, these couples return in ceremonial robes to escort the boy and girl who have led them. The diaphanous ceremonial robes of the girl flow behind her as the boy lifts her in a dance of praise. But love here is as ritualistic as the setting. The attendants remove the ceremonial robes of the couple. They continue their dance, now unencumbered by the costumes. Their dance is a *pas de deux* of discovery. After the adagio, the girl dances joyously, then the boy, but then the music slows down. The attendants return to dress them again in their robes and there is a stately procession at the end of which all kneel.

THE CAGE

Ballet in one act. Music by Igor Stravinsky (Concerto Grosso in D for Strings). *Choreography by Jerome Robbins. Costumes by Ruth Sobotka. Lighting by Jean Rosenthal. First presented by the New York City Ballet at the City Center, New York, June 10, 1951, with Nora Kaye as the* Novice, *Yvonne Mounsey as the* Queen, *and Nicholas Magallanes and Michael Maule as the* Intruders.

This ballet is a dramatic demonstration of a phenomenon common to insect and animal life and to Western mythology too: the phenomenon of the female considering the male as prey. The mantis devours her partner after mating; the spider kills the male unless he attacks first; and the Amazons, in Greek mythology, were a cult of warlike females who did not associate with men, except for procreation. The Amazons despised their male children and maimed or destroyed them. Woman was sufficient; Man was accidental. *The Cage* shows us such a tribe of women.

Before the ballet begins, the auditorium is completely dark. The footlights come up before the curtain, then go out; the lights in the orchestra are extinguished. There is no music. The curtain rises. The light is obscure and misty, but we see hanging over the stage a tangle of multicolored strands, like the web of some huge spider. Mysteriously, as if it were a living thing, the web rises, stretches, and hangs over the floor. On the left stand a group of female figures arranged in a tight tableau; they are clustered together like bees in a hive.

The music begins with three notes sounded sharply on the strings. The women stir. In the center of the group sits the queen of the tribe. The lights come up gradually. A still, shrouded creature is drawn out from between the queen's legs; the novice has been born. The queen strips the confining membrane from the novice's body. The new member of the tribe crouches slightly. Her body is marked with endless, tangled viscera. Her face is still covered. She is motionless. The queen stands behind her, extending her arms grotesquely, seeming to enclose the novice with her long talons.

The orchestra begins a vibrant march. The twelve members of the tribe turn their backs, rise on point, and commence a grotesque ceremonial dance. As their bodies turn, we see that their backs are insectlike: strands reach out from their black spines to cover their backs, and they seem to resemble scuttling beetles. The queen leaves the novice and dances among the tribe. The women circle her and bow low obediently as she dances. The novice remains inert.

Now two of the women go to the novice and drag her to the center, before the queen. The queen tears off the membrane covering her face. The novice's hands reach up to protect her eyes from the sudden light. Her face is a mask; her hair, dark and wet, clings to her head. The queen is well pleased at her ugliness. The birth rite is over; the queen and her creatures leave to watch the novice from the surrounding darkness. Just as she departs, the queen touches the novice's dark head in blessing.

The melody changes; the music slows in tempo. The novice's untrained limbs do not yet know how to move and she squats alone. She tests her arms and legs, pushes her body up on them, rises on point. Her gestures are sudden and sharp, her body angularly contorted. Her fingers are clawing and knifelike blades cutting at the air tentatively; her arms are sinuous, serpentine. She walks with knees open and bent, arms ready to enlace her prey.

The music breaks into a loud, rapidly rhythmic burst of sound. A man rushes in and seizes the novice by the waist. She twists away in revulsion. The intruder attempts to pull her close to him and falls to the ground. The novice falls upon him, and they roll over together. The exhausted intruder lies quiet as the novice rises and steps upon his chest with the sharp point of her foot. Now she straddles his body, grabs his head between her legs, clenches her fists, tightens and twists her body, and cracks his neck with her knees. He is dead.

The music quietens. The novice kicks the body over on its face. As the orchestra resumes the opening march, she dances alone, her knees rising high, driving her feet hard against the ground. Her head is thrown back and her mouth hangs open in a shriek of triumph.

The queen leads the tribe back to the novice. The hideous women stalk into the light, surround the novice, and congratulate her. She has met the test, her instinct has obeyed the law of the tribe: she has killed her first male. The novice kicks at his body contemptuously, and he is dragged off.

The queen embraces the novice. Other women in the tribe pair off and rest together. The women are content with their own society and relax without fear of intrusion. Then the music sounds a warning. The couples separate. The light dims. The queen signals the others to hasten away. The novice, suddenly afraid, is running off after them as her swift body is caught up in the arms of a dark, handsome intruder. Her legs try to kick her body free as he holds her, but she cannot loosen his grasp. The warning in the music ceases; the melody flows yieldingly. The novice is now unsure. Gradually she succumbs to the superior strength of the intruder and dances with him a romantic love duet. He holds her on his knee, and she sharpens her claws together, not for battle now, but for love. Their bodies separate and their fingers approach and entwine like bristling antennae. She tries to make herself graceful as she dances and falls back into the intruder's arms. He catches her body between his legs; her face turns up toward his, and their arms embrace in a cocoon. The novice's feet beat at the floor as the intruder becomes her lover.

The lights go down for a moment. The music whirrs ominously. The frightened intruder moves and the woman falls to the ground. The two lovers cower together, trying to conceal each other in the darkness, as the queen and the tribe enter. Then, as the intruder sees the women who would claim the novice, he revolts and pushes the woman, now hideous to him, into the arms of her Amazon queen.

This is what the tribe have waited for. The queen directs her creatures to attack the intruder as the novice is held secure. The women climb upon the intruder like ants on a stick of candy. He is released briefly and rolls helpless on the ground. The novice's native instinct begins to return. She falls upon him, straddles him, and slides her body over the passive male. She squats guiltily as the women seize him and carry him aloft. The queen orders her fellow creatures to carry the novice on their shoulders and hold her poised above him. The novice's claws are straight and sharp for the kill. She aims carefully and deliberately and slashes.

The body of the intruder lies again on the ground. The hungry women crawl over him, devouring his limbs. The novice strangles him between her knees. His body curls for a moment, then straightens. He is dead. His body is rolled across the stage. The victorious women leap over it as they dance triumphantly.

The novice cleans her talons. The queen joins her to accept her as a true member of the tribe. The two grotesque figures whirl together, then stand motionless, their deformed bodies dominating the dark cage. The music stops. The great spidery web loosens and falls about them to the ground.

NOTES   When *The Cage* was presented during the New York City Ballet's Stravinsky Festival in June 1972, the critic Sam Norkin wrote in the *Daily News:* "A hit since its premiere 21 years ago, this ballet is a 16-minute spellbinder . . . The driving music that accompanies the ballet was danced sensationally by Melissa Hayden as the novice. Here was a great ballerina in full mastery of her role. Gloria Govrin and Nicholas Magallanes were convincing in their roles as the queen and intruder respectively."

CAKEWALK

Ballet in three parts. Music adapted and orchestrated by Hershy Kay after music by Louis Moreau Gottschalk. Choreography by Ruthanna Boris. Scenery and costume by Robert Drew. Lighting by Jean Rosenthal. First presented by the New York City Ballet at the City Center, New York, June 12, 1951, with a cast headed by Janet Reed, Patricia Wilde, Yvonne Mounsey, Herbert Bliss, Frank Hobi, Tanaquil LeClercq, and Beatrice Tompkins.

Cakewalk is an American ballet based on the minstrel shows. The great era of the minstrel show began to end toward the turn of the century, but this ballet reminds us of why this form of entertainment, native to America, was once so universally popular: like the original, it has humor, sentiment, magic, and liveliness. *Cakewalk,* being a ballet, doesn't have the two sets of bones, the two banjos, the two tambourines, and the singers that every real minstrel show used to have. These musical elements are taken care of by the orchestra, which plays in special arrangements a group of pieces and songs by Louis Moreau Gottschalk, the American composer and pianist whose music was so popular among original minstrel show artists: such works as "Bamboula," "Maiden's Blush," and "Won't You Buy My Pretty Flowers?" On stage, the dancers imitate the conventional minstrel show turns in dance terms that combine folk dancing with an enlivened classical technique. Like all proper minstrel shows, *Cakewalk* is divided into three parts.

PART ONE   The orchestra strikes up a loud, ebullient overture. The curtain rises. At extreme left and right are entrance doors on to the stage. In the back hangs a drop curtain that shows a huge Mississippi side-wheeler plying up the stream. Already, before the dancers appear, we have a vivid sense of the atmosphere in which the original minstrel show flourished.

One by one, the performers make their entrance to begin the "Grand Introductory Walkaround." They strut across the stage rapidly, led by the interlocutor, giving us a hint of the novelties to come. Finally, when all have disappeared in the door at the left, the drop curtain rises and we see the stage set for the minstrel show. In the back stands a long platform with ramps leading forward down to the stage. Gold chairs and torches are lined up on stage and platform. The "Grand Introductory March" reaches a climax of happy anticipation, and the artists—the center performers, the semicircle, the auxiliary ladies and gentlemen, and the two end men—move to their seats. A tambourine claps for order as all sit down at the interlocutor's signal.

The interlocutor leads forward a dainty girl, whose old-fashioned curls and somber countenance presage a dance of great seriousness. The orchestra sounds the first notes of a "Pathetic Ballad" in slow waltz time; the girl moves forward on point and renders a dance of absurd tragedy. She is all alone; the four boys who dance with their partners in a semicircle around her will not pay any attention to her. She is doomed to be a perpetual wallflower. Yet all the time the girl maintains in her steps and gestures an indifference to ordinary mortals that exposes her addiction to pathos. She loves to be sad, and sad in the grand manner. She clasps her hands and raises them in supplication; she kneels, begging for help in her distress; she turns beseechingly to the happy couples for succor. No one will help her! The girl raises a pointed hand to her temples and fires. The saccharine music expires, and the unfortunate creature is free to be happy again. She takes her seat, rises disconsolately to the audience applause, and sits down again, her eyes downcast.

The interlocutor, his black cane in hand, comes forward and performs "Sleight of Feet," a rhythmic jumping specialty that makes him a magician in movement. He tries to attract our attention to his hands, his coattails, and his cane as his feet perform quick marvels. The end men run forward with a chair, and he falls back, exhausted by triumph.

The interlocutor is followed by the two end men, one short, the other tall, who rise from their places at each end of the line and dance "Perpendicular Points." This number displays their adroit sharpness in dancing almost continually on their toes to curtly paced music that would trip them up if it could. Their long swallow-tailed coats bounce in the air as their points hit every beat of the music. As their number ends, they rush over to the left and end up sitting in the lap of the surprised interlocutor.

The lights go down. A bright spotlight catches a girl in a shining red dress who rushes out and dances a vigorous "Freebee" to a fresh, rousing theme. All the performers clap their hands in rhythm to the music; the girl dances faster; the whole troupe catches the contagious liveliness of her movement and the members come forward to join her. They parade across the platform as the girl in red is lifted high between two boys and carried around the stage. But the instant her feet touch the floor, she is on fire again with movement and leads all in a jumping, turning ensemble that increases in speed and dizziness. All fall flat on the floor, exhausted.

PART TWO The dancers rise and carry out the chairs and benches. The drop curtain falls, and some of the performers come forward and sit to watch the show themselves. The stage is now empty and dark. The music warns of mysterious events. Three capes—red, green, and purple—seem to move across the stage unsupported, sweeping the air before them. Then the capes are dropped and we see that they are worn by Louis, the Illusionist, and his two assistants, Moreau and Lessau—the interlocutor and the two end men in disguise.

Louis and his two assistants make magic signs, gather close in a line, their capes before them. The drop curtain rises. The three cloaked figures slide off into the wings, miraculously leaving before us, in the center of the stage, the goddess Venus, gamboling on the green with three Graces. When they have danced their bit, the magician and his helpers return. They enclose the four mythical figures in their capes and they disappear.

Next Louis brings forth a wild pony, transmigrated from its native hills. The wild pony, danced by the leader of the frenzied "Freebee," cavorts and bucks about her unnatural surroundings with stubborn, bold abandon. The magician tries to tame her, pulling the reins taut, but the pony's mane switches the trainer's face and he at last releases her.

Tinkling music is heard. Perched on a seat hung with flowers, Hortense, Queen of the Swamp Lilies, swings into view and off again. Her garlanded swing brings her back, however, and she is lifted down to earth by Harolde, the young poet, who joins her in a pas de deux. To the music of a solo violin and the harp, the idealized lovers dance with considered, prolonged languor, never hurrying, never reaching their goal.

PART THREE The lights come up. The magician has materialized his last illusion and he and his assistants leave the scene stealthily, their cloaks wrapped about them. The orchestra begins a catchy march, and all the participants parade the stage in a spirited, strutting, gala cakewalk that moves rapidly to a boisterous, rollicking conclusion. All the dancers wave responsive greetings to the audience as the curtain falls.

CAPRICCIO ESPAÑOL

Ballet in one act. Music by Nikolai Rimsky-Korsakov. Choreography by Leonide Massine, with the collaboration of Argentinita. Book by Leonide Massine. Scenery and costumes by Mariano Andreù. First presented by the Ballet Russe de Monte Carlo at the Théâtre de Monte Carlo, May 4, 1939, with a cast that included Argentinita, Alexandra Danilova, Michel Panaieff, and Leonide Massine. First presented in the United States by the Ballet Russe de Monte Carlo at the Metropolitan Opera House, New York, October 27, 1939, with Mia Slavenska, Alexandra Danilova, André Eglevsky, and Leonide Massine in the leading roles.

Capriccio Español is a ballet about Spain, rather than a Spanish ballet. Just as Spanish dance themes provided Rimsky-Korsakov with melodies for a bright and colorful orchestration, the choreography here uses Spanish dance steps to create a romantic and colorful representation that some of us might imagine to be Spain. The ballet, therefore, has no particular story to tell; instead, it tries through a series of dances to create an atmosphere, a feeling that something real has been touched.

The ballet begins with a dance called the alborada, a morning serenade. We find ourselves in the public square of a small Spanish town whose inhabitants are preparing for a festival. The music is almost uncontrolled in its loud, blaring enthusiasm. Boys of the village dance with wild abandon to this music. Soon they are joined by a group of girls. But instead of choosing the boys for their partners, the girls turn to the elders of the village and dance with them playfully and charmingly. The girls are aware that only these older men, who have seen so many beautiful women in their lives, have a real and knowing appreciation of their loveliness, and the older men, in turn, are charmed by the fact that the girls know this. The music is quieter, occasionally bursting into crescendos, as it varies the more gentle secondary theme.

The turbulent first movement is now repeated, and the boys again take up their dance. There is a roll on the drum, which the brasses build into a fanfare, and a stunning gypsy comes into the square. This is the fortuneteller. She begins to dance, enchanting all the village with her fiery, sinuous movements. A gypsylike melody inserts itself between solos for various instruments as the fortuneteller continues to hold everyone's attention. She is joined by a partner and in the rapid stampings, quick whirls, and persistent rhythms of their dance, the bodies seem to make the whole square vibrate. The strings are plucked like guitars, and the couple bring their duet to a close with a fandango.

Another couple come forward and, in the midst of the excited crowd, now overflowing with the spirit of the festival, this peasant boy and girl lead all the

natives in a tempestuous ensemble. The fortuneteller returns with her partner
to join the peasant couple as the festival reaches a peak of excitement. All the
people have now forgotten that they are moving in a dance, for their dancing
derives from a holiday impulse that makes everything but dashing and turning
movement impossible. Inspired by the dazzling display of the two lead couples, the villagers become intoxicated with joy at their own brilliant facility
and dance with their leaders a final, uproarious ensemble as the opening theme
of the ballet triumphantly returns.

CAPRICHOS

*Ballet in four episodes. Choreography by Herbert Ross. Music by Béla
Bartók. Costumes by Helene Pons. First presented by the Choreographers'
Workshop at the Hunter Playhouse, New York, January 29, 1950. Presented
by Ballet Theatre at the Center Theatre, New York, April 26, 1950, with
Charlyne Baker, Jenny Workman, Nana Gollner, John Kriza, Ruth Ann
Koesun, and Mary Burr as the principals.*

This ballet derives its inspiration from the comments the Spanish artist Goya
made on a series of his etchings. The choreographer has taken four of these
comments and visualized opinion. The ballet is performed to Béla Bartók's
Contrasts for Piano, Clarinet, and Violin. A blue backdrop is the only scenery.
   There are two girls on stage as the curtain rises. They are dressed in brief
white nightgowns. They wear black crucifixes about their necks and long black
gloves. Goya's comment is: "These good girls have seats enough and nothing
to do with them better than carry them on their heads." The girls are not good
at all. Their principal pleasure consists in pulling their dresses up to their
necks as often as possible. They carry two stools and try to amuse themselves
by playing with them as they cavort about the stage. Finally the girls realize
that they are boring themselves to death. One stands holding a stool on her
head; the other falls to the ground in an idiotic posture.
   "No one ever escapes who wants to be caught" is Goya's second comment.
The two girls remain on stage to watch. One fans her dress back and forth to
cool her body; the other relaxes with her head in her hand. A woman in black
enters, her head concealed by a blue shawl. She is followed by two men in
cloaks. The woman moves over to the two girls, who observe her with preoccupied, gum-chewing expressions. The woman begins to dance. The men close
in. She pretends to detest them and to want to be alone. The men are
delighted by the pretense at resistance and allow her to fascinate them. They
move in and caress her boldly, and the three dance together, the woman clapping her hands with simulated Spanish pleasure. The two men lift her up to
their shoulders, then each holds her and swings her body around and around.
As one of the men embraces her, the other picks up her feet. They lay the
woman on the ground. Now something has happened that the two girls can
understand; they move over to the woman. The men walk away. The girls

frolic about the stage. The woman rises and disappears, her blue shawl whirling with her movement.

The girls are dejected again. A young widower enters. He mourns his dead wife and holds his hand before his eyes as he sees the lascivious girls. He moves over toward them, his face determined to be sad. Then he goes to the back of the stage and stands close to the wings. He holds out his arms in supplication. Suddenly, as if he were holding out his arms to catch a potato sack, his dead wife falls into his arms. Her body is limp, absolutely lifeless. The man kneels. He attempts to bring his love to life, but her loose body resists his efforts. If he does not hold her, the girl falls over on her face. The young man gets a little annoyed and tries to dance with his rag doll of a wife. He is forced to push her legs ahead of him. Now he is embarrassed. He shows the girls that his wife really is dead. There is no use pretending. Goya's comment is: "If he were more gallant and less of a bore, she would come to life again." He carries his wife off.

The color of the backdrop changes to a bright green. The two girls rise from their siesta as four hooded figures enter slowly, carrying long brooms of straw. The girls are suddenly respectful in the presence of these mysterious, religious men. Two of the men carry a plank; a woman sits upon it, resigned to her fate. ". . . They are determined to kill this saintly woman. After judgment has been pronounced against her, she is dragged through the streets in triumph. She has indeed deserved a triumph, but if they do it to shame her, they are wasting their time. No one can make her ashamed who has nothing to be ashamed of . . ."

The triumphal procession is over. The men stand the plank upright and fix its base in the ground. The girls stand on their stools at the back to see better. The saintly woman is tied to the plank. Red light appears at her feet, and from the movement of her toes it is apparent that she is uncomfortable. She tries to escape the licking flames by lifting one tortured foot, then another away from the fire. One by one, the four men toss their brooms of straw at her feet. The woman trembles all over. The light on the backdrop becomes brilliantly red. With a hideous gesture, the woman at the stake claws at her flesh, seeming to pull it up over her face like a mask. One of the men stands behind the stake and extends his arms straight out, sanctifying the project. The woman's body falls forward. Her bonds still hold her to the stake. Everyone is still but the two girls, who move about slowly. One finally rests on her stool and amuses herself alone. The other girl, on the right, imitates crudely the sufferings of the saintly woman. The curtain falls. A voice says, *"El sueño de la razón produce monstruos"* ("The dream of reason produces monsters").

CAPRIOL SUITE

Ballet in one act. Music by Peter Warlock. Choreography by Frederick Ashton. Scenery and costumes by William Chappell. First presented by the

Marie Rambert Dancers at the Lyric Theatre, Hammersmith, London, February 25, 1930. First presented in the United States by the Sadler's Wells Theatre Ballet at the War Memorial Opera House, San Francisco, California, December 5, 1951, with a cast that included Patricia Miller, Donald Britton, and David Poole.

This entertainment ballet is a twentieth-century version of dances that were popular four hundred years ago. In 1588, the Frenchman Thoinot Arbeau set down in writing a record of sixteenth-century dances with the music that accompanied them. This book, called *Orchesographie* (writing dancing), appeared seven years after the presentation of the first modern ballet, the first ballet to unify in one entertaining spectacle the theatrical elements that had amused the courts of Europe for many centuries.

Arbeau's book is a dialogue, in the classical manner. He and a novice at the dance, a young man named Capriol, talk about dancing—how it came to be so popular among mankind, the different kinds of contemporary dancing, and the proper music to accompany the different forms. Peter Warlock, the English composer, arranged a number of the tunes set forth by Arbeau in an orchestral suite, and Frederick Ashton, in turn, devised the appropriate sixteenth-century dances as described by Arbeau to young Capriol.

The curtain rises and the orchestra begins a sprightly tune. The setting is simple and formal: a low stone railing topped with urns curves about the back of the stage. The back cloth is light green. Two couples dressed in the sixteenth-century French fashion perform a basse danse, a light but dignified measure. When they finish, the lights dim and two boys lead on a girl dressed in a long skirt. The orchestra plays a stately pavane, and the girl begins to dance between her escorts. Soon she pauses and sits on the knee of one of the boys. He presents a red rose to her. She sweetly refuses to accept it and when the other boy offers her a scroll, upon which he has written a poem to her, she will have none of him. She rises, and the boys stand on each side of her contemplating the gifts she has rejected.

The lights brighten, and to gay, bouncing music a girl and a boy dance a tordion, a court dance that is nevertheless playful and uninhibited in enthusiasm. The dancers who performed the pavane watch the dancing couple. Another girl enters. When the tordion finishes, those two couples come forward. The dancing, which has mostly been confined to the floor, now rises as the boys perform *pieds en l'air* to entertain the girls. When the dance is over, the boys kneel and the girls fall back over their shoulders. They leave the stage.

The music becomes bright and brisk. Four boys jump out onto the stage and dance a mattachins, a vigorous sword dance. Three of the boys lift the victor high over their heads as this dance ends. Gradually all the dancers return and perform different versions of the branle, a sixteenth-century court dance so popular that there were different versions for different age groups. The music increases in gaiety. The more ebullient dancers enclose in a moving circle the more stately couples, and the curtain falls.

CARACOLE (*see* DIVERTIMENTO NO. 15)

CARD GAME (Jeu de Cartes)

Ballet in three deals. Music by Igor Stravinsky. Choreography by George Balanchine. Book by Igor Stravinsky, with the collaboration of M. Malaieff. Scenery and costumes by Irene Sharaff. First presented by the American Ballet at the Metropolitan Opera House, New York, April 27, 1937.

The characters in this ballet represent the cards in poker hands. There are twenty-six cards for the whole ballet, representing portions of the four suits, plus the joker. Fifteen of these cards—one always the joker—are dealt out to make up three separate hands of poker for each of the three scenes in the ballet. The ballet is prefaced by this translation from a poem by La Fontaine:

One should ever struggle against wrongdoers.
Peace, I grant, is perfect in its way,
But what purpose does it serve
With enemies who do not keep faith?

FIRST DEAL   The orchestra plays a sonorous and playful march. The curtain rises on an empty stage. The scene is enclosed in a green felt façade. A great crystal candelabra stands at the left, representing one corner of a card table. The green tabletop stretches back up against the backdrop, where another candelabra is suspended at the opposite corner of the table; the stage thus becomes the table itself.

Fifteen dancers trip out from the right and form in a line straight across the stage. All hold large yellow-striped cards before them, concealing their identity. The joker is among them. Easily identified by his yellow costume striped with bright orange and his silly fool's cap, he steps out of line and runs about, trying to find the best hand. The cards turn and move close together in a shuffling movement. Then the hands are dealt out by an invisible player. The first five cards on the left jump out of line over to the left; the remaining cards form hands at the center and on the right. All the characters still hold the cards before them, but the joker can be distinguished in the hand on the left.

The hand on the right throw the placards over their heads to reveal themselves as the Ace and Queen of Hearts, the Queen of Clubs, the Jack of Spades, and the Jack of Diamonds—a two-pair hand. All the cards are easily identifiable in their resplendent costumes. The Ace of Hearts, his head covered like some medieval armored knight, flourishes his powerless sword in the air, and the smiling Queen of Hearts is surrounded by her dancing partners. The cards fall back in line and bow to the hand at the left.

The second hand turns out to be two kings and two eights—with the joker, a full house. The four cards and the joker step out proudly, the joker flagrantly boasting about the two kings. Now the members of the back hand throw off their placards. The joker holds his nose in contempt as he sees a pair of sevens, but he is stunned along with everyone else as they see three aces with the two sevens—another full house, which beats the joker's hand unaided! The joker comes forward, laughing hilariously to music that accompanies his dance. He grips his sides and bends over as he laughs. His loose, disjointed figure cavorts about the stage in short, jerky steps, running to the left, then to the right. He pirouettes like a top and circles the stage in wide, distorted leaps, turns in the air, slaps the table with his hands, and exits. The three hands spread out and close. All the cards choose partners and slowly dance off. The last couples to leave the stage are the two disconsolate kings with their two eights hanging limply on their arms.

SECOND DEAL   The introductory march to the ballet heralds the second scene. A new line of cards run out from the left, holding up before them large blue-striped placards. They form in a line down the center of the table, shuffle, and form three hands as before. From the hand at the left two jacks step out and dance. They bow and scrape before the three kings in their hand, carrying their trains and saluting them endlessly to a comic martial tune. They fall back into line and bow ceremoniously to the right after they have danced a courtly measure.

The Queen of Hearts steps out of the second hand, bounces in royal attitude, and dances a sprightly variation to a vivacious tune while throwing kisses gaily to everyone. She resumes her place, and the Queen of Clubs emerges and dances alone. She spins rapidly with her arms extended and as the whirring tune finishes, she stands with her hands on her hips while the Queen of Diamonds performs a difficult series of steps to a fresh melody. The Queen of Spades follows her, and then all four queens stand and watch the Jack of Hearts, their one remaining card, perform his variation. He bows to the queens; they all dance together and resume their places. They gesture toward the hand arranged in the center. Four aces and the ubiquitous joker come forward, the joker walking arrogantly, congratulating himself on the good luck he brings. But his hand has won the deal on its own merit, without his help.

The joker dances with the four queens as all the other cards leave the stage. He pulls them around in a line as he kisses the hand of the Queen of Hearts, then tags onto the end of the line. The joker stands in the middle of the line and dances lackadaisically with the queens, amusing himself at their silly posturings and leading them in a dance that burlesques their charm. Finally he pushes them all into the wings.

THIRD DEAL   The same march begins the third deal. A line of cards, their identities concealed as before, file out from the right; the cards are dealt into three hands. The hand on the left—a flush of Hearts, the five, six, seven, eight, and nine—walk to the front and dance pertly but modestly. They retire, and the joker dances forward with the hand on the right—the seven, eight, nine, and ten of Spades—with the joker, a higher flush than the first hand. The joker tries to play off his Spades against the Hearts, but the first hand moves away to stand in front of the final hand, which is still unrevealed. The joker and his Spades form a huddle to decide on the best method of play, then the five cards form a line, with the joker at the end. He bumps the girls forward and dances with them playfully as the orchestra mimics a bright melody of Rossini's.

The Hearts move forward; the joker and his Spades run back to see the final hand and stand aghast as they behold a royal flush: the ten, Jack, Queen, King, and Ace of Hearts! The joker grips his head in despair: he can laugh no longer when the joke is on him. He falls on his back, the music laughs at him, he rolls over and crawls off.

The royal flush marches forward to a delightful tune. The jack holds up his hand, trumpeting their arrival; the king and queen raise their hands in greeting and congratulate each other that the royal family is reunited. The queen jumps and everyone jumps. All the cards in the three deals gather behind them. They blow kisses to all her family and everyone else in sight and they all bow to her in mock humility. The other cards come to shake the hands of the lucky hand, and the king and queen welcome them. The king orders all the Hearts in the deck to come forward with the royalty. The other suits form lines behind the Hearts and all dance a courtly measure to the king's command. The deck of cards form a tableau about the queen. She is lifted high above them; the surrounding multitude fall forward in obeisance to her; and as the lights go out, all the cards are seen scrambled together in the middle of the table, shuffled together for a new game.

NOTES *Card Game* was the first collaboration between Stravinsky and myself in the United States. In 1936, when Lincoln Kirstein and I decided upon a Stravinsky Festival for the American Ballet, we wanted to present a new Stravinsky ballet. We wrote to Stravinsky in Paris, commissioning him to write a new ballet. We told him to write anything he wanted. He decided on a dance with playing-card characters, a poker-game ballet.

Soon after the score arrived in New York and I had begun rehearsals on the new ballet, Stravinsky himself arrived. As always, the ballet was a collaboration. Lincoln Kirstein has noted that Stravinsky possesses "the profound stage instinct of an amateur of the dance, the 'amateur' whose attitude is so professional that it seems merely an accident that he is not himself a dancer."

In *Card Game*, Stravinsky and I attempted to show that the highest cards— the kings, queens, and jacks—in reality have nothing on the other side. They are big people, but they can easily be beaten by small cards. Seemingly powerful figures, they are actually mere silhouettes.

Card Game was revived by the Ballet Russe de Monte Carlo at the Fifty-first Street Theatre, New York, October 14, 1940, with Frederic Franklin as the joker and a cast that included Alexandra Danilova, Nathalie Krassovska, Alicia Markova, André Eglevsky, and Igor Youskevitch. In the most recent revival by the New York City Ballet (first performance February 15, 1951), Todd Bolender and Janet Reed have danced the joker and leading parts have been danced by Janet Reed, Patricia Wilde, Doris Breckenridge, Jillana, Francisco Moncion, Frank Hobi, Michael Maule, and others.

Another version of Stravinsky's score was choreographed in 1945 by Janine Charrat and had its first performance by the Ballets des Champs-Élysées in Paris, with Jean Babilée as the joker.

John Cranko's production of *Jeu de Cartes* was first presented at the Württemberg State Theatre, Stuttgart, January 22, 1965, with scenery and costumes by Dorothee Zippel and lighting by Gilbert V. Hemsley, Jr. The ballet, introduced to the United States by the Stuttgart Ballet at the Metropolitan Opera House, New York, June 17, 1969, has been staged by the City Center Joffrey Ballet.

CARMEN

Dramatic ballet in five scenes inspired by the opera by Meilhac and Halévy. Music by Georges Bizet. Choreography by Roland Petit. Scenery and costumes by Antoine Clavé. First presented by Les Ballets de Paris de Roland Petit at the Prince's Theatre, London, February 21, 1949, with Renée Jeanmaire and Roland Petit in the principal roles. First presented in the United States by Les Ballets de Paris at the Winter Garden, New York, October 6, 1949, with the same principals.

SCENE ONE: A PUBLIC SQUARE IN SEVILLE   What seems to be a building with an outside staircase stands at the back of the square, and from it a long clothesline hung with multicolored garments suggests that it is a cheap public square. Three men play at cards on a plank that has been set up between two high ladders. Couples mill about the square in a casual and desultory manner, smoking, dancing occasionally with simulated high spirits, but in general implying that if they wait about long enough, something important may happen. They are not disappointed. Upstairs in the building someone is making a ruckus. Everyone listens attentively. Down the stairs runs an unfortunate girl who is clearly having difficulty with her pursuer. We understand why when we see that her pursuer is Carmen.

Everyone in the public square knows Carmen, every woman and especially every man. By experience and reputation fierce in love, Carmen is also fierce in jealousy, and although no one knows or cares what she is fighting with this other girl about, all the people in the square assume that the fight is worth watching. They take sides. Between two groups who egg them on, Carmen and the girl scratch each other and tear each other's hair out and kick each other around. The crowd is delighted with their ferocity and cheers spitfire Carmen when she succeeds in throwing her opponent to the ground. Just as they begin to express their enthusiasm for her victory, Don José, cape flying, enters on the run. Everybody seems to know him, too.

Don José is an official of some sort, a man from another part of the town, perhaps a policeman in mufti. He does not approve of what is going on and tries to break up the crowd. He takes pity on the prostrate girl, but then he sees her conqueror. The music sounds an ominous theme; the drum beats warningly. Don José is transfixed, immediately attracted to Carmen, as all the men seem to have been. He takes in her long and supple body, her boyish bob, her defiant eyes, her wide red mouth that seems a brilliant slash across her white round face, and doesn't know what to do. Then he remembers his duty. He seizes Carmen by the shoulder, coldly, officially, to admonish her. Carmen responds by glaring up at him and yanking down her blouse to expose the voluptuousness of her other shoulder. Don José is confused. Instead of arresting her, he allows Carmen to make a rendezvous with him. He dashes off, and the spectators nod to themselves knowingly.

SCENE TWO: A TAVERN   The stage is dark as the curtain rises on the second scene. Gradually a line of paper lanterns light up across the scene, and behind the lanterns is a tavern: tables and chairs, a bar in the back, and steps leading to an upstairs room. A number of steady customers are disposed about the tavern. A couple are making love, indifferent to their surroundings, and other habitués sit on the wooden chairs in an attitude of boredom. Some of them get up and start a kind of dance—wiggling and stomping and turning cart wheels and revolving the chairs on one leg—signifying their willingness to make the evening a deliberate, if not a spontaneous, success. Back near the bar, a man cloaked in black dozes.

Don José enters the room. He enters it just as he entered the public square: officiously, disapprovingly. But in the tavern, he senses that this will not be tolerated. After all, he has come on his own account, not on any official business, and everyone happens to know his particular business. And so, he joins the steady customers to prove that he is a regular fellow. He dances all by himself to prove also that he is a dashing fellow, while the crowd stands back and sings to the rhythm of his stomping the "Habañera." Although this song, with its warnings of rebellious love that can never be tamed, accompanies Don José's solo, he is sensitive only to its rhythms, which the spectators accentuate with militant clapping of hands. Don José is thinking of his meeting with Carmen.

Carmen has apparently been hiding behind the bar all this time. Suddenly, we see her sitting on top of it. Two gallants lift her down, and she commences a dance of her own. She carries a small black fan, which she holds close to her breasts. Her naked shoulders and her hair are covered with shiny spangles that fall from her body as she turns in powerful spins. Carmen's dance has more dash and strength than Don José's, and everyone watches her long legs as she traverses the tavern with steps that reveal her character as an untamable lover. Don José observes her more intently than the rest. At the end of her dance, Carmen kneels at his feet, her arms open in a gesture of welcome that is both public and intimate.

Don José goes to her. Carmen pretends that she is indifferent and fans herself nonchalantly. A pickpocket tries to rob Don José, but he brushes him aside. He picks Carmen up, holding her knee in his arm. He carries her closely, possessively, as if she had never been carried by a man before. He turns and carries her upstairs; Carmen relaxes in his arms.

When the two lovers have disappeared, two men and a girl begin a tempestuous dance that attracts all the customers. All join in the dance and whip themselves into a frenzy of happiness. Carmen's rendezvous has been a success, Don José has been seduced, and there is cause for rejoicing: they need fear officials no more. Carmen and Don José run down the stairs and lead the dance. The crowd fall on their knees around the lovers and beat the floor to the hysterical rhythm of their feet. At the climax of the music, Don José enfolds Carmen in his cape and runs off with her.

SCENE THREE: CARMEN'S ROOM; IT IS THE MORNING AFTER Don José pulls back the yellow curtains that conceal the boudoir from the audience, and bright sunlight from an open window fills the room. Carmen lies on a disordered iron bed, sucking a plum. She rises lazily, stretches, and slowly goes into a dance. Don José pours water in a basin, washes his hands, dries them on the curtains, and seems not to notice the increasing sensuous pleasure Carmen derives from her own seductiveness. He sits and watches her disinterestedly. She caresses her body, her hands moving from her hair over her face to her shoulders, her breasts and her thighs, and up again to her face. Don José shows no signs of interest and, tired of self-love, Carmen turns away with disgust toward the balcony outside the window. The noise of the street attracts her. Instantly, Don José is on his feet. Really, he isn't tired at all. He wishes her to stay! Carmen moves to leave the room, but Don José pulls her back. Carmen, however, will be detained only by love. The lovers kiss and begin a dance together.

Don José lifts Carmen up to his shoulder, then holds her as her body comes down full length in his arms. Carmen's interest in him is renewed and gradually she compels Don José to share her passion. His body falls back to the floor and he braces himself on his arms and legs as Carmen poses aggressively above him, her knee resting between his. Carmen's breathing is now as lusty as her movements, and Don José responds fully. The climax of her passion approaches. She lies upon him. Don José raises his knees, and Carmen's legs stretch out straight from her curved body in an attitude of diving. The tenseness in their bodies relaxes as the music ends and the two lovers lie exhausted.

Barely has their passion subsided than three of Carmen's friends enter to persuade them to come out into the street. The friends whisper secretively to Carmen, and she motions to Don José to follow them. Now he will follow her anywhere.

SCENE FOUR: A STREET IN SEVILLE It is night again. The scene is abandoned. Old cart wheels stacked against posts constitute the only scenery. Carmen and Don José, followed by her friends, walk on carefully, not wishing to be overheard. Cloaks disguise their identity. There is a brief conference. They are giving Don José his final instructions. Carmen puts a dagger in his hand. He listens and nods; the others leave and he is alone. The orchestra again sounds the theme that marked the first, fateful meeting of Carmen and Don José, and the drum now beats the rhythm of death. Don José stomps his feet in unison with the drum and waits. On the right, a man in a purple cloak enters. Don José seems to recognize him, stands motionless as he passes, then throws himself upon him. He stabs the man in the back. The man falls flat on his face. Don José reaches for his purse. Carmen and her bandit friends run out from hiding, grab for the money, and run off. Don José kicks the body over and follows them.

SCENE FIVE: IN FRONT OF THE PLAZA DE TOROS   Now that Don José has become a part of Carmen's life and has made the ultimate sacrifice and killed for her, Carmen begins to lose interest in him. She must always be taming someone to her will; once they have given in, she must seek new conquests. At the beginning of the fifth scene a crowd of lovely girls dressed colorfully but formally stand outside the arena, the Plaza de Toros, waiting for the bullfight to start—but waiting, too, for the arrival of the handsome toreador. The toreador, brought in on the shoulders of his admirers, gets down smartly and welcomes the greetings of the girls. As he flirts with them, he notices Carmen standing away from the crowd. She stares at him. She wears a veil, and the toreador prefers her indifference to the open affection of the young ladies. Don José enters and observes this silent exchange between Carmen and the toreador. The bullfight is about to begin; the toreador turns away from Carmen regretfully, and the crowd follows him into the arena. Carmen starts to join them.

Don José rushes up to her, tears off her veil, and grasps her throat in a passion of jealousy. He holds her face between his hands, and Carmen defies him. They separate, take positions at either side of the stage, and stand for a moment facing each other with so deep an anger that they become animal in their hatred. One of them must tame the other. The drum sounds slowly in a staccato beat; spotlights magnify and double the shadows of Carmen and Don José against the side of the arena. They approach and separate in a manner very similar to the fight in progress inside the ring, daring each other on, determined that one of them shall die. The drum beats faster and louder; Carmen circles Don José. He pulls out the dagger, rushes her quickly, and stabs her in the heart. He holds her about the waist as her body writhes back. She reaches up a trembling arm and caresses the face of her lover. She can stand no longer. Don José holds her to him still, and her legs vibrate with her heart's last beat. She falls limp. The music sounds brilliantly. Hats are thrown in from the arena. The fight has been won. The love has been lost.

Ballet in two acts. Music: a Bizet collage by Wolfgang Fortner in collaboration with Wilifried Steinbrenner. Choreography by John Cranko. Scenery and costumes by Jacques Dupont. Lighting by Gilbert V. Hemsley, Jr. First presented by the Stuttgart Ballet at the Württemberg State Theatre, Stuttgart, February 28, 1971, with Marcia Haydée, Egon Madsen, and Richard Cragun in the principal roles. First presented in the United States by the same ensemble at the Metropolitan Opera House, New York, April 28, 1971, with the same principals.

The ballet, in seven scenes, conveys in dance terms the plot of Bizet's opera. The locale is Spain, about 1820. The first scene takes place in a cigarette factory where Carmen, a beautiful, sultry girl who works there, has an argument with the woman in charge and scratches a cross on her back. She is arrested by a sergeant, Don José, a country boy who is immediately attracted to her. In the next scene, at the barracks jail, Carmen gets Don José to free her. He is stripped of his rank and jailed. In Scene Three, at a gap in the town wall of

Seville, Carmen persuades Don José, who is on guard, to let the smuggler band to which she belongs pass out of the city. Don José follows them. In the final scene of the first act, in the gypsy camp of the smugglers, there is a love scene between Carmen and Don José. Soldiers arrive to arrest Don José, who has deserted. He stabs the officer in charge.

Act Two of the ballet opens at an inn on the beach. Here Carmen dresses for her dance and sends Don José away on an errand. The toreador arrives with a group of friends and is fascinated by Carmen. Don José returns and is fiercely jealous. The desert region is the next scene, where Carmen's fate is revealed to her in a game of cards. Don José feels that he is losing her. A traveling Englishman is robbed and killed by the smugglers. Now an outlaw and a murderer, hunted by soldiers, nearly rejected by Carmen, Don José becomes desperate as he watches Carmen leave on the arm of the torero. In the final scene, outside the arena in Seville, Carmen accompanies the torero to the bullfight. She sees Don José there and has a presentiment of her fate. After the corrida has begun and they are alone, Don José pleads with her to come back to him. Knowing her fate, she still refuses. Don José stabs her.

CARMEN SUITE

Music by Rodion Shchedrin. Choreography by Alberto Alonso. First presented by the Bolshoi Ballet at the Bolshoi Theatre, Moscow, in 1967, with Maya Plisetskaya in the leading role. First presented in the United States by the same ensemble at the Metropolitan Opera House, New York, 1974.

The first ballet to be choreographed especially for the celebrated Soviet ballerina Maya Plisetskaya, *Carmen Suite* presents the familiar story of Mérimée's novella as a mortal combat in a simulated bullring. It emphasizes character rather than plot. While we see Carmen, Don José, and the toreador assume their expected roles, the ballet is dominated throughout by Fate in the form of a bull. A huge head of a bull painted on a backdrop high over the arena dominates the decor. The program says: "Carmen is a beautiful woman who is free, true to herself, and completely honest. Don José lies, and thus he loses her. The Bull represents Fate. Therefore Carmen and the Bull die at the same time because she and her Fate are one." The final *pas de deux*, a danced contest between Carmen and Don José, is a simulated bullfight in which the ballerina assumes the combined roles of heroine and Fate in the form of a bull.

CARMINA BURANA

Music by Carl Orff. Choreography by John Butler. First presented by the New York City Opera at the City Center, New York, September 24, 1959, with Carmen de Lavallade, Veronika Mlakar, Scott Douglas, and Glen Tetley in the principal roles.

Carmina Burana, a choral theater piece based on poems discovered in the library of an ancient Bavarian monastery, is a secular rather than a sacred work. The thirteenth-century poems and songs composed by minstrels and monks who had freed themselves of monastic discipline were set by Carl Orff to vigorous, compelling music. The chorus of monk-clad singers stands at both sides of the stage.

The ballet, which begins after the First Chorus, is an abstract landscape of movement, not a realistic retelling of the poems. The Prologue regrets the ever-changing fate of man, first riding the Wheel of Fortune with success, then ground under by it. The first part relates the joys of spring. The second celebrates the pleasures, extravagances, and despairs of tavern life. The third part is a series of love poems. The Epilogue returns to the plaintive bemoaning of the ruthless Wheel of Fate.

Leopold Stokowski, a champion of the score, characterized it as "a synthesis of beauty of melodic line, remarkable rhythmic variations; lusty vitality; immense range of mood, humor, frenzy; folk-like simplicity, satire, mystery, spontaneous eloquence and tranquility . . ."

Fernand Nault created a *Carmina Burana* for the Colorado Concert Ballet in Denver, in 1962. This version, with decor by Robert Prevost, was presented by Les Grands Ballets Canadiens at the Salle Wilfred Pelletier, Montreal, June 24, 1967.

Writing of the first presentation of John Butler's ballet, the critic Arthur Todd in *Dance Observer* said that "All of the movement for the four dance principals is composed in honor of eroticism . . . Most notable of the four is Scott Douglas, notable heretofore chiefly for his classical balletic style."

CARNAVAL

> *Romantic ballet in one act. Music by Robert Schumann. Choreography by Michel Fokine. Scenery and costumes by Léon Bakst. Book by Michel Fokine. First presented at Pavlova Hall, St. Petersburg, 1910, with Tamara Karsavina as Columbine, Vera Fokina as Chiarina, Ludmilla Shollar as Estrella, Bronislava Nijinska as Papillon, Leonide Leontiev as Harlequin, Vsevolod Meyerhold as Pierrot, Enrico Cecchetti as Pantalon, and Joseph Kchessinsky as Florestan. First presented in Western Europe by Diaghilev's Ballets Russes at the Théâtre National de l'Opéra, Paris, June 4, 1910, with the same principals except for the following substitutions: Vaslav Nijinsky as Harlequin, Adolph Bolm as Pierrot, and Ivan Kussov as Florestan. First presented in the United States by Diaghilev's Ballets Russes at the Century Theatre, New York, January 1916.*

First performed as a *divertissement* for a benefit in St. Petersburg, *Carnaval* was later revived and presented in Paris by Diaghilev. It became one of the most popular ballets in his repertory and one of the most popular works in the repertories of ballet companies that have since performed it, though it must be admitted that contemporary revivals have hardly retained the spirit of the original. The music is an orchestration of Schumann's *Carnaval* Suite for piano. The principal characters—Pierrot, Columbine, etc., are drawn from the *commedia dell' arte,* the popular early Italian street comedies.

The scene is an antechamber to a ballroom. At the rise of the curtain, we are introduced to the atmosphere of the ball that is taking place in the next room. Girls run by, pursued by their escorts. Dancing couples from the ball take refuge in the empty spaces of the anteroom and waltz. Chiarina and Estrella, two charming girls, enter with their partners. Two lovers kiss in passing and return to the ball.

Pierrot, the sad clown, pokes his head into the room. He steps into the room carefully, lest anyone hear or see him, his long, loose sleeves flapping dejectedly at his sides. He moves with slow melancholy; he seems to be saying that he is the only one in the world who will not dance and enjoy himself at the ball. Aware of his ugliness and awkwardness, he is filled with self-pity.

Harlequin bounces in, notes the melancholy Pierrot, and taunts him for not joining in the fun the music calls for. Unmercifully the energetic Harlequin pokes at the helpless clown, who falls to the floor. The irrepressible Harlequin leaves him in disgust.

Couples from the ball dance through the anteroom again. Pierrot looks at them and takes himself off before he can be chided once more.

Now the romantic poet Eusebius enters. He sits on a settee and wistfully contemplates a vision he has of an ideal lady. The lady materializes in the form of Chiarina, who gives him a rose. Estrella, ambitious and flirtatious, enters pursued by the eager Florestan, who beseeches her to grant him the favor of some small attention. Estrella pretends to disapprove of his advances, but then links her arm in his; the two exit for a dance.

Eusebius and Chiarina dance, or rather Chiarina dances and Eusebius observes her with adoring eyes. They leave the scene together.

Papillon, a girl whose varied, busy movements suggest a perpetual giddiness, rushes in. Pierrot discreetly follows her, hoping to make a conquest at last. He watches her from behind a settee, then bounds out into the room to catch her. When poor Pierrot thinks he has finally found a partner, Papillon escapes his grasp and leaves. The helpless clown is alone again.

Now there is an interval of dancing by Chiarina and two of her girl friends, who are masked. Florestan, still in pursuit of the coquettish Estrella, comes into the room. The girls playfully try to detain him, but the determined youth flees.

Columbine, gay and flirtatious, enters with Harlequin. They play together amorously. Though she seems to like him very much, the girl refuses Harlequin's invitation to elope. Their rendezvous is interrupted by the foppish Pantalon, who sits on a settee and reads with relish a note. Columbine goes to the back of the settee and puts her hands over Pantalon's eyes, while Harlequin snatches the note away from the intruder.

Pantalon, who was only reading the note to attract attention, tries to ingratiate himself with Columbine, who toys with him amusingly and then suggests that he join her and Harlequin in a *pas de trois.* At the end of the dance, she and Harlequin send Pantalon on his way.

Harlequin sits on the floor and indicates to Columbine that his heart lies at her feet. The fickle girl goes to the settee, where Harlequin sits adoringly in front of her.

The dancers return and, observing Harlequin and Columbine, congratulate them on their love. Columbine is suddenly nice to everyone. She comforts the pompous Pantalon and permits poor Pierrot to kiss her hand. All join in a happy dance.

The joviality is cut short by a crowd of busybodies, proper people who think that the people in the anteroom are not behaving with decorum. The gay dancers mock them and shove them about until they take flight. In the melee, the trickster Harlequin sees that Pierrot and Pantalon are pushed together. Before the two can separate themselves, Harlequin has tied Pierrot's long sleeves together around Pantalon. While Pantalon tries to release his bonds, all the other dancers gather about Columbine and Harlequin to form an admiring tableau.

CELEBRATION

Ballet by Jerome Robbins. Music and choreography as specified below. Scenery by Rouben Ter-Arutunian. First presented by the Festival of Two Worlds at the Teatro Nuovo, Spoleto, Italy, July, 1973, with Antoinette Sibley and Anthony Dowell (England), Violette Verdy and Jean-Pierre Bonnefous (France), Carla Fracci and Paolo Bortoluzzi (Italy), Patricia McBride and Helgi Tomasson (United States), and Malika Sabirova and Muzafar Bourkhanov (Soviet Union).

Subtitled "The Art of the *Pas de Deux*," *Celebration* combined in a few historic performances classical *pas de deux* of the past with contemporary dance. The basic idea was to show the classic *pas de deux* in all its glamor but to show, too, the depth of feeling of contemporary ballet duets. The original intention was for *Celebration* to begin with a brief talk and demonstration of the art of the *pas de deux* by Anton Dolin, the famed partner of many ballerinas. Jerome Robbins decided instead to introduce his ballet himself, saying simply that it would be a "celebration of dancing by dancers."

The dancers are five couples from England, France, Italy, the United States, and the Soviet Union. Heralds carrying flags introduce the action. All five dancers enter to a fanfare and dance to the music of a Tchaikovsky waltz. Then one by one, the couples performed some of the great *pas de deux*. First, Sabirova and Bourkhanov in *The Corsair Pas de Deux*, then Fracci and Bortoluzzi in the love duet from *La Sylphide*, the oldest work of the evening. A *grand pas classique* for Verdy and Bonnefous came next, followed by Robbins's own *Afternoon of a Faun* by McBride and Tomasson. The *grand pas de deux* from the final act of *The Sleeping Beauty* by Sibley and Dowell concluded the first act of the presentation.

The second part consisted of the Balanchine *Tchaikovsky Pas de Deux* (McBride and Tomasson), the Ashton *Pas de Deux* from *Thaïs* (Sibley and

Dowell), the Petipa/Minkus display piece from *Don Quixote* (Sabirova and Bourkhanov), Robbins's new *Bagatelles* to music from Beethoven (Verdy and Bonnefous), and the celebrated final *pas de deux* from the Mérante/Delibes *Coppélia*.

The finale was an arrangement by Jerome Robbins for all five couples of the Ivanov adagio from *Swan Lake*, Act Two.

NOTES   Robbins's *Bagatelles*, called then simply *A Beethoven Pas de Deux*, had been performed initially at a preview in New York, May 16, 1973, at the New York City Ballet's Annual Spring Gala. It was danced by Violette Verdy and Jean-Pierre Bonnefous to *Four Bagatelles* of Beethoven, played by the pianist Jerry Zimmerman: Nos. 4, 5, and 2 from *Opus* 33 and No. 4 from *Opus 126*. The costumes were by Florence Klotz and the lighting by Ronald Bates.

Reporting to the New York *Times*, the critic John Gruen wrote of the première of *Celebration* at the Spoleto Festival: "Bringing together five celebrated ballet couples (by no means an easy feat), and devising a work that would focus on international ballet styles, Robbins made clear both his magnetism as one of the world's great choreographers and his deep love of classical traditions."

The Ashton *pas de deux*, to the Meditation from the opera *Thaïs* by Jules Massenet, was first performed by Antoinette Sibley and Anthony Dowell at a gala ballet performance at the Adelphi Theatre, London, March 21, 1971. The critic Peter Williams wrote about the performance in *Dance and Dancers* magazine: Ashton "has created one of those oriental dream sequences that so reflect the whole mood of occidental awakening to the orient of the mid-nineteenth century. At least I imagine that Sibley must have been a dream figure, since she first appears with a light veil over her face as she approaches the kneeling Dowell. Everything about this dance evoked Pavlova, whom Ashton adored without reservation and whom he delighted in imitating until once, while staying at a country house, he seriously damaged his foot in an impromptu performance of *The Dying Swan*. But although the accident put a stop to any further imitations, Pavlova continued to cast a loving shadow over his life. This new *pas de deux* is all drifting and swooning and some fiendishly difficult lifts which have to look as though she is a wraith, and in which Dowell managed to make Sibley look as though she was. . . . It was lovely, and they were lovely, and to those that remembered, it must have brought on waves of nostalgia for Pavlova with Mordkin. . . ."

Writing after the first repertory performance of *Four Bagatelles* by the New York City Ballet, January 10, 1974, with Gelsey Kirkland and Jean-Pierre Bonnefous, Anna Kisselgoff said in the New York *Times*: "The very structure of *Four Bagatelles* follows the conventional sequence of the nineteenth-century classic *pas de deux*: adagio, variation for the man, then the woman, coda. In the first part, Mr. Robbins throws out almost subliminal quotes from three styles. A fleeting reminder of Denmark's Bournonville school, as in *Flower Festival at Genzano*, occurs in the beginning with the girl's *penchées arabesques*, head tilting and the man's leaps. Later, as Miss Kirkland slowly extends her leg to the side from on-toe position, while Mr. Bonnefous supports her in an image directly culled from the *grand pas de deux* of *The Sleeping Beauty*, there is a flashing allusion to the Russian style of Petipa.

"The adagio ends with Miss Kirkland down on one knee and Mr. Bonnefous behind her, in a reversal of the traditional pose that closes the adagio of Act Two of *Giselle*—a nod toward French Romantic ballet.

"These are, of course, whiffs of history wafting through a contemporary work, and the allusions are absent from the solos. Mr. Bonnefous's variation has folk touches that are echoed in the coda and some interesting experiments in phrasing. It is a tricky solo, somewhat short on transitional steps, and Mr. Bonnefous could not quite conceal the effort involved. Miss Kirkland, obviously most suited to the Robbins choreography, danced with brilliant technique and demure appeal. Mr. Zimmerman played with his customary excellence."

CELLO CONCERTO

Music by Antonio Vivaldi. Choreography by Gerald Arpino. Lighting de-sign by Thomas Skelton. First presented by the City Center Joffrey Ballet at the City Center, New York, September 6, 1967. Cellist: Nellis De Lay. Conducted by Seymour Lipkin.

A dance ballet to Vivaldi's *Concerto for Cello, Strings, and Continuo in E Minor*, this is Gerald Arpino's second work to the music of Vivaldi for the City Center Joffrey Ballet. It is in four movements.

While an ensemble figures at the beginning of the first movement, it is in fact dominated by the adagio *pas de deux* of the girl and boy who finish it. The second movement, brisk in style, is again an ensemble, led at first by a girl who performs a brilliant variation.

The third, quiet, movement is danced by two couples, who perform two adagios to the lyric score; the girls are lifted high into the wings at its close.

Bright again in tempo and atmosphere, the final movement features brisk variations by a boy and his girl against the animation of the ten supporting dancers.

CHABRIESQUE

Music by Emmanuel Chabrier. Choreography by Gerald Arpino. First pre-sented by the City Center Joffrey Ballet at the City Center, New York, Feb-ruary 1, 1972.

A dance ballet to Chabrier's *Trois Valses Romantiques, Souvenirs de Munich,* and *Cortège Burlesque, Chabriesque* is arranged for fourteen dancers. Writing of the ballet's performance in Chicago, the critic Ann Barzell said in *Dance News*: "*Chabriesque* is a classical suite in the high key of exhilarating virtuosity to which Arpino stretches his most virtuosic dancers. The choreographer delights in spaciousness and his fourteen dancers are seldom on stage all at the same time. His designs are not group tableaux, but groups flowing in ever-changing patterns. Arpino's inventiveness is boundless as he finds new ways to fly and whirl, to lift a partner or catch her coming or flipping from on high. There are new combinations of steps, new interweavings and through it all he maintains a style, romantic in mood and airy in movement. The girls wear white leotards with a cloud of sequin-spattered tulle for skirts. The men are in dark-blue tights and shirts.

"No matter how many unique roles dancers star in they feel the need to appear in what is nearest to them, the basic classicism of the daily class. So, it is understandable that Christian Holder has a pivotal role in *Chabriesque*, perhaps to prove that serenity of classicism is in his range. He danced with exemplary style, partnering the excellent Pamela Johnson. Starr Danias and Glenn White were notable throughout and after one stunning *pas de deux* set audiences cheering into the next dance. Francesca Corkle, recovering from an injury, brought her special bounce to several dances partnered by Scott Barnard, always excitingly precise."

CHACONNE

Music by Christoph Willibald Gluck. Choreography by George Balanchine. Lighting by Ronald Bates. First presented by the New York City Ballet at the New York State Theatre, Lincoln Center, January 22, 1976, with Suzanne Farrell and Peter Martins in the leading roles. Conducted by Robert Irving.

It is no secret that I have loved Gluck's music for *Orpheus and Eurydice* almost all my life. Soon after I came to America, when Lincoln Kirstein and I took our new, young American Ballet to the Metropolitan Opera, I did a ballet to all of his music for the opera. The opera became, in fact, a ballet, with the dancers taking the stage and the singers performing with the orchestra from the pit. That production, designed by Pavel Tchelitchew with settings and costumes we could never produce today, is part of history. My next involvement with *Orpheus* was with Stravinsky, with whom I did the ballet of that name in 1948. But I returned to Gluck and his opera in Hamburg, in November 1963, when Rolf Liebermann of the Hamburg Opera kindly invited me to stage the work there. To conclude the production of the opera, which was brilliantly designed by Rouben Ter-Arutunian in a high baroque style of extraordinary extravagance, I had an opportunity again to do dances to Gluck's music. I repeated them in 1973, after Liebermann moved to the Paris Opéra and invited me to produce *Orpheus* there, too. The present ballet is an adaptation of what was first done for Hamburg, plus the introductory *pas de deux*. Brigitte Thom, who danced in the Hamburg production, helped me to revive it.

The chaconne of the title of course refers to an old-style dance, now centuries old, but it also was the popular name for ballet music used to end an opera. Basically, the ballet is a set of two *pas de deux* with other *divertissements*—a duet, a trio, a dance for five, with an ensemble. There is no story. Listen to the music first, if you can. Words you might try to use to describe it— mysterious, reflective, contemplative, plaintive, noble, etc.—are not enough for Gluck's lyric masterpiece.

The critic George Jackson has written: "Vainest endeavor, to try to document dance, the most ephemeral of the arts."

CHANSONS MADÉCASSES

Music by Maurice Ravel. Choreography by Jerome Robbins. First presented at the New York City Ballet's Hommage à Ravel at the New York State Theatre, Lincoln Center, May 28, 1975, with Patricia McBride and Helgi Tomasson, Debra Austin and Hermes Conde. Conductor: Robert Irving.

The music here is three songs for soprano, piano, flute, and cello. The work was commissioned by Elizabeth Sprague Coolidge of Washington, D.C., and first performed in 1926. Ravel used poems by the Creole poet Evariste-Désiré de Parny, who lived in India and collected folk songs of Madagascar: "which may give an idea of their customs and habits. They possess no verse; their poetry is nothing but an elaborate prose. Their music is simple, gentle and always melancholy."

Ravel once said he believed this music introduces a "new element, dramatic —indeed, erotic, resulting from the subject matter of Parny's poems."

Jerome Robbins set the three songs in an individual way. The first is a love song; the second, where the action of the ballet principally focuses, expresses doubts about the white man and his role in Madagascar's past; and the third song depicts a hero husband lying in the heat of the shady tree, wondering what's for dinner.

CHECKMATE

Dramatic ballet in one scene with prologue. Music by Arthur Bliss. Choreography by Ninette de Valois. Scenery and costumes by E. McKnight Kauffer. First presented by the Sadler's Wells Ballet at the Théâtre des Champs-Élysées, Paris, June 15, 1937, with June Brae as the Black Queen, Robert Helpmann as the Red King, Pamela May as the Red Queen, Harold Turner and William Chappell as the Red Knights, Richard Ellis and Michael Somes as the Black Knights, Frederick Ashton and Alan Carter as the Two Players, and a cast that included Margot Fonteyn and Leslie Edwards. First presented in England by the Sadler's Wells Ballet at the Sadler's Wells Theatre, October 5, 1937, with the same principals. First presented in the United States by the Sadler's Wells Ballet at the Metropolitan Opera House, New York, November 2, 1949, with Beryl Grey as the Black Queen, Leslie Ed-

wards as the Red King, *Gerd Larsen as the* Red Queen, *Alexis Rassine and John Field as the* Red Knights, *Kenneth Melville and Philip Chatfield as the* Black Knights, *and a cast that included Pauline Clayden, Rosemary Lindsay, Rowena Jackson, Kenneth MacMillan, and John Cranko.*

Checkmate is an allegory, a story of the battle between love and death told in terms of a chess game. It is apparent from the beginning who will win, but the contest, with its determined conflicting forces, creates a dramatic situation that often precludes prediction and the spectator, like the quiet chess player, finds himself deliberating the outcome.

The terms of the allegory are introduced in a prologue. The music is ominous, doomful, without relief in its projection of the battle to come. The curtain rises on a chess game. Two players in armor, Love and Death, sit opposite each other at a small table in the center of the stage. The chess game begins as Love makes a move. Death watches, deliberates, and moves his skeletonlike hand over the table. He moves. Love tries to analyze the situation, will not move again as he sees that the situation is hopeless: it is checkmate and there has not been any game at all. Blackout.

A backdrop rises, and we see that the stage is covered with black and white squares, as on a chessboard. The red chessmen enter and begin to take their places on the board. First come the eight pawns, danced by girls, gay and lighthearted pages to the royalty to come. The two red knights march in from opposite sides of the board and practice their fierce skill in combat. Two black knights, sent by the enemy to report on the strength of the other side, herald the entry of the black queen, whose omnipotence over all the pieces on the board is soon apparent. She beats off one of the red knights who will not submit to her attractions. To make himself attractive to her, the other red knight dances a vigorous mazurka. When he finishes, she rewards him with a red rose —Death's symbol of the blood she will spill before she is through. The pawns leave the board, followed by the conquering black queen and the black knights. In their absence, one of the red knights dances the praises of the black queen. Two red bishops parade in ceremoniously, followed by two red castles. Finally the red king and queen enter. Both knights salute them. The red king, old and doddering, can hardly make his way about the board and it is clear he can win nothing, while the queen is anything but a matriarch. The red pieces are now all in place, and the game begins in earnest.

The black queen leads the onslaught. The red king tries to maneuver his forces to prevent a frontal attack, but the black queen sees an opening and dashes through the enemy line. Even the two red bishops cannot hold off the black pieces. The red queen begs for mercy for her king, but the relentless black queen delivers her into the hands of her two knights.

The red knight, who imagined himself powerful in love, even with the black queen, attempts to rally his king's forces. For a time the contest is equal, for the knight's love of his king appears to be a match for his passion for the enemy queen. But when he must choose, when he has the chance to slay the queen, when she is kneeling helpless before him, he naturally hesitates. The black queen laughs in his face and cuts him down. The red king despairs.

Death enters. The body of the defeated red knight is held high by the red pieces, and Death leads the cortege off the board.

The red king has been abandoned; he is alone on the board with the black queen. She toys with him like a snake. He cannot escape: wherever he turns, a new black piece appears to block his path. He makes a pathetic figure—but then, from the beginning he has seemed weak and powerless—and the black queen's game with him becomes a protracted mercenary exhibition of power. She looks at him as if wondering whether the game were worth winning after all, he being such a contemptible creature. He is backed into his throne. Now, with nothing to lose, the king fights back with vigor for a brief moment. The black queen admires his mettle so much that she condescends to kill him. It is checkmate indeed.

CHOPINIANA (see LES SYLPHIDES)

CHORAL VARIATIONS ON BACH'S "VOM HIMMEL HOCH"

Music by Igor Stravinsky. Choreography by George Balanchine. Scenery by Rouben Ter-Arutunian. Lighting by Ronald Bates. First presented by the New York City Ballet at the Stravinsky Festival, 1972, at the New York State Theatre, Lincoln Center, June 25, 1972, with Karin von Aroldingen, Melissa Hayden, Sara Leland, Violette Verdy, Anthony Blum, and Peter Martins in the principal roles.

The Christmas hymn *"Vom Himmel Hoch Da Komm' Ich Her"* is familiar today as it was in Bach's own time. Its inspiriting music derived from a time during the Reformation when popular feeling gained an ascendancy in church music, and even today it is possible to find reflected in its melody an open, confident, but at the same time tender conviction to match the words:

Vom Himmel hoch da komm' ich her,	From heaven high I come to you,
Ich bring' euch gute neue Mähr.	I bring you tidings good and new,
Der guten Mähr bring' ich so viel,	Good tidings of great joy I bring:
Davon ich sing'n und sagen will.	Thereof will I both say and sing.

In 1747, Bach wrote canonic variations on the hymn for two-manual organ and pedals as a submission to a learned society. In 1955, Stravinsky began to compose instrumental and choral variations on Bach's masterwork. The score, for mixed chorus and orchestra, was dedicated to Robert Craft, who conducted its first performance at Ojai, California, May 27, 1956.

I myself first learned about the music from Stravinsky when he was working on the first two variations in New York at the end of 1955. When we were planning the Stravinsky Festival at the New York City Ballet after the composer's death, in 1971, one of the first works that I wanted very much to include was this one. Robert Irving conducted the first performance at the last night of the festival.

Those who will want to know more about the music will wish to read Robert Craft's exposition for Stravinsky's own recording of the work. As for the ballet, it is very simple.

There are five variations in the score. Brass proclaims the melody of the hymn as twelve young girls dance. All wear white. The background is a high chevron of white and brass rods, an imaginative simulation of pipes of the baroque organ.

In the four variations that follow, one is led by a ballerina and eight girls; another by four couples in which a *pas de deux* figures; another by a girl and boy against a background of twelve boys; and a finale with four *pas de trois* and eight girls, ending with the entire group of forty-six dancers. All forty-six dancers are on stage throughout the ballet, those not participating in the action standing aside.

It is boring, I think, to describe in any kind of detail what appears on the stage in a ballet that has only the music as its subject. What matters is the music itself and the more we can all be familiar with it, the better we are, both before seeing and afterward, too. This score is such an especially beautiful one that I hope you will hearken to it, but as always it is perhaps best to like it first without caring to, without preparation. I mean, many of the loveliest works of art are surprises we enjoy because we like them themselves, not because others alert us to them. Which is, of course, the point of the open mind, the open ear, the open eye!

CHOREOGRAPHIC OFFERING

Music by Johann Sebastian Bach. Choreography by Ballet of the Twentieth Century. First presented by that ensemble at the Brooklyn Academy of Music, New York, January 25, 1971.

The Artistic Director of the Ballet of the Twentieth Century, Maurice Béjart, has written in his *Notebook* about the philosophy behind this and other works by his company:

"Dancer-Choreographer collaboration / Choreography, like love, is done in pairs / In a choreographic work, the dancer is more important than the choreography, for it is the dancer who is author of the work; the choreographer merely fits it together / To the extent that the choreographer strives to understand the shape, rhythm and will of the body one may create a work that appears original. The dancer's body, which is the interpretator, is always right. When I say body, I mean the whole intuitive and spontaneous being, and not the mind of the dancer. The dancer should be carefully observed, not only for the steps he makes, which he believes favor him, but because, despite what he says or thinks, his whole being is impelled to express itself in that very particular way / By listening to both the music of the bodies and that of the musical work, one could very well create a work. But taken on the whole, the work is not one's own, since it exists only because of its parts: the music and dancer / After all is said and done, the important thing is that something happens, regardless of who creates it / The dance is visual music."

The music for *Choreographic Offering* consists of eight canons from Bach's *Musical Offering,* orchestrated by Münchinger, with percussion episodes. Bach composed his work on a theme by King Frederick of Prussia. For almost a full hour, the regal theme supports a prodigious suite of canons, which imitate the theme, fugues and sonatas. Bejart's ballet, choreographed by his dancers, uses as its theme an adagio exercise used by the great Italian dancer and ballet master Enrico Cecchetti (1850–1928), teacher to pre-eminent Russian dancers. Béjart writes: "Within the eight central canons of the work there is a development which takes the form of a musical discourse; a countersubject, which is developed by the dancers and the percussion, follows; the theme meshes with a classic dance motif, modifying, supplementing and parodying it. These two basic elements seem to struggle to dominate the work, which appears about to fall apart. 'Life' enters and supplies a conclusion. This ballet has no other meaning, no other purpose, than to present, or to 'offer' the public the quality called 'Twentieth Century Ballet.'"

Following Béjart's scenario, the theme is danced by a boy, classically presented, but at once there is an "anti-theme" by another boy, who dances in a completely contemporary way, in vivid contrast, to the music of drums, chimes, and an "Iguanaphone." The ballet is full of surprises, seemingly improvised by the dancers, although there are the expected sequences in canon, with couples repeating dances by their predecessors. The contrast between the old and the new would appear to be the point, plus a useful and novel way to introduce a ballet company to a new public who might wonder what it represents.

Interviewed in *The New Yorker* magazine (February 6, 1971), the choreographer said of *Choreographic Offering:* "It's a discourse between the two main elements in my work—classical ballet, which is choreographed to Bach's *Musical Offering,* and modern dance, which appears during percussion passages, to interrupt and parody the traditional steps. There is a struggle between the two styles but we don't resolve it. We end with a young girl holding out a rose to the audience. That's our way of saying, 'In New York, you have the best choreographers and dancers, so we don't dare offer you a finished ballet. Come to your own conclusions.'"

CINDERELLA

Ballet in three acts and seven scenes. Music by Sergei Prokofiev. Choreography by Rotislav Zakharov. Libretto by Nikolai Volkov. First presented by the Bolshoi Ballet at the Bolshoi Theatre, Moscow, November 15, 1945, with Olga Lepeshinskaya in the title role. Designed by Pyotr Williams. Presented in a new version with choreography by Konstantin Sergeyev at the Kirov State Theatre of Opera and Ballet, Leningrad, April 8, 1946, with

Natalia Dudinskaya in the title role. A new production, revised by Sergeyev, was presented at the Kirov Theatre, July 13, 1964, with Irina Kolpakova. Designer: Tatiana Bruni. This production was first presented in the United States by the Kirov Ballet at the Metropolitan Opera House, New York, September 11, 1964, with Irina Kolpakova and Yuri Soloviev.

Prokofiev wrote that he conceived of *Cinderella* "as a classical ballet with variations, adagios, *pas de deux*, etc. I see Cinderella not only as a fairy-tale character but also as a real person, feeling, experiencing, and moving among us." The Russian composer began work on the score in 1940, but because of other commitments during World War II did not finish the orchestration until 1944.

ACT ONE: A ROOM IN CINDERELLA'S HOUSE　It is evening and Cinderella's stepsisters—Krivlyaka (Affected) and Zlyuka (Furious)—are embroidering a silk scarf while their mother dotingly looks on. Cinderella sits alone at the fireplace, polishing a pot. The two sisters begin to quarrel over the scarf; their tempers are so bad that the mother can resolve the fight only by cutting the scarf in two. They now tease Cinderella, whom no one, not even her loving father, will defend. When they leave her alone finally, she sets about her routine of cleaning up the room. She finds a piece of the scarf and, forgetting herself, dances. But a mirror brings her back to reality; she sees her miserable dress and realizes that such a scarf is not for her. Her sadness induces memories of her beloved mother; she shuns the portrait of her cruel stepmother and tries to cover it with a curtain.

Her father returns and wants to comfort Cinderella. She sits on his knee and cries. But he fears his wife more than he loves his daughter, and, observing the covered portrait of his spouse, is apprehensive. Meanwhile, Zlyuka and Krivlyaka, who have been watching, alert their mother, who rushes in in a rage. She attacks her husband and taunts Cinderella mercilessly, finally collapsing in a fit of anger.

A beggarwoman appears, asking for alms. While the stepmother and the two sisters want to chase the woman away, and the father is too frightened to do anything, Cinderella turns and gives her a piece of bread.

Now preparations begin for the gala ball to which the family—all except Cinderella—have been invited. Dressmaker, hairdresser, dancing master, and musicians come to prepare the ladies. When everything is ready, they all depart for the castle, and Cinderella is alone.

Wishing also to be at the ball, Cinderella lets herself be carried away by unattainable dreams. She curtsies, as if before the prince himself. Suddenly the old beggarwoman appears again, but this time as Cinderella's fairy godmother. She promises to make the girl's dreams come true in gratitude for Cinderella's kindness. The fairy presents the girl with a pair of crystal slippers and orders four fairies representing the seasons of the year to prepare and dress Cinderella for the ball. The fairy of Spring brings her a gossamer dress, light as a cloud; Summer brings lovely roses; Autumn a splendid cloak glowing like the sun; and Winter diamonds and jewels, glistening like icicles. Dressed and ready now for the ball, Cinderella is truly a princess out of a fairy tale.

Before she leaves for the castle, however, the fairy godmother warns her that she must return home exactly at twelve o'clock, or she will turn back into her original state forever. She will be reminded of the approach of midnight by twelve dwarfs whom the fairy godmother will cause to emerge from the ancient clock at the castle. The fairy godmother wishes her godspeed and leaves, as a golden coach magically appears before Cinderella to take her to the ball.

ACT TWO: THE BALL AT THE PRINCE'S CASTLE   While waiting for their host to appear, the splendidly dressed ladies and gentlemen dance a stately measure. The stepmother and her two daughters arrive and, grotesquely imitating the manners of their betters, attract considerable attention. Two men are finally persuaded to ask the two sisters to dance.

The prince appears, greets his guests, and ascends the throne. As the ball continues, a new strain of enchanting music is heard, and, accompanied by attendants, a lovely young girl enters. The prince cannot take his eyes off her, and asks her to dance. The court is curious about her identity. No one, not even her own family and least of all the ugly stepsisters, realizes that the beautiful guest is Cinderella.

When Arab boys present Cinderella with three oranges, she is so moved by the envious glances of Krivlyaka and Zlyuka that she gives the fruit to them. The prince and Cinderella are then briefly alone. They have both fallen in love at first sight and dance together to declare their love.

When the guests return, the court festivities continue. But at the height of the celebration, before she has even contemplated that such an evening should ever end, the clock strikes twelve. True to the fairy godmother's word, twelve dwarfs emerge from the clock. Cinderella, terrified, flees the castle. The prince runs after her. The prediction of the fairy godmother is fulfilled: Cinderella is again as she first was, and only the crystal slippers remain from her ball dress. She loses one slipper as she dashes home, and the prince, as he pursues her, finds it. He comforts himself that to find the girl all he has to do is find the owner of the slipper!

ACT THREE, SCENE ONE: COURTYARD OF THE CASTLE   In an effort to find the maker of the shoe, the prince summons cobblers throughout the kingdom. No one can name the shoemaker and the prince decides to set out himself on his search for his beloved.

ACT THREE, SCENE TWO   The prince searches far and wide, and every lovely girl in the land weeps that the slipper will not fit. The prince remains determined to find his true love.

ACT THREE, SCENE THREE: A ROOM IN CINDERELLA'S HOUSE   Cinderella sleeps, pressing the remaining slipper to her breast. The slipper falls to the floor. Waking up the next morning, she recalls the splendid ball and her meeting with the prince. She decides that it must all have been a dream. But in the course of going about her daily chores, she finds the glass slipper. So it was not a dream after all! She cannot believe it.

The stepsisters come and relate the fine time they had at the ball, how popular they were, and how a princess gave them oranges.

Noise from the street heralds the arrival of the prince, who is going from house to house in search of the unknown beauty. When he enters, both stepsisters try in vain to force their feet into the shoe, and even their mother tries her luck. Then the prince notices Cinderella standing in the corner. She is so stunned by her lover's presence that she does not know what to do. She becomes so confused that she drops the other slipper. There is now no doubt as to who she is! Her fairy godmother appears and blesses Cinderella and her prince.

ACT THREE, SCENE FOUR: A FLOWERING GARDEN   Cinderella and the prince have found each other. They celebrate their reunion and live happily ever after.

Ballet in three acts. Music by Sergei Prokofiev. Choreography by Frederick Ashton. Scenery and costumes by Jean-Denis Malclès. First presented by the Sadler's Wells Ballet at the Royal Opera House, Covent Garden, London, December 23, 1948, with Moira Shearer as Cinderella, Michael Somes as the Prince, Robert Helpmann and Frederick Ashton as Cinderella's Stepsisters, Pamela May as the Ragged Fairy Godmother, Nadia Nerina, Violetta Elvin, Pauline Clayden, and Beryl Grey as the Fairies, and Alexander Grant as the Jester. First presented in the United States by the Sadler's Wells Ballet at the Metropolitan Opera House, New York, October 18, 1949, with Margot Fonteyn as Cinderella and the same principals.

Cinderella is a story everybody knows and in the past it has attracted a great number of choreographers—French, Russian, and English. This particular ballet on the story, however, is important for a special reason: it is the first classic English ballet in three acts, the first full-length English work in the style and manner of the great nineteenth-century classics. But *Cinderella* is entertaining as well as important. Here the familiar tale is embellished with dramatic and comic differences, with *divertissements*, and with the grace and warmth of the grand academic style.

ACT ONE: A ROOM IN THE HOUSE OF CINDERELLA'S FATHER   The curtain rises on a somber scene. Cinderella crouches on the hearth of a high stone fireplace on the right. On the left, at a plain table, her father sits reading. Near him sit Cinderella's two stepsisters, busily sewing a scarf. They are elderly and hideous, and there is an obvious tension in the room. Cinderella is sitting by the fireplace because she is not allowed to sit anywhere else. Dressed in worn, unbecoming brown, she makes a pathetic figure. The light shines on her face and, despite her sadness, we note that she is beautiful. The music is quiet but expectant; strings are plucked rapidly to sound curiously like the clicking of knitting needles.

The stepsisters, old maids that they are, have been invited to a ball this very night and they work at their sewing with some haste. They finish the scarf and begin to fight about who shall wear it. Cinderella glances at them as if their bickering were all too familiar: in this house there is either quarreling or silence. But she is afraid to interfere. She is no longer the daughter of the house but its servant. The daughters of her father's second wife now rule the house, and she, like her father, can exist only by conforming to their wishes.

The father tries to calm his stepdaughters, but abandons hope when they ignore him. Each tugs at her end of the scarf, and it is torn in two. The stepsisters leave the room, still quarreling, and he follows after them despondently. Cinderella is alone. She takes up a broom and moves wistfully about the room, posing gracefully. She is thinking of happier days, when her mother was alive and there was love for her to respond to. She picks up a piece of the scarf her stepsisters have left behind and puts it around her shoulders: now she is a lady, the lady her mother would have wanted her to be. She takes a candlestick from the table, crosses the darkened room, lights the candle at the fireplace, and holds it high to look upon her mother's portrait, which hangs above the mantel. The father returns, sees his daughter's despair, and attempts to cheer her. But he, too, is sad. The ugly stepsisters come in and reprimand him for keeping Cinderella from her housework. They warn the girl to return to her cleaning.

The orchestra sounds a new, magical melody. The stepsisters hear it, too. Cinderella looks up expectantly, and into the room hobbles a hunchbacked woman in rags. Her face is grotesque, her rags are filthy, but Cinderella seems to welcome her. The old hag begs for money, and the two stepsisters go into a tizzy of silly fear, running away to the other side of the room. Cinderella would like to comfort the old hag, but she knows that she has nothing to give. When the woman begs from her, Cinderella can only give her a bit of bread. The elder stepsister is annoyed at this generosity and threatens the woman. But, like an omen fulfilled, she is suddenly seized with a toothache and flees back to her sister. As Cinderella watches, wishing she could help more, the old hag glances at her gratefully and gently and disappears.

No sooner has the father reminded his two stepdaughters that they must begin to dress for the ball, than purveyors arrive—a tailor, dressmakers, a shoemaker, a jeweler, a hairdresser, a dancing master, each taking advantage of the sisters' new-found popularity to sell all their wares and talents. The old women are delighted at this attention, costly as it may be, and titter constantly like debutantes. Soon they are decked out in extravagant dresses. At this point the dancing master reminds them of the courtly steps in which they must be perfect. The women practice their bows and try to dance, as two violinists play a gavotte. The elder stepsister, old as she is, manages to execute the gavotte more or less to the dancing master's satisfaction, while the meek, shy sister despairs of learning. The dancing master sees that neither will ever learn and finally pretends that both are perfect.

The time of the ball is drawing near, and the stepsisters hurry with their makeup, primping extravagantly, as if all the powder and rouge in the world would reduce their ugliness. Their coach is announced, there is a final flurry of activity, and the sisters, absurdly proud in their bearing, depart.

Again Cinderella is alone. She looks into the fire. The women did not even bother to say good night to her. She wonders what the ball will be like, what any ball is like. She dances again with the broom, holding it before her as if she were not waltzing alone, and moves happily about the room, imagining herself at the ball. Soon she sees how silly she is being, puts the broom down, and goes back to sit at the hearth.

The harp is plucked gently, and again the eerie, high, piercing cry that heralded the arrival of the old beggarwoman causes Cinderella to look up and smile. The music is magical, like the loveliness of a dream; it grows in volume as the lower strings sound a full, promising melody. The room in which Cinderella sits seems to disappear, its walls vanishing. The old woman stands in the center of the room. She looks at Cinderella, and then something more extraordinary happens. In a flash, the old hag is transformed into a lovely, kind fairy: the ragged cretin becomes a beautiful creature dressed in a shimmering gown.

Cinderella cannot believe her eyes and when her fairy godmother tells her that she must prepare for the ball, that now, really, she *is* going to the ball, the lonely girl almost cries with happiness. The fairy godmother waves her wand, calling forth four fairies to dress Cinderella for the ball.

First comes the fairy Spring, then the fairies Summer, Autumn, and Winter. One by one, the fairies each dance a variation. After each one appears, the accompanying backdrop vanishes and Cinderella's room stretches back into the distance farther and farther. The scenery is transformed completely for each fairy, changing in color from green to icy blue, in surroundings from abundant garlands to a pinnacle of ice, and the fairies and their attendants are dressed charmingly in the habits of their seasons.

Cinderella sits on the floor at the feet of her fairy godmother, taking in the full magic of her great powers. Now she understands. The fairy godmother tells her to bring a pumpkin. Before the girl's astonished eyes, she changes the pumpkin into a magnificent coach. Cinderella is surrounded by the fairies, who present gifts to her and dress her for the ball. Almost at their touch, the lonely girl becomes as beautiful as a fairy tale princess, dressed splendidly in white and gold, wearing a crown and a long, flowing cape with a high pearl collar that encloses her shining face.

Her godmother tells Cinderella not to delay, that a newfound happiness awaits her at the ball. But she warns the girl that she must leave the ball before the clock strikes twelve. If she remains after midnight, the magic will vanish as mysteriously as it came and she will be just a lonely girl again, dressed in shabby clothes. Cinderella promises that she will not tarry and bows to her in gratitude. The fairies and a multitude of stars surround Cinderella as she goes to her coach and proceeds to the ball.

ACT TWO: A BALL AT THE PALACE   The ball has already begun when the curtain rises. Members of the court are dancing a formal measure in a ballroom that has been set up in the palace garden. Two great trees and their overhanging branches enclose the festive scene. To the left and right, spectators watch the ball in low stage boxes. In the back, on either side of a flight of low steps, are two high elegant structures, pavilions set up especially for the ball. On the ground floor of these pavilions we can see other guests amusing themselves. Farther back, by the light of a distant chandelier, we can make out a splendid formal garden. At the top of the steps is the prince's throne. The prince has not yet arrived, and the court jester sits on the royal stool.

Cinderella's stepsisters make an absurdly grand entry in keeping with the elegance they have assumed for the occasion. Cinderella's father accompanies them and is made visibly ill at ease by their pretensions. The older sister is determined to enjoy herself and acts unimpressed by the beauty of the palace garden: it is all her due, designed for her enjoyment, and she imagines herself attractive. The younger sister is more honest and cannot so easily disguise the fact that all this elegance is strange to her. She tugs plaintively at her sister's dress and wants to go home. She is, of course, refused and resolves to see the evening out only when a courtier begins to pay her some attention, thus reviving her spirits. She is disenchanted when her jealous sister takes her suitor away.

Now, as another courtly dance commences, the two sisters have a chance to perform the measures the dancing master taught them. The older sister watches with disgust as the younger dances. She starts out well, and for a moment we think she is really going to make it, but her steps become tentative and it is apparent that she's forgotten every step she knows. The older sister laughs, executes the dance with grotesque accuracy, and then, to show off, tries to balance on one foot. The younger sister is terrified, and, of course, the show-off begins to topple over. The jester catches her as she stumbles about trying to keep from falling flat on her face.

Four friends of the prince enter and prepare the guests for the arrival of their host. The handsome prince enters with a regal but lively flourish, and all the guests bow to him. The two sisters attempt to make their reverence so that the prince will take particular notice of them, but he does not even glance at them. The prince's companions dance a *pas de quatre*, which is followed by another general dance by the court.

One guest has not yet arrived. The light, mysterious music that heralded the first appearance of Cinderella's ragged fairy godmother interrupts the court music, and everyone pauses. The jester, at the prince's order, goes to welcome the newcomer in the garden. The twelve girls representing stars and the four fairies with their pages enter at the rear, and the court wonders what to expect with such an elaborate preparation. All look toward the entrance to the ballroom as the prince awaits the guest. Finally the royal coach of Cinderella draws up to the garden gate. The girl steps out, and all are dazzled by her natural beauty and the loveliness of her costume. The prince, who is immediately charmed, takes Cinderella's hand and leads her forward. Two pages hold Cinderella's train while the stars and fairies kneel about their mistress. Wishing to discover more about this ravishing girl, the prince escorts her for a walk through the palace grounds.

The other guests, who have watched the entrance of Cinderella from the boxes at the sides of the ballroom, now mingle on the dance floor and begin a masked dance. The ugly stepsisters, of course, have not recognized Cinderella and accept her simply as visiting royalty. Soon the prince returns alone and dances a variation, after which he leaves the scene. Now Cinderella dances and in her movements she conveys the youthful and tender joy she feels at the ball. It is as if she belonged there, for she is unembarrassed and confident in her natural graciousness.

The two sisters, alone for a moment, spend their time gossiping about the unattractive girl who has gained the prince's favor. The two lovers return. The harp is plucked against a deep, flowing melody, and they begin a *pas de deux*. The dance is soft and considerate, yet strong in its regal elegance and the personal elegance of the handsome young pair. The prince kneels before Cinderella as their dance finishes. She responds to his love by dancing a variation that reflects her new-found pleasure in loving and being loved. She is so happy that she has no memory of her misery at home; she pirouettes rapidly, and her two stepsisters are a million miles away.

A Negro page brings to the prince an orange on a silver tray. This is the most highly prized fruit in all the kingdom and the finest gift he can give Cinderella. She accepts it graciously. Then the prince turns to the ugly stepsisters and bestows an orange on each of them. Instantly they begin to quarrel about whose orange is larger, and the dominating sister snatches the choice one away from the timid creature.

Cinderella and the prince lead the court in an ensemble dance. The music is a bright, sparkling waltz that gradually gains in sonorous force, and all the guests are caught up in the spirit of romance. Suddenly—as the waltz gains relentless force, cymbals shimmer, and we hear the loud ticking of a clock—a flourish of trumpets announces the approach of midnight. The cymbals crash, to warn Cinderella that she must hasten. The girl rushes from the prince's arms. He watches, astonished, as she tries to make her way through the crowded guests to the gate. The girl is desperate lest her secret be discovered. When she arrives at the gate, midnight has come. Her beautiful dress becomes her ragged work clothes, and she flees into the night, leaving behind one of her slippers. The prince cannot understand; he looks after her as the orchestra restates the theme of their *pas de deux* and the curtain falls.

ACT THREE, SCENE ONE: AFTER THE BALL   When the curtain rises on the first scene, again Cinderella is seen sitting by the fire in her father's house, just as she was at the entrance of the fairy godmother. She is asleep. She wakens, looks about, and thinks she has dreamed of the ball. Only the slipper she finds hidden in her apron convinces her that she really was there, that there was a handsome prince, and that he did love her. She dances again with the broom, reflecting in her steps her unhappiness before the ball, her recollection of her first love, and her resignation to her everyday life.

Her sisters return. They are so tired that they don't even wish to gossip until they have undressed and cast off the weight of their excessive finery. They sigh as they remove their shoes from their swollen feet. But soon they are taunting Cinderella with tall tales about the ball, the prince, and his attentions to them. They toy with the oranges he gave them, and Cinderella is thinking too much of what the ball was really like to care much about their prattling.

The women hear a disturbance in the street. Townswomen rush in and excitedly announce that a royal procession is waking everyone up, that the prince, enamored of a girl he cannot find, is determined to discover the owner of a shoe left behind at the ball. He vows that he will marry the girl whom the shoe fits.

The sisters are apprehensive lest the prince visit their house when they are not fully dressed and scurry about putting on their formal gowns and their tight shoes again. The prince enters with the jester and an entourage. He holds Cinderella's lost slipper in his hand and declares that the woman it fits shall become his wife. He does not notice the girl in rags who crouches at the fire. The stepsisters do obeisance before the prince, who responds to them so graciously that they imagine one of them might be the chosen one. First, the shy stepsister tries on the shoe. She knows it is silly to pretend that it will fit and gives up wistfully. The other sister is delighted at her failure, but has no more luck herself, despite much straining and pinching in an effort to force her foot into the shoe.

When it is apparent that she, too, is a misfit, Cinderella helps her pull the shoe off. As the girl kneels before her sister, the other slipper falls from her apron pocket. The prince sees it and asks the girl if she will try on the shoe. Her stepsisters rail at her, but the prince insists. The shoe fits perfectly. At first the sisters cannot believe it, but when the prince announces that Cinderella will be his bride, they attempt in several reverential gestures to make up for the years of misery they have caused the girl. Cinderella understands them, pities them, and touches them lovingly as they bow before her. The prince and Cinderella embrace. The fairy godmother appears and raises her wand.

ACT THREE, SCENE TWO: AN ENCHANTED GARDEN   The scene is transformed. We find ourselves in a magical place, a colorful garden where the light seems to sparkle. There a great boat awaits the arrival of the lovers. The prince's friends and the fairies dance together, and Cinderella and the prince enter. Six of the stars surround them as they dance, the fairies pose gracefully with their cavaliers, and the music sounds soaringly the theme of ideal romance that marked the couple's first recognition of love. The fairy godmother and all the magical creatures wish the lovers godspeed, and they step into the waiting ship. The surging music falls off into soft measures that predict eternal joy. The prince holds Cinderella in his arms as they sail off on a happy voyage that will never end.

Yet another important version of this ballet came into the American repertory in 1970:

Music by Sergei Prokofiev. Staged and choreographed by Ben Stevenson. Scenery by Edward Haynes. Costumes by Norman McDowell. First presented by the National Ballet at the Lisner Auditorium, Washington, D.C., April 24, 1970.

The synopsis of this version of the ballet is close to others, but has some important differences:

ACT ONE   Cinderella's father watches his two stepdaughters embroidering scarves to be worn to a ball given that evening by the prince. The cruel stepdaughters tease their stepfather with the scarves. Cinderella enters and stops them. The stepsisters are furious and order Cinderella to clean the kitchen as they drag their father from the room. Her only friend now seems to be the broom.

Cinderella, remembering a picture of her mother, takes it from its hiding place and sits gazing at it. Her father enters and is overcome with remorse when he sees how much Cinderella resembles his first loving wife. She tries to comfort him when the stepsisters enter and are enraged to see Cinderella in her father's arms. They pull them apart and snatch the picture away. Suddenly the door opens and an old beggarwoman enters. The stepsisters decide to give her the picture, but the old woman sees the resemblance between the picture and Cinderella and returns it to Cinderella. Cinderella gives the old woman her last crust of bread.

The dressmaker and the wigmaker arrive to ready the stepsisters for the ball. A dancing master also arrives with the impossible task of teaching the stepsisters how to dance. Cinderella is alone again, pretending she is at the ball, and dances with the broom, then bursts into tears realizing it is only a daydream. The old beggar returns and much to Cinderella's amazement is transformed into a beautiful fairy godmother. The kitchen changes into a magic glade with dragonflies swooping among the trees. The fairy godmother asks Cinderella to find a pumpkin and four lizards and gives them to one of the dragonflies, who darts off into the trees. The fairy godmother gives a pair of glass slippers to Cinderella. The fairies of Spring, Summer, Autumn, and Winter arrive and dance for Cinderella, changing the seasons as they do. Cinderella's rags become a beautiful dress. The fairy godmother shows Cinderella a magic clock and warns her that at midnight her magic clothes will turn again into rags. The fairy godmother changes the pumpkin and lizards into a coach and horses and Cinderella drives to the ball like a princess.

ACT TWO   A jester greets the guests as they arrive in the ballroom. The guests are amazed when the ugly stepsisters arrive. The prince enters, and he too is amused by the sight of the sisters; however, he asks them each in turn to dance with him to the amazement of the crowd. Cinderella arrives in her coach, and the prince falls in love with her at first sight. He offers his guests oranges, as they are the very rarest fruit in the land. One of the sisters is left without an orange; Cinderella sees this and gives up her own. The stepsister accepts without recognizing Cinderella.

While the prince and Cinderella are dancing together, the clock strikes midnight and Cinderella's beautiful clothes turn to rags. The prince rushes after her to find only one of her glass slippers on the stairs.

ACT THREE   Cinderella waits among the cinders in the kitchen thinking the ball only a dream until she finds the other glass slipper in her pocket. She quickly hides it as the ugly sisters arrive. They show Cinderella the oranges they received from the prince. Suddenly the jester enters the room, heralding the arrival of the prince and two of his friends who have with them the glass slipper. The stepsisters vainly try to squeeze their big feet into the tiny slipper. The prince sees Cinderella sitting by the fire and asks her father if she may try it. As Cinderella gets up from the stool, she drops the other glass slipper. The prince is overjoyed! The stepsisters beg Cinderella's forgiveness and the fairy godmother arrives, accompanied by the fairies of the seasons.

The prince returns the glass slippers to them and the kitchen once again changes into a magic glade. Cinderella and her prince dance a romantic *pas de deux,* and at its conclusion, the guests arrive for the coronation of Cinderella, the cruelly mistreated girl who rose from the cinders to a royal throne.

NOTES Reviewing this production of *Cinderella* in the British magazine, *Ballet Today,* Kay Rinfrette wrote: "Ashton's *Cinderella* for the Royal Ballet influenced Stevenson's ballet in several aspects. Like Ashton, Stevenson employs the English pantomime tradition by having the stepsisters played *en travesti,* and he excludes the stepmother who usually appears in Russian productions. Also, Stevenson omits the prince's search around the world. Unlike Ashton, Stevenson changes the sequence of musical numbers in the ballroom scene to give the *grand pas de deux* a traditional, formal structure. (The adagio is followed by the man's, then the ballerina's variation.) The choreography, especially effective in solos and group work, and character development are Stevenson's exciting, original conceptions (with only a few distant reverberations of some Ashton choreography).

"The choreographic structure of the ballet—Stevenson's use of thematic materials—is magnificent. Two primary movement themes (motifs), used separately and in combination, are introduced in the four-seasons sequence in Act One: (1) sudden or unexpected changes in direction of movement, and (2) traveling lifts which give an impression of weightlessness. The feeling of lightness created in this sequence emphasizes a fairy-tale quality and contrasts to the heaviness of the previous fireside scene (the cumbersome, heavy awkwardness of the stepsisters, the figurative 'burden' falling on Cinderella's shoulders).

"Specifically, the thematic movements include the 'dragonflies' transporting the fairy godmother in multiple traveling lifts with quick changes of direction —at one point she is carried back and forth across the stage three times without pause—and the sudden direction changes in the solos for Spring and Autumn. The same movement themes appear in the ballroom scene, especially in the *corps de ballet* work: many lovely lifts in unexpected directions, often backwards; at the waltz's climax, the girls, arching their backs, fall forward sequentially into their partners' arms, only to be weightlessly lifted and wafted away. The ballroom grand adagio, with its many extend traveling lifts (in fact, some lifts looked awkward and unnecessarily difficult), is also a part of weightless fantasy—the ballerina is swept away by the fairy-tale grandeur both literally and figuratively.

"The adagio in the last act is less involved with fantasy, closer to a real-life love relationship. This meaning is underscored by the choreography which includes thematic elements but in different combinations: there are fewer lifts, more *terre à terre* work, including swift runs with sudden direction changes, as if the lovers were blown by the wind. Structurally, this adagio is the climax of the ballet, combining and reconciling the literary themes of fantasy versus reality and the choreographic motifs of floating lightness versus heaviness or a sense of weight. In the final coronation scene, heavy-looking imperial crowns are placed on the heads of Cinderella and the prince—the fantasy (lightness) becomes a reality (weight).

"Character and dancing aspects are well balanced in this production, meaning that the stepsisters do not monopolize the show. Their hilarious antics are most clever in sequences with the dancing master and at the ball when they 'send-up' ballet steps—such as one sister holding an *attitude* for several seconds and then collapsing in a heap. The polarization of characters is clearly established in the beginning, when the stepsisters angrily snatch away from Cinderella a painting of her mother, and when Cinderella is kind to the old hag visitor (fairy godmother in disguise). The father, depicted as a multiple-henpecked man unable to cope, is a kind of transition figure between the 'good' Cinderella and the 'evil' stepsisters. Even minor characters are sharply drawn— the snobbish, prim dancing master and the eccentric, dissatisfied wigmaker."

Reviewing this new production of *Cinderella* in the New York *Times,* the critic Clive Barnes wrote: "The result is most pleasing. This is a good *Cinderella*. The settings by Edward Haynes and the costumes by Norman McDowell are simple but elegant, and Mr. Stevenson's unaffectedly classical choreography is a model of good taste.

"This is a formidable undertaking for a small company—it does not have so many dancers as the City Center Joffrey Ballet—and it survived grandly. Mr. Stevenson's choreography is strongly influenced by Frederick Ashton—Mr. Stevenson being a former member of the Royal Ballet—yet not slavishly so. Often he has gone to some lengths to be different from the Ashton version of the score, and his concept is always attractive.

"It is the kind of choreography that suits dancers—graceful and understated. He is not afraid of virtuosity, and certainly Mr. Stevenson has made more demands upon these Washington dancers than any previous choreographer. He cannot prevent the first scene of Cinderella and her sisters from appearing prosey—it always does in any production—but he does give his two lovers the most intricately stylish *pas de deux.*

"The dancing was splendid. Mr. Stevenson has mounted his ballet on two couples, Gaye Fulton and Desmond Kelly, and Marilyn Burr and Ivan Nagy. At the performance I saw it was given by Miss Fulton and Mr. Kelly.

"Miss Fulton, a delicate figurine of a princess in hiding, made an enchanting Cinderella, and Mr. Kelly, elegant and assertive, was the most perfect of Princes.

"Another young man of more than usual promise is Kirk Peterson, from the Harkness Youth Company, who was dancing the Jester. He had a brilliant technique and was very cleverly used by Mr. Stevenson. I also admired the roistering humor of Frederic Franklin (the company's director) and Larry Long as the Ugly Sisters, and the style of Judith Rhodes and Christine

Knoblauch among the fairies. But the entire company extended and excelled itself."

CIRCLES

Music by Luciano Berio. Choreography by Glen Tetley. Decor and costumes by Nadine Baylis. First presented by the Netherlands Dance Theatre at the Royal Theatre, The Hague, March 5, 1968. First presented by the same ensemble at the City Center, New York, April 19, 1968.

This dance ballet uses the Luciano Berio score *Circles* for female voice, harp, and two percussion. The score's libretto is three poems by e. e. cummings (*Numbers 25, 76,* and *22*). The ballet is for six dancers, all of whom appear at the beginning of the piece, moving, exercising, warming up in silence. A boy and girl separate themselves from the group and, to the first of the three songs, dance together. Another *pas de deux* accompanies the second song while the third is more of an ensemble that recalls what has gone before.

Reviewing the ballet after its American premiere, Clive Barnes said in the New York *Times:* "Mr. Tetley's *Circles* is a lovely work. It is curious—perhaps shameful—that while Mr. Tetley has an enormous reputation in the Netherlands and England, in his native land he goes as a prophet if not unhonored at least remarkably unrecognized . . .

"The dancing flickers, ebbs and flows in all directions at the happily wayward command of the music. The six dancers interweave their patterns with a kind of creative expertise, certain in its technique yet diffident in its artistic assurance. The impression is of golden people dancing in a golden landscape, yet a gold not without the threat of devaluation and a landscape not without the danger of erosion. Nothing here is quite so certain as the actual dancing—what lies behind could be another story."

CIRCUS POLKA

Music by Igor Stravinsky. Choreography by Jerome Robbins. First presented by the New York City Ballet at the Stravinsky Festival, 1972, at the New York State Theatre, Lincoln Center, June 23, 1972.

Stravinsky's *Circus Polka* was composed precisely for the circus—for the Ringling Brothers, Barnum and Bailey Circus in 1942. The circus impresarios wanted to do a ballet for elephants. They asked me to arrange the dance and told me I could choose the composer. Who else but Stravinsky? I telephoned him, not giving away the whole story. "What kind of music?" he asked. "A polka," I said. "For whom?" he wanted to know. "Elephants." "How old?" "Young!" "Okay, if they are very young, I'll do it." What he did served its purpose very well, and our ballet for *Fifty Elephants and Fifty Beautiful Girls,* staged by John Murray Anderson, with costumes by Norman Bel Geddes, and

Vera Zorina riding at the head of the troupe at the first performances, was done no less than 425 times.

Jerome Robbins in his ballet took an entirely new direction, and the work was one of the happiest inventions during our Stravinsky Festival at the New York State Theatre in 1972. Robbins chose for his cast young girls from the School of American Ballet and put them, the youngest first, through their paces. As ringmaster of the troupe, in formal top hat and swallow-tail coat, he led forty-eight of our talented children to Stravinsky's brisk measures. At the end, at his direction, the children formed the Stravinsky initials, *I. S.*, with periods. The ballet was such a hit that the whole piece had to be repeated at once.

CLOCKWISE

Music by Jean Françaix. Choreography by Bruce Marks. Costumes by Stanley Simmons. Lighting by Jules Fisher. First presented by the American Ballet Company at the Brooklyn Academy of Music, New York, October 24, 1970, with Karen Kelly, Christine Kono, Elizabeth Lee, Christine Sarry, Cristina Stirling, Larry Grenier, Edward Henkel, Daniel Levans, Richard Munro, John Sowinski, Kenneth Hughes, Kerry Williams, Olga Janke and Eve Wallstrum.

This first ballet by a premier danseur of American Ballet Theatre is a dance work arranged to a composition about a clock of flowers, by the French contemporary Françaix. The piece is in seven parts, as is the ballet, where different combinations of dancers suggest the fleeting passage of time. A central *pas de deux*, to a pensive romantic melody, suggests permanent affection, too, but that soon yields to convivial ensemble, and the work ends as it began, with a simulation of a clock.

NOTES   The critic Clive Barnes, in the New York *Times*, said that Bruce Marks "has produced a graceful, charming work . . . that bodes well for his future as a choreographer. This elegant first ballet . . . was neatly danced, with Christine Kono, Christine Sarry, Daniel Levins, Elizabeth Lee and John Sowinski all to the fore."

THE CLOWNS

Music by Hershy Kay. Choreography by Gerald Arpino. Costumes by Edith Lutyens Bel Geddes. Lighting by Tom Skelton. Assistant to Mr. Arpino: James Howell. First presented by the City Center Joffrey Ballet at the City Center, New York, February 28, 1968, with Robert Blankshine, Frank Bays, Erika Goodman and Maximiliano Zomosa in principal roles. Special effects by Vernon Lobb and Kip Coburn. Conducted by Hershy Kay.

The Clowns is a dramatic metaphor about life as it is lived by those perennial reflectors of the human spirit—the floppy white clowns of the *commedia dell' arte.* The piece begins with a bang, as if all the world had exploded, and a lone clown, battered and bruised, appears to be the only remnant of civilization. But he is not quite alone, for bodies begin to fall out of the sky like hail, bodies of fellow clowns. Mournfully but doggedly determined and not stopping to grieve, the survivor piles them all up into a kind of pyre. But mysteriously, at least one of them is alive, for a girl emerges to join the clown. The two clowns dance together joyously. Their dance is a dance of renewal and liveliness and the life is contagious: before we know it, the whole pile of bodies is revived and the clown tribe lives again.

Not content, however, with renewal and resumption of their old funny and antic roles, the clowns now reveal their human side, too. They begin to plot against each other and to employ weapons—big balloons that seem to envelop the opposition. The original survivor, however much he tries not to get involved in this dark side of human nature, is soon caught up in it, too. The fellows he has helped revive turn hostile and he is the victim. In retaliation, he brings in the biggest balloon imaginable, a huge, long cylinder that becomes a transparent tunnel. What this instrument soon becomes is a clown catcher and all the opposition are entrapped in it, beating against its walls, helpless to get out. They can *see* out and the walls of the prison are soft but they cannot penetrate them. They are all sucked down into it. Except for one. The first survivor, who again survives.

LE COMBAT (*see* THE DUEL)

CON AMORE

Classic ballet in three scenes. Music by Gioacchino Rossini. Choreography by Lew Christensen. Libretto by James Graham-Luhan. Scenery and costumes by James Bodrero. Scenery executed by James Martin. First presented by the San Francisco Ballet, March 10, 1953, at the War Memorial Opera House, San Francisco, with Sally Bailey, Nancy Johnson, and Leon Danielian in the principal roles. Presented by the New York City Ballet at the City Center, New York, June 9, 1953, with a cast headed by Sally Bailey, Nancy Johnson, Herbert Bliss, and Jacques d'Amboise.

Con Amore is a ballet about love as it was frequently depicted in nineteenth-century European engravings. It is about love as it was regarded a hundred years ago and about love as it is frequently still regarded today. The ballet is in three scenes, each of which has for its music an overture by Rossini: the overtures to *La Gazza Ladra, Il Signor Bruschino,* and *La Scala di Seta.*

SCENE ONE: THE AMAZONS AND THE BANDIT After a musical introduction, the curtain rises on a stylized rustic scene. Here a company of Amazons, handsome and robust girls in smart military uniforms, are drilling under the command of their captain and her lieutenants. The girls move briskly and sharply, and it is apparent from their severe military bearing that they have never known love and wouldn't even entertain the idea of it. They are perfectly happy watching their beautiful captain as she sets an example of the brilliant skill in dancing and drill that they themselves hope to attain.

Love, however, asserts itself. A bandit invades the wood and dances among them. The girls treat the handsome intruder with disdain at first, but his uncontrolled gaiety and charm eventually pierce their hearts. But the vagabond bandit will have none of them. He will not be tied down by love and spurns their affections. He even dares to resist the charms of the lovely captain. At this point the perennial wrath of woman scorned holds the bandit at bay. The Amazons aim their muskets at him and he kneels before them, helpless. Blackout.

SCENE TWO: THE HUSBAND'S RETURN   After a short musical interlude, the curtain rises on the boudoir of a fashionable lady. She is alone in the room and is obviously preparing for a tryst. This turns out to be a series of trysts. The lady's husband is away at the moment, and all of her suitors have chosen this night to visit her.

First, a man about town knocks at her door. The lady admits him. The man attempts to embrace her, but the lady eludes him. It is clear, however, that she does not wish to elude him long. But before she can succumb, there is another knock at the door. The man about town hastily conceals himself, and the lady admits a sailor, who relentlessly chases her about her apartment, breathing lustily. He has almost worn down the lady when there is still another knock. The lady hides the sailor in her closet and admits a young student. This lad, instead of being eager for the lady's affections, finds her charms distasteful. She is obliged to make the advances, which the young man, knees quivering, just manages to escape. The man about town and the sailor, who have been watching all this, emerge from their hiding place to berate the student and resume their attack. There is another knock at the door. The lady's husband enters. He sees his wife with the three men and stares at them with his mouth open in astonishment. Blackout.

SCENE THREE: A TRIUMPH OF LOVE   In the final scene, we return to the finale of Scene One, where the bandit still kneels at the mercy of the angry Amazons. Amore (Cupid) enters in a chariot and with her skill attempts to remedy the situation. Hardly has she begun to do so than we are again presented with the dilemma of the finale of Scene Two. What is Amore going to do with all these men who seem to be in love with the same woman? But Amore solves everything. She draws her bow; her arrows pierce the hearts of all the men. As the curtain falls, the bandit, smitten finally with love for the Amazon captain, holds her in his arms; the lady is reunited with her husband; the man about town and the sailor embrace the Amazon lieutenants; and the timorous student, struck by love at last, rushes to claim Amore herself.

THE CONCERT

A charade in one act. Music by Frédéric Chopin. Choreography by Jerome Robbins. Costumes by Irene Sharaff. First presented by the New York City Ballet March 6, 1956, at the City Center, New York, with Tanaquil LeClercq and Robert Barnett in principal roles.

Jerome Robbins subtitles this ballet "The Perils of Everybody" and writes in a program note: "One of the pleasures of attending a concert is the freedom to lose oneself in listening to the music. Quite often, unconsciously, mental pictures and images form; and the patterns and paths of these reveries are influenced by the music itself, or its program notes, or by the personal dreams, problems, and fantasies of the listener. Chopin's music in particular has been subject to fanciful 'program' names such as the Butterfly Étude, the Minute Waltz, the Raindrop Prelude, etc."

During the overture to the ballet, we look at an amusing drop curtain, by Saul Steinberg, depicting the interior of an old-fashioned concert hall. When the curtain rises, a pianist crosses the stage, dusts the piano, and slumps down in meditation. Finally, he begins to play, and the audience begins to arrive, each carrying a folding chair: a man in a scarf who sits and meditates seriously, then two girls who clearly disturb him, then a girl in a huge wide-brimmed hat. She is so enthralled by the music that she snuggles right up to the piano and embraces it. A very serious student indeed follows, and then a husband and wife and a man on tiptoe. An usher tries to straighten out a mix-up over seats. When everyone is quieted down a bit, their fantasies begin to take over.

The husband envisages the murder of his wife and dreams of her substitute nearby. As the pianist pounds out a Mazurka, he sees himself as a brave hussar carrying off his beloved. His beloved, meanwhile, only wants to be a poor butterfly and acts that way. The wife intervenes, the poor girl is put down, and her husband is compelled to back down.

These are but some of the jokes that are played and acted out by these people to Chopin's music. To reveal all of them is to miss the fun of seeing the ballet, called by Patricia Barnes, in *Dance and Dancers,* "dance's funniest creation."

NOTES *The Concert* was extensively revised for Jerome Robbins's Ballets U.S.A. presentation at the Spoleto Festival June 8, 1958, with settings by Saul Steinberg that were used in the New York City Ballet revival (first presented December 2, 1971, at the New York State Theatre with Sara Leland, Francisco Moncion, Bettijane Sills, Shaun O'Brien, Robert Weiss, Bart Cook, Stephen Caras, Gloriann Hicks, Delia Peters, and Christine Redpath in principal roles. Jerry Zimmerman was the pianist).

The Concert was mounted for the Royal Ballet at the Royal Opera House, Covent Garden, London, on March 4, 1975, with frontcloths designed by Edward Gorey. Principal roles were taken by Lynn Seymour, Michael Coleman, and Georgina Parkinson. Writing in *Dance and Dancers* magazine, the English music critic Noël Goodwin said: "When I first saw *The Concert* in the inaugural Festival of Two Worlds at Spoleto in 1958, I ventured the opinion that this was one of the few deliberately comic ballets which could round off a program without anticlimax . . . Let me now amend that in the light of later experience and its welcome addition to the Royal repertory: *The Concert* is one of the few successful comic ballets on any count, and one that I still find the most hilarious I have ever seen."

CONCERTO

Music by Dimitri Shostakovich. Choreography by Kenneth MacMillan. First presented at the Deutsche Oper, West Berlin, November 30, 1966. First presented in the United States by American Ballet Theatre at the New York State Theatre, New York, May 18, 1967, with Eleanor D'Antuono and Scott Douglas, Toni Lander and Bruce Marks, and Cynthia Gregory in the principal roles. Decor and costumes after designs by Jürgen Rose. Lighting by Jean Rosenthal.

This is a dance ballet arranged to Shostakovich's *Concerto No. 2 for Piano and Orchestra*. Its plot is the music. The choreographer has said: "I just listen and listen and dig into the music. I don't do any actual preliminary work at home like some other choreographers, and so it can be a tricky business. Every choreographer has his own method of working, but I invent my ballets directly, in the rehearsal room. When there, I again listen to the music, this time with the dancers, and then start experimenting and inventing."

The first movement is led by a brightly dancing girl and boy, the second is dominated by a serious dance for two lovers, while the third is led by a charming girl. The mood and temper of the dances reflect a vision of the music.

The British critic Clement Crisp has written that *Concerto* has "a fresh, 'open' style that matches the exhilarating textures of the score with complete assurance."

CONCERTO BAROCCO

Classic ballet in three movements. Music by Johann Sebastian Bach. Choreography by George Balanchine. Scenery and costumes by Eugene Berman. First presented by the American Ballet at the Theatre of Hunter College, New York, May 29, 1940, with Marie-Jeanne, Mary Jane Shea, and William Dollar in the principal roles.

The only preparation possible for this ballet is a knowledge of its music, for *Concerto Barocco* has no "subject matter" beyond the score to which it is danced and the particular dancers who execute it. Set to Bach's *Concerto in D minor for Two Violins,* the ballet tries to interest the audience only by its dancing, its treatment of the music, just as Baroque art and architecture interested people not because of their subjects but because of the decorative treatment that embellished those subjects.

Bach's great concerto can stand alone. Some people then wonder, why arrange a ballet to such music? Why not arrange ballets to music that is more dependent, music that dancing can "fill out"? The answer is that bad music often inspires bad dancing, bad choreography. It is not an accident that the dance masterpieces of Saint-Léon, Petipa, and Fokine all have scores that are also masterworks. *Coppélia, The Sleeping Beauty,* and *Petrouchka,* with their scores by Delibes, Tchaikovsky, and Stravinsky, suggested to each one of these choreographers an advance in the development of ballet.

Choosing pieces of music for dancing is a matter for the individual choreographer. A choreographer disinterested in classical dancing will not care to use scores by Bach and Mozart except for theatrical sensational reasons; he will select music more to his immediate purpose. But if the dance designer sees in the development of classical dancing a counterpart in the development of music and has studied them both, he will derive continual inspiration from great scores. He will also be careful, as he acts on this inspiration, not to interpret the music beyond its proper limits, not to stretch the music to accommodate a literary idea, for instance. If the score is a truly great one, suitable for dancing, he will not have need of such devices and can present his impression in terms of pure dance.

FIRST MOVEMENT: VIVACE   The curtain rises. The music begins. There are eight girls on stage. Dancing variously as one group, as two groups, and in duets, the girls correspond to the music the orchestra plays, but not in any strict or literal sense; they do not mirror the music, rather they move in accordance with its length, the space between its beginning and end being filled by a dance picture of the music. Just as the portrait is different from the news photograph, so the dance picture tries to tell something independent of an exact, bar-by-bar, rhythm-by-rhythm, mirror image of the music.

As the two violins take up their parts in the music, two soloists enter. Singly, together, and with the *corps de ballet,* they become a part of the dance orchestration. They support each other as the music of one violin entwines the other; they depict and develop dance themes that recur with the repetition and development of themes in the orchestra.

SECOND MOVEMENT: LARGO MA NON TANTO   Now the soloists leave the stage. The orchestra sounds the touching, lyrical melody. One of the soloists returns, accompanied by a male partner, who lifts her softly and slowly, turns her as the *corps de ballet* bend low before her, and leads her in and out of a maze formed by the *corps.* The music is tender, but it possesses a warm nobility and strength that the ballerina's partner allows her to imitate as its development proceeds. When the music gathers toward a full statement and the theme repeats again and again, climbing with each repetition to a climactic rest, the ballerina's partner lifts her without pause high over his head, over and over again, to the accumulating sound. Then, toward the end of the movement, the boy slides the girl low across the floor in three daring movements. The ballerina rises each time in an open pose that reflects the strength underlying the lyricism of the theme.

THIRD MOVEMENT: ALLEGRO The music is now quickly rhythmic. All ten dancers seem to respond to it spontaneously, marking the beat of the music with soft, light jumps, crisp arm gestures, and syncopated groupings. As the joyous music ends, all the dancers kneel.

CONCERTO FOR JAZZ BAND AND ORCHESTRA

Music by Rolf Liebermann. Choreography by Arthur Mitchell and George Balanchine. Lighting by Ronald Bates. Conducted by Robert Irving. First presented by the New York City Ballet at the New York State Theatre, Lincoln Center, May 7, 1971, with dancers from the Dance Theatre of Harlem and the New York City Ballet.

This ballet, which received its one and only performance at a special gala occasion, will never be done again in all probability but is worth remembering and recording. It was a wonderful thing for me to collaborate on the choreography with Arthur Mitchell, who had become, in the New York City Ballet, our first black *premier danseur,* the first black first dancer in *any* major ballet company.

In 1968, at the time of the assassination of Martin Luther King, Jr., I did a memorial ballet, for one performance, to Stravinsky's *Requiem Canticles.* Arthur Mitchell, at that time disturbed by King's death and its meaning, determined that he would make it possible for other blacks to become fine dancers. The Dance Theatre of Harlem, and its associated school which he subsequently founded, is one of the great breakthroughs in the arts in America. To work with his dancers and our own on one ballet was, therefore, a special pleasure.

The music for the ballet, by the distinguished impresario and musician Rolf Liebermann, alternates a big jazz band (Doc Severinsen and the *Tonight Show* Orchestra) with a symphony ensemble. It is in six parts: *Introduction and Jump, Scherzo I, Blues, Scherzo II, Boogie Woogie,* and *Interludium.* Those who saw the ballet that night seemed to enjoy it very much and to appreciate the special quality of the occasion. It made me, personally, as it did Lincoln Kirstein, prouder than ever to be an occupant of the New York State Theatre.

CONCERTO FOR PIANO AND WINDS

Music by Igor Stravinsky. Choreography by John Taras. Costumes by Rouben Ter-Arutunian. Lighting by Ronald Bates. Pianist: Gordon Boelzner.

*Conducted by Robert Irving. First presented by the New York City Ballet
at the Stravinsky Festival, 1972, at the New York State Theatre, Lincoln
Center, June 20, 1972, with Bruce Wells in the leading role.*

This wonderful score by Stravinsky, too seldom heard in the concert hall, has
been used twice by John Taras for ballet. His first version, *Arcade,* was done
for the New York City Ballet at the City Center, New York, March 28, 1963,
with Suzanne Farrell and Arthur Mitchell in the leading roles. His second
ballet to this music was presented during the Stravinsky Festival at the New
York City Ballet in June 1972.

The ballet starts shortly after the orchestra begins, the curtain rising on
fourteen boys, all in red costume. Different groupings take up the accent of
the music, precise and percussive, as the piano, like a percussive instrument,
plays a toccata-like theme. There are no strings in this orchestra, we remember, as the definitive gesture and movement point to vital and supple action rather than reaction.

The second movement, which is very slow and pulsating, has an entirely
different character. The stage darkens and three spotlights point to three boys
kneeling. They rise slowly in answer to the music, as do the lights, and in
poses and groupings complement the piano and wind instruments' accompaniment. At the end, they again kneel in the dark.

Under bright lights, the dancers to the music perform a variety of brisk response that includes references back to the first part, a fugue, and a lively
finale.

CONCERTO FOR TWO SOLO PIANOS

*Music by Igor Stravinsky. Choreography by Richard Tanner. Costumes by
Stanley Simmons. First presented by the New York City Ballet at the New
York State Theatre, Lincoln Center, January 21, 1971, with Gelsey Kirkland and John Clifford, Colleen Neary and James Bogan, and David Richardson as principals.*

This work, the first by Richard Tanner for our repertory, was later performed
at the New York City Ballet's Stravinsky Festival, on February 23, 1972.
Stravinsky's music had its first performance in 1935, with the composer and his
son Soulima as soloists. The concerto is in four movements: 1. *Con moto,* 2.
Notturno—Adagietto, 3. *Quattro variazioni,* and 4. *Preludio* and *Fuga;* the
ballet follows this same pattern, basing its movement on the score's development. The plot of the music is the ballet's narrative.

One of the remarkable aspects of the score, as Eric Walter White notes in
his indispensable volume on Stravinsky, is its second movement, the *Nocturne*
—"a slow movement of exquisite tenderness and feeling, closely related in style
to the slow movements of the Piano Sonata and the Capriccio."

CONCERTO GROSSO

Music by George Frederick Handel. Choreography by Charles Czarny. Costumes by Joop Stovkis. First presented by the Netherlands Dance Theatre at the Circustheatre, Scheveningen, Holland, January 29, 1971. First presented in the United States by the same ensemble at the Brooklyn Academy of Music, New York, April 1, 1972.

Handel's music for the *Concerto Grosso No. 5* and the *Allegro* from the *Concerto Grosso No. 12* accompany this dance ballet based on gymnastics and athletics. The first part, begun by four boys in gym suits, is a warm-up for exercises and games to come. Four girls join them. The second part, *Obligatory Exercise,* is for three dancers. In *Shadow Boxing,* in silence, eight dancers wearing red mittens fight with each other in a gentle way. Following a sequence for skating, a line is drawn on stage to represent a tightrope, on which the dancers balance and perform. Next, in bright striped costumes of red and white, two boys play at soccer, each embodying opposing sides. All four couples join together again for the finale, a *Karate Minuet.*

CONCERTO IN G

Music by Maurice Ravel. Choreography by Jerome Robbins. Sets and costumes by Rouben Ter-Arutunian. Lighting by Ronald Bates. First presented by the New York City Ballet at the Hommage à Ravel at the New York State Theatre, Lincoln Center, May 14, 1975, with Suzanne Farrell and Peter Martins as principals. Conducted by Manuel Rosenthal.

One of the real hits of the New York City Ballet's Ravel festival in 1975, *Concerto in G* is danced to music that has an association with the United States. Ravel, at the peak of his fame and popularity, had just returned from a triumphant American tour when he began work on the piece. His hope was to compose a work that he could play himself, in order to fulfill the many requests that had accumulated for personal appearances. In the end he asked Marguerite Long, an old friend, to play as he conducted. Together they performed the concerto to great acclaim throughout Europe.

Janet Flanner attended the first performance and reported, under her pen name "Genêt," enthusiastically to *The New Yorker,* as Irving Drutman has recalled in *Paris Was Yesterday, 1925–39* (The Viking Press, New York, 1972).

Robbins's ballet to the *Concerto in G* is a dance piece without a story. There are three movements. While the first and third parts of the ballet, like the music, respond to jazz influences, a central sinuous adagio for the two principals creates an enduring impression.

Frances Herridge in the New York *Post* called *Concerto in G* "another gem for the repertory in a class with Robbins's *Dances at a Gathering.*"

Writing in *Dance and Dancers* magazine, the critic Patricia Barnes wrote that Robbins's "opening and closing movements, inventive, fresh and lively, used the ensemble of boys and girls with a vitality that earlier characterized his *Interplay* and in its jazz-tinctured rhythms showed Robbins in his very best Broadway mood; but it was the adagio movement for Suzanne Farrell and Peter Martins that was the work's real heart. Robbins has used Farrell's exquisite body to fabulous effect, exploiting her length of limb, her whole-hearted approach to dancing, in a pas de deux of genuine tenderness. The blend of daring lifts, swoops and swirls is contrasted with wonderfully effective little pauses, moments of telling stillness."

THE CONSORT

> *Music by Dowland, Neusidler, Morley, and anonymous composers. Orchestrated by Christopher Keene. Choreography by Eliot Feld. Costumes by Stanley Simmons. Lighting by Jules Fisher. First presented by the American Ballet Company at the Brooklyn Academy of Music, New York, October 24, 1970, with Marilyn D'Honau, Christine Kono, Elizabeth Lee, Olga Janke, Cristina Stirling, Larry Grenier, Kenneth Hughes, Daniel Levans, Richard Munro, and John Sowinski.*

Seventeenth-century music, mostly English, with some bawdy German songs for salt, provides the musical base for this dance ballet, orchestrated by the then musical director of the American Ballet Company, Christopher Keene. There is no plot here, and at first it appears that we shall be watching simply a stately but vigorous period piece, expressive of the Elizabethan age. But a curious thing happens. The long, formal dresses of the girls yield to short shifts, and before we know what has happened, the boys are whirling them about, courtiers have become peasants and, perhaps, themselves. While the stylization of the dances suggests a time long ago, the best of the orchestration and its demanding rhythms suggest the music of our own time, too, which is reflected in a rustic dance difference. Set for ten dancers, there are combinations of ensembles, boys and girls alone as well as *pas de deux* and solos, that merge the two styles of dancing.

NOTES   Writing about *The Consort* in the *Village Voice*, the critic Deborah Jowitt said: "The first part of *The Consort* is courtly, restrained, with that faint undercurrent of unpleasantness that you feel in a real pavane. Within the elaborate ritual, everyone is sizing up his partner and engaging in an almost invisible thrusting and parrying. Feld keeps the feeling of social dance; many instances of couples doing unison movement based—very remotely—on period dances. There are a few interludes that are more irregular. For example, there's an interesting bit in which Olga Janke dances very slowly and minimally, involved with her own skirt and a path that she is not quite progressing along, while John Sowinski keeps circling her lightly, but not lightheartedly—doing some of the subtly complex Feld steps that Sowinski performs with such luminous intelligence. They are aware and yet not aware of each other, and you are not quite sure which is the moth and which the star.

"As the court section ends, some of the women begin to help each other undress on stage. Quietly and naturally, they remove headdresses, take off boleros, loop their skirts up to above their knees. Daniel Levans examines and strokes his feathered cap for quite a time before tossing it into the wings. Again there is something faintly sinister in the air. When all the dancers are ready, the peasant section begins and begins mildly, with some of the same steps from the court part. You almost feel that these could be the same aristocrats playing at being peasants. Yet the stage gets more crowded (five couples as opposed to the three who began the piece), the dancers' bodies begin to look more weighty and sprawling, the harp (Keene's lute surrogate) is less noticeable, and the brasses begin to bray. These are still social dances, but with a coarseness and an increasingly ribald air. Two men do a fast rowdy dance, each with two girls, to Hans Neusidler's marvelously strange "Der Juden Tanz." *The Consort* ends with a debauch—the men wobbling like scarecrows, clutching the women to them; just drunk enough to be singlemindedly lecherous and with enough control left to do something about it. As the curtain comes down, the women have their legs about the men's waists and are being tossed and worried at. It reminded me of one of those Breughel scenes: you feel that because most of the time the peasants must have worked so hard, their appetites for play and drunken oblivion must have been immense, simple, and quickly sated."

COPPÉLIA (The Girl with Enamel Eyes)

Classic ballet in three acts. Music by Léo Delibes. Choreography by Arthur Saint-Léon. Book by Charles Nuitter and Arthur Saint-Léon, after a story by E. T. A. Hoffmann. First presented at the Théâtre Impérial de l'Opéra, Paris, May 25, 1870, with Giuseppina Bozacchi as Swanilda and Eugenie Fiocre as Franz. First presented in the United States by the American Opera at the Metropolitan Opera House, New York, March 11, 1887, with Marie Giuri and Felicita Carozzi in the leading roles. First presented in England at the Empire Theatre, London, May 14, 1906, with Adeline Genée as Swanilda.

Just as *Giselle* is ballet's great tragedy, so *Coppélia* is its great comedy. Both ballets are love stories and both have their roots in real life as well as in fantasy. In *Giselle* there are ghosts to test the quality of the hero's love for the heroine, and in *Coppélia* there is another romantic device by which the heroine makes sure of her lover's devotion. This device is the beautiful, lifeless doll, whose quiet, mechanical beauty contrasts with the charming liveliness of the real-life heroine. Because the hero in *Giselle* can only meet his lost love briefly in fantasy, and thereafter she is lost to reality, the ending of the ballet is tragic. But in *Coppélia* the inadequacy of the fantastic wax doll leads the hero back to his real love, and the ending is happy. And where Albrecht in *Giselle* learns an unhappy lesson from which he will never completely recover, Franz in *Coppélia* learns a lesson that makes his life happy forever after.

ACT ONE: THE SQUARE A spacious overture sets the tone for the whole ballet. The music begins with a melody of quiet dignity, first stated by the horns, then swept up by the strings. A muffled drum sounds, and the mood changes spontaneously to open gaiety as the orchestra plays a spirited robust mazurka. At its conclusion, the curtain rises.

The scene is a square in any small town in Central Europe; the time is a sunny afternoon several hundred years ago. A small house in the back faces the audience; on the side, a higher dwelling with a balcony projecting from the second floor dominates the street. Other buildings cluster about the square in a pleasantly haphazard fashion. All the façades are clean and painted in bright colors, and the walls and roofs seen in the background confirm our impression of an old village whose charm has not been worn away by changing times. The square is empty. An old man, bent with age, hobbles out of the door of the house on the right. This is Dr. Coppélius, the town's most mysterious citizen. He is said to dabble in alchemy and magic, but no one knows precisely what he does. Coppélius looks up at the balcony of his house, and we see that a lovely young girl is sitting there, reading a book. She is hidden a little from the full light of the sun, is wholly preoccupied with her reading, and takes no notice of the old doctor. Coppélius points up at the studious girl, rubs his hands with satisfaction as if he were a delighted chaperone, and re-enters his house.

The door of the little house in the back opens in a moment, and Swanilda emerges. She is dressed in bright colors particularly becoming to her dark beauty. From her movements we know almost immediately that she is very young and very much in love. The music to which she dances is piquant in the unembarrassed fullness of its melody, and Swanilda dances to it with obvious pleasure at some inner happiness. She walks rapidly on point, looking about the square anxiously to see that she is alone. She is expecting someone, but has some business of her own to attend to first. She glances up at the balcony of the large house and sees there the charming young girl, just as attractive as she is. The girl is intensely occupied and, holding the book rigidly before her, she does not look down to see Swanilda waving to her. Swanilda is annoyed. First of all she is annoyed because the girl is clearly snubbing her, but she is chagrined mostly because she has noticed that Franz, her fiancé, has also waved at this strange girl and has never mentioned it to her. Everyone calls the girl Coppélia. She is said to be the old man's daughter, but Coppélius has never appeared with her in the streets of the town and their relationship is just as unfathomable as Coppélius himself. Swanilda imitates her, holding an imaginary book before her. Then she bows low to Coppélia, in mock ceremony. Still the girl will not notice her. Swanilda stamps her foot in annoyance and dances briefly. She does not understand why Coppélia sits there reading on such a beautiful day and suspects she might be in a trance. On the other hand, she might be waiting for Franz! Swanilda approaches the house to see the girl more closely, shakes her fists at her, but quickly turns away as she hears Franz coming down the street. She is carefully hidden by the time he enters and she observes him secretly.

Franz is a high-spirited young peasant dressed in country costume. Like Swanilda, Franz is open and carefree by nature, but his heartiness masks a certain conceit: he seems not to have a care in the world and would not think it odd if every girl in the village adored him as much as Swanilda does. He does not go directly to Swanilda's door, but strides over to the house of Coppélius. After making sure that he isn't being watched, he glances up at the balcony. He waves to Coppélia flirtatiously, but also casually, as if he were in the habit of greeting her every time he passed. He points to Swanilda's door and remembers his love for her in the midst of this new infatuation. He clearly enjoys not knowing which lovely girl to choose. He clutches his heart as he looks up at Coppélia, then blows a kiss to her. Swanilda's worst suspicions of Franz's fickleness seem to be justified. Her suspicions become fears when Coppélia looks up from her book and waves back to Franz. Neither she nor Franz can see that behind the girl Coppélius stands concealed. He watches the flirtation with obvious disapproval, steps forward quickly, and closes the window curtains in Coppélia's face. Franz is abashed by this sudden disappearance of his new love. He is so distressed that he doesn't notice Swanilda, who has come into the square and stands right behind him. Swanilda refuses to attract his attention when he won't even turn away from the balcony; she walks off.

Now Franz consoles himself by remembering his rendezvous with Swanilda. But he does not have time to reach her door before Swanilda returns, bringing a beautiful butterfly she has just caught.

Franz takes the butterfly from her and pins it to his shirt. To Swanilda, this harmless gesture is a stab at her own broken heart. She bursts into tears and angrily accuses Franz of being unfaithful to her. He demurs, but she has no patience with his offhand answers and suggests that they come to him just as readily as his flirtations. Now that he sees how serious she is, Franz sincerely denies that he loves anyone else. But Swanilda is firm in her disbelief; she will not listen. Now Franz begins to lose his temper: how can she fail, he wonders, to see that he loves only her? Swanilda leaves the square, and Franz hails a party of peasants, their friends, who are unaware of the tension between the two lovers. They dance the rollicking mazurka that the orchestra first played in the overture, and when Swanilda joins them, her anxieties are momentarily dispelled. But she is determined to keep clear of Franz and, even at the sacrifice of her happiness, will accept no explanations.

The dancing of the peasants halts as the burgomaster enters the square. Everyone stands aside to make room for him and listens attentively as he tells them that on the next day the village will receive a great new bell for the town clock as a gift from the lord of the manor and that they must prepare themselves for the celebration attendant upon the ceremonies. The peasants are delighted at the idea of an unexpected festival. Their pleasure is so great that they do not pay much attention to strange noises emanating from the house of Coppélius.

The burgomaster goes on to say that the gracious lord will present handsome dowries to the girls who marry on the festival day. Several couples look at each other expectantly, but Swanilda is unmoved. Franz watches her closely. The burgomaster turns and asks her if she will be wed tomorrow. Unwilling to expose her broken heart to her friends and perhaps still hoping that she may be wrong about Franz's love, Swanilda resorts to fate and takes up an ear of wheat which the burgomaster offers her and shakes it near her ear, looking at her fiancé. The custom is—if she hears anything, her lover "loves her true"; if the wheat is silent, her lover "loves her not." Franz supports Swanilda in lovely deep poses as she bends low to listen to the wheat. Swanilda hears nothing. Franz, who thinks this pretense is silly, also hears nothing. She beckons to a friend and shakes the wheat again. The friend claims there is a sound, but Swanilda will not believe it. She throws the straw to the ground and announces that she and Franz are no longer engaged. Franz stalks away in disgust at the ways of women, while Swanilda joins her friends to dance a bright, gay tune as if nothing had happened to disturb their good time. A drum roll sounds, and Swanilda's friends dance a czardas, a Hungarian folk dance that starts out with slow, formal dignity and then increases in both speed and humor to become delirious with joy. The light grows darker and the group soon disbands. The stage is empty as night falls.

The door to Coppélius's house opens, and the wizened old man totters out. He pulls out a large key, locks the door, tries it several times, puts his key away, pats his pocket, and proceeds slowly across the square, leaning heavily on his cane. Obviously reluctant at leaving his house, Coppélius is easily frightened by a band of pranksters who rail at him good-humoredly, dance about him, and boisterously try to overcome his reluctance to join in. He loses his temper, which only encourages the fun. As they push him about, Coppélius drops his key. The villagers do not notice this and soon leave him. He shuffles across the street on his errand, shaking his head at their impertinence.

Swanilda and a group of her friends pass him as they enter on their way to supper. Swanilda is delighted to find that he has lost his key. She looks back toward Coppélius, who has now disappeared, and then at his house. Her friends easily persuade Swanilda to try the key in Coppélius's door. At last she will discover the illusive Coppélia alone! She goes to the door, fits the key to the lock, and signals pleadingly to her friends to follow. She steps in. She backs out hurriedly, frightened at her own audacity and the dark interior. Her friends line up behind her in single file, trembling with fear, and one by one they enter the house.

The square is deserted for a moment, then Franz comes in, armed with a ladder. The petulant youth is determined to have his love acknowledged by Coppélia, now that Swanilda has renounced him, and he places the ladder against the house. He is climbing up to a window when Coppélius, who has finally missed his key, rushes in to look for it. He apprehends Franz, attacks him with his walking stick, and chases him off. He then continues to search for the key. When he fails to find it and discovers that his door is wide open, he throws up his hands in despair and with great agitation runs into the house. The persistent Franz re-enters, places his ladder again, and climbs toward the mysterious Coppélia. The curtain falls.

ACT TWO: COPPÉLIUS'S HOUSE   The scene is a large room with dark walls. There is a large window at the back, and on the left is a curtained enclosure. Curious immobile figures, staring straight ahead, sit and stand about the stage in fixed attitudes, each as if cut off in the middle of a gesture. But there is not time to observe them before Swanilda and her friends walk in on tiptoe. The girls take in the weird room and are clearly sorry that they have let Swanilda talk them into coming. A small light throws their shadows against the walls, and they retreat into the center of the room. More curious than afraid, but still treading softly, Swanilda roams about looking at the woodenlike characters.

They seem to be dolls, but they are all life-sized and the suspended gestures in which they are fixed are alarmingly human. On the right, seated on a cushion, sits a tall Chinaman dressed in a richly embroidered native costume. A one-man band in resplendent parade dress stands with arm out, ready to strike the huge drum he carries. An astronomer in long black robes and a high, peaked hat, a poised juggler in the middle of one of his tricks, a Harlequin in typical diamond-patched costume, and a king holding scepter in hand—all these characters occupy Coppélius's room as if it were their home. [In the Sadler's Wells Theatre Ballet production, the figures are a Chinaman, a Crusader, Pierrot, an astrologer, and an Oriental dancer.] They are all individuals, each seems to exist apart from the others, yet to Swanilda and her friends the silent, still figures have no animate existence at all and resemble nothing so much as oversized dolls. Still, the girls are terrified by the darkness and the strange silence. Swanilda is instinctively moved to investigate the curtained alcove, for nowhere does she see Coppélia. She goes over, starts to peep through the curtain, and then runs back to her friends. Her knees are trembling so much that one of the girls holds her shaking legs. The girls force Swanilda to return to the curtain, and this time she is a little bolder. She looks behind the curtain, runs back to her friends, and gestures with automatic movements to music that might accompany the dance of a mechanical toy! Coppélia is a doll! One of the girls accidentally collides with the sitting Chinaman, and the interlopers are aghast as the Chinaman throws out his arms like an automaton, wags his head knowingly, and does a little rhythm act. The terrified girls approach him carefully, but the Chinaman does not change his position. He is a doll, too, but a wonderful mechanical doll, so close to reality that the girls have never imagined his like before. They stare rapturously at his jerky, automatic gestures, laugh delightedly, and search for the hidden clockwork that makes him move. They find nothing. The music peters out. The doll stops as he began.

Swanilda and her friends examine the doll Coppélia. Swanilda reaches out tentatively and touches her. Coppélia is cold as ice, utterly lifeless, a wax doll like all the rest! Swanilda takes her book away, and the frozen girl sits as before, her stilted hands grasping nothing. Swanilda can make neither head nor tail of the book and turns back to be absolutely certain that the lovely girl will not look up and wave to her, as she did to Franz. She leans over to feel her heart. She feels nothing. Sure now that the charming creature of whom she was so jealous is merely an absurd doll, Swanilda gathers her friends about her and laughs with glee at the prospect of Franz paying court to her.

All the girls are tremendously relieved that they have no one to fear in the empty house and prankishly run to each one of the dolls. They wind the dolls up, and soon all the mechanical creatures are in motion. The one-man band plays his music, the juggler commences his act, the astronomer lifts a telescope to his eye—and the fascinated girls can't decide which they like best. They are so enchanted by the dolls that they do not hear Coppélius enter. The music imitates his fierce anger.

He runs in, cape flying behind him, speechless with rage. He shakes his stick at the intruders and rushes about to catch them. All the girls retreat toward the door—all of them except Swanilda, who sneaks into Coppélia's booth while the toymaker shakes his stick at her fleeing friends and pulls the curtains closed. Coppélius comes back into the room and makes straight for the curtains to see if the girls have harmed his most cherished creation. A window opens at the back, and Coppélius stops. Another intruder! He stands close against the back wall, ready to pounce on the stranger. Franz climbs into the room. Coppélius waits patiently until the youth cannot return to the window and then sets upon him. Franz pleads that he means no harm, that he has entered merely to see the girl he loves, and that he will die unless he talks with her.

Gradually Coppélius realizes that Franz is quite serious and he ceases to threaten him. He wants to hear more and astonishes Franz by becoming quite friendly. Coppélius insists that he stay, telling him that his daughter will be in very shortly, and invites the unbelieving youth to sit down and have a drink. When the drink is poured, Franz has no more apprehension and accepts it with relish. The toymaker chatters constantly, pretends to drink too, and Franz —gloriously happy now that he has neared his goal—fails to see that Coppélius is providing him with one drink after another. He tries to describe the beauties of Coppélia to the old man with drunken gestures, and his host nods repeatedly in agreement as Franz's intoxication is increased by a potion he has poured into the drink. Franz's head falls back against the chair, his arms hang limp in sleep, and in this room filled with dolls he is almost like a doll himself.

Coppélius checks to be sure that he is unconscious and wrings his hands in glee in anticipation of his next move. He takes out a huge leather volume, puts it down on the floor, and hurriedly leafs through the pages looking for a secret formula he has never used before. He finds it, leaps up, looks back at Franz, and approaches the drawn curtains of Coppélia's closet. He yanks back the curtains, peers in, and examines carefully every feature of Coppélia's face and dress. The clever Swanilda no longer resembles herself as she sits rigidly in Coppélia's costume, holding up her little book. Coppélius goes behind her chair and wheels Swanilda into the middle of the room as the orchestra sounds a beautiful melody on piercing, muted strings. He glances down at the book and makes magical gestures in Swanilda's face. Swanilda does not blink. Now the toymaker runs over to Franz and, moving his hands down the youth's body from head to foot, seems to pull the power of life from him like a magnet. Coppélius holds the life force tight in his hands and goes back to the doll, whom he tries to endow with this potency. He consults the book again and repeats the ritual. To his astonishment and happiness, Swanilda tosses away the book, and Coppélius believes his wooden doll has actually come to life.

Swanilda's arms move stiffly as the music mimics the mechanics of her strength. She raises her head and stands up, her body still bent over in a sitting position. The delighted Coppélius straightens her up, and she stands still for a moment. Her face is expressionless. Then she begins to try out her arms and legs, pushing her feet out before her in a simulated walk. Coppélia's master encourages Swanilda's every step with more incantations; the girl is excited at her success in deceiving him. She looks over at Franz and can hardly wait until he wakens. Meanwhile she lets Coppélius imagine that he alone is responsible for her new-found vitality. Her stance is rigid and her face assumes an equally artificial smile. At Coppélius's command, her legs move less mechanically, and soon she is dancing to a light, sparkling waltz, perfecting her steps as she circles about. Now that he has taught her to dance, the toymaker wishes her to continue showing off his magical powers. The doll smiles ingratiatingly, but instead of dancing she walks about the room, as if she were exploring it for the first time. She goes over to Franz, shakes him, sees the discarded wine mug, and raises it to her lips. Coppélius snatches it from her in the nick of time. He is beginning to find out that this live doll can be as exasperating as any young girl.

Swanilda keeps up her fun with him, but still maintains her mechanical characteristics. Like a child, she pretends in each one of her tricks merely to be doing what her teacher has told her to do in the first place. The tormented Coppélius beseeches her to dance again; she stares at him dumbly. Finally, to keep her out of any more mischief, he distracts her by placing a black mantilla about her shoulders. Swanilda responds instantly by dancing a bolero. The music is subdued, but the girl intensifies the impassioned Spanish dance as the tempo mounts. Coppélius now supposes that there is nothing he cannot make her do; he experiments further by investing the doll with a Scottish plaid. Sure enough, as the orchestra pipes a sprightly jig, she follows its rhythms like a good Scottish lass. At the end of this dance, however, Swanilda has had enough. She kicks the pages of his magic book and runs berserk about the room.

She tries to awaken Franz from his stupor. Coppélius, fraught with anxiety lest she harm herself as well as the other dolls, finally succeeds in grabbing her. He sets her down hard on her chair, shakes his finger in her face, and rolls the chair back into the curtained alcove. Franz stirs, stretches, and looks about. Coppélius allows him no time for questions and tells him to get out. Franz leaves eagerly, climbing back out of the window. Swanilda, no longer a doll, pushes the curtains aside and dashes about the room knocking over every one of Coppélius's precious toys except the king, who stands in ridiculous majesty over the chaotic scene. Then, all too lifelike, Swanilda escapes through the door to catch up with Franz.

The shocked Coppélius cannot believe his eyes. He pulls back the curtains, and there, thrown across her chair, he sees the naked, limp body of his beloved Coppélia.

ACT THREE: THE WEDDING   The festival day has arrived, and all the villagers have gathered in the sun on the manor house lawn to take part in the celebration. The town's new bell has been blessed, and the lord of the manor awaits the presentation of dowries to those who will marry on the holiday. Swanilda, radiant in her wedding costume, and Franz, also in formal array, approach the lord with the other couples. Franz cannot take his eyes off Swanilda, who has taught him the lesson he unconsciously yearned to know. He knows now that, as his wife, she will be to him all women—all the other girls the beautiful Coppélia represented. The assembled villagers share the exuberant joy of Franz and Swanilda. The lord of the manor congratulates them and presents the dowries.

The irate and pathetic Coppélius marches in and upsets the happy throng by reminding them of the damage he has sustained. Coppélius is so intent on securing compensation, rather than explanations and apologies, that the crowd does not sympathize with him readily. The only one who sympathizes is Swanilda, who steps forward understandingly and offers him her dowry. The sullen Coppélius is about to take it, but the lord of the manor motions Swanilda away and rewards the toymaker with a bag of gold. The old man leaves the scene, wondering whether it will ever be possible for him to create a doll as lovable as his ill-fated Coppélia.

The pageant of the day now commences. The peasants dance the familiar "Dance of the Hours," in which the arrangement of the performers imitates the progress of the hours around an enormous clock as the hurdy-gurdy music tinkles the time away. The twelve girls form a circle like the face of an enormous clock, kneel toward the center, and one by one rise, pirouette, and kneel again, telling the time away.

Soft woodwinds herald the arrival of Dawn, danced by a lovely young girl. Her dance, with the music, is at first slow and tentative, like the gradual approach of light; then her body responds to bright wakening music and she celebrates the rising sun.

Now Prayer—a demure girl who clasps her hands before her and turns slowly in deep arabesques—delights the villagers. She kneels as the harp ends the music for her dance.

A peasant couple perform a vigorous betrothal dance to rhythmic, piping music. They bow to the lord of the manor, and all await the arrival of the bride and groom.

Franz bows and holds out his hand to Swanilda. Together they dance a moving adagio to a deep melody from the strings. Franz carries Swanilda high on his shoulder, sets her down gently, and the girl kneels before him. She rises on point, pirouettes swiftly in his arms, is lifted again, released, and caught as her lover holds her across his knee. He turns her in arabesque, and the dance that symbolizes their reconciliation and pledged happiness comes to an end. Their dance together and the variation each now performs alone reveal the youthful strength and tenderness each possesses for the other. When they have

finished, all the villagers join the smiling couple in a fast, constantly accelerating dance in which the whole company becomes a part of the breathless
happiness reflected in the shining faces of Swanilda and Franz.

American Ballet Theatre revived *Coppélia*, in a new production by Enrique
Martinez, during their 1968 season at the Brooklyn Academy of Music in New
York. Carla Fracci and Erik Bruhn danced the first performance. Others dancing the principal roles were Cynthia Gregory and Gayle Young, Alexandra Radius and Ted Kivitt, and Eleanor D'Antuono and Ivan Nagy. When she joined
the company, Natalia Makarova danced the role of Swanilda.

In 1974 I decided that we should stage *Coppélia* at the New York City
Ballet (we needed another evening-long ballet) and asked the ballerina and
teacher Alexandra Danilova, celebrated for many years for her Swanilda, to
collaborate with me on the choreography. Rouben Ter-Arutunian designed the
scenery and costumes, which were executed by Karinska. The ballet was first
presented by the company July 17, 1974 at the Saratoga Performing Arts Center, the New York City Ballet's summer home at Saratoga Springs, New York.

Coppélia was first danced, of course, in France. It was introduced in Russia
in 1884, with Marius Petipa's own version of Saint-Léon's original choreography. I remember very well performances by the Russian Imperial Ballet of
Coppélia and as a member of the company danced in the mazurka. (It is said
that the czardas and the mazurka were first introduced into ballet in *Coppélia*
and, from then on, divertissements based on national and folk dances became
very popular in ballet.)

I have often said that Delibes is one of my favorite composers for dance. In
our new *Coppélia*, we used the entire score of the three-act version. The first
dance drama of really uniform excellence deserves no less! No part of the
ballet is subordinate to any other; most important of all, ballet music in
Coppélia participates in the dance drama as never before, Delibes' charming,
melodic music assisting the plot and unifying the music and dance. As we
know, Tchaikovsky was directly inspired by Delibes' scores to write his own
ballet music. Delibes is the first great ballet composer; Tchaikovsky and
Stravinsky are his successors.

The first American performance of *Coppélia*, though greeted with applause
by press and public in 1887, was not as memorable as a later one, when Anna
Pavlova, making her début in the United States, appeared as Swanilda at the
Metropolitan Opera House, New York, February 28, 1910.

Most major ballet companies round the world dance *Coppélia* and many distinguished dancers have performed its leading roles. The Ballet Russe de
Monte Carlo staged the ballet for Alexandra Danilova who was identified with
it for many years. The noted dance critic and poet Edwin Denby called her
"the most wonderful *Coppélia* heroine in the world." Madame Danilova now
teaches at the School of American Ballet in New York, where we began our
work on our production.

Writing of the first performances at Saratoga, the critic Arlene Croce said in
The New Yorker:

"In the New York City Ballet's new *Coppélia*, which had its première at the company's summer home in Saratoga, Patricia McBride gives a great and a great *big* performance—big in scale as well as spirit. The role comes as a climax to the present and most exciting phase of her career. The scale on which she has been dancing this year is a new development in her style, and to reach it she hasn't sacrificed any of her speed or sharp-edged rhythm or subtlety of intonation. And although the role of Swanilda gives her plenty of unaccustomed material (such as extended pantomime), she sweeps through it without ever once looking like anyone but herself. She persuades you that Swanilda is Patricia McBride and always has been. This is a remarkable triumph for an artist whom the world knows as the flag-bearer of the New York City Ballet, the embodiment of its egoless-star ethic. McBride is fundamentally inscrutable. She doesn't exist outside her roles, and when you try to place her among her peers in world ballet—Gregory and Sibley and Makarova and the other great Russians whose names mean more to the public than McBride's does—her image dissolves in a succession of ballets: *Donizetti Variations, Rubies, La Valse, Brahms-Schoenberg Quartet, Who Cares?, Dances at a Gathering, Harlequinade.* McBride doesn't throw us cues to let us know how we ought to take her; she doesn't comment, doesn't cast herself as an observer of life. All she knows about life she seems to have learned through dancing, and all she has to tell she tells through dancing. How durable a bond of communication this is she proves once again in *Coppélia*, and in the very first moments.

"Swanilda's *valse lente* is the opening dance. By custom, it's a straight classical solo, and it gives us the ballerina in full flight almost as soon as the curtain has gone up. But in the New York City Ballet version McBride runs down to the footlights and, on the first notes of the waltz, addresses the audience in a passage of mime. 'This one up there,' she says, pointing to Coppélia on her balcony, 'she sits and reads all day long. That one, who lives over there, is in love with her, but she never notices him. Me, I just play.' And she plays (dances), first for her own pleasure, then for Coppélia's, with enticing steps that seem to say, 'Come down and play with me. See how nicely I play.' The structure of the waltz is mime, dance, dance-mime; in one stroke the means by which the story of *Coppélia* will be told are laid before us, and the fact that it's all done to an unvarying waltz rhythm lets us see easily how these different effects—of a mime gesture or a dance movement or a dance movement that functions as a mime gesture—depend for their force and clarity on having a different relation to an over-all rhythm. 'Mime' time is not 'dance' time, and each has to be established to musical time in a different way. This isn't as elementary as it sounds. The big catch in keeping the time values disparate is that the rhythm which connects them may disintegrate, and the worst danger of *that* is that the dancer will seem to be switching personalities on us, much as if she were a singer whose speaking voice didn't resemble the voice she sang with. (A lot of the modern distrust of mime comes from the schizoid effect of miscalculated rhythm.) In McBride's variation, and through her whole radiant performance, she plays excitingly close to the danger point. But the values of dance and mime, distinct in their time sense, are equalized in their scale—the largest scale that one could hope to see. So the meanings that are conveyed by all these sharply differentiated rhythms are always absolutely clear; they fly at you and away, or loom and settle, but there's no break in her consistency. She 'reads' at every moment. She is a character. McBride has never struck me as a particularly strong actress, and her method baffled me for years. How else, if not by acting, could she have made her character in 'La Valse' so vivid—a character unlike anyone else's who does the part? But for McBride acting is not the key; dancing is. And now that she's become so grand I don't see how anyone could miss that. She is a great dancer and a great star.

"The new production of *Coppélia,* staged by George Balanchine and Alexandra Danilova, is a combination of old and new choreography, the old being a first and second act built largely around the excellent 'after-Petipa' version in which Danilova used to star for the Ballet Russe de Monte Carlo, and the new being a glittering Act III, all of it Balanchine's except for the grand adagio and the ballerina's variation, which belong to Danilova-Petipa. Balanchine's dances are not uniformly masterpieces, but, taken all together, they ought to extend the life of this ballet another hundred years. In their unique blend of light irony and ingenuousness, they are a mirror of the music—serious music that was not meant to be taken too seriously.

"For his third act, Delibes envisioned a village wedding, with the villagers putting on an allegorical pageant of man's works and days. Most productions get through Dawn and Prayer and then give up in confusion, either reassigning the rest of the music (Work, Hymen, Discord and War) or dropping it altogether. Balanchine uses all the music Delibes wrote, and he does not mistake its spirit. His choreography really does present a plausible (though not a realistic) village pageant stuck together with metallic threads and parchment and candle wax, but noble nonetheless, with an anti-grand-manner grandeur. The Waltz of the Hours, that sublime gushing fountain of melody, is danced by twenty-four grinning little girls in gold tunics, who line the path of the soloist, Marnee Morris, and form choral borders for the solos that follow: Dawn (Merrill Ashley), Prayer (Christine Redpath), and Work, or La Fileuse, here called Spinner (Susan Hendl). The entrance of these three graces—posed motionless as beauty queens in a carriage that circles the stage twice—is one of the most piercing visions in the ballet. And the solos for Ashley and Hendl are outstanding—complete summations of their gifts. There's a dance for Four Jesterettes in padded motley sewn with bells. (In the Monte Carlo production, this entrée—originally Hymen—was called Follies, which seems more to the allegorical point than Jesterettes.) Discord and War is a romp for boys and girls in horned helmets, a flourish of capes and spears waved as idly as pickett signs—a witty number, shakily danced. Then, after the bridal *pas de deux,* comes an exhilarating finale, with climax piled on smashing climax. Best of all is the ballerina's fish dive into her partner's arms, instantly followed by the only thing that could top it—the return of the twenty-four golden tinies cakewalking on in a wide curve, with Morris in the lead tearing off *piqué-fouetté* turns.

"Balanchine's hand is evident elsewhere in the production, too—in that first-act entrance of Swanilda, and in the Mazurka and Czardas, which surely have never before been so thick and bushy with (musical) repeats, so fertile with invention. Their one weakness is that they are isolated from the action and don't serve any purpose. But the weakness is very likely not a permanent one.

This is not a finished production, and by the time it reaches New York, in November, Balanchine is sure to have taken over more of it—filling up gaps in the staging, refurbishing or replacing some of the less effective old dances, and straightening out a few discrepancies, such as the sudden, unmotivated shift to a sunnier mood that follows Swanilda's solemn ear-of-wheat dance. Possibly he'll find more for the hero to do, too. At present, Franz has only one dance— an interpolation in the third act which old-timers will recognize as Eglevsky's variation from the *Sylvia Pas de Deux*. It's nice to have this great solo back again, especially as danced by Helgi Tomasson, but Tomasson, who is a charming Franz, doesn't get a chance to display his true dance power until the finale. I hope, too, that a way can be found to make the meaning of the ear-of-wheat episode (a direct descendant of the petal-plucking scene in *Giselle*) at least as clear to a modern audience as it is in the Ballet Theatre version.

"The part of the ballet that is, right now, just about perfect is the second act. Here, again, Balanchine has obviously been at work; you can almost feel him assuming command of the action the moment Coppélius enters his workshop to find it overrun by Swanilda and her friends. Coppélius is Shaun O'Brien, giving the performance of his career. He is not a buffoon, and Swanilda is not a zany. He's a misanthrope, a tyrant, believably a genius who can create dolls everyone thinks are alive. She is a shrewd, fearless girl who grows into womanhood by accepting as her responsibility the destruction of Coppélius. She must break his power over gullible, romantic Franz, who has chosen the perfect woman, the doll Coppélia, over the natural woman, herself. The conflict between idealism and realism, or art and life, is embedded in the libretto of *Coppélia*, and Coppélius's passion is in the music. I enjoy burlesque versions of the second act (and in this tradition there's no Swanilda more enjoyable than that gifted zany Makarova), but the heart of the music isn't in them. Balanchine's Coppélius is kin to other Balanchine artist-heroes—not only Drosselmeier of *The Nutcracker* but Don Quixote and Orpheus and the Poet of *La Sonnàmbula*. And when he raises Swanilda-Coppélia onto her points and she remains locked there, upright or jackknifed over them, he's the strangest of all alchemists, seeking to transform his beloved twice over: doll into woman, woman into ballerina. Swanilda must become as totally manipulatable, totally perfectible, as a Balanchine ballerina. She must be a work of art, and then burst out of her mold. I once saw a brilliantly horrifying performance given by the Royal Danish Ballet, in which Solveig Østergaard and Frank Schaufuss confronted each other as monsters equal in might if not in cunning. But there was nothing in it like Shaun O'Brien's 'speech' to McBride, conveyed in a paroxysm of joy: 'I have made you and you are beautiful.'

"Rouben Ter-Arutunian's costumes are attractive, and his scenery is modest and quite pretty in several styles. Act I is like a child's pop-up picture book, with exaggerated perspectives. Act II, a cutaway of Coppelius's lab, ranges from Ensor to Burchfield, but the backcloth for Act III looked sketchily realized. A number of bells hanging above the stage (the pageant celebrates, along with everything else, a *fête de carillons*) bear the monograms of those associated with the original production—the choreographer, Arthur Saint-Léon; the librettist, Charles Nuitter; and E. T. A. Hoffmann, whose tale of Coppélius inspired the ballet—and those responsible for the present one. The largest bell, for which I forgive this somewhat presumptuous idea, is inscribed 'J'étais créé par Léo Delibes, 25 Mai 1870.' It is Coppélia herself who speaks. G.B., for George Balanchine, happen to be the initials also of Giuseppina Bozzacchi, who has no bell of her own. She was sixteen when she made her début at the Paris Opéra, appearing as the first Swanilda. Giuseppina took Paris by storm. Then Discord and War came in earnest. Six months later, in the siege during the Franco-Prussian War, she died of smallpox on the morning of her seventeenth birthday."[*]

In February 1975 Erik Bruhn, Resident Producer of the National Ballet of Canada, mounted for that company a new production of *Coppélia* which Clive Barnes in the New York *Times* (March 2, 1975) described as "unusual in its style and manner." This *Coppélia* was first presented in the United States by the same ensemble at the Metropolitan Opera House, New York, July 24, 1975, with Veronica Tennant, Rudolf Nureyev and Jacques Gorrissen as the principals.

Reviewing a performance in January 1975 of *Coppélia,* the critic Robert Greskovic wrote in *The Soho Weekly News:* "Swanilda, the lead in Balanchine/Danilova's *Coppélia,* was made on McBride. At this matinee she was sensational. The lusciously brocade layers of her dancing and the free, spunky spirit of her manner make hers the yardstick of interpretation for this role. McBride's physical response to the role's musical and choreographic demands is immediate and enchanting. She's the 'favorite daughter' of the village by virtue of the mental and physical prowess she brings to her almost constant presence in all three acts. Her mime, simple and clear with opera-house scale, is melded, like her dancing, with spontaneity, giving a fully articulated account of the music. McBride doesn't now act and then dance her characterization—she is always this Swanilda.

"Her large dark eyes create a focus that comments on her dancing. She *takes* everyone in, onstage and off, as she 'tells and shows' us what she's up to. Her strong and accentuated arm and leg joints stretch, curl and angle her limbs in a constant state of flirtatious flux. She elaborates her story as she responds to her music. As McBride's *batterie* cuts the air along a diagonal line, she proudly rivets her attention to the precise and generous activity of her feet. As she maintains her place to execute a series of multiple and varied turns, she sparkles, glances up and out; each time her head snaps around, she reverberates another wave of ecstatic after-energy.

"By the time she's dancing in celebration as the guest of honor at 'The Festival of the Bells' (Act III), she's fully matured. She doesn't rest on her laurels, her dancing scatters them in the wind of her joyous triumph. The conflict of her emotions in Act I and the calculation of her scheme in Act II are clearly behind her, here she's free and riding the crest of her popularity. This role is richly designed with some of Balanchine's finest dancing ideas, and McBride's

[*] "I Have Made You and You Are Beautiful" by Arlene Croce. Reprinted by permission; © 1974 The New Yorker Magazine, Inc.

pungent glamour and full-range dance power yield a Swanilda who is at home and home free."

LE CORSAIRE

Music by Adolphe Adam. Choreography by Mazilier. Scenery by Desplechin, Cambon, Thierry, and Martin. First presented at the Théâtre Impérial de l'Opéra, Paris, January 23, 1856, with Carolina Rosati, Mlle. Couqui, and Segarellu in the leading roles.

Based on Byron's poem, *Le Corsaire* was originally a three-act ballet that served as a useful vehicle for ballerinas such as Taglioni, Pavlova, and Karsavina. It was long in the repertory of the Russian theatres. Over the years, the work was much revised, with new music by Minkus and Drigo as well as new choreography by Marius Petipa and Vakhtang Chabukiani. A *pas de deux* from the complete ballet has frequently been performed by Soviet companies and by the Royal Ballet. Chabukiani's version, after Petipa, was first performed in the United States at Madison Square Garden by soloists of the Mali Opera Theatre, Leningrad, in July 1959. Margot Fonteyn and Rudolf Nureyev introduced the work to London at the Royal Opera House, Covent Garden, November 3, 1962.

In her *Autobiography* (1976), Margot Fonteyn describes the first performance of the *Corsaire pas de deux* with Rudolf Nureyev in New York in 1964. The applause lasted at least twenty minutes. "No one has ever danced *Corsaire* like Rudolf, and it is permissible in this case to use the adjective 'sublime.'"

When the Dance Theatre of Harlem took its version (by co-director Karel Shook) of the *Corsaire pas de deux* to London for a season at the Sadler's Wells Theatre in 1974, Peter Williams wrote in *Dance and Dancers* of the performance by Paul Russell and Laura Brown: "Russell gave one of the most exuberantly extrovert performances I have ever seen in this showy pas de deux. Looking for all the world like the Gold Slave from *Scheherazade* (naked torso, glittering baggy pants and bandeau round the brow), he bounds about, ripples his muscles, dives into head-to-floor back-bends in a manner which I feel Fokine originally intended for his Slave . . . Laura Brown had a few tricks in store, particularly in a dazzling manège of turns and a remarkable extension . . . At every performance I saw, this duet justifiably brought the house down in a manner I have seldom known in Rosebery Avenue."

In a long essay on the Dance Theatre of Harlem in *Ballet Review*, in 1974, the critic Robert Greskovic commented on this ballet:

"Shook's restaging is splendid. Laura Brown's princess manner is delicate enough to convey her character and strong enough to configure her choreography. The most finished of her 'finished' manners are showcased here. She projects smiles and knowingly wondrous eyes that gleam their brightest satisfaction at the top of her balances, lifts and posé arabesques. Her ear-high développé à la seconde reaches its height quickly as she holds a sharp steady balance. Her manège of: piqué turn, piqué (changing arms), piqué again, and fouetté turn in the coda is a clearly spotted and securely jumped ride around the world. In Russell's extraordinary, steady one-handed lifts, she's relaxed and regal.

"The delicacy and finesse of her performance is a perfect counterbalance and motivation for Russell's pirate. Paul Russell is Le Corsaire—Russian, French, exotic and proud, with a touch of American athleticism. The only other American dancers I've seen who succeeded in impersonating this swash-buckling bandit have been John Prinz and Edward Villella. Prinz ultimately failed by his lack of technical control and I've seen Villella only on television, but Russell is completely alive and breathing, full on stage. His rush-on en-trance is immediately authoritative. His alert, darting eyes are seeing his space before they're looking for a partner. He takes us all in before he takes flight. His enthusiasm and freedom on stage suggest someone who's been on the seas for months and this is his first return to solid earth. He's found one of earth's treasures, and, as Brown enters, rises through ¾ point and folds himself to the ground in a sinking révérence. He approaches her and handles her with won-dering care. The mechanics of the partnering gain drama from Russell's daz-zling concentration. He must handle this beauty, now. He must lift her, he must catch her, he wants to hold her. He makes his job his passionate desire. And when he's alone and in his variations he's wanting to celebrate. When he takes his first attitude balance atop strong ¾ point, he dégagés back for a spinning cocked-leg double tour, landing on one knee with the other leg ex-tended; then whips around a twisting sous-sus turn to stand full height again. These sous-sus turns with his hands on his shoulders are lusciously plastic in the smooth, changing tilt his shoulders take to propel his turn and stop it at an opposite angle to its beginning. Shook has set a clearly musical series of embo-îtés en tournant that travel into preparation for the long spine-tingling axis of Russell's double tours. Coming out of even chaîné turns there is a tour that folds kneeling to the floor and unfolds instantaneously as, with a brazen slap of one hand to his stage, Russell springs to arabesque posé on ¾ point, perfectly placed, leanly arced—like an arrow's vibrating contact with the bull's-eye of a target. This is no formidable youthful debut as Le Corsaire, it's an electrifying (by any standards) triumph of theater."

CORTÈGE BURLESQUE

Music by Emmanuel Chabrier, orchestrated by Hershy Kay. Choreography by Eliot Feld. Decor by Robert Munford. Costumes by Stanley Simmons. Lighting by Jules Fisher. First presented by the American Ballet Company at the Festival of Two Worlds, Spoleto, Italy, June 27, 1969, with Christine Sarry and John Sowinski. First presented in the United States by that en-semble at the Brooklyn Academy of Music, New York, October 21, 1969, with the same dancers. Conductor: Christopher Keene.

A *divertissement* to Chabrier's *Cortège Burlesque* and *Souvenirs de Munich,* arranged for orchestra, this ballet featured the dancing of the two principals of the new American Ballet Company, Christine Sarry and John Sowinski, when the group made its debut. The *pas de deux* is danced against a fantastic backdrop that recalls the circus, its animals and amusements. The dance reflects the circus atmosphere as the boy and girl dance their bouncing display piece in open competition, the boy supporting the girl but acting, too, very much the soloist who won't be upstaged by any ballerina, however famous. Not as often as he can help it, that is, which isn't much, for the girl takes over the scene steadily, yielding only to real perseverance from her partner.

NOTES   Reviewing the ballet in *Dance and Dancers,* Patricia Barnes wrote that "*Cortège Burlesque* is one of those ballets that laughs at itself while exploiting the technical skill of its dancers. Sarry was a joy . . . and in the New York performances the two dancers really went to town, sending up the manners and egos of ballerinas and their partners with wit and some bold, assertive dancing. The piece is enhanced by yet another excellent backdrop by Robert Munford, portraying a circus atmosphere precisely right for its purpose."

CORTÈGE HONGROIS

Music by Alexander Glazunov. Choreography by George Balanchine. Decor and costumes by Rouben Ter-Arutunian. Lighting by Ronald Bates. First presented by the New York City Ballet at the New York State Theatre, Lincoln Center, May 16, 1973, with Melissa Hayden and Jacques d'Amboise, Karin von Aroldingen and Jean-Pierre Bonnefous in the leading roles. Conducted by Robert Irving.

I did this ballet for Melissa Hayden, who had been dancing with our company twenty-four years—when she decided in 1973 to retire. "Why not stop before you begin making excuses?" she said. "Why not stop when you're still enjoying everything?" The idea behind the ballet was simply to give Melissa Hayden yet another opportunity to enjoy herself and give our audiences pleasure.

The music is a collection of pieces by Glazunov (1865–1936), best-known for his ballet *Raymonda.* The finale of the ballet features a *pas classique hongrois,* where Hungarian gesture and dance are combined with the academic classic dance.

There is no story to *Cortège Hongrois:* it is simply, as its name suggests, a procession of dances in the Hungarian manner. There is a grand promenade at the start, which introduces two sets of dancers—first a group in colorful peasant costume, and then a group of courtiers led by the ballerina and her cavalier. The scene is a large formal ballroom.

Four of the courtly couples begin a dance in which others join. Next, eight couples, to a plaintive melody, dance a supported adagio.

In vivid contrast, the peasants, led by a vigorous couple, dance a czardas, a

Hungarian folk dance of perennial popularity. Four of the courtly girls follow, for a whirring, accelerating *pas de quatre*.

Variations for some of the courtiers are now presented; first one for a girl, another for four of the boys, a third for another girl, and the finale, what we have been waiting for, a *pas de deux* for the leading courtly couple. Dressed in white embellished with gold and wearing a crown, the ballerina performs in the grand manner, dancing with her partner to a deep, stirring melody that gradually builds. There are variations for the two dancers, hers a character dance with much folk gesture. The courtiers rejoin the royal couple; the peasants come, too, to participate in the festivities, and there is a flourishing finish.

Finally, the two groups combine in a folk dance, heels and spurs clicking, and that seems to be the end. But there is another promenade, the lights go down, and only on the ballerina does the spotlight shine. A crown of lights illumines the stage and all kneel, acknowledging her radiance.

NOTES   At the time of the ballet's premiere, when ballerina Melissa Hayden was presented by Mayor Lindsay with the Handel Medallion, New York City's highest cultural award, Lincoln Kirstein wrote of her career in the New York City Ballet's program: "If one had to define one essential gift with which a dancer needs to be endowed, there might be a rush of answers. A beautiful body, grace of line, graciousness of spirit, joy in the work, ability to please, unswerving integrity, relentless ambition towards some abstract perfection. Certainly all these factors determine a dancer's character, and every element exists in some combination within the performing artist's presence. These factors and elements are never evenly, nor even justly distributed. The first lesson dancers approaching any wisdom about themselves learn is how little they can depend on any single attribute or even combination of a few of them.

"Perhaps the most essential gift donated by those forces who care for careers, cosmically or supernaturally, is an ability to animate, magnetize and dominate those factors which one likes least in oneself. The mirror is the first to tell us no one is perfect, but there is always a terrible temptation to whittle down our notions of perfection in order to accommodate what we imagine our mirrors reflect. Dancers are accustomed to look to their mirror for correction, criticism and even comfort from their earliest days in a classroom. Strong dancers never succumb to the blindness of narcissism. Dancers are not narcissistic; their selves are their material. These must be kept under constant scrutiny; their own eyes and minds are finally their closest friend and severest critic. The best performers know themselves better than anyone else. Whatever face they may put upon their image, they know exactly what face, best face and worst fits them.

"This kind of realism is not easily endured. In the best sense, it becomes a method, an analytical attitude towards performance. It is a strict school, a stoic attitude, but it has advantages. It permits survival. Of all the dancers with whom I've had the honor and pleasure of working, Melissa Hayden has been strongest and lasted longest. In the twenty-two years that she has been associated with Balanchine and myself, there has been no one whose strength surpassed hers. This is not alone in muscle, although one can mark little deterioration in her fantastic energy since the first season we danced at Covent Garden in 1950. To say that she has never missed a performance is less important than to realize that no single performance has ever been below her extraordinary level of efficiency. Whether or not the audience recognized it, her steely spine and wiry resilience, even under the attack of cruel strain or sprain, gives stamina to colleagues who know only too well what pain and strain are.

"Melissa has been the nearest thing to a 'star' in our starless company. We have never encouraged stardom on programs, posters or publicity; managers can't make stars; the public does. There has been a good deal of unobservant cant about a creature vulgarly entitled 'the Balanchine dancer.' When one takes the trouble to inspect the personnel of our company as it is now constituted, one can easily mark the corporeal distinction between Gelsey Kirkland and Gloria Govrin, between Peter Martins and John Clifford, between Karin von Aroldingen and Helgi Tomasson. Melissa Hayden was never a Balanchine-dancer, but she supported his repertory for over twenty years. In consideration of his much bruited intolerance or prejudice, this must mean something; Milly must have been doing something right.

"What she has given, and still victoriously gives, is a sense of security, a conviction that she knows what she's doing, how it should be done, and to what complete degree of energetic expenditure she can do it. The ballet, like *bel canto* voice production, is an area of extreme virtuosity; remove the element of physical electricity and acrobatics, the hazards of the arena overcome, and you delete most public curiosity. Ballet is a spectator sport; its very economics depend on mass appeal. For more than a century, whatever its association with kings and queens, courts lost or in decline, it is the big opera-house public that has justified its expense and problems. Intellectuals may analyze their pleasure, but it is fortunately not left to their tender mercies. Melissa Hayden is and has been a popular figure; she pleases, satisfies, thrills and amuses a big public which may make no very delicate judgment, but which in its instinct can not be fooled into thinking that boredom or dissatisfaction with emptiness is entertaining or instructive.

"From her own account, she has been dancing for forty years in schools and on stages, all over the world. Mathematically, considering the hours of practice, rehearsal, performance—plus a private life with a family, children and friends—this is staggering. Less accident-prone than almost any professional, she has probably made more appearances before a public than any other performer of the period. Her pleasure in performance has been so complete that it has been transmitted to her muscular organism like some blessed sun lamp, to keep her fit in spite of any mischance or fatigue.

"To stop dancing, to abandon the habit of a lifetime, to foreswear performance in a frame that has become familiar as one's bed and breakfast, is not the worst thing that can happen to a dancer. When the decision is made, as in the case with Melissa, there is the new adventure of energy reapplied. Her energy is no less; it will simply be channelled otherwise. Anyone who has heard her demonstrate in lectures knows that charm is a weak word for her didactic method. She has been a crusader for ballet as a language and a skill and now she will direct her experience, taste and information towards a wholly new audience—that of potential students, scholars and enthusiasts. The husbanding of energy that has been her greatest gift permits no waste of effort. Hysteria is an artificial additive that lack of control sometimes substitutes for temperament. Hysteria is not part of her nature, since she has always been a realist and she realizes, from observation of colleagues less fortunate than she, that irrational indulgence costs mind and muscle of which no one has too much to spare. Her warmth is humane; she has had her fair portion of the world's grief. She has not been given everything she may have desired or even deserved. However, in situations in which she has found herself, and indeed in which she has chosen to find herself content, she did better than most."

DANCES AT A GATHERING

Music by Frédéric Chopin. Choreography by Jerome Robbins. Costumes by Joe Eula. Lighting by Thomas Skelton. First presented by the New York City Ballet at the New York State Theatre, Lincoln Center, May 8, 1969. Pianist: Gordon Boelzner. Dancers: Allegra Kent, Sara Leland, Kay Mazzo, Patricia McBride, Violette Verdy, Anthony Blum, John Clifford, Robert Maiorano, John Prinz, and Edward Villella. Dedicated to the memory of Jean Rosenthal.

Dances at a Gathering is a ballet for ten dancers to piano pieces by Chopin. Five girls and five boys dance in an open space as a pianist plays to the left of the stage. He plays mazurkas, waltzes, études, a scherzo, and a nocturne— eighteen pieces in all—as the dancers, distinguished in the program by the color of their costumes, respond to the music.

The curtain goes up on a bare stage with a background of blue sky and amorphous clouds; we are outdoors in a clearing, a field, a meadow, a grove. A boy enters on the right, informally dressed in open white shirt, brown tights, and boots. He walks slowly, quietly looking the place over, glancing up at the sky, thinking. Then he is lifting his arm and his walk becomes a stride, a dance, as the piano begins, *Mazurka, Opus 63, No. 3*. His dance reflects a pleasure in being where he is on a day like this. As the music ends, he leaves, meditating.

A girl and a boy enter and dance to the *Waltz, Opus 69, No. 2*, moving arm in arm, at first a bit tentatively as if nothing will come of it, but the music changes all that as they follow its flow in lifts, leaps, and a rushing exit with the girl poised high on the boy's shoulder. Another girl and boy come in and dance a little more formally, responding to the character of the *Mazurka, Opus 33, No. 3*, with arm gestures, too. But they, too, get carried away with the music and she, too, is lifted off in a rushing conclusion.

A girl enters alone and dances fast to the staccato beat of a new, more demanding *Mazurka, Opus 6, No. 4*. She is still on stage as the next part begins.

Six dancers in different groupings respond to the music of four fresh *Mazurkas, Opus 7, Nos. 5* and *4, Opus 24, No. 2* and *Opus 6, No. 2*. There are two boys, dancing back to back in a kind of jig, one of the boys interested in one girl, who watches, the other in another. And not the same ones they were dancing with earlier. Rhapsodic as particular partnerships become, in the group commitments dissolve with no regrets and everyone begins again. In the dancing and watching of dances, in the joining in, partnerships shift. The dances become full of character and there is a feeling that we are in real Mazurka country as gesture identifies with music and place. There are friendships between the girls, too, and both boys and girls play at posing each other in groups for photographs.

Now to the *Waltz, Opus 42*, a girl and boy try to outdo each other in speed and virtuosity, each showing off to the other, he cartwheeling to victory, all of it a serious but affectionate competition. She touches his hand and he lifts her up to his shoulder, wrapping her about his head closely as they leave.

Three girls dance the *Waltz, Opus 34, No. 2*, entering in a dim light, strolling, doing solos, then all three dancing together. A boy comes to lift one girl away. They dance together as the other two watch. These two look into the distance. Then as quietly as he came the boy is gone, leaving his girl kneeling. She rises to join her two friends, they pose in a group, then separate with separate dreams, only to join arms and leave together.

The lights come up and two boys compete now to the music of *Mazurka, Opus 56, No. 2*, each trying to outdo the other, throwing each other about, making dramatic exits backward.

As the lights fade, a girl enters to dance thoughtfully alone to the *Étude, Opus 25, No. 4*.

To the big *Fourth Waltz, Opus 34, No. 1*, six couples dance, responding dramatically to the pulse of the music. There is an exhilarating series of slides and lifts, at the end of which the boys line up to pass the girls down a diagonal line, lifting them so that the next boy lifts them higher still to the demanding rush of the piano.

Now in dimmer light come a boy and girl. She clearly likes him and tries to make it clearer. He leaves her but another boy enters. She dances all around him, surrounding him with attention but he ignores her and goes off. With a third boy she has the same result, but more amused than despairing, she flicks her wrist and goes off.

Next a *pas de deux* to the *Étude, Opus 25, No. 5*, then a fast solo for a boy to the *Étude, Opus 10, No. 2*. The *Scherzo, Opus 20, No. 1* involves six dancers in dramatic declarations, fulfillments, and disappointments. As the three girls fall back in the boys' arms, they are a bit embarrassed and leave in a rush.

For the final piece, the *Nocturne, Opus 15, No. 1* and its slow melody, the lights come down. Gradually all ten dancers appear, singly and in couples, together now for the first time. One of them, the boy who began the dances at this gathering, touches the ground of the place. They all look at him and then up at the sky, which they watch intently. They pair off then and walk away. All move forward as the music dramatizes their situation. Then they look to the ground and raising their arms start a dance that does not develop. They go to the back of the stage, the boys to one side, the girls on another, and bow. The curtain falls.

NOTES *Dances at a Gathering* came about in an interesting way. "I started out to do a *pas de deux* for Eddie Villella and Pat McBride," Jerome Robbins told Hubert Saal of *Newsweek.* "Then I got turned on by the music. It all started to pour out as if some valve inside me had opened up and the purity of working with dancers took over. I had to find the form. Usually I work with a structured music, as in Stravinsky's *Les Noces,* where the literary material is built in. In this case I took whatever appealed to me and let it happen, trusting it. It's nice to work loosely and intuitively."

Shortly before the première, Robbins said to Clive Barnes of the New York *Times,* "I'm doing a fairly classical ballet to very old-fashioned and romantic music, but there is a point to it. In a way it is a revolt from the faddism of today. In the period since my last ballet (*Les Noces,* 1965), I have been around looking at dance—seeing a lot of the stuff at Judson Church and the rest of the avant-garde. And I find myself feeling just what is the matter with connecting, what's the matter with love, what's the matter with celebrating positive things? Why, I asked myself, does everything have to be separated and alienated so that there is this almost constant push to disconnect? The strange thing is that the young people are for love. Is that bad?"

Shortly after the première of *Dances at a Gathering,* Robbins was interviewed for *Dance Magazine* by the critic Edwin Denby. The complete text of the article, reprinted by courtesy of *Dance Magazine,* follows: "Robbins's *Dances at a Gathering* is a great success both with dance fans and the general public. And it is a beautiful piece. But it wasn't planned as a sure-fire piece—it wasn't planned at all beforehand and began by chance, as Robbins explains in the interview (taped shortly after the official première) which appears on the pages that follow.

"The ballet is set to Chopin piano pieces and the program lists ten dancers but tells you little more. The curtain goes up in silence on an empty stage. It looks enormous. The back is all sky—some kind of changeable late afternoon in summer. Both sides of the stage are black. Forestage right, a man enters slowly, deep in thought. He is wearing a loose white shirt, brown tights and boots. He turns to the sky and walks slowly away from you toward center stage. You think of a man alone in a meadow. As he walks you notice the odd tilt of his head—like a man listening, inside himself. In the silence the piano begins as if he were remembering the music. He marks a dance step, he sketches a mazurka gesture, with a kind of pensive vigor he begins to improvise and now he is dancing marvelously and, in a burst of freedom, he is running all over the meadow at its edge. Suddenly he subsides and, more mysterious than ever, glides into the woods and is gone. Upstage a girl and boy enter. At once they are off full speed in a double improvisation, a complexly fragmented waltz, the number Robbins speaks of as the 'wind dance.'

"As one dance succeeds another—the ballet lasts about an hour—you are fascinated by the variety and freshness of invention, the range of feeling, and by the irresistibly beautiful music which the dance lets you hear distinctly—its mystery too. You see each dancer dance marvelously and you also see each one as a fascinating individual—complex, alone, and with any of the others, individually most sensitive and generous in their relationships. The music and the dance seem to be inventing each other. For a dance fan, the fluid shifts of momentum are a special delight. For the general theater public, Robbins's genius in focusing on a decisive momentary movement—almost like a zoom lens—makes vivid the special quality of each dance, and all the charming jokes.

"But it is a strange ballet.

"Our talk began before the tape machine arrived. Robbins had been telling me how the ballet developed. He had been asked whether he would care to do a piece for the 25th Anniversary City Center Gala, May 8. Delighted by the way Patricia McBride and Edward Villella had been dancing *The Afternoon of a Faun,* he thought he would like to do a *pas de deux* for them—perhaps to Chopin music—and he accepted. As he listened to records and became more and more interested in the possibilities—it occurred to him to add two more couples—and he began rehearsal. In the course of rehearsals, however, all the six dancers he had chosen were not always free, so he went on choreographing with four others, using those who happened to be free. Gradually he made more and more dances, but without a definite plan for the whole piece. When about two-thirds of the ballet was done, he invited Balanchine (who had just returned from Europe) to rehearsal. At the end of it he turned to Mr. B and said, 'Don't you think it's a bit long?' Mr. B answered, 'More. Make more!' He did.

"Robbins said to me, 'As you see, there are still never more than six dancers dancing at once.' He told me that as the dances and relationships kept coming out of the different pieces of music and the particular dancers available, he began to feel that they were all connected by some underlying sense of community (he said, laughing, 'Maybe just because they were dancers') and by a sense of open air and sunlight and sudden nostalgia perhaps.

"We spoke of one of the many lovely lifts—this one at the end of Eddie's *pas de deux* with Pat where it looks as though he were lifting a sack onto his shoulder and, up on his shoulder, the sack suddenly changes into a beautiful mermaid. Robbins explained how it came out of a sudden metamorphosis in the music. And he illustrated how the lift is done.

"We were talking of Villella's gesture of touching the floor in the final minutes of the ballet, and Robbins mentioned that he was perhaps thinking of the dancers' world—the floor below, the space around and above. I was saying that I liked that gesture better the second time I saw it because it was slower and I wondered if he (Robbins) had changed it. At that point the tape begins:

"ROBBINS No, that's just a very subtle thing of acting and where the human being is at the time. I think two weeks ago at the preview, Eddie was under more difficulties and pressures—down more—and perhaps that made the difference.

"I think the ballet will seem different in almost every performance, not vastly, but shades like those you saw, they will happen, depending on the dancers. You said it, I remember, way back—the dancers read (in a review) what the ballet is about, then they change because now they *know* it (they know it in words)—before they just *did* it. And that can happen—there was a modesty and a sort of not knowing in the first showing. They may start to think now that maybe they should do it more like what everyone says it is. I don't know what to do about that except to ask them not to.

"I always tell them to do it for themselves, and to think of 'marking' it— Don't think of doing it full out.

"DENBY   Well, that's another quality the ballet has. I was very happy to see that with Eddie, who is used to 'doing it full out'—he does that very beautifully, it's not vulgar selling at all—he's not forcing it. But the inner business he also does very well—in *Giselle*. He's remarkable, you know, wonderful.

"ROBBINS   I like watching ballets, anyway, best of all at rehearsals when a dancer is just working for himself, really just working. They are beautiful to watch then. I love to watch George's (Balanchine) work that way. Just love to.

"DENBY   How beautiful everything is before it gets its name. Did I hear you say that Melissa (Hayden) will be covering Violette (Verdy)?

"ROBBINS   Yes, I think she'll be marvelous.

"DENBY   And so is Verdy. Someone told me that you're working to add a much longer number for her. So I said, 'Oh, wonderful.'

"ROBBINS   I haven't been around ballet for so long, I forget how scuttlebutty it gets around here. If you say to someone, 'I want to work with you tomorrow,' the next day someone asks you, 'Are you doing a new ballet?' It already has gotten that big.

"But it was nice working with them. I did enjoy it very much. Patty McBride, I just *love* working with her.

"DENBY   Yes, she's remarkable. . . . And I am very happy about what you did with Bob Maiorano. Because this year he's suddenly become a very good dancer wherever I look at him. He was beginning last year and, all of a sudden, there he is—now you can really see it.

"ROBBINS   Yes.

"DENBY   He has a marvelous Italian beauty of gesture. Maybe he was afraid of it all this time. The arm is so heavy the way he moves it. But the weight is right for all of them—the boys especially.

"ROBBINS   Bobby Weiss, have you seen him? In one of the performances he is going to do Johnnie Clifford's part.

"DENBY   He was wonderful in a school performance last year, too. Especially in the end of *Sylphides*, when he lost his nervousness in the finale. He looks as though he were not letting go as much as is his nature.

"ROBBINS   He is beautiful when he lets go. In rehearsal, I just made him go.

"DENBY   Clifford was remarkable too; he is so positively there. But it's not so simple. There is also something private about it. And Tony's (Blum) great— so much livelier than he's been . . . often.

"ROBBINS   That's the fun of having another choreographer work with the dancers. Like in Ballet Theatre, Eliot Feld was doing a ballet, and I looked at his dancers and thought, Now, those are people I bypassed, but he saw something in them and brought out another whole aspect of them. It's always charming. But every choreographer—Agnes (de Mille) has people she works with I can't see—people I work with that she can't see. That's nice for the dancers, isn't it?

"DENBY And for the choreographers if you are going to travel around. You should try out your dances on the Russians. I'm sure they would like to have a dance of yours, they like to gather things—archives in their minds. It would be so much fun.

"ROBBINS I'm going to Russia. I *would* like to see if I can get it either to the Bolshoi or Kirov. I would like to see them dance this. I really would. It might finally turn out to be a peasant parody, you never know (*laughter*)—that folk part of it—I was surprised.

"DENBY I was surprised that people made so much of it, because the dancers are always so elegant. They might be landowners, if they were anybody in Europe.

"ROBBINS At first I also thought they were very elegant people, maybe at a picnic, maybe doing something—their own thing.

"And also to me—and this I'm very careful about—I don't want it to be a big thing—but the boys and the whole period are very hippie-ish.

"DENBY At first you had the beards, I was quite pleased with that.

"ROBBINS The boys still had them at rehearsal because of the long lay-off. Tony had long hair and a moustache and John Prinz had long hair and a beard and it was marvelous looking. It really affected what I was doing. I liked the boots—and the sketches are much more hippie than they appear on stage, in the sense of belts and open blouses for the boys and long hair and ballooning sleeves. There is something in the nature of knowing who they are and having love and confidence in them.

"DENBY Competence? . . .

"ROBBINS Confidence—which I feel is in the work, finally. Loving confidence in themselves and in the other people.

"DENBY That is in there very strongly.

"ROBBINS It has some strangenesses in it too, I'm sure, but I can't yet quite see it. Every now and then I look at a step and think that is a very odd step. There is a strange step that Eddie does in his solo—he should play with it the way one does this (*hand gesture*).

"DENBY There was an eight-year-old Negro boy in the street and he was running; he suddenly started throwing his feet around—with such pleasure.

"ROBBINS I saw something nice in the park. Near Sheep Meadow there was a black boy and a white boy, both happened to be wearing blue. The black boy had a blue sweat shirt and the white boy had a blue sweater and open collar. They were running toward each other and it was more than a game. They ran and reached out hands. Not just shook hands, because that's what it was about, but they took hands and swung around each other with their heads thrown back with laughter. And then let go and embraced each other. Oh, it was so beautiful, I was thrilled by it. There was so much rapture and ecstasy and friendliness and openness about it. Then they quieted down and began talking, (*laughs*).

"DENBY There are things in the ballet that are a bit gruesome. And, you know, very interesting.

"ROBBINS Gruesome?

"DENBY   It's partly in the lifts, partly sometimes in the way the boys treat a girl.

"ROBBINS   Well, opening night there was an accident. I want to be sure you know that it was an accident. There was a place where Sally (Sara Leland) was being swung around and they fell off the lift and it turned into a—it looked like she was in outer space—like she'd been released from a capsule. She was just swirling around. Horrifying for a moment. But there are?—I don't know, I can't tell.

"DENBY   It's definitely in the music. It's much stranger than one. . . .

"ROBBINS   Yes, than one thinks.

"DENBY   Than one is supposed to think.

"ROBBINS   There's a nocturne. I began late listening to one nocturne—it was like opening a door into a room and the people are in the *midst* of a conversation. I mean, there's no introduction, no preface; it's like a cut in a film; it's almost like Chopin had finished the previous nocturne, finished it properly, and there was a fade-out. And suddenly (*clap*) you're on somebody's face who's talking. But in the middle of a sentence! You don't even get 'and then,' it's right in the middle of a word and he's very strange, really quite strange. He knew a lot, I think. Much more than I thought before I began. It was fascinating that way—just like some connection happened between all those sounds that he thought of, and where I was at.

"DENBY   The movement through a piece is always so interesting, and that you catch so well and do so many things with.

"ROBBINS   I listened to a lot of recordings, different people playing the same piece. I used mostly Rubinstein and Novaes and some Brailowsky. I listened to some of the Dinu Lipatti. Then it was enough for me and after that I knew I would start to get confused. There are hardly any liberties taken at all —I would say none. Only one where at the end of Eddie's first dance it's marked *fortissimo*—da da da *whoosh*—I don't even know if it's Chopin's indication—I choreographed it that way—and Eddie was gone, *whoosh*. I didn't like it, it was a little obvious, like I was trying for a hand and the piece was trying for a hand, I thought there was something else there, so I took it on retard and soft, and let him take that poetic thing he does there. The dancers are beautiful.

"DENBY   Gordon (Boelzner) plays it very well because he also plays it for movement, without those extra questions of pianism.

"ROBBINS   There are no sentimentalities.

"DENBY   If you were listening to the music at a concert you might want more nuances, but this way you don't because the dancers are doing it, the nuances.

"ROBBINS   And he's tireless, that boy. It's fantastic. He plays it all day long, and does the other rehearsals, too. Some of those pieces are killers. I suddenly thought, Look at a Chopin concerto—they play a piece and go off and rest. They do maybe half an hour or twenty minutes and go and have a fifteen-minute intermission. But he's tearing off those *Études* written for these two fingers. You know about the one Eddie dances to—the little fast one—sort of chromatically going up and down the scale? Well, Chopin devised it to give these two fingers which are the weakest, a workout.

"DENBY   I am so glad you didn't orchestrate it. Not that it would be possible, but there's that temptation.

"ROBBINS   I got worried for a while before we got it down on the big piano because it began to sound very hollow to me. And I thought, Well when people come to this big theatre and they have just seen a big ballet with a lot of marvelous sounds, the piano is going to sound like a little rehearsal piano. But it doesn't, where it is. It seems it fills the house and sustains—a good combination, I think, between what you are seeing and what you hear.

"DENBY   It isn't miked?

"ROBBINS   No, not at all!

"DENBY   And you're so glad to see him, too. I wondered whether he can see the dancers.

"ROBBINS   Most of them, but not the ones on the side of the stage he is on. But there is a place where we have a mirror—rigged way up high on the wings so that if he looks up he can see someone come in for just a cue. And I thought Tom Skelton did a very good job in a very little time. He did the lighting.

"DENBY   Some of it looks ominous, sometimes. I mean weather. It changes. I suppose you wanted that too. I liked it.

"ROBBINS   I didn't mean it to look ominous, but I suppose that vast sky, it is almost like nature changing on you. You're a little worried about what is going to happen next, it doesn't matter if it goes up or down. It's just that it changes. Everything changes.

"I didn't know it was going to be that long a ballet or what it was going to be. I originally thought, we'll do it using the wings and the cyclorama because it's just going to be a *pas de deux*. But by the time it was all done, I thought, Wow, who should do a set? Is it Jane Freilicher, or is it one of those watery sort of places, or is it—? Now I'm used to the way it is. I don't know if I want a set, or anything softer around the edges. That's a very hard line, those black wings. But once it starts, I don't suppose you are particularly aware of it any more.

"DENBY   When you watch you realize that there are woods there, and you're in a meadow and there are trees.

"ROBBINS   Isn't that funny, odd how that all got evoked. My names for the dances themselves, for instance, the second dance for John Prinz and Allegra (Kent), I call it 'wind waltz' because to me they are like two things that are on the wind that catch up with each other. There is something about air—breezes which are clawing them and pushing them almost like two kites. And 'walk waltz' or 'the three girls' to me is somehow in the woods. On a Chekhov evening. It just is. I can't see it any other way. It has that quality.

"DENBY   The whole piece is a Chekhov piece. There are so many things suggested and not explained. The business of looking around at the end is the trickiest. I didn't like it at all the first time. Yesterday I didn't mind it so much. It is like looking at an airplane, I think of missiles and war.

"ROBBINS   They must do it very softly. That is almost one of the hardest parts to be able to do. It is very hard for them just to walk on and be confident and just raise their heads or eyes and look at something without starting to make it dramatic. I keep telling them, 'Relax, don't be sad, don't get upset, just see it, just whatever you want to pick, just see. It's a cloud passing, if you want. Take it easy on it, don't get gloomy.'

"DENBY   It's because they all do it together.

"ROBBINS   Together—right—they all follow one thing. And that upset you? You thought it was airplanes and missiles?

"DENBY   The atom bomb comes in and everything else. The sort of thing about Hitler attacking Poland. Your mind gets full of ideas that you don't want, that don't have anything to do with the piece.

"ROBBINS   If I had to talk about it all, I would say that they are looking at —all right—clouds on the horizon which possibly could be threatening, but then that's life, so afterwards you just pick up and go right on again. It doesn't destroy them. They don't lament. They accept.

"DENBY   That's what I told myself. It must be that they are looking at clouds—clouds rarely go that fast, but it might be a storm coming up and they're wondering if it's going to happen.

"ROBBINS   That section, it was the last piece I did, though. I spent about two weeks after I finished the bulk of the choreography—it was almost all done about two weeks before the eighth of May. But that last two weeks I spent in arranging, trying to get the right order. Not only who danced what, but also that sense of something happening—making the dances have some continuity, some structure, whether I knew specifically what it was or not. At one point I had the scherzo finishing the ballet and the grand waltz opening it. All different sorts of ways. It was just—it was a marvelous sort of puzzle. Here I have all these people and these situations and I know they belong to each other—now let me see how. It was almost like rearranging *things*. And suddenly a picture was there. I am surprised by a lot of it. I am very surprised by the reaction to it. I didn't expect it at all. Something is there that I didn't know I was doing.

"DENBY   The reaction?

"ROBBINS   To the ballet.

"DENBY   That everybody liked it so much.

"ROBBINS   So much. The questions you are asking me about it seem to—I was originally going to call it *Some Dances*. That's all they are, just a series of dances. But something else takes over.

"DENBY   I don't know that the title is exactly the best.

"ROBBINS   It's a hard one to find. I was going to say *Dances: Chopin, In Open Air,* but that isn't the right title. In French *Quelques Danses* is nice, but in English *Some Dances* is sort of flat. If you say *Eighteen Dances* or *Nineteen Dances,* it divides them into compartments.

"DENBY   And it's of no consequence. Once you see the piece, you figure it is a piece. That end is quite prepared for all along when it happens. You really didn't want a big dance at the end. Since they are walking so much anyway, it is natural to make the end out of that.

"ROBBINS   Also the end of it had to come out of the scherzo, that very restless piece which ends with them all sort of *whoosh* running out—disappearing like cinders falling out into the night, and it couldn't end there, either. That's not the end of it, that's not how I feel about these people—that they went *whoosh* and disappeared. They are still here and they still move like dancers. They are a community. They take—what's the Italian word?—'a *passegiata*'— they take a stroll, like in an Italian town, around the town's square at sundown. They may have felt a threat, but they don't panic, they stay.

"I was very touched by Maria (Tallchief) last night. She was moved by the ballet, and I suddenly realized how much it meant to me that she *was* and that it pleased her, because she is such an image in my mind of what a dancer should be, and I can't think of her as a cinder which went *whoosh* and was gone.

"So coming back after the scherzo to the stage and the floor that we dance on, and putting your hand on it—if it's the earth or a ballet dancer's relationship to a wood floor—*that* somehow is the ending I knew I had to get to somewhere. Very little of this was conscious, Edwin. I don't like to make theory afterwards. I'm just trying to get at it—there may be seven other reasons I'm not mentioning, well, you understand.

"DENBY   I don't want to pull it out of you—

"ROBBINS   Well, besides, you have your thoughts about it anyway.

"DENBY   Of course. Everyone is very happy that you've done a ballet again.

"ROBBINS   So am I.

"DENBY   And the dancers are happy. And it's nice you want to do some more.

"ROBBINS   I'm surprised. I didn't know which I would do or how I would do. It's almost like an artist who has not been drawing for a long time. I didn't know how my hand would be. And I was so surprised that the dances began to come out and began to come out so gushing, in a way. And I worked in a way I hadn't worked before. Whether I knew the details or not, I pushed through to the end of the dance. I sort of knew where it was going, and then I'd go back and clean it up and fill it up. Quite often the dancers weren't even sure how they got through the steps to the next step. But they went with me. Well, what I started to say was that I was pleased to be choreographing again and to have it coming out, and it's given me a sort—it's unplugged something. And I want to do a lot of ballets. I want to go on and see if I can work a little bit more the way I've worked this time—that sort of trusting the intuition more than self-controlling the intuition. I'd like to see what happens with some other kind of music now. That music I feel I am very identified with and always have been. It may go all the way back to my sister's dancing days as a Duncan dancer. I think a lot of that's in there.

"DENBY   I imagined you and your sister at the piano—you were seven or eight. The first thing that came from it was *The Concert* which, the first time, I was quite offended by.

"ROBBINS   (*laughs*) I made up for that.

"DENBY   I miss it now. I'd love to see it. But your jokes this time are adorable.

"ROBBINS   I love them in the section where they're posing, just love them. . . . I had a researcher call me from a magazine to ask me some questions. The first one was something very close to this: 'Where do you place your newest ballet in the mainstream of the trend of abstract dancing today?' (*laughter*) I've also been asked, 'What is the relationship between *Les Sylphides* and your ballet?' Well, I guess we used the same composer.

"DENBY   Did you use any of the same pieces?

"ROBBINS   No, I didn't, except one, the adage that Tony and Pat do, the third dance. Evidently, that music was used as the man's variation at one point, which I didn't know. It's a lovely piece.

"DENBY   You told me that you are going to do another Chopin ballet.

"ROBBINS   I've finished one nocturne and I've about three-quarters of another one, and I have an idea for a third. I've started them and want to see how they come out. One for Millie, one for Allegra, and I think one for Kay Mazzo.

"DENBY   She's beautiful.

"ROBBINS   Isn't she lovely?

"DENBY   Sally is wonderful. She gets more and more of that giving-without-thinking.

"ROBBINS   She has a kind of toughness, not tough as much as a practical quality. But then I'll say something and can see in her eyes that she's suddenly grasped it, and you can see it explode inside her—such joy.

"DENBY   The dance of the girls comes off so wonderfully. Allegra is wonderful all through.

"ROBBINS   That's the way about all of them. At so many rehearsals, they didn't dance all out. They sort of walked. That's how I got Eddie to do that first variation the first night. He came into rehearsal and had to save himself for the performance and just marked through it. I ran back and said, 'Now, that's what I want.' The same with Allegra—when she marks something, she shows you what it is. I don't think they realize how trained they are—so clear. Like someone with a great voice who can whisper and you hear it. And that's what you see. And that's what they do.

"DENBY   They are so completely clear, it's extraordinary how clear they are because whatever is passing through is never a blur or an uncertainty or a conventionalism.

"[Postscript from Robbins to Denby (sent the following day from Stockholm where Robbins was supervising final rehearsals of *Les Noces* for its June 6 première with the Royal Swedish Ballet. He went from there to Moscow to attend, by invitation of the U.S.S.R., its International Ballet Competition.)]

May 27, 1969

"Dear Edwin:

"Something bothered me terribly after we met—one of your remarks about the people looking up and watching something cross the sky at the end of the ballet. You said something about planes—A bomb—war today, etc., and it jarred me very much. I couldn't figure out 'the why' right away—but then I did on the trip over. First of all I feel you are imposing a terribly out-of-context meaning to what they are seeing. The ballet stays and exists in the time of the music and its work.

Nothing is out of it, I believe; all gestures and moods, steps, etc. are part of the fabric of the music's time and its meanings to me. I couldn't think of planes—A bomb, etc. Only clouds—and the flights of birds—sunsets and leaves falling—and they, the people's reactions are all very underplayed, very willing to meet whatever threat is *in the music.*

"Well, those people knew their disasters—felt them, maybe felt that at a certain time their being would come to an end—but they faced it as a part of living.

"I hadn't thought of *all* of this when I did it. All I knew is that they weren't afraid, had no self-pity, and stayed—didn't leave.

"And I do feel that last piece is the logical end of the whole ballet. To me it is very much the only possible result of all that's come before.

". . . Stockholm is lovely, limpid skies at midnight—looking clear and blue as a New York fall—It was so good to see you—J"

Dances at a Gathering has been acclaimed in the United States and in London, where it was first performed by the Royal Ballet, October 19, 1970. Marcia Marks in *Dance Magazine* found it "the most significant work for many a season. For Robbins, it is the most spontaneous outpouring of sheer creative force in his balletic career, and for the dancers, it is an unexpected revelation." Patricia Barnes in *Dance and Dancers* magazine said, "*Dances at a Gathering* is, by general consent, a masterpiece. . . . It has been interpreted by different people in different ways, but all seem agreed on one aspect. This is a ballet about people, recognizable human beings rather than mere ciphers. There is no story, but a strong mood and atmosphere are present. There are ten dancers, five boys and five girls—they could be Americans, Poles, Danes or Russians. Their nationality is unimportant. What is significant in the fluent, utterly captivating series of dances is a love of humanity, an observation and understanding that is remarkably conveyed by the dancers involved. It seems impossible to leave the theatre having seen *Dances at a Gathering* and not feel one's soul uplifted."

In London, where the first performance was danced by Rudolf Nureyev, Monica Mason, Antoinette Sibley, Anthony Dowell, Laura Connor, Ann Jenner, David Wall, Lynn Seymour, Michael Coleman, and Jonathan Kelly, the editor of the *Dancing Times,* Mary Clarke, wrote: "Genius is a word to be used sparingly in the small artistic world of ballet but genius is the only word for Jerome Robbins, as choreographer and man of the theatre. . . . It may sound exaggerated to say that this ballet, just about people dancing, is profoundly moving but it is true. There is more dancing than in some three-act ballets and certainly more emotion because it is happening here and now. It is an hour of delight and if you catch it on a program with Ashton's *Enigma Variations* or *The Dream,* your faith in ballet will be restored. The Press has been unanimous in praise. I echo Clement Crisp of *The Financial Times:* it is a ballet 'that will enrich our lives for years to come.' "

In 1972, Jerome Robbins wrote to *Ballet Review* the following letter, which is of general interest:

To the Editor:
    For the record, would you please print in large, emphatic and capital letters the following:

THERE ARE NO STORIES TO ANY OF THE DANCES IN DANCES AT A GATHERING. THERE ARE NO PLOTS AND NO ROLES. THE DANCERS ARE THEMSELVES DANCING WITH EACH OTHER TO THAT MUSIC IN THAT SPACE.

Thank you very much.

New York, N.Y.

Jerome Robbins.

The pianist Gordon Boelzner, interviewed by Arlene Croce and George Dorris in *Ballet Review* (Vol. 3, No. 4.), has many interesting comments on *Dances at a Gathering*, *In the Night* and *Who Cares?*

DANSES CONCERTANTES

Classic ballet in five parts. Music by Igor Stravinsky. Choreography by George Balanchine. Scenery and costumes by Eugene Berman. First presented by the Ballet Russe de Monte Carlo at the City Center, New York, September 10, 1944, with a cast headed by Alexandra Danilova and Leon Danielian.

Stravinsky's *Danses Concertantes* was first performed as a concert piece, but the composer had conceived the work with the choreographer and had intended his score to be used in the theatre. When the work was first played (1942), it was apparent that the music embodied dancing—not only dance rhythms, but specific poses and gestures for a group of dancers—so that to hear *Danses Concertantes* was also to visualize a ballet. The plot of the ballet *Danses Concertantes* is the plot of the score: "Introductory March," "Pas d'Action," "Four Variations on a Theme," "Pas de deux," and "Concluding March."

The curtain rises on a handsome, ornate drop curtain. Between two high columns draped in rich cloth, the legend of the ballet is sketched out and we read the name of the ballet, its composer, choreographer, and designer. The orchestra commences a rhythmic, witty march. The dancers, in bright costumes, parade before the curtain at the music's command. There are fourteen of them—eight girls, four boys, and the *premier danseur* and the ballerina, who enter toward the end of the march and finish it with a flourish.

The drop curtain rises. The ballerina dances before the *corps de ballet,* which is arranged in four groups, in each of which a boy partners two girls. The colorful, spangled figures of the dancers are outlined boldly against the dark back cloth. The ballerina dances with sweet, lyric grace, but also with humor, for the music contrives to interrupt and cut short its soft melody with sharp accents in surprising places. You get the impression that you might get from reading a lyric poem whose lines are sometimes truncated in the middle of words but nevertheless flow on to graceful conclusion.

The majestic opening of this second section is heard again, and the full orchestra plays a lively, precisely accented conclusion that merges directly into a new theme that is quiet, tender, and romantic. The ballerina has left the stage, and each of the four groups of dancers comes forward and dances a *pas de trois* to variations on the theme.

The first and second variations are rigorous in rhythm, and the musical phrases seem to balance about a center, as the two girls cluster and move away from the boy. The third variation, Andantino, is softer, more wistful; the fourth, happy and boisterous.

The dancers now leave the stage to the ballerina and her partner, who dance a *pas de deux*. The dancers are almost personified in the music, which demands at first beauty in slowness, then a quiet, pointed wit that ascends to an elevated, noble manner. The *pas de deux* ends on a note of tenderness.

All the dancers return. The opening march is resumed, and the entire group dances to its buoyant rhythm. The music ends sharply and unexpectedly. All rush forward and bow low to the audience as the curtain falls behind them.

NOTES Frederic Franklin later took the role first danced by Leon Danielian. Maria Tallchief, Ruthanna Boris, and Mary Ellen Moylan were among the dancers in the first performance.

In 1972, for the Stravinsky Festival at the New York City Ballet, which we planned in order to celebrate the composer's ninetieth birthday, I did a new version of *Danses Concertantes*. It was not only that I did not remember what I had done the first time; it was that I wanted, with the new dancers I was working with, to do something different.

It often happens: we forget. I don't think that is so bad when we have in the present so much to do! How in the world is it possible—really for me, it is not—to create a ballet first done many years ago, with young dancers who are very different? Writers think with words; I think with bodies and the ballets I work on necessarily have a great deal to do with the here and now, not a recollection or a notation or someone's idea of accuracy of the past. That is perhaps a proper function in a ballet company for some ballet masters, to reconstruct, but it is not for me; I am too busy making for now. I think ballet is now. I remember saying to an interviewer, Louis Botto, as we were preparing for the Stravinsky Festival, precisely this—that ballet is about people who are now, not about what will be. Because as you don't have these bodies to work with, it's already finished. This is not a question of what the story is, or what the costumes are, or preserving the ballet of 1972 for future generations. I'm staging ballets for today's bodies. For people who are here now. And you admire the way he or she looks and how they move. It's this person today—not just *anybody*.

And so I enjoyed very much doing *Danses Concertantes* again.

The outline of the ballet is just as it was in the first version, but the details are radically different. The first performance of the new *Danses Concertantes*, by the New York City Ballet at the New York State Theatre, was danced by Linda Yourth and John Clifford, with a group of twelve dancers. The orchestra was conducted by Robert Irving. Scenery and costumes, as before, were by Eugene Berman.

DANTE SONATA

Dramatic ballet in one act. Music by Franz Liszt. Choreography by Frederick Ashton. Scenery and costumes by Sophie Fedorovitch. First presented by the Sadler's Wells Ballet at the Sadler's Wells Theatre, London, January 23, 1940, with Margot Fonteyn and Robert Helpmann among the principal dancers. First presented in the United States by the Sadler's Wells Ballet at the Metropolitan Opera House, New York, September 23, 1950, with Margot Fonteyn, Moira Shearer, and Michael Somes among the principals.

This ballet is based on appreciations of Dante's *Divine Comedy* by the poet Victor Hugo and the composer Franz Liszt. Liszt used Hugo's poem "After a Reading of Dante" as an eloquent statement of his own appreciation of that poet and wrote a composition for piano on its theme. This ballet, like Liszt's music, depicts an embattled conflict between the forces of good and the forces of evil.

The curtain rises on a decorative backdrop that indicates with a few white lines the fiery fumes of purgatory hovering above parallel lines reminiscent of ascending steps. There are two groups of people in the ballet: the Children of Light and the Children of Darkness. The former are dressed in innocent white, most of the latter in black. Black, shining snakes coil about the bodies of the two principal Children of Darkness, a man and a woman.

The Children of Light, apparently those who have understood their sins and repented, dance joyfully alone. Soon they are invaded by the Children of Darkness. The evil men and women attack the purified ones with determined concupiscence. The Children of Light try to beat them back, but some are seduced.

The Children of Light move flowingly, without suddenness, while their opposites fill the stage with violence. The efforts of the innocent to save themselves, to prevent any one of their number from yielding to this violence, enforce a constant tension. But finally their resistance is in vain: physically they become slaves to the powers of evil.

The Children of Darkness are not enlightened by their triumph and regard it with displeasure even as it is achieved. The curtain falls as the leaders of the Children of Light and the Children of Darkness, on opposite sides of the stage, are held up by their fellows in simulated crucifixion, their limbs twitching with agony.

DAPHNIS AND CHLOË

Dramatic ballet in three scenes. Music by Maurice Ravel. Choreography by Michel Fokine. Book by Michel Fokine. Scenery and costumes by Léon Bakst. First presented by Diaghilev's Ballets Russes at the Théâtre du Châtelet, Paris, June 8, 1912, with Tamara Karsavina as Chloë, Vaslav

Nijinsky as Daphnis, *and Adolph Bolm as* Dorkon. *Revived, with choreography by Catherine Littlefield, for the Philadelphia Ballet, 1937. Revived, with choreography by Frederick Ashton, by the Sadler's Wells Ballet at the Royal Opera House, Covent Garden, London, April 5, 1951. Scenery and costumes by John Craxton. Margot Fonteyn, Michael Somes, Violetta Elvin, John Field, and Alexander Grant danced the principal roles. This is the version described below.*

The two orchestral suites *Daphnis and Chloë,* now so familiar to us, are derived from an original ballet score designed for this ancient tale of youthful romance. Actually, two suites Ravel made of this music were performed in concert form before the ballet was produced. *Suite No. 1*—"Nocturne," "Interlude," and "Warriors' Dance"—begins at the end of Scene One of the ballet, after Daphnis has collapsed, and concludes with the end of the general dance of the pirates in Scene Two. *Suite No. 2*—"Daybreak," "Pantomime," and "General Dance"—is the music for the whole of Scene Three.

In its outlines, *Daphnis and Chloë* is not radically different from many ballets with stories that relate the love of young people who are finally reunited after some difficulty, some obstruction, has seemed to rule out a happy ending. This is naturally the way of ballet stories, as it is with all fiction, for unless there is some kind of obstruction, we are not apt to have a story: love, alone, is not enough. But it is the different quality of the love—the difference in the affection of Tristram for Iseult in *Picnic at Tintagel,* of Franz for Swanilda in *Coppélia,* of Amyntas for Sylvia in *Sylvia,* and in the way these lovers react to any interference—that make all these stories interesting. If we care about the kind of affection these lovers have for each other, what their gestures are, and how they look together, we are apt to be disturbed if any obstruction is put in their way and we are delighted at the end if the lovers seem to be happy and forgetful in their understanding of what has come between them. The two lovers in the story *Daphnis and Chloë* are very young; they are youthful innocents. We are made to see this and resent immediately the interference they endure. We are happy at the end because their initial innocence is not seriously violated: they still love, but with a difference that will make them happier.

SCENE ONE: A SACRED GROVE   On this day young people of a Mediterranean isle are paying tribute to the god Pan and his nymphs, whose grotto stands at the left. Daphnis, the handsome shepherd, and Chloë, the girl he has loved all his life, are among the worshipers. Their affection has become so accepted by the other young people that some of the maidens don't seriously believe in it. Still hoping that Daphnis will notice one of them, the maidens join him in a dance. Chloë reacts with appropriate jealousy and does not repulse the advances of another shepherd, Dorkon. All this is in the spirit of fun; the lovers have taken a vow to be faithful to each other, and their friends are amusing themselves a little because of the seriousness of the romance. Dorkon, however, is serious too, and Daphnis tells him to leave his girl alone. But Dorkon is not to be easily routed. Daphnis becomes angry, and his friends try to make light of the situation by suggesting that the two begin a dancing contest for Chloë's favor.

Dorkon's dance is as crude and awkward as his advances toward Chloë have been, and Daphnis, in a splendid dance with his shepherd's crook, easily defeats him. Chloë rewards Daphnis with a kiss, Dorkon departs, and her friends take Chloë away.

Daphnis is alone. He lies down on the ground and daydreams of his perfect love. He has almost fallen off to sleep when he is joined by the temptress Lykanion. Daphnis is indifferent to her beauty, but strangely attracted also. Lykanion is sure of her knowledge of love, and the inexperienced youth is disturbed. But Lykanion is too anxious to instruct Daphnis. He senses instinctively the evil in her advances and dismisses her.

Now the youth is roused by a battle cry. A band of pirates have invaded the island, and the natives have risen in arms against them. The defenseless girls seek the safety of Pan's grotto, but the pirates, disrespectful of the god, pursue them. Bryaxis, leader of the pirates, captures Chloë and carries her off swiftly before Daphnis can act. Daphnis cannot understand how this has happened. He despairs and rails at the power of gods who would permit her abduction.

The music is quiet and mysterious. Suddenly one of the stone nymphs of the grotto comes to life in a magical blaze of light. As the chorus begins to chant along with the music, this girl and two other nymphs begin to dance. Daphnis does not see them. Now they go to him, rouse him, and lead him before the grotto of Pan. At the nymphs' call, an image of the god fills the sky. Daphnis prays that the powerful god will restore Chloë to him.

SCENE TWO: THE PIRATES' HIDE-OUT   On the shore of another island, the pirates are celebrating their victory at night. They dance joyfully and divide among themselves the day's profits. Chloë, her wrists bound together with rope, is brought in, and Bryaxis, the pirate captain, commands her to dance. The helpless girl is afraid to refuse, but soon, as she dances, she lifts her bound wrists in supplication, begging to be released. Bryaxis only laughs at her. The terrified girl trembles at the thought of intimacy with such a man. Bryaxis is about to approach her when the seacoast is suddenly illuminated by brilliant, flashing light. The pirates cower at this miracle and stare, astonished, as the great god Pan appears in a vision. He orders the pirates to free Chloë. The brigands flee to the hills.

SCENE THREE: ANOTHER PART OF THE SACRED GROVE   The orchestra is silent as the curtain rises. Daphnis, lying alone, grieves over Chloë's loss. Gradually the music imitates the sounds of the breaking day; the sun rises. Fellow shepherds come seeking Daphnis. But he does not wish to join them; only by praying to the god may he help his love to be rescued. Chloë's friends appear and tell him that she has returned. The ecstatic Daphnis searches for her. At first sight of Daphnis, Chloë runs into his arms, and the two lovers rejoice.

Lammon, an old shepherd, tells Daphnis that his prayers have indeed been answered but that Pan acted in his favor because of the god's memory of his own love for the Syrinx. Daphnis and Chloë, in their gratitude for Pan's intervention, re-enact the god's romance for their friends. Daphnis, as Pan, vainly pursues the lovely nymph, who flees from him. He pleads with her, but she will not acknowledge him. She hides and, at Pan's persistence, casts herself into a brook and drowns. The god takes a reed from the brook and makes of it a flute, which he names for Syrinx. He plays upon the flute. At its sound, Chloë begins to dance with tenderness and joy.

The ensemble joins the two lovers in a final general dance that celebrates their reunion and their lasting love.

NOTES   Serge Diaghilev commissioned Ravel to compose a ballet in one act on the story of Daphnis and Chloë. The work was to be performed in 1911, and during the ensuing delay, Ravel arranged two suites from his score, both of which were performed in the concert hall before the ballet's first performance. The ballet at last saw the stage June 8, 1912, with Tamara Karsavina and Vaslav Nijinsky in the title roles. Fokine, the choreographer, had had in mind a ballet on the Daphnis and Chloë legend for eight years. In 1904, in St. Petersburg, he had submitted a scenario for such a work to the director of the Imperial Theatre, along with a preface that detailed the reforms to be embodied in his work, reforms that he regarded as crucial for the art of ballet: "The dance need not be a mere *divertissement*, introduced into the pantomime. In the ballet the whole meaning of the story can be expressed by the dance. Above all, dancing should be interpretive. It should not degenerate into mere gymnastics. It should, in fact, be the plastic word. The dance should explain the spirit of the actors in the spectacle. More than that, it should express the whole epoch to which the subject of the ballet belongs . . . The ballet must no longer be made up of 'numbers,' 'entries,' etc. It must show artistic unity of conception . . . a unity which is made up of the three elements—music, painting, and plastic art . . . The great, the outstanding feature of the new ballet . . . shall be but one thing—the aspiration for beauty . . ."

But the reforms suggested in Fokine's manifesto were largely ignored and his project for a ballet was refused. Part of his original scenario was staged for the Diaghilev Ballets Russes after many of his reforms had been realized, in *Les Sylphides, Firebird,* and *Petrouchka.*

This production of *Daphnis and Chloë* was a considerable success. Tamara Karsavina, who created the part of Chloë, has written that the ballet was, to her mind, Fokine's masterpiece. "In it, Fokine explored to the full the recesses of neo-Greek choreography as originally revived by Isadora Duncan."

Successful as it was, however, the production of *Daphnis and Chloë* created a quarrel between the choreographer and the impresario. Fokine had difficulty obtaining adequate rehearsal time and new costumes for his new ballet, and since Nijinsky, in his staging of *The Afternoon of a Faun,* was being rewarded with both, the older choreographer felt slighted. Soon after, he left the Diaghilev company for two years.

The *Daphnis and Chloë* of Catherine Littlefield, pioneer in American ballet, was a completely new choreographic venture, first produced in 1937 for her Philadelphia Ballet.

Two new productions of *Daphnis and Chloë* were given in New York in

1975. The first, with choreography by John Taras, costumes and production by Joe Eula, and lighting by Ronald Bates, was part of the New York City Ballet's Hommage à Ravel and received its first performance at the New York State Theatre, Lincoln Center, New York, on May 22, with Robert Irving conducting. Peter Martins, Nina Fedorova, Karin von Aroldingen and Peter Schaufuss were the principals.

The second new production, choreographed by Glen Tetley for the Stuttgart Ballet and first presented at the Württemberg State Theatre, Stuttgart, May 17, 1975, with scenery and costumes by Willa Kim and lighting by John B. Read, was first presented by the same ensemble in the United States at the Metropolitan Opera House, Lincoln Center, on June 12, 1975 (lighting executed by Gilbert V. Hemsley, Jr.), with Stewart Kershaw conducting the orchestra and chorus. Richard Cragun, Marcia Haydée, Birgit Keil, and Egon Madsen were the principals.

DARK ELEGIES

Music by Gustav Mahler. Choreography by Antony Tudor. Scenery and costumes by Nadia Benois. First produced by the Ballet Rambert at the Duchess Theatre, London, February 19, 1937, with Maude Lloyd, Antony Tudor, Walter Gore, John Byron, Agnes de Mille, Hugh Laing, Daphne Gow, Ann Gee, Patricia Clogstoun, Beryl Kay, and Celia Franca. First presented in the United States by Ballet Theatre at the Center Theatre, New York, January 24, 1940, with scenery and costumes by Raymond Sovey after the Benois originals. The principal dancers were Nina Stroganova, Miriam Golden, Antony Tudor, Hugh Laing, Lucia Chase, and Dimitri Romanoff.

Dark Elegies is a dance ballet to the Kindertotenlieder (Songs of Childhood Death) of Mahler. The singer on stage tells of the grief of a father over the death of his children. The setting is somber, rough, jagged, with lowering clouds over water and mountains and trees that seem to have been lashed relentlessly by the wind. As the music laments, a small group of villagers begin to dance. Their grief over a disaster that has befallen them all is communal and also private. We do not know what the tragedy is, there are no specifics, but with the expression and gesture of the dancers, we have no need. Their movement universalizes the particulars of Mahler's songs and we watch, as at a religious rite, the unfolding of desperate grief to mourning, to resignation and perhaps hope.

Dame Marie Rambert, in whose ballet company this ballet was created, has recalled in her biography Quicksilver: "Tudor told me he was anxious to do a ballet to Mahler's Kindertotenlieder. He had already suggested it two years before, but at that time I did not think he was mature enough to tackle such a tragic subject. I had also been perturbed by the main idea of a disaster that would kill all the children and leave the parents alive. I kept reasoning with Tudor that except for the Massacre of the Innocents such a special calamity

had never happened and would seem *too* contrived. But now in 1937 he
seemed very sure of the way to treat it. I asked him to show me one finished
song and realized how profound the choreography was. He had seen at an exhibition of Nadia Benois a landscape which he was sure would be the right
setting, and when I saw the painting I agreed with him. So we invited her to
design the scenery and the costumes, which she did perfectly. The ballet was
not purely realistic. It had lovely words and music, and the dances were classical for the soloists and in folk-dance style for the ensemble. Yet he managed to
keep the style homogeneous.

"He called this ballet *Dark Elegies*. It was in two scenes: 1. Bereavement;
2. Resignation. It was like a mourning ritual accompanied by a singer on the
stage. Singly or in groups, the bereaved parents express their sorrow in a slow
dance at having lost their children when their village was stricken by calamity.
They try not to show their pain, but it breaks through at moments. All was
said in classical language, and this severe form made the expression more
poignant when despair burst through it.

"When we performed this ballet in 1966 to a new young public, many of
them thought that it was all about the Aberfan Disaster, to such a degree had
the most unforeseen of calamities happened in reality.

"*Dark Elegies* was Tudor's masterpiece and has remained the greatest tragic
ballet of the English repertoire so far.

"In addition to our own dancers he used a guest dancer, the American
Agnes de Mille, a most remarkable artist."

Agnes de Mille's own recollections of *Dark Elegies* are recorded in a long interview with the critic Clive Barnes (see his book *Inside American Ballet
Theatre*, 1977).

NOTE   *Dark Elegies* has been in the active repertory of the Ballet Rambert
since it was first performed. It is now danced by the National Ballet of Canada
and other companies. Jerome Robbins has said: "Fokine inspired me as a performer; he made me feel I could really dance. Tudor didn't; he made it complicated. He brought psychological motivation into ballet; he conveyed
through movement emotions that could not be put into words. And he had the
courage to persevere along this line in the face of adverse criticism. But he did
wonderful things in pure dance, as well. *Gala Performance* and *Dark Elegies*
stand alone, and I think they will last longest because they are more formal in
structure . . . Tudor had a great influence on my early work and a great
influence on all contemporary ballet."*

LES DEMOISELLES DE LA NUIT (The Ladies of Midnight)

*Dramatic ballet in three scenes. Music by Jean Françaix. Choreography by
Roland Petit. Book by Jean Anouilh. Settings and costumes by Léonor Fini.
First presented by Les Ballets de Paris at the Théâtre Marigny, Paris, May
21, 1948, with Margot Fonteyn, Roland Petit, and Gordon Hamilton in the*

* From "Antony Tudor" by Selma Jeanne Cohen, in *Dance Perspectives 18*, 1963.

leading roles. First presented in the United States by Ballet Theatre at the Metropolitan Opera House, New York, April 13, 1951, with Colette Marchand, John Kriza, and Eric Braun.

This ballet rightly assumes that when a young man marries a cat, things are going to be pretty difficult around the house. How the young man meets the cat, how he is enamored of her feline grace, how his love transforms her for a time into a beautiful young girl, and how, despite his love, his wife is unable to conquer an irresistible inclination to scamper on the rooftops, the ballet chooses to relate in three scenes.

SCENE ONE: A HOUSE IN THE COUNTRY Low, moaning music is heard from the orchestra as a brief overture begins. The curtain rises. The scene is a large, high room whose walls are papered with yellowing, peeling newspapers. Cats sit about the room in relaxed attitudes: some polishing their nails, some resting against a ladder. A black kitten reclines on a white couch at the right. On the wall, partially obscured by a wispy rag, hangs a portrait of a big, beautiful white cat. A doorway in the center is hung with tattered and torn cloth; innumerable cats must have sharpened their claws on it.

A young musician enters. He pushes aside the dusty drapes and steps carefully into the room. He has been invited to this house in the country to play at a wedding and is astonished to see that no ordinary preparations for such an occasion have been made. He observes the curious cats and walks over to the portrait. He turns in the air in surprise at what he sees there. The entire house is occupied by cats!

Two black-and-white cats in handsome livery, pages to the household, dart out and grab the musician's hat. The tempo becomes brisk. The light brightens. He chases after them unsuccessfully. The black cat rises from the couch; she and three of the kittens surround the musician. The cats dance about the boy, scratching at his face. The black cat curls up at his feet. He dances for a short time with the kittens. They leave. Agatha, the beautiful white cat at whose portrait the musician has marveled, enters quickly, expectantly. Agatha is the bride of the month. The cat baron who rules over the house marries one of his harem every month, and it is Agatha's wedding that the musician has been invited to attend. Tall and graceful, with long, lithe legs, she immediately attracts the young man. She is dressed in white, with short gloves; a blue ribbon is tied about her throat. The music changes; an oboe plays a wistful, yet playful, melody to the accompaniment of plucked strings.

Agatha begins to dance. The musician watches, fascinated. The music becomes rhythmic. He compares the cat to her portrait. He goes up to Agatha. She circles him on point, and the strings commence a flowing theme. The boy turns swiftly and kneels at her feet. Now he rises and holds her close. The cat responds experimentally. Gradually Agatha becomes as interested in the musician as he is in her. He lifts, holds, and embraces her for a duet that lasts five minutes. The music whines plaintively. The other cats look on with horror. What will the cat baron do? They attack the boy and try to pull him away, but

Agatha climbs up on his back. Cymbals and brass simulate the contest. The boy embraces the cat. The music is silent for a moment.

The cat baron enters, his fur bristling. A lovely black cat, whose costume is embellished with the skeleton of a fish, separates the lovers rudely. She is evidently the cat baron's principal aide. Footlights throw the shadows of the two lovers and the jealous cat baron against the back wall. The baron dances in gleeful anticipation of his wedding. Agatha dances with him, not unwilling at first, but she breaks away and gestures to the boy, who stands on the opposite side of the stage, holding out his arms to her plaintively. She goes to the boy. The cat baron pulls them apart and dances furiously. He threatens the musician with his long claws.

The black cat takes Agatha's hand and pulls her toward the baron. A white veil is thrown over the bride's head before she can protest. Daringly she pulls it off and rejoins the boy. The cat baron makes a last effort to dominate her passions. The pages hold the cat couple high on their shoulders in a wedding parade. But Agatha falls down into the musician's arms. The desperate cats scuttle off. Suddenly Agatha is no longer a kitten; her face is the face of a beautiful girl.

SCENE TWO: AT HOME   The orchestra plays a protracted interlude of hurried music. The curtain rises on a boudoir scene. A white bed canopied in white gauze stands on the left. At the right is a large window, looking out on to a dark-blue night. A bird cage stands near the window. Agatha, in a becoming white costume, her light hair shining, stands alongside her new husband. They embrace. The girl goes over to the bird cage, takes out a bluebird, fondles it, and dances as she holds it before her. The boy sits at the foot of the bed and watches her adoringly. Odd, this passion of hers for birds.

He rises, stands by the window, then goes over to the right wall. As he steps back into the room, the cat baron follows him closely. Agatha is agitated. Her lover tries to throw the intruder out, but the baron is so delighted to see his sometime fiancée again, even if she is a real girl now, that he forces her to dance with him. When the boy separates them, the cat jumps up onto his back and scratches at him fiercely. Both claim Agatha. Finally the musician succeeds in throwing the baron out.

Agatha seems to be grateful. To a quiet, deep melody, she stands behind the boy and wraps her arms about his neck. They begin to dance. In the midst of their *pas de deux*, the girl's limbs seem to quicken. The boy takes her to the bed. There he lifts her high on his shoulder. He lets her down slowly, and the girl's body curves backward. He rocks her back and forth, his knee a fulcrum to her seesawing body. The boy falls back, exhausted. Agatha falls over his knees.

Prolonged, mournful cat calls are heard. Agatha raises her head. The sounds persist. As she moves off the bed onto the floor, a cymbal crashes. Her movements are catlike. She looks back at her lover, despairs, and climbs out the window. The musician awakens. The orchestra plays the haunting music of the ballet's overture. Where has Agatha gone? Out on the roof again, presumably. He takes a candle and follows her.

SCENE THREE: THE ROOFTOPS   The theme of the overture persists throughout the interval. The scene, as the curtain rises, is a red rooftop against a blue sky. Four dormer windows penetrate the roof from within. There is a gutter at the front. Agatha and the cat baron stand poised against two of the windows. They run to each other and embrace in the gutter. The musician climbs onto the roof through the window at the left. Other cats crawl over the roof and stand ready to attack him behind the window. They pounce on him. The boy falls. Agatha and the cat baron lead a train of cats over the roof, in and out among the windows. The boy tries to follow and slides into the gutter. When he rises, the cats gather behind each of the windows and menace him as he tries to gain the top of the roof. He holds Agatha desperately for a brief moment. The cat baron pulls her away and leads her to the peak of the roof. There the other cats place her on the baron's back. He races down toward the gutter. Agatha falls. The musician has been slapping about in the gutter like a fish fresh out of water. He squirms over to the girl. He sits up. Agatha poses against him; then both fall back. Their bodies arch away from each other, their hands and feet joined. They move close and lift their legs so that their toes touch. The boy dies. The girl looks down at him and dies. Their heads fall back and their arms dangle over the edge of the roof. Their curious love is happy in death.

NOTES   After its performance by Ballet Theatre, *Les Demoiselles de la Nuit* was called by John Martin of the New York *Times* "in many ways the best of Petit's ballets to be seen in this country. Though it has his characteristically theatrical approach, it has also much more of a choreographic basis than any of his other pieces." Petit had originally planned to include this ballet in the repertory of his own Ballets de Paris during one of its New York seasons, but had been unable to do so. Colette Marchand had succeeded Margot Fonteyn in performances of the principal role in Paris when the ballet was first produced; in New York, Marchand repeated her earlier success. The ballet has been considerably revised since its first American performance. Mary Ellen Moylan has danced Agatha with both critical and popular approval.

DESIGNS WITH STRINGS

Music by Peter Ilyich Tchaikovsky. Choreography by John Taras. First presented by the Metropolitan Ballet at Wimbledon, England, February 6, 1948. First presented in the United States by Ballet Theatre at the Center Theatre, New York, April 25, 1950, with costumes by Irene Sharaff.

Designs with Strings is a dance ballet to the second movement of Tchaikovsky's *Trio in A minor*, arranged for piano and string orchestra. Instead of a story it has a mood, a character that arises from the dancing. There is no scenery; all the dancers wear simple black classical costumes and it is only in what they dance that they become individuals rather than performers.

The piano plays the stately, sentimental opening theme. There are six

dancers—two boys and four girls. When the curtain rises, they are grouped together and stand motionless in silhouette against a plain backdrop. Their arms
are extended slightly as they stand together; all the dancers appear to have a
common relation and when they respond to the music and begin to move
slowly in and out among themselves, they create an impression of unwinding
of latent, quiescent energy.

The lights come up, the full string orchestra takes up the theme, and three
of the dancers leave the stage. The remaining three, a boy and two girls, dance
softly to the music. Their movement, like the melody, is romantic—a little sad,
a little wistful. Their three companions return and circle the stage rapidly, as if
to show that there is happiness in romance also. All six dance together briefly,
and suddenly the melody quickens and the music becomes tinkling and light
and gay. The dancers duplicate this change of pace and temper with whirling
acceleration and with steps that are sharply fast and precise.

At the climax of this openly joyous sequence, the dancers leave the stage
and a girl dances with a boy alone. The theme changes for this *pas de deux,*
which is not at first so much romantic as it is matter-of-fact. But the dancing
soon alters this, and we see as they move together that the girl and the boy are
surprised and pleased to be by themselves, apart from the group. He lifts her
off into the wings on the left; the first theme returns accompanied by a newly
accented rhythm. Three girls rush out and dance brightly for a moment, to
break the romantic spell, and leave the stage.

Another theme, noble and lowing, is heard on muted strings. The ballerina
returns with two boys, who support her in a short dance. The wistfulness and
playfulness have disappeared; the ballerina and her partners display a proud,
youthful dignity. The new-found dignity breaks into pathos, however, upon
the return of the other dancers. The six try to dance together as before, first
the girls, then the boys. The first theme is heard again, poignantly on piercing
strings. The ballerina separates herself from the group, and a boy supports her
in a series of slow, extended movements across the stage. The other dancers
move forward and separate them. The girl runs to the boy, seeming to plead
with him and to claim him. But when she places her arms on his shoulders, he
slips away from her and goes to rejoin the others. Slowly the girl follows him.
The lights go down. The dancers stand as they were at the beginning, their
figures silhouetted in a close group that seems now inseparable.

DEUCE COUPE

*Music by the Beach Boys. Choreography by Twyla Tharp. Setting by
United Graffiti Artists. Costumes by Scott Barrie. Lighting by Jennifer Tipton. First presented by the City Center Joffrey Ballet at the City Center,
New York, March 1, 1973, with Erika Goodman, Twyla Tharp, and dancers
from the Joffrey Ballet and the Twyla Tharp Company.*

Described as a juxtaposition of classical ballet and choreography based on social dances of the 1960s, *Deuce Coupe* was the first major work to be staged

with an important ballet company by the modern dancer and choreographer Twyla Tharp, who appeared in the piece with members of her company. The title refers both to an automobile and to the piece *Little Deuce Coupe* by the Beach Boys, the rock group whose music, on tape, is featured in the ballet. Another major feature of the ballet is the setting—a background of three high strips of translucent paper (at first they look like windows we can't see out of) that a group of young people gradually fill with graffiti. As they inscribe the long sheets of paper, the paper is rolled up until the full height of the stage reflects their handiwork.

What happens on stage can be simply suggested but inadequately described. While a ballet dancer, Erika Goodman, performs an alphabetical but not-so-straightforward rendition of steps from the classical ballet dictionary, beginning with *Ailes de pigeon,* the rest of the dancers, in various combinations and permutations, perform dances both ancient and modern.

There are nineteen dances: *Matrix I, Ailes de pigeon* through *Attitude,* for the ballerina type and a couple; *Little Deuce Coupe, Balancé* through *Ballon,* with eighteen dancers and the persistent ballet performer; *Honda I, Balloné battu* through *déboulés,* for a *pas de trois* and the ballet girl; *Honda II, Changement de pieds* through *Dégagé à la quatrième devant en l'air,* for a couple and the girl; *Devoted to You, Dégagé en tournant* through *Failli,* for two couples and the girl; *How She Boogalooed It, Faux* through *Manège,* for the girl and a large ensemble; *Matrix II, Pas de basque sur les pointes* through *Pas de chat,* for the girl and six; *Alley Oop, Pas de cheval* through *Répétition,* for the girl plus eight; *Take a Load Off Your Feet, Retire* through *Sissone Tombée,* for three girls and two boys; *Long Tall Texan, Six* through *Suite,* for three girls; *Papa ooh Mau Mau,* for six; *Catch a Wave,* for five; *Got to Know the Woman, Temps de cuisse* through *temps lié,* for two girls; *Matrix III, Temps lié grand* through *Voyage,* for the ballet girl; *Don't Go Near the Water,* for six girls; *Matrix IV,* for a girl and boy; *Mama Says—"Eat a Lot, Never Be Lazy,"* for five boys and a girl; *Wouldn't It Be Nice,* for ten; and *Cuddle Up,* a finale for the whole company.

NOTE   Writing on the première in the *Daily News,* the critic Joseph Gale said that *Deuce Coupe* "is all the sadness, joy, cynicism and flavor of the beat generation . . . and the ballet is a smash.

"It is never less than exciting in crazy whorls of frenzied choreography that races, expires, picks up, jets ahead, pauses, and finally lays itself bare in unshed tears of last hopes.

"Through it all, there is the shining thread that holds it together and is the ballet's signature. That is Erika Goodman, unruffled and serene, who goes through a fair lexicon of classical dance, from *ailes de pigeon* through *pas de cheval,* while the world breaks up around her. She is the symbolic glory and salvation, the one who, after all else has failed, proffers hope in the palm of her outstretched hand. . . .

"There is also the schizoid passion of Miss Tharp's own dancing and, too, the United Graffiti Artists, who scrawl up a wall with the best decor of the season."

See comments on *As Time Goes By*, another Twyla Tharp ballet, for other views of this choreographer.

In the City Center Joffrey Ballet's spring season, 1975, the ballet became *Deuce Coupe II*, with the removal of Twyla Tharp's own dancers from the ensemble, a revision of the dances, and a new backdrop. Writing in *New York* magazine, the critic Alan Rich said that "the new work creates its own joy. Its scenario is entirely new; instead of being a work about pure dance, with its central soloist re-enacting the classic steps in alphabetical order, it is now a work about style. It spends its 40-or-so minutes as a steady wash, its pop steps from early on slowly oozing into romantic elegance as its dancers learn to unbend their knees and walk upon earth as adults. It is also, therefore, about growing up. Its music track, still a pastiche of the Beach Boys's greatest hits, is stronger, more poignant, altogether splendid."

DIM LUSTRE

Music by Richard Strauss. Choreography by Antony Tudor. Scenery and costumes by Motley. First presented by Ballet Theatre at the Metropolitan Opera House, New York, October 20, 1943, with Nora Kaye and Hugh Laing in the leading roles.

The dancer Hugh Laing has defined the theme of this ballet to Richard Strauss's *Burleske in D minor* for piano and orchestra: "Two people find they have been caught up with memories, not with each other, and they part." The scene is a ballroom. The atmosphere is heavy with recollection of another era. There a couple are attracted to each other and dance. He kisses her on the shoulder, she recalls the past, the action freezes, there is a blackout, and a girl dancing a reflection of the lady relives her first innocent romance with a young boy. When the young boy kisses her on the shoulder, the past dissolves and the present dance resumes. Now the man is reminded suddenly by a tap on the shoulder of a time spent with three coquettish girls. The action dissolves again into the past and we see his double relive the earlier time (which was the one he loved?). This emerges again into the present at the tap of a shoulder. Other memories converge upon the dance of the couple, there are flashbacks of a girl with an unforgettable perfume, of a man with a white tie. In the end, the lovers part, aware that what attracts them to each other is not themselves so much as pieces of the past. They cannot make for themselves a new memory.

Dim Lustre was revived by the New York City Ballet on May 26, 1964, with costumes, scenery, and lighting by Beni Montressor. Patricia McBride and Edward Villella danced the principal roles.

DIVERTIMENTO NO. 15

Music by Wolfgang Amadeus Mozart. Choreography by George Balanchine. Costumes by Karinska. Scenery by David Hays. First presented by the New York City Ballet at the American Shakespeare Festival Theatre, Stratford, Connecticut, May 31, 1956, with Tanaquil LeClercq, Diana Adams, Patricia Wilde, Melissa Hayden, Allegra Kent, Nicholas Magallanes, Herbert Bliss, and Roy Tobias in principal roles.

This ballet is a complete reworking of *Caracole*, a ballet to the same music, Mozart's *Divertimento No. 15 in B flat major* (*K. 287*), that was first presented by the New York City Ballet in 1952. Although *Caracole* had real success when it was first done, we did not dance it for several years and when the dancers and I began to work on a revival in 1956, we found we could remember very little of the original. So many new ballets had intervened that I had to start work all over again! That was not altogether a misfortune, for this score is one I admire most in the world.

Mozart wrote the *Divertimento* when he was twenty-one. He composed many similar works, pieces designed for special social occasions, large garden parties, carnivals, balls. All of these pieces were written to divert and charm audiences that expected to be entertained. Very often people danced to them. This particular divertimento is probably the finest ever written.

The ballet follows the different movements of the score. There is no story. It is designed for five principal girls, three boys, and a *corps de ballet* of eight girls. First movement—Allegro. Second—Andante Grazioso—Theme and Variations. Third—Minuet. Fourth—Andante. Fifth—Allegro Molto—Andante.

The ballet was danced for the first time at the bicentennial celebration of Mozart's birth that Lincoln Kirstein arranged at the American Shakespeare Festival Theatre. It then became a part of the repertory of the New York City Ballet.

DONIZETTI VARIATIONS

Music by Gaetano Donizetti. Choreography by George Balanchine. Costumes by Karinska. Lighting by David Hays. First presented by the New York City Ballet at the City Center, New York, November 16, 1960, with Melissa Hayden and Jonathan Watts in the leading roles.

This is a dance ballet, pure and simple, to some pleasant music by Donizetti. It was originally produced as part of "Salute to Italy," a dance program at the New York City Ballet honoring the one-hundredth anniversary of the formation of the Italian state. The program was planned around works with music by Italian composers, beginning with *Con Amore* (Rossini) and continuing with *Monumentum* (Stravinsky/Gesualdo) and *La Sonnambula* (Bellini). To contrast with the seriousness of these last two, we needed another, cheerful and sunny work. We found just what we wanted in music from a little-performed opera by Donizetti, *Don Sebastian*. The ballet features a central *pas de deux* for a ballerina and her partner—entrée, adagio, two variations and coda, plus variations and ensembles for the corps of six girls and three boys.

DON JUAN

Ballet by John Neumeier. Music by Christoph Willibald Gluck and Tomás Luis de Victoria. Choreography and staging by John Neumeier. Decor and costumes by Filippo Sanjust. Text by Max Frisch, translated by John Neumeier. Narrated by Sir Ralph Richardson. First presented in New York by the National Ballet of Canada at the Metropolitan Opera House, Lincoln Center, April 26, 1974, with Rudolf Nureyev in the leading role.

The romantic hero Don Juan is no stranger to ballet. Gluck's great music, so important for its time, is thought to be the first truly dramatic score for dance, designed to conform to a projected scheme of character, time, place, and situation. The first choreographer for the score was Angiolini (Vienna, 1761). Michel Fokine staged it for René Blum's Ballet Russe in London in 1936, with Anatole Vilzak as the hero and André Eglevsky as the Jester. Sir Frederick Ashton also choreographed a *Don Juan*, but to the score of Richard Strauss. This production, with Robert Helpmann, Margot Fonteyn, and Moira Shearer, was staged by the Sadler's Wells Ballet in London in 1948. Its theme was "The love that caught strange light from Death's own eyes," taken from Gautier's poem *"La Morte Amoureuse,"* and Ashton depicted the hero pursuing many loves but discovering that Death is his true beloved.

John Neumeier's ballet pursues a similar conception in a dramatic narrative accompanied not only by Gluck's music but also by the *Requiem Mass* of Victoria. Like a contemporary film, the ballet cuts back and forth in theme and music in such a way as to suggest motivations and insights the choreographer wishes to bring out, interweaving solemnity and celebration, action and passion, love and death. The context of the narrative is the familiar aftermath of Don Juan's murder of the father of a girl he has seduced.

When the curtain rises we discern behind a scrim a Lady in White. She is watched by a man who stands with his back to us, a mysterious creature in a long black cloak and black hat. It is November 2, the Day of the Dead in the Spanish calendar. A funeral procession passes. Commander Don Gonzalo de Ulloa is being carried to his grave, mourned by his daughter Doña Ana. After the bier has passed, the man in black reveals himself as Don Juan Tenorio, her father's killer. Doña Ana, still beguiled by the Don, is heartbroken as he rebuffs her. The Don proceeds to a banquet, accompanied by his servant and collaborator Catalinon.

In the next scene, a huge ballroom, Catalinon engages a troupe of dancers to present, in a series of *divertissements*, the amorous adventures of his master. Catalinon himself assumes the role of the legendary seducer, Don Juan. The

Don and the ladies of the party watch with amusement as a placard announces the theme of the play, "Don Juan and the Ladies," which is enacted on a small stage at the back of the hall. There the Don is observed in successful pursuit of three girls. Next, in the scene "Don Juan Serenades Doña Ana," we flash-back to his conquest of that lady, whose fierce passion soon exhausts him. When her father enters unexpectedly, sword in hand, a duel ensues. After he has killed her father, Don Juan wipes his sword on Doña Ana's skirt.

Now the Lady in White appears, but only to Don Juan, who reaches out to her. They dance, he fascinated by her blond coolness, in a duet in which she rejects him. She seems to be leading him away in a direction he cannot deter-mine. For the first time, a woman has not succumbed to his charm. Mysteri-ously, she disappears and there is no one in his arms. In one of the moments of silence in the ballet, the hero composes himself. A voice says, "Don Juan is a narcissist who loves only himself . . . He is not a lover, he remains alone . . . Disguising his true self, Don Juan is his role."

Then the music resumes and Catalinon is organizing things again, this time with "A Peasant Wedding," where the rustic lovers dance a *pas de deux*. Watching the dance and eying the peasant girl, Don Juan, to reassure himself after the incident with the Lady in White, determines to seduce her. In the midst of the Don's conquest of the girl, Doña Ana enters and watches. She knows everything that is happening at once but is so in thrall to the Don that it does not seem to matter. The Don amuses himself by playing the two ladies against each other.

As a climax to his satirical presentation, Catalinon and the dancers present "The Damnation of Don Juan," which develops into an orgy involving all the guests.

Don Juan leaves the party, pursuing the Lady in White. He passes a proces-sion of mourners carrying the empty bier. Doña Ana is there, weeping. Gradu-ally he realizes that this is his own funeral cortege. As the Lady in White now beckons to him, he recognizes her as the Angel of Death.

Clive Barnes wrote in the New York *Times* after the New York premiere that "Mr. Nureyev is superb as Don Juan—from the nervous, preening way he pats his hair, to his smiling yet supercilious disdain, to his slightly nervous pride . . . The entire portrayal, morose, disenchanted and just a little foolish, is remarkable.

"The ballet shows the National Ballet of Canada at its very best and the whole performance could not have been bettered."

DON QUIXOTE

Ballet in four acts, eight scenes, and a prologue. Music by L. Minkus. Chore-ography by Marius Petipa. First presented by the Bolshoi Theatre, Moscow, December 26, 1869. First presented in the United States by the Bolshoi Ballet at the Metropolitan Opera House, New York, April 21, 1966, with Petipa's choreography revised by Aleksandr Gorsky and Rostislav Zakharov. Scenery and costumes by Vadim Rindin. Maya Plisetskaya appeared as Kitri,

Vladimir Tikhonov as Basil the barber, Pyotr Khomutuv as Don Quixote, and Nikolai Samokhvalov as Sancho Panza.

Miguel Cervantes's masterpiece *Don Quixote* has a long ballet history. Beginning with a danced version by Noverre in the mid-eighteenth century, the story has attracted dancers and choreographers many times. The two principal versions of Cervantes's novel are described below.

PROLOGUE: DON QUIXOTE'S STUDY   Don Quixote's servants, anxious about his growing obsession with ancient chivalry, are seen trying to throw his books away. He enters, reading, and sits at his table. He rejoices in heroic tales of brave knights and beautiful ladies. In a vision, he beholds the lady of his dreams, Dulcinea. Sancho Panza enters, pursued by angry shopkeepers from whom he has stolen a goose. The Don rescues him, appoints him his squire, and sets out on his adventures.

ACT ONE: THE SQUARE IN BARCELONA   Basil, a barber, is in love with the innkeeper's daughter, Kitri, but her mother wishes her to marry Gamache, a foppish nobleman. Don Quixote arrives with Sancho. The Don assumes that the inn is a famous castle. Sancho is teased by the townsfolk and tossed in a blanket. Don Quixote rescues him. Don Quixote now sees the beautiful Kitri. He is bewitched and acclaims her as his Dulcinea.

ACT TWO, SCENE ONE: INSIDE THE INN   Kitri's mother, still determined to marry her daughter to the nobleman, so distresses Basil that he pretends to stab himself. As he lies dying, he begs Kitri's parents to unite them.

ACT TWO, SCENE TWO: A GYPSY ENCAMPMENT   Gypsies and strolling players, alerted to the imminent arrival of Don Quixote and Sancho, prepare to trick the knight. Don Quixote enters and pays homage to their leader as king. The leader then calls for dances to begin. This is followed by a command performance of the puppet theater. Watching the play, Don Quixote mistakes the heroine for Dulcinea, sees her under attack, and rises to assault the puppet stage. Pursuing her further to windmills nearby, he imagines Dulcinea is being concealed. Mistaking the windmills for menacing giants, he tilts at them, only to be caught up in one of the wings and tossed in the air. Sancho revives and comforts him.

ACT THREE, SCENE ONE: A FOREST   The Don and Sancho lie down to rest in a wood. But still stunned from his fight with the windmill, the Don is troubled by fantastic dreams where he sees himself a knight in shining armor surrounded by lovely ladies.

ACT FOUR: PROLOGUE   Hunting horns proclaim the arrival of the Duke of Barcelona, who has heard about Don Quixote and wishes to see the curious knight himself. He awakens the Don and invites him to accompany a *fiesta*. The Duke then persuades Basil to dress up and pretend to be a Knight Errant to play a trick on Don Quixote.

ACT FIVE: THE MAIN SQUARE OF BARCELONA   It is *fiesta* time. The Duke and the Duchess and the Don watch the dancing. Suddenly the Don thinks that he recognizes his Dulcinea in a girl carried on by mysterious figures guarded by a strange knight. The Knight challenges the Don to a duel and the old man is soon vanquished. His opponent, removing his disguise, reveals himself as Basil the barber. The Don is so crestfallen by this trickery that the Duke and Duchess have pity and comfort him. Kitri and Basil then celebrate their betrothal in a *grand pas de deux*. Don Quixote realizes that he has not yet found his Dulcinea and with Sancho sets off for more adventures.

NOTES   This *Don Quixote* includes the *grand pas de deux* that is often presented independently in various versions on ballet programs. The part of Kitri has been performed over the years by many famous ballerinas, Pavlova and Karsavina among them. Pavlova produced a shortened version of the ballet for her tours. Rudolf Nureyev produced his version of the Petipa ballet for the Vienna State Opera on December 1, 1966, himself appearing as *Basil* with Ully Wuehrer as *Kitri*, Michael Birkmeyer as *Don Quixote*, and Konstantin Zajetz as *Sancho Panza*.

In 1970, Nureyev staged his version of the ballet with the Australian Ballet in a production designed by Barry Kay. This production was first presented in the United States by the Australian Ballet in San Francisco, January 4, 1971. In 1972, Nureyev and Robert Helpmann made a film of this production.

Interviewed by Laura Bell for *Show* magazine in 1971 about certain aspects of his production of *Don Quixote*, Nureyev commented about the duel between the Don and his foppish rival Don Gamache: "The duel is mine but the stabbing is all in the original Petipa, and in the book. There, you may remember, it is even broader. Basilio has a bladder of sheep's blood hidden under his arm and when he stabs it, blood spurts everywhere. I decided this was going a bit far in literalness, and it would be messy. The duel, though, was originally between the knight and the heroine's father, an innkeeper. But I think it proper Don Quixote should fight his own kind, not a commoner, so I have him fight Don Gamache, who, in the bargain, is wearing the proper white gauntlets to throw down. I try all through to keep the six main characters together, playing off each other, as in *commedia dell'arte*—you can even match up characters. Quixote is Pantalon, Kitri is Columbine; Basilio, Pierrot, and so on. I wanted the story not to be about Don Quixote but about how people react to him, how they take advantage of him and devise ways to mock and laugh at him. Yet they go crazy doing this, they are as fanatic as the knight is.

"And Don Quixote himself . . . At first, I hated him quite a lot. I didn't understand for a long time. I was on the side of the people. To me he was just a clown. And then I read the book! There is so much there, but in a ballet you can only skim the surface. I tried to put in a lot of things I felt about the book, like impressions of the Callot lithographs, but you daren't put too much comment in. It really is largely a lot of dances and great zest and comic spirit . . . and yet, everybody seems to think of this ballet as kind of foolish.

"I can't take any credit for these productions which I do only to provide another vehicle for myself and to preserve what is left of Petipa. With *Don Qui-*

xote I wanted a comic part and since no choreographer has ever offered me one, I did this. With original choreography you have to sit down and think and spend a lot of time. I do *not* like improvisations. If you want to create a ballet, you have to have a certain point of view, something you want to say, not just steps or variations that just 'come' to you. And even with *Raymonda* and *Don Quixote*, they took a lot of working out and research. Perhaps in time . . ."

A film of Nureyev's production of *Don Quixote* was made in Australia in 1972 with the Australian Ballet. Codirected by Nureyev and Sir Robert Helpmann, the film starred Lucette Aldous as Kitri-Dulcinea and Nureyev as Basilio. It was first presented in the United States, November 1, 1973, at a Gala Benefit for the Dance Collection of the New York Public Library.

Ballet in three acts. Music by Nicolas Nabokov. Choreography by George Balanchine. Scenery, costumes, and lighting by Esteban Francés. Assistant to Mr. Francés: Peter Harvey. Costumes executed by Karinska. First presented by the New York City Ballet at the New York State Theatre, May 27, 1965, with George Balanchine as Don Quixote, *Suzanne Farrell as* Dulcinea, Deni Lamont as Sancho Panza, *and the entire company.*

I first read Cervantes in Russian, but I have read parts of *Don Quixote* many times since, in English and French as well. The idea of doing a ballet about the Don has always seemed to me natural and inevitable, something I would want to do whenever time and opportunity came. Other ballets to *Don Quixote* I had perhaps seen but scarcely remembered. The Petipa ballet, with music by Minkus, was in the repertory of the Maryinsky when I was a boy (I danced in this production in 1916, when I was twelve), but it was not a serious work and not one of my favorites. Twenty years ago I discovered that my friend the composer Nicolas Nabokov had a similar enthusiasm for *Don Quixote*. He had written an orchestral suite on the Don and Dulcinea which I liked. We then spoke of doing a full-scale ballet on the subject one day, but it was some years before this came about. We began to work out a scenario in detail. We did several scenarios, in fact, arriving at a final one in June 1964. Throughout the composition of the score we were in frequent communication and saw each other as often as possible to discuss the music and the action. As a musician with a deep knowledge of ballet, Nabokov knew what he was getting into. Three-act ballets are difficult compositions. Nabokov's score has everything, it *has* to have everything to do its job properly, for music written to accompany a danced narrative with *divertissements* cannot preserve the unities designed for the concert hall. Nabokov worked within three traditions, the musical one, the ballet tradition, and the dramatic. His score in essence amounts to symphonic dance variations.

The action of the ballet follows closely the scenario Nabokov and I worked out together.

The form the novel took for us naturally does not follow the sequence of the book, but I must say we never had any difficulty in our ideas. The problem was always what we had to cut and put aside. Don Quixote's anguished search

for human perfectibility, the intricate shifts from fantasy to reality that take
place in his mind, are vividly expressed through his adventures and the dream
of the Lady Dulcinea, who appears in many guises to him. Guises these always
are—the Magdalen, the Virgin Mary, the Shepherdess Marcela, the Lady
of the Silver Moon—and although he gives his whole life for her, he never really sees her. He is, if you like, a kind of secular saint whom no one believes
in. Finally, his death brings him face to face with himself, seemingly defeated,
but having lived as he believed.

PROLOGUE: DON QUIXOTE'S STUDY   Don Quixote sits alone and reads his
books about chivalry. He searches through them for the answers to his dreams
of knight errantry. He falls off to sleep. A mist covers the stage and strange
figures from his dream take over the scene: a girl seems to materialize right out
of the pages of a book; a dragon appears. The Don rescues the girl. He rests.
A young girl, a maidservant, enters and washes his feet, drying them with her
hair. He kisses her forehead and she leaves and Don Quixote rises.
Sancho Panza enters carrying the Don's clothes, does a pratfall but quickly
rises to dress his master. The Don, with sword held high, follows the girl toward the brilliant sun she has let into the room. This is the only sun he will
see. As Cervantes said, "Misfortunes always pursue men of talent." Don Quixote's study is now transformed, becoming:

ACT ONE, SCENE ONE: LA MANCHA   Don Quixote stands alone surrounded by
earth and sky. Windmills in the distance. In the piercing light of midday there
appears to him a vision of the Madonna, a girl with a resplendent headdress
standing on a cart much as if a statue of the Virgin being carried in a village
procession has suddenly come to life. It is the servant girl of the Prologue. He
kneels before the vision, takes the oath of a knight, and receives the Madonna's blessing.
Don Quixote encounters a child being beaten by a man. He challenges the
man and chases him off. The rescued child runs away, mocking the Don. Next
he comes upon a group of prisoners being led in chains. He attacks the jailers
and frees the men, who thereupon set upon the Don and Sancho and give
them a good trouncing.

ACT ONE, SCENE TWO: A VILLAGE SQUARE   There are folk dances in front of
an inn. Sancho runs out, pursued by guards and fishwives from whom he has
stolen a huge fish. He is caught, beaten up, and tossed in a blanket. Don Quixote appears on his horse, dismounts and liberates Sancho. Sancho kneels at his
feet, weeping. The Innkeeper brings food and the Don comforts Sancho. A
cortege enters. A poet is being mourned. A beautiful country girl, Marcela, is
seized and accused of causing his death. We see that she is the same girl as in
the first scenes, dressed now as a shepherdess with a long crook. She is grateful to the Don and dances. In Cervantes, she explains that she is not to be
blamed for the poet's death: "If every beauty inspired love and won hearts,
men's fancy would become vague and bewildered and not know where to stop,
for as beauty is infinite, desire must likewise be infinite. If this is so, as I be-

lieve it to be, why do you ask me to surrender my will under pressure for no other reason than that you say you love me? For beauty in a modest woman is like distant fire or a sharp sword; the one does not burn, the other does not cut the man who does not go near it. Now if modesty is one of the virtues and the fairest ornament of the body and the soul, why must the woman who is loved for her beauty lose it to gratify the desires of a man who, for his pleasure alone, tries with all his strength and ingenuity to rob her of it? I was born free, and to live free I chose the solitude of the fields. The trees of those mountains are my companions; with the trees and the brooks I share my thoughts and my beauty. I am the hidden fire and the distant sword . . ."

Now a puppeteer comes into the courtyard with his cart and arranges his puppet show. In the midst of the show Don Quixote becomes indignant about what he sees. Here again is the tiny blond heroine who emerged from his books. To him, she is Dulcinea and when he sees her being persecuted by Saracens, he charges the puppet show with his sword. The puppet theater falls down on his head. Just then, to solemn music, heralds announce the arrival of the Duke and Duchess of the region. The Duchess observes the wreckage of the theater and orders it cleared out. She congratulates the Don on his victorious adventure with the puppet. Supported by Sancho, Don Quixote kneels before her. Recognizing him from Cervantes's book, the Duchess gives him wine and invites him to come to the castle. He is lifted onto his horse, Sancho mounts the donkey, and the villagers wave them farewell.

ACT TWO: THE PALACE   The curtain rises on the sumptuous ballroom of the Duke's palace. Don Quixote enters with the Duchess, who places him to her right as she sits on the throne. He stands by her side like a true gentleman. Courtiers enter and as they bow to the royal couple, they also pay mocking deference to Don Quixote, sensing the joke the Duchess is playing on the knight. The courtiers and their ladies now dance a stylized courtly ballet: first, a sarabande by the entire assembly, then a series of danced *divertissements: a danza della Cacia*, a *pas de deux Mauresque*, a *Courante Sicilienne*, a *Rigaudon Flamenco*, and a *ritournel*. Now eight masked men enter. The Duchess whispers to the Duke. All salute as Don Quixote escorts the Duchess down to the dance floor to dance a *pavane*. The court has decided to end the charade they have been playing with the Don. Sancho senses this and tries to take the Don away, but the courtiers close in on them. They are blindfolded, tickled by ladies' fans, pricked by swords. A wooden horse is brought in, they are placed on it, fireworks are set off in its tail and at the explosion Don Quixote and Sancho fall to the ground, where they are beaten. There then appears to Don Quixote a vision of Dulcinea. The whole court freezes like waxworks. She gestures to him, seems to be calling to him to renew his adventures. He lays his sword at her feet and kneels before her. Dulcinea helps him up and just as Don Quixote is about to follow her, a masked lady approaches and beards him with whipped cream, a final mockery. He ignores her scorn and in a trance stumbles after Dulcinea to start again on his quest.

ACT THREE, SCENE ONE: A GARDEN OF THE PALACE   The Don and Sancho enter. They lie down to rest under an old oak tree. He sleeps and begins to dream. Masked courtiers arrive and cover him with a fishing net. Dulcinea appears. In his dream he sees a ballet in the Elysian fields. In the midst of the dancing is the Lady of the Silver Moon in whom is embodied "all the impossible and chimerical attributes of beauty which poets give to their ladies." There follows a classical *pas d'action,* consisting of a set of four variations, a *pas de deux* and a coda. Dulcinea is challenged by a girl in black, the Night Spirit, reminiscent of the Duchess, and tormented by the magician Merlin. She goes to Don Quixote, and he rouses himself to help her. As he does so, dragging the net behind him, the magic landscape of his dream vanishes. He is alone on an empty field with mills turning their big wheels in the wind and seeming to move ominously toward him and Dulcinea.

ACT THREE, SCENE TWO   A huge giant bears down on Don Quixote as high as a windmill. The Don attacks him but his long lance is caught in a sail of the windmill and he is tossed high into the air and falls back to earth. Sancho runs to him and binds his head. Strange creatures cross the stage; like pigs they swarm all over the place. Now four courtiers of the Duchess disguised in masks bring in a wooden cage. Don Quixote crawls into it like a wounded dog. Weeping, Sancho follows, holding his master's sword.

ACT THREE, SCENE THREE: DON QUIXOTE'S STUDY   To a *pavane funèbre* the Don is carried to his home. He is taken from the cage and undressed for bed. He asks for the last rites of the Church. In his delirium he sees a procession of Bishops, Cardinals, monks, earls, and dukes, all hooded figures, march in to a Gloria. His books are burned by these Inquisitors. Then, in another vision, he sees again the vision with which his adventures began, the Madonna of the cart, the lovely blond girl with a halo. He reaches out to her yearningly, rises high in his bed as if by a miracle, she looks at him, then vanishes. The hooded figures are grouped around his bed as in the painting of the burial of the Count d'Orgaz by El Greco. But in a changing light, they are changed into the simple people of his village, the serving girl, the priest, Sancho. He recognizes them, blesses them, and dies quietly as the first lights of dawn come through the open window. The servant girl makes a cross of two sticks, places it on his body, and kneels to weep at his side. ". . . If he like a madman lived, at least he like a wise man died," said Cervantes.

NOTES   My interest in *Don Quixote* has always been in the hero's finding an ideal, something to live for and sacrifice for and serve. Every man has a Don Quixote in him. Every man wants an inspiration. For the Don it was Dulcinea, a woman he sought in many guises. I myself think that the same is true in life, that everything a man does he does for his ideal woman. You live only one life and you believe in something and I believe in that.

For criticism of this ballet, readers may wish to consult "The Story of 'Don Quixote'" by Elena Bivona in *Ballet Review,* Vol. 2, No. 2; and Andrew Porter's review of the 1973 performances of the ballet in *The New Yorker,* reprinted in his book *A Musical Season.*

The composer Nicolas Nabokov contributed to the January 1973 edition of the New York City Ballet program *Playbill* an entertaining and informative essay about his career and our collaboration on this ballet. His autobiography *Bagazh*, like his earlier book of recollections, *Old Friends and New Music*, is a fascinating account of his remarkable career.

DOUGLA

Music by Geoffrey Holder, arranged by Tania Leon. Choreography by Geoffrey Holder. Scenery and costumes by Geoffrey Holder. First presented by the Dance Theatre of Harlem at the ANTA Theatre, New York, April 20, 1974.

Dougla is a colorful, exotic dance ballet about an Asian and African marriage—a mix of Hindu and African ritual set to drumming music. The theme is: "Where Twains meet, where Hindu and African tangle, their offspring are called Dougla."

There are five parts to the ballet: "Dougla People," "Woman in Green," "Pas de Deux," "Women in Black," and "Acrobats," with the full company again on stage for a "Dougla People" finale.

When the Dance Theatre of Harlem conquered London in their first appearances there in 1974, the critic Peter Williams wrote in *Dance and Dancers* magazine: "What was shown during the season was quite enough to prove Arthur Mitchell's point which is that black dancers *can* take their rightful place in all areas of dance; it also proved what an incredible feat it was to have achieved all this in five years."

THE DREAM

Ballet in one act. Music by Felix Mendelssohn, arranged by John Lanchbery. Choreography by Frederick Ashton. Scenery by Henry Bardon. Costumes by David Walker. Lighting by William Bundy. First presented by the Royal Ballet at the Royal Opera House, Covent Garden, April 2, 1964, with Antoinette Sibley as Titania, Anthony Dowell as Oberon, Keith Martin as Puck, Alexander Grant as Bottom, Carole Needham as Helena, Vergie Derman as Hermia, David Drew as Demetrius, Derek Rencher as Lysander, and Alan Bauch as the Changeling Indian Boy. First presented in the United States by the Royal Ballet at the Metropolitan Opera House, New York, April 30, 1965, with the same cast, with Rennie Dilena as the Changeling Indian Boy.

Frederick Ashton arranged his ballet to *A Midsummer Night's Dream* for the Royal Ballet's observance of the four-hundredth anniversary of Shakespeare's

* See also A MIDSUMMER NIGHT'S DREAM.

birth. Based on Shakespeare's play, using Mendelssohn's music, the ballet tells the magical story of the quarrel between the King and Queen of Fairyland and its outcome.

The King and Queen, Oberon and Titania, quarrel over the Changeling Indian Boy. Whom shall he belong to? Oberon sends his sprite Puck through the forest to pluck a strange flower, the juice of which when dropped in the eyes during sleep brings love for the first living thing seen on waking. Oberon plans to use this drug to spite Titania. Into the forest meanwhile have strayed a happy pair of lovers, Lysander and Hermia, and their unhappy friends Helena and Demetrius. Helena's desire for Demetrius is unrequited, for he mistakenly desires Hermia. Oberon has watched these mortals, and when Puck returns with the magic flower he sends him with the potion to charm Demetrius into love with Helena.

Now Oberon drops some of the charm into his Queen's eyes and causes her to be awakened by a rustic called Bottom on whom the returning Puck, to heighten his master's revenge, has fixed an ass's head. On waking, Titania at once falls in love with Bottom the Ass, but Puck, for all his cleverness, has complicated the affairs of the other, mortal lovers by charming the wrong man, Lysander, into love with Helena. Oberon commands Puck to create a fog, under cover of which all that is awry is magically put right. Titania, released from her spell, is reconciled to her master and the mortal lovers are happily paired off. Bottom, restored to human form but with dreamlike memories of what lately happened to him, goes on his puzzled way.

NOTES   *The Dream* was staged by John Hart for the City Center Joffrey Ballet in 1973. The first performance, at the Wolf Trap Performing Arts Center in Virginia, near Washington, D.C., August 9, featured Rebecca Wright, Burton Taylor, Russell Sultzbach, Larry Grenier, Alaine Haubert, Charthel Arthur, Robert Talmage, Robert Thomas, Richard Coleman, Robert Estner, Phillip Hoffman, Jeffrey Hughes, Ted Nelson, Donna Cowen, Denise Jackson, Eileen Brady, Diane Orio, and Vinod Sahl. Writing of this production after its first New York performance (October 9, 1973), Clive Barnes said in the New York *Times:* "Ever since Ashton created *The Dream* for Britain's Royal Ballet nearly ten years ago, it has been one of that company's special treasures. This new production, authoritatively staged by John Hart, is a charmer, full of the original's mixture of Shakespeare, poetry, Mendelssohn, moonshine and fun. It is an extraordinarily English ballet, but the New York dancers have adopted it for their own.

"The costumes, fanciful and glamorous, are the same as David Walker designed for the original production, but Mr. Walker has devised a completely new setting to replace the earlier scenery by Henry Bardon. The setting, a sylvan glade, looks appropriately Victorian, but does not have the full romantic exuberance of the Royal Ballet's first staging. Yet what is more important is the style of the dancing, and here the Joffrey company does splendidly.

"Rebecca Wright made a Titania of glistening eyes and the most entrancing delicate footwork. It was a performance of gossamer and thistledown. As Oberon, Burton Taylor—making his welcome return to the stage after nearly two years off through injury—danced cleanly and forcefully. His presence was admirable, his partnering secure and his elegance always completely natural."

DRUMS, DREAMS AND BANJOS

Music by Stephen Foster; variations and orchestrations by Peter Link. Choreography by Gerald Arpino. Set by Rouben Ter-Arutunian. Costumes by Stanley Simmons. Lighting by Thomas Skelton. Vocalist: Charles Leighton. First presented by the City Center Joffrey Ballet at the City Center, New York, October 9, 1975, with a cast headed by Charthel Arthur and Dermot Burke. Conductor: Seymour Lipkin.

"He set a nation singing," wrote Harold Vincent Milligan in his biography of Stephen Foster; *Drums, Dreams and Banjos* is the Joffrey Ballet's bicentennial tribute. In 1951, President Truman issued a proclamation designating January 13, 1952, and each succeeding January 13 throughout the years as Stephen Foster Memorial Day, calling upon all to observe that occasion with appropriate ceremonies, pilgrimages to the shrines of this beloved composer, and musical programs featuring his compositions. Gerald Arpino's ballet celebrates the Stephen Foster achievement, expressing in both dance and music the sentiment as well as the energy and ebullience of his work.

A Joint Resolution of the House of Representatives some years ago referred to Foster and his work as "a national expression of democracy through his clear and simple embodiment of American tradition" and called him the "father of American folk music and the true interpreter of the fundamental spirit of music."

Recalling as it does the charms of an earlier America, Foster's music has extraordinary appeal. Born in Pittsburgh on the fiftieth anniversary of the Declaration of Independence, Foster lived to hear his music flourish throughout the land. His infectious songs, introduced by such groups as the Christy Minstrels, quickly became a part of our heritage. They were sung by pioneers on the long trek westward, hummed by harvesters in the fields and by workers laying the first railroad lines. The forty-niners whistled "Oh! Susanna" while prospecting for gold in California; his songs were favorites of soldiers on both sides during the Civil War.

Besides his own large body of work, Foster arranged the songs of some of the great European contemporaries—Bellini, Donizetti, Strauss—for inclusion in his anthology *The Social Orchestra*. One of the aims of that successful volume was to "improve the taste of the community for social music."

The Stephen Foster songs that are danced to in the ballet are "Angelina Baker," "Old Folks at Home," "Oh! Boys Carry Me 'Long," "Nelly Bly," "Farewell My Lilly Dear," "Plantation Jig," "Open Thy Lattice, Love," "Anadolia," "Some Folks," "I Will Be True to Thee," "Ah, May the Red Rose Live Alway," "Eulalie," "Oh! Susanna," "Camptown Races," "Jeannie with the Light Brown Hair," "Old Black Joe," "Ring de Banjo," "My Old Kentucky Home," "Beautiful Dreamer," "Soiree Polka," and "Tioga Waltz." Taken from

The Social Orchestra are "Oh! Summer Night" by Donizetti and a waltz by Strauss.

The dance and dramatic action of the stage panorama to the vivid score that was arranged to this memorable music reminds us not only of the familiar tunes but the times they were created in and the times they have lived through. As such, it reminds us of years of war as well as peace, years that Foster has made memorable.

THE DUEL (Le Combat)

Ballet in one act. Music by Raffaello de Banfield. Choreography by William Dollar. Costumes by Robert Stevenson. Lighting by Jean Rosenthal. First presented by the New York City Ballet Company at the City Center, New York, February 24, 1950, with Melissa Hayden and William Dollar, Val Buttignol, Walter Georgov, Shaun O'Brien. This ballet is an extensive revision of the same choreographer's Le Combat, which was performed for the first time in the United States by Les Ballets de Paris at the Winter Garden, New York, October 6, 1949.

This short, dramatic ballet tells the story of the brave Christian warrior Tancred and the pagan girl Clorinda: how they meet, fall in love, separate, and meet again for a final, fatal encounter. A low beating of the drum and subdued fanfares—heard as if from some distant battlefield—introduce the warlike rhythms that dominate the ballet.

The curtain rises on a scene that might represent any barren field. Rocks are clustered on the left, there are no trees, and a bright sky exposes the wasteland. Four Crusaders stand poised for action against any intruder. All are armored and wear high-plumed helmets with visors that conceal their faces. One of them, the warrior in red, is the leader, Tancred. They begin to dance, holding out their arms to control invisible reins, jumping and turning, practicing their skills in battle. They are all obedient to Tancred's command.

A strange warrior enters and approaches. The four Crusaders stand in line, ready to attack. The stranger is dressed in black. This is Clorinda, the beautiful Saracen. From her golden helmet streams a green scarf lined with red. Her movements are direct and unafraid; she is not in the least terrified of the enemy. She comes nearer to the group. The men stand motionless until finally the daring Clorinda challenges one of the Crusaders. He moves out of line and engages her in battle; the other men observe their code of honor by refusing to assist him. The two warriors rush each other swiftly, jumping high as they pass back and forth. Clorinda gains the upper hand and wounds her opponent mortally; and he falls over on his face. She dances around his body on firm points, her head held high. During the duel, her helmet had fallen off, and the long black hair that hangs down to her shoulders accentuates her proud beauty. Tancred walks toward her, obviously moved both by her bravery and her loveliness. He takes off his helmet and bows in tribute. Clorinda does not respond. She leaves the scene. Blackout.

Tancred enters alone. He dances, to reveal his superior strength and agility as a prince of warriors, and exits. Clorinda follows him. Now she is dressed in full battle array, with a visored helmet topped with a black plume. She leaps around the stage lightly, glorying in her own adroitness. Suddenly she stops; she senses danger. Two Christian warriors appear before her. She leaps into the air as they rush by closely, trying to enclose her. The drum beats in staccato rhythm. Clorinda does not hesitate in her attack, and soon the Crusaders weary of their effort to maneuver her into a dangerous position. She drives them off.

Clorinda relaxes for a moment and briefly shows herself to be a beautiful and pathetic girl, exhausted by the strenuousness of war. She holds her hand up beseechingly and opens her arms wide, as if she were praying for relief from the life she has chosen. She holds her head in her hands despairingly for an instant, but then she is alert again, listening for anyone who might be watching her. She crosses the stage slowly in an arrogant posture. A drum beats, loudly and suddenly. Clorinda leaps off.

Tancred enters, seeking out the enemy. He follows Clorinda. She reenters the field, the Crusader close behind. Neither recognizes the other. They begin to fight, standing close together at first, then separating to each side of the stage, then approaching each other warily. Tancred supports Clorinda and turns her as she assumes first a tight, aggressive pose, then an open arabesque. Now the duel becomes earnest as the two adversaries dodge and jump aside from their strong thrusts. Clorinda wounds Tancred, but this only encourages the Crusader. He stabs the girl as they engage in close contest. She falters in pain. They separate, preparing for the finish. They approach slowly. The girl falls. Tancred stands back. She pulls off her helmet. He sees her face; his own face is shocked with recognition. He holds out his hands helplessly, then takes off his own helmet and goes to her. He lifts her to him, and in her agony and love Clorinda's body curls in his arms. Tancred stands and pulls Clorinda up. She leans against him, her head on his shoulder, and he turns her in arabesque. Her movements are now automatic. She seems not to have the strength to move at all, and yet she wishes to reassure Tancred of her own love. But she is tired. He carries her in his arms; her body stiffens, her legs beat in a final spasm, and she is dead. Tancred places her body on the ground softly and stands over her. As he grieves, he remembers the long battle he has just begun. He picks her up and carries her off.

DUMBARTON OAKS (A Little Musical)

Music by Igor Stravinsky. Choreography by Jerome Robbins. Costumes by Patricia Zipprodt. Lighting by Ronald Bates. First presented by the New York City Ballet at the New York State Theatre, Lincoln Center, June 23, 1972, with Allegra Kent and Anthony Blum in the leading roles.

Dumbarton Oaks is the name of a nice old house in Washington, D.C., with magnificent gardens. Actually, all the house is not old, only a bit of it, but there have been important additions (the place houses a superb museum of pre-Columbian sculpture, a center for Byzantine studies, and a great library). Mr. and Mrs. Robert Woods Bliss, who bought this property and endowed it, were wonderful patrons of the arts for Washington and for the nation. In 1937 they commissioned Stravinsky to write a piece for their thirtieth wedding anniversary. The first performance was led by Nadia Boulanger at Dumbarton Oaks, May 8, 1938, and Stravinsky's *Concerto in E Flat* for chamber orchestra has been named for the place ever since.

The score is in three movements. The instruments of the chamber orchestra are treated as solo instruments and there is much variety in what Eric Walter White calls a work that "is gay and exhilarating in its effect."

The ballet is a dance to this music, with a theme. The theme is a recollection of time past, perhaps the 1920s, when a house like Dumbarton Oaks enjoyed a new lease on its lively history. The setting is wicker chairs, garden trellises with Japanese lanterns, and a tennis court in the background.

The piece begins with an ensemble of six couples, boys and girls in various combinations, who wear typical sporting dress of the 1920s (headbands for the girls, etc.). As they leave, a couple keen on tennis come into the picture. They put aside their tennis rackets and dance a vivacious *pas de deux*, syncopated and responsive to the music of the score's *Allegretto*. What starts out to be, at one point, sentimental, in the love duet returns to the flirtatious. From a recumbent posture, the girl picks up her tennis racket again and, as if a match were ended, shakes hands with her partner. Serious though it has seemed to be, the game is still the thing.

In the last movement, marked by Stravinsky *Con moto*, six boys tap-dance to a march with six girls. The lead boy then rushes in, finds the lead girl, and together they and the ensemble conclude a brisk finale to a *Fugato* climax.

NOTES   It is of interest that during the composition of this work, Stravinsky studied and played Bach regularly. He was greatly attracted, he writes in *Themes and Episodes*, to the Brandenburg Concertos, especially the third, "which I have also conducted. The first theme of my concerto is, of course, very much like Bach's in that work, and so is my instrumentation—the three violins and three violas, both frequently *divisi a tre*, though not chordally as in Bach. I do not think, however, that Bach would have begrudged me the loan of these ideas and materials, as borrowing in this way was something he liked to do himself."

The original costumes for this work were abandoned soon after its first performances during the New York City Ballet's Stravinsky Festival. It has been performed since in practice clothes.

Reviewing the ballet's entry into the regular repertory of the New York City Ballet, February 9, 1973, Clive Barnes wrote in the New York *Times*:

"On Friday night the New York City Ballet at the New York State Theatre gave everyone a surprise. A small surprise, but a surprise. It was the first repertory performance of Jerome Robbins's ballet *Dumbarton Oaks*. When this was originally given last summer at the Stravinsky Festival, it had an anyone-for-tennis setting. Now the work has been transposed to the ballet studio. Tennis rackets are out, and toe shoes are in.

"This strong but lighthearted work has taken the transposition well. The setting, which had a definite air of improvisation to it, could be improved and should be, for this is a most agreeable work. There is a playful flirtatiousness to the choreography, which is perfectly apt for this breezy, jazz-tinctured score. The ballet was fluently danced by a cast led by Allegra Kent and, dancing the role for the first time, Jean-Pierre Bonnefous."

DUO CONCERTANTE

Music by Igor Stravinsky. Choreography by George Balanchine. First presented by the New York City Ballet at the Stravinsky Festival, 1972, at the New York State Theatre, Lincoln Center, June 22, 1972, with Kay Mazzo and Peter Martins as the dancers, Lamar Alsop and Gordon Boelzner as the musicians. Lighting by Ronald Bates.

This work for violin and piano was composed by Stravinsky in the early thirties. It is a short piece in five movements and a marvelously lyrical one in several of its parts. It is not surprising that the composition of the *Duo Concertante* was associated in Stravinsky's mind with a book on the classical poet Petrarch by his friend Cingria, which appeared about the time he was writing this music. Stravinsky in one of his recollections quotes this passage from Cingria: "Lyricism cannot exist without rules, and it is essential that they should be strict. Otherwise there is only a faculty for lyricism, and that exists everywhere. What does not exist everywhere is lyrical expression and composition. To achieve that, a craftsman's skill is necessary and that must be learned."

This is exactly a thought I have tried so unsuccessfully to say myself on a number of occasions and it is wonderful to find it so finely expressed in connection with a composition I so much admire.

I am trying to recall the first time I heard the *Duo Concertante*. It was, I think, in France in a performance by Samuel Dushkin, the violinist, and the composer himself, both of whom in the early thirties toured Europe performing Stravinsky's music. It has always been a favorite of mine and when we were planning the Stravinsky Festival at the New York City Ballet, I decided to make a ballet to the music.

The less I say about the ballet, the more I think you may enjoy watching it. It is nothing very unusual, only two dancers, a girl and a boy, standing on stage next to a piano, where the two musicians begin to play. The dancers listen intently; we listen to them. The music for piano and violin is questioning at first, then declarative, open; it then tightens in rhythm and assertiveness of melody. Before we know it, the dancers are moving to the music. Sometimes they stop to listen. The second movement, Ecloque I, begins with a jocular tune and develops into a brisk dialogue between the two instruments. In Ecloque II, the violin takes the lead and in a slowly paced cadenza sings an idyll. For the fourth movement, there is a vigorous and lively Gigue. The stage darkens for the finale, the Dithyramb. Eric Walter White calls this a "noble rhapsody . . . a movement of grave beauty. The high-pitched violin part leads the piano into an increasingly elaborate passage. . . . The effect is that of an exalted threnody." The stage darkens for this music, one spotlight shining on the two musicians, another on the two dancers. The lights close down about the artists as the music ends.

A girl and a boy, a piano and violin. Perhaps, as Lincoln Kirstein says, that is what ballet is all about.

NOTES   Reviewing this ballet in *The Nation*, Nancy Goldner wrote: "*Duo Concertante,* for piano and violin, is one of the most beautiful duets Balanchine has ever done. As a metaphor on the idea that the festival celebrates music, Mazzo and Martins listen to the musicians, who are on the stage, almost as much as they dance. Watching them listen is a theatrical experience in itself. Their faces speak a multitude of unknown thoughts, but the intensity and sweet concentration with which they listen suggest that the notes are running through their bodies. Finally, they are moved to dance. At first they stick closely to the music's beat, almost 'conducting' it with arms and legs; torsos are still.

"Becoming more free, the dance turns into a melting duet, each phrase winding down on slightly bent knees, as in a whisper. They dance with seeming spontaneity. Even when Balanchine arranges an unusual means of partnering—as when Martins scoops her from the floor holding only the underside of her thigh—the movement spins off them with utter simplicity and naturalness. In other sections, they occasionally stop dancing to listen. At those times, Martins firmly takes hold of her hand or slips his arm around her waist. She is shy, but the music pleases her and so does he. She does not move away. They listen in repose, arm in arm. In the last part, the stage darkens except for a white spotlight. She places her arm in the light and raises it above her head. No longer is it her arm; it exists independently, like a segment of a statue. He kisses the back of her hand, a supplicant at the throne of beauty. She is now a goddess-ballerina; he, her servant. She steps out of the light. He steps into it. Not finding her, he leaves. She returns. He kisses her hand again. The jump from intimate hand-holding to ceremonial hand-kissing is theatrically daring. It is also inevitable, and those who cannot accept the leap or the brazen display of sentiment cannot ultimately accept one of the underlying themes of Balanchine's work. In his most noble ballets, he elevates the dancer into an image of love, a Muse-ballerina who inspires but is unreachable. And so this ending is an apotheosis of Balanchine's art."

DYBBUK VARIATIONS

Music by Leonard Bernstein. Choreography by Jerome Robbins. Scenery by Rouben Ter-Arutunian. Costumes by Patricia Zipprodt. Lighting by Jennifer Tipton. First presented by the New York City Ballet at the New York State

Theatre, Lincoln Center, May 15, 1974, with Patricia McBride and Helgi Tomasson as the principals and a cast headed by Bart Cook, Victor Castelli, Tracy Bennett, Hermes Conde, Daniel Duell, Stephen Caras, Nolan T'Sani, Peter Naumann, Muriel Aasen, and Stephanie Saland. Conducted by Leonard Bernstein. Baritone: David Johnson. Bass: John Ostendorf.

The composer Leonard Bernstein and the choreographer Jerome Robbins first conceived of the idea of a ballet to the dybbuk theme in 1944, at the time of their first brilliant collaboration, *Fancy-Free*. A dybbuk, in Central-European Jewish folklore, is a dead but restless spirit that enters and persists in the body of a living person. The possessed body acts and speaks with the voice and behavior of the dead one. The most famous treatment of the theme is the play by S. Ansky, *The Dybbuk*, renowned in its original Yiddish version and through many subsequent international productions, among them the Habimah presentation in New York in the 1940s. The restless spirit dominates the action.

Jerome Robbins has said that the ballet is not a retelling of Ansky's play, "but uses it only as a point of departure for a series of related dances concerning rituals and hallucinations which are present in the dark magico-religious ambience of the play and in the obsessions of its characters."

An understanding of the play is useful background to the ballet. It tells the story: In friendship, two young men pledge that their children will wed each other, should one have a son and the other a daughter. The friends part and go out into the world, where each marries and has a child, boy and girl, as hoped for. Chanon and Leah meet when grown and, unaware of their parents' commitment, fall in love. But because Leah is from a wealthy family and Chanon is a poor but devoutly orthodox theological student, their love is undeclared. Chanon is also regarded as a wanderer and seeker of truths that are perhaps best always hidden.

Leah's father arranges a suitable match for her; Chanon desperately turns to the Kabbala, book of mystic wisdom and dark magic. (This text, developed by rabbis from about the seventh to the eighteenth centuries, was based on a mystical technique of interpreting Scripture; by this method the initiated were empowered to foretell the future and penetrate sacred mysteries.) He seeks in the Kabbala for a way in which to win Leah for himself. As a last resort, he invokes the powerful but dangerous other-worldly formulae of ancient usage. At the supreme moment of discovering the secret words that unleash the dark forces, he is overwhelmed by the enormity of it, faints and dies.

At Leah's wedding, Chanon returns to her as a dybbuk and, claiming her as his rightful bride, clings to his beloved. Finally, through prescriptive counterrituals instituted by elders of the religious community, Chanon is placed under formal ecclesiastical curse and the dybbuk is expelled. Leah, unable to survive without her predestined bridegroom, dies to join him.

Throughout the Ansky play, a supernatural being called "The Messenger" is an omniscient and prophetic witness to each evolving phase of the drama.

The action of the ballet is divided into eleven parts: 1) IN THE HOLY PLACE: Variations for Seven Men; 2) THE PLEDGE: Male duet; two couples; three couples; 3) ANGELIC MESSENGERS: Variations for three men; 4) THE DREAM: *Pas de*

deux; 5) INVOCATION OF THE KABBALA: the quest for secret powers; VARIATIONS:
a. Solo with six men; b.c.d.e. Soli; f. Solo with six men; 6) PASSAGE; 7)
MAIDEN'S DANCE; 8) TRANSITION; 9) POSSESSION: *Pas de deux:* allegro, adagio;
10) EXORCISM: Entire cast; 11) REPRISE AND CODA.

NOTES   Talking with *The New Yorker* about the ballet shortly before its
première, the composer, Leonard Bernstein, described how he and Jerome
Robbins had approached the dybbuk legend. "Ansky's story is a kind of ghetto
version of *The Ring of the Nibelung.* Greed versus love. A compact that is broken. Two young men pledge that their children will marry, but one of them
eventually disregards the oath because he wants a wealthy husband for his
daughter, Leah. Chanon, the son of the other man, becomes a wandering
scholar, a very *farbrente* Talmudist, and a Cabalist. He comes to this little
town, sees Leah, and, even though he doesn't know about the pledge, falls in
love and desperately tries to find Cabalistic ways of winning her. In (one)
dance . . . Chanon calls on the dark powers to help him, and at the moment
of revelation he dies, because no human vessel can contain that much fire and
knowledge and survive. His soul becomes a dybbuk and finds its resting place
in the body of his beloved. And when the rabbi exorcises the dybbuk from her
body, Leah joins him in oblivion.
". . . You have to remember that this is a story about ghetto people who
have nowhere to go, no professions they can be in, no place in the world except the isolated provincial town in which they live. They are forced in on
themselves, and they turn to their Torah and live their whole lives in terms of
that. And they get to such a point of intensity, of concern, of concentration on
their relationship with God that they come to believe the whole universe
depends on it. That is the reason behind all the diagrams, the mysticisms, and
the calculations. Where else could these people look except to heaven? Jerry
suggested a marvellous line for the program note. He said that this ballet deals
with the visions, hallucinations, and magical religious manifestations of an
oppressed people. And that's exactly it. All they had for centuries was a book
with the words of God."*
Writing after the première of *Dybbuk Variations* in *Newsweek,* the critic
Hubert Saal said: "Robbins's ballet does not tell the detailed story . . . of
S. Ansky's 1914 play, a classic of the Yiddish theatre . . . but extracts highlights
of the drama, making a superdrama of such abstractions as the conflict between light and dark, the individual and society, love and law. Sometimes what
occupies a long scene in the play takes a moment in dance—and vice versa. In
reorganizing what Ansky called a 'realistic play about mystic people,' Robbins
and Bernstein have created a work that is theatrical without being showy,
stylized without being stilted and Hebraic without being parochial.
"The eleven scenes, starkly and effectively designed by Rouben Ter-Arutunian, begin with the important mood setter, the dance of the seven elders,
who with pious grace assume the shape of a Menorah, the Jewish candela-

* From "Possession" by Jane Boutwell in "The Talk of the Town." Reprinted by
permission; © 1974 The New Yorker Magazine, Inc.

brum. Throughout the ballet they act as an irresistible force in their faith and fanaticism, embodying the inexorable power of Jehovah's Law and of social custom. Among the most dramatic scenes are the brilliant, complex variations for Chanon and his fellow scholars, who vainly try to dissuade him from the cabalistic investigation that ends in his death. Of all the dance sequences, perhaps the most satisfying is the long *pas de deux* in which the dybbuk takes possession of Leah. Their agitated bodies, trying to adjust to the violent collision of two souls, gradually fuse into one, through their love for each other.

"The climax is spine-tingling, with some magical stagecraft, as the exorcising elders force Chanon to leave the body of Leah and she abandons her own flesh to join him as pure spirit in the hereafter. As this Jewish Romeo and Juliet, the brilliant Helgi Tomasson and the radiant Patricia McBride dance with fire and tenderness.

"No one could have provided Robbins with a more resilient musical floor than Bernstein, who has remained in close touch musically with his Jewish origins. His first symphony, the 'Jeremiah,' was dedicated to his father, a noted Talmudic scholar, and his third symphony is called 'Kaddish.' With obvious eagerness, Bernstein has seized this opportunity to invent music with old-fashioned Hebrew lilt and cadence, an intonation that is part laughter, part tears, and a range from simple folk tunes to complex inversions of tone rows. . . .

"Robbins and Bernstein, two 55-year-old partners and friends, are complementary opposites. . . . Robbins emphasized that the new work is a ballet, not a play. It says things that the play doesn't. There are whole areas in the play that are non-verbal.' Bernstein was amazed by the performance of the New York City Ballet Orchestra. 'They're fantastic,' he exclaimed, 'the most wonderful theatre orchestra in the world.'

"Both men remembered the time 30 years ago when the idea for *Dybbuk Variations* came to them—standing on the stage of the old Metropolitan Opera House after the triumph of *Fancy Free*. 'I love the dark, lyric quality of Ansky's play,' says Robbins. 'The astonishing faith. Of all kinds.' Two years ago they isolated themselves in Jamaica and devoted a concentrated three weeks to finding an approach that lay between Robbins's feeling for the abstract and Bernstein's for the concrete drama. 'After that,' Bernstein says, 'I just wrote music and played it for Jerry and he would say that excites me or it doesn't.'

"Earlier Robbins had said, 'Choosing the *Dybbuk* had nothing to do with my being Jewish.' Now Bernstein said, 'In a larger sense what success we've had is based on our experience of Jewishness. Isn't that right, Jerry?' Robbins paused and said, 'I don't know,' and then smiled and added: 'But we are what we are and that feeds into it.'"

THE DYING SWAN (Le Cygne)

Music by Camille Saint-Saëns. Choreography by Michel Fokine. First produced at a concert in the Nobleman's Hall, St. Petersburg, Russia, in 1905, with Anna Pavlova. First presented in the United States at the Metropolitan Opera House, New York, March 18, 1910, by Anna Pavlova.

Perhaps the most famous of all dramatic solos for the ballerina, *The Dying Swan* shows the last minutes in the life of a stricken swan. Slowly, trembling, trying to hold on to life for a brief last flight but then giving up, she dies. It only takes about two minutes to perform. When Pavlova first danced it at the Metropolitan, Carl Van Vechten wrote that it was "the most exquisite specimen of her art which she has yet given to the public."

The choreographer, Michel Fokine, recalled that the dance was composed in a few minutes. One day Pavlova came and asked him to do a solo for her for a concert being given by artists from the chorus of the Imperial Opera. She had just become a ballerina at the Maryinsky Theatre. Fokine was at that time a mandolin enthusiast and had been playing at home—to the piano accompaniment of one of his friends—Saint-Saëns' *Swan*. He said right then, "What about Saint-Saëns' *Swan?*" She immediately realized, Fokine wrote, that a swan would be a most suitable role for her. "As I looked upon the thin, brittle-like Pavlova, I thought—she is just made for the *Swan.*" A rehearsal was arranged and the dance completed very quickly. "It was almost an improvisation. I danced in front of her, she directly behind me. Then she danced and I walked alongside her, curving her arms and correcting details of poses.

"Prior to this composition, I was accused of barefooted tendencies and of rejecting toe dancing in general. *The Dying Swan* was my answer to such criticism. This dance became the symbol of the New Russian Ballet. It was a combination of masterful technique with expressiveness. It was like a proof that the dance could and should satisfy not only the eye, but through the medium of the eye should penetrate into the soul" (*Dance Magazine*, August 1931).

In 1934 in Paris, Fokine told Arnold Haskell (see his *Balletomania*): "Small work as it is, and known and applauded all over the world, it was 'revolutionary' then, and illustrated admirably the transition between the old and the new, for here I make use of the technique of the old dance and the traditional costume, and a highly developed technique is necessary, but the purpose of the dance is not to display that technique but to create the symbol of the everlasting struggle in this life and all that is mortal. It is a dance of the whole body and not of the limbs only; it appeals not merely to the eye but to the emotions and the imagination."

The French critic André Levinson has written of *Le Cygne:* "Arms folded, on tiptoe, she dreamily and slowly circles the stage. By even, gliding motions of the hands, returning to the background from whence she emerged, she seems to strive toward the horizon, as though a moment more and she will fly—exploring the confines of space with her soul. The tension gradually relaxes and she sinks to earth, arms waving faintly as in pain. Then faltering with irregular steps toward the edge of the stage—leg bones aquiver like the strings of a harp—by one swift forward-gliding motion of the right foot to earth, she sinks on the left knee—the aerial creature struggling against earthly bonds; and there, transfixed by pain, she dies."

The dancer and teacher Hilda Butsova, who became Pavlova's leading

dancer (1912–25) in the company that toured the world, has recalled with
Marian Horosko in *Dance Magazine* the joy and hardships of those days: "It
was not that she wanted to make money or had a big ego. She wanted people
to see dance. . . . It was Anna Pavlova, and no one else, who opened the
world to ballet. It was she who did the back-breaking work of pioneering. It
was Pavlova who found and cultivated audiences for contemporary ballet companies. Her service to ballet is priceless. No other single human being did
more for ballet than she. To all the millions of people for whom she danced,
she brought a little of herself; she brought a little happiness to them all. Her
genius was as intangible as the legacy she left behind. What remains of
Pavlova today is not a movement in the art, not a tendency, not even a series
of dances. It is something far more concrete, but possibly far more valuable:
inspiration."

EARLY SONGS

*Music by Richard Strauss. Choreography by Eliot Feld. Costumes by Stan-
ley Simmons. Lighting by Jules Fisher. First presented by the American
Ballet Company at the Brooklyn Academy of Music, New York, April 5,
1970. Soprano: Eileen Shelle. Baritone: Steven Kimbrough. Pianist: Gladys
Celeste Mercader.*

Early Songs is a dance ballet arranged to fourteen songs by Richard Strauss,
songs of the composer's youth, when he wrote with fervor and passion to accompany poems he admired about love, dreams, separation, longing, despair,
night. *Early Songs* can be said to be about love and the way different young
couples are involved in it, how they show it, hide it, seek it, find it, languish in
it, rejoice in it. There is no story, only the dance and gestural images we seek
on stage. Sometimes they are reflective of the music; sometimes they suggest
things beyond the music.

The music is sung by a soprano and a baritone, accompanied by the piano.
The words are not directly relevant to the danced picture which is best seen
beyond words, in the theater. Successful dance ballets are the hardest things in
the world to describe outside their own language!

The ballet is in fourteen parts that flow together, accompanying the Strauss
songs. While an understanding of the words of the songs, which are sung in
German, is certainly not essential to enjoyment of the dances, you may wish to
listen to recordings before coming to the theater.

The curtain rises in silence on two boys and a girl. The music is quiet as the
baritone starts to sing of meadows at twilight and the pursuit of a beautiful
woman "Dream at Twilight." As the song continues in that vein, rising slowly
in intensity, one of the boys, in green, responds to the girl and the others
among the couples who materialize about him. He would be with them, but
is not, as they come and go. He is left, seeking but not finding, but not absolutely forlorn; after all, they have not rejected him: perhaps it is the other way
round.

To the tempo of the rapid "Serenade," sung by the baritone, the boy dances with a girl quick in movement and flirtatiousness. He kneels at her feet and they dance together. Her legs tremble at the beauty of it. Two other couples, the girls responding similarly to the romantic ambience, appear to attend them; the boy then lifts the girl to his shoulder and takes her off into the wings. It is not surprising that the song should invoke the nightingale dreaming of kisses and a rose that, in the morning, should remember and shine with the recollection of the night.

Four couples dance pensively to a poem about "The Star." Next, in the fourth dance, again a *pas de deux* ("Tomorrow"), a young couple move quietly together as the soprano sings of a tomorrow that will unite happy persons, who will look into each other's eyes with muted recognition of their joy. Gently, the boy carries the girl off into the wings.

The baritone sings now a bright tune ("To What End, Maiden?") in which he wonders amusingly at the deceitfulness of a young maiden. There is a dance for three couples, then just one, where the boy seems to question the girl and to find her wonderful at the same time.

"Strolling at Night" follows, under a silvery moon, where an enraptured couple dance of their intense happiness. He falls at her feet. Now, two boys and a girl, hand in hand, dance to a song ("Beautiful, Yet Cold"); the soprano sings about the beautiful but cold stars of heaven that cannot compare to the eyes of the beloved.

Next, a girl moves toward dancing couples, seeming to see a vision of her own ideal and truly finding him in her thoughts, if not in reality ("Rest, My Soul"). The girl in lonely torment is joined by a boy who makes an effort to make her forget. Gentle at first, he fails to comfort her and then almost forces her to forget. She is then in torment, held by him agonizingly and turning her face from him. They leave, her arms folded and her hands curled over her face.

Bright light comes up and five couples rush on to celebrate with the baritone the coming of spring ("Sir Spring"). Next, a boy alone dances, introspectively and thoughtful ("All My Thoughts"). Then he faces three girls. He tries to lead them in a dance ("Ah, Woe Is Me, Unhappy Man!"), partnering them one after another, but does not succeed. He is alone again at the end.

A radiant couple swirl to a song by the baritone about the uselessness of descriptions of his beloved ("Nothing"). What do we know about the sun, the giver of life and light?

Two other lovers dance their joy as the soprano recalls the magic of the time they first looked into each other's eyes and love showered down on them ("Ever Since Your Eyes"). The girl leans against the boy as the lights dim. He touches her hand. Other lovers join them as the song speaks of night, which may steal one's love away ("Night").

NOTES Writing about *Early Songs* in the New York *Times*, the critic Clive Barnes said that the ballet "is a picture of a world lost, a world full of gentle nuance, of literary feeling, of a rapture impassioned by the poetry of poetry rather than the poetry of life. Love is pure here, and its heartbeat is a kind of exquisite stylization of lust. It is the end of a civilization, and empty-handed cavaliers bearing silver roses are about to be everywhere. . . . It is a fantastically beautiful work; it lilts, it rises, it flies like a kite above our all-too-average dance works. . . . Feld offers a choreographic viewpoint that extends our view of the dance."

Walter Terry wrote in *The Saturday Review*: "*Early Songs*, tastefully costumed by Stanley Simmons and sensitively lit by Jules Fisher, is a work of superior craftsmanship choreographically, but more, it is an art experience that lifts the spirit. At its première, it was faultlessly danced by its cast of thirteen, including Feld himself, (Christine) Sarry, Elizabeth Lee, John Sowinski, and Richard Munro among the most impressive."

ECCENTRIQUE

Music by Igor Stravinsky. Choreography by Eliot Feld. Scenery by Oliver Smith. Costumes by Frank Thompson. Lighting by Jennifer Tipton. First presented by American Ballet Theatre at the City Center, New York, January 18, 1972, with Elizabeth Lee, Christine Sarry, and John Sowinski in leading roles.

This is a dance ballet to two works by Stravinsky—the *Four Studies for Orchestra* (1928) and the *Orchestral Suites 1 and 2* (1917–25). The first part of the ballet is for a group of girls and a leading dancer; the second, in a setting inspired by the image of Harlequin, is for a boy and girl and accompanying corps de ballet.

ECHOING OF TRUMPETS

Music by Bohuslav Martinů. Choreography by Antony Tudor. Scenery by Birger Bergling. First presented by the Royal Swedish Ballet at the Royal Opera House, Stockholm, September 28, 1963. First presented in the United States by the Metropolitan Opera Ballet at the Metropolitan Opera House, New York, March 27, 1966.

The theme of *Echoing of Trumpets* is closely related to another composition by Martinů, *Memorial to Lidice,* but the choreographer, Antony Tudor, was not aware of this until later. He chose instead Martinů's *Symphonic Fantasies Symphony No. 6* for his ballet about domination and war, about humanity under the heel of the conqueror.

The action takes place in an occupied village that has been ravaged by war. There the women whose husbands have been killed are in immediate conflict with the invaders. They are violated and killed. A refugee returning to the village to see his sweetheart is caught and killed. The girl dances a lament with her dead lover.

Many have seen in this ballet resemblances to the destruction of Lidice by the Nazis. The choreographer has denied that this is the theme of his work. "Perhaps it's more about how people always seem to want to dominate people. Everyone knows that's a stupid thing to do. Yet they keep on doing it. They never stop torturing each other with a kind of mild viciousness."

ELITE SYNCOPATIONS

Music by Scott Joplin and others. Choreography by Kenneth MacMillan. Costumes by Ian Spurling. First presented by the Royal Ballet at the Royal Opera House, Covent Garden, London, October 7, 1974, with Merle Park, David Wall, Monica Mason, Michael Colman, Jennifer Penney, Carl Myers, Vergie Derman, Wayne Sleep, Wayne Eagling, Jennifer Jackson, Judith Hower, David Drew, and David Adams in leading roles. First presented in the United States by the same ensemble April 27, 1976, at the Metropolitan Opera House, New York.

This is a dance ballet to Scott Joplin's music. The pieces that are illustrated by dance are the *Sunflower Slow Drag, Elite Syncopations, The Cascades, Hothouse Rag, Calliope Rag, Ragtime Nightingale, The Golden Hours, Stop-time Rag, The Alaskan Rag, Bethena*—a Concert Waltz, *Friday Night,* and *Cataract Rag.*

EMBRACE TIGER AND RETURN TO MOUNTAIN

Music by Morton Subotnick. Choreography by Glen Tetley. Decor by Nadine Baylis. First presented in the United States by the Royal Swedish Ballet at the City Center, New York, November 21, 1974.

Fourteen centuries ago, the Chinese developed a system of calisthenics and shadowboxing called T'ai-Chi. The object in T'ai-Chi is to empty out all extraneous thoughts in order to gain an intense inner concentration. Today in China and on Taiwan persons gather in parks every morning to do these thirty-seven exercises. In the West, too, T'ai-Chi has become extremely popular with persons who seek a thoughtful but not exhausting form of exercise. The names of the thirty-seven exercises typify the action so that participants will remember the sequence. The seventeenth exercise is called Embrace Tiger and Return to Mountain. It is this that the choreographer Glen Tetley has seized upon in order to evolve a work that fuses Eastern and Western attitudes to movement. It is danced to an electronic score by Morton Subotnick and performed on a mirrored floor that adds a further dimension to the visual impression of the piece. What the dancers do is not determined by a story. The stances they take, the gestures they make, and the steps they perform suggest variations on exercise (for combat?), shadowboxing (illusions?), tracking (prey?), and hunting.

Embrace Tiger is also part of the repertoire of the Eliot Feld Ballet.

L'ENFANT ET LES SORTILÈGES (The Spellbound Child)

Lyric fantasy in two parts based on a poem by Colette. Music by Maurice Ravel. Choreography by George Balanchine. First presented by Raoul Guns-bourg at the Théâtre de Monte Carlo, March 21, 1925. Conducted by Victor de Sabata. First presented in New York by Ballet Society at the Central High School of Needle Trades, November 20, 1946. Costumes and scenery by Aline Bernstein. Conducted by Leon Barzin. The Child: Joseph Connolly. Presented in a third version by the New York City Ballet at the Hommage à Ravel, May 14, 1975, at the New York State Theatre, Lincoln Center. Costumes and sets by Kermit Love; supervising designer, David Mitchell. Orchestra, singers, and chorus conducted by Manuel Rosenthal. The Child: Paul Offenkranz.

"The essence of Ravel's genius is found in this sympathetic and somewhat sentimental masterpiece," writes the musician Arbie Orenstein in *Ravel: Man and Music* (1975). I very much agree, as will probably be clear from the number of times I have worked on this opera-ballet! The title has been variously translated—everything from *Dreams of a Naughty Boy* to *The Spellbound Child*, but I have preferred to stay with the original. Which is where I began, having worked on the first production with Ravel. The composer has always meant a great deal to me.

Ravel, who was fond of George Gershwin's music, wrote that *L'Enfant et les Sortilèges* "was composed in the spirit of an American musical comedy." The hero of the piece, a young boy, both sings and dances. He is about six or seven years old. Colette's text sets the scene in a country house in a room looking out on a garden. There are a large Armchair, a tall Grandfather's Clock, a round squirrel cage by the window, a boiling kettle in the fireplace, and a purring Cat. It is afternoon.

The boy is supposed to be studying, but he is bored and would rather do anything else. His Mother comes in and scolds him but he sticks out his tongue at her. For punishment, she gives him bitter tea and dry bread and says he has to stay alone until dinner. Alone, the boy stamps his foot and shouts that he hates everyone and will be as naughty as he likes. Proving it, he breaks the teapot and Cups, tries to torture the squirrel, pulls the Cat's tail, overturns the kettle, rips the wallpaper, stops the Clock and tears up his schoolbooks. He declares that he may be naughty but he is also free!

What he has also done, however, is to free the room and the objects in it. Animated by his naughtiness, they all begin to come to life and to sing and dance. First the Armchair, then the Grandfather's Clock, then the Teacups followed by the figures on the wallpaper, Shepherds and Shepherdesses. A Princess emerges from one of his schoolbooks, complaining, "Now that you have torn up the story, what will happen to me?" He vows to protect her from evil enchantment but she disappears. As he despairs, other books come to life and the Child is suddenly faced with arithmetic and other problems! This is followed by a duet for two Cats, who retreat into the garden. The boy follows them.

Now the room disappears, the walls giving way, and the boy is alone in the garden with the Cats. There the music of Dragonflies, Moths, Bats, Frogs, and rustling Trees greets him. Much as he wants to join in the enchanted world of the lively garden, he sees that they delight in their freedom and in their love for each other. He realizes that they are forgetting him; he cries, "I'm alone! . . . Mother!"

In chorus the Animals turn on the boy, attacking him as the naughty lad who had always tormented them. They are so anxious to strike him and to get in the first blow that they begin to fight each other. In the process a small Squirrel is wounded. He goes to the Child, crying in pain. The boy puts a bandage on him. The Animals observe this and are astonished at his kindness. They cannot believe it. Then they observe that they have hurt the boy, too. As they wonder what to do they recall that he was calling someone. Who? Mother! They encircle the hurt Child and all call "Mother! Mother!" Then, getting no response, they take him to his nest. Dawn begins to rise. Proclaiming the boy to be good and kind and their friend, they leave him as he reaches out for home and his Mother.

ENIGMA VARIATIONS

Music by Edward Elgar. Choreography by Frederick Ashton. Scenery and costumes by Julia Trevelyan Oman. First presented by the Royal Ballet at the Royal Opera House, Covent Garden, London, October 25, 1968, with Derek Rencher, Svetlana Beriosova, Stanley Holden, Brian Shaw, Alexander Grant, Robert Mead, Vyvyan Lorrayne, Anthony Dowell, Georgina Parkinson, Desmond Doyle, Antoinette Sibley, Wayne Sleep, Leslie Edwards, and Deanne Bergsma in the principal roles. First presented in the United States by the same ensemble, with the same cast, at the Metropolitan Opera House, Lincoln Center, April 22, 1969. Conducted by John Lanchbery.

Subtitled, in the composer's words, "My Friends Pictured Within," *Enigma Variations* is a dance portrait of the artist among friends and family in Victorian England. The ballet is based on its score, which characterized thirteen friends and relations "who were there," and a fourteenth, "absent on a sea voyage" at the time, who remains the "enigma."

Describing one aspect of his composition, Elgar said it was "written at a time when friends were dubious and generally discouraging as to the composer's musical future." The action of the ballet, which is set in an English country house in the Cotswolds in 1898, occurs at a point when the composer needed friends most. It follows very closely the true story that Elgar had sent the completed score of his *Variations* to the celebrated Viennese conductor Richter, in the hope of interesting him in the work. Elgar's various friends, who visit him during the trying period of his awaiting a reply, pass an afternoon in the customary, relaxed pursuits of a Victorian autumn day. Only his wife, a constant source of inspiration and encouragement throughout his life, understands and watches over him to offer comfort. One by one the friends enter the action, identifying their separate personalities with each danced variation to the music Elgar wrote to characterize them. A chamber-music comrade, an amateur cellist, a tricycle-riding crony, a contemplative scholar, a romantic young girl, a gracious and sedate lady, and an eccentric dog lover all pass in review. Those closest to him, his wife and his friend "Nimrod" (who also knew the conductor Richter), continually reflect their understanding and the significance of the anxious waiting period. From time to time, Lady Mary Lygnon appears and reappears as a mysterious background figure, symbolic of the enigma of the long anticipated reply. At the end of the ballet, a telegram arrives for "Nimrod" from Richter, announcing that he will indeed conduct the first performance of *Enigma Variations*.

NOTES   Unanimously regarded as a masterpiece when it was first presented in England, the ballet was called by John Percival, in the *Times*, "a rare and moving expression of the quality of friendship." It received wide acclaim after its U.S. première. Writing in the *Village Voice*, the critic Deborah Jowitt said: ". . . I am astonished at its power to move me. The key—or one of them—to the enigma of the ballet's beauty is the nostalgia inherent in certain things. Lorca once wrote that a flock of sheep bears nostalgia about with it; it need not matter whether one has longings at all relevant to a flock of sheep. I don't think that one needs to have known era, place, or people involved in Ashton's ballet to be beguiled.

"The setting is Elgar's house in Worcestershire in the late years of Victoria's reign and of the nineteenth century. Everything about the ballet has an air of lateness: the composer's lateness in achieving recognition, the ripe late-Romantic music, the autumn garden, the amber of the sunlight. Julia Trevelyan Oman's set and costumes are carefully and poetically authentic. It's the kind of set I loved as a child—so super-real that it's hard to believe that there actually is a backstage area and not just more lawns and paths. There is a brick entrance, a cutaway view of an interior stairway, hammocks, bicycles, trees from which occasional yellow leaves float. Those friends of Elgar's cryptically enshrined in the musical variations are conveniently brought together. . . . They wander about . . . each emerging to do his (or her) variation and then strolling off. At the end a telegram is brought. . . . Elgar's friends rejoice in his good fortune.

"I see most clearly in this ballet what Ashtonophiles rave about. He is best at being quiet; his effects are modest, unflamboyant, but extremely sensitive to the nuances of character. . . . Sometimes he creates character through rhythm and through subtle gestural grafts onto the ballet vocabulary. Other times . . . he suggests eccentricities by requiring an eccentric manner of performing straightforward classical steps. He has a fine way with small understated lifts that seem to come with no preparation; the girl's feet make shy conversational steps barely off the ground. There are several of these in the bittersweet duet for Elgar and a very young girl (beautifully done by Derek Rencher and Antoinette Sibley), and in one of more promise of fulfillment between Matthew

Arnold's son and Isabel Fitton (Robert Mead and Vyvyan Lorrayne). I especially liked two delightfully brusque, erratic solos performed by Alexander Grant and Anthony Dowell; some affectionate conjugal passages between Elgar and his wife (Svetlana Beriosova); and a dignified . . . touching duet between Elgar and a friend (Desmond Doyle) to the famous *Nimrod* variation."

In a long essay on the work of Frederick Ashton in *Ballet Review* (Vol. 3, No. 4), the critic Jack Anderson has written:

"Man is capable of being better: he can dream, he can work, he can try harder. Such assumptions may seem old-fashioned and unduly optimistic. But they have not yet been proven totally wrong, and I can conceive of no satisfactory social relationships without them.

"One of Ashton's most unusual ballets on these themes is *Enigma Variations*. Formally, *Enigma* is daring—much more so than many ballets which ostentatiously proclaim their originality. For one thing, it is filled with "nondance." Elgar studies a manuscript. Two eccentrics ride bicycles. Lady Elgar examines a score. Nevinson yawns. Elgar and Jaeger gesticulate as though actually conversing in the "Nimrod" variation, which concludes with the men and Lady Elgar walking, arms linked, backs to the audience. The telegraph boy is tipped and the ballet ends with the taking of a photograph. Amidst these gestures—distillations of character traits akin to those Ashton uses in his comedies—passages of heightened movement occur like surges of feeling, as in "Nimrod" where the weighted stride of "real" walking gives way to low lifts and the long, eloquent line of classical ballet, only to subside back into walking. A master of choreographic repose, Ashton knows when not to move a dancer. In the passages for Elgar and his wife a movement is usually allowed to come to rest before a new movement begins, which makes these actions seem to arise from deep founts of emotion.

"The ballet is a quiet ode to friendship, to people one loves. The characters are not necessarily Elgar's friends as they were historically, they are his friends as he might have remembered them—an altogether different matter, since we glorify their virtues and convert their failings into eccentricities. And we see all in the light of affection.

"The hero is a successful artist. What an unlikely subject for a ballet! For, as Ashton shows, artistic creation is untheatrical—a matter of solitude, work, and worry, interspersed with conversations with neighbors and confidences shared with wife and friends. Elgar is often alone. But his work and solitude are not in vain. The telegram from Richter arrives. A party is held and friends take photographs. And tomorrow the new work begins.

"Art. Friendship. Meaningful work. Graciousness. Tranquility. These are some of the things Ashton's ballets celebrate."

In a long interview with Don McDonagh in *Ballet Review* (Vol. 3, No. 4), Frederick Ashton was asked if he had a preference for works with a narrative continuity or works that are lyrical abstract statements.

"A: No, it depends on the music. For instance in *Enigma Variations* I could have taken the music and done a series of dances. But this somehow didn't appeal to me. Then I hit upon the idea of using the actual people who were written about musically and this began to fascinate me. I did a lot of study on them and read biographies to try and get under the skin of it. When Elgar's daughter, who is now a very old lady, came to see it she said, 'I don't understand how you did it because they were exactly like that.' And she said, 'I never liked any of them except Troyte.'

"McD: There is very little dancing by Elgar himself and yet he is apparent everywhere. Just his presence as he stands upstage is very important. It focuses the piece.

"A: He needs to be that kind of solid character. I started by making him dance more but it seemed wrong, so I cut it out. Even when he does a few steps it kind of jars on me. When he and Jaeger have the conversation they're supposed to have had, about Beethoven's quartets, they do a bit of dancing there, and I tried to do it like question and answer. Even that I kept to minimal dancing."

David Vaughan's complete account of the creation of *Enigma Variations* in the book *Frederick Ashton and His Ballets* is strongly recommended.

EPILOGUE

Music by Gustav Mahler. Choreography by John Neumeier. Costumes by Mitchell. Lighting by Nananne Porcher. First presented by American Ballet Theatre at the New York State Theatre, Lincoln Center, New York, July 9, 1975, with Natalia Makarova and Erik Bruhn. Conducted by David Gilbert. Dedicated to Vera Volkova.

Epilogue, as the title suggests, is a dance narrative supplementing an earlier dramatic action. What that action was is never made clear. What is clear, as the curtain rises, is that there has been Trouble in the autumnal years. There is as yet no music. A spotlight shines from above and in it brown leaves can be seen to fall to the ground. A girl crouches. A man stands nearby. There appears to be no communication between them; but then the visible tension suggests these two know each other, are lovers in fact, and have had a serious quarrel that disallows contact. They want to make it up, but how? They bow to each other in curious ways, without acknowledgment. Then, as the man stands with his back to the girl, she goes to him, standing close. The music starts: the *Adagietto* of Mahler's *Symphony No. 5.* The dance now recapitulates the Effort at Reunion, the Difficulty in Giving In, Making Allowances, Permitting Forgiveness. Yet tensions persist. Long dances by each display varying degrees of anguish and being wronged; sometimes neither sees what the other suffers. Toward the end, in capitulation, the man falls at the girl's feet. She touches his head. As she falls back in his arms, the leaves again descend.

EPISODES

Music by Anton Webern. Choreography by Martha Graham and George Balanchine. Scenery and lighting by David Hays. Costumes by Karinska. First presented by the New York City Ballet at the City Center, New York, May 14, 1959. Episodes I, with choreography by Martha Graham, was danced by Miss Graham, Bertram Ross, Sallie Wilson, Helen McGehee, Ethel Winter, Linda Hodes, Akiko Kanda, Richard Kuch, Dan Wagoner, David Wood, Kenneth Peterson, James Gardner, and Robert Powell. Episodes II was danced by a cast headed by Violette Verdy and Jonathan Watts, Diana Adams and Jacques d'Amboise, Paul Taylor, Melissa Hayden, and Francisco Moncion.

In the 1950s Stravinsky began to tell me about the music of Anton Webern, the Austrian composer (1883–1945). Stravinsky called him a great composer and was so enthusiastic that I thought he must be very good indeed, although I was not then much interested in atonal music, except maybe Schoenberg's. To me, Schoenberg was the Einstein of twelve-tone music; I didn't see how he could be surpassed. But within the next few years, Robert Craft, Stravinsky's friend, recorded all of Webern's work. Everyone who cares about music must always be grateful to him. I listened to everything and liked it. The songs were the best of all, but they were written to be listened to. The orchestral music, however, fills air like molecules: it is written for atmosphere. The first time I heard it, I knew it could be danced to.

To understand Webern better, I transcribed several of the instrumental pieces for piano and played them over and over. The music seemed to me like Mozart and Stravinsky, music that can be danced to because it leaves the mind free to *see* the dancing. In listening to composers like Beethoven and Brahms every listener has his own ideas, paints his own picture of what the music represents. Beethoven did not have this in mind, I am sure, but he does seem to be painting a picture and people like to put themselves in that picture. Now how can I, a choreographer, try to squeeze a dancing body into a picture that already exists in someone's mind? It simply won't work. But it will with Webern. This kind of music, which Mozart and Stravinsky have also written, is like a rose—you can admire it deeply but you cannot inject your personal feelings into it.

Lincoln Kirstein shared my interest and admiration for Webern and we thought we should try to do dances to all of the orchestral pieces. They are not many and last altogether less than an hour. We decided to invite Martha Graham to collaborate on the undertaking and she happily agreed. We accordingly divided the scores and got to work. Miss Graham did her dance on a theme of Mary Queen of Scots while I began to do a ballet without a story. Miss Graham's part of *Episodes* has unfortunately not been seen for some years. It is our hope that one day it will be danced again.

EPISODES I   The music is the *Passacaglia, Opus 1,* and the *Six Pieces for Orchestra, Opus 6,* both composed in 1909 before Webern had used Schoenberg's idea of the twelve-tone row. The dance is based on the final moments of Mary Queen of Scots. It recapitulates her last thoughts as she mounts the scaffold.

The setting is austere, a black platform across the back of the stage with steps on both sides approaching it; in the center of the platform stands a black box and a high halberd-like heraldic device. The music begins with an ominous plucking of strings. Mary, in black, stands below, tense. Her stiff dress seems both to armor and to imprison her. Suddenly high on the platform, she is free of it, stepping out as a young girl in white to meet her lover Bothwell. She comes down again and her black dress remains standing like an empty cage, on the platform accusing her worldliness. She rejects the crown-craving Bothwell, the love of her life, and is in torment.

Four girls now dress Mary in blood red and she begins her long contest with Queen Elizabeth of England. The music shifts to the *Six Pieces for Orchestra.* The black box on the platform becomes a throne. Elizabeth sits there in burnished gold. She descends. The two queens play a fateful game of tennis, a formal court tennis.

As Elizabeth wins, she is lifted high. Mary then sits for a moment on the throne. But now the throne is the scaffold. Mary kneels before it, the tall halberd, now an ax, turns in the air and a bright red light illumines her cast-off queenly garb.

EPISODES II   The music for this part of the ballet, which, like the first part, can stand alone, consists of Webern's other orchestral works.

To the *Symphony, Opus 21,* there is an ensemble. The curtain rises before the music begins. Four couples stand on stage. As the music starts, dryly and carefully, the boys touch the girls on the shoulder; they join hands then, pose briefly, and begin to'move together. One couple leads the others but soon, just as the instrumentation shifts and develops, the other pairs react to the music differently. The dance is about the music; it is meant to look that way. Stravinsky has said that nothing in contemporary music has haunted him more than the coda of this symphony.

The second part, to the *Five Pieces, Opus 10,* is a *pas de deux.* The lights dim to darkness. Two figures emerge in spotlights, a boy dressed in jet black, a girl in white. She moves toward him slowly. He catches her, her body collapses over his arm and stays there, bent over, as he moves away. He leaves her there, then goes to find her again. Schoenberg said of Webern's music that it expresses an entire novel in a gesture, a joy in a breath. Although I did not know he had said that when I was working on this ballet, I believed it myself.

Some people watching this part of the ballet in the theatre laugh a little. That is, here at home, not on our tours of Europe or Russia. I sometimes think Americans feel obliged to laugh too much when there is not any reason to.

The third part, to the *Concerto, Opus 24,* is again a *pas de deux* for another couple, with four girls accompanying them. The boy moves the girl as the composer moves his instruments. Speaking of some of Webern's music, Robert

Craft says that "at first the listener might be reminded of a switchboard sporadically lighting up, but the plot of wires between the lights is what must be illuminated." Which is what I try to do.

The Variations for Orchestra, Opus 30. The original production of *Episodes* continued at this point with a dance performed by Paul Taylor, then appearing as a guest artist with our company. Just as Sallie Wilson from the New York City Ballet appeared in Miss Graham's part of *Episodes*, Mr. Taylor appeared in mine. The piece consists of a theme and six variations. Webern wrote of the *Variations:* "The motivic development uses much crab-wise movement with augmentation and diminution . . . By changing the center of gravitation within the two forms by augmentation and diminution the character and meter of the piece is constantly changing . . ."

The final part of *Episodes* is performed to Webern's tribute to Bach, the *Ricercata for Six Voices from Bach's Musical Offering.* The dances here, as elsewhere in this work, praise the music. The further Webern goes, the more active and lean the music becomes. The energy it has is that of free polyphonic voices, each equally individual and expressive. They keep shifting in balance and so do the dances. In Virgil Thomson's phrase, the music turns out to be "a dialect of Bach."

EPITAPH

Music by György Ligeti (Atmosphères *and* Volumina). *Choreography by Rudi van Dantzig. Scenery and costumes by Toer van Schayk. First presented by the Dutch National Ballet, June 25, 1969, in Amsterdam, Holland. First presented in the United States by the same ensemble at the Minskoff Theatre, New York, November 9, 1976.*

The Dutch critic Luuk Utrecht has rightly observed that *Epitaph* is "a gloomy comment on the life of man, like an inscription on a tomb." Love and death govern the action and there is never any doubt that the latter will win out. Two brides in spotless white symbolize, according to the choreographer, Rudi van Dantzig, "the illusions and ideals after which mankind always strives; sometimes unattainable, then senseless or cruel, sometimes ridiculous and often so overwhelming that generations sacrifice themselves or are offered to them." The two boys who devote themselves to the two brides perish, dancers are encased in black boxes and to the sound of a roaring organ all the ensemble collapses in a heap. The brides tidily close them all up in a box and kneel to weep at the loss.

L'ESTRO ARMONICO (Cycle of Harmony)

Music by Antonio Vivaldi. Choreography by John Cranko. First presented by the Stuttgart Ballet at the Württemberg State Theatre, Stuttgart, Ger-

many, April 27, 1963. First presented in the United States by the Stuttgart Ballet at the Metropolitan Opera House, New York, May 30, 1973.

L'Estro Armonico ("Cycle of Harmony") is a dance ballet to three concerti by Antonio Vivaldi, arranged by Kurt-Heinz Stolze, the *Concerto in A Major*, the *Concerto in A Minor*, and the *Concerto in D Major*. The choreographer, John Cranko, said of his ballet that it "uses a selection from the twelve concertos of Vivaldi. Personally I should have liked to choreograph all twelve, but to avoid boring the public I have chosen three. These concertos have been choreographically linked: the themes propounded in the first two concertos have been taken up and developed in the third." A woman is the center of the ballet, the male soloists supporting and revolving about her.

THE ETERNAL IDOL

Music by Frédéric Chopin. Choreography by Michael Smuin. First presented by American Ballet Theatre at the Brooklyn Academy of Music, December 4, 1969, with Cynthia Gregory and Ivan Nagy.

A romantic narrative ballet, *The Eternal Idol* is appropriately set to the *Larghetto* of Chopin's *Concerto No. 2 in F Minor*. The theme and inspiration for the ballet is Rodin's famous sculpture "The Eternal Idol," where a boy kneels at a girl's feet and rests his head on her breast. The ballet begins that way, reminding us of the pose of the sculpture. It then explores in a *pas de deux* for the lovers the beginnings and growth of their love for each other. As the critic Walter Terry has noted, the ballet evokes such images as Bernard Champigneulle speaks of in his book *Rodin:* ". . . Songs and sighs of love, cries of pleasure and pain, cries of pain and pleasure mingled, the eternal call of woman, the call of man . . . all found expression in Rodin."

ÉTUDES

Music by Knudager Riisager (after Czerny). Choreography by Harald Lander. Scenery by Erik Nordgreen. First presented by the Royal Danish Ballet at the Royal Theatre, Copenhagen, January 15, 1948. First presented in the United States by the American Ballet Theatre at the Metropolitan Opera House, New York, October 15, 1961, with Toni Lander, Royes Fernandez, and Bruce Marks in the leading roles. Scenery and costumes by Rolf Gerard.

This ballet is the choreographer's tribute to the dancer and may perhaps be considered as a representation of the work that must be accomplished by young dancers throughout the long and difficult preparatory years. We see in the ballet the first elementary exercises at the *barre* by young pupils, then work in the center of the stage, away from the *barre*, followed by a *pas de trois,* a *pas de deux,* a *pas de quatre,* a *pas de six,* and ensemble work. At the end of the ballet, the soloists display their skill individually and collectively.

EUGENE ONEGIN

Ballet in three acts and six scenes after Alexander Pushkin. Music by Peter Ilyich Tchaikovsky, arranged and orchestrated by Kurt-Heinz Stolze. Choreography by John Cranko. Scenery and costumes by Jürgen Rose. First presented by the Stuttgart Ballet at the Württemberg State Theatre, Stuttgart, Germany, April 13, 1965, with Marcia Haydée and Heinz Clauss in the principal roles. First presented in the United States by the same ensemble at the Metropolitan Opera House, Lincoln Center, New York, June 10, 1969.

The ballet tells the story of Pushkin's great poem. The music, by Tchaikovsky, is not from that composer's opera *Eugene Onegin,* but has been arranged from his lesser-known compositions.

How is it possible for me to speak of Pushkin's poem *Eugene Onegin* without emotion? It is like asking an Englishman to speak of Shakespeare without emotion. Alexander Pushkin produced the first great Russian poem, or "free novel" in verse, in *Eugene Onegin* (1823–30). His work is the beginning of greatness of the Russian language. There are problems about the translation of *Eugene Onegin* into English. Many have tried to render the poem into English. Vladimir Nabokov's complete version is the best we have, but for the reader with no Russian, it is difficult to explain the poem's greatness. For it is not what we think of as an epic or a huge, classic poem. It is a story, first of all, a work in poetry in a language that was unknown before, a language that became with Pushkin the Russian language of literacy and spoken liveliness. At any rate, John Cranko chose to make a ballet of this narrative, having known it as a poem, and also as an opera in Tchaikovsky's profound version. He arranged his ballet not to the music of Tchaikovsky's opera, but to other work by Tchaikovsky researched, arranged, and orchestrated by Kurt-Heinz Stolze.

Interviewed by *The New Yorker,* Cranko spoke of his ballet: " 'I see *Onegin* as a myth in the same way that Charlie Chaplin is a myth. . . . Myths always have double meanings, and in this sense Chaplin is both funny and terrifying. Onegin is a young man who has everything—good looks, money, charm—and yet he adds up to nothing. Which makes *him* terrifying. His problem is a very contemporary one—lack of recognition. Then, of course, the plot of the Pushkin poem is balletic—explainable in three different dance styles. The first act is a youthful peasant dance, the second is a bourgeois party, the third is an elegant St. Petersburg ball. And like a thread going through the labyrinth you have your soloists, with their problems, their stories.'

"Mr. Cranko . . . added that when he choreographed a ballet he tried to create visual images that speak for themselves. 'A diamond has no color, but it takes light, and when you look at it you see red, blue, green, and yellow,' he said. 'A ballet image should be like a diamond. No meaning. No color. But hard, not sloppy. I have a specific feeling which maybe I can only shape for myself. So the ultimate definition of the images comes from the eyes of the public, not from my eyes.'"

A synopsis of the ballet follows:

ACT ONE, SCENE 1: MADAME LARINA'S GARDEN   Madame Larina, Olga, and the nurse are finishing the party dresses and gossiping about Tatiana's coming birthday festivities. Madame Larina speculates on the future and reminisces about her own lost beauty and youth. Girls from the neighborhood arrive, their greetings and chatter are interrupted by gunshots.

Lensky, a young poet, engaged to Olga, arrives and tells them there is no cause for alarm; he was hunting with a friend from St. Petersburg. He introduces Onegin, who, bored with the city, has come to see if the country can offer him any distraction. Tatiana, full of youthful and romantic fantasies, falls in love with the elegant stranger, so different from the country people she knows. Onegin, on the other hand, sees only a coltish country girl who reads too many romantic novels.

ACT ONE, SCENE 2: TATIANA'S BEDROOM   Tatiana, her imagination aflame with impetuous first love, dreams of Onegin and writes him a passionate love letter which she gives the nurse to deliver.

ACT TWO, SCENE 1: TATIANA'S BIRTHDAY   The provincial gentry have come to celebrate Tatiana's birthday. They gossip about Lensky's infatuation with Olga and whisper prophecies of a dawning romance between Tatiana and the newcomer. Onegin finds the company boring. Stifling his yawns, he finds it difficult to be civil to them: Furthermore, he is irritated by Tatiana's letter which he regards merely as an outburst of adolescent love. In a quiet moment, he seeks out Tatiana and, telling her that he cannot love her, tears up her letter. Tatiana's distress, instead of awaking pity, merely increases his irritation.

Prince Gremin, a distant relative, appears. He is in love with Tatiana, and Madame Larina hopes for a brilliant match; but Tatiana, troubled with her own heart, hardly notices her kindly and elderly relative.

Onegin, in his boredom, decides to provoke Lensky by flirting with Olga who lightheartedly joins in the teasing. But Lensky takes the matter with passionate seriousness. He challenges Onegin to a duel.

ACT TWO, SCENE 2: THE DUEL   Tatiana and Olga try to reason with Lensky, but his high romantic ideals are shattered by the betrayal of his friend and the fickleness of his beloved; he insists that the duel take place. Onegin kills his friend and for the first time his cold heart is moved by the horror of his deed. Tatiana realizes that her love was an illusion, and that Onegin is self-centered and empty.

ACT THREE, SCENE 1: ST. PETERSBURG   Years later, Onegin, having traveled the world in an attempt to escape from his own futility, returns to St. Petersburg where he is received at a ball in the palace of Prince Gremin. Gremin has recently married, and Onegin is astonished to recognize in the stately and elegant young princess, Tatiana, the uninteresting little country girl whom he once turned away. The enormity of his mistake and loss engulfs him. His life now seems even more aimless and empty.

ACT THREE, SCENE 2: TATIANA'S BOUDOIR   Tatiana reads a letter from Onegin which reveals his love. Suddenly he stands before her, impatient to know her answer. Tatiana sorrowfully tells him that although she still feels her passionate love of girlhood for him, she is now a woman, and that she could never find happiness or respect with him. She orders him to leave her forever.

NOTES   The critic Walter Terry, reviewing a performance of *Eugene Onegin* in New York in 1971, wrote in *The Saturday Review:* "How Cranko tells a story in dance! He is a theater man through and through, as was his illustrious predecessor of two centuries ago in Stuttgart, Jean-Georges Noverre, whose revolutionary esthetics carried the ballet away from mere steps to *ballet d'action*—that is to say, to dramatic ballet, to movement with dramatic meanings.

"Cranko's *Onegin* has its virtuosic steppings—the cross-stage leaps by the company at the close of Act One, Scene 1, or the great pinwheel pattern in the ballroom scene—but of equal importance are the acted, not danced, duel and death scene that takes place way at the back of the stage (the late Doris Humphrey, among the great choreographers of our age, once stated that tragedy worked best in upstage remoteness and that comedy was for downstage familiarity), the finale in which the heroine stands alone center stage, and the remarkable mirror dance that combines acting and dancing as Tatiana literally draws her dream lover from the image in her mind and has him step from behind her own reflection in the mirror and into her arms.

". . . Marcia Haydée was Tatiana, a role identified with her very special artistry as both an actress and a dancer, and Heinz Clauss was Onegin, stern, strong, remote yet romantic. . . ."

EVENING DIALOGUES

Music by Schumann. Choreography by Jonathan Watts. First presented by the Joffrey City Center Ballet at the City Center, New York, October 22, 1974, with Francesca Corkle, Beatriz Rodriguez, Russell Sultzbach, and Burton Taylor as principals.

One of Schumann's great works for piano, the *Davidsbündlertänze*, is played throughout this ballet to inspire and accompany dances by vulnerable and susceptible young persons who listen and respond. They care deeply about what they hear and react with fervor to the intensity of concentration of the short, vivid dance pieces. Their dances express the joy and disappointments of love and youth.

AN EVENING'S WALTZES

Music by Serge Prokofiev. Choreography by Jerome Robbins. Costumes by Rouben Ter-Arutunian. First presented by the New York City Ballet at the New York State Theatre, Lincoln Center, May 24, 1973, with Patricia Mc-Bride and Jean-Pierre Bonnefous, Christine Redpath and John Clifford, Sara Leland and Bart Cook in leading roles.

The music for this dance ballet is five waltzes by Prokofiev from his *Symphonic Suite of Waltzes*. There is no story, only these persons dancing to these waltzes. Each of the waltzes is different, and a different atmosphere and mood are established for the dances. The three leading couples as well as the soloists and *corps de ballet* are formally dressed, as if they were attending a formal party.

Writing in the *Wall Street Journal* about the ballet, Peter J. Rosenwald said that "it has so much beautiful movement that it could almost bring back ballroom dancing as a national pastime. . . . From beginning to end it has that Robbins romantic style, warm and eloquent, full of effortless and thrilling lifts which are never showy for their own sake."

Deborah Jowitt in the *Village Voice* wrote: "Over the decorous unison waltzing of the *corps,* pairs of soloists enter one at a time to make violent small talk in dance. Small outbursts of movement, sudden changes of heart and direction interrupt the smooth surface of the waltzing. These couples are, perhaps, dancing out the thoughts and the verbal exchanges that occur at grand parties such as these, where a current of fashionable melodrama flows through the ballroom. The duet for Redpath and Clifford (replacing the injured Gelsey Kirkland and Helgi Tomasson at the last minute) is particularly effusive, with a hint of drastic coquetry."

EVERY NOW AND THEN

Music by Quincy Jones. Choreography by William Scott. Costumes designed by Hutaff Lennon and Jack Cunningham; costumes executed by Zelda Wynn. Lighting design by Gary Fails. First presented by the Dance Theatre of Harlem at the Uris Theatre, New York, April 26, 1975.

The ballet *Every Now and Then* was made by the ballet master of the Dance Theatre of Harlem, William Scott. His dances play with black folk dance, jazz, and ballet, mixing them together and merging the styles. Designed and laid out to be danced, the steps often appear spontaneous and improvised, like sudden expressions of a personal fantasy. The critic Arlene Croce of *The New Yorker* once noted in young amateur dancers on the "Soul Train" television program: "Every now and then, one of the boys will hurl himself into a *saut de basque*—playing at ballet."

FAÇADE

Ballet in one act. Music by William Walton. Choreography by Frederick Ashton. Scenery and costumes by John Armstrong. First presented by the Camargo Society at the Cambridge Theatre, London, April 26, 1931, with a cast that included Lydia Lopokova, Alicia Markova, and Frederick Ashton. First presented in the United States by the Sadler's Wells Ballet at the Metropolitan Opera House, New York, October 13, 1949, with Moira Shearer and Frederick Ashton in featured roles.

The music to *Façade* was originally written as a setting to certain poems by Edith Sitwell. The poet recited her verses accompanied by the music. The ballet has nothing to do with the poems and uses only the music, to which the choreographer has arranged a series of nine comic *divertissements* that poke fun at their subjects. The scene shows the façade of a large, light-colored house of the Victorian era.

First, two girls and a boy amble out on stage and dance a "Scottish Rhapsody" in appropriate native costume. This is followed by a number called "Yodeling." A milkmaid enters with a stool. Soon she is disturbed by three mountaineers, who turn her around as she stands posed on the stool and pay tribute to her fresh beauty. There is a yodeling contest, in which the girl enters with gusto. The music ripples and laughs with the happy young people. Next comes a "Polka," danced by a smart young lady.

Now two couples dance a "Fox Trot," which is followed by a "Waltz" executed by four girls. Two vaudeville dandies take up the "Popular Song" and perform it with quick, funny precision. The "Country Dance" features a silly country girl, a yokel, and an irate squire. A gigolo, overslickly dressed in evening clothes, and a debutante, who wears a long red dress and an absurd feather in her hair, now come forward and dance the "Tango." The gigolo bends the debutante backward, dips her low, runs a scale down her back with his fingers, and with a devilish air tries to overexploit her good nature. The debutante is amenable to any treatment, however, and finishes the dance considerably disheveled. All the dancers come forward now and join in a "Tarantella Finale."

FACSIMILE

Choreographic observation in one scene. Music by Leonard Bernstein. Choreography by Jerome Robbins. Scenery by Oliver Smith. Costumes by Irene Sharaff. First presented by Ballet Theatre at the Broadway Theatre, New York, October 24, 1946, with Nora Kaye, Jerome Robbins, and John Kriza.

A naturalistic ballet of ideas, *Facsimile* takes up a problem which is not only contemporary, but ageless. It is the problem of what modern man shall do with his time. Often apparently immune to authentic feeling, he takes refuge in the constant company of his fellow men, where he can conceal his lack of security. He arranges his life not only to conceal his real identity from his friends, but to hide it from himself. The ballet's program note reads: "Small inward treasure does he possess who, to feel alive, needs every hour the tumult of the street, the emotion of the theatre, and the small talk of society."

The scene of the ballet is a lonely stretch of beach. There is an improvised bathing tent at the left. On the right, disappearing in the distance, is an irregular line of pilings, marking the shore line. When the curtain rises, there is but one figure on stage: a woman in a bathing suit, who is idling away her time. The music is quiet and as lonely as the scene.

We see that the woman is bored. She seems to have nothing to wait for and walks about trying to find something to amuse her. She takes no pleasure in the scene and tosses away inanimate objects. Finally she goes over to her bathing tent, pulls the awning across it, and amuses herself slightly by watching her own shadow. Her own shadow is better than no society at all.

The woman turns and looks down the beach. Someone is coming! She is delighted and childishly runs behind the awning to surprise the stranger. A man strolls onto the scene. He does not see the woman and, just as she has done, tries to find something to amuse him. He plays with his beach towel, looks up and down the beach, thinks of nothing. He wonders why he is there. Now he sees the woman's shadow on the awning.

She steps out coyly. Both these vacuous personalities try to make something of themselves. Alone, they may be nothing, but together, they must pretend that this is not true. They introduce themselves, chatter, begin to flirt. They have nothing else to say to each other and grasp at flirtation like a straw. They therefore take their love very seriously.

But soon they tire even of this recourse. They come to life again as another man strolls toward them. Both imagine that the newcomer might be self-sufficient enough to amuse them. He turns out to be just as insecure as they are.

Now that they are a triangle, one woman and two men, the idlers try to make something out of nothing. The first man pretends to be annoyed at the intrusion of the second and claims the girl's whole attention. The girl plays along with him, and the intruder sees that this might be an interesting game after all. He flirts with the woman and tries to win her from his rival.

The woman now has a situation that amuses her immensely. She plays with the two men adroitly and watches closely to see their reactions. She knows that the important thing is to be so charming that the game will never end, for if either suspects that she is insincere, both will desert her. The men participate in the game for a short while, but the first man finally insists that she stop this nonsense and be his. The woman says, "No." Finally she has to take some way out and confesses that she likes the second man best. Her first lover storms at her and acts furiously jealous. He takes the woman and his rival and drags them across the beach. Soon all three are fighting together, their bodies tied in a writhing knot on the beach.

The woman is through. She cries out, "Stop!" The three figures untangle themselves, and when they see that the girl is really serious and actually prefers neither one of them, the two men leave the scene. The first man acts as if he had been hurt and misunderstood; the second tries to shrug off the incident: what difference could it possibly make to him? Now the woman is alone again. The incident has not made any difference to her, either. As she strolls away from the beach, there is a real question as to whether anything will ever make any difference to her.

FALL RIVER LEGEND

Ballet in eight scenes, with prologue. Music by Morton Gould. Choreography by Agnes de Mille. Scenery by Oliver Smith. Costumes by Miles White. First presented by Ballet Theatre at the Metropolitan Opera House, New York, April 22, 1948, with a cast headed by Alicia Alonso, Diana Adams, Peter Gladke, and John Kriza.

This modern melodrama is founded on fact. Fall River, Massachusetts, in the summer of 1892 was the scene of a hideous crime that attracted the attention of the nation. In that city, a respectable spinster by the name of Lizzie Borden was said to have hacked to death with an ax her father and her stepmother. Lizzie Borden was subsequently tried for this double murder. The jury, however, acquitted her, and she went back to her father's house and lived as a recluse until she died. The murderer was never found.

In *Fall River Legend*, Lizzie Borden is hanged. Here she is called the Accused, and in the prologue of the ballet she faces the gallows.

PROLOGUE Before the curtain rises, the music begins with loud shrieks of sound that forebode terror. The orchestra quiets down, the curtain rises, and we are about to be witnesses at an execution.

The gallows stands stark and bare, its rope dangling, against a dark, blue-green sky. The Accused, in black, stands on the right with her pastor. Near them is a black, leafless tree. On the left, the speaker for the jury mechanically intones the jury's bill: that the jurors on oath present that on August 4, 1892, the Accused with a certain weapon, to wit, an ax, did assault and kill her stepmother and father with twenty mortal wounds. The Accused stands in a spotlight on the right. She holds the pastor's hand and seems immune to feeling. The speaker for the jury recalls aloud that the house where she committed these murders was the house where she was born. As he remembers that she lived there once with her father and mother in happiness, the drop curtain rises, the gallows slides back to support a corner of the house, and the lights rise on a typical Victorian home set back off the street. Except for the stoop and the front door, the façade of the house is torn away to expose the interior. On the left, we notice a tree stump set for chopping wood. We are to see the Accused in her childhood.

SCENE ONE: THE HOUSE OF THE ACCUSED—THE PAST   The sky that hangs over the house is washed in hideous green. The Accused, dressed now in dark green, stands before her room and watches time go back to the days of her girlhood. Old neighbors and townspeople pass by. Her father and mother are there. The Accused holds out her hands to them longingly, trying to claim their attention, but they do not notice her. A young girl in white appears. We know immediately that she is the Accused as a child. The Accused goes to her, hovers over her as if to protect her, and follows her girlish dance steps to hurdy-gurdy music.

The child runs to her mother. The mother caresses her daughter; the Accused pathetically fingers her mother's white shawl. A strange woman enters. Her back is straight as a ramrod, her chin is held high; she is dressed in severe black with a black boa about her shoulders. This woman marches, rather than walks, and watches with the determined interest in everyone else's business that only the spinster can have. The child is frightened of this woman; the Accused articulates this fright in a sudden tightening of her gestures: as the mature child, she is not only afraid, she knows why she fears. Instinctively the Accused goes to her father and kneels before him to guard him against this woman. But the adamant spinster comes forward; the father welcomes her and shakes her hand, not seeing his daughter as she kneels between them.

The spinster turns on the child and scolds her, apparently for no reason at all, but we see instantly that the spinster is acutely aware of the child's hatred that the Accused has expressed. Just as we note the woman's rudeness in scolding the girl in the presence of her mother, we see that the mother is indifferent. She is ill. She clutches at her heart and faints. A crowd gathers. The father and the child rush to her and hold her lovingly; they are helpless in their fear and shock. The spinster orders the child away from her mother and takes charge like a schoolteacher. The Accused, who has seen it all before, trembles; she holds her hands in front of her face to erase this memory. The child cries.

The mother recovers slowly from the attack, and the father leads her to the house. He turns at the door and bows to the spinster. The crowd disperses. The spinster walks proudly and primly down the street alone. The Accused turns her back on this woman.

The lights go down and a little time passes. When the stage is lit again, we see the child sitting on the steps by the door watching her mother and father dance. The Accused watches, too, as her parents move gracefully in a soft love duet. The child goes to her father, who holds her tenderly; then the mother lifts the girl into her arms. We are watching the ideally happy family. The Accused joins in the reliving of her childhood and with the girl dances gaily about her loving parents. She seems to lose all her hardness and bitterness; she forgets about the future as she and the child become one in their movements and one in their affection for the mother and father.

But the joyous dance is too much for the mother. She has another attack. Two passers-by run for help. The father lifts her carefully and carries her into the house. The Accused and the girl pray together for their mother. The spinster enters and goes immediately into the house. Two women come to the girl and dress her in black: her mother is dead. The Accused clutches the side of the house, hides her agony, and represses the hatred that must soon be asserted.

The father comes out into the street, looking for his daughter. The spinster stands beside him. The child runs to her father's arms and weeps. He attempts to console her, but the child breaks away from him and moves to enter the house. She cannot go in: the spinster, now in complete control, stands in the doorway.

The child returns to her father and kneels at his feet, begging him to allow her to see her mother. The woman in black marches up to the child and, taking her shoulders in her hands, shakes her viciously. The grieving father does not understand. He tries to separate them, then buries his face in his hands. He bows to the woman's authority and falls on his knees at her feet.

In the background, the Accused has turned to watch. Her grief and indignation are uncontrollable; her body writhes obscenely. The spinster sees the mother's white shawl lying on the ground. She goes to pick it up. As she does so, the Accused runs across the stage and leaps to her father's back, claiming him, denying him everything but grief. But he does not feel her presence. The spinster puts the white shawl over her shoulders. The father lifts her in his arms and takes her across the threshold. The door slams shut in the face of the Accused.

SCENE TWO: THE HOME OF THE ACCUSED—THE PRESENT   Many years have passed. The child has disappeared, and the Accused now lives her own part in the tragedy. She is a woman now, a young woman who ought to have been married years ago. As the lights come up, we see her father and her stepmother in the living room of the house. They sit opposite each other, rocking back and forth, reading books that they hold out stiffly in front of them. There is no music. In this oppressive silence, the Accused enters. She takes a chair between the two. All three rock in unison. The silence becomes taut and music begins quietly.

The house is moved forward to the front of the stage. The Accused rises from her chair and snaps her fingers desperately, demanding an end to this sitting and staring. Her father and stepmother do not pay any attention to this outburst. For a moment the Accused sits down again, then, nervously, almost without control, she runs up the stairs and down again, apparently for no reason at all. The stepmother glances up knowingly from her book and whispers to her husband. The Accused returns to sit and rock and stare. She gets up to look out of the window, but the woman in black follows her and snaps the window shade shut in her face. The Accused goes to her father and embraces him, but the woman pulls her away.

The Accused can bear it no longer; she goes out into the yard. The suspicious stepmother follows her for a moment, but sees she is alone and returns to the sitting room. Her husband places the white shawl about her shoulders and stands behind her chair.

In the yard the Accused meets her pastor. He is young and pleasant-looking, slightly deferential to her, and she is plainly attracted to him. They dance together, the girl participating in the dance with a kind of desperate and abandoned joy. She has no other companionship, no one knows the secret agonies and longings of her heart, and she does not know how to be happy in a normal way. The pastor is sufficiently acquainted with her family situation to be sympathetic and kind. The dance over, the two shake hands formally, both of them a little conscious of the absurdity of this convention.

The father opens the door and comes out to look for his daughter. He has acquired now the sternness and brusqueness of his wife. He disapproves of the rendezvous and tells the girl to come in. She does so reluctantly, and the pastor leaves the scene.

Back in the parlor, the family sit rocking again. The Accused moves from her chair and goes into the back hall. She re-enters the room with an ax in her hand. The orchestra sounds a sharp shriek on the strings. The stepmother cringes and seeks protection from her husband. The girl does not understand why she should be afraid and smiles to herself. She goes out into the yard, chops wood, and buries the blade of the ax in the chopping block. She goes back into the house with the wood, wipes her hands, and sits down again. Everything is still the same.

SCENE THREE: THE STREET BEFORE THE HOUSE   The house is moved back. We hear light and gay music, and young happy couples fill the street and dance together. The Accused opens the door and comes out to watch; her family remain seated in the parlor. Sitting on the doorstep, the girl observes wistfully the open happiness of youth. A soft and romantic *pas de deux* is danced by one couple who find themselves alone for a moment; then they are joined by other couples and leave the stage.

The Accused is alone and despondent. She thinks she must hate what she cannot have. The music snarls; she rises, leaps, and turns down the stage in a rapid diagonal. She almost runs into the ax, which still stands buried in the tree stump. She touches the handle. The music cries out in warning, and the girl creeps away from the ax in terror. She falls to the ground. As she rises, her eyes turn, fascinated, back to the ax. She moves toward it; her hand trembles. She is revolted by her thoughts and moves away.

Just as she does so, the young pastor enters with a bouquet of red roses. The music is low and tender. The girl takes the flowers and smoothes her hair. The pastor picks her up and holds her briefly as if she were a child. They begin to dance, and the girl forgets that romance seemed impossible for her five minutes before. The pastor asks her to come with him on a church picnic, and the girl responds eagerly.

Her happiness is short-lived. Her father and stepmother come out of the house and see her with the pastor. The parents creep up on the innocent lovers. The stepmother stares at the girl. The Accused falls to the ground and kicks her feet in an uncontrolled, childish tantrum. She rolls across the stage and finds herself looking straight at the ax. Meanwhile the stepmother is whispering to the pastor about the girl's abnormalities, telling him that she is perhaps insane. The pastor is respectful to the woman, but disbelieves her. The Accused rushes at her stepmother, scratching at the air in front of her. The woman accepts this as but another sign of the girl's insanity and threatens her. Then she and her husband beckon to the girl to come with them back to the house. The Accused gives them a quick look of appraisal, glances at the house, hesitates, and quickly, spasmodically, grabs at her mother's white shawl. Placidly she now goes to the pastor and takes his arm. They walk off together. For the first time in her life, the Accused has defied in action what she has always defied in her mind.

SCENE FOUR: A PRAYER MEETING   The lights go down; the house turns. Over the house, the green sky darkens ominously. But when the lights come up, we find ourselves at a prayer meeting. The pastor stands in the midst of his congregation. The Accused looks on like an outsider: these happy people are like the lovers she saw dancing in front of her house, and she doubts that she can become one of them. The pastor perceives her thoughts, welcomes her, and the women of the church gather about the Accused and befriend her. One of the women kisses her and smiles. The Accused cannot believe her eyes. The congregation divides into two groups, dancing joyously to simulated organ music. The Accused hesitates to participate, but no longer watches as if she were an outsider.

Suddenly the congregation leaves the scene. The Accused and her pastor are alone. The music becomes dispassionately sentimental. The Accused falls to the floor and curls up like a child: never since childhood has she known such kindness as this. She rises; the pastor goes to her and takes her hand. Still the girl is afraid. The Accused looks into his eyes and sees there none of the deception, none of the duplicity she fears. Now she submits wholly to the young man's tender feeling for her and, all doubt gone, allows him to give her hope in a triumphant dance. The music mounts steadily in volume; the two figures move faster, circling and leaping. Then, with a quick cut in the music, the melody becomes soft and yielding. The girl kneels against her lover. He lifts her in his arms, and she curls up against him. He releases her for a moment, and they stand together, side by side, as the other couples in the congregation return.

To fresh, vibrant music, the Accused dances among the other lovers in an ensemble dance strongly reminiscent of a country revival meeting. She is carried high off the ground by two boys and shakes hands with the girls. Knowing happiness, she now has the right to participate. Her joy is open and she moves with quick spontaneity.

Her stepmother enters. When the Accused sees her, her body stiffens, her face contorts in pain, as if her heart were slashed with a knife. She falls to the ground, hysterical in her agony. The pastor reaches out to help her, but the woman in black draws him aside. The Accused sees them whispering together and, losing all control, seems to become as mad as her stepmother imagines her to be. The music whirls insanely. The congregation closes in on her in a semicircle of slow motion. The Accused writhes on the ground, rises, and walks in a trance.

The stepmother and the pastor come to her. The pastor puts her mother's white shawl about her shoulders and politely says good-by. The girl turns to stare after the pastor. She holds out her hand to him in one last plea. He does not see her. The stage darkens. The church turns, to become the house again. The stepmother leads her to the door. Her last hope is gone.

SCENE FIVE: INSIDE THE HOUSE   When the lights come up, the stepmother has gone into the house. The Accused remains on the doorstep. From this position she watches the happy young couples of the town move before her. Changed entirely, she observes them from the private distance of her mind. Her face is a mask. Her father and stepmother sit rocking in the parlor. She can no longer envy the lovers, because the possibility of being like them has been destroyed. Now she moves like an automaton, as if her every step were predetermined. She walks directly to the chopping block. Two cheerful girls walk down the street. The girl does not know they are there. She touches the ax, then picks it up and turns back toward the house. She has no doubt about what she must do. When she enters the parlor, her father and stepmother jump up in terror. The Accused merely looks at them. As the scene blacks out, her free hand moves up to cover her face.

SCENE SIX: THE PRESENT AND THE PAST   A drop curtain falls, to enlighten us on the goriness of the crime. We see depicted here the parlor suspended in mid-air, its chairs overturned; on the floor of the room streams of blood meet to form a red flood.

The Accused enters. She has removed her dress; her petticoat is spattered with blood. Her mother appears. The Accused begins to act out the wish she imagines to be fulfilled by her terrible crime. The mother must approve of the double murder; it is for her that the Accused has killed.

Her mother embraces her, and the girl rests content in her arms. But then the mother notices the red stains. The girl, now again the small child of the ballet's first scene, tries to hide the stains with the hem of her skirt. The mother slaps her hand. She examines the stains and sees that her daughter is covered with blood. She slaps the girl's cheek and pushes her forward. The child's arms hang limp, her fingers flutter. The mother rocks the naughty child against her breast. She smiles a little as she upbraids the Accused and vanishes in the night.

SCENE SEVEN: THE HOME OF THE ACCUSED   The drop curtain rises and the house is seen again. In time, this scene follows immediately after Scene Five. No longer dark, the sky in back of the frame dwelling is now hideously and grossly red. There is no sound, yet the atmosphere is tense, expectant. Neighbors are running up and down the street, frantically trying to locate the source of the ghastly outcries they have heard.

The Accused can be seen emerging from the back hall under the stairs. The orchestra is still quiet. She tries to straighten up the parlor hastily, but stops when she sees that people are looking in the window at her. Then quickly, in a desperate rush, she dashes for the front door. When she appears on the doorstep, the orchestra crashes and blares. The girl runs into the crowd and circles the street. The orchestra continues to play fortissimo as the girl cries out to the world the horror of her home.

Meanwhile townspeople have entered the house. Two men bring forward the bloody ax and the mother's white shawl, laced now with blood. They confront the girl. Her hands quiver before her face. Moving as in a dream, she takes her mother's shawl and holds it to her lips.

The pastor makes his way through the crowd to the Accused. He holds her, lifts her gently as if to protect her. The girl's feet kick at the air in a spasm of desperation. Then she collapses at the pastor's feet.

SCENE EIGHT: THE GALLOWS   The house of the Accused disappears except for a piece of its framework, which forms the gallows we saw in the prologue. She stands with the pastor, awaiting her execution. The people of the town pass by and stare at her. She is not disturbed, for she is preoccupied with her own frantically rapid memories of her crime and what led up to it: the blissful childhood, the loving mother, the father destroyed in his weakness by the demon spinster, the love she has wanted to give all her life, and the love that must now die. She holds out her hand, grasping at her memories, kneels, and opens her arms. The pastor comforts her.

A mother and her small daughter, perhaps the Accused herself, come to see the condemned woman. Ironically, the child shakes her fists at the Accused. Contented couples pass and watch. The Accused lets her head rest briefly on the pastor's shoulder. There is not much time left. He kisses her and leaves her alone. The girl turns to the gallows and opens her arms, as if to welcome the hangman's noose. Her body twitches grotesquely; her neck breaks. The music finishes like thunder. The Accused has been hanged until she is dead.

FANCY FREE

Ballet in one act. Music by Leonard Bernstein. Choreography by Jerome Robbins. Scenery by Oliver Smith. Costumes by Kermit Love. First presented by Ballet Theatre at the Metropolitan Opera House, New York, April 18, 1944, with John Kriza, Harold Lang, and Jerome Robbins as the three Sailors; Muriel Bentley, Janet Reed, and Shirley Eckl as the three Passers-by.

This modern American ballet tells what happens to three sailors who go out on liberty in New York City. The time is "the present": any hot summer night. The scene is a side street in Manhattan.

The music is quiet when the curtain rises. Outlined against the dark city night is the interior of a bar. The entrance to the bar, on the right, leads out onto a street corner. There a bright street lamp shines down on the sidewalk. Inside the bar there are no customers; the lone bartender lazily dries and polishes beer glasses. He begins to read a newspaper. In the background the myriad lights of distant skyscrapers penetrate the sultry night like stars.

Through the side windows of the bar we can make out three sailors walking toward the corner. The music blares out. They rush toward the corner, pivot on the lamppost, and begin to dance in the street in front of the bar. Dressed in clean summer whites, the sailors are out to make the most of the night. They preen a little, adjust their hats to jazzy angles, and strut along the pavement in anticipation of the good time that must naturally come their way. Their dance is like an improvised vaudeville act; it's clear that the three are friends and that they can kid each other and laugh about it. If they have their way, this is going to be an evening to beat all the rest. They try to outdo each other with brief trick dance steps and laugh. Two of them push the third high up in the air between them. Inside the bar the bartender smokes and reads his paper.

The rowdy music that accompanies the sailors' dance slows down and softens. The three men know from experience that simple determination isn't going to get them a good time. They straighten their jackets, readjust their hats, and wonder what to do next: which do they want first—women, drink, or music? One of the sailors leans against the lamppost to consider the problem seriously. One of his pals joins him. Before these two have made up their minds completely, the third sailor enters the bar. His friends race in after him.

The three sailors strut up to the bar with a special salty air for the bartender's benefit. They order three beers, clink their glasses together, down the drinks in unison, and slam the glasses back down on the bar. The bartender eyes them suspiciously: who's going to pay? The sailors look at each other as if such a thought had never entered their heads. Finally one of them is tricked into paying by the other two. As he puts down the money, he tries to shrug off the fact that he always ends up with the short end of the stick.

Now that they've had one drink, the sailors remember that they don't want to drink alone. They look around the empty bar with amused disgust, hitch up their pants, and head for the door. The music is moody, waiting for something to happen. The sailors are getting slightly tired of each other; they wonder if the evening is going to turn out to be a bust, after all. One of them pulls out a stick of gum. He starts to unwrap it, then remembers his friends and splits it with them. The three chew thoughtfully and, one by one, flick the pieces of gum wrapper out into the street to see which one can flick it farthest. The winner wonders what difference it makes.

At this point, just as the three are about to relax into boredom, they straighten up as if lightning had struck. The music breaks out into loud, rhythmic boogie-woogie, and a terrific-looking girl walks by. She wears a tight-fitting blouse and skirt, high patent leather shoes, and carries a red handbag. The girl knows she is being watched; she smiles and by her walk suggests all the things the sailors are imagining. The sailors are struck numb; standing close together, they move as one body—bending so far forward to watch the girl that they almost fall on their faces.

The girl pretends that she hasn't seen them, which sends the boys into action. Suddenly they are three very different individuals, each trying to interest the girl in his own special way. They imitate her walk, laugh at her, grab her purse and toss it around, and all but lie at her feet to get the girl to recognize their existence. The girl wants to be angry and tries to act as if she is, but the boys sense that she's just kidding. When she laughs in warm, friendly recognition, the three sailors smile back and wonder—who saw her first? A small fight breaks out. Two of the boys lift the girl high. She kicks free and stomps off impatiently. The battle has left one sailor lying in the street. He watches as his two friends follow the girl, then lazily picks himself up.

He smoothes out his uniform and starts to go back into the bar. Then, as in a dream, he bumps into a small, cute girl, younger than the first. He apologizes for his clumsiness, smiles winningly, looks her up and down adroitly, and introduces himself. The girl smiles back. The sailor looks over her shoulder to be sure his friends have disappeared and asks her into the bar for a drink. The girl consents.

Inside, the bartender is still reading. The sailor and his girl climb up on two stools and order drinks. He is feeling his way with the redhead, but decides on the old routine. The music stops as he gives her a dazzling, rapid display of What-I've-Been-Through. His hands circle the air and zoom down to attack imaginary ships, and his body vibrates to machine-gun fire as he describes the terrors of life at sea. When the girl takes this in and doesn't laugh at him, just watches, the boy decides that she's not only cute, she's adorable. He asks her to dance.

The orchestra plays a low blues number as they move together slowly. The *pas de deux* they dance is instinctively intimate, and the intimacy—their mutual liking and attraction—is so natural and unforced that formality and doubt would be out of place. This is a made-for-each-other dance that makes sense in its alternate casualness and conviction. He dances with her as he would with any girl, then holds her closely, and she responds warmly to this way of showing how special she is. When the dance is over, he bends down and kisses her softly. The girl smiles and wipes her lipstick off his face. They move together back to the bar.

The sailor picks the girl up and sits her on a stool. He has started to pay for the drinks when a roaring rattle of sound breaks the romantic spell and ushers in his two friends. The two gobs barge into the bar with the first girl and stop dead in their tracks when they see him with a date. He grabs his girl and pulls her toward the door to avoid the intruders. But the girl stops him. The girls are old friends, apparently, and begin to carry on together as girls will.

The boy sees that the situation is hopeless and goes to join his pals at a table. More drinks are ordered. The girls sit down. There are only four chairs, and one of the sailors is left standing. He tries to sit on the first girl's lap—she seemed more experienced and tolerant—but she pushes him off. Two of the sailors dance with the girls, and the boy who found the redhead sits alone for a moment. Now he cuts in. The snare drum signals the quarrel that ensues: who's going to dance with whom? The situation is hopeless. One of the boys has got to clear out or the night will be ruined.

The three sailors finally get together and agree that they'll have a contest to see which one of them can dance best. The girls will be the judges of the two winners, and the third man will scram. Two of the sailors join the girls at the table, and one of the boys begins a solo.

His dance is rowdy and energetic as he tries to outdo all the steps he thinks his friends might try. The girls are delighted at his fresh and arrogant skill and begin to applaud as he finishes his number by jumping up on the bar with one leap. There he poses for an instant, then jumps down, grabs up a beer, and flourishes his glass. The other two sailors razz him as the girls clap their hands.

The next variation is danced by the cute girl's first partner. His dance is subtler, relying more on sinuous, flowing rhythm than boisterousness, more on false modesty than overt bragging. The girls respond to his quiet dance with a sigh, and his friends hold their noses. He lies on the floor with his legs in the air as his number ends. The last sailor tries to combine the two styles of his friends and succeeds brilliantly in a snaky, Latin dance at the end of which he jumps down from a bar stool to kneel on the floor before the girls.

The girls don't know which ones to choose! They argue about it; then the boys argue with them and start to fight among themselves. The competition that began when the first girl passed by on the street turns into anger and rage, and they begin to tear each other apart. The girls cringe against the bar, thinking at first that this can't be serious, but as the battle goes on in earnest, they decide to get out of there fast. The sailors dive behind the bar in a tussle and don't notice that the girls have walked out on them. When they pause and wake up to this fact, they look at each other frantically and dive for the door. Out on the street they can't find the girls. They look at each other with amused disgust, straighten out their uniforms, nurse their aches and pains, and relax again.

What are they to do now? Maybe another drink will help. They re-enter the bar, down a drink apiece, and again the same sailor pays. The friends head back for the street. They stand there under the lamppost, as they did before they first entered the bar at the beginning of the evening. They split another piece of gum three ways; they tear off the paper and flip it into the street.

The music sounds noisily, and a beautiful babe promenades across the street —terrific, you understand? As before, the three bodies slant in unison as they follow her every step and wiggle. The girl struts off down the street on the left. The sailors seem to recover from her fascination and remember the bruises of the battle royal the last girls got them involved in. Each watches the others carefully, to be sure that this feeling is unanimous. This is just a stall. They begin to idle away from each other, laughing the blonde off, when one sailor strikes off like a streak of lightning after the girl. His friends follow. The cycle is endless.

NOTES   Lincoln Kirstein, in his book *Movement and Metaphor* (1970), which analyzes fifty seminal ballets in the history of the art, reminds us that *Fancy Free* "remains the sturdiest characteristic national work" in the American repertory.

FANFARE

Classic ballet in one act. Music by Benjamin Britten. Choreography by Jerome Robbins. Lighting by Jean Rosenthal. First presented by the New York City Ballet at the City Center, New York, June 2, 1953, with a cast headed by Yvonne Mounsey, Todd Bolender, Frank Hobi, and Michael Maule.

Fanfare, which had its first performance on Coronation Night 1953, is a visualization of *The Young Person's Guide to the Orchestra,* a well-known work by the contemporary English composer Benjamin Britten. Britten's score consists of variations and a fugue on a theme by Henry Purcell, from *Abdelazor.* These variations and the final fugue illustrate, one by one, the different musical instruments, or group of instruments, that make up the modern symphony orchestra. The ballet is a set of dances arranged to these variations and fugue. A narrator stands at the side of the stage to introduce the ballet and the different instruments.

When the curtain rises, all the dancers who will later represent the different instruments of the orchestra are gathered together on stage under heraldic flags that depict ancient instruments. As Purcell's theme is played by the orchestra, the dancers imitate by noble gestures and attitudes the solemn dignity and nobility of the music. The dancers' costumes differentiate by color the four families of the symphony orchestra: the woodwinds are dressed in blue, the strings in orange, the brass in yellow, and the percussion in black. Each dancer's costume is embellished with a design that identifies the instrument portrayed. Each wears a crown.

After the opening theme has been stated, all the dancers exit. Now the narrator introduces the instruments. First, the woodwinds. The variation of piccolo and two flutes is characterized by a *pas de trois,* danced by three girls. Next, the clarinets, who are represented by a *pas de deux* for a boy and a girl. A lone girl dances to the music of the oboe. She moves in slow, beautiful adagio to its music. Next, two boys dance comically to the variation for two bassoons.

The strings now take the stage. The first and second violins are represented by groups of girls. They are followed by a girl and a boy who dance to the music of the violas. Two girls depict the cellos, while a boy mimes and dances the difficulties of the double bass. Finally the harp, represented by a ballerina all in white, fills the eye with precise and flowing grace to tingling arpeggios.

Next the brass—horns, trumpets, tuba, and trombones—are depicted. Finally, the percussion—drums, cymbals, gongs, etc. The variation which these instruments play is represented by three boys who characterize by horseplay and wit the sudden booms, rattles, crashes, and slaps of the percussion instruments.

Now that all the instruments of the orchestra have been demonstrated, the narrator tells us: "We have taken the orchestra to pieces. It remains to put it back together again. We shall do this in the form of a fugue."

The first voice of the fugue is taken by the woodwinds, one by one; next come the different strings; then the brass; and, at the end, the percussion. The four great families of the orchestra mingle on stage, depicting by a massive dance the cumulative power of all the instruments. The original theme by Purcell is again sounded by the entire orchestra, and all the dancers accompany the music with triumphant, noble flourishes.

Fanfare was revived by the New York City Ballet January 15, 1976, at the New York State Theatre, Lincoln Center, New York.

FANTASIES

Music by Ralph Vaughan Williams. Choreography by John Clifford. Costumes by Robert O'Hearn. Lighting by Ronald Bates. First presented by the New York City Ballet at the New York State Theatre, Lincoln Center, January 23, 1969, with Kay Mazzo, Sara Leland, Conrad Ludlow, and Anthony Blum.

A dramatic dance ballet for two couples, *Fantasies* is about reality and the ideal—the real persons we meet and the imagined ideal we sometimes make them into. The music is Vaughan Williams' *Fantasia on a Theme by Thomas Tallis.*

The Chicago critic Thomas Willis said: "The ballet is at once tender and passionate, joyful and wistful, *Romeo and Juliet* in a skewed mirror."

Writing after its première, Clive Barnes said in the New York *Times* that the twenty-one-year-old John Clifford, "the City Ballet's wunderkind, produced his second work for the company and it fascinated . . . It is a very good piece . . . and reveals a choreographer of more than usual interest . . . Here he is concerned with choreography that combines Soviet-style partnering with a very Tudoresque awareness of the psychological motivation of movement. It is a good work, arresting and moving . . . It was a privilege to be there in the theatre when Mr. Clifford's future first became apparent."

FEAST OF ASHES

Music by Carlos Surinach. Choreography by Alvin Ailey. Costumes by Jack Venza. First presented by the Robert Joffrey Ballet at the Fashion Institute of Technology, New York, September 30, 1962, with Françoise Martinet, Lisa Bradley, and Paul Sutherland in leading roles.

This dramatic ballet is based on García Lorca's famous play *The House of Bernarda Alba.* The story, narrated in modern dance techniques, tells the tragic plight of a young girl, Adella, who tries to escape the fatal decisions of her matriarchal family. Her love for her elder sister's fiancé causes a family disaster.

The music for the ballet is Surinach's *Doppio Concertino* and part of his *Ritmo Jondo.* The choreographer has said that he chose these scores "because of their texture, rhythm, color, and dynamics in relation to the theme of the dance drama. Also because, like the work itself, they are a stylization of real Spanish themes—both secular and religious. I have tried in the texture of the movement to re-create, with stylized modern movements, the quality of Lorca's drama—to start as the playwright and actor do with the natural gesture and meaning and to extend these into the intense and telling emotional language of modern dance. I have tried to suggest and comment upon Lorca's view of his Spanish milieu rather than imitate it. I have also tried through this movement to universalize this drama of matriarchal domination. And, last of all, I have tried to remain as faithful as one can in a transposition of this sort to the great play upon which it is based."

Reviewing *Feast of Ashes* in the Washington *Post*, the critic Jean Battey found it "a stunning work of theatre . . . It is magnificently conceived, moving from the daughter's relationship to her mother and family to the inner torment of her lover . . . The dance idiom is strongly that of modern dance (no one is on point), with strong use of Spanish dance to underline the brooding Spanish mood."

LA FÊTE ÉTRANGE

Ballet in two scenes. Music by Gabriel Fauré selected by Ronald Crichton. Book by Ronald Crichton. Choreography by Andrée Howard. Scenery and costumes by Sophie Fedorovitch. First presented by the London Ballet at the Arts Theatre, London, May 23, 1940, with Frank Staff, Maude Lloyd, and David Paltenghi in the principal roles. First presented in the United States by the Royal Ballet at the Metropolitan Opera House, New York, with Donald MacLeary, Anya Linden, and Ronald Hynd in the principal roles.

Based on an episode in a chapter in Alain Fournier's novel *Le Grand Meaulnes*, *La Fête Étrange* is a ballet about "the tragedy of sensitive adolescence, symbolized not only by the sequence of events, but by the gradual though pronounced change of mood; anticipation leading through happiness to ecstasy, which in its turn fades into sadness and disillusion." These words by Ronald Crichton, whose idea the ballet was, reflect the narrative action, which shows an adventure a country boy has one winter day with the inhabitants of a strange château.

There he wanders early one morning and is fascinated to find a lovely young girl, who mistakes him for a moment for her fiancé, a young nobleman she has come out of the house to meet. She returns to the house, her fiancé arrives, and the boy is about to leave when he meets with guests on their way to the wedding at the château. He joins them and in the second scene, on the terrace of the château, he again meets the lovely young girl. She and all the guests are kind to him, and excited by their warmth and elegance, the boy is happier than he has ever been. But this cannot last. The fiancé, jealous of the bride's kindness to the boy, denounces her and leaves her. The boy is heartbroken and tries in vain to console the girl, who goes into the house alone. The boy leaves and goes back into the country.

Reassessing this ballet after many years, the critic James Monahan wrote in *The Dancing Times* that it was still a beautiful work because "it carries just the sort of 'story-line'—and no more—which a ballet can well support. Ballet is the lyric poetry among the dramatic arts; it is at its weakest when it tries to be most dramatic and at its strongest either when it relies most on 'pure' dance or when, like lyric poetry, it is evoking mood and atmosphere rather than telling a story. There is very little story in *La Fête Étrange;* it is all, or almost all, mood and atmosphere—wonderfully evoked by Fedorovitch and Fauré, gracefully sustained by Andrée Howard."

FÊTE NOIRE

Music by Dimitri Shostakovich. Choreography by Arthur Mitchell. Scenery and costumes by Bernard Johnson. Lighting by Fred Barry. Pianist: Craig Sheppard. Conducted by Isaiah Jackson. First presented by the Dance Theatre of Harlem.

When the Dance Theatre of Harlem presented *Fête Noire* at the Spoleto Festival in July, 1971, the critic William Weaver called the ballet "a kind of black version of *Graduation Ball,* danced with precision and brio," and so indeed it is. The music is the *Concerto No. 2 for Piano and Orchestra* by Shostakovich. The setting is a huge ballroom where, responsive to the developing themes and moods of the music, the dancers celebrate an important occasion that demands of them their very best.

FIELD FIGURES

Music by Karlheinz Stockhausen. Choreography by Glen Tetley. Scenery and costumes by Nadine Baylis. First presented by the Royal Ballet, November 9, 1970, at the Theatre Royal, Nottingham, England. First presented in the United States by the same ensemble at the Metropolitan Opera House, Lincoln Center, New York, May 22, 1972, with Deanne Bergsma, Rudolf Nureyev, Vergie Derman, Michael Coleman, Sandra Conley, Wayne Eagling, and Peter O'Brien.

A dramatic dance ballet, *Field Figures* is performed to two pieces of music by Karlheinz Stockhausen: *Setz die Segel zur Sonne* ("Set Sails for the Sun") and *Verbindung* ("Connection"). They consist of instrumental improvisations that are variously processed by electronic techniques at the time they are played.

The setting is an abstract one of vertical rods and there is about the piece a sense of the magnetic field—what happens when certain bodies in certain situations attract and repel, satisfy and frustrate. The three girls and the four boys in the ballet are variously paired but there is one principal couple.

Writing in *The Times* of London, the critic John Percival said: "There is nothing pretty about *Field Figures,* but it is, to my mind, extraordinarily beautiful."

Richard Buckle in the *Sunday Times* of London said that *Field Figures* "is one of the most important creations of our time." Writing in the *Financial*

Times, Andrew Porter called it "one of the most perfectly shaped, impressive and enthralling works in the repertory."

LA FILLE MAL GARDÉE (The Unchaperoned Daughter)

Ballet in three scenes. Music by Ferdinand Hérold. Choreography by Jean Dauberval. First presented at Bordeaux, France, 1789, and at the Grand Theatre, Paris, July 1, 1789. First presented in the United States in various versions beginning in 1794. Revived by Ballet Theatre, with music by Wilhelm Hertel and choreography restaged by Bronislava Nijinska and Dimitri Romanoff, at the Center Theatre, New York, January 19, 1940, scenery and costumes by Serge Soudeikine.

Many people who go to the ballet and chance to come across a work that was originally presented more than a hundred and fifty years ago imagine that such a ballet must be sad—perhaps an antique tragedy. But *La Fille Mal Gardée* is a comedy. The earliest of all the ballets in the current repertory, its universally comical situations are no doubt responsible for its survival.

Soon after the music begins, a painted drop curtain depicts the principal characters of the ballet. On the left are Lisette and Colin, the two lovers. A rotund Cupid painted at the top of the scene directs a pointed arrow at the heroine. Lisette's mother, Madame Simone, dominates the scene, trying to watch her daughter and be pleasant to the suitor she has chosen for her. The story contained in this picture gradually unfolds as the drop curtain rises. The ballet is set in a small provincial French town. The time is about two hundred years ago.

SCENE ONE: THE FARM OF MADAME SIMONE   Alongside the steep-roofed house of Madame Simone, a "rich farmerette," is the family barnyard. In back, a rushing stream cascades down a hill. Madame Simone sits on a bench at the left, whiling away the time of day. Two neighbors join her to gossip. She bustles off with them.

The music suggests the arrival of the heroine, and Lisette enters on the left. Dressed in a light-blue skirt with a red bodice, with blue ribbons in her hair, she is the picture of innocent, country prettiness. The day has just begun, and because she is supposed to be busy at one task or another, Lisette pretends to arrange several flowerpots on the bench. She bows to several of the village boys, bound for the fields with their scythes, as she waters the flowers. Colin, a good-looking farmer, enters on the left, carrying a rake. He sits down on the bench, and Lisette, anxious to be surprised by his arrival, absent-mindedly waters his head. Colin jumps up, and he and Lisette immediately begin to dance together. Their dance reveals that the two have been attracted to each other for some time, that this is not their first rendezvous. Colin lifts Lisette boldly, yet gently.

The love duet is interrupted by Lisette's mother. Directly she approaches, the two lovers rush to hide behind the bench. Madame Simone discovers them, however, and chases Colin around the stage. Hastily he embraces Lisette and rushes off. Madame Simone, in a high temper, proceeds to lecture her daughter on her duty to make a proper marriage. Lisette protests that she is absolutely innocent of any flirtation, but her mother persists in her rage. The two neighbors come in to watch the scene. Lisette finally secures her mother's forgiveness by offering her, with a sweet smile, one of her own flowers.

Trumpets announce the arrival of four of Lisette's friends. They are followed by a group of villagers. The young people want Lisette to join them. Dutifully she asks her mother's permission and she begins to dance. Colin sneaks in at the back and conceals himself in the crowd. He runs out and takes Lisette's hand when her mother stalks off. The two dance a lively duet, surrounded by their friends. The music is gay and sparkling. The conviviality is short-lived, however, for Madame Simone returns, sees Colin, and sends him packing. She makes a point of her daughter's idleness by presenting scythes to her four friends.

Lisette attempts to console herself by dancing with her friends as they celebrate the harvesttime. She tries to leave with them when they go, but her mother pulls her back. Lisette herself is now in a temper. She stomps, shakes her fists pathetically, cries, and hides her face in her hands. Her mother takes her hands away and tries to make amends. Colin has entered quietly and stands in back of Madame Simone. That is consolation enough for Lisette. She waves to him. Her mother notes the gesture, but cannot find a reason for it. Colin does not conceal himself for long, however. The impetuous girl rushes to him. They embrace briefly before Madame Simone leaps at them to drag Lisette back toward the house.

She sits her daughter down on the bench. Lisette rises and brings out a butter churn. Her mother fills the churn with cream and orders her daughter to work. Lisette churns away, and her mother leaves the scene. Colin leaps in behind Lisette. He places his hands on hers and easily persuades her to stop her work. He sits down on the bench beside her; Lisette, suddenly embarrassed at being alone with her lover, rises and dances. She turns softly and slowly, beguiling Colin with her sweet motion. When she finishes her dance with a series of rapid turns, Colin throws out to her a long blue ribbon. Lisette catches it and, holding the flowing ribbon above their heads, the two dance together romantically. Lisette tosses the ribbon back to Colin, who fixes it halter-fashion around her shoulders, after which the girl performs her steps as if by his command. Lisette pirouettes into his arms, Colin ties the ribbon about her, and the girl poses against her lover. The two then leave the stage.

Thomas, a vinegrower, enters with his son, Alain. Come to see Madame Simone by appointment, the obese Thomas is decked out in a bright-green suit; he is determined to be formal and correct. His son, determined to be playful and completely oblivious to his surroundings, leaps about the stage trying to catch butterflies in a net. Thomas reprimands him and pulls him to a bench.

Madame Simone, dressed in her best purple, arrives to greet the guests. With ceremonious gestures, she and Thomas discuss the suitability of a marriage between their children. Madame Simone is readily persuaded of Alain's eligibility when Thomas dangles a bag of gold in her face. The woman approaches to examine the young man, ascertains that he is sound of limb if not of mind, and gives her approval. She drags Lisette out to meet her fiancé. Dutifully the girl has changed her clothes for the occasion, but she has no idea of its real meaning. Both parents push their children toward each other. Both children step back in horror as they realize the meaning of their parents' interview. Each tries to escape, but the parents hold them secure. The curtain falls as they both kneel, their faces turned away from each other. Lisette's white dress and pink ribbons are for the wrong man. Madame Simone stands over them in an attitude of supreme happiness. During the scene change, Thomas and Madame Simone, accompanied by the neighbors, drag the engaged couple off to the village notary to make the marriage settlement final.

SCENE TWO: THE VILLAGE GREEN   On the painted backdrop, wheat fields are seen in the distance. Sheaves of freshly cut wheat are propped up where the workers have left them. A windmill stands over the fields on a hill at the back. On the right is a great tree; two cows meditate nearby. The workers of the village, colorfully dressed girls and their companions, pause for a general dance. Lisette and Alain are pushed into the scene by their parents. Despite all their complaining, the two are made to stand close together. They are able to separate only when Thomas asks Madame Simone to dance. The aged couple cavort grotesquely about the green; it has suddenly occurred to Madame Simone that she, too, might be quite a match, and she flirts with the vine-grower.

Meanwhile Colin has entered quietly on the right. He sees that his sweetheart has been promised to another and turns away. Madame Simone and Thomas race off to pursue their flirtation elsewhere, and some of Lisette's friends, noticing Colin's plight, encourage the girl to comfort the poor lad. Lisette touches his arm. By her soft, endearing gestures the girl convinces him that she herself has had nothing to do with the proposed match. Colin puts his arms about her, and their foreheads touch. He kneels, and the two begin an adagio to the melody of solo strings and an accompanying harp. The villagers sit on the ground to watch the lovers. Lisette leaves the scene after the dance is over, and Colin performs a bright, dazzling variation. Lisette returns for a winsome, engaging dance in which she lifts her skirt softly, with innocent coquetry. Her variation increases in momentum; at the end she turns brilliantly and cuts her movement off suddenly with a swift, pert pose.

Alain, who has been off chasing after butterflies, runs onto the scene, brandishing his net before him. He circles the stage in long, high leaps. Two of the girls try to engage his attention. The youth ignores their flattery, but the girls persist and dance on either side of him. Alain abandons them, jumping off into the wings in pursuit of his hobby.

Thunder is heard and the scene darkens; lightning flashes illumine the hurried dashing back and forth of the villagers. Lisette and Colin follow as their friends run for cover. Alain rushes in, trembling with fright at the lightning. He hides his head under a girl's skirts and pushes her off toward safety. The drop curtain falls.

SCENE THREE: MADAME SIMONE'S HOUSE   Lisette enters quickly to escape the storm. Her mother follows and bustles about the room. Lisette pours coffee for her, then sits at her feet as Madame Simone begins to work at her spinning wheel. Lisette tries to sneak away, but her mother orders her to read a book she gives her. Lisette looks at a page or two, then asks her mother the meaning of one of the words. Madame Simone is horrified: she has given her daughter the wrong book! A romantic novel, no less! The girl succeeds in crawling away a few feet until Madame Simone seizes her from behind and draws her back to her chair. She takes up her sewing again.

Colin opens the transom above the door and throws in a flower to Lisette. Lisette turns around and sees him. Immediately her mother senses her agitation and commands her to be still. Colin, by passionate signs, beseeches her to dance for him. The girl persuades her mother to play the tambourine so that she can practice her dancing. Lisette dances flirtatiously for Colin's benefit. The old woman tires of the tambourine and falls off to sleep. Lisette approaches her on tiptoe. As the girl takes her key, her mother wakens and beats the tambourine. Lisette continues her dance, and at its conclusion Madame Simone kisses her in reward.

Boys and girls of the village enter, bringing with them sheaves of wheat, which they stack against a table. Lisette would like to follow them off, but her mother commands her to take her turn at the spinning wheel. Lisette stamps her foot and throws herself down in the chair to sulk. Her mother leaves the room.

The orchestra repeats the melody to which she and Colin danced so happily, and Lisette imagines what it would be like to be married to the man of her own choice. She puts her hands on her heart and blows a kiss toward the door. She sees herself surrounded by Colin's children, whom she scolds; she rocks her arms as if they held a child.

To Lisette's embarrassment, Colin is there in the room watching her. The sheaves of wheat are thrown aside, and her lover sits smiling at her. She sits beside him for a moment, then jumps up as he proposes to her seriously. Colin pleads with her—after all, she has just imagined herself as his wife—but the girl in her embarrassment and confusion denies her love and shoves the boy toward the door. Colin begins to lose his temper at her stubbornness and is delighted to find her even more flustered when she finds that the door is locked!

Lisette runs to the chair and sees that she can keep up the pretense no longer. Colin kneels at her feet and places his head in her lap. The two trade their scarves as a pledge of their love. Madame Simone can be heard approaching. Lisette tries to hide Colin—under the little table, in a small chest. In desperation, she pushes him into the hayloft and slams the door shut just as her mother enters.

Lisette thinks she is safe but she has forgotten Colin's scarf. Madame Simone spots it instantly and fetches a large switch to beat the girl. Lisette runs, but the old woman catches up with her, spanks her soundly, and, as an additional penalty, locks her in the hayloft!

Visitors are heard outside. Madame Simone admits Thomas and Alain, the village notary and his secretary following in their wake. Villagers accompany them to witness the marriage contract. The notary buries his face in his registry, the parents rejoice, and the preoccupied Alain toys with the spinning wheel. Madame Simone presents him with the key to the hayloft and tells the youth where to find his bride. Alain unlocks the door. Lisette and Colin step out sheepishly, their clothes and hair covered with hay.

Madame Simone is scandalized. Before all the village, her daughter has ruined the family's reputation. Lisette begs her to understand. Colin joins Lisette, and both lovers kneel before her. At first Madame Simone refuses to listen. Then she realizes that the notary can quite easily make another marriage contract and consents. Lisette kisses her joyfully. Colin kisses her. The two lovers kiss, and Madame Simone embraces them both.

Ballet in two acts. Music by Ferdinand Hérold, freely adapted and arranged by John Lanchbery. Choreography by Frederick Ashton. Scenery and costumes by Osbert Lancaster. First presented by the Royal Ballet at the Royal Opera House, Covent Garden, January 28, 1960, with Nadia Nerina, David Blair, Stanley Holden, and Alexander Grant in the principal roles. First presented in the United States by the Royal Ballet at the Metropolitan Opera House, New York, September 14, 1960, with the same principals.

Although other versions of the ballet are often danced, Frederick Ashton's re-creation of *La Fille Mal Gardée* is now permanent in the modern repertory. In 1960 Tamara Karsavina, the ballerina who danced in the ballet in Russia, recalled an earlier production in the Covent Garden program: "This production we now regard as the turning point in the history of ballet; a break-away from the formal, pseudoclassical tradition; a ballet of action instead of a succession of conventional dances which use the plot as a peg on which to hang a succession of *entrées, pas seuls, pas d'ensemble* . . . The story lends itself admirably to ballet treatment; there is not a dance in it that does not flow directly out of a natural situation. It is a charming period piece singularly compatible with the artistic trends of today . . ."

The music for the ballet, entirely restudied and arranged by John Lanchbery after consulting varied scores for the ballet by Hertel, Feldt, and others, is based on the 1828 score of Ferdinand Hérold, then chorus master of the Paris Opéra. After a pleasant overture, the curtain rises. An inner drop curtain depicts a charming rural landscape with a village in the distance. Arnold Haskell in the Covent Garden program describes the action when this inner curtain rises:

ACT ONE, SCENE ONE: THE FARMYARD   "Lise, the only daughter of Simone, a widow and owner of a prosperous farm, is in love with Colas, a young farmer, but her mother has more ambitious plans.

"The dawn of a busy day on the farm is heralded by the cock and his attendant hens. Lise, disappointed at not seeing Colas, leaves a ribbon tied in a lover's knot, as a token of her devotion. He finds it and ties it to his staff. The lovers meet, but are interrupted by Simone, who sets her daughter a task of churning butter. Colas, in hiding in the loft, joins her. The work is shared and then forgotten as they declare their love.

"The farm girls summon Lise to play, but her mind is elsewhere. Her suspicious and ever-watchful mother catches hold of her and chastises her. Just then Thomas, the prosperous and wealthy proprietor of a vineyard, arrives with his son Alain. Simone, aware of their mission, dismisses Lise. Thomas asks her hand for his son, and when Lise returns, Alain, coy and clumsy, shows off his paces. She is amused and a little shocked by his antics, but definitely not interested. They set off for the harvest.

ACT ONE, SCENE TWO: THE CORNFIELD   "It is harvest time, and after working in the fields the harvesters, led by Colas, relax in a joyful dance. Lise and Alain dance, but Colas intervenes, and the young girl makes it clear where her preference lies. One of the harvesters plays the flute to the general merriment, and Alain thinks he will have a turn, but the harvesters mock him and he is rescued from their horseplay by his indignant father.

"The field is now left for the triumphant Colas, who dances with Lise. Simone joins in the merriment. But suddenly they are interrupted by a storm that drenches them, scattering them far and wide.

ACT TWO: INTERIOR OF THE FARM   "Mother and daughter, soaked by the storm, return to the farmhouse. They sit down to spin: work, thinks the mother, should keep Lise out of mischief. But she is overcome by sleep and Lise, who has seen Colas through the gate, tries to take the key from her. Simone awakes and, in order to remain watchful, plays the tambourine for Lise to dance. But the tap grows feebler, she begins to nod, and now she is fast asleep. Lise runs to the door and makes love to Colas through the unfriendly bars. The knocking of the harvesters, coming for their pay, awakens Simone. Colas enters with them and conceals himself in a pile of straw. Simone tells her daughter to get on with her chores as she leaves to give the harvesters a drink. Lise, thinking she is alone, dreams of the delights of married life. Colas cannot resist, and comes out from hiding. She is bashful at first having been taken by surprise, but once again they declare their love, exchanging scarves as a token.

"As Simone reappears, Lise hustles Colas into her bedroom. The ever-suspicious mother realizes that the lovers have been meeting, and in her turn hustles Lise into the bedroom, locking the door.

"Alain and his father now arrive with a notary to complete the marriage contract. When it is signed, Simone hands Alain the key to the bedroom. After a moment of idiotic indecision, he opens the door, and to everyone's dismay, Colas and Lise emerge. The lovers fall on their knees to ask Simone for forgiveness and a blessing. In spite of the fury of Thomas and Alain, urged on by the notary and the villagers, she finally gives in amidst general rejoicing."

NOTES   Andrew Porter, music and dance critic of *The Financial Times*, London, has said of this ballet: "The first act, in two parts, lasts just over an hour; the second, thirty-six minutes. There is not an ounce of padding. Invention tumbles on invention, and the whole thing is fully realized in dance. The second act, in fact, is continuous, *durchkomponiert;* there is no possible break for applause except between the sections of the *grand pas de deux* just before the final gigue. The choreography is wonderfully fresh, and the shape of the scenes is beautifully balanced.

"There is comedy, sentiment, jollity, romance, flowing one into another. There is a clog dance for Widow Simone, brilliantly sustained; a 'parade' before the drop curtain which must be the most delightful of its kind ever done; a *valse des moissoneurs* in the first act which one would like to be twice as long; a stave dance; breathtaking 'Russian' lifts; passages which seem to be inspired by the virtuosity of the Georgians.

"Ribbons run like a motif through the first two scenes. They are used in a score of ingenious and beautiful ways, reaching their climax in a great maypole where the fleeting kaleidoscope of stage patterns is recorded by the plaited thread.

"To a far greater extent than any of the classics as we now know them, *La Fille Mal Gardée* seems to be all 'highlights,' without any of the stretches that we sit through for the sake of the best bits. And this cunningly varied and ceaseless flow of dance is constantly enlivened by the most brilliant inventions by the way, comic or touching, that give fullness to the ballet—far more of them than can be taken in at once."

Interviewed by the critic Don McDonagh in *Ballet Review* (Vol. 3, No. 4), Frederick Ashton observed that *La Fille Mal Gardée* is a really English work. "It has the Lancashire clog dance which is almost like a folk dance. *Fille* came about in a very odd way because of Karsavina. She was always after me to do it. I didn't particularly like the idea and I didn't like the music to the traditional version, by Hertel. I went back to Hérold, who did it originally . . . It was mostly a matter of selecting and curtailing. I always work out the structure of a ballet before I start—who's doing what and for how long. I don't do any steps until I'm with the dancers. The structure for *Fille* I worked out with John Lanchbery, marking the music. I have a great instinct for the right length of things. And I set that very tightly. It's a kind of minutage. And after I set that, in the case of *Fille* at least, it went very easily. Everything just flowed."

Readers are referred to David Vaughan's *Frederick Ashton and His Ballets* for more details on the genesis of *Fille Mal Gardée.* Vaughan has written in *Ballet Review* about Ashton and this ballet:

"He is a great comic choreographer. *La Fille Mal Gardée* is a perfect expression of his artistic benevolence. The dramatic complications are ingenious and of great concern to the characters involved. Yet the problems can be solved, the mistakes can be mended and the mistaken forgiven. As in Molière, all balance which can be attained is attained (the lovers marry) and any remaining sources of imbalance are neutralized (Molière's hypochondriac becomes a doctor himself, Ashton's Alain goes off with his umbrella).

"Each set of characters has its distinct style. The young lovers dance in a now playful, now softly melting classicism. The farmers' choreography combines classicism with folk dance borrowings to suggest the union of man with nature and a love of meaningful work. Simone, Thomas, and Alain derive from farce, pantomime, and music-hall. The dancing chickens, which some ballet-goers find annoyingly "unrealistic," may be there to be deliberately artificial, to emphasize right from the start that this ballet, however homely its subject, is not photographic naturalism, but instead uses the exaggerations of comedy to point to certain human truths."*

FILLING STATION

Ballet-document in one act. Music by Virgil Thomson. Choreography by Lew Christensen. Book by Lincoln Kirstein. Scenery and costumes by Paul Cadmus. First presented by Ballet Caravan at the Avery Memorial Theatre, Hartford, Connecticut, January 6, 1938, with Lew Christensen, Marie-Jeanne, Erick Hawkins, Michael Kidd, Todd Bolender, Eugene Loring, and Fred Danieli in the principal roles.

Filling Station is not only one of the first modern ballets on a familiar American subject, but one of the first ballets to employ American music, scenery, and costumes by an American, and American dancers. It was the first ballet on an American subject commissioned by Lincoln Kirstein for his Ballet Caravan, a small American company founded in 1936 which, with the Balanchine-Kirstein American Ballet, was to be the precursor of the present New York City Ballet.

Filling Station is an attempt to discover an American hero, a hero equivalent to the heroes of classical European ballets. The makers of the ballet have chosen a filling station attendant as their hero. The fact that the ballet succeeded in its aim was recently demonstrated by the marked success of its revival, which clearly indicated that the popular American myth of 1938 was still viable fifteen years later.

After a robust overture, the curtain rises on the interior of Mac's filling station. It is night. A neon sign advertising gas is seen in reverse against the large plate-glass window on the left. In the rear, there is a door leading to the station rest room.

Mac, the station attendant, is whiling away the lonely hours of the night reading a tabloid. He puts down the paper and begins to dance. He moves about the stage with vigorous leaps and turns. His dance is interrupted by a motorist who comes into the station to ask for directions. The motorist is dressed like a golfer in a comic strip: he wears violently colored checkered knickers, straw hat, and smokes a cigar.

Mac tries to direct him to his destination by pointing out the route on a map. When the motorist fails to understand, Mac produces a huge enlargement of the map to set him right. Behind this map, two truck drivers, friends of Mac, sneak into the station while Mac gives the motorist final directions.

As soon as the motorist departs, the two truck drivers greet Mac and the three men dance an athletic *pas de trois* that features cartwheels and somer-

* Reprinted by permission of *Ballet Review,* Marcel Dekker, publisher.

saults. Their good fellowship is cut short by the arrival of a state trooper, who accuses the truck drivers of speeding. The men deny this, and the state trooper leaves after warning them severely.

The motorist in knickers returns, this time with his family and his golf gear. His wife, a huge blonde in unbecoming slacks, towers over her husband and constantly berates him. Their daughter, a constantly whining child, is clearly in need of the rest room. While his wife and daughter disappear into the rear of the station, the motorist entertains Mac and the truck drivers by practicing golf. He is not happy for long, however. When wife and daughter return, they combine to make life so miserable for him that he happily leads them back to their car outside.

Now an intoxicated young couple drop by on their way home from a party at the local country club. The girl stumbles in first, followed by her escort. She is in no condition to dance, but insists on doing so. The boy supports her in adagio poses, holding the girl's almost limp body upright when she collapses in his arms.

As the couple finish this comic adagio, they are joined by Mac and the truck drivers. By this time, the girl wants to dance with everybody. All the men join her in a dance that is climaxed as she is tossed from one man to another and thrown high into the air. When the unhappy motorist, who has momentarily escaped from his wife and child, re-enters the station, the dance is at fever pitch. Noting the newcomer, the girl jumps into his arms just as his wife comes in 'after him.

The motorist tries to stay on the opposite side of the stage from his wife as all join in the "Big Apple." But the celebration is soon broken up. A gangster enters. He lines all the people up and instructs them to place all their jewelry and cash in a bag he snatches from the motorist's wife. Everyone conforms to his wish except Mac, who sneaks outside and turns out the lights.

Directly the lights go out, the stage is in confusion. Mac enters with a flashlight, and soon the stage is filled with the beams of flashlights carried by the others as they try to help Mac track down the gangster. Blinded by their lights, the gangster shoots.

When the lights come up, it can be seen that the girl from the country club is dead. All gather around her body. The state trooper enters and takes the gangster off to prison. The girl's body is lifted high and carried off in solemn procession. Just as the ballet seems about to end in a tragedy, the girl wakes from the dead and waves at Mac as her cortege moves out of the station. Mac saunters about for a moment, then returns to his newspaper.

NOTES *Filling Station* was revived by the New York City Ballet on May 12, 1953, at the City Center, New York. Jacques d'Amboise, Janet Reed, and Michael Maule danced the principal roles.

FIREBIRD

Dramatic ballet in three scenes. Music by Igor Stravinsky. Choreography by Michel Fokine. Scenery and costumes by Golovine and Bakst. First presented by Diaghilev's Ballets Russes at the Théâtre National de l'Opéra, Paris, June 25, 1910, with Tamara Karsavina as the Firebird, Michel Fokine as Prince Ivan, and Enrico Cecchetti as Kastchei.

Firebird marks Igor Stravinsky's entry into the field of ballet music. Perhaps his most famous score, the original ballet to the music remained dormant for many years. In 1954, to commemorate the twenty-fifth anniversary of the death of Diaghilev, under whose auspices the original had been created, the Royal Ballet produced in London a reconstruction of the original, with scenery and costumes by Natalie Gontcharova. This was made possible by Serge Grigoriev, Diaghilev's régisseur for many years, Lubov Tchernicheva, and Tamara Karsavina. The revival was first presented at the Empire Theatre, Edinburgh, August 23, 1954, with Margot Fonteyn as the *Firebird,* Michael Somes as *Prince Ivan,* Svetlana Beriosova as the *Tsarevna,* and Frederick Ashton as *Kastchei.* This production was first given in the United States at the Metropolitan Opera House, September 20, 1955, with the same principals.

Fokine has described in his book *Memoirs of a Ballet Master* how he envisaged the action of the ballet, and the background to the collaboration that produced the final work. In the Royal Ballet revival, the curtain rises on the enchanted garden of the sinister Kastchei. A high golden fence protects his golden fruit and the lovely princesses he has captured. The Firebird now appears, followed by Prince Ivan. The Firebird attempts to steal the golden apples from Kastchei's magic tree but Ivan captures her. He vows that he will not let her go unless she gives him one of her feathers. With her feather as talisman, he is assured of her magic intercession if he should ever need it. The Firebird yields to his entreaties and leaves.

Now in the growing darkness Ivan learns from the most beautiful of the captive maidens held prisoner by Kastchei how the evil magician entraps innocent travelers and turns them into stone. Ivan is attracted to the lovely creature who tells him this strange story and they dance. At dawn they kiss and part, the girl warning him not to follow her.

Ivan does not heed the warning. Following after his beloved, he opens the gate to Kastchei's magic garden and alarms sound, bells peal, and swarms of monsters rush out. Kastchei emerges, his enslaved creatures do him homage, and he approaches Ivan menacingly. The wicked magician tries to turn him to stone but just then Ivan remembers the Firebird's feather. He waves the feather in Kastchei's face and the Firebird instantly reappears. She compels Kastchei's monsters to dance until they collapse. Then, remembering the great egg that holds the soul of the magician, she orders Ivan to steal it. Finding it, Ivan throws the egg into the air. As it falls and breaks, Kastchei dies. Ivan then is free to marry his princess. All at the ceremony rejoice. The Firebird flies away forever.

Music by Igor Stravinsky. Choreography by George Balanchine. Setting by Marc Chagall. Lighting by Jean Rosenthal. First presented by the New York City Ballet at the City Center, New York, November 27, 1949, with Maria Tallchief as the Firebird *and Francisco Moncion as* Prince Ivan.

The composer of *Firebird,* Igor Stravinsky, once said that Russian legends have as their heroes men who are "simple, naïve, sometimes even stupid, devoid of all malice, and it is they who are always victorious over characters that are clever, artful, complex, cruel and powerful." Prince Ivan in this ballet is such a hero: he is a simple hunter who stumbles into the eerie garden of an evil monster, there falls in love with a beautiful princess held captive by the ogre, and rescues her with a supernatural power granted him by a magical bird of fire.

SCENE ONE: A FOREST   As the music to the ballet begins, we have that first suggestion of the mystery and magic that will control Ivan's destiny. No sooner has the orchestra—with its low, throbbing strings and baleful trombones—given us a hint of darkness and foreboding, than the curtain rises to present us with an enormous painting of the ballet's heroine, the Firebird who will help the prince to free the world of one of its monstrous evils. The Firebird is depicted as bright, glorious, and triumphant—a fantastic creature, half bird, half woman. She has the face and arms of a charming young girl and a body of shimmering feathers that tapers off in orange-speckled flame. This colorful figure is painted against a background of amorphous, purple shapes. The music now suggests unimagined giants plodding across the earth and a fairyland peopled with primeval beings sadly singing an accompaniment.

Now the painted curtain rises. It is dark, and as the stage brightens slightly, we can see in the background trees so thickly crowded that the sun can scarcely penetrate. Here in the forest we are transported visually to the world of fantasy at which the music has hinted, and when the prince enters, his bow stretched tightly, ready to destroy any creature concealed in the thicket, we understand why he hunts with care. Ivan wears a costume more becoming to an untutored Russian peasant than to a royal prince, but this serves only to remind us that we are watching a story of a time before the primitive court of the Tsar was altered by European opulence.

Subdued, half-uttered cries come from behind the dark trees. Ivan looks about him, searching for the beasts that may lie waiting in the shadows, when a low, steady drum, followed by an answering horn, indicates that he is about to meet his prey. Suddenly the music whirs rapidly and brightly and from above a bright amber light races around and around the prince. Ivan, almost blinded, throws up his arms in astonishment and tries to avoid the shadow the light makes of his startled figure. He runs off, seeking the safe darkness. The music increases its speed, and on stage to its swift accompaniment dances the dazzling Firebird.

Her entrance is as strong and brilliant as the bright red she wears. As she crosses the stage in a series of swiftly executed leaps and poses, followed by that same amber light which announced her arrival, glints of light catch her figure in various attitudes to reveal the long red feather that rises high on her head. Her arms and shoulders are speckled with gold dust, and the shimmering red bodice reflects spangles of brilliance about her moving form. She dances frantically, in continuous movement, to music that mirrors her great joy in displaying vivid images of flight. Even here, in the secluded forest, the Firebird refuses to be earth-bound and seems to resist nature by performing dashing movements that whip the very air about her.

The prince emerges from the shadows to watch unseen. Wishing to capture this creature who moves so magnificently, he reacts with wonder as he discovers that this marvelous bird is also a ravishing woman. He follows her surreptitiously while the Firebird, unaware of the hunter who pursues her, darts about the stage climaxing her solo with rapid turns on point across the stage. This movement increases in momentum with the music, and just as her accelerating spin reaches its fullest force and the music its highest pitch, Ivan dashes forward and reaches out to catch the Firebird about the waist. Brought down to earth, she freezes at his touch, all movement ceasing. Slowly she backs away, in terror of the hunter, in modesty at sight of the man. She turns to escape, but Ivan, fascinated at her daring now that she is in his power, holds her secure. The Firebird, rigid with fear, her arms stiff across her body, falls back against him reluctantly, apparently resigned, but now her arms fly out and beat the air in a frantic effort to free herself.

Ivan will not release his prey, and the frightened Firebird, certain of death by his hand, pleads for mercy. The prince is moved to pity by this appeal for freedom and gently loosens his grasp. He holds out his arm, and the Firebird, in extended arabesque, falls across it, bending her head so that her headdress almost touches the floor at the prince's feet as she bows in tribute to his pity and courtesy.

Encouraged now by the prince's tenderness, the Firebird moves back to dance again. When she turns full circle, Ivan comes forward to support her. Moved by his compassionate strength, as Ivan is moved by her unclaimed love, the Firebird walks toward this man so strange to her. He holds her hand high, then she runs toward him, her body falling back full-length in mid-air. Ivan catches her swooping body and supports her again, as she repeats this movement of ultimate sacrifice and trust. Assured of his sympathy, the Firebird now dances with the prince.

Standing behind her, Ivan supports her arms with his own as the Firebird, standing on point, bends her knees to the floor, then rises to his embrace. Legs spread wide, she slides across the stage as Ivan holds her. The haunting melody of their *pas de deux* soars to its height as the Firebird is held motionless on point, her right leg extended in stillness. Then she falls back, and Ivan swings her around and around in great circles as her free arm flutters in flight. Reminded by this of her greater freedom in the air, the Firebird moves as if to leave the prince. He bows to her formally in homage, and in gratitude for his generosity in releasing her, the Firebird takes from her breast a brilliant red feather. She indicates to the prince that this feather is a magic charm: he need only wave it in the air and she will come to his aid, should he ever require it. Ivan, in respectful deference to the truly supernatural being he now understands the Firebird to be, thanks her and watches regretfully as she turns and leaps gloriously into the wings. The prince follows, transfixed as the music ends in enchanted serenity.

SCENE TWO: KASTCHEI'S GARDEN   While Ivan remains in the shadows, marveling at his encounter with the Firebird, we hear a gay melody from the orchestra. Ten young princesses run in, happily dancing to its tune. They wear long peasant dresses with little caps, and their innocent, carefree gambols make it impossible for us to believe that they are, in reality, captives of the monster Kastchei who rules over the forest. Two of the young girls carry scarves and, as the group dances with simple but elegant grace, these two playfully direct the dancing of the others. They are all dancing together when Prince Ivan startles them. Shocked at the intrusion of a stranger in their dangerous world, the princesses gather together and whisper excitedly. Ivan is amused at their fear and approaches them. From a respectful distance, in mock seriousness and formality, he beckons one of the maidens to come to him. The princesses are agitated by this request and wonder at Ivan's audacity. Ivan insists, and one of the girls at last leaves the group. Ivan bows to her, then whispers softly in her ear. The girl is shocked by what he says to her and runs back to tell her friends. The maidens confer, and then the most beautiful one of them all, in sweet and nervous modesty, steps forward to greet the prince.

The two bow formally and, linking hands, lead the group in a *khorovod* or Russian round dance, to the accompaniment of folklike themes. The chorus of girls become so entwined about their two leaders that it is impossible for the prince and the princess to remain long together. They close their arms about one another, but their partners come amusingly to break their embrace. The two lovers dance with their friends until the light begins to fade. A trumpet is heard in the distance, and the girls gather together quickly in fear. The princess then hastily bids Ivan farewell and runs off with her companions. Ivan stands alone, bewildered at their behavior, as the music takes on mysterious darkness and hints of things unseen.

Ivan stares into the dark thicket about him and is suddenly afraid, but before he can leave the threatening darkness that seems to close in on him, a sharp crash of sound comes from the orchestra and dozens of weird monsters leap with a single bound into the stage and surround him. Green, brown, and multicolored creatures with hideous features and maimed limbs cavort about Ivan to fierce, militant beats from the orchestra. The monsters—some masked with the head of animals—divide into four groups and race backward and forward and sideways, each group trying to outdo the others in grotesque gestures of threat. One of the creatures is held upright, then thrown straight up into the air and caught by the others, only to be tossed up again. The music subsides, and all the creatures of this fantastic underworld fall on their faces as their master, Kastchei, enters menacingly. He is surrounded by the princess and her friends. Kastchei flourishes his dark cap at his creatures, and we glimpse his skeletonlike body. On his head he wears a spiked crown of burning gold. His fingernails, long as his hands, clutch at the air for victims to satisfy an insatiable appetite.

As Kastchei's slaves surround him in frantic attitudes of homage, Ivan moves to flee. But then he remembers the pledge of the Firebird, remembers that he need fear no danger, and brings out the magic feather. He runs, weaving in and out among the monsters, waving the charm in the air. The monsters try to close in on him. Kastchei stamps the earth in indignation and vows to kill the prince. To the theme to which they danced so playfully just a few moments before, the princesses encircle their evil lord and plead for mercy for Ivan. Kastchei dismisses them with curt disgust, but the prince, encouraged by the confusion he is causing among the monsters, races about with the brilliant red feather. The ogres step back, astounded at his fearlessness in the presence of the all-powerful Kastchei. Enormous snarls from the orchestra follow the prince as he provokes the demons to madness. Kastchei moves in to attack. Then a quick whir in the music proclaims the imminent arrival of the Firebird, come to Ivan's rescue.

The Firebird runs onto the scene with a magnificent leap, carrying over her head a naked golden sword. She hurriedly presents the sword to Ivan, then circles the stage in so rapid and fierce a spin that all the monsters are set to twirling with her. She exits quickly as Ivan falls upon Kastchei with the golden sword. The monster falls dead and Ivan, bathed now in the Firebird's brilliant light, holds the gleaming sword high in triumph as the music sounds his victory in a final crescendo.

The stage is dark. The prince stands alone among the fallen bodies of the monsters. The Firebird approaches. Harp strings are plucked gently. The prince finds the princess; he helps her rise. Both bow low before the beautiful Firebird, thanking her for saving their lives. The princess' friends rise and do obeisance before the magical bird, and the Firebird bows to them in return.

Free now of mortals, the Firebird dances alone. The stage is completely dark save for the light that follows her. She rises on point, extends one leg straight out, and whips the air in daring turns. The Firebird now revives the fallen monsters. She gestures over them as the harp sounds swooping arpeggios and consigns them to an endless sleep. The orchestra plays softly a flowing lullaby. The mysterious eerie forest of Ivan's adventure becomes serene as she sets all at peace with graceful, birdlike movement. Her mission over, the Firebird moves across the stage in a flowing dance, now turning, now stepping softly. Her feet tremble to release her body back into the air. Compelled to leave the earth, she moves away, her body thrown back. The last we see of her is her golden hand fluttering against the dark curtain at the side of the stage. The scene blacks out.

SCENE THREE: THE COURT OF PRINCE IVAN   The music begins a quiet, subdued statement of an ancient Russian folk song. The melody that seems simple

at first is changed gradually into a majestic song of thanksgiving. The music
mounts in dignity and volume as light slowly comes up to show us a blue-
green drop curtain. On this curtain are represented all those figures in fairyland who never will have any trouble in living happily ever after. Now that
the music has asserted itself fully in praise and gratitude, we see two guards
enter. They stand at attention in front of the curtain. The stage is fully lighted.
Courtiers enter and bow to each other with each mighty chord from the orchestra, then join hands with the princesses who trip in to meet them. Now the
drop curtain rises. Before another curtain of magical deep red, Ivan and his
princess stand together. Pages enter with royal standards. A crimson carpet is
pulled down the center of the stage, and onto it step Prince Ivan and his
bride, in regal costume. All pay homage to the royal couple, and a page comes
running out to present to the prince and princess a great wedding cake, aglow
with hundreds of candles. The curtain falls as he kneels before them with his
gift.

NOTES   The New York City Ballet production of *Firebird* has been revised
over the years, like all ballets of any interest, and most importantly perhaps by
Jerome Robbins and me at the New York State Theatre, May 28, 1970. Marc
Chagall had wanted for some time to do new designs for the costumes and to
make other changes. The new *Firebird* was an attempt, in fact, to present
Chagall's paintings in action, with Stravinsky's accompaniment. This provided
an opportunity to make changes, too, in the choreography. Jerome Robbins
and I shared the work, he taking responsibility for the scenes involving large
ensembles. Gelsey Kirkland, Jacques d'Amboise, and Gloria Govrin were the
principal dancers in this revival. Barbara Karinska's costumes to Chagall's
designs were acknowledged masterpieces of art and craft, like all her marvelous work. Karinska's supremacy was appropriately acknowledged at this period by an exhibition of her designs at the Library and Museum of the Performing Arts, New York Public Library, Lincoln Center.

*Music by Igor Stravinsky. Choreography by Maurice Béjart. First presented
by the Paris Opéra Ballet at the Palais des Sports, Paris, October 31, 1970,
with Paolo Bortoluzzi in the principal role. First presented in the United
States by the Ballet of the Twentieth Century at the Brooklyn Academy of
Music, New York, January 25, 1971.*

To the choreographer Maurice Béjart, *Firebird* is a revolutionary act, a Maoist
gesture. Béjart writes: "The Firebird is the Phoenix reborn from ashes. The
Bird of Life and Joy, immortal, whose splendor and strength remain inde-
structible, untarnishable. . . ."
Referring to the original version of the *Firebird*, Béjart says: "Since then,
the . . . ballet seems lame. What remains now is pure music that is true to a
certain choreographic vision, but inappropriate to the complicated wanderings
of the complete scenario" of the original. "There is no question about replacing one story with another or even transforming the original. Instead, let us try

to free the emotion that fills the succession of scenes in a reduced version, and therein find the two major elements that startled at the creation: Stravinsky, Russian musician; Stravinsky, revolutionary musician. Let the dance become the abstract expression of these two elements that are always present in the music: a profound feeling of Russia and a certain rupture with traditional music, translated above all by an inhabitual rhythmic violence. The Firebird is the Phoenix reborn from ashes. The Poet, like the revolutionary, is a Firebird."

Interviewed in *The New Yorker* magazine (February 6, 1971), Béjart was even more specific about his viewpoint on *Firebird:* "The music is so strong, so modern, so full of life, but the Russian legend on which the ballet was based—the magical Firebird who enables a Prince to rescue a Princess from a wicked sorcerer—is impossible to translate on the modern stage. So I thought there must be a way to reach the spirit of the music. The ballet was composed shortly before the Russian Revolution, and as I started to read revolutionary poets such as Esenin and Mayakovsky, I discovered that there was a small group of avant-garde writers, artists, composers, and dancers working in this period who called themselves the Firebird. So I did an abstract ballet but tried to give the feeling of young intellectuals grouped around one boy searching for something new in life. The Firebird leader is a phoenix. He is destroyed, but he rises from the ashes and lives again. That is why we have two men dancing the Firebird instead of one ballerina. . . . Ballet has been a woman-dominated art since the middle of the nineteenth century, but in every folklore the male dancer is more important. In seventeenth-century France and Italy, where ballet was born, women were at first not even allowed to participate. For example, Louis XIV was a very good dancer, but never his queen. They called him the Sun King because he always took the part of the sun in his ballets. In the classic repertoire, we have the *entrechat,* the jump in which the dancer changes the position of his feet several times. The *entrechat-trois* is always called *le royal,* because the Sun King performed it exceptionally well. I think the day of the prima donna in dance, theater, and opera has passed into the history of our civilization. Now we begin to go in the other direction."[*]

Following this conviction, the action of the ballet depicts the history of a vigorous revolutionary band: their rise, fall and, miraculously, their rise again at the will of a dynamic boy. A group of young partisans in dungarees declare their faith in a revolt, making a pledge of faith in blood in a red spotlight. One of the group, a vigorous boy, discards his denims for a red costume and asserts leadership. He is hailed by the group and leads them in battle. While he loses the fight and his army is defeated, he rises from the dead, hailed by his band of Firebirds.

In his book *The World of Ballet*, the English critic Oleg Kerensky describes another version of *Firebird:* "John Neumeier, a young American dancer and choreographer who became director of the ballet in Frankfurt in 1970, launched his regime with a new version of Stravinsky's *The Firebird* in a science-fiction, outer-space setting. The translation of the wicked Kastchei

* From "Béjart" by Jane Boutwell in "The Talk of the Town." Reprinted by permission; © 1971 The New Yorker Magazine, Inc.

from a sinister Russian magician into an enormous robot with a television screen for a face, and of the hero from a peasant-prince into a white-suited space explorer, gave the ballet a new life, creating much the sort of shock and naive fantasy effect which the original Fokine-Golovine production must have had in Paris sixty years ago. Neumeier, who is still in his twenties, resembles John Clifford in his versatility as a choreographer (he has also done an abstract Bach ballet for Frankfurt) and as a dancer (he replaced Richard Cragun in Cranko's difficult Webern ballet, *Opus I*)."

The Harkness Ballet presented a production of *Firebird* at the Kennedy Center, Washington, May 24, 1972, with choreography by Brian Macdonald and settings and costumes by Rouben Ter-Arutunian. Jeanette Vobdersaar and Manola Asensio alternated in the title role.

FIRST AERIAL STATION

Music by Louis Spohr. Choreography by Toer van Schayk. Scenery and costumes by Toer van Schayk. Lighting by Howard Eldridge (Theatre Projects Services Ltd.). First presented by the Dutch National Ballet at Amsterdam, Holland, October 6, 1976. First presented in the United States by the same ensemble at the Minskoff Theatre, New York, November 9, 1976.

A vivid contrast between a forgotten time and the present, *First Aerial Station* tells the story of a minor revolution in the dance world. The past is represented by the phrase *First Position on Point*, what the choreographer, Toer van Schayk, calls "an antiquated and obsolete ballet terminology from the early years of the past century." The time is around 1813, when Louis Spohr wrote the *Nonet in F Major* that accompanies the ballet. The contrast here, before the triumph of the romantic ballet later in the nineteenth century, is between the leftover "genre noble" dancers who hang on tenaciously to the rigid, frozen style of performance established since the days of Louis XIV, and the "genre/grotesque," the avant-garde dancers who were determined to seek new ways of moving.

The action all takes place in a ballet classroom, where a portrait of Napoleon on the wall comes and goes as victory follows defeat. The eventual victory of the avant-garde permits the dancers to leave the earth and take off in flight.

FIVE DANCES

Music by Sergei Rachmaninoff. Choreography by Christian Holder. Costumes by Christian Holder. Lighting by Jennifer Tipton. First presented by the City Center Joffrey Ballet at the City Center, New York, October 16, 1975, with Denise Jackson and Russell Sultzbach. Pianist: Stanley Babin.

The dancer Christian Holder for his first ballet chose some wonderful piano pieces by Rachmaninoff. The five dances arranged to them are for a girl and a boy, alone and together, in moods and transports that show different aspects of character. Each dances alone, for the first four dances, so that we have an idea of their personalities before they meet for the final *pas de deux*. The focus at the beginning is on the girl who appears in a long dress in a spotlight, her back to us. She responds to the elegiac music of the piano with a dance of some passion and then rushes off. Next, the boy, in white, dances lyrically on a bright stage. His dance becomes tempestuous, then assumes a stillness, and the lights fade. To fast, rippling music the girl returns. The boy's second dance which follows is decisive and assertive in strength and confidence. Now, on a darkened stage, the boy carries the girl. She turns softly in his arms and to quiet music that grows in intensity of passion they dance. At the end, the boy lifts the girl high in declaration of his love and the light fades.

The music by Rachmaninoff for *Five Dances:* Élégie and Mélodie, Op. 3, Nos. 1 and 3; Preludes No. 9 in E flat minor, Op. 23, No. 6 in F minor, Op. 32, No. 1 in F sharp minor, Op. 23.

In a review entitled "Aptly Original" in the New York *Times,* Clive Barnes said that "clearly Mr. Holder has a choreographic fluency, and it was particularly obvious in the gentleness and intricacy of the final duet."

FLAMES OF PARIS

Music by Boris Asafiev. Choreography by Vasili Vainonen. Book by Nicolai Volkov and Vladimir Dimitriev. Decor by Vladimir Dimitriev. First presented at the Kirov Theatre, Leningrad, November 7, 1932, with Vakhtang Chabukiani, Olga Jordan, Nina Anisimova, and Galina Ulanova in principal roles.

Long celebrated in the Soviet Union as a full-length four-act ballet, *Flames of Paris* tells a story that takes place at the time of the French Revolution of 1789. Full of revolutionary fervor, the ballet features not only the march of the Marseillais on Paris but the storming of the Tuileries. The decadence of the court of Louis XVI is portrayed, counterrevolution is exposed, and a brave young girl personifies the triumph of the people.

Scenes from the ballet have been seen on film, one of them featuring the Soviet virtuoso danseur Chabukiani in a popular *pas de deux* from the last scene of the ballet. It is this *pas de deux* that American Ballet Theatre introduced on January 13, 1973, at the City Center, New York, in a version staged by David and Anna-Marie Holmes. The costumes were by Marcos Paredes, the lighting by Nananne Porcher, and the conductor was Akira Endo. Eleanor D'Antuono and John Prinz were the dancers. The central dance takes place in the atmosphere of a celebration over the taking of the Tuileries. The *pas de deux* is ebullient and pyrotechnic in character, political but personable.

LES FLEURS DU MAL (The Flowers of Evil)

Music by Claude Debussy. Choreography by Maurice Béjart. Scenery and costumes by Joëlle Roustan and Roger Bernard. First presented by the Ballet of the Twentieth Century, September 3, 1970, at the Théâtre de la Monnaie, Brussels. First presented in the United States by the same ensemble at the City Center, New York, January 26, 1971, with Suzanne Farrell, Jaleh Kerendi, Angela Albrecht, Jorge Donn, Floris Alexander, and Dyane Gray-Cullert.

In 1968 the choreographer Maurice Béjart created a full-evening ballet, *Baudelaire*, in which seven dancers played the part of the poet Charles Baudelaire and attempted to re-create his world. *Fleurs du Mal* ("Flowers of Evil," the title of the French poet's masterpiece) is an adaptation of part of that ballet. Set to *Le Jet d'Eau* ("The Fountain") as arranged by Debussy, the ballet treats different aspects of love.

There is a floorcloth of black, swirling waves on a white background that climbs up into the backcloth. Large mirrors right and left reflect the movement as dancers emerge to respond to the poem that is being recited. The girls wear long, trailing dresses and in the atmosphere there is a feeling of a bygone era. The girls discard the trains of their gowns and join three boys in a dance as the music begins. They dance in pairs, a girl and boy, then girl and girl, boy and boy. What we have is three impassioned *pas de deux*. The dancers cluster together at the end.

LES FORAINS (The Traveling Players)

Ballet in one act. Choreography by Roland Petit. Music by Henri Sauguet. Book by Boris Kochno. Scenery and costumes by Christian Bérard. First presented by Ballets des Champs-Élysées, Paris, March 1945, with Roland Petit, Janine Charrat, and Ethéry Pagava in principal roles. First presented in the United States by Les Ballets de Paris at the National Theatre, New York, October 8, 1950, with Polajenko, Belinda Wright, Danielle Darmance, Simone Mostovoy, Jack Claus, Gordon Hamilton, Elise Vallée, and Nina Bibikova.

The overture to *Les Forains* blares out with trumpets, drum rolls, and crashing cymbals—appropriate music for a parade, a vaudeville show, or a circus. The ballet that follows is something like all of these things. Although never familiar in America, bands of strolling players have entertained people in Europe for centuries, performing on street corners, on highways, and in remote villages, attracting such crowds as they could and living as their casual audiences rewarded them. *Les Forains* shows us what happens to one particular group of such players one night in a city street.

The stage is dark as the ballet begins. There is no decoration, only a plain backdrop. From the left, a young girl enters. She wears a simple costume, but carries a black-and-silver fan and dances across the stage oblivious of anyone who might be watching her. A troupe of poorly dressed young people trudge wearily onto the scene behind her, pulling along with them a battered wheelbarrow packed high with what seems to be a rolled-up tent. One man follows a little behind, supporting with his left arm a girl who sits on his shoulder. He appears to be the leader of the group. He lets the girl down, consults with the others, claps his hands, and the relaxed scene is transformed instantly into breathless activity.

The wheelbarrow is moved toward the back of the stage; several of the men begin to unpack it hurriedly while the other members of the troupe energetically practice their routines. They throw off their overcoats, and we see that they are wearing costumes. We see a clown and several acrobats; the rest are dancers. The boys support the girls as they warm up for performance; one of the acrobats cartwheels around the stage; while in the back a primitive stage is constructed of crude lumber and cloth. There is a white curtain across the stage proper; colored curtains conceal the wings. Several passers-by pause to watch. The company runs in back of the miniature stage, the lights are lowered, and our attention is fixed on the white curtain.

An intense green light is thrown against the curtain from behind, and we see the silhouettes of a man and a woman engaged in amorous dalliance. The light changes; a clown and a girl come out, bringing with them a chair; and there is acrobatic display. The girl does a running jump onto the chair, where the clown catches her and lifts her down. Next there appears a girl wearing a long white dress of gauze, with long, full sleeves. She dances slowly, to accentuate her movements with the airy movement of her costume. Then the clown enters again, this time to do his specialty, which consists of brisk acrobatics executed as clumsily and as amusingly as possible. Now the curtains part for the Siamese twins, two girls bound together in what appears to be one *tutu*. They step down from the stage and dance side by side, each indicating hopelessly the impossibility of ever dancing otherwise.

The magician who now takes his turn we recognize as the leader of the troupe. He is dressed formally now, in long black evening coat. He waves his wand, and the stage is filled with confetti and paper streamers. Then he approaches the stage, pulls the curtains aside, and brings to life a beautiful girl who lies there motionless in a glass case. The girl is under his power and obeys the magician, with the stiff movements of a mechanical doll. The magician now does his final trick: two live doves fly from his hands and circle the stage until they are retrieved by one of the men.

The whole company joins in for a finale. Each of the performers dances a short variation alone, then all participate in a final chorus, surrounding the magician, whose rapid spins in the air set an increasing tempo for the others to follow. The dance ends with everyone in the group cheerfully exhausted. The small crowd that has been watching applauds lightly, and the magician passes his hat. But each member of the audience turns away as he approaches, and soon the players are left alone.

The youthful ebullience with which they had produced their show collapses almost at once; they are angry because they have received nothing for their entertainment and sad at their public's indifference. They take down the stage, pack up the cart again, and move off in the same melancholy manner with which they entered. The troupe seems to have forgotten the two white doves, which flutter against their cage as the light darkens. One of the girls comes back to find them, picks up the cage, and runs with it back to her friends.

FORCES OF RHYTHM

Music: traditional and contemporary. Choreography by Louis Johnson. Costumes by Zelda Wynn. Lighting by Fred Barry. First presented by the Dance Theatre of Harlem at the Hunter College Playhouse, New York, December 11, 1971.

The dance audience has often imagined a work that would combine the styles of classical ballet, modern and ethnic dance. The choreographer Louis Johnson has made such a piece using the gifts of the Dance Theatre of Harlem. The choreographer's idea here is to capture the essence of ballet and ethnic dancing styles in such a way as to display the rapport, beauty, and relationship between the two. This is accomplished in a number of ways.

The curtain rises on twelve dancers as a voice speaks above the music, "We're in a difficult situation. We're going to have to live together." Some of the girls are in long white cotton dresses with bandannas in the hair, an attire reminiscent of the old South; others are in toe shoes and short white ballet costumes; while the boys, too, are in ballet rehearsal costume, T-shirts and tights. This costume combination reveals the ballet's content as the three groups dance together. It is enlarged in the next part, "Roots and Rhythm," by four boys in red loincloths who display the vigor of native African dance.

The sixteen dancers play a kind of counterpoint against each other with the music. Ranging from the heroic measures of affirmation in the Tchaikovsky symphonies to folk, blues, rock, and jazz, the dances reveal variations on these musical themes in dance expression. Six movements follow: "Rhythm and Strings," to Tchaikovsky's music; "Distress," for four girls; "Shout," a solo for a girl to a plaintive, demanding rhythm; "Forces of Rhythm," a dance for three; "Harlem Rhythms," for a boy soloist; and a "Coda" for all sixteen dancers. From bare foot to toe shoe, recollections of minstrel days with derby hats and white socks, the ballet traces a historical development within a dance entertainment.

Arlene Croce wrote of Paul Russell's performance in *Forces of Rhythm*, in *The New Yorker* in 1973: "Russell is the greatest performer the company has . . . He has the greatness and the naturalness to remind you of something in real life."

Writing of *Forces of Rhythm* as it was performed in 1974, the critic Robert Greskovic said in *Ballet Review*: "Using a tape track that sounds patched together from twirling a radio dial, the dances range from soul-felt, revivalist surges through Balanchinian concerti forces to mimetic African arm-flapping rituals. The costumes match each dance's style with long, white ruffled muslin shifts and kerchiefed heads for the revivalists, basic black and white dance-wear for the Balanchinians, and loin-bikinis, ankle bells and head bands for the tribal artists. There is a jumbled pas de trois for McKinney and Williams (as a *Barocco* couple) with Bryant in his red loin wrap. The joke here is a 'ballet' one with McKinney distracted from her lyric duet with Williams by the foot-stomping and arm-waving Bryant. We've seen partners compete for the ballerina before, but never with such outrageous contrast. And, of course, in 'There Is a Rose in Spanish Harlem,' Paul Russell, in loincloth, derby, socks and ballet slippers, provides one of the most delicious performances of the season. I saw Russell in '72 and again (twice) this season, and it amazes and thrills me every time to see him take this recorded music and fill it out to bursting with show biz know-how and genuinely amusing style. During his dancing, which is a cross between bravura pyrotechnics and gyrating Broadway jives, he has some 'takes' that confront his audience with generous wit and unabashed joy. He is a comic and a comet; his body is all singing, all dancing. He's a genius. There is an interchangeable male/female solo for either V. Johnson doing a sweetly abandoned skirt-whirling freak-out à la Jamison in *Revelations,* or William Scott biting the music with purposeful rock/bop attack. It has something from (for) everybody and all of it's dancing by a company that loves what (ever) it's doing."*

THE FOUNTAIN OF BAKHCHISARAI

Choreographic poem in four acts. Music by Boris Asafiev. Choreography by Rotislav Zakharov. Book by Nikolai Volkov, based on the poem by Alexander Pushkin. Scenery by V. M. Khodasevich. First presented by the Kirov Ballet at the Kirov State Theatre of Opera and Ballet, Leningrad, September 28, 1934.

This ballet in four acts follows closely the action of Pushkin's poem. The action takes place in Poland and Bakhchisarai during the eighteenth century.

ACT ONE: AN ANCIENT PARK NEAR THE CASTLE OF THE POLISH PRINCE POTOTSKY The prince is celebrating the birthday of his beautiful daughter Maria by giving a ball. Maria and Vatslav, a young nobleman, dance together, oblivious to their surroundings. Hand in hand they go off into the park.

Out of the darkness a scout from the army of the Crimean Khan Girei steals into the park. He is not observed.

The prince and his daughter lead their guests in a polonaise, which is followed by a lively kracovienne. The guests enjoy themselves hugely. Vatslav plays the harp and to its song Maria dances. He responds with a dance of his own. At the conclusion of a *pas de deux,* the guests join in a mazurka. The

* Reprinted by permission of *Ballet Review,* Marcel Dekker, publisher.

merriment of this dance is quickly dispelled, however, by the sound of an approaching army on horseback. The castle guard, mortally wounded, enters to warn the prince of a surprise attack by the Tartar horde:

> . . . multitudes of Tartars
> Pour forth into Poland like a river;
> not with such terrible swiftness
> does fire spread through the harvest.

The guests disperse and return to engage the forces of Girei in combat. Many are slain and the Poles are soon overwhelmed. The castle is ablaze. Vatslav attempts to lead Maria to safety, but the khan himself blocks their escape. Vatslav challenges Girei and appears to succeed, but then we see that he has been stricken by a blow from a concealed dagger. Maria, in despair, hides her face in her scarf. Girei tears it away and, dazzled by her beauty, adores her.

ACT TWO: GIREI'S HAREM IN BAKHCHISARAI, CAPITAL OF THE CRIMEAN TARTARS   The many lovely young wives of the khan play and chat in the morning sunlight. The khan's favorite, the Georgian girl Zarema, "star of love, beauty of the harem," demands the attention due her position. She and the other wives impatiently await the khan's return and prepare themselves excitedly when trumpets announce the arrival of Girei and his troops from Poland.

Warriors rush in. Maria is carried in on a litter. Girei enters, takes off his armor, dons a golden robe and reclines on his couch. Zarema dances for him, but he is indifferent to her. The girl is distraught, but persists; she cannot believe that he has lost interest in her.

Maria enters, carrying the harp Vatslav played for her. With her fair hair and delicate features she is a curiosity to the other women. Absorbed with her own thoughts of home, of her lost lover, she ignores Girei, who cannot comprehend her aloofness. The other wives try to divert the khan, but neither they nor Zarema can claim his attention. He thrusts Zarema aside and leaves the room. The other wives ridicule the rejected Zarema and rejoice in her downfall. When Girei returns and she embraces him, he again repulses her, this time more coldly.

ACT THREE: MARIA'S BEDCHAMBER IN GIREI'S PALACE   Alone with an old servant, Maria strums the harp that Vatslav left behind. Girei, transfixed by an unearthly love unknown to him, enters the room. Haunted by her presence, wishing to possess her, but realizing also that as the murderer of her beloved he cannot hope to win her, Girei does not know where to turn. Maria, appalled by the force of his desire, is desperately afraid. He sees her fear and spares her, leaving the room.

Maria, relieved and alone, dreams of the past, of her lover Vatslav, of their longed-for marriage. The old servant takes her to bed, and, falling asleep on a carpet at the door, stands guard over the girl.

Zarema, the favorite of the harem, enters, skirting the old woman's carpet. She begs Maria to return the khan to her, his rightful beloved: she cannot live without him. The servant wakens and summons the khan. He enters the room with a guard just as Zarema threatens to stab Maria to death. Girei, in a frenzy, dashes to Zarema, trying to catch her hand, but she eludes him and stabs Maria, who dies like a flower cut off in full bloom. Maddened by this act, the khan threatens to kill Zarema. But the girl, welcoming death as an alternative, goes to meet his blow. He then instructs the guard to take the girl away.

ACT FOUR: A FOUNTAIN COURT IN THE PALACE   Girei watches as one of his generals returns from a fresh campaign with trophies, banners, and new captives for the harem. He is unmoved by these triumphs. Zarema is dragged before him. He is merciless, thinking only that Maria one day would have yielded to him except for this girl's wicked jealousy. She begs him for mercy with her eyes but he cannot bear to look at her. She is led across to the battlements and forced over the steep precipice to her death. A fierce dance by the khan's warriors does not assuage his grief. He finds solace only at the "fountain of tears," which he has erected in the courtyard to the memory of his "sorrowful Maria."

The water murmurs in the marble
and drops like cold tears,
never falling silent.

In the magical sound of the fountain Girei seems to see the image of Maria. But when he reaches out to touch her, she is not there.

FOUR LAST SONGS

Music by Richard Strauss. Choreography by Maurice Béjart. First presented by the Ballet of the Twentieth Century. First presented in the United States by the same ensemble at the Brooklyn Academy of Music, February 10, 1971.

While Richard Strauss did not write his four last songs to be performed as a group, that is the way they have turned out in musical history. Not so much in subject matter as in temper and retrospective attitudes to life, the four songs lend themselves to appreciative contemplation. Dancers have found that, too, and to the fancy of Maurice Béjart the four songs—*"Frühling"* ("Spring"), *"September," "Beim Schlafengehen"* ("Going to Sleep"), and *"Im Abendrot"* ("In the Evening")—suggest the four loves of a dying man.

The curtain rises in silence and we see a boy in the distance in a spotlight. As he walks toward us, four girls, from the four corners of the stage, approach him. All five join hands, the music begins, and he in the midst of the girls is caught up in recollection of his past loves. A series of *pas de deux* then follows, each recalling the drama of a particular passion, while the other girls watch from a symbolic distance. His final love and partner is Death.

The critic Don McDonagh in the New York *Times* wrote that "The ballet beautifully succeeds in detailing each encounter with respect for and rapport with its music . . . Each of the duets displays the tonality of the Strauss song that accompanies it and conveys its romantic interlude with soft spoken surety."

Music by Richard Strauss. Choreography by Lorca Massine. First presented by the New York City Ballet at the New York State Theatre, January 21, 1971.

The first of Lorca Massine's ballets in America (the dancer and choreographer had previously composed fifteen ballets for his own company in Europe), *Four Last Songs* was first arranged for students at the School of American Ballet, a number of whom appeared in the ballet's performances. Writing of the ballet, Nancy Goldner, dance critic of the *Christian Science Monitor,* described it as "an utterly strange and utterly beautiful ballet . . . The music is Richard Strauss; it is perhaps the most difficult kind of music to work with, for it lacks a tight rhythmical structure. Dynamically, the music ebbs and crests."

So does the action, taking place in a rehearsal studio where small and larger groups of dancers move together, break apart, recombine, isolate each other, come together again. There is a feeling of community achievement but of great individuality, too. Art is a product of being alone and working and the beautiful dances we sometimes see emerge from such a place as this.

Persons who saw *Four Last Songs* as it was first done with students at the School of American Ballet in New York say they will never forget it.

FOUR SCHUMANN PIECES

Music by Robert Schumann. Choreography by Hans van Manen. Scenery and costumes by Jean-Paul Vroom. First presented by the Royal Ballet at the Royal Opera House, Covent Garden, London, January 31, 1975, with Anthony Dowell in the principal role. First presented in the United States by the National Ballet of Canada at the Metropolitan Opera House, New York, August 4, 1976, with Rudolf Nureyev in the principal role.

Danced to the music of Robert Schumann's *String Quartet in A Major,* Op. 141, No. 3, which is played in the orchestra pit, *Four Schumann Pieces* is a dramatic ballet without a story. It shows a man who stands alone but who is surrounded by persons he would wish to know, though he often has strength only to ignore them. Of the five couples who dance with him, he appears to know none. Gradually, however, his courage is emboldened and he tries to join them. He despairs, however, at the first opportunity and just keeps on watching. Later, he dances with one of the girls, then with one of the boys, and appears to be bereft, preferring a lone splendor until he again goes back to join the group.

FOUR SEASONS

Music by Antonio Vivaldi. Choreography by Flemming Flindt. Scenery by Jorgen Mydtskov. Costumes by Charlotte Clason. First presented by the Royal Danish Ballet at the Royal Theatre, Copenhagen, April 10, 1975. First presented in the United States by the same ensemble at the Metropolitan Opera House, New York, June 5, 1976.

Vivaldi's great musical work, envisioned by many as *musique dansante,* has attracted many a choreographer. The Danish ballet master first essayed a ballet to this score in 1971 but revised his conception definitively four years later. Commencing with the open expressiveness of the "Spring" concerto, the action in dance/dramatic terms moves to the harmony and invention of an impassioned "Summer." The color of the scene shifting into "Autumn," the dances take on a commitment to hunting, and in "Winter" there is dedication by the assembled dancers to the omnipotent Snow Queen that melts into a renewed expectation of "Spring" and the circle of the year is closed.

THE FOUR TEMPERAMENTS

Classic ballet in five parts. Music by Paul Hindemith. Choreography by George Balanchine. Scenery and costumes by Kurt Seligmann. Lighting by Jean Rosenthal. First presented by Ballet Society at the Central High School of Needle Trades, New York, November 20, 1946, with Gisella Caccialanza, Tanaquil LeClercq, Mary Ellen Moylan, Elise Reiman, Beatrice Tompkins, Todd Bolender, Lew Christensen, Fred Danieli, William Dollar, José Martínez, and Francisco Moncion as the principal dancers.

Subtitled "A Dance Ballet Without Plot," *The Four Temperaments* is an expression in dance and music of the ancient notion that the human organism is made up of four different humors, or temperaments. Each one of us possesses these four humors, but in different degrees, and it is from the dominance of one of them that the four physical and psychological types—melancholic, sanguinic, phlegmatic, and choleric—were derived. Greek medicine associated the four humors and temperaments with the four elements—earth, water, fire, and air—which to them composed the human body as well as the world.

Although the score is based on this idea of the four temperaments, neither the music nor the ballet itself make specific or literal interpretation of the idea. An understanding of the Greek and medieval notion of the temperaments was merely the point of departure for both composer and choreographer.

The ballet is in five parts that correspond to the divisions of the score. The first section, Theme, features three couples, who dance three *pas de deux* to different statements of the basic musical theme. The music is languidly paced at first; the strings carry the melody carefully, but effortlessly. The bright assertiveness of the piano interrupts this passage, and the music becomes syn-copated, with a quick, tinkling brilliance. In the third statement the string or-chestra and the piano combine to state the theme fully.

Melancholic, the first variation on the theme, begins sadly and slowly; a solo violin sings despondently against the piano's accompaniment. A dancer per-forms a helpless, despondent, and lonely variation. The tempo changes, and he is joined by two girls as the full orchestra plays with muted strings. Four mys-terious girls stalk in fiercely, majestically, to the tune of a strong and vibrant march in which the piano joins percussively.

The second variation, Sanguinic, is bright and effusive in its waltz tempo. A ballerina and her partner dance with open gestures that are alternately sharp and flowing. A secondary group of four dancers accompanies them.

To the third variation, Phlegmatic, a dancer dances at first alone. His mood changes suddenly with the music. He is joined by four girls and with them dances a sequence of adroitly measured lightness to a gay, humorous melody.

After a brief variation by a ballerina who represents the choleric tempera-ment, the entire ensemble returns to the stage for a recapitulation of their dances; this merges with the music for a finale characterized by high, extended lifts.

NOTES Arlene Croce, in *The New Yorker,* December 8, 1975, reviewed at length the New York City Ballet revival of *The Four Temperaments* with Bart Cook in Melancholic, Merrill Ashley in Sanguinic, Jean-Pierre Bonnefous in Phlegmatic, and Colleen Neary in Choleric.

GAÎTÉ PARISIENNE

Ballet in one act. Music by Jacques Offenbach. Choreography by Leonide Massine. Book by Comte Étienne de Beaumont. Scenery and costumes by Comte Étienne de Beaumont. First presented by the Ballet Russe de Monte Carlo at the Théâtre de Monte Carlo, April 5, 1938, with Nina Tarakanova as the Glove Seller, Eugenia Delarova as the Flower Girl, Jeannette Lauret as La Lionne, Leonide Massine as the Peruvian, Frederic Franklin as the Baron, and Igor Youskevitch as the Officer. First presented in the United States by the Ballet Russe de Monte Carlo at the Metropolitan Opera House, New York, October 12, 1938, with Alexandra Danilova as the Glove Seller; the other principals were the same as those who danced the première in Monte Carlo.

The trumpets and snare drum, which begin the overture to this ballet with loud and persistent good humor, proclaim a tale of the night life of old Paris, a story of romance, convivial dancing, and perpetual high spirits. The jubilant rhythm and sparkling melody of the music remind us of a time when love was brief and casual, but intense, of a time when the day began at nine o'clock in the evening.

The curtain rises on the most popular room of a fashionable restaurant in

nineteenth-century Paris. High green draperies are looped back against brass
pillars; brass chandeliers flood the room with light. Marble-topped tables and
gold chairs stand at the back. Four waiters and four cleaning girls are preparing the *salon* for the evening's entertainment. The boys flick the tables and
chairs with their towels and dance comically to amuse the girls. They run forward and sit at the front of the stage at the end of their act.

A girl with flowers in her hair enters gaily. She shakes hands with the
waiters, who gather around her adoringly. This is the flower girl. She presents
each boy with a bouquet. They reward her with a drink, and the flower girl
joins them in a dance in which she toasts her admirers. One of the boys lifts
her up to his shoulders and another kneels below her.

Three ladies of easy virtue—the *cocodettes*—enter with their escorts. The
girls are dressed cheerfully in loud, candy-striped dresses; their companions
wear black jackets and berets. The flower girl sets up her tray of flowers and
leaves with the waiters. The *cocodettes* dance a lively mazurka with their partners. The waiters return to watch, but soon the company is distracted by the
entry of the ballet's heroine, the beautiful glove seller. The men desert their
partners and cluster around her. She carries a basket of gloves on her arm and
tries to attend to her business, but the men insist that she dance with them.
She is lifted high, then circles the stage as all stop to admire her. The glove
seller is not as pert and flirtatious as the flower girl, yet her beauty is more
striking.

Everyone is watching her when the gay Peruvian, just arrived in Paris, hustles in to a whistling tune. He has been so eager to get to the café and enjoy
the proverbial night life that he has brought his bags with him. He scuttles
about the stage in uncontrollable excitement at the possibilities of the evening,
amusing the girls, who know that—though his pockets may be filled with gold—
he is incapable of stopping long enough to spend it on any one of them: he
will always pursue pleasure, but never enjoy it. Finally he drops his bags and
goes over to the flower girl, who places a *boutonnière* in his white lapel. He
wiggles with delight as the girls watch him. Only the glove seller does not notice him. The Peruvian is fascinated. He sneaks up on her and asks for a pair
of gloves. The girl obliges and tries to fit him. The Peruvian dances even as he
stands still.

The baron enters. A waiter takes his cape, and the flower girl, attracted by
his handsome uniform, immediately goes over to him. The baron, however, has
seen the glove seller; gently ignoring the other girl, he turns to her, introduces
himself modestly, and asks her to dance. The glove seller responds graciously,
and the guests retire as the two come forward and dance to a romantically
rhythmic waltz. The couple move together not as if they had just met, but as if
they were predestined to know one another; their dance is touching, in its
quiet, flowing warmth.

In the background the jovial Peruvian entertains the *cocodettes*. With a
flourish, he ceremoniously orders a bottle of champagne. He sips a glass, spits,
and stamps his feet. The girls encourage him as he orders another bottle. He
approves the new wine and offers it to the ladies. His flirtations are interrupted
by the arrival of five soldiers and an officer, who strut into the café as if they

expected all the girls to notice only them. The girls oblige them. The couples perform a martial dance at the conclusion of which the girls hang about the soldiers' necks in mock farewell as the soldiers salute them.

All are startled by the sudden entrance of La Lionne, the fashionable beauty of the day. She sweeps into the café in her red velvet dress and greets the group condescendingly; the girls are furious, the men anxious to please her. La Lionne's escort, the duke, is unable to make up his mind whether to be pleased or annoyed. Her companion, the lady in green, seeks an alliance among the men.

La Lionne makes eyes at the officer, who abandons his attempt to take up with the beautiful glove seller. The Peruvian returns. He douses himself liberally with perfume and approaches the glove seller. As he whispers in her ear, she plagues the baron by pretending to agree to the Peruvian's suggestion. The baron is furious with her. The duke is furious with La Lionne. Both fight with their rivals, and the guests, who seem to have been waiting for such an outbreak, take sides and join in the contest. The scene becomes riotous. It is too much for the Peruvian, who crawls under a table, his limbs quaking. The restaurant is cleared. The waiters return and see the Peruvian, who doesn't dare look up. They pound on the table, and the terrified playboy rushes off, carrying the table on his head.

The baron and the glove seller re-enter and, to a sumptuous waltz, dance together. Their mutual love now assured, the two dance in reunited harmony. No sooner have they finished than the café comes to life again. The dazzling cancan dancers enter with their dancing master, and all the guests regather to watch them display their high, bold kicks. The girls form in a line as the dancing master commands, one by one they fall to the floor in a split. The crowd is delighted and everyone joins in the boisterous dance, some taking the cancan girls for their partners. The Peruvian enters with his top hat. The girls circle him and rotate his hat about their slippers.

The whole cast is assembled on the stage for the finishing bars of the heated dance. All the girls are lifted high; their legs fall back in the air. The girls fan themselves briskly. The lights dim; wraps are brought. The girls take their partners' arms; the music becomes soft and mellifluous; and the couples glide away as if they were carried by quietly moving gondolas into the night—the baron with the glove seller, the flower girl with the duke, La Lionne with the officer. The glove seller, her hair covered with a black mantilla, waves farewell and falls back in the baron's arms. The Peruvian is left alone. The couples wave at him. He sulks.

GALA PERFORMANCE

Ballet in two parts. Choreography by Antony Tudor. Music by Sergei Prokofiev. Scenery and costumes by Hugh Stevenson. First presented by the London Ballet at Toynbee Hall, London, December 5, 1938, with Maude Lloyd, Gerd Larsen, Peggy van Praagh, Hugh Laing, and Antony Tudor in principal roles. First presented in the United States by Ballet Theatre at

*the Majestic Theatre, New York, February 11, 1941. Scenery and costumes
by Nicolas de Molas. The cast was headed by Nora Kaye, Nana Gollner,
Karen Conrad, Hugh Laing, and Antony Tudor.*

Gala Performance is a comedy, telling a joke about ballet and three different
ballerinas. Today many of us are inclined to stay away from ballet because we
think it's made up of silly mannerisms. *Gala Performance* shows us these mannerisms (exaggerates them in the style of its period) and makes us laugh.
Three famous ballerinas—the Queen of the Dance (from Moscow), the Goddess of the Dance (from Milan), and the Daughter of Terpsichore (from
Paris)—are performing on the same stage for the first time in their lives. In
their attempts to outdo each other, the dancers invoke every trick of their
trade: they not only compete in respect to their dancing, but resort to any ruse
that will secure the most applause.

The time of this *Gala Performance* is about sixty years ago; the place is the
Theatre Royal in London. The music is by Prokofiev: the first movement of the
Concerto No. 3 in C for Piano (for Part One) and the *Classical Symphony* (for
Part Two).

PART ONE   The curtain rises on a backstage scene. The closed curtain of the
Theatre Royal is the backdrop of the setting, and in the harsh light before the
performance begins we watch the nervous, hurried preparations for an unprec-
edented program of ballet. Two *coryphées* come out through the wings and
begin to warm up. Others join them. These girls are members of the Theatre
Royal's *corps de ballet,* the chosen few who will have the honor of appearing
with the three guest ballerinas. They are quite naturally frightened and wait
apprehensively for the arrival of the great dancers. They practice dance steps,
turn their backs to us, and pose in the direction of the audience behind the
curtain. Other girls and a number of boys—attendant cavaliers to the ballerinas
—come on stage.

A woman in black, the theater dresser, enters and adjusts the costumes of
the *coryphées.* Next comes the ballet master, who watches the *corps de ballet*
as they quickly run through the steps they will dance when the curtain rises.
All the company turn expectantly as the Russian ballerina approaches the
stage. She walks commandingly. Everyone on stage is beneath her notice, and
she accepts the homage of the company with marked indifference. Then, as
she scrutinizes the *corps de ballet,* she notices that one of the *coryphées* is
wearing a necklace. She motions to the girl, reprimands her, and orders her to
remove it. She herself is loaded down with jewelry, to which she now directs
her attention while the distraught girl dashes off, weeping.

The ballet master and the conductor hover about the ballerina. The conductor promises to heed her warning about the proper tempo, while the ballet
master can only assure her that his *corps de ballet* will be impeccably unob-
trusive. The Queen of the Dance makes final adjustments in her richly embroidered red dress, fixes the high feather in her hair, and turns toward the curtain
to rehearse her bows. Her way of acknowledging applause seems to be more
important than the dance that will apparently receive it, and the girls and boys

are secretly amused at the number of kisses she expects to throw to her audience. She is watching out of the corner of her eye, however; she snaps her fingers at the *corps* and orders them to practice their routine.

This severe scene is interrupted by the arrival of the Daughter of Terpsichore, the sparkling French ballerina, who bounds onto the stage in a fluffy, delicate costume appropriate to her exuberance. She can hardly keep still long enough to be introduced to her Russian peer, who naturally scorns her, and has no time to be regal and domineering. But she has time to be demanding and takes the conductor aside to instruct him about the tempo *she* will require. Where the Russian ballerina will make her every wish a command, the scatterbrained French dancer imagines that everything will be all right because everyone loves her and wants to please her. We are suddenly thankful that this is a ballet and not a play, for the silly French ballerina must surely never stop talking.

But if we think that the Russian and French ballerinas are vain and absurd, we have not yet seen their peer in mannerism. The Italian ballerina, the famed Goddess of the Dance, now enters. She is dressed in dignified black and walks across the stage with slow, studied elegance; her steps are carefully measured: every time she puts a foot forward, it seems to hesitate, as if it were considering the worthiness of the floor she deigns to walk upon. Automatically she holds out her hand to be kissed. The cavaliers, prompted by the ballet master, pay tribute to her. Now she orders the dresser to hold up a mirror so that she can make final adjustments to her coiffure and elaborate headdress. The dresser's attention wanders for a moment, and the Goddess of the Dance rewards her with a smack.

The ballet master huddles with the *corps de ballet,* giving them their final instructions. The stage lights come up; some of the dancers make a final rush to the rosin box so that their shoes will not slip on stage; others wish themselves luck by repeating private superstitious gestures; and one wonders how the performance will ever begin. But suddenly everyone is miraculously in place. The drop curtain rises, and the scene blacks out.

PART TWO: GALA PERFORMANCE   When the lights come up again, we are the audience at the Theatre Royal. Instead of the backstage picture, we now see an ornate setting, draped in orange and red, that might represent any regal hall. Eight *coryphées* are on stage. They wait tremulously for their cue and begin to dance. They are nervous, but not too nervous to try to ingratiate themselves with the audience: each tries to outleer the others with absurd chorine smiles.

Four cavaliers lead the Russian ballerina on stage. They bow and leave the stage. The ballerina comes forward slowly, almost to the footlights, and begins to dance when she has played upon the anticipation of the audience to establish what she doubtless imagines is a personal, lovable relation. In her dance she attempts to hit the audience between the eyes with the most elementary pirouettes, staring them down, *daring* them not to like her. And she wins our applause. When she leaps off into the wings, one of her cavaliers, invisible to the audience, catches her, and she poses in endless midflight. She accepts applause with no modesty whatsoever and finds it difficult to leave the stage for an instant while it continues.

Now the Italian ballerina comes on. She comes forward to the footlights, tantalizing us with possibilities, rises on point as if it were the supreme sacrifice, and nods curtly at the conductor. The dance she executes is an adagio, in which she eschews the assistance of her partner. No one can serve her great art but herself; the audience should be grateful to be watching her. She balances as long as possible in every pose and is coldly indifferent to gasps of amazement from the audience: to her, nothing is impossible. When her dance ends, she allows a cavalier to lift her off into the wings. As she returns for her curtain calls, she walks with the measured steps of her backstage entrance. After obligingly taking applause with the company and her cavaliers, she finally shoos them off so she can acknowledge her due alone.

The French ballerina now takes the stage and covers it with rapid leaps. She responds to applause by inflicting upon the audience an ingratiating and somewhat irritating charm.

The solos are over, and the three ballerinas appear together in the coda. They come out on stage and stand together and for a moment they are equals, but directly they begin to dance, competition is rampant. The French and Russian ballerinas try every means to attract the attention of the audience and thereby lose the contest, for the Italian "goddess" makes the audience love her by treating them as if they were idiots. She is surely in command of the whole situation and only at the final curtain does she give any sign of respecting any gift the audience might bestow on her. When the three ballerinas receive flowers, she manages to grab more bouquets than the other two. Not to be outdone, the French ballerina steps in front of the curtain to pick up more bouquets which the audience has thrown to her. But when the curtain rises again, the Italian still has the most flowers. The other two ballerinas look at her and then at us and smile and smile and smile.

GAMES

Choreography by Donald McKayle. Decor by Paul Bertelsen. Costumes by Remy Charlip. First presented at the Hunter College Playhouse, New York, May 25, 1951, with Esta Beck, Eve Beck, Louanna Gardner, Remy Charlip, John Fealy, George Liker, John Nola, and Donald McKayle.

The music for this dance is traditional songs, sung at the first performance by June Lewis and the choreographer. Donald McKayle has divided *Games* into three parts—Play, Hunger, Terror. "The streets are their playground, through all their play runs a thread of fear—'Chickee the Cop.'"

Writing of *Games* in *Dance Magazine*, the critic Doris Hering said: "In his group work *Games*, Mr. McKayle captured with uncanny perception the shadowed happiness of little children in the city." Seven children play, get frightened, terrified, fantasize, find their own kind of happiness.

Games was revived by Eliot Feld's American Ballet Company at the Brooklyn Academy of Music, New York, October 22, 1969.

GARTENFEST

> *Music by Wolfgang Amadeus Mozart. Choreography by Michael Smuin. Scenery by Jack Brown. Costumes by Marcos Paredes. Lighting by Jean Rosenthal. First presented by American Ballet Theatre at the Brooklyn Academy of Music, December 18, 1968, with Sallie Wilson and Paul Nickel, Ted Kivitt and Ivan Nagy, and Cynthia Gregory in principal roles. Conducted by Jaime Leon. Solo violinist: Guy Lumia.*

Gartenfest is a dance ballet to Mozart's early *Cassation No. 1 in G* (he was but thirteen at the time), music suitable for use in the open air, where much great eighteenth-century music was performed. The scene is appropriately, therefore, a garden, where dancers perform a series of diversions, varying in character with the music. There is no plot, only the inherent dance quality of the score and its design. The ballet is in six movements: *Menuetto,* for a lead boy and girl and four couples; *Allegro,* a bright and vigorous dance for two boys who compete in varied complex combinations of steps, beats, and jumps; *Andante,* a solo for a ballerina, supported by an ensemble of six girls; *Menuetto,* a dance for three couples; *Adagio,* a *pas de trois* for a ballerina and two boys; and *Finale: Allegro assai,* a dance for the ballerina who introduced the ballet, with the entire cast.

NOTES Reviewing *Gartenfest* in *Dance and Dancers* magazine, Patricia Barnes said that "Ballet Theatre has been lucky enough to find within its ranks another young man, Michael Smuin, who with his latest work shows himself to have genuine choreographic potential. . . . *Gartenfest* was a genuine success, most notable for the way in which it exploited the talents of its dancers, mostly drawn from the younger principals and the most promising soloists. . . . The choreography had the same fluent charm as the score."

GASPARD DE LA NUIT

> *Music by Maurice Ravel. Choreography by George Balanchine. Scenery and costumes by Bernard Daydé, execution supervised by David Mitchell. Lighting by Bernard Daydé in association with Ronald Bates. Solo pianist: Jerry Zimmerman. Conducted by Robert Irving. First presented at the New York City Ballet's Hommage à Ravel at the New York State Theatre, Lincoln Center, May 29, 1975, with Colleen Neary, Victor Castelli, Karin von Aroldingen, Nolan T'Sani, Sara Leland, and Robert Weiss as principals.*

Gaspard is a manifestation of the evils of Night. Lincoln Kirstein has written that this composition was the first of Ravel's major works in which "he expressed his attraction to the turbulent, mysterious, bewitched world of the supernatural." Robert Craft has said, too, that Ravel "is essentially a musical story teller, more inspired by poetry, and more inspired by words, syllables, literary programs, than by the problems of traditional musical form."

The music accompanies three poems: "Ondine," "The Gibbet," and "Scarbo." "Ondine" evokes the spirit of the water nymph in her enchanted watery kingdom where "each current is a path that winds its way towards my palace, and my palace is built aqueously at the bottom of the lake, in a triangle of fire, of earth and of air."

"The Gibbet" recalls the sounds of night "or the hanged man who breathes a sigh on the forked gibbet . . . and the corpse of a hanged man that is reddened by the setting sun."

The poem of Scarbo, who is an obscure devil-dwarf, begins with "O, many a time have I seen and heard him, Scarbo, when at midnight the moon shines in the sky like a silver shield upon an azure banner sown with golden bees."

The celebrated French pianist and conductor Alfred Cortot said that "these three poems enrich the repertory of our time by one of the most astonishing examples of instrumental ingenuity ever contrived by the industry of a composer."

The ballet I made to these songs is not a narrative affair illustrating each poem but an attempt to complement the music and works by visual gesture.

GEMINI

Music by Mahler. Choreography by Vicente Nebrada. First presented by the Harkness Ballet at Brooklyn College, New York, October 7, 1972, with Christopher Aponte and Darrell Barnett.

A *pas de deux* for two boys to the *Adagietto* from Mahler's *Fifth Symphony*, *Gemini* explores varied aspects of the relationships between the protagonists. Writing in *Dance and Dancers* magazine, the critic Patricia Barnes wrote: "Undeniably evoking homosexual love, the bodies of the two men twine and curve around each other. Numerous lifts are used but I found it neither acrobatic nor vulgar. Aponte and Barnett brought a control and strength to their movements that prevented the work from descending to sensationalism or sentimentality."

Music by Hans Werner Henze. Choreography by Glen Tetley. Scenery by Nadine Baylis. First presented by the Australian Ballet with Marilyn Rowe, Alida Chase, John Meehan, and Gary Norman. First presented in the United States by American Ballet Theatre at the City Center, New York, 1975, with Cynthia Gregory, Martine van Hamel, Jonas Kage, and Charles Ward.

The twins of this *Gemini* are two couples who resemble each other. Often the dances they do appear to be a kind of mirror-image. But it is not always so and, like true twins, there is a similarity of movement but an inner difference of feeling that materially alters behavior. No two couples can be the same, love in the same way, make the same commitments, or fulfill their destinies identically. The ballet shows us variations on these themes.

Writing of the performance of July 9, 1975, the critic Anna Kisselgoff reported in the New York *Times:* "Mr. Tetley works in a totally international style . . . *Gemini* is one of the best examples of this genre, and it was danced on this occasion with a thrilling blend of virtuosity and emotional depth by Cynthia Gregory, Martine van Hamel, Jonas Kage and Charles Ward."

GISELLE

Fantastic ballet in two acts. Music by Adolphe Adam. Choreography by Jules Perrot and Jean Coralli. Book by Vernoy de Saint-Georges, Théophile Gautier, and Jean Coralli. Scenery by Pierre Ciceri. Costumes by Paul Lormier. First presented at the Théâtre de l'Académie Royale de Musique, Paris, June 28, 1841, with Carlotta Grisi as Giselle, *Lucien Petipa as* Albrecht, *Adèle Dumilâtre as* Myrtha, Queen of the Wilis, *and Jean Coralli as* Hilarion. *First presented in England at Her Majesty's Theatre, London, March 12, 1842, with Carlotta Grisi and Jules Perrot in the principal roles. First presented in Russia at the Bolshoi Theatre, St. Petersburg, December 30, 1842, with Elena Andreyanova as* Giselle. *First presented in Italy at the Teatro alla Scala, Milan, January 17, 1843, with choreography by A. Cortesi and music by N. Bajetti. First presented in the United States at the Howard Atheneum, Boston, January 1, 1846, with Mary Ann Lee and George Washington Smith in the leading roles.*

Giselle is such an important and popular ballet that people who know something about dancing are always talking about it. They speak of Pavlova's Giselle, Karsavina's Giselle, Spessivtzeva's Giselle, Markova's Giselle, and those who are unfamiliar with ballet think it strange: it's as if the habitual theatregoer spent all of his time talking about *Hamlet,* without paying much attention to modern plays.

But there is good reason for the balletgoer to be preoccupied with *Giselle.* Like *Hamlet, Giselle* is a classic: it is not only important historically, it also happens to be good. It is just as popular today as when it was first performed, more than 130 years ago. People go to see *Giselle* and to see new ballerinas dance it for the same reason we go to see new interpretations of *Hamlet:* the work is such a good one that we always discover something in it we hadn't seen before, some variation in performance that brings out an aspect that seemed previously concealed; we learn something new.

There are many ballets important to history: the ballet in which the ballerina first discarded her heeled slipper, the ballet in which she first stood on the tips of her toes, and the ballet in which she jumped dangerously but effortlessly from a height of twenty feet to be caught in her lover's arms. But these ballets, with all their innovations, haven't come down to us; they are important only in a narrow academic sense. *Giselle* has come down to us, has been performed by one ballet company or another ever since its first performance, because it combines innovation with drama and dancing that make us forget all about history.

Giselle's innovation is its summing up of what we know as the Romantic ballet. To be romantic about something is to see what you are and to wish for something entirely different. This requires magic. The mysterious and supernatural powers that romantic poetry invoked to secure its ideal soon became natural to the theatre, where dancers attired in billowy white seemed part of the world and yet also above it. Marie Taglioni in the ballet *La Sylphide* (see page 459), popularized this fashion so completely that the sylph became ballet's symbol for romantic love—the girl who is so beautiful, so light, so pure that she is unattainable: touch her, and she vanishes.

Poets and novelists of the time were all interested in stories of the romantically supernatural, stories that told of lovely young girls whose love was never fulfilled because of intervening powers. One of these stories told of girls known as Wilis, who were engaged to be married yet died before their wedding days. In the evening they rose from their graves and danced alone in the moonlight. Their dancing was impassioned with their anger at death; but, dressed in their flowing bridal gowns and endowed with unearthly gifts of movement, their ghostly forms seemed never to touch the ground.

The Wilis were so beautiful that it was simple for them to attract young men into their midst. But they were as dangerous as they were irresistible. They danced with the young men who came only to trap them: their suitors were compelled to dance until they died.

This story of the Wilis seemed to be ideal for ballet: it made the story of *La Sylphide* look like merely the first step in the attainment of the romantic ideal. For the heroine of that ballet was purely a creature of the imagination, a figure in the hero's dream. We had admired her beauty and pitied her, but she was too illusory a character to make us feel deeply. What would accomplish this, what would make us care about such a character, would be to give her a basis in real life, to make her real and unreal at the same time—like the Wilis.

The poet, novelist, and critic Théophile Gautier read the story of the Wilis as it was related by Heinrich Heine, and thought it would make a good ballet and would be particularly fine for Carlotta Grisi. Gautier had seen Grisi's début in Paris and had fallen in love with her. Under the tutelage of her husband, Jules Perrot, the great dancer and choreographer, she had become the potential rival of Marie Taglioni and Fanny Elssler.

However, the story of the ballet required considerable work before it was resolved. There was the problem of how the heroine would become a Wili, under what circumstances would she die? Gautier presented this difficulty to the popular librettist Vernoy de Saint-Georges. Within three days they had contrived a suitable story and the libretto had been accepted at the Paris Opéra. Within a week the score had been written and the ballet was in rehearsal. At its first performance, a few days later, *Giselle ou les Wilis* was proclaimed the triumphant successor to *La Sylphide* and the greatest ballet of its time. For the Giselle he created for her, Grisi owed Gautier her greatest triumph and Gautier's attachment later obliged the ballerina to leave Perrot.

ACT ONE: A VILLAGE ON THE RHINE   The first curtain is preceded by a brief overture. The contrast between the strong, virulent opening measures and the light romantic melody that follows gives us an indication of the pitiless fate that will govern this love story. When the curtain rises, we see a part of a wooden village on the Rhine. It is vintage time, and the people of the village are preparing to celebrate. Peasant couples cross the stage, talking to each other affectionately; a few girls enter alone, wave in greeting to their friends, link arms, and follow them off to the left, near the entrance to a cottage. This is the cottage of Giselle, the lovely village maiden who lives with her mother, Berthe. On the right we discern the entrance to another cottage.

The stage is empty for an instant. Trumpets sound a warning. Hilarion, a gamekeeper, enters. He is dressed somewhat rudely and his gestures are not refined, but he is a man of genuine feeling. Almost directly he walks over to the door of Giselle's cottage. He is in love. Hilarion is about to knock on the door when he hears someone approaching. He looks around hurriedly and hides behind Giselle's cottage to watch.

Two men enter. They are Albrecht, Duke of Silesia, a handsome young man who wears a royal cape over his peasant clothes, and his squire, Wilfrid. Albrecht, too, goes to Giselle's door. Hilarion, who watches the scene jealously, is interested in the cape and sword that Albrecht wears, for Hilarion, like Giselle, knows this young man only as Loys, a peasant. Albrecht stands before Giselle's cottage and holds his hands over his heart. He, too, is in love and has put on peasant disguise in order that his love may be returned. Wilfrid, his attendant, is not in favor of his master's love for Giselle and begs him to come away. Albrecht refuses. He gives his cape and sword to Wilfrid and dismisses him. Wilfrid conceals the cape and sword in the cottage on the right and reluctantly withdraws.

Albrecht, at the door of Giselle's cottage, listens, then knocks. The music anticipates. He runs and hides. Giselle emerges from the house. She is expecting Albrecht and runs out happily. She dances joyfully and beautifully, as if she wanted to be watched. But no one is there! She looks about, acts as if she were indifferent, and begins to dance again. Now she hears something. She stops and poses as she listens carefully. Albrecht is blowing kisses to her! But still he will not show himself. Giselle is annoyed at this teasing, stamps her foot impatiently, and prepares to go back into the house. At this point Albrecht steps out before her. Giselle frowns and pretends that she is not glad to see him. He nudges her shoulder, and she bows low before him, still unsmiling. She runs to the cottage door, lest her pretense break down. Albrecht stands before the door to prevent her escape, then reaches out and gently takes her wrist. Now she smiles, looking up at him with amused reproach.

The two lovers dance across the stage together and sit on a crude wooden bench at the right. Albrecht tries to sit close to Giselle, but she edges away every time he moves closer. Again she tries to go back into the house, and again Albrecht prevents her.

Suddenly Albrecht is completely serious. He expresses to Giselle his eternal love and vows that he will always be faithful to her. Giselle acts as if she did not take him at his word and, to prove this, she picks a flower and begins to pluck its petals in a game of he-loves-me-loves-me-not. Albrecht vigorously nods his head when the petals say he-loves-me, but the last petal she chooses to pick turns out to be loves-me-not. Giselle throws the flower to the ground and begins to cry. To comfort her, Albrecht picks up the flower again and declares that the last petal is really he-loves-me. Giselle is fully consoled and, linking her arm through Albrecht's, dances again with him.

The lovers are so absorbed in each other that they do not notice Hilarion, who has emerged from his hiding place. The gamekeeper boldy interrupts their rendezvous and separates them. Before they know what has happened, Hilarion is attacking Albrecht and warning him not to make love to Giselle. Giselle thinks that Hilarion is simply jealous and upbraids him for eavesdropping. Hilarion kneels before her and assures her that he alone truly loves her. Her anger mounting, Giselle dismisses Hilarion with rude laughter. The gamekeeper regards Albrecht with suspicion and hatred and, as he leaves the scene, shakes his fists at him.

Giselle is still shaken by this scene. Albrecht holds her in his arms and reassures her softly. They walk together. Village girls now enter, carrying huge baskets of grapes. They are all friends of Giselle's, and when they begin to dance, she joins them, dancing in their midst to a bright, melodious waltz. Albrecht watches Giselle from the bench nearby. She soon runs over and asks him to join in. Boys join the girls as Albrecht and Giselle dance around the stage. The two lovers blow kisses to each other as the music accompanies their dance with a soft, hesitant theme that tinkles gently. The waltz ensemble ends as Albrecht holds Giselle on his knee.

Berthe, Giselle's mother, opens the cottage door and steps out. She does not wish to interfere with the festivities, but she is genuinely worried. Giselle playfully hides behind her friends, but her mother discovers her. She upbraids her daughter for dancing so much and reminds her that her heart will fail. Berthe attempts to impress Giselle with the truth of what she says by warning her that if she dies, she will become one of the Wilis, one of those creatures doomed to dance forever, even in death.

Giselle's friends take Berthe's tale more seriously than her daughter does. She wishes to dance again and goes to Albrecht. Berthe, however, takes her by the hand, and together they go into the cottage. The door closes. The disappointed Albrecht wanders off, and the villagers disperse.

Now that the stage is empty, Hilarion, bent on vengeance, approaches Giselle's cottage. He does not know how he can convince the girl that she is being deceived. A hunting horn sounds in the distance. Hilarion hears a hunting party come his way and seeks concealment in Albrecht's cottage.

Wilfrid, Albrecht's squire, is the first of the hunting party to enter. He looks about apprehensively, lest his master still be present. The prince of Courland and his daughter, Bathilde, follow with huntsmen and members of the court. The prince gestures to Wilfrid that they are in need of refreshment and rest and orders him to knock at Giselle's door.

Berthe responds to Wilfrid's knock. Seeing the prince and his daughter, she bows low before them and invites them to partake of whatever humble refreshment she can offer. She signals inside the house, and two girls bring out a table and stools, metal goblets, and a pitcher of wine.

Giselle steps out of the house and is astonished to see the royal party. She bows to Wilfrid, thinking him a prince. Wilfrid indicates the true prince; Giselle curtsies to him and his daughter and tries to assist in their entertainment. Bathilde is kind to the girl and indicates to her father, "How beautiful she is!" Wilfrid pours the wine, and the prince and Bathilde drink. While they sit at the table, Giselle kneels surreptitiously at Bathilde's feet and touches the hem of her long dress. Giselle has not seen such expensive fabric before and remarks its beauty when Bathilde looks down and sees her. Bathilde takes Giselle aside and asks her how she spends her day. "Weaving and spinning," Giselle replies. "But are these the things you like to do best?" Bathilde wonders. "No," Giselle indicates, "I like best to dance," and so saying dances several steps before Bathilde.

Giselle's mother disapproves and is about to reprimand her daughter, but the dance is quickly over. Bathilde wishes to express her admiration for the peasant girl by giving her a present. With the prince's consent, she takes off her necklace and, calling Giselle to her, places it about the girl's neck. Giselle, in rapture, kisses her hand and proudly shows the necklace to her mother.

The hunting party now accepts Giselle's invitation to rest within the cottage. Wilfrid remains without, ready to rouse the prince with the hunting horn should there be good cause for the hunt to continue. Wilfrid dismisses the huntsmen and follows after them.

Hilarion comes forth from Albrecht's cottage. He carries Albrecht's sword in his hand. He looks about quickly, sees no one, and gestures in triumph: now perhaps Giselle will believe him! He exits as the peasant girls and boys return to resume their dancing. They knock at Giselle's door and finally persuade her mother to allow her to join them. The girls and boys recline in a semicircle about Giselle, who dances a brilliant solo. Albrecht appears as the girls dance. He and Giselle join her friends, and as the dance ensemble ends, the lovers embrace.

The music crashes ominously. Hilarion runs out, tears the lovers apart, and tells Giselle what he has learned: "You might love this man, but he is an impostor." He rushes out, retrieves Albrecht's sword, and places it in Giselle's hand. Albrecht is motionless with horror. He knows that the gamekeeper is right, but he knows that this is not the way for Giselle to learn the truth. She will never believe him again, never believe his love. Giselle seems to think Hilarion is lying; it does not occur to her that her lover has wronged her.

Wilfrid enters and attempts to protect his master. Hilarion persists in reminding Giselle that the sword is Albrecht's. She goes to Albrecht. With great faith she asks him if the gamekeeper is speaking the truth. Albrecht bows his head; he cannot speak. Then, looking up at Hilarion, who imagines that a duke cannot love as truly as a gamekeeper, seizes the sword and attacks him. Only Wilfrid prevents him from murdering the gamekeeper. The sword falls to the ground. Hilarion is glorying in his revenge so much that he does not notice what he has done to Giselle. He takes down the hunting horn and blows on it to summon the prince. Sobbing in her mother's arms, Giselle cannot yet believe what she has learned.

The prince and his daughter come out of the house with their party. The prince is surprised to see Albrecht in peasant's clothes; Bathilde goes to Albrecht and asks him what is wrong, why he is dressed like this? Giselle watches him closely. When he kneels before Bathilde and kisses her hand, Giselle tears herself from her mother's arms and accosts Bathilde. Albrecht tries to caution Bathilde, but before he can prevent it, she has pointed to the ring on her finger: she is engaged to Albrecht, Duke of Silesia.

Giselle, her heart broken, is so defenseless that her reason begins to disintegrate. Fiercely she tears the necklace Bathilde gave her from her neck and dashes it to the ground. She falls before her mother. Berthe comforts her as best she can and tries to quiet her and loosens her hair. Albrecht attempts to speak to her, to assure her of his love, but she will not listen. The girl is so stricken with grief, so helpless without the love she lived by, that all present, courtiers and peasants alike, pity her.

Giselle staggers to her feet. She moves about the stage slowly and pathetically, reliving her moments of happiness with Albrecht. With her reason gone, this is all she can think of. She picks up an imaginary flower and to herself plays another game of he-loves-me-loves-me-not. She circles the stage, and all the people stand back. Suddenly Giselle sees Albrecht's sword lying forgotten on the ground. She runs to it and, taking it up at the pointed end, holds it in front of her. Hypnotized by her madness, her friends do not move. Giselle bends low and drags the sword about with her, its handle rattling as she trails it around the stage at the feet of her friends. Then, before anyone can move, she raises the sword high and forces its point into her heart. Albrecht leaps across to her and seizes the sword.

The prince and Bathilde withdraw. Here they can only cause agony. Giselle, dying in her mother's arms, rises and goes to Albrecht. Her mind is now completely gone and she imagines that there has never been anything wrong, that he is her lover as before. She begins to dance with him, and again the soft, hesitant theme of romance that accompanied one of their happy dances together is repeated. Giselle awkwardly, falteringly, repeats the steps that she formerly danced with such grace. Then, in the midst of the dance, she is frightened. She runs to her mother, but falls to the ground before she can reach her embrace. Albrecht despairs as Berthe bends over her daughter. But Giselle asks for him. He comes to her and looks down into her eyes, which even now seek only his. He declares again his imperishable love. Giselle reaches up to touch his face in a gesture of forgiveness; then her hand falls. She is dead.

Albrecht rises and drags Hilarion to see what his jealousy has accomplished. As the gamekeeper weeps and kneels beside Giselle, Albrecht seizes the sword and again tries to kill him. Wilfrid again prevents him. Albrecht weeps beside Giselle. The dead girl lies before him, her arms crossed on her breast. The villagers turn their faces away to hide the grief they share.

ACT TWO: WITHIN A FOREST GLADE AT MIDNIGHT   In the second act we pass to a scene and a mood entirely different from that of Act One. Our first hint of this comes in the music. The strings sing softly against a rippling harp; all is quiet and ethereal. The curtain rises on a scene misty with the dewy night. The moon penetrates the thick trees occasionally; its light is reflected in a nearby lake, and in this dimness we discover Giselle's grave at the left. Her name is inscribed on a large cross that stands above the grassy mound. In the dark-blue sky, small shimmering lights appear.

Three huntsmen with a lantern enter to rest. They sit down near the lake. Hilarion joins them. Soon the men are disturbed by the eerie atmosphere of the place. They have heard tales that Wilis danced here and they fear the place is haunted. The lights in the sky are not constant, they appear to shimmer at will. Hilarion, aware that Giselle's grave is close by, becomes apprehensive. He approaches the grave. The men warn him to leave. Hilarion is reluctant, but joins his friends as they depart.

Across the back of the stage a veiled figure in a long white dress moves flowingly. She is Myrtha, Queen of the Wilis. She enters, crosses the stage rapidly, and again appears at the back. At her second entry, she has removed her veil. She bows, poses in deep, still arabesque, and begins to dance. Her movements are confident, controlled, beautiful, but they possess no warmth. The supernatural powers Myrtha possesses allow for nothing but perfection. She moves more rapidly now; the quickness of her dancing is brilliant and hard, like a diamond. She gathers two fern branches from the lakeside, throws them into the forest to dedicate the place to her awful purpose, and circles the stage in a brilliant display of virtuosity.

Now, with her wand, she calls forth the Wilis. Instantly obedient to her command, they appear on either side of the stage, their hands crossed over their breasts. Myrtha orders them to remove their white veils. They obey her and arrange themselves for a dance. Led by two attendants to the queen, the Wilis move with a perplexing, almost automatic, grace, as if they danced only at Myrtha's will. Myrtha dances among them, dances with relentless, abandoned force, as if she could not restrain herself, then orders the dancing to end. All the Wilis turn toward Giselle's grave, kneel, and bend low. A new creature is to be initiated.

Myrtha bends over the grave with a magical branch. The earth parts, and Giselle rises from the mound. She is dressed in white, veiled, her arms crossed over her breast. Instinctively, as if hypnotized, she responds to Myrtha's commands. She walks toward the queen and stands motionless as Myrtha removes her veil. Now Giselle opens her eyes. Following Myrtha's example, she begins to dance, imitating her movements exactly. Myrtha declares that she is now a member of the ghostly tribe and orders Giselle to dance alone. The girl suddenly seems to come to life and, turning around and around, rejoices in her liberation from the grave.

Surrounded by her sisters, Giselle dances as they, too, have danced at their first appearance from their graves—before the dreadful power of the queen dominated them completely. Giselle leaves the scene at the end of her dance, and Myrtha orders the Wilis to conceal themselves.

The stage is empty when Albrecht enters. He moves slowly, dejectedly. He has come to visit the grave of his beloved and is filled with memories of her tragic death. Wilfrid follows his master and attempts to dissuade him from reminding himself of Giselle. Albrecht dismisses him and kneels before Giselle's grave. As he thinks of her, Giselle appears. Albrecht cannot believe it; he looks again; she was not there, after all. He rises and looks about the scene. Now Giselle runs fleetingly in a swift diagonal before him. Albrecht catches her in his arms briefly, lifts her in midflight, and again she disappears. Albrecht's brief touch is like a glance; he thinks that he must be dreaming, yet prays that the dream is true.

As he kneels in prayer, Giselle re-enters and dances about him. He does not see her. Then Giselle walks up in back of him and lovingly touches his shoulder. Albrecht rises and watches her. Joyful that his prayer has been answered, he wishes to touch her. They begin to dance together, Giselle leading the way. Then suddenly she vanishes.

She returns, picks two white lilies, and, dancing in swift diagonals, throws the flowers back over her head. Albrecht, pursuing her closely, picks up the flowers and follows her into the forest as she exits.

Hilarion returns to the scene. No sooner has he done so than Wilis appear before him. He turns to escape them, but in every direction other winged creatures enter and surround him. Myrtha enters with her attendants to examine the captive. At her command, all the Wilis encircle Hilarion, then stand in a long diagonal line, reaching from the right front of the stage to the lakeside. Myrtha stands at the right, at the head of the line. Hilarion, now sure of her intent, begs her for mercy. The queen gestures grandly, "No." Hilarion rushes down the line, beseeching the Wilis to intervene for him. They all refuse. Myrtha declares that he must die. She points to the lake. Hilarion is turned around and around as he is thrust down the long line of Wilis. At the end, two Wilis seize him and cast him into the lake.

Myrtha, unrelenting and triumphant, crosses the stage in light, unremembering leaps and exits at the rear. Two by two, all the Wilis follow her, imitating her step precisely. When Myrtha leads them back on stage, Albrecht confronts the queen. He, too, asks that his life might be spared, and again the queen denies the request. Giselle pleads in his behalf, but her intervention serves only to increase Myrtha's anger. Giselle, determined to save Albrecht at all costs, gestures to him to take refuge beneath the cross at her grave. Myrtha quickly orders the Wilis to intercept Albrecht, but he succeeds in reaching the cross in spite of their efforts to ensnare him. Giselle stands before him in an attitude of protection, and the queen is helpless.

Determined that Albrecht shall die, and offended at this sudden curtailment of her power, the queen orders Giselle to descend from the cross and dance. The girl obeys her, dancing alone between the Wilis, who are arranged in lines down the sides of the stage.

At the conclusion of the dance, Albrecht leaves the protective cross, steps down, and the two lovers go down the lines of Wilis, pleading for their intercession. All obstinately refuse. Now Giselle and Albrecht begin a *pas de deux*. As Albrecht supports Giselle in the adagio, Wilis contrive to come between them and separate them. But the two are now so reunited, so reassured of their lasting love, that they escape these Wilis without even noticing them.

Myrtha commands Giselle to dance alone again. This is followed by a variation for Albrecht. Giselle rejoins him. He lifts her again and again, higher and higher, straight into the air, her phantomlike body seeming a part of the air. Giselle dances another solo. The queen of the Wilis knows that Giselle will never tire, that, like all Wilis, she has a passion for dancing. She knows also that Albrecht will wish to please Giselle and will dance with her. Albrecht will dance to his death.

Albrecht commences another variation. When he has finished, he pleads with the Wilis to make him dance no longer. They ignore his request and, in the midst of continuation of the dance, he falls exhausted to the ground. Giselle tries to help him up, but he cannot move. Giselle turns to the queen and dances to divert her. Finally Albrecht stirs as Giselle beckons to him. They resume their dance; Albrecht makes a new plea to Myrtha, and the dance is resumed as she again denies him. When Albrecht collapses and kneels on the ground, Giselle stands over him protectively. She humbly approaches Myrtha and when the queen obstinately rebuffs her, Giselle asks each of the Wilis to help her. They can do nothing; they are all in the queen's power.

Albrecht attempts to leave the scene, but the watchful Wilis prevent his escape and force him to dance again. He leaps again and again high into the air, then falls to the ground.

Dawn approaches. Four o'clock sounds in the distance. The Wilis must vanish, for with the coming of day, they are powerless. Giselle rejoices that Albrecht has been saved! The Wilis again bow at Giselle's grave, consigning her back to the earth. Giselle embraces Albrecht as she kneels beside him. She knows that this is farewell. The Wilis rush away into the coming dawn, followed by their queen. Albrecht succeeds in rising. Giselle, with mysterious longing, yearns to return to the earth. She goes to her grave. Albrecht follows her, but before he reaches the tomb, she has fallen back and been covered with earth. Albrecht despairs and falls to the ground where he first knelt beside the grave of his beloved.

NOTES   Two recent performers of the title role in *Giselle* have attracted special attention, both in the Royal Ballet's production. Writing in the New York *Times* of Merle Park's performance of May 10, 1970, at the Metropolitan Opera House, New York, Clive Barnes said: "She is gorgeous—one of the greatest Giselles I have ever seen and to be ranked with Ulanova, Markova, Alonso, or Chauviré. Miss Park conveys all of Giselle—her innocence, her simple love of play-acting, her vanity, her nervousness, her compassion. Her portrayal is not only beautiful in its dramatic detail—never in my life have I seen a more consummately convincing mad scene—but is also marvelously danced. Once again, as with Antoinette Sibley, with these classic English ballerinas, one looks to Leningrad for their peers, and here you find Natalia Makarova. Makarova has more elevation, more ethereality. Park has more force, more honesty, and more technical finesse. Miss Park is a Giselle for people who never want to see that ballet again."

In June 1972, Natalia Makarova danced *Giselle* with the Royal Ballet in London. Peter Williams reviewed her performance in *The Observer:* "The first time that Natalia Makarova ever danced *Giselle* with her parent company, the Kirov, was in London. In this city, some years later, she broke the umbilical cord and decided to remain in the West. It was right that in *Giselle* she should return to dance as guest with the Royal Ballet at Covent Garden, since the company has its roots deep in the Leningrad School.

"Giselle is probably the most deceptive role in all classical ballet since sheer dancing ability is simply not enough to make it work. The ballerina has to be totally convincing as a human and, later, as a supernatural being. It is the conviction Makarova brings to both aspects of the part, combined with her great schooling, that makes her possibly the finest interpreter of our time.

"She *is* the simple village girl, overpowered by the attentions of Albrecht, whom she believes to be a swain of peasant stock; her trust in him is complete and touching. Her madness, following the moment of truth, is achieved by none of those contrived ballerina gestures but with the inconsequential movements of a deranged mind—she scrabbles at the ground for imagined flowers; in her aimless wandering she already imagines the Wilis; she is a lost soul with just the right glimmer of confused recognition as she confronts one of the figures in her tragedy.

"In the opening moments of the first act, Makarova had a bit of trouble with the tempi; gradually, as the ballet progressed, she and conductor Lanchbery moved together until, in the second act, any disparity was smoothed out. Her control, never overstepping the bounds of the role, is wonderful: slow turns which even leave time for extra beaten steps in their progress; a softness that is never coy; a quiet exultation in all her phrasing. Her arms are so expressive that, in the second act, their fluidity seemed to become a part of the mists encircling her unhallowed grave.

"There is no doubt that Makarova's performance was enriched by the accord which existed between her and Anthony Dowell's anti-hero Albrecht. What for him started as a flirtatious game gradually developed into true tenderness; his partnering all through became a moving expression of a love that believably went beyond death and the grave. Dowell's dancing and subtle playing matched so perfectly with Makarova's that this might well be the beginning of an historic partnership."

Writing of his famous roles, the *premier danseur* Erik Bruhn recalled his impressions of Albrecht in the essay "Beyond Technique" for *Dance Perspectives:* "I think I consider Albrecht as something of a playboy, with a definite background that James (in *La Sylphide*) does not have. He is just James. He could be a peasant boy from the country with not much sophistication. Albrecht belongs to the aristocracy. A marriage has been arranged for him, as was customary at that time, and he accepts this without protesting or rebelling. At the same time he feels that he is free to do what he wants to do as well. So here is this playboy playing with something as lovely, as innocent, as serious as Giselle. Yet there is a certain innocence in Albrecht too, or he would have been smart to conceal the fact of his disguise as a peasant and nobody could have discovered that he had a fiancée already. His fancy for

Giselle is earnest enough as long as he can keep it secret. For he is quite prepared to do what he is supposed to do and marry his proper fiancée and continue the family tradition. He does not dream that Giselle will take his attentions so seriously.

"She is attracted to him because he is different. After all, she has plenty of peasants to choose from. Whether the audience sees him first dressed as a count or as a peasant does not matter. There is something different about him. It is like we see someone on the subway and he may stand out because of his mod clothes and long hair (though even that we pass by now), or he may dress like anyone else and we don't know why but suddenly we turn and look. Giselle recognizes his difference though she doesn't know where he comes from.

"After she dies from the shock of Albrecht's deception, he realizes some sincerity in life that he might not otherwise have known. His awareness of guilt makes him mature. His going to her grave at night is like a nightmare. The wilis, of course, are not real because today we cannot believe in terms of wilis flying around. They are in Albrecht's mind. They are all the things we are afraid of, that we have tried to escape. In his nightmares a man's wrong deeds come back to him, carrying a message that he must look at right in the face. Then he can accept his guilt without pushing it away; he can face reality. Albrecht survives because he can admit his guilt and realize his responsibility. After that night he will go into the future with an awareness that makes him mature. And this proves a strength in him too.

"My first *Giselle* was with Alicia Markova in 1955 and, unlike my first *La Sylphide,* it was a success. We did it in three days. I had never done *Giselle* before but I had seen it and maybe I wanted to do it for years. Markova was so clear in what she told me about the ballet that I felt ready to go on stage that night after only one rehearsal. She never had to repeat herself and she said once, 'We seem to speak the same language.' Thanks to her, it worked out just right. Some things were sketchy because we had worked alone and there was just one runthrough before the performance with everyone on stage, and suddenly I realized that people were there in those places and they were all moving. I chose to do nothing rather than try to act something I didn't know anything about. Yet I later relied on the work I had done with Markova and based my future performances on it.

"It seemed there was nothing wrong with my first *Giselle;* in fact it set me up like I was supposed to be *the* Albrecht. But if I had not on occasions revived my idea about Albrecht, I couldn't do the character today and the memory of my Albrecht would belong to the books. It had only a momentary truth that worked for a time as life. Now I can bring more to a role. I can go back to roles I have done for ten years to get a picture of how I see James or Albrecht today. When I first did them I had less of a past to return to and therefore was not able to give that much to a role. I think the more experience you have got the more need there will be for you to use it. And there will be a youth and vitality in the characterization that it didn't have originally. In a more mature state, one has more imagination as to what a youth would do. When I was his age I could only be me which was the beginning of a James. Now I can give a more complete portrayal of James and Albrecht because I have used my imagination. And the portrayal of the character is always true as long as we bring to it what we have within us."

In a review headlined "Fairy-Tale Debut," the critic Clive Barnes wrote in the New York *Times* of Gelsey Kirkland's first performance in this role with American Ballet Theatre at Washington's Kennedy Center, May 18, 1975: "Partnered by Mikhail Baryshnikov, she made her debut in the title role of *Giselle* and the debuts of few ballerinas can have been more memorable. It was the coming together of a dancer and a role that had been made for each other . . . Since her school days, Miss Kirkland has understandably been the darling of the ballet's cognoscenti, but here irrefutably was the emergence of a great American ballerina. She did not put a foot, a hand or even a gesture wrong—it was the fairy-tale debut little girls dream about . . ."

The Kirkland-Baryshnikov *Giselle* was reviewed in detail by Arlene Croce in *The New Yorker* after its New York presentation in August 1975. The critic, pointing out that we have lacked a great American-born Giselle ever since the ballet became a part of the active repertory in the United States, said that Gelsey Kirkland "may be the first totally creditable Giselle since the ballet was first danced here," in 1846.

When Galina Ulanova visited New York in 1975 with the Bolshoi Ballet, whose young dancers she enjoys training, the critic Anna Kisselgoff interviewed her in the New York *Times*:

". . . The difference between Miss Ulanova's approach to a ballet and that of a younger generation was illustrated during the interview when she cleared up a specific dramatic point in the Bolshoi's current production of *Giselle* that is not included in Western productions.

"At the close of the second act, Giselle (a peasant girl who is now a spirit) is cradled by Albrecht, the aristocrat who has betrayed her. The action seems puzzling. Is the ghost of Giselle so corporeal that she can be picked up like a parcel?

"No, replied Miss Ulanova, explaining that the original dramatic meaning of the moment had been lost.

" 'In the original production by Leonid Lavrovsky, it was different. Giselle had returned from the grave and was joyful. She was a live spirit, as there are in fairy tales.

" 'As dawn breaks, however, she must leave and it was then that Albrecht tried to prolong this moment. She would lean back and it was here that he would carefully pick her up as she was "fading away."

" 'He would touch her skirt'—here Miss Ulanova moved her arms and lifted her head in an instant that brought the action to life—'and Albrecht would feel Giselle's presence as if it were a breeze.

" 'Now they pick Giselle up and just rock her. Well, you know young people —they are lightheaded.' Miss Ulanova smiled as she used a Russian expression that could be literally translated as 'They have the wind blowing through their heads.' "

Readers interested in discovering the motivations and rationale of dancers will wish to know that Mikhail Baryshnikov, in his book *Baryshnikov at Work*, has described with Charles Engell France the background of his first appearances as Albrecht. He analyzes *Giselle* in detail from the point of view of the part as he sees it—a man in love, caught up by fate, innocent, not a faithless, plotting aristocrat.

Shortly after the Kirkland-Baryshnikov *Giselle*, another debut in the title role was given by Bronwyn Thomas, aged fifteen, in the U. S. Terpsichore production at the Marymount Manhattan Theatre, New York, on August 13, 1975. Her Albrecht was Daniel Levans, the Myrtha Marrisa Benetsky. The role of Giselle's mother was taken *en travestie* by David Vaughan. This modest presentation, with piano accompaniment, was modeled after Anton Dolin's production, made so familiar in performances by that *danseur noble* and Alicia Markova.

On June 2, 1977, the American Ballet Theatre production of *Giselle*, with Makarova, Baryshnikov and Van Hamel, was seen live on PBS television direct from the Metropolitan Opera House in New York.

GLINKAIANA

Music by Michael Glinka. Choreography by George Balanchine. Scenery, costumes, and lighting by Esteban Francés. First presented by the New York City Ballet at the New York State Theatre, Lincoln Center, November 1968, with Violette Verdy and Paul Meija, Mimi Paul and John Clifford, and Patricia McBride and Edward Villella in the principal roles.

Glinka is the Mozart of Russia; before him there was no real Russian music. From my earliest years I have always loved his music. In the New York City Ballet's days at the City Center Theatre, we did a ballet, a short one, the *Mazurka* from *A Life for the Tsar*, one of Glinka's great operas, which Vida Brown and I danced in. But I go back further than that with Glinka, having danced in his opera *Russlan and Ludmila* at the Maryinsky Theatre in St. Petersburg when I was a student. I remember those days (this was during the Revolution or just afterward) very well: sometimes it was so cold the men in the orchestra wore overcoats and mittens without fingers. We froze on stage. Still, I loved every note of that music.

Glinkaiana is simply a series of dances to four works by Glinka: a *Polka*, orchestrated by Vittorio Rieti, *Valse Fantasie* (this music was used for an earlier New York City Ballet production, in 1951), *Jota Aragonesa*, and *Divertimento Brilliante*.

THE GODS AMUSED

Music by Claude Debussy. Choreography by Eliot Feld. Costumes by Frank Thompson. Lighting by Jennifer Tipton. First presented by the American Ballet Company at the Brooklyn Academy of Music, New York, April 28, 1971, with Daniel Levans, Elizabeth Lee, and Christine Sarry.

The Gods Amused is a dance ballet for three deities set to Debussy's *Danses Sacrée et Profane*. A young god and two young goddesses disport and amuse themselves on a day brilliant with light and reflection. The boy is the leader, and the girls are watchful of him. The nobility of these Olympian creatures gives them a certain detachment and while they might openly admire each other, there is no commitment in a personal sense; after all, all gods are beautiful. When the game is over, the three rest a bit, but at the end remind us in a statuesque pose of their immortality.

GOLDBERG VARIATIONS

Music by Johann Sebastian Bach. Choreography by Jerome Robbins. Costumes by Joe Eula. Lighting by Thomas Skelton. First presented by the New York City Ballet at the New York State Theatre, Lincoln Center, May 27, 1971. Pianist: Gordon Boelzner. Part I: Theme, Renée Estopinal and Michael Steele. Variations, Gelsey Kirkland, Sara Leland, John Clifford, Robert Weiss, Robert Maiorano, and Bruce Wells; Bryan Pitts, David Richardson, Delia Peters, Christine Redpath, Bettijane Sills, Stephen Caras, Hermes Conde, Richard Dryden, Francis Sackett, Suzanne Erlon, Gloriann Hicks, and Virginia Stuart. Part II: Variations, Karin von Aroldingen, Susan Hendl, Patricia McBride, Peter Martins, Anthony Blum, and Helgi Tomasson; Merrill Ashley, Rosemary Dunleavy, Renée Estopinal, Johnna Kirkland, Deborah Koolish, Gail Kachadurian, Colleen Neary, Susan Pilarre, Giselle Roberge, Polly Shelton, Marjorie Spohn, and Lynne Stetson; Stephen Caras, Victor Castelli, Hermes Conde, Richard Dryden, Bryan Pitts, David Richardson, Francis Sackett, Nolan T'Sani.

Because this dance ballet is based on its music, Bach's *Goldberg Variations*, it might be well to consider the score first. The popular name of *"Goldberg" Variations* attached itself to the work because of the circumstances of its composition. It was hoped that they would be a sure cure for the insomnia of one Count von Kayserling. As the story goes, Bach was commissioned by the count, the Russian ambassador to the Dresden Court, who suffered badly from insomnia, to write some pieces "of a smooth and lively" character in order to relieve the tedium of his sleepless nights. Johann Theophilus Goldberg, a pupil of Bach, was harpsichordist to the count. He was the one who played the finished variations for the count and his name has attached itself to the work ever since.

Published in 1742, the *Goldberg Variations* consist of an aria or theme and thirty variations. It is the only work of Bach's in the form of a theme and variations. But it differs from most compositions of this work in an important respect. We usually think of a series of musical variations as an exploitation or development of a theme or melody that is stated at the beginning of the piece; we expect the same music to appear again and again in different dress. Bach's variations, however, are harmonic variations, rather than melodic; they develop the bass of the original aria rather than its melody. The result is that in the thirty variations that follow, the melody of each is always fresh while the original bass accompaniment is developed anew underneath. The fundamental pattern in the bass can be heard in the first few bars of the aria, a *sarabande* that Bach wrote for his wife.

But first of all, the *Goldberg Variations* are a pleasure. The pianist Charles Rosen writes in the notes to his recording: "It is the most open and public of Bach's keyboard works, the one that most absorbs and transforms the popular styles of his time. The *Goldberg Variations* are, in fact, an encyclopedia: a survey of the world of secular music . . . a social work: it was meant mainly to delight, and it instructs only as it charms. . . . There are canons, a fugue, a French overture, a *siciliana*, a *quodlibet*, accompanied solos and a series of inventions and dance-like movements."

A hearing of a recording of the work is certainly not essential before seeing the ballet (Bach's music is immediately likable in any case), but it is enjoyable to listen to so entertaining and danceable a masterpiece. Come to think of it, I would suggest, if the piece is not familiar to you already, that you hear it first as you see the ballet. In this case, both what you see and what you hear will be marvelous.

What you see begins, and ends, with a *sarabande* or stately dance. Two dancers in eighteenth-century costume perform an elegantly simple *pas de deux* at the beginning. They are still as the curtain rises, posing formally, then they step toward us as the music begins. Their somewhat courtly manner of movement and gesture sets the style for much that follows. Their dance is slow, a bit grave, "yet happy, tranquil and at the same time vibrant with internal life," as Wanda Landowska described the music.

The theme stated, dancers in modern attire come to accompany the inventiveness of the score: there is a trio for a girl and two boys, then a series of variations for different groupings—solos, quartets, *pas de deux*, a sextet, in a continuing flow of dance discovery of the music.

After the fifteenth variation, a middle point is reached. The second part of the ballet has a different character from the first, as do the costumes, which become more formal. Dominated by the dancing of three couples, with solos by the principals, and a *corps de ballet* of twenty, the new part is an exploration of the classic *pas de deux* and concentrates more on the few rather an the many. Just before the end, all the dancers return, and in costumes recalling eighteenth-century court dress, celebrate the final variation. The restatement of the opening aria at the end is danced by the couple we saw first at the start of the piece, but dressed now in contemporary costume. The circle is closed.

The general outline I have tried to give here is all you need, assuming, in fact, that anything is needed but open eyes and ears. Those who want to recollect some details after they have seen *Goldberg Variations* may find the following map useful:

The piece begins, and ends, with an aria, a *sarabande*. The harpsichordist Ralph Kirkpatrick calls the whole work "an enormous *passacaglia* . . . framed as if by two monumental pylons, one formed by the aria and the first two variations, the other by the two penultimate variations and the *quodlibet*, the variations are grouped like the members of an elaborate colonnade."

Galina Ulanova in *Swan Lake*. Collection of Rosemary Winckley.

Alicia Markova and André Eglevsky in *The Nutcracker*. Photo by Maurice Seymour, from the Dance Collection, N.Y.P.L.

Vyacheslav Gordeyev. Photo by Kenn Duncan.

Rudolf Nureyev in *Petrouchka*. Photo by Rosemary Winckley.

Jerome Robbins in *Prodigal Son*. Photo by George Platt Lynes, from the Dance Collection, N.Y.P.L.

Vladimir Vasiliev in *Spartacus*. Photo by Rosemary Winckley.

Merle Park and David Wall in *Walk to the Paradise Garden*. Photo by Anthony Crickmay.

Margot Fonteyn and Rudolf Nureyev in *La Bayadère*. Photo by Anthony Crickmay.

Lynn Seymour and Anthony Dowell in *A Month in the Country*. Photo by Beverley Gallegos.

Karin von Aroldingen in *A Midsummer Night's Dream*. Photo by Costas.

Suzanne Farrell in *Union Jack*. Photo by Beverley Gallegos.

Peter Martins in *Tchaikovsky Pas de Deux*. Photo by Costas.

Paolo Bortoluzzi and Jörg Lanner in *Nijinsky, Clown of God*. Photo by Rosemary Winckley.

Suzanne Farrell in *Nijinsky, Clown of God*. Photo by Rosemary Winckley.

Starr Danias and Dennis Wayne in *Sacred Grove on Mount Tamalpais*. Photo by Herbert Migdoll.

Gelsey Kirkland and Mikhail Baryshnikov in *La Sylphide*. Photo by Beverley Gallegos.

Martine van Hamel in *The Sleeping Beauty*. Photo by Martha Swope.

After the aria is stated by the piano, the curtain rises on a girl and boy, she in a white ballet dress, he in eighteenth-century attire with black knee britches, white stockings, and a white ruffled shirt. They are quite still for a moment, posing formally, then they move toward us. Their dance is slow, a bit grave, yet, in Wanda Landowska's words about the music, "happy, tranquil and at the same time vibrant with eternal life." The boy kneels before the girl briefly.

1. A girl in a light olive-green tunic and two boys in tank suits replace the first couple as the introductory aria finishes and we are in another century altogether. The music is brisker, too, within the flowing melodic line and after the girl begins, the boys dance too, at her signal. She joins them at the close.

2. In what Landowska calls a "serene and pastoral mood," a girl in violet and two other boys dance; it is a friendly, thoughtful occasion, both boys lifting the girl to the trills of the score.

3. A boy, like a watchful teacher, leads four couples in an ensemble. One of the girls joins him. As he takes her off, the music changes, becoming openly declarative, with a kind of flourish.

4. These "jocose imitations" (Landowska) are danced by three couples and a boy who gesture in formal greeting and thanks.

5. The music, very fast, a contest for the performer, is for crossed hands (crossed keyboards on the harpsichord), an "outburst of irrepressible joy," in George Malcolm's words; two boys compete in the dance.

6. To new, slower music, the boys rest, lie down, stretch, look up briefly at the sky, then at each other. Then they sit up, rise, approach each other in a friendly way and begin to dance.

7. Their dance is a *saltarella*, a kind of jig, the rhythms of which were very popular in old French ballets. They greet a group of newcomers.

8. Six boys who watch a girl dance to tripping rhythms. She bows to them and goes. A boy in green leads the boys in a dance, girls join them and there is an ensemble.

9. As the music slows down four beats to the bar, the lead boy moves toward the lead girl, as do other couples in the group. They face each other across a circle of dancers. They simply walk, aimlessly, without any intention. The circle is broken; they are individuals again, then the walk becomes a promenade and they are all moving together and it is a dance. For twelve dancers.

10. A *fughetta*. Here, as George Malcolm puts it, the solemn *aria* melody is "slyly turned into a lithe and witty subject" for a little fugue. A dance for four boys, somersaults, cartwheels, and rolls.

11. To very rapid runs on the keyboard, three girls and three boys dance like the wind.

12. Three other couples dance to a stately measure in a dim light, then the six dancers from (11) return for varied combinations and separations. The boys watch the girls a bit and there is a final ensemble.

13. To a *cantilena* with a delicately ornamented upper melodic line, two girls and two boys dance. The light is subdued, the atmosphere friendly and thoughtful. There, hinting, in the words of the critic Emory Lewis, "at the

differing ways of love," the two boys dance together, as the girls watch, then the girls dance together, as the boys relax. Then again the boys dance with the girls.

14. Again the boys dance with the girls. The lights come up. To brilliant music of crossed keyboards, there is an ensemble led first by the boy in green.

15. The mood quietens again and the first of the variations in a minor key is danced by six girls, who back in from the right, and six boys, who back in from the left. They become a group of varied partnerships. The girls are lifted off gently into the wings at the close.

16. One boy remains, his arm raised before his face when suddenly to the right, to flourishing music, a phalanx of twelve girls ushers in three couples. In George Malcolm's words, this is "a specially grand variation and acts as a prelude to the second half, taking the form of an overture in the French style with the typical pompous opening and lively fugato. The aria is transformed by great technical skill into a splendid piece of Baroque grandeur."

17. A group of girls in blue begins this sparkling variation in which the music seems to cascade across the stage. The three couples who are to dominate this last half of the ballet take over but the girls return to finish the dance.

18. To a marchlike rhythm, a girl in pink and her partner dance an exhilarating, witty *pas de deux* in which the two dancers openly enjoy the mocking laughter in the music. Four boys and four girls watch.

19. Another *pas de deux* to music of gentle syncopations that floats, in Landowska's phrase, "like a barcarolle."

20. Excitement returns and the same two dancers seem to counteract the impulsive rhythm of the music by deliberately slow movement. The lights dim and before we know it they seem to have caught up with the music in rapid combinations of motion and gesture. The dancers perhaps embody George Malcolm's description of the music here, where "differing voices take up a living pursuit of each other."

21. The light darkens. A supported adagio for the third couple, this variation in G minor is reflective of the tragedy and pathos implied in the score.

22. A "massive" variation to Landowska, "its voices interlacing after the fashion of Palestrina," is danced by the boy who, left alone, dejected, seeks comfort in expression, then returns to his memories.

23. The lights come up. Brilliant again and almost "vertiginous in its joy" (Landowska), this variation accompanies a swift dance for four couples; the boys, then the girls racing diagonally across the stage, then all leaving together.

24. Calm again and in a stately dance rhythm, the music accompanies the girl who left the boy. She dances a variation. Three of her friends are with her and appear to want to be soloists, too.

25. The last variation in a minor key, somber, restless, romantic, a "richly ornamented adagio that overwhelms us" (Landowska), is danced by the girl in pink and her partner.

26. This sparkling variation is a combination of 18/16 time in one hand and 3/4 in the other, the two hands temporarily changing places once in a while.

Girls and boys in new costumes, like the eighteenth-century couple at the start, enter and watch as the other two lead couples dance.

The 27th variation (Landowska saw "humor and malice" here), the 28th (memorable for its tinkling trills), and the joyful 29th bring all six of the principals before us as each dances before the *corps de ballet*. All now are dressed in eighteenth-century costume.

For the 30th variation, a *quodlibet,* or fantasia, involving two folk tunes as well as the fundamental base melody, the dancers cluster at the center of the stage. They stand there briefly in a quiet pose. The lights come down; they all seem to promenade off. But as the aria is played again, the first two dancers, now in modern dress, come back to show again the beginning.

NOTES Few ballets have been so praised, and at such articulate length, as *Goldberg Variations.* After a performance of what the choreographer called a "work in progress" at the Saratoga Performing Arts Center on July 23, 1970, Don McDonagh wrote in the New York *Times* that "the New York City Ballet has presented many premières in its history but none has had the informal and charming intimacy of *Goldberg Variations.*"

After the New York première, *Variety* said the ballet was not only "a pinnacle of 20th century art but gave rise to the notion that it may be the most perfect dance work ever made. No better dancing can be seen than in this work. . . . Few other companies could have provided such superior execution by 42 dancers. . . . It is difficult to overestimate the contribution of pianist Gordon Boelzner, who played the immense work with brilliance, insight and rhythmic subtlety."

Winthrop Sargeant in *The New Yorker* called *Goldberg Variations* "a magnificent spectacle. . . . The ballet is abstract in the sense that music is abstract, but, like music, it contains moods ranging from sombre to playful. Mr. Robbins's feeling for the music is extraordinarily sensitive, and his treatment of rhythmic movement is—like his treatment of stage space—fluid, sometimes eccentric, but always deeply conscious of musical values. The première of the *Goldberg Variations* was to me the high point of a busy ballet season, and it places Mr. Robbins among the great, original masters of the art."

In *The Saturday Review,* the critic Walter Terry, admiring the ballet, recalled that Jerome Robbins had used the harpsichord at the working rehearsal of *Goldberg Variations* at Saratoga. "At a subsequent matinee, the harpsichord was tried again. In both forms of accompaniment, Gordon Boelzner was the admirable, laudable musician. Robbins himself says that he prefers the support of the piano since 'I worked with the piano in rehearsal when the ballet was being created, and it is closely related to those sounds. As for the length of the ballet . . . I could not violate the music. It is there, all there, and if the mind wanders, let it rest and then come back.'"

Writing in *Dance and Dancers* magazine, the critic Patricia Barnes described many of the performers:

"The first variations are dominated by the performances of the six soloists—among the company's most brilliant. The two girls are rewardingly contrasted. Sara Leland, lithe, daring and intensely musical, has an abandon and fearlessness that is exciting to watch; while Gelsey Kirkland, more restrained in her personality, offers us dancing that is as delicately precise as the finest embroidery. Her manner is touching too. Just 18, she is poised on the threshold of womanhood, but retains the charming innocence of a young girl. She has one solo, outstandingly danced, sympathetically watched by six young men casually seated on the floor, that perfectly catches in its unselfconscious coquetry her individuality and special grace.

"John Clifford, Bruce Wells, Robert Weiss and Robert Maiorano have equally enhanced their reputations. Each has had his artistry extended in this work. Clifford has never looked so elegant, while losing nothing of his appealing ebullience. Wells, a sure *premier danseur* in the making, is superb, smooth and effortless in everything he does, demonstrating a perfect line, buoyant elevation and a radiant personality.

"Another dancer who has caught the eye ever since he joined two years ago has been Robert Weiss. His brio, neat footwork and fine *ports de bras* are always in evidence, and Robbins has here exploited his mercurial gifts to splendid advantage. A slight stiffness in his upper torso at present prevents this slim and promising young dancer from total elegance, but this should come.

"One of Maiorano's first major opportunities came with *Dances at a Gathering*, and he has once more found himself in a Robbins ballet that gives him a chance to shine. His developing stage presence and ever-improving technique need this sort of exposure, for when given the opportunity he has shown himself most capable. . . .

"It would be impossible, in this dense and lengthy ballet, to describe fully the variations in detail, so isolated examples must suffice. One particularly striking section for four dancers, two boys and two girls, stands out. The two boys (Bryan Pitts and David Richardson) dance together, watched by the two girls (Leland and Kirkland), and while they relax the two girls dance.

"My own favorite variation is performed by two couples. Maiorano with Leland and Weiss with Kirkland, while Wells and Clifford slowly, in musical counterpoint, walk around them. The dance turns into two pas de trois, as the two boys weave their way in and out of the dancers to form two trios. The subtle transition is so beautiful, natural and elegant that one almost holds one's breath at Robbins's dazzling craftsmanship. . . .

"The final half of the ballet revolves around the six dancers, supported by the ensemble, and is far more formal in its construction while the choreography is more intricate. There is room only for the mention of highlights.

"The opening couple, McBride and Tomasson, backed by the ensemble, reflect in their pas de deux something of the bucolic humours of the 18th century, as hands on hips, backs to the audience, their bodies seem to shake with merriment, but this humour is touched with a 20th-century jazziness that perfectly fits the music's rhythms. The pas de deux from Blum and Hendl, at the start cool and classical, deploys Hendl's clean lines and Blum's strong presence. There is a gradual and subtle change of mood as the choreography becomes more sensual. The convolutions of the two dancers as they entwine around each other, while within the framework of the classic technique, succeeds in looking very new and very arresting.

"The loose-limbed and pliant qualities of von Aroldingen are shown off well in her quirkily individual solo, backed by three girls, but even better is the appearance of Peter Martins. He has never seemed more spirited, more dexterous. He was a joy to watch as he revelled in the musical rhythms and choreographic complexities. This elegant and beautiful dancer has sometimes in the past appeared a little too reserved. In *Goldberg* he was a powerhouse of excitement and physical strength. . . .

"Musically the work is yet another gift to City Ballet by its remarkable pianist, Gordon Boelzner. As in the previous Robbins masterworks, Mr. Boelzner, calm and implacable, is at his keyboard on a platform to the left of the proscenium arch and, as always, playing with modest majesty. He has become one of City Ballet's gilt-edged assets. Typically, when for one performance he was asked as an experiment to play on the harpsichord rather than the piano, he was willing, able and of course brilliant."

Admirers of *Goldberg Variations* must also be referred to Elena Bivona's indispensable essay on the ballet in *Ballet Review*, Vol. 3, No. 6, 1971.

GRADUATION BALL

Ballet in one act. Music by Johann Strauss. Choreography by David Lichine. Scenery and costumes by Alexandre Benois. Book by David Lichine. First presented by the Original Ballet Russe at the Theatre Royal, Sydney, Australia, February 28, 1940, with Tatiana Riabouchinska and David Lichine in the leading roles. First presented in the United States by the Original Ballet Russe at the Fifty-first Street Theatre, New York, November 6, 1940, with the same principals.

Graduation Ball is the story of a party. Young girls at a fashionable school in Vienna put on a gala entertainment to fete the graduates of a nearby military academy. The girls and boys meet, amuse themselves by performing a series of *divertissements*, discover a secret romance, and dance until the headmistress of the school ends the party. The music for the ballet—chosen, arranged, and orchestrated by Antal Dorati—is selected from the works of Johann Strauss.

The ballet is set in the high, formal drawing room of the girls' school. There the girls are excitedly preparing for the ball, which is clearly their one real social occasion of the year. The senior girls primp excessively and try out their newly acquired fashionable manners, while their more numerous juniors, in simple frocks and pinafores, laugh at their affectations. Soon they are all ready to receive their guests from the local military school. The headmistress, an absurd and bustling busybody danced by a male dancer, rushes in and makes sure that her pupils look their very best.

Loud martial music announces the arrival of the cadets, who march in boldly to the staccato drums. Although the boys stand rigidly at attention when they halt, and face straight forward, their roving eyes size up their young hostesses in short order. The elderly general who leads the boys finally allows them to relax, and the young people are suddenly embarrassed: with all their pretense at worldly knowledge, they don't really know how to get the ball under way. The boys stay on one side of the room, the girls on the other, and there is a momentary stalemate.

The pompous old general has been immediately attracted to the headmistress and escorts her off for a rendezvous. The young people are unchaperoned and don't know quite what to do. A young girl, deciding to give the senior girls their comeuppance, leaves her friends and approaches the formation of boys. The cadets greet her with such loud heel-clicking and deference that the girl is terrified: she finds herself sitting smack in the middle of the floor.

The ball at last gets under way when the cadets elect a leader and order him to choose a partner and begin the first dance. Of course, he is more timid than his fellows and steps out of line only because of military discipline. The girls feel so sorry for him that before he can really make a choice, a partner is dancing with him. With this example, the other cadets take partners and all dance.

The headmistress and her general return to supervise the entertainment they have so carefully rehearsed—first comes a *divertissement* by one of the cadet drummers, then a romantic Scottish *pas de deux* that recalls the spirit of such old ballets as *La Sylphide*. The young girl who tried to start the dance is enchanted by this dance of ethereal love and improvises an impromptu dance of her own.

Next comes a dance-step competition in which the girls try to outdo each other in the number of *fouettés* they can execute, and there is a final *perpetuum mobile* in which all dance. The romance of the headmistress and the general has progressed during these entertainments, which they have hardly watched. The girls and boys leave the room seeking refreshments; the older people dance together and declare their love. They are in the midst of a passionate embrace when their students come back. The young people laugh and congratulate them, and the party hastens to a high-spirited conclusion. Despite their discovered romance, the headmistress and the general are compelled to end the dance. The cadets bid the girls a fond farewell and sadly take their leave. The lights dim.

The ballroom is now deserted. One of the cadets is seen trying to sneak back, to bid his girl a more private farewell. We are a little amused to see that this is the same cadet who was so hesitant about beginning the ball; no longer bashful, he is now bold. For a moment it appears that he'll be able to effect his rendezvous, but the headmistress darts out and shoos him off. He was only trying!

GRAND PAS ESPAGNOL

Music by Moritz Moszkowski. Choreography by Benjamin Harkarvy. Costumes by Joop Stokvis. First presented by the Netherlands Dance Theatre at the Empire Theatre, Sunderland, England, November 7, 1963. First presented in the United States by the Harkness Ballet at the Music Box Theatre, New York, January 17, 1969, with Elisabeth Carroll, Marina Eglevsky,

Lone Isaksen, Finis Jhung, Helgi Tomasson, and Lawrence Rhodes. Conducted by Krasimir Sipusch.

This *divertissement* in the Spanish manner is a dance ballet for three girls and three boys. The music, by a German composer much admired in Russia, recollects, like the style of movement and gesture, familiar Spanish attitudes from folk dance and bullfight that recall, too, an affection the Russian classic dance developed for Spain. There are opportunities for vivid ensembles, a pensive duet for two of the girls, a vigorous trio for all three boys, and a flourishing finale.

Grand Pas Espagnol was presented by the City Center Joffrey Ballet at the City Center, New York, October 12, 1972. Lighting by Jennifer Tipton. Seymour Lipkin was the conductor and the dancers were Francesca Corkle, Rebecca Wright, Pamela Nearhoof, Glenn White, Paul Sutherland, and William Whitener.

Writing in *Dance and Dancers* magazine, Patricia Barnes wrote of the first performances by the Harkness Ballet: "This is an excitingly conceived *pas de six* reminiscent of the days of Petipa and Minkus—a display of that ballet—Spanish variety of classical dancing that can still be seen in such ballets as *Don Quixote . . .* To ensure that these classical variations should have the authentic flavor of the Imperial Russian Ballet, Harkarvy studied for a period with Madame Anderson Ivantzova, a former ballerina of the Bolshoi, who taught him the particular style he required as his base."

THE GREEN TABLE

Dance of Death in eight scenes. Book by Kurt Jooss. Music by Fritz Cohen. Choreography by Kurt Jooss. Costumes by Hein Heckroth. First presented by the Jooss Ballet at the Théâtre des Champs-Élysées, Paris, July 3, 1932. First presented in the United States by the City Center Joffrey Ballet at the City Center, New York, March 9, 1967.

One of the most renowned dance works of the century and now a part of the American repertory, Kurt Jooss's ballet about war and death was first performed in the United States by his own company in the 1930s. Memories of World War I were still fresh and apprehensions of another war dominated many people's thoughts. Although naturally influenced by the time of its creation, *The Green Table* has been successfully presented ever since, testifying to the power of its theme and presentation. The English critic John Percival has written: "*The Green Table* must be one of the most *shocking* ballets ever created, in the proper sense of the word, but its impact remains the same after repeated performances."

Subtitled "A Dance of Death," the ballet is about diplomacy and war, the seeming uselessness of talk, the horror of battle. The table of the title is the green baize table to be found in a diplomatic conference room, where the ballet begins. There men in morning dress negotiate at the table. The two sides cannot agree about the matter under discussion, evidently one of great seriousness. Formal pleasantries persist for a while as each side takes up a series of attitudes, but it is clear that they are getting nowhere. In the final argument, the diplomats pull out guns and fire them across the table, and war is declared.

We now see the result of the fruitless discussions and watch as Death, stalking throughout the ballet like a relentless demonic force, claims his victims. There is a scene of parting, as soldiers leave for war, scenes of carnage in battle and refugees fleeing, a scene in a brothel and the home-coming of the few survivors. Death claims everyone: the fighting men, an old mother, a young girl in a brothel, a war profiteer. Then the action returns to the beginning and we are at the conference table again. Signifying peace, the diplomats fire their revolvers into the air and get on with the discussion.

GROSSE FUGE

Music by Ludwig van Beethoven. Choreography by Hans van Manen. Scenery by Jean-Paul Vroom. Costumes by Hans van Manen. First presented by the Netherlands Dance Theatre at the Circus Theatre, Scheveningen, Holland, April 8, 1971. First presented in the United States by the same ensemble at the Brooklyn Academy of Music, New York, April 1, 1972.

This dance ballet arranged to the *Great Fugue* of Beethoven and the *Cavatine* from the *B Flat Quartet* is for eight dancers, four boys and four girls. While there is no narrative, the ballet develops a set of themes established by the dancers. At first, apart, the girls and boys seem not to care about each other while in fact that is what their dancing is about—display pieces to excite interest. That accomplished, the four couples pair off, the girls attaching themselves to the boys, clinging to large buckles that hang from the waists of the boys' trunks. Together, each pair of lovers celebrates the joy found in sensuality.

NOTES   The dancer and choreographer James Waring reported from Europe to *Ballet Review* in 1971: "Hans van Manen has made a ballet to the "Great Fugue" of Beethoven, with a postlude, a slow movement from one of the late string quartets. It looks nothing like Ashton's *Symphonic Variations*, yet it has a similar kind of watertight construction. Hans's style is not so lyric nor so expansive, yet, after Ashton, he is the best choreographic craftsman I've seen in Europe. *Great Fugue* . . . is a formal piece, very musical, a very personal kind of musical response. The dancing observes the rhythms of the music, but with constant slight shifts of focus in and out of Beethoven's phrases. The Netherlands Dance Theatre dance it beautifully, with passion and precision. An elegant piece."*

* Reprinted by permission of *Ballet Review*, Marcel Dekker, publisher.

THE GUARDS OF AMAGER

Music by V. C. Holm. Choreography by Auguste Bournonville. Scenery and costumes by Bjorn Wiinblad. First presented by the Royal Danish Ballet at the Royal Theatre, Copenhagen, February 9, 1871. Revived for the contemporary repertory by Hans Brenaa, assisted by Lizzie Rode. First presented in the United States by the Royal Danish Ballet at the Metropolitan Opera House, New York, June 3, 1976.

A ballet about a forgotten incident in history, *The Guards of Amager* takes us back to 1808, when Napoleon had all Europe in thrall. Determined to protect themselves against a menacing English fleet, the Danes set up a volunteer corps to protect themselves. The story of the ballet, a *demi-caractère* comic affair, deals with the possible unfaithfulness to his wife of a young lieutenant posted on the island of Amager to protect Copenhagen. Enamored of the peasant girls there, Edouard seems to have another alternative when his wife, Louise, on a visit, perceiving this possibility, disguises herself to become the belle of a local ball. When Édouard fails to recognize her, despite his enchantment with her charms, she reveals her identity but forgives him. The atmosphere of this ballet and the design of its choreography suggest an achievement of *ballet comique* unimaginable a hundred years ago, much less today.

THE GUESTS

Classic ballet in one act. Music by Marc Blitzstein. Choreography by Jerome Robbins. Lighting by Jean Rosenthal. First presented by the New York City Ballet at the City Center, New York, January 20, 1949, with Maria Tallchief, Nicholas Magallanes, and Francisco Moncion in the principal roles.

This ballet concerns itself with prejudice: with "the patterns of adjustment and conflict between two groups, one larger than the other." What happens when these two groups meet and find themselves absolutely opposed? The ballet presents this problem socially, at what seems to be an ordinary party.

The curtain rises on a formal setting. High black columns in the back suggest a large ball. The host comes forward formally and prepares to welcome a group of guests. The guests enter in two distinct groups. At first it would seem that they are not distinct at all, for the boys and girls wear the same kind of clothes and move in the same way, but gradually we see that they never commingle, that the dances that now get under way are arranged in block patterns, and that the two separate groups instinctively avoid close contact. The host is not disturbed by the difference between the two. He leads the party on without nervousness, aware that the two groups have lived amicably side by side for a long time and cannot possibly achieve closer contact. Both sides of the party feel this almost naturally, the girls dancing only with partners from their group, gathering together and speaking together, but never paying attention to what the other side might be doing; they do not even acknowledge each other's existence beyond politely moving aside when they wish to pass each other. It is apparent, however, that the smaller group is more deferential to the larger.

The party proceeds. The host brings out masks and passes these favors out to members of the larger group of guests. Several masks are left over and put aside. The masked couples begin to dance, while the smaller group stands aside and watches. The dance has not proceeded long before we notice that the discarded masks have disappeared; two of the dancers are obviously wearing them. But the host does not note this breach of etiquette, and the dancing couples, unaware of true identities, continue to enjoy themselves.

One girl and boy in particular are strangely attracted to each other. They move together with a soft, relaxed ease as if they had been dancing together all their lives. The boy steps forward slightly and reaches out his hand, pointing the way to some distant happiness. The girl imitates this gesture. They stand facing each other; when their hands touch, the contact is electrically romantic. Yet their dance is not intimate; it is, rather, the dance of two people who are living a dream. There is no sudden passion, no questions need to be asked; the boy supports and lifts the girl tenderly, and she responds to this with soft grace.

The ensemble dance ends, and the host orders the guests to remove their masks. The guests discover that the boy and the girl who are so much in love belong to different groups; one of them has worn the mask in error! Chaos breaks out. The two groups drag the boy and the girl apart and make them dance separately. When the two groups pass, the boy and girl hold out their hands to each other longingly.

Finally they can bear the separation no longer. They defy convention and meet. The boy lifts the girl high and carries her away into the distance. The astonished guests look at each other in horror. The curtain falls.

HAMLET

Dramatic ballet in one act. Music by Peter Ilyich Tchaikovsky. Choreography by Robert Helpmann. Scenery and costumes by Leslie Hurry. First presented by the Sadler's Wells Ballet at the New Theatre, London, May 19, 1942, with Robert Helpmann as Hamlet and Margot Fonteyn as Ophelia. First presented in the United States by the Sadler's Wells Ballet at the Metropolitan Opera House, New York, October 12, 1949, with the same principals.

This *Hamlet* is not an adaptation of Shakespeare's play for ballet; rather, it is a ballet version, a ballet interpretation of Shakespeare's subject. It does not follow the action of the play precisely, but rather recollects the plot of the play in its own drama. The ballet *Hamlet* is prefaced by these lines from the play:

> For in that sleep of death, what dreams may come
> When we have shuffled off this mortal coil
> Must give us pause.

These lines warn us to expect dreams, impressions, perhaps even flash backs of Hamlet's life and tragedy. The music for the ballet is Tchaikovsky's fantasy-overture *Hamlet*.

At the rise of the curtain we see a ghostly sight. A thin, bright shaft of light shines down on Hamlet's face. He is dead. Four pallbearers carry him slowly to his grave; the end of the play is the ballet's beginning. And still it is different, for the pallbearers are not the captains appointed by Fortinbras to bear Hamlet; they are hooded monks.

The monks bear Hamlet off, and the scene brightens. The scene is not literal, not so much a section of a Danish castle as a projection of Hamlet's imagination. It is ghastly and bloody and mad. A huge creature depicted on the backdrop rushes toward murder, a jagged knife poised in readiness. Over a portal at the left, a great detached hand holds a dagger casually, as if it were a cigarette. The scene is possessed with violence.

One by one, characters familiar to Hamlet appear—first the gravedigger. As we are remembering what he said to Hamlet and what Hamlet said to him, the Prince of Denmark himself enters. He watches the scene as we watch it; he is observing himself. Detached in death, he looks back over his life.

He does not like what he sees; his anticipation of vile deeds suffered and vile deeds done causes him to hide his face from view. Now he watches the gravedigger play with Yorick's skull, throwing it into the air, rolling it along the ground.

A crowing cock heralds the arrival of the ghost of Hamlet's father, who instructs Hamlet in the manner of his death: how he was murdered by his brother with the connivance of his queen. Hamlet's guesswork has proved true in a way he had not imagined, and the evil of the present king and Hamlet's mother, the queen, has new justification. Hamlet promises the ghost that he will seek revenge.

Old Polonius and Laertes appear, followed by the king and queen. The lusty king makes love to the queen while her son rages openly. But the king ignores him and turns his attention to Laertes, granting the youth permission to go to France. Polonius warns the king to beware of Hamlet. When the doddering chamberlain has promised him to spy on Hamlet, the king departs.

Hamlet watches his mother and approaches her. Mysteriously, Ophelia steps before the queen, and the two women are confused. Hamlet falls to the floor, moves his hands frantically in front of him as if to separate this double image, but still the two women shift before his eyes. When they leave the scene, Hamlet prays.

Now Laertes dances gaily with his sister, Ophelia. Soon they are interrupted by Polonius, who wishes his son a lengthy Godspeed. Laertes departs for France, and Polonius takes his daughter to Hamlet. He wishes to observe them and conceals himself as the prince courts his daughter sweetly and sincerely. But then Hamlet senses that something is rotten; he catches the king spying on him with Polonius and throws Ophelia to the ground.

Next Hamlet watches the play-within-a-play. All members of the court enter, and a page announces that the entertainment is about to begin. In the play, parts are taken not by professional actors but by the creatures of Hamlet's imagination: Ophelia is the player queen, the ghost of Hamlet's father is the player king. When the player king is to be murdered, both Hamlet and Claudius approach his sleeping figure. Both pour poison in his ear.

The king, again the spectator and no longer the murdering actor, is horrified at this re-enactment of his crime and goes to pray. Hamlet is about to seize this opportunity to kill his archenemy, but then rationalizes that it is the wrong occasion. But there is occasion for another death: Polonius is plotting with the queen; Hamlet stabs him.

Laertes returns to avenge his father's death and accuses the king. The queen points out the youth's error, and all turn to watch sadly the beautiful Ophelia, gone mad with grief at her father's death and her lover's inconstancy. Ophelia's madness spurs Laertes to seek out Hamlet.

Hamlet stands aside to watch a funeral procession. Ophelia is dead, and he would accompany her to her grave. But the pallbearers are not carrying Ophelia, his dead love; it is the queen they carry. Again Hamlet cannot distinguish the two in his affections. Laertes, who is marching in the procession, sees Hamlet and immediately attacks him. The prudent king pulls Laertes back and suggests to him another plot.

This plot is now set in motion. We watch another courtly scene, where all the principals are present. The king and Laertes are in concert, while Hamlet is apparently reconciled with his mother. Now the king offers Hamlet wine, which is poisoned. Hamlet will not accept it and turns away in wrath at such a social grace from such a man. The queen attempts to pacify her son by drinking a toast to him with the wine. The king, paralyzed with anxiety at her foolish act, draws her aside.

Laertes sneaks up on Hamlet and stabs him in the back. The wounded prince returns the thrust, and Laertes dies. Now Hamlet attacks the king. The queen watches, horrified, as her son kills her husband. Then she, too, dies.

The gravedigger returns, and the ballet has come full circle. Now that there is no need for him to live, now that revenge is done, Hamlet succumbs to his wounds. He falls to the ground. The monks come in, take up his body, and raise it high over their heads. The scene grows dark. Soon all we can see is Hamlet's face, ghostly white in the pin-point spotlight; his beginning is, after all, his end.

HARBINGER

Music by Sergei Prokofiev. Choreography by Eliot Feld. Setting by Oliver Smith. Lighting by Jean Rosenthal. First presented by American Ballet Theatre at the New York State Theatre, New York, May 11, 1967, with Christine Sarry, Edward Verso, Paula Tracy, Cynthia Gregory, Marcos Paredes, and Eliot Feld in leading roles.

Harbinger tells no story; its plot is outlined by the music of Prokofiev's *Concerto No. 5 in G for Piano*. Usefully for the listener and spectator, both the composer and the choreographer have given notes on their own impressions of this work.

Prokofiev writes: "The first movement is an *Allegro con brio* with a *Meno mosso* as middle section. Though not in sonata form, it is the main movement of the concerto and fulfills the function and maintains the spirit of the traditional sonata form. The second movement has a march-like rhythm. I would not think of calling it a march because it has none of the vulgarity of commonness which is so often associated with the idea of march, and which actually exists in most marches. The third movement is a toccata. This is a precipitate, displayful movement of much technical brilliance and requiring great virtuosity; it is a toccata for orchestra as well as for piano. The fourth movement . . . is the lyrical movement of the concerto. It starts off with a soft, soothing theme; grows more and more intense in the middle portion, develops breadth and tension, then returns to the music of the beginning. The finale has a decided classic flavor. The coda is based on a new theme, which is joined by the other theme of the finale. There is a reference to some of the material of the preceding movements in the finale."

The choreographer and dancer Eliot Feld described his view of the work in an interview with Jack Anderson in *Dance Magazine*. He said that in choreographing *Harbinger*, he wishes to "explore certain patterns of human relationships. . . . The first movement, in which a solo boy ambles lazily among a group of girls, is about 'being by yourself and having fantasies.' The impetuous second movement is conceived as a chase. The third movement is a slightly melancholy duet with *corps de ballet* serving as background. . . . The fourth movement, a competitive trio for two boys and a girl, is 'just what it appears to be.' The finale is composed of movement motifs taken from the preceding sections. 'I guess that in all of *Harbinger* I'm talking about myself and the people I know. It's like showing some of the kinds of personal games we play.'"

Harbinger attracted considerable attention when it was first presented in New York. Clive Barnes of the New York *Times* wrote that Mr. Feld was "the most important indigenous talent in classic ballet since Jerome Robbins."

Interviewed by the British magazine *Dance and Dancers*, Eliot Feld was asked when, as a dancer in American Ballet Theatre, he got the idea of doing choreography. He replied: "I don't really know. When I started to try out choreography I really had no idea of doing a ballet. I had listened to the Prokofiev fifth piano concerto for some time and I had the idea of doing this duet—very allegro, very short. I worked with a dancer just as a favour and we choreographed this dance, which turned out to be the eventual duet in *Harbinger*, my first ballet. It took us about 300 hours of rehearsal time to choreograph two minutes of choreography. I don't indulge in that way of working any longer. Then I got another idea for another of the movements and I began to choreograph that, but it became difficult because I needed three people, and Royes Fernandez helped me out at that time. Gradually I realised that I had a ballet, but I don't really think that I had thought of myself as wanting to be a choreographer before that. Before *Harbinger* I had never put any steps

together. I have a lot to thank Robbins for, because after I had completed
about four minutes of choreography he came in and saw what I had done
and seemed very excited about it. He asked me what I intended to do, and
I told him it depended a lot on what he could do for me; would he be willing to speak to Lucia Chase about producing the ballet? He did, and on the
basis of his approval it was put on by Ballet Theatre."

HARLEQUINADE

*Ballet in two acts. Music by Riccardo Drigo. Choreography by George Bal-
anchine. Scenery, costumes, and lighting by Rouben Ter-Arutunian. First
presented by the New York City Ballet at the New York State Theatre, February 4, 1965, with Edward Villella and Patricia McBride in the leading
roles.*

Most of us know the old *commedia dell'arte* story of how Harlequin wins
Columbine from her rich father.

The original ballet to this story, *Harlequin's Millions*, was first presented at
the Hermitage Theatre in St. Petersburg in 1900. It was the last success of the
brilliant creator of dance, Marius Petipa. I remember very well dancing in this
production when I was a student at the Imperial Ballet School. What I
liked about it was its wit and pace and its genius in telling a story with clarity
and grace. It was a very different kind of ballet from *The Sleeping Beauty*,
and showed the range of his genius.

Les Millions d'Arlequin had a great deal of influence, I think, on ballet history, becoming the model for comedy narrative. It is the other side of the coin
from *Swan Lake*, if you like. I don't of course remember details of the old
production. In 1950 I arranged a *Harlequin pas de deux* for Maria Tallchief
and André Eglevsky that used some of Drigo's music in a *demi-caractère* display piece. I remember thinking at the time that one day we should try to do
the whole ballet. That came about in the usual accidental way when it was
suggested that the settings Rouben Ter-Arutunian had designed for the New
York City Opera production of Rossini's *Cenerentola* might be usable for a
full-length *Harlequinade*. We were able to borrow the scenery, which the
designer adapted for the ballet, and I began to work.

During the overture we see a drop curtain painted in the style of Pollock toy
theaters with boxes right and left and a paper proscenium. When this rises the
scene shows the exterior of the house of the rich merchant Cassandre, father of
the beautiful Columbine. The action shows how Harlequin, helped by La
Bonne Fée, succeeds in rescuing Columbine from the wealthy suitor her father
has picked out for her. The enraged Cassandre tries to have Harlequin killed
but is foiled. The Good Fairy brings a cornucopia of gold pieces, Harlequin
outbids his rich rival, and the lovers are united. There is a dance celebration of
their love in an enchanted park.

NOTES   When I was studying ballet in Russia, I much admired Petipa's original version of this ballet (*Les Millions d'Arlequin*, first performed at the Hermitage Theatre, St. Petersburg, February 10, 1900). The fun and slapstick as well as the occasional deeper meaning of the popular Italian comedy, the *commedia dell'arte*, have always appealed to me with their strength and warmth, and in *Harlequinade* I have attempted to remain faithful to the spirit of Petipa's dances and drama without reproducing any of the actual steps of his time. Who, in fact, remembers them?

As I often do with my ballets, I changed *Harlequinade* somewhat in 1973, adding sequences at certain points and filling out the piece so that, hopefully, with one intermission, it makes for an evening-long diversion. Among the additions are a tarantella in Act One and a polonaise in Act Two. Children are used among the dancers, and the music is now the complete score by Riccardo Drigo.

The critic Nancy Goldner described the revision in *Dance News:* "*Harlequinade* is now filled out so that it fills an evening. The main addition is a 'ballabile des enfants' for polichinelles, little harlequins, scaramouches, and pierrots and pierettes—in other words, small editions of all the adult roles. They do a series of *divertissements* in the beginning of Act II, and, as is his way, Balanchine gives them simple but utterly charming steps. Their dances most closely resemble the polichinelle dance in *Nutcracker;* in fact, the *Harlequinade* polichinelles are now wearing the *Nutcracker* costumes. At the end of the variations, all the children do a grand polonaise, and they do it with more style and belief than the adults. Watching all 32 children dancing with proper deportment and happy faces is enchanting. Inevitably, it reminds one of Balanchine's childhood and his statements about how exciting it was to appear on stage. So here is Papa giving his kids what he had. That knowledge gives an extra charm to the ballet.

"There is also a new blaze-of-color ensemble dance for adult revelers in the first act. The idea is to cram hordes into a small area, so that all you see are many bright colors in squished motion. But the costumes are garish, the paper lanterns carried by the dancers kept falling off, and it went on too long.

"Gelsey Kirkland was beautifully shy and sweet in her solemn way as Columbine. Her delicate articulation suits the choreography well, yet this is still Villella's ballet. His brute strength is here quieted by humor and something that is almost lyricism, especially in the beautiful serenade dance. His strength is still felt, but from the underside. It is very compelling."

HARLEQUIN IN APRIL

Pantomime with divertissements in two acts, with prologue, entr'acte, and epilogue. Music by Richard Arnell. Choreography by John Cranko. Scenery and costumes by John Piper. First presented by the Sadler's Wells Theatre Ballet at the Sadler's Wells Theatre, London, May 8, 1951, with David Blair as Harlequin, Patricia Miller as Columbine, and Stanley Holden as Pierrot. First presented in the United States by the Sadler's Wells Theatre

Ballet at the Eastman Theatre, Rochester, New York, October 25, 1951, with the same principals.

This dramatic ballet tells a modern story in terms of old characters. Here the old, typed characters—Harlequin, Columbine, and Pierrot—who have come down to us from Greek mythology and the *commedia dell'arte* and who figure in such ballets as *Carnaval*, are used to represent new notions while at the same time preserving much of their original symbolism. Here Harlequin is human aspiration reborn after fire and devastation. Harlequin returns to life among the flowers of April, earth-bound and self-sufficient creatures from whom he escapes. Columbine is Harlequin's love, the representation of the ideal he aspires to. Pierrot stands between the two; he is the perpetual fool, and we laugh at him until he interferes too much.

PROLOGUE   The curtain rises on an inside drop that depicts another, smaller stage hung with a tattered curtain. This interior theatre has not simply fallen into disrepair through age and use; it has been burned out and destroyed, and stands as a symbol of human wreckage where no human can flourish.

Pierrot, superhuman fool of the gods, ambles in carrying a bag. His face is painted white to match the loose white costume that hangs about his loose-jointed figure. He takes a sheet of music from the bag and opens his mouth to sing. When he discovers that he cannot sing, that he can make no sound, he hides his face behind the music. Now he tries again, a little more successfully, then puts the music back in his bag of tricks and exits. The lights grow dim.

ACT ONE: APRIL   When the lights come up, the drop curtain has disappeared and we are backstage in the interior theatre. Groups of girls dressed like plants lie about the stage. Pierrot enters with a watering can and goes about watering the plants. One of the groups begins to rise; the center group stirs. There is a fluttering of hands, and the plants in the center group huddle together closely, as if protecting something. Now the girls kneel, and Harlequin rises in their midst, born anew in the ashes of destruction. Naked to the waist, Harlequin wears a black mask across his eyes. He walks in and out among the flowers and plants, who celebrate his birth.

Pierrot takes from his bag a jacket for Harlequin. Harlequin puts on the coat and removes the mask. Now fully dressed in his traditional diamond-patched costume, Harlequin comes fully to life. A drum sounds loudly; he chases Pierrot off and dances, turning again and again to a persistent drum roll. The plants, which have remained lifeless, now rise and leave the scene. As the last plant moves off, Harlequin restrains her and the two dance a *pas de deux*. This is largely a dance of resistance, as the self-sufficient plant struggles to be free of this strange being who demands and requires her company. Harlequin tears the flowery mask from her face and for a moment she is just a young girl, but she reaches out trembling hands to retrieve the mask.

Harlequin kicks at the mask and throws it aside. The other plants begin to return; they find the mask and place it again on the face of the frightened girl, after which they form a line and leave the scene. Harlequin kisses the last girl, the girl he has danced with, and finds himself alone.

Harlequin is angry. He falls to the ground in his rage. Pierrot comes and tries to comfort him. Harlequin, armed now with a sword, watches astonished as a unicorn, traditional guardian of chastity, crosses the stage. Even now, Harlequin is aware that the unicorn will attempt to separate him from his ideal. He threatens the strange animal, but the proud unicorn stalks away. The drop curtain falls.

ENTR'ACTE Pierrot comes out before the drop curtain and dances. Then he takes from his white bag a violin and a bow and plays the instrument. Like the song he tried to sing at the beginning of the ballet, Pierrot's violin concerto is not of high quality. Rather impatient with the unobliging violin, he kneels and plays it as if it were a cello. Then he thrusts it aside, returns it to the bag, and leaves the scene.

ACT TWO: THE SKY The light is dim when the drop curtain rises again. Gradually the light rises. Now the interior backdrop is streaked with clouds. Harlequin, still carrying his sword, enters and watches the unicorn. Pierrot hides behind Harlequin, egging him on. The unicorn nods its head in assent to a command that Harlequin has made to it and returns, carrying on its back a lovely young girl—Columbine. Immediately in love, Harlequin kisses her. Pierrot pulls him away from the girl, and Columbine comes down from the unicorn's back. She seems to have some power over the creature, for at her order the unicorn goes to sleep.

Columbine goes directly to Harlequin and they dance. Harlequin pushes Pierrot away when he attempts teasingly to interfere. Columbine falls back in Harlequin's arm, and he buries his face in her breast. The two lovers fall to the ground and kiss. Columbine's arms reach up around Harlequin's head, and Pierrot rushes in to pull them apart. They are separated for a moment, but again Harlequin embraces the girl. He lifts her, and as he holds her aloft, her extended leg trembles. The lovers lie down again to fulfill their passion.

Pierrot, now fully alarmed, wakes the sleeping unicorn. The unicorn, militant and unfeeling, pulls Columbine from Harlequin's close embrace. Harlequin stabs at the unicorn, but the scene is filled with magical duplications of the unicorn and Harlequin is helpless against this multiple representation of chastity. Some of the unicorns claim Columbine as others stalk Harlequin down and stand over him. She is lifted onto the back of one of the unicorns, then lifted high into the air by the others. Harlequin climbs up on the strange creatures to reach her; at the pinnacle he is pushed off and falls to the ground.

Columbine disappears. Harlequin goes off in search of her as the unicorns leave the scene. Harlequin returns, with a rag-doll representation of Columbine in his arms. Pierrot bows to him, and Harlequin begins a wild, frantic dance that expresses his rage at his loss. He beats Pierrot, the interfering fool who has deprived him of the ideal, and chases him off.

To quiet, moving music, Harlequin holds the model of Columbine in his arms and kisses its hands. The plants return, gather about Harlequin, and enfold him. They place the black mask about his eyes and take off his jacket. The plants huddle over him closely, and as they kneel, he disappears in their midst.

EPILOGUE Pierrot returns. He sees Harlequin's jacket lying on the ground and picks it up. For a moment he considers the loss of his friend, but not for long. He begins to try on the jacket. It is too small for him, he can get only one arm in, but so dressed he poses arrogantly, an absurd masquerade of Harlequin, while the real Harlequin sleeps.

THE HAUNTED BALLROOM

Dramatic ballet in three scenes. Music by Geoffrey Toye. Choreography by Ninette de Valois. Book by Geoffrey Toye. Scenery and costumes by Motley. First presented by the Vic-Wells Ballet at the Sadler's Wells Theatre, London, April 3, 1934, with a cast that included Robert Helpmann, Alicia Markova, and William Chappell. First presented in the United States by the Sadler's Wells Theatre Ballet in Buffalo, New York, October 23, 1951, with David Poole in the principal role.

The drama of this ballet is based on its mysterious locale and the destiny that haunts the people who inhabit it. Set in the ancient ballroom of a Scottish castle, the ballet calls up those venerable but terrifying demons and ghosts which control the fate of a family. In two graphic scenes, *The Haunted Ballroom* displays the inscrutable power of these creatures and the helplessness of those who live in perpetual dread of their appearance.

The overture is low in volume, eerie and mysterious in mood. The music warns us of incipient danger—a danger that does not come suddenly, but quietly and patiently waits to pounce upon its helpless prey. There is a rush of sound from the harp, the orchestra plays a low, murmuring waltz, and the curtain rises.

The scene is dark, almost pitch-black. Slanting wings enclose a large, cavernous space. At the back, centered in the black wall, is an arched doorway. From the ceiling hangs a chandelier festooned with cobwebs. Long strips of rotting black cloth are draped from the chandelier to the corners of the room.

We are in an abandoned ballroom, a place seldom used by its owner. In the back, the door opens. Young Tregennis, son of the master of the house, enters. He is dressed in black velvet with a red sash about his waist. The youth looks about the room apprehensively, and we sense that even in some typical childish prank he would never choose to enter it alone. Three ladies in long, trailing evening dresses follow him into the musty ballroom. They flutter their large fans nervously and examine the ballroom with no little curiosity; it is clear that, during a ball that is being held elsewhere in the castle, they have asked the boy to show them this hidden room.

One by one, the ladies tap the boy on the shoulder with their fans, playfully commanding him to dance with them. As he moves about the dark ballroom with the ladies, the trains of their dresses drag along the floor and whirl the dust about their waltzing figures. But the youth is in no mood for dancing. He breaks away from the women and stands with his head in his hands. He seems to be aware of something the women cannot see and trembles like a small child.

The ladies still wish to be amused, however, and again tap him with their fans. The boy remains motionless. He knows that he should never have given in to their whim and, most of all, that he should not have come here himself. As the teasing women begin to lose all patience with their young host, his father is seen standing in the doorway.

The master of Tregennis is astonished to find the door open and shocked to find his guests in this part of the house. He observes his son standing in the corner. The youth cowers away from his father. He orders the boy to leave the room. The boy runs to his father, begging for forgiveness, but imperiously the father gestures him away. The boy flees.

Now the master of Tregennis turns and bows to the ladies. A waltz melody is heard. The master apologizes to his guests for his strange behavior and tells them the cause of his anxiety. He indicates to them that this is truly a haunted ballroom: his father died here and his father before him—indeed, all of his family have perished in this room. The ladies cover their faces with their fans to conceal their embarrassment and fear. Now that they understand, they bow to the master of Tregennis, take up their trains, and leave the room.

Alone, the man stands in the center of the haunted ballroom and stares into the dark corners. He is afraid and fascinated at the same time; he cannot move. The room darkens and a light shines upon him. He looks into the light, trying to control his fear, but his hand reaches out to ward off some unseen terror. The light has caused his frightened figure to be thrown against the back wall in immense silhouette. The curtain falls as he stands helpless in the sight of the fate he must someday meet.

During a brief interval, the orchestra recapitulates the happy dance theme to which the three ladies danced with young Tregennis. The harp interrupts this music to sound a warning, there is a muffled trumpet call, and the curtain rises again.

The ballroom is now almost completely dark. Gradually the lights come up, and we note that the door in the back wall is open. Into the room dances a strange figure dressed in somber black with a black mask. He plays upon a flute and then thrusts the flute into the air as if it were a sword. Ghostly creatures in white follow him and form a tableau. Their faces are veiled, their long white sleeves dangle from their arms to give their figures a disjointed, unearthly quality. Two veiled women, dressed similarly to two of the ladies who invaded the ballroom in the first scene, enter and dance at the command of the strange figure in black.

Just as we are wondering where the counterpart to the third lady might be, she enters and dances as the masked stranger plays upon his flute. The ghostly creatures collapse and form weird groupings that remain still throughout her demoniac dance. She is joined by the other two women, and all three move together until the strange player halts the dance suddenly: at his command, each ends her movement in an arabesque.

Now the strange player moves about the room, obviously preparing the scene for some portentous event. The master of Tregennis stumbles into the room. He wears a long white dressing gown, and a mysterious call seems to have demanded his return to the room. He observes his uninvited guests and rudely asks the strange player for an explanation. The master of Tregennis is told that a group of dancers have come to his ballroom and that they are eager to dance if he will be good enough to lead them.

The master apparently accepts this explanation, for he bows to the ghostly creatures. The music roars in violent crescendo. The master takes off his dressing gown to move more freely and enters into a violent dance. His strange guests surround him like flies, encouraging him to increase the tempo of his movements. The master is tired and wishes to stop, but is helpless to do so. Finally he collapses in the stranger's arms.

One of the ladies encourages him to renew his dance, and he moves with her about the room as figures cloaked in white robes weave in and out between them. The orchestra sounds the music of the dance fiercely and relentlessly. The master of Tregennis can move no more. He falls to the floor, dying. The lady is held poised above him. He reaches out and is caught up in the arms of the ghostly creatures. He struggles helplessly in their grasp. Weird women gather close about him; the music cries out with piercing pathos. He is carried aloft.

For a brief moment the master manages to free himself. He rushes away from his attackers, running to the front of the stage to cling to the proscenium. He knows now who they are and that he must soon be one of them. The time for his own death in the haunted ballroom has come, and he is powerless to resist.

A clock begins to clang. The ghosts who have made him one of themselves form a final tableau, and he dies. The curtain falls. The strange player in black emerges with three creatures in white and across the front of the stage, in step with the striking clock, they carry the body of the master of Tregennis to his forebears.

Once more the curtain rises on the ballroom. Two footmen enter by the door, carrying lanterns. A butler follows them, and the three men search the room for their master. When they discover his body, his son, dressed in a white dressing gown similar to his father's, stumbles into the room. He hastens to his father and turns away in grief and terror. The master of Tregennis, his lifeless arm dangling in the air, is carried out by his two footmen.

Three women, evidently members of his family, try to comfort the boy. He accepts their condolences, but then turns away from them. They know what he is thinking—that he will be next. They leave him alone. The light that shone upon his father makes of his startled figure a frightening silhouette against the dark wall of the ballroom; he clutches at his throat in terror and acknowledges his destiny.

HELEN OF TROY

Comic ballet in three scenes, with prologue. Music by Jacques Offenbach. Choreography by David Lichine. Book by David Lichine and Antal Dorati. Scenery and costumes by Marcel Vertès. First presented by Ballet Theatre in Detroit, Michigan, November 29, 1942, with a cast headed by Irina Baronova as Helen, André Eglevsky as Paris, Jerome Robbins as Hermes, and Simon Semenoff as Menelaus.

This ballet is a comic treatment of the legend of Helen of Troy: how the beautiful queen deserted her aging husband, Menelaus, and sailed away with Paris to far-off Troy. The music, by Offenbach, was arranged and orchestrated by Antal Dorati.

PROLOGUE   After a jubilant, rousing overture, the curtain rises on a mountain scene. A drop curtain depicts rocks and trees. Half a dozen sheep kneel about the youthful Paris, who is sleeping. The shepherd rises, yawns, stretches, and begins to dance. A lamb joins him, and Paris holds her lovingly in his arms. Now all the sheep sit in a semicircle about Paris as he displays his youthful vigor. They applaud him when the dance is over.

Hermes, messenger of the gods, enters, idly chewing an apple. Three goddesses accompany him. The great Zeus, apparently, has a problem. Each one of these goddesses, Hera, Pallas Athena, and Aphrodite, has claimed a golden apple inscribed "To the fairest," and since only one of them can finally possess the apple, the ladies have been brought before Paris. Hermes tells him he will judge for Zeus which is the fairest.

Paris doesn't have much trouble making up his mind. Hera is the oldest and a little too grimly determined. Pallas Athena can't take her nose out of a book. Aphrodite, the goddess of love, promises Paris that he shall have the fairest of all women for his wife, and the shepherd immediately rewards her with the golden apple. The sheep circle about them, and Paris starts to leave with Aphrodite. But he has forgotten the lamb, who runs up and reminds Paris not to forget her. Paris takes her by the hand, and all exit. Hermes is left alone, still eating his apple. He reaches up and pulls down the curtain.

SCENE ONE: THE COURT AT SPARTA   Under the patronage of Aphrodite, Paris has come to Greece. We are at the palace of Menelaus. The aged king sits on his throne as the court entertains him. His beautiful wife, Helen, dances before him. Paris watches her closely. This must be the woman Aphrodite promised him! When her dance is over, Helen runs to the throne and kisses Menelaus, but it is clear that she has eyes only for the strange shepherd.

She dances again, this time with garlands. Paris comes forward and supports her in the dance. Menelaus is preoccupied with court business and only waves to her from time to time. All the men of the court seek to partner Helen, but she always chooses Paris. The two lovers approach Menelaus. Helen kisses her husband, and the jealous old man shoves Paris aside.

Courtly couples in white dance before the king and queen. Helen is bored. When the time comes for Menelaus to dance before his court, she ridicules him like all the rest. His absurd exhibition is cut short by a cramp. Paris is amused and comes forward to dance. The brilliant strength and graceful ease of his dance dazzle the court. He kneels to Helen.

There follows another courtly entertainment, in which Paris' pet lamb participates. Helen is now sitting at Menelaus' feet. The old man has dozed off. Hermes jumps into his lap, and the king embraces him. Helen is delighted at the success of this idiotic ruse and joins Paris for a *pas de deux* in which they acknowledge their love for each other. Paris lifts her high, to his shoulders, and carries her across the stage.

Menelaus is warned that his country is at war. He wakes up, pushes Hermes off his lap, and tries to recover his dignity. He straightens his crown and staggers blindly across the stage. His men drive on the stage in a chariot, and Menelaus, hastily decked out in battle dress, drives off to battle. All wave to him. Hermes sits on the royal throne of Sparta.

Paris caresses Helen. The members of the court form a great semicircle, and Helen, in their midst, dances. Now Hermes presents Helen with a duplicate to the key to her chamber. Helen gives it to Paris, who kneels before her. Helen's lady in waiting presents another duplicate to another adorer of her mistress, Orestes. Now that the stage is set for further complications, Hermes, back on the throne, gestures in comic triumph.

SCENE TWO: HELEN'S BEDCHAMBER   Before a drop curtain, the lady in waiting hastily provides Orestes with a dress similar to her own. Then she peeks behind the curtain. She takes Orestes by the hand, and the curtain rises. We are in Helen's private apartment. There is a screen on the left; the darkened room is dominated by a great canopied bed.

Helen enters, dressed in diaphanous white. The two maids help her prepare for bed and go behind the screen. Now Orestes declares himself. Discarding the attire of a lady in waiting, he assures Helen of his love, embraces her, and forces her to dance with him. Helen protests. Hermes wanders in, reading a book. When he sees what's going on, he wonders where the devil Paris is. He draws his arm back as if to strike Orestes, and the intruder, stricken by this godlike gesture, falls to the ground. Hermes pushes him out of the room.

Helen sprays herself liberally with perfume and is ready now for her true lover. Hermes unlocks the door, and Paris comes in. His pet lamb scurries behind the screen as he takes Helen in his arms. Hermes starts to knit. At first he pays no attention to the lovers, but when their mutual demonstrations become passionate, he rises and discreetly places the screen in front of them. The screen begins to vibrate.

And who should come in at this point but good old Menelaus, back from the wars. He carries a bouquet of roses for Helen. He assaults Hermes and tells him to get out. Then he observes the trembling screen. He rushes behind the screen. Paris runs out, followed by Helen, disguised in the lamb's coat. The poor lamb shivers in her underwear as Menelaus pursues Paris vainly, dashing hither and thither about the room. Paris and the pet lamb escape. Hermes blows a policeman's whistle to direct the busy traffic, stands behind Menelaus, and Helen pushes her deluded husband over his back. She stands over him as Hermes sits knitting on her bed. The drop curtain falls.

SCENE THREE: THE PORT   Menelaus emerges from his wife's boudoir and weeps despairingly. Ladies of the court join him, wring out his wet handkerchief, and try to cheer him up.

The drop curtain rises on a seaside scene. Ladies of the court gambol about the beach. A girl enters, leading a faun on a leash. The faun cavorts across the beach obligingly among the ladies and leaps off into the wings when they have had enough.

Courtiers come onto the scene, followed by Helen. She dances, surrounded by all the sheep in Paris' flock, who lift her to their shoulders. Menelaus puffs in and pleads with her.

Now Hermes sails up in a great barge of war. He takes out a Yo-yo and plays with it adroitly as Helen and Paris are confronted by Menelaus. The music laughs and chortles, and all the courtiers gather for a razzle-dazzle dance of farewell to the lovers. Menelaus is carried helplessly above the swirling crowd, and before he knows what has happened, Paris and Helen have climbed into the barge and set sail for distant Troy. All wish them Godspeed save Menelaus, who vainly tries to board the vessel.

HI-KYO

Music by Kazuo Fukushima. Choreography by Jaap Flier. Costumes by Joop Stokvis. First presented by the Netherlands Dance Theatre at the Stadsschouwburg, Amsterdam, Holland, June 30, 1971, with Arlette van Boven and Hans Knill. First presented in the United States April 1, 1972, by the same ensemble at the Brooklyn Academy of Music, New York, with the same principals.

There are at least eight meanings for the Japanese *hi-kyo*, and this ballet is about all of them: hidden place, place where no one lives, the moon, flying mirror, sly, unfair, adversity, and distress. *Hi-kyo* is a dance for two people, an extended *pas de deux*, with the flutist on stage with the dancers. The music is a work of the same title for flute, piano, and strings by the contemporary Japanese composer Kazuo Fukushima. *Hi-kyo* was the first new work created by the dancer and ballet master Jaap Flier after he became artistic director of the Netherlands Dance Theatre.

The dance takes place in a setting hung with black rope so that we seem to be in an impenetrable forest. A boy enters and appears to move easily through the thicket. A girl, who enters from the opposite side, encounters difficulty but pulling herself up on the strands of rope, seems to swim among the branches. The boy joins her now and the two become close and inseparable, tangled like the ropes they dance among. They wish to escape, are captured again by the ropes, but then the girl is released and leaves the scene. The boy remains, caught in the forest, which now, the ropes still, looks like a cage.

L'HISTOIRE DU SOLDAT (The Soldier's Story)

Narrative ballet in five scenes; to be read, played, and danced. Music by Igor Stravinsky. Words by C. F. Ramuz. Choreography by Ludmilla Pitoev. First presented at Lausanne, Switzerland, September 28, 1918, with Gabriel Rossel, George Pitoev, and Ludmilla Pitoev in the principal roles. Scenery and costumes by René Auberjonois. First presented in the United States by the League of Composers at the Jolson (later Century) Theatre, March 25, 1928. Pantomime by Michio Ito. Scenery and costumes by Donald Oenslager. Tom Powers was the Reader; Blake Scott and Lilly Lubell were the principal characters.

L'Histoire du Soldat is a composition for eight instruments, a narrator, and dancers. The small orchestra and the narrator are on stage with the dancers, who perform in a separate central area. The story is taken from an old Russian fairy tale which tells of a soldier who gives up his violin, the instrument that "speaks like his own heart," to the devil.

SCENE ONE: A WOOD   Before the action begins, the narrator tells us that there is a soldier who is going home to his village on leave. He has walked all the way.

The scene reveals a wood, through which there runs a stream. The soldier enters. From his gear he takes out a holy medallion, a snapshot of his girl back home, and a violin, his favorite personal possession. He begins to play, sitting idly by the stream.

The devil comes to him, disguised as a harmless elderly man. He asks if he may buy the violin. The soldier, who knows that the instrument is really a poor one, cannot understand; he does not want to sell it anyhow. The man insists, and the soldier finally agrees to trade his violin for a book the man tells him is of great value. The soldier is illiterate and does not know whether this is true, but the man's claim that the book will surely make him rich convinces him that the exchange is a good one. The man persuades him to teach him how to play the violin and to visit his home for several days.

SCENE TWO: THE VILLAGE   The narrator informs us that Joseph, the soldier, visited the devil and then resumed his homeward march. But when he got home, no one welcomed him. His girl had married someone else and had two children, and his mother was so frightened of him she would not come near him.

The action is renewed. The devil, disguised now as a cattle merchant, stands in the center of Joseph's native village. Joseph, outraged at his unpleasant homecoming, blames the barter of his violin for the mysterious book on the stranger. He attacks him with a sword. The devil, unmoved, commands him to become a civilian and to find the valuable book. As he takes out the book, the devil takes out his violin.

The narrator goes on to tell us how Joseph became a wealthy man by following the lessons of the devil's book. He is wealthy but miserable, able only to take money for additional orders for business.

SCENE THREE: JOSEPH'S OFFICE   Joseph is seen behind a great desk, reperusing the devil's book. A ragged old woman, the devil in disguise, enters and tries to sell him junk from her scavenger's bag. She lays before him his holy medallion, the photo of his girl, and his violin. He demands to know the price of the violin. The old creature tells him he'd better try to play the violin first: maybe it doesn't work well. Joseph takes up the instrument, but though he bows the strings frantically, no sound emerges. The hag has disappeared. Joseph destroys the violin and the book he received for it from the devil.

SCENE FOUR: A FOREIGN LAND—THE PALACE   The march that heralded the beginning of the soldier's story is heard again, and the narrator tells us that Joseph has tried to begin life anew. After destroying the book, he abandoned his wealth and went to a new country near by. There, in Joseph's new land, the king's daughter is dying of an unknown disease. The king has promised that the man who cures her shall marry her, and Joseph hopes to do this. Briefly the devil appears, this time as a gentleman in evening dress.

Joseph is seen sitting in a room at the palace, trying to determine what he should do by consulting a deck of playing cards. The cards augur well for him, but he is certain that he has not escaped Satan.

The narrator interrupts and tries to persuade Joseph to put up everything he has and gamble, all or nothing, with the devil. The soldier agrees and sits down to a game of cards with the devil. Although the devil wins each draw, he becomes strangely tired. Joseph forces him to drink, and he passes out in a stupor. Joseph seizes his violin and plays upon it the old, familiar music.

The narrator now tells us that Joseph will surely cure the ailing princess. Joseph is seen playing his violin before the princess, who lies back on a couch. She is revived by the music and rises to dance with him. Joseph embraces the princess.

Satan, all disguise thrown off, enters and demands the violin. Desperately, on all fours, the devil tries to snatch the instrument. Joseph begins to play upon it. The devil dances to this music until he collapses. The princess and Joseph drag him away.

They return to talk of their love. The devil, from outside, vows vengeance. He indicates that if Joseph remains in the princess' kingdom, he will survive, but that if he goes beyond the borders of the land, he will again be Satan's victim.

Again the narrator intervenes. He tells us how the princess, wishing to know more about her beloved, persuades him to take her on a visit to his native village. He realizes that this trip outside the kingdom will be fatal, but he cannot resist her demand.

SCENE FIVE: THE VILLAGE In this scene, the soldier's old village and the border of his new home are both seen. When Joseph crosses the border of the princess' kingdom, the devil attacks. The devil now plays upon the violin. The princess calls to Joseph, but he cannot answer. He is now the devil's perpetual slave.

NOTES Notable among the many other ballets to this score is that of Eliot Feld, who abandoned the original libretto for a new one. This depicts the sexual initiation of a young soldier as it is manipulated by a pimp and two whores. The soldier here is not only the victim of the military situation but also the victim of a human situation war has encouraged and accelerated.

Music by Igor Stravinsky. Choreography by Eliot Feld. Costumes by Frank Thompson. Lighting by Jennifer Tipton. Conductor: Akira Endo. First presented by American Ballet Theatre at the City Center, New York, January 7, 1972, with Daniel Levans, Eliot Feld, Sallie Wilson, and Paula Tracy in leading roles.

Reviewing Eliot Feld's version of the ballet in *Dance News*, the critic Nancy Goldner wrote: "It is a true theater piece, perhaps the purest of its genre. In place of the traditional story, Feld has substituted the theme of corruption, and the ballet ends with a strong anti-war statement. The corruptors are the pimp (Feld) and his whores (Sallie Wilson and Paula Tracy); they do in the soldier (wonderfully done by Daniel Levans). The dance style is as stylized as can be without becoming mimetic. Character is introduced and almost mercilessly sustained by emblematic movement, the most pungent of which is the pimp's rolling palms. Even the soldiers' dance, because it is repeated several times, becomes emblematic . . ."

Eliot Feld presented a revised version of his ballet *A Soldier's Tale* at the New York Shakespeare Festival Public Theatre, October 18, 1976. Lighting was by Thomas Skelton, costumes by Theoni V. Aldredge.

HOLBERG SUITE

Music by Edvard Grieg. Choreography by Arthur Mitchell. Costumes by Zelda Wynn. Lighting by Gary Fails. First presented by the Dance Theatre of Harlem at the Festival of Two Worlds, Spoleto, Italy, in June 1971.

When Arthur Mitchell founded his Dance Theatre of Harlem, he was concerned to show the great gift his dancers have for classical ballet. *Holberg Suite* happily accomplished that result for the company's first performances and the work soon entered the repertory. *Holberg Suite*—named in honor of Norway's great playwright, for whom Grieg wrote the music as a tribute—is a dance ballet in five parts: a lyric "Opening" (for nine dancers); "pas de

Neuf"; a quick and playful "Pas de Trois"; a moody "Pas de Deux"; and a jolly "Finale."

NOTES Writing of the production by the Dance Theatre of Harlem in *Ballet Review*, the critic Robert Greskovic said: "'Holberg Suite' (like 'Fête Noire') is one of Mitchell's program openers and as such it remains his best suite. It's a solid, varied and impressive introduction of the company to its audience. In addition to its lineups of group work, it contains some perky solos for dancers who, grateful for the chance, take it with daring aplomb. With the men in pale blue blouses, darker tights and light knee socks, and the women in filmy pale blue shifts, there is a Bournonville brightness to the stage which re-states itself in the hops, beats and jumps of the ensemble sections. The dances are bright and fluid presentations of this sunny, 'up' music by radiant young performers. Dances for nine, three, and two precede a group finale (with a lead couple). Virginia Johnson's largesse of stature proves accomplished and virtuoso-sweet in some cool, breezy pirouettes and sparkling batterie. The easy manners she projects as Russell and Bryant carefully support her in the pas de trois prove her power to enchant. She has opportunities to release (and quick change) her long legs in lifts and splits. Russell and Bryant present her with smiling authority and individual, double-escort manners. There is some sound and articulate supported work in the pas de neuf with Raines, Gerald Banks, and Scott handling two ballerinas each with deft calm. Susan Lovelle's upcurv-ing back and star-reaching gaze as she's transported in arabesque look superb. She reposes in stilled flight with a proud, private smile from her pixie face, her eyes glistening competition with her rhinestone earrings. In moments like this I want to say 'Hold it. You're there!' Here she was, not just a gifted dancer's body, but a young ballerina-hopeful. Ronald Perry and Roslyn Sampson lead the Finale with knowing-we-made-a-conquest ease. By this time the audience is theirs, and Sampson and Perry gratefully respond by not resting on their predecessors' laurels. They seize the chance with gracious attack, Sampson springing jumps and flashing sous-sus turns with impish glee, and Perry, ice-blue sleeves billowing, taking to the air with easy legs and carefully pointed sharp, multiple beats.

"'Holberg Suite' is a clear, handsome piece that makes suitable demands on the company and breezes about the stage with musical authority and theatrical purpose."*

HOMAGE TO ISADORA

Music by Brahms. Choreography by Frederick Ashton. First presented at the Hamburg Ballet's Nijinsky Gala, Hamburg, Germany, June 22, 1975, with Lynn Seymour. Pianist: Christoph Eschenbach. First presented in the United States with Lynn Seymour by American Ballet Theatre at the Ken-

* Reprinted by permission of *Ballet Review*, Marcel Dekker, publisher.

nedy Center of the Performing Arts, Washington, D.C., April 6, 1976. Pianist: Howard Barr.

Initially called *Brahms Waltzes*, this work is Frederick Ashton's recollection of the impression made by Isadora Duncan as he saw and admired her. Set to the Brahms Waltzes No. 15, Op. 39, which are played by the pianist on stage, the dances re-create a memory of a legend. John Percival wrote in *Dance and Dancers* that Ashton told the opening of the ballet, "with Seymour coming forward and scattering flower petals, was exactly as he remembered Isadora, the rest being a re-creation based on his memories. It certainly had an entirely authentic look to it, bringing the beautifully curved line of the many Duncan drawings into a seamless flow of movement . . ."

In an interview with Don McDonagh in *Ballet Review* (Vol. 3, No. 4) Frederick Ashton recalled what Isadora Duncan was like "in London, in 1921, I think. It was before she went to Russia. She did a series of matinees in London at the Prince of Wales Theatre to practically empty houses. She was a marvelous mover. She ran wonderfully. Even when she was galumphing around she was still very impressive. I must have been about fifteen or so when I saw her and that's a very bad age at which to see an aging, fat woman. I was completely taken by her. I saw about three or four performances. She would do a whole program of Wagner one afternoon, and then she would do a whole program of Chopin another afternoon, and then she would do Schubert or Liszt. She had a very good pianist who would play pieces while she got into another drape. She had a marvelous tragic impact and she had enormous grace. Marvelous use of the head and arms. The hands were beautiful. I don't think she did very much, I'm sure she didn't. And it's quite difficult to do a recital, you know. You have to be somebody pretty big to interest an audience for a whole afternoon . . . She had a quality I can only describe by saying that when she moved she left herself behind. And she did very simple things. In one Brahms waltz I remember she had her hands full of petals and as she ran forward the petals streamed after her. It sounds terribly corny but it was wonderful. Then she could be quite dramatic. In Chopin's Funeral March she would come in with a huge cloak around her and would just stand there. And you'd think, My goodness, how much longer is she going to stand there. Then slowly she would open the cloak and she had a whole armful of lilies inside. She had grace and she had power. She was also like a sort of highbrow striptease, because she would start her program in a great long garment and then after she did a dance she would take something off and hang it on the piano and so on 'til she finally ended up in a short thing up to here. Big legs, she had."

Anna Duncan's recollections of Isadora, as recorded in an interview with Parker Tyler in *Ballet Review* (Vol. 3, No. 1), are also of interest to those who would wish to know more about the great American dancer.

HOMAGE TO THE QUEEN

Music by Malcolm Arnold. Choreography by Frederick Ashton. Scenery and costumes by Oliver Messel. First presented by the Sadler's Wells Ballet at the Royal Opera House, Covent Garden, London, June 2, 1953, with Nadia Nerina, Violetta Elvin, Beryl Grey, and Margot Fonteyn in leading roles. First presented in the United States by the Sadler's Wells Ballet at the Metropolitan Opera House, New York, September 18, 1953.

Presented in London on Coronation Day, 1953, *Homage to the Queen* was ballet's tribute to Queen Elizabeth II. Arranged in four tableaux and an apotheosis, the Queens of the four elements, Earth, Air, Fire, and Water, enter with their consorts and attendants. Then in separate scenes the monarchs dance, epitomizing their special characteristics. Their attendants also perform a *pas de six*, a *pas de trois*, and a *pas de quatre*. At the end, in an apotheosis, Queen Elizabeth I is seen in gold brocade at the top of a flight of steps, where she gestures to the young queen who stands below.

ILLUMINATIONS

Dramatic ballet in one act. Music by Benjamin Britten. Words from Arthur Rimbaud. Choreography by Frederick Ashton. Scenery and costumes by Cecil Beaton. Lighting by Jean Rosenthal. Soprano soloist, Angelene Collins. First presented by the New York City Ballet at the City Center, New York, March 2, 1950, with a cast headed by Nicholas Magallanes as the Poet, Tanaquil LeClercq as Sacred Love, Melissa Hayden as Profane Love, and Robert Barnett as the Dandy.

A sequence of danced pictures or charades, *Illuminations* was inspired by prose poems written in 1871–72 by the French symbolist poet Rimbaud and by certain incidents in the short, violent life of the poet. Rimbaud lived to be thirty-seven, but he wrote no poetry we know of after he was nineteen. What he wrote before then is contained principally in two works, of which *Les Illuminations* was the first.

The title of this book and its meaning relate not only to the poems, but to the poet. For it was Rimbaud's special idea that the poet should be a seer, a visionary, one who arrived at a new, fresh illumination through the disordering of the senses, one who participated fully in darkness in order to see the light. His poems recollect the process by which this light is discovered, and in them we see sudden flashes of light illuminating the darkness the poems enclose. Throughout the ballet, selections from *Les Illuminations* are sung in French.

FANFARE   The music begins with loud, strident cries from the strings. The curtain rises. About the stage, reclining in various postures, are mysterious white figures. All of them are asleep. In the center, in waistcoat, high white collar, and striped pants, lies the poet. The soloist sings:

"J'ai seul la clef de cette parade sauvage."

The poet rises, falls back, rises again, and wakes, wakes the sleepers, turning their drowsy bodies. Now he puts on a hat and encourages the strange people to dance. The soloist sings portions of these impressions of the poet.

Now the people leave the stage and the poet is alone. The music is quiet and expectant. The poet throws gold stardust into the air to the song:

"J'ai tendu des cordes de clocher à clocher; des guirlandes de fenêtre à fenêtre; des chaînes d'or d'étoile à étoile, et je danse."

Stars glow brightly on the backdrop as the poet seems to string pearls between the distant steeples.

Two women come to the poet. One is all in stark white—even her face is a white mask; the other, also in white, wears her clothes loosely, voluptuously. The pure white figure, Sacred Love, leaves the poet alone with her opposite. Profane Love and the poet join in a ferociously passionate dance to a new song:

"Gracieux fils de Pan! Autour de ton front couronné de fleurettes et de baies, tes yeux, des boules précieuses, remuent. Tachées de lie brune, tes joues se creusent. Tes crocs luisent. Ta poitrine ressemble à une cithare, des tintements circulent dans tes bras blonds."

As the lovers embrace, they look up and see a parade enter, led by a drummer and a trumpeter. There follow two acolytes, a bishop, and a royal couple whose long trains are held out behind them. The parade moves to the center, and the royal pair are crowned king and queen by the bishop. They kneel together. The poet watches this procession and ceremony as if he couldn't believe it. The soloist sings:

"Un beau matin, chez un peuple fort doux, un homme et une femme superbes criaient sur la place publique: 'Mes amis, je veux qu'elle soit reine!' 'Je veux être reine!' Elle riait et tremblait. Il parlait aux amis de révélation, d'épreuve terminée. Ils se pâmaient l'un contre l'autre.

"En effet, ils furent rois toute une matinée, où les tentures carminées se relevèrent sur les maisons, et tout l'après-midi, où ils s'avancèrent du côté des jardins de palmes."

Finally the poet can bear it no longer. When the procession begins to leave the scene, he rushes upon it, throwing himself on the king's back. He knocks off the crowns of the royal pair and sends the whole parade packing. Alone, he takes up the king's crown and puts it on his head. Profane Love enters and throws herself at his feet. The poet ignores her. The girl grovels in the dirt for a moment, then reaches out her hands and tries to crawl up to his shoulders. The poet repulses her and begins to walk away, and the girl, refusing to give up her hold on him, is dragged along behind him. The poet, now enraged, strikes her in the face. She leaves the stage, promising vengeance. The poet lies at the front of the stage.

The scene darkens. Two spotlights show us the figure of Sacred Love, who enters with four men. The song is renewed as the poet lies dreaming.

Supported by the four men, Sacred Love is turned around and around in graceful poses, lifted high above the stage, and carried across it as the men form a chariot beneath her. As the dream subsides, she is lifted off in a long, quiet rush toward the wings.

The poet rises. He tosses his crown away. The curious crowd that peopled the stage in the first scene now fills the stage. Its members grab the poet, toss him about, turn him upside down and attack him.

The strange creatures chase the poet and surround him. Hidden for a moment in their midst, he is then lifted high above them. Profane Love enters to watch the scene with pleasure. Back in the distance we see the figure of Sacred Love soaring across the landscape. The poet is helpless and beckons to Profane Love for help. She laughs and orders one of the men to shoot the poet.

A man draws a pistol, aims it, and fires. The poet is wounded in his wrist, just as the real poet, Rimbaud, was wounded by his sometime mentor and guide, the poet Verlaine.

Profane Love, now wishing to be forgiven, falls at the poet's feet. He does not even look down at her. He grasps his wounded arm and steps over her body. Blood spills from the wound. The poet turns and slowly moves backward toward the transparent backdrop, where Sacred Love can still be seen in flight. The poet steps through the backdrop, the front of the stage darkens, all the curious people collapse again in sleep, and we see the hero walking alone beneath a blazing sun.

IMAGINARY FILM

Music by Arnold Schoenberg. Choreography by Glen Tetley. Designed by Nadine Baylis. First presented by the Netherlands Dance Theatre at the Circustheater, Scheveningen, Holland, May 5, 1970. First presented in the United States by the same ensemble at the Brooklyn Academy of Music, March 28, 1972.

The titles of the pieces of music by Arnold Schoenberg used for the ballet give us an indication of things to come: Danger Threatening, Fear and Catastrophe; Forebodings, the Past, Climax or Turning Point. The Schoenberg scores are *Incidental Music for a Film Scene* (*Begleitungsmusik zu einer Lichtspielszene*, Op. 34), which is played through twice in the ballet, and *Five Pieces for Orchestra*, Op. 16.

Imaginary Film's title tells its story, in fact a free fantasy on film drama and melodrama and also on what dance sometimes imagines itself to be when it takes itself too seriously. Everything seems to happen in it: a girl in evening dress on roller skates shoots one of two struggling men; a huge shaggy creature like King Kong moves in and out, even umpiring a tennis match. The choreography catches the action and violence we are used to in films and stops it down, as it were, to comedy, so that we can reflect on it, and ourselves.

INCUBUS

Music by Anton Webern. Choreography by Gerald Arpino. Costumes by Lewis Brown. First presented by the Robert Joffrey Ballet at the Fashion Institute of Technology, New York, September 28, 1962, with Lone Isaksen, Brunilda Ruiz, Paul Sutherland, Helgi Tomasson, Nels Jorgensen, Suzanne Hammons, and Lawrence Rhodes in leading roles.

"According to a legend originating in medieval times, a demon or spirit was thought to lie on sleeping persons, especially young women, inducing agonizing nightmares." The ballet, set to Webern's *Six Pieces for Orchestra*, is a journey into madness for such a young girl, who goes to sleep in torment one night, having been rejected by her mother. She clutches a rag doll. She dreams of others with whom she might identify—and whom she fears: a boy who wants to kiss her, a minister intent on dealing with the devil, a group of acrobats who seem to represent the free spirit she wishes to become. The lead acrobat falls and dies. The girl collapses into madness, indifferent now even to the rag doll. She is taken away and the doll alone remains.

The choreographer has said that he chose Webern's music "because he anticipated his time in music, and today I feel his music in 'our time.'"

INITIALS R.B.M.E.

Music by Johannes Brahms. Choreography by John Cranko. Décor by Jürgen Rose. First presented by the Stuttgart Ballet at the Württemberg State Theatre, Stuttgart, Germany, January 19, 1973, with Richard Cragun, Birgit Keil, Marcia Haydée, Heinz Clauss, and Egon Madsen in principal roles. First presented in the United States by the same ensemble with the same principals at the Metropolitan Opera House, New York, May 30, 1973. Conducted by Stewart Kershaw. Piano solo by Katsurako Fujiwara.

This dance ballet is named for its principal dancers—Richard Cragun, Birgit Keil, Marcia Haydée and Egon Madsen, the stars of John Cranko's Stuttgart Ballet. Cranko called it "a ballet for four friends to music of Johannes Brahms, whose passionate feeling for friendship and love is confirmed by his compositions, in his letters and by the testimony of others."

The first movement of the Brahms *Piano Concerto No. 2*, to which the ballet is arranged, was set for Richard Cragun; the second for Birgit Keil. Marcia Haydée and Heinz Clauss are featured in the third movement and Egon Madsen in the fourth. Each of the sections is supported by the *corps de ballet*.

NOTES Writing of this ballet's success on the Soviet tour of the Stuttgart Ballet (1973) in *Dance Magazine*, Lydia Jaffe notes that each of the four stars of *Initials R.B.M.E.* are "all dancers with whom Cranko has had a long and friendly association at the Stuttgart. They started with him as beginners, and his guidance brought them to artistic accomplishment.

"The ballet was enthusiastically acclaimed, and Vera Krasovskaya, the Soviet ballet critic, remarks: 'What a wealth of fantasy! The dancers execute these virtuosities with precision, discipline and feeling. It is an homage to the whole company.'"

IN NIGHTLY REVELS

Music by Bach. Choreography by Peter Darrell. First presented by the Jacob's Pillow Dance Festival, Lee, Massachusetts, July 3, 1973, with Margot Fonteyn. Harpsichordist: Jess Meeker.

In Nightly Revels is a dramatic dance for a lady. A harpsichord is at the left; three candelabra stand in what appears to be a deserted ballroom. A boy enters with a taper to light one of the candelabra. A man enters then and sits at the harpsichord. He begins to play music, from Bach's *Well-Tempered Clavier.* Now comes a beautiful lady, rushing on in a black cape. She wears a tiara and a pink gown. Expectant, she gestures graciously for the other candles to be lit and signals to a boy to take her cape. She seems to have arrived at a party; no one else is there; it is perhaps her own.

Now pensive, the woman nods at the harpsichordist, who begins to play. The measures he plays are sad and stately, and the woman reaches up her arms as if sacrificing something. Her hands descend down her body as if bathing it in her own tears as the dance threnody continues. She seems to be recovering from an experience that still controls her being. It is the reverse of another ballet, *Le Spectre de la Rose,* where a young girl returns from a ball to fall asleep in a chair to dream of a spectral hero. This woman of experience has had her dream, and there is a suggestion that it is one of many broken ones. She consoles herself with the music and the luxury of her surroundings. The back of the room disappears and the forest surrounding the room beckons to her. Looking out on the birch trees in the soft moonlight, she is renewed in body and spirit. A new experience awaits her. She again takes up her cape, stands briefly at the harpsichord, thanks the player, and disappears into the night.

INTERMEZZO

Music by Johannes Brahms. Choreography by Eliot Feld. Costumes by Stanley Simmons. Lighting by Jules Fisher. First presented by the American Ballet Company at the Festival of Two Worlds, Spoleto, Italy, June 29, 1969, with Christine Sarry, Elizabeth Lee, Cristina Stirling, David Coll, John Sowinski, and Alfonso Figueroa. Pianist: Gladys Celeste Mercader. First presented in the United States by the American Ballet Company at the Brooklyn Academy of Music, New York, October 23, 1969, with Olga Janke replacing Cristina Stirling in the original cast.

Intermezzo is a set of dances to piano music by Brahms—the *Op. 117* and *118 intermezzos* and some of the *Op. 39* waltzes. The piano is on stage to accompany the dances throughout the ballet. The story is what the dancers do.

They are seen entering gradually onto a darkened scene, three couples in formal dress. They listen to the first bars of the music as the light rises. Then a girl begins to move to the music. The others follow, responding to the flow of the music in speed and stillness. Two couples leave, and the remaining one dances a *pas de deux* to a romantic sequence. They yield the stage to another, faster duet, this one buoyant and full of brio; then the third couple returns and all six finish the piece.

This is the ballet's pattern, a series of duets and ensembles, all of them distinct in character with the music, all of them a contrast. There is a tempestuous waltz, and, in one duet, the boy is distracted by the girl so much that she seems to blind him. After another duet in which the dancers appear to be driven in the demanding pace of the music, a girl dances pensively alone. The *pas de deux* resume, their variety accumulating with shifts in the music. Toward the end, as the lights begin to fade, the three girls are cradled in their lovers' arms. They realize it is late and say good night.

NOTES *Intermezzo* was the new major work created by Eliot Feld for the first performances of his American Ballet Company. Writing about these performances in *Dance and Dancers*, Patricia Barnes said:

"For a choreographer still only in his middle 20s to create within a couple of years six ballets is an achievement in itself; that they should all be interesting, and at least three of them major works by any standard, sets Feld up in the ranks of the leading contemporary choreographers. Choreographed during the spring of 1969 and seen for the first time in Spoleto, *Intermezzo* is a real beauty. Performed to a backdrop of curtains and with the piano placed to the left of the stage, the dances have a flow and musicality that is both subtle and natural. Using just six dancers and varying his work with ensemble, *pas de deux* and solos, the choreography has an ecstasy and technical dexterity that is gorgeous . . . it is Feld's genuine invention and originality that make *Intermezzo* so rewarding. He dares a great deal in his choreography and asks almost impossible things of his dancers. Lifts abound in his work, some like none I have ever seen before. When performed by dancers such as the nimble Christine Sarry and David Coll, who is, quite simply, one of the best partners I have ever seen, the effect is dazzling.

"Another striking *pas de deux* is that created for Elizabeth Lee and John Sowinski, which is strongly atmospheric, a tiny choreographic gem almost complete in itself. With Sowinski's arm protectively round her waist, Lee seems to perceive strange and fearful visions. Sowinski gently removes her hands from her eyes and tenderly, reassuringly, he helps her face life. This small sequence is danced with a beauty, gravity and compassion that is altogether memorable."

Writing of the ballet in the *Village Voice*, the critic Deborah Jowitt said, "*Intermezzo* . . . is all ardent swoops and dips, runs and waltzes, light and breathless lifts. Occasionally a mysterious melancholy comes in like gathering dark. John Sowinski reaches toward the invisible while his partner, Elizabeth Lee, tries gently to turn him back toward her. They and the other two couples (Christine Sarry and David Coll, Olga Janke and Alfonso Figueroa) do not so much formally replace each other on stage in *pas de deux* as sweep in and out as if flashing different facets of a relationship between two people."

INTERPLAY

Ballet in four movements. Music by Morton Gould (American Concertette). Choreography by Jerome Robbins. First presented by Billy Rose, in Concert Varieties, at the Ziegfeld Theatre, New York, June 1, 1945, with a cast headed by John Kriza, Janet Reed, and Jerome Robbins. First presented by Ballet Theatre at the Metropolitan Opera House, New York, October 17, 1945, with settings by Oliver Smith and costumes by Irene Sharaff; Janet Reed, John Kriza, and Harold Lang headed the cast of dancers.

Interplay is an American ballet for eight dancers: four boys and four girls. It has no subject matter and no locale; but directly the dancing and music begin, it is apparent that it could only be an American work. The setting is simple: a plain colored backdrop and wings of differently colored cloth. The costumes are informal. So is the music. Loud and brassy at the beginning, the score is overtly raucous and playful.

FIRST MOVEMENT: FREE PLAY   A boy dances out onto the stage. He is followed by three companions. He dances alone for a few seconds, showing off. The others join him. The boys take turns jumping over each other's backs and horsing around. They all end up lying on the floor with their legs in the air.

A girl enters. The boys sit and marvel at her. Three other girls follow, and now the boys are moved to action. They get up, take partners, and the four couples, one after the other, execute a number of turns in a quick, graceful, athletic fashion. The lead boy runs through, under the arms of the dancers, and takes them to the front of the stage. There are no footlights, and the modern jive motions of the couples are silhouetted against the backdrop.

Now the couples move back and form a wide circle. The boys toss the girls around, and the music becomes quieter as the dancers stand in a straight line. The dancers seem to be playing a game that they all understand. There is some competition among the couples in the execution of conventional pirouettes and arabesques, but the game isn't really that serious. They are all having a jazzy good time. They all clap hands, the boys roll the girls over their backs, and the first dance ends with the four boys sitting on the floor; their girls stand in back, holding their hands.

SECOND MOVEMENT: HORSEPLAY   After a brief pause, the music resumes.

Though still modern in its rhythm, the melody now has a buoyant lightness. A few of the couples sit lazily on the stage; the others stand apart. One of the boys begins to dance alone. His solo is quietly comic, like the music, and amusingly impertinent in its imitation of some conventional movements in classic ballet. The dance increases in pace. The boy circles the stage, spins rapidly in the air, and finishes his solo. He kneels and opens his arms to two of the girls.

THIRD MOVEMENT: BYPLAY   The lights dim, and the piano begins a slow, sentimental blues. All the couples stretch and rearrange themselves about the stage. The lead boy and lead girl commence a *pas de deux*. Their dance is openly romantic, but has no particular intensity. Love is a game, too, they seem to say. The boy lifts the girl high over his head as she maintains an open position, pushes her forward across the floor on her toes as if she were a toy cart, then holds her close. The girl wraps herself around the boy, then both sit down on the floor and hold hands, like two children sitting on the beach.

FOURTH MOVEMENT: TEAM PLAY   The light brightens; the music returns to a fast, vigorous tempo. Now the dance becomes a contest. Two of the boys choose sides, and the two sides go into huddles to decide on tactics. They line up opposite each other. All turn cartwheels, then soloists from the two sides try to outdo each other in complicated movements. The boys vie with one another to see who can do the most turns in the air without stopping. Two girls, one from each side, begin to turn around and around on point as the game comes to a heated close. All the boys and girls run back and turn about the stage in a circle. The girls dash forward to the footlights. The boys sprint after them. With the last crash of the music, the boys take a running fall on the floor and slide under the girls' legs. Blackout.

IN THE NIGHT

Music by Frédéric Chopin. Choreography by Jerome Robbins. Costumes by Joe Eula. Lighting by Thomas Skelton. Pianist: Gordon Boelzner. First presented by the New York City Ballet at the New York State Theatre, Lincoln Center, January 29, 1970 with Kay Mazzo and Anthony Blum, Violette Verdy and Peter Martins, Patricia McBride and Francisco Moncion.

At the time of his ballet *Dances at a Gathering*, Jerome Robbins said, "There is more Chopin that I like—the nocturnes, for example—that I may use for another ballet." *In the Night* continues the exploration of Chopin's music, using for its score the Chopin *Nocturnes, Opus 27, No. 1; Opus 55, Nos. 1 and 2;* and *Opus 9, No. 2.*

When we speak of a nocturne, the critic Harold Schonberg has pointed out in his fine book on Chopin and Schumann, we think automatically of Chopin's "night pieces." They were, in the composer's lifetime, his most popular compositions, captivating all of Europe from the amateurs who found them comparatively easy to play, to the connoisseurs who liked their dreamlike form. "We live in a non-sentimental age, or pretend to," Schonberg remarks, and the nocturnes are not now so much played. Perhaps after this ballet we will listen to them more. Many consider the first nocturne used in the ballet to be Chopin's greatest; the last, *Opus 9, No. 2*, is surely the most popular of the twenty works in this genre.

In the Night consists of dances for three couples. They dance in sequence and then appear together briefly. The curtain rises on a starry night. A boy and a girl enter to the slow introductory music. Their dance develops with the pulse of the score, which quickens dramatically, then returns to simplicity and melody. The boy lifts the girl into the wings.

There is a more formal atmosphere for the second *pas de deux*, a suggestion of chandeliers above the stage. The music is tender, but in the midst of the dance the girl breaks away from the boy. When she returns, their dance has a real abandon until holding the girl upside down as her limbs tremble, passions subside. At the end, he lifts her, facing him, and away.

In the third *pas de deux*, almost melodramatic in response to the piano, there are declarations, rejections, pleadings, rapid swings from one emotion to another. She hangs onto the boy. He leaves her and she seems helpless. But after a short reunion, both leave. She returns, to walk across stage, kneel before him, and touch him. He cradles her in his arms.

To the most familiar nocturne, the three couples enter, meeting as if accidentally at a dance. The girls acknowledge each other, then the boys, but all clearly have eyes only for each other and do not know quite what is happening. Each couple goes its own way.

Deborah Jowitt wrote in the *Village Voice:* "I shall not vex myself with wondering whether Jerome Robbins intended his new ballet, *In the Night,* as a companion piece to his *Dances at a Gathering* or as a sequel, prelude, epilogue, cadenza. I think that it is probable that Robbins simply had more Chopin in his ears and more movement ideas in his head so he made another ballet—not as long as *Dances at a Gathering* but equally astonishing.

"The two ballets are certainly related. The movement has the same beautiful ease in space. We do not notice 'choreography,' but see dancing. Even ballet steps that we know melt into the long phrases before our eyes can freeze them. The special kind of contemporary Romanticism that Robbins is interested in is expressed in dance that burgeons and branches and grows like leaves— startling, perhaps, by its eventual shape, but never seeming inorganic. . . .

"Kay Mazzo and Anthony Blum perform the first duet. The gracious rapture of their relationship is punctuated by little confrontations. They appear to leave each other for the pleasure of rushing together again.

"The chandelier projection creates a half-indoor feeling—a ballroom with all the doors and windows flung open. In this duet for Violette Verdy and Peter Martins, there is a delight in each other, but also a slight and charming decorousness. Occasionally they do little steps arm in arm as if they were at a dance, or remembering a dance. She looks very small, very trusting beside him.

"The third duet is full of passion and artifice. The lovers, Francisco Moncion and Patricia McBride, are being melodramatic for each other. One minute they are involved in flashy, tempestuous lifts; the next minute one of them disappears from sight. Their very anger seems to be exciting them. Even her final kneeling at his feet to touch him is extreme as well as truly humble.

"At the end the three couples, still alone, occupy the same fragrant patch of night. The women come together and are surprised to see each other: you can almost see them blinking awake. The men greet each other. Then the couples separate and again take their own paths.

"The choreography serves the dancers, and they in turn serve it beautifully. Each seems completely real in what he is doing. Ballet technique disappears as artifice and becomes—as it rarely does—a means to dancing, a transparency for spirit to be seen through."

In the Night has also been described, with an interesting commentary, by the critic Robert Sealy in *Ballet Review*, Vol. 3, No. 3.

INTRODUCTION AND ALLEGRO FOR HARP

Music by Maurice Ravel. Choreography by Jerome Robbins. Costumes by Arnold Scassi. Lighting by Ronald Bates. First presented by the New York City Ballet at the Hommage à Ravel at the New York State Theatre, Lincoln Center, May 22, 1975, with Patricia McBride and Helgi Tomasson as principals. Solo harp: Cynthia Otis. Conducted by Robert Irving.

A dance ballet to some lovely music composed by Ravel in 1905–6, this work is arranged for a girl and a boy and six couples. A small-scaled work for harp, string quartet, flute, and clarinet, the *Introduction and Allegro* has a bright, luminescent lyricism. The harp seems to ask a question the dancers attempt to answer in a rush of delight.

THE INVITATION

Scenery and costumes by Nicholas Georgiadis. Music by Matyas Seiber. Choreography by Kenneth MacMillan. First presented by the Royal Ballet at the New Theatre, Oxford, November 10, 1960, with Lynn Seymour, Christopher Gable, Anne Heaton, and Desmond Doyle in the principal roles. First presented in the United States at the Metropolitan Opera House, New York, May 10, 1963, with the same principals.

Speaking about his ballet, the choreographer Kenneth MacMillan has said, "The story is realistic, set at the beginning of this century. I combined two ideas—from a South American book called *House of the Angel* and Colette's *Ripening Seed*. But I made the characters people I know, not the characters in the books. An older, unhappy married couple meet two young people whose love for each other is gentle and tender. The older couple destroy this innocence. The story does not resolve itself. When one loses innocence and grows up, it can be a shattering experience without resolution. I hope the spectators may see things in the ballet which they've felt in their lives."

The scenario for the ballet follows: "In a grand house live a wealthy widow and her three daughters. The two elder daughters of marriageable age are strictly guarded by their mother. The youngest daughter has invited her boy cousin and some young friends to stay with her, along with their parents. In the party there is an unhappily married couple who were friends of the widow's husband.

"The youngest daughter and her cousin are drawn towards each other, but she is also attracted to the married man after dancing with him. After the children have gone to bed, entertainers arrive to perform for the guests. The girl creeps down and secretly watches. At the end of the performance the married couple quarrel and the man rushes off in anger followed by the girl. The cousin appears in search of the girl but instead finds the wife alone. Timidly he succumbs to her. At the same time the girl discovers the man walking by the lake, but his affectionate approach to her changes to violence and she is left weeping.

"The house party ends and the married couple continue their indifferent relationship. The boy tries to resume his courtship of the girl but she rejects him."

IRISH FANTASY

Music by Camille Saint-Saëns. Choreography by Jacques d'Amboise. Scenery and lighting by David Hays. Costumes by Karinska. First presented by the New York City Ballet at the Greek Theatre, Los Angeles, August 12, 1964, with Melissa Hayden, André Prokovsky, Anthony Blum, and Frank Ohman in the leading roles. First presented in New York at the New York State Theatre, October 8, 1964, with the same principals.

Irish Fantasy is a dance ballet on an Irish theme set to music from Saint-Saëns's opera *Henry VIII*. The opening music even has occasional strains of the traditional Irish tune "Johnny I Hardly Knew You." A lace-curtain drop curtain sets the light, bantering tone of the piece, which is dominated by girls in green, boys in brown, and a girl in pink, the heroine. The girl in pink is admired by several of the boys, but is finally won, after a vigorous dance of conquest, by the leading *danseur*. The quality of the movement tells the story of the piece, which is bright, competitive, and ebullient.

IVAN THE TERRIBLE

Ballet in two acts. Music by Sergei Prokofiev, arranged by Mikhail Chulaki. Scenario and choreography by Yuri Grigorovich. Scenery and costumes by Simon Virsaladze. First presented by the Bolshoi Ballet at the Bolshoi Theatre, Moscow, February 20, 1975, with Yuri Vladimirov and Natalia Bess-

mertnova in the principal roles. First presented in the United States by the same ensemble at the Metropolitan Opera House, Lincoln Center, New York, April 29, 1975. Conducted by Algis Zhyuraitis.

Persons unacquainted with Russian history and knowing no Russian might suppose that Ivan was a terrible Tsar. Actually, the Russian word *grosniy* means formidable, threatening, menacing, stern, as well as terrible. This ballet about his life goes back to sixteenth-century Russia to provide the background for what we know of his character. The action tells of a difficult and troubled time when, torn apart by civil strife and foreign invasion, "Russia rang like an alarm bell with a call to unite the country." The scenes of the ballet tell of the young Tsar Ivan IV, of his beloved Anastasia who was poisoned by treacherous Boyars, and of Prince Kurbsky who betrayed his homeland. They tell of "the Russian people, who withstood all the ordeals, survived and emerged victorious."

The choreographer Yuri Grigorovich has said that the ballet is not a literal representation of history but "seeks to re-create an image of the period. The essential theme is the nature of the Russian character, the traditions of loyalty and heroism, the ethics and morals of the individual Russian . . .

"Many aspects of Ivan's complex nature are portrayed. On the one hand he is shown as a man who passionately and faithfully loves his wife Anastasia, and detests the treachery of the Boyars. On the other hand, he is shown as the mighty Tsar, himself treacherous and cruel.

"The ballet is conceived as a historical chronicle in which the action develops through the juxtaposition of contrasting scenes, which are not necessarily subject to the strict development of the plot. Lyric, dramatic, even humorous scenes, set side by side, reveal a many-faceted panorama of the period. Thus the ballet becomes not 'episodes in the life of a Tsar' but scenes of a complex and tormented time in sixteenth-century Russia."

The action of *Ivan the Terrible* is presented in two acts of nine scenes each.

ACT ONE, SCENE ONE: INTRODUCTION; THE BELLRINGERS SUMMON THE PEOPLE   Agitated chords commence the action. Six Bellringers holding ropes that ascend to huge bells overhead are encircled by crowds of people. The Bellringers kneel. In the back behind a scrim, we discern leading members of the Tsar's court, all dressed in long robes.

ACT ONE, SCENE TWO: THE BOYARS AND IVAN   The scrim opens. On a high throne sits Ivan. He rises. All kneel as he dances. His movements and gestures are as percussive as the declarative music that accompanies them; we witness an assertion of power so strong it appears to be a natural force. At the end he climbs back up to the throne as if it were Everest to conquer.

ACT ONE, SCENE THREE: IVAN'S ENCOUNTER WITH ANASTASIA   Girls in diaphanous gowns decorated with pearls approach the throne. Fierce in his black and gold robes, the Tsar grips the arms of his throne but watches. Soon he descends. Enthralled with one of the girls, he touches her head. She is frightened and backs away but the Tsar is transfixed and will not let her go. Prince Kurbsky, a leading courtier and chief of the Boyars, instinctively kneels to the Tsar's new favorite and with the others discreetly withdraws. Alone with the Tsar, Anastasia kneels before him. He declares his love openly. They bow deeply to each other, then walk toward us to begin a dance of quiet joy at his discovery.

ACT ONE, SCENE FOUR: KURBSKY'S DESPAIR   The leading courtier is outraged at Anastasia's sudden ascendancy and mimes his displeasure at being side-tracked after all he has done for the Tsar in the past. Alternately whining and attacking, tearing his hair and banging on the door, Kurbsky finally determines to get even with the Tsar and attack him where it will hurt most. He is deflected by an invasion from abroad.

ACT ONE, SCENE FIVE: THE BATTLE WITH THE FOREIGN ENEMY   The Bellringers return in red boots, sound their bells, and cluster in the center. Crowds of people enter to lament the coming war but the invaders must be repulsed. Now the very battle comes onto the scene, Kurbsky leading the Russians in pursuit of the Moslems. Ivan even more vigorously at the head of the battle declares his will for victory and kisses his sword as trumpets blare. Among scythes of death which surround him as he dances, he proceeds to battle and overcomes the enemy in a blaze of glory.

ACT ONE, SCENE SIX: ANASTASIA'S MEDITATION   In the throne room of the Kremlin, Anastasia descends to dance to lyric strings of an increasing fear. She is afraid for her husband and the country and longs for his return.

ACT ONE, SCENE SEVEN: VICTORY CELEBRATION   The Bellringers, now in the white of peace, lead the victory parade. The Boyars are welcomed home by their ladies, then Anastasia greets Ivan. They dance jubilantly in a *pas de deux* at the end of which he carries her off into the wings. Kurbsky and the others continue the celebration.

ACT ONE, SCENE EIGHT: IVAN'S ILLNESS   The courtiers kneel before Ivan, who is seated on his throne in torment. Anastasia is at his feet. In severe exhaustion he rises. She tries to help him and he leans on her.

ACT ONE, SCENE NINE: THE TSAR'S ANGER   Emboldened by the Tsar's illness, a group of Boyars plot together. In the Tsar's absence, one of the wily courtiers goes to the throne. Ivan suddenly appears in back of the throne, seizes him, throws him down the high flight of steps, following him as he falls. The Tsar then turns and climbs back up to the throne as if he were making an attack on a craggy mountain. At the top he confronts the revolting courtiers and hurls down in their midst his golden spear. They cower in terror.

ACT TWO, SCENE ONE: IVAN'S HAPPINESS   This is a dance of love to quiet music in the royal bedchamber. Treacherous Boyars watch and wait for the time to strike.

ACT TWO, SCENE TWO: THE BOYARS' CONSPIRACY   The wily courtiers assemble with their women and plot against the Tsar. In a drink that is passed among them, they pledge their new allegiance. Kurbsky enters. They hold out the cup to him. He cannot take it. Yet in an ensuing dance, he deliberates the alternatives and succumbs, seizing the cup in a frenzy.

ACT TWO, SCENE THREE: ANASTASIA'S DEATH   The Tsarina Anastasia is now given the cup. She drinks, is poisoned, and begins to die. She dances limply, helplessly as all watch in despair, collapsing finally in Kurbsky's arms. All shun him. Kurbsky puts down the body. Incredibly, Anastasia rises. She reaches out for vengeance and dies as Kurbsky trembles.

ACT TWO, SCENE FOUR: THE PEOPLE'S REVOLT   Again in red boots, the Bellringers return. The people who surround them cry havoc and protest.

ACT TWO, SCENE FIVE: IVAN MOURNS FOR ANASTASIA   Alone, the Tsar gives himself up to grief and despair, an intensification of his earlier illness. Voices sing as he lies spread-eagled. In the midst of the choir and candles, Anastasia seems to come back to him. She kneels to bless him.

ACT TWO, SCENE SIX: KURBSKY'S ESCAPE AND THE ROUT OF THE BOYARS   Ivan attacks the drunken, celebrating Boyars, cracking a long rope like a whip. There is a frenetic chase but with halberds and axes the traitors are closed in.

ACT TWO, SCENE SEVEN: THE OPRICHNIKI   A dance of death re-enacts the murder of Anastasia and the Boyars are ensnared by the Tsar's private secret police and vigilantes, the Oprichniki. The Devil forces Kurbsky, who has finally been caught, to drink from the cup of poison he had given to Anastasia. Devilish minstrel clowns, the Skomorokhi, hang the Boyars. The Devil himself, his jaw wagging hideously, suddenly tears off a mask and rips off his costume. It is Ivan.

ACT TWO, SCENE EIGHT: IVAN'S MEDITATION   The Tsar appears to be exultant in victory over his enemies but we see at once, as he pounds his staff into the ground, that his life force has begun to leave him. The scepter of power has now become a burden, weighing him down, oppressing him beyond measure. He lies again spread-eagled on the ground. Figures presaging death torment him but miraculously he rises. He dances with a newfound ferocity and is determined to persevere.

ACT TWO, SCENE NINE: FINALE. THE TRIUMPH OF THE RUSSIAN PEOPLE   The Bellringers return, leading a mass of people. As the bells resound, Ivan seizes the ropes and is pulled up by them toward the bells. Ensnared there, he glares out at us, implacable, unforgiving, determined on yet another victory.

NOTES   The Soviet composer Mikhail Chulaki, who arranged Prokofiev's music for the ballet, has recalled that the idea for a dance-drama about Ivan came originally from the conductor A. L. Stasevich, who had worked on Prokofiev's music for the Eisenstein film *Ivan the Terrible*. Stasevich had arranged the film music as a cantata and drew Grigorovich's attention to its great potential as a ballet score.

Chulaki continues: "Unfortunately, Stasevich died before he could evolve the score for the ballet. But Grigorovich's imagination had already been fired by this deeply expressive music. The ballet began to form in his mind as an independent work, which did not slavishly follow the plot of the film, but drew its theme from the quality of Prokofiev's music.

"The thematic material from the film *Ivan the Terrible* became the basis for the ballet score. In certain episodes other stylistically related works by Prokofiev were used: The *Russian Overture*, three sections from the *Third Symphony*, and a fragment from the cantata *Alexander Nevsky*. This additional music gave Grigorovich a broader psychological spectrum to work with— from Ivan's unbounded happiness with Anastasia, to his horrifying visions."

The choreographer Yuri Grigorovich has said that "Prokofiev's music for the film *Ivan the Terrible* is an outstanding achievement . . . I considered it essential that this music, so full of vivid imagery, lyric beauty, and heroic grandeur, be brought back to life; not only to be heard again, but this time to be interpreted choreographically because Prokofiev's music seems to demand expression in direct, human terms."

Writing in *Ballet Review* (Vol. 5, No. 2), the critic Robert Greskovic commented on a performance of *Ivan the Terrible* in 1975 by Vladimir Vasiliev: "Vasiliev is magnetically magnificent. He has both a manly and a boyish quality that makes him unique. He represents the first male Bolshoi dancer to have the charisma heretofore held by Bolshoi ballerinas. Though the Bolshoi is touted for the power of its male dancing, it has not, like the Kirov—which has produced stars aplenty starting with Nijinsky—produced a male classical star of household-word stature. Vasiliev gives off a personable power that keeps his audience as interested in him as in what he's doing. You can almost sense the audience around you growing more keenly perceptive as Vasiliev grows more potent. If he were to become a regular visitor to our country, Vasiliev could develop a following similar to that of Nureyev."*

IVESIANA

Music by Charles Ives. Choreography by George Balanchine. Lighting by Jean Rosenthal. First presented by the New York City Ballet at the City Center, New York, September 14, 1954. Janet Reed and Francisco Moncion, Patricia Wilde and Jacques d'Amboise, Allegra Kent and Todd Bolender, Diana Adams and Herbert Bliss, Tanaquil LeClercq and the entire company.

* Reprinted by permission of *Ballet Review*, Marcel Dekker, publisher.

The great American composer Charles Ives died May 19, 1954, at the age of seventy-nine. Four months later, our company performed for the first time a ballet of some of his music, music that was then little known. Fortunately that situation has since changed and with fine performances and recordings of Ives's major works, most of us know something about the music that was seldom played during the composer's lifetime. I remember hearing about Ives's music in 1934, I think from Roger Sessions, but it was then almost impossible to hear his music. Leon Barzin gave me my first chance with a performance by the National Orchestral Association. Fascinated as I was by the music, it seemed to me incredibly difficult, far too complex for dancing. Some years later, however, after refreshing myself with the music of Schoenberg, Berg, and Anton Webern, I turned again to Ives. After finishing a ballet to Schoenberg's *Opus 34,* I began to work my way into Ives's music and with increasing respect and admiration. It saddens me that I never met him or told him I wanted to use his music: he seemed inaccessible. Lincoln Kirstein brought Mrs. Ives to the first performance of our ballet and I was very moved.

Ives's music is most interesting to me for its rhythms. The choreographer has little music that can twist him out of his habitual methods of design, but I found in Ives's work the shock necessary for a new point of view. Since the ballet was first done, I have revised it several times, adding a new piece I have discovered, omitting another. The music I find hard *not* to work with. In homage to the composer, we called the ballet *Ivesiana.*

1. *Central Park in the Dark.* As the names Ives gave to his music so vividly describe them, I would hope that they also tell what the dance might be about. Ives wrote that this piece "purports to be a picture in sound of sounds of nature and of happenings that men would hear . . . when sitting on a bench in Central Park on a hot summer night. The strings represent the night sounds and silent darkness—interrupted by sounds from the Casino over the pond—of street singers coming up from the Circle, singing— . . . of pianolas having a ragtime war in the apartment house 'over the garden wall' . . . a streetcar . . . a fire engine . . . wayfarers shout—again the darkness is heard . . ." That is the musical background to the dance event, which is a meeting between a girl who is lost and a boy and how they become lost together, in the dark in a place like Central Park.

2. *The Unanswered Question* calls for a double orchestra. "The strings . . . are to present 'The Silences of the Druids' who know, see, and hear nothing. The trumpet intones 'The Perennial Question of Existence' and states it in the same tone of voice each time. But the hunt for the 'Invisible Answer' undertaken by the flutes and other human beings becomes gradually more active, faster and louder. The 'Fighting Answerers,' as time goes on . . . seem to realize a futility, and begin to mock 'The Question'—the strife is over for the moment. After they disappear, 'The Question' is asked for the last time, and the 'Silences' are heard beyond in 'Undisturbed Solitude.'" The dance of course does not follow these interesting remarks of the composer but from them and from the music, which is in effect a dialogue or argument between the trumpet and the woodwinds against the background of the strings, I derived the idea of

a girl all-knowing like a sphinx to whom a man might turn. But I try to say too much and in words begin to limit what I hope the dance conveys.

3. *In the Inn*. This is as informal as its music, with a dance by two young people. As the music echoes old-time dance rhythms, the dancers' steps do too. They act exhausted at the end, shake hands and part.

4. *In the Night*. This short piece of Ives's composed in 1906, and what I have arranged to it, must speak for themselves in the theatre.

Other music by Ives that has been used in *Ivesiana* includes "Hallowe'en," which was originally the second of the danced pieces; "Over the Pavements," originally the fourth (after "The Unanswered Question"); "Arguments," which replaced "Hallowe'en" in 1955; and "Barn Dance," which in 1956 replaced "Arguments."

LE JEUNE HOMME ET LA MORT (The Young Man and Death)

Dramatic ballet by Jean Cocteau. Music by Johann Sebastian Bach. Choreography by Roland Petit. Scenery and costumes by Georges Wakhevitch. First presented by Ballets des Champs-Élysées at the Théâtre des Champs-Élysées, Paris, June 25, 1946, with Jean Babilée and Nathalie Philippart in the title roles. First presented in the United States by Ballet Theatre at the Metropolitan Opera House, New York, April 9, 1951, with the same cast.

This modern fable of love pictures the plight of a young man whose passion for a girl is requited only in death. The boy is the typical young romantic Parisian painter, thinking and dreaming only of the girl who does not love him: of the girl who never comes, but for whom he constantly waits. The ballet is performed to an orchestration of Bach's *Passacaglia and Fugue in C minor*.

The orchestra states the music's dominant theme deeply and softly. The curtain rises. The scene is a corner of a Paris garret. Dirty walls on both sides converge at the rear. In the center, a high stanchion supports a rafter. A rope hangs down from the rafter, tied in a noose at the end. Alongside it stands an iron stove. There is a door at the left. The stark furnishings of the room—a bare table, a stool, half a dozen old wooden chairs—are illuminated by the harsh light of a bare electric bulb shaded with newspapers. Against the right wall stands a cot, partially covered with a red silk cloth. A young man in paint-covered overalls lies sprawled back on the cot, smoking slowly, languidly, apparently relaxed. His body tightens, becomes tense. He looks at his watch, sits up. His eyes watch the door as he mashes out the cigarette; his feet move restlessly. The boy rises and moves toward the door, where he poses adroitly and turns swiftly in the air to indicate his increasing anxiety. When he has examined his watch again, he turns away angrily and throws himself on the cot.

The door opens slowly. A dark girl in a yellow dress and black gloves stands there in the doorway. Her feet vibrate against the floor arrogantly as she watches the boy across the room. There is a brief moment of recognition, and he runs across the room to leap to her side. He attempts to embrace the girl;

she is reluctant, cold in his grasp. They begin to dance together around the room. The boy is indifferent to anything but the girl. They move rapidly and roughly, banging chairs aside. The girl dances with fierce stiffness, like a violent mechanical doll.

The girl pushes the boy away and sits down on a chair and crosses her legs. He stands in back of her, declaring his love for her with generous, open gestures. The girl ignores him. The boy tries to force her to dance with him again. The girl joins him for a moment, but it is apparent that he is not content merely to dance. The girl turns stiff in his embrace and pushes him to the floor. She dances over to the table. He jumps onto the table and crouches for an instant above her. The girl shoves him to the floor and sits nonchalantly against the table, watching him writhe on the floor.

The boy reaches out for a chair, pulls himself up, and sits with his back to the girl. She lights a cigarette. The smoke drifts over to him. He points his leg out toward her and rises, hypnotized. He moves toward her like a toy soldier, his movements imitating the quality of the girl's gestures. He stands close, his face against hers. The girl blows smoke in his face. The boy angrily knocks the cigarette out of her hand and stamps on it. Now the girl moves around the table, and he cannot seem to catch her. He decides on a more careful approach.

The girl sits in a chair, absolutely oblivious to him, as if she were at a cocktail party and he was only one of the many people who were quite naturally looking only at her. The boy takes a chair and walks it over beside her. He steps up on the chair, and the girl moves away. He chases after her and dances with bold, desperate leaps in the air, pleading for her love. The girl does not notice. He turns rapidly and comes close to her. The girl slaps him off fiercely, and he falls away in the slow motion of agony. Now he moves about the room frantically—back to the corner and to his love again. Kneeling behind her, he embraces her legs. The girl wrenches herself free and pushes him away. The boy falls against the table.

He has lost control of his will and only wishes to be close to her. He lies on the floor and reaches out to caress her. She kicks him in the face savagely. His body reacts in agonizing, painful slow motion as his face falls against the floor and his feet describe a high arc in the air. Twice more he attempts to touch her, and twice more she kicks him away.

The boy rises and chases the girl back to the corner of the room. The music approaches a crescendo. They meet and move forward. The music softens. Suddenly the girl responds to the boy's embrace. She caresses his face softly; he is motionless in her gentle arms, oblivious to the violence they threaten. She leads him to a chair. The boy moves in a dream. He sits down, his head falls forward, and the girl raises his arm high in a wide arc of slow movement. She moves away. The boy seems to be asleep; his arm hangs pendulously over the back of the chair.

The girl moves a high stool to the foot of the post in the center of the room, steps up on it, and adjusts the noose that hangs from the rafter. Carefully she sets the noose swinging. Then she moves back to the boy. Her cold hands touch his neck. The boy wakens, startled. She twists his head around toward the noose. As he lifts his arms in terror, the girl pushes him backward. The chair clatters to the floor. The boy's foot trembles. The girl runs through the door, triumphant.

The boy leaps after her, but she has vanished. He takes a chair, swings it wide, and throws it against the wall. He jumps upon the table, turns briskly in his anger and fear, then falls, helpless. He rises. He is standing beside the table, and his line of sight crosses the swinging noose. He drags the table with him as he moves forward stiffly. His body arches back as he holds the table, and he topples to the floor. He rises, leaps boldly and assertively to regain his courage, and moves stiffly toward the noose. He grabs the stool and backs away, circling the post. His frantic, nervous shadow is seen reflected against both converging walls. Slowly, inevitably, he sets the stool down firmly at the foot of the post. He climbs up, fixes the noose about his neck, and pushes the stool away with his feet. The stage darkens. Two crossing beams of light are focused on his hanging body. His leg trembles spasmodically as he dies.

Mysteriously, the walls of the garret fall back and the night sky line of Paris is seen in the distance. The room is illumined by the light of the city. A woman wearing the white mask of death enters on the left from over the rooftops. Her arm points forward. As if by her command, the boy's body stirs. He releases the noose and slides down the post to stand beside her. The strange figure removes her mask and places it on the boy's face. Her own face is revealed as the face of the girl he loved. The girl points forward, and the boy moves magically through the wall before her. As the curtain falls, the two are seen moving against the rooftops of the dark sky line.

Le Jeune Homme et la Mort was revived for Mikhail Baryshnikov and Bonnie Mathis by American Ballet Theatre at the City Center, New York, 1975.

JEUX (Games)

Ballet in one act. Music by Claude Debussy. Choreography by Vaslav Nijinsky. Book by Vaslav Nijinsky. Scenery and costumes by Léon Bakst. First presented by Diaghilev's Ballets Russes at the Théâtre des Champs-Élysées, Paris, May 15, 1913, with Tamara Karsavina, Vaslav Nijinsky, and Ludmilla Shollar. First presented in the United States by Ballet Theatre at the Center Theatre, New York, April 23, 1950, in a new choreographic version by William Dollar, with Nora Kaye, Igor Youskevitch, and Norma Vance. Scenery and costumes by David Ffolkes.

For his second ballet, the famous dancer Vaslav Nijinsky chose a modern subject. Today, when we are accustomed to ballets about garden parties (*Lilac Garden*) and sailors on liberty (*Fancy Free*), the new ballet without a modern subject is a rarity, but in 1913 the opposite was the case. Nijinsky was the first choreographer to create a ballet related to the modern world. His subject is love as it is revealed in a tennis game.

The curtain rises on a formal garden of a large estate. The sky is dark-blue; it is almost night. A tennis ball bounces onto the stage, and after it comes a young man leaping in pursuit. He is dressed in tennis clothes and carries a tennis racket, but is clearly somewhat bored with the game. He searches half-heartedly for the ball and welcomes the distraction of two girls who enter the garden. With the approach of night they, too, have left off a game of tennis.

The boy begins to flirt with the girls, at first casually, then more seriously. He dances with them playfully, as if he were continuing with each of them a game of tennis. After he has partnered the two girls singly, he dances with both of them together. He lies down on the grass between them and then, rising, touches their faces tenderly.

Now the boy does not know which girl to choose. He wants both; both are beautiful. The girls long for him to make a choice, but at the same time know how unhappy such a choice will make one of them.

Another tennis ball bounces in from the nearby court. The boy leaps to retrieve it, and the girls follow him as he abandons the game of love for tennis.

NOTES   *Jeux* has been restored to the modern repertory in a production by John Taras for the New York City Ballet. The ballet, with choreography by Mr. Taras to Nijinsky's original libretto, was first presented at the New York State Theatre on April 28, 1966, with Edward Villella, Allegra Kent, and Melissa Hayden. Scenery and costumes were by Raoul Pène du Bois, lighting by Jules Fisher, and the costumes were executed by Karinska. Writing about the ballet in the New York *Times*, Clive Barnes said that the choreographer "has managed to sustain the mood of a hot summer evening, where secrets are told and emotional corners turned, one of those evenings with thunder in the air . . . Interestingly, the one major change Mr. Taras has made in the Nijinsky scenario is to make the relationship between the girls more serious than in the original . . . While flirtation still abounds, the relationship of the girls is no longer merely flippant."

For a full understanding of this ballet of Nijinsky's, the account in Richard Buckle's biography of the dancer-choreographer and that in Lincoln Kirstein's *Nijinsky Dancing* are recommended.

JEWELS

Ballet in three parts. Music by Gabriel Fauré, Igor Stravinsky, and Peter Ilyich Tchaikovsky. Choreography by George Balanchine. Costumes by Karinska. Scenery by Peter Harvey. Lighting by Ronald Bates. First presented by the New York City Ballet at the New York State Theatre, April 13, 1967, with Violette Verdy and Conrad Ludlow; Mimi Paul and Francisco Moncion; Patricia McBride, Edward Villella, and Patricia Neary; and Suzanne Farrell and Jacques d'Amboise in the leading roles.

This is a dance ballet in three parts to music by three different composers. The music for the three parts is very different and so are the dances. The dancers for each part of the ballet are dressed like jewels, emeralds for Fauré, rubies for the Stravinsky, and diamonds for the Tchaikovsky. (I thought of using sapphires, too, and had Schoenberg in mind, but the color of sapphires is hard to get across on stage.) The idea for a new ballet using jeweled costumes came about some years ago when my friend Nathan Milstein introduced me to Claude Arpels, the jeweler. I saw later the splendid stones in his collection in New York. Of course I have always liked jewels; after all, I am an Oriental, from Georgia in the Caucasus. I like the color of gems, the beauty of stones, and it was wonderful to see how our costume workshop, under Karinska's direction, came so close to the quality of the real stones (which were of course too heavy for the dancers to wear!).

The first part, "Emeralds," is arranged to music by Fauré, from *Pelléas et Mélisande* and *Shylock*. It is danced by two leading couples, three soloists, and a *corps de ballet* of ten girls. There is first of all a *pas de deux* to soft, melodious strings with eight girls accompanying, then a variation for a girl to light, lilting music. This is followed by a dance by the other leading girl. There is a *pas de trois* and then to music of muted strings another *pas de deux*, quiet and alone. All the dancers join in the finale.

To try to describe for you the dances themselves would be boring, for they have no literary content at all. I suppose if this part of the ballet can be said to represent anything at all, it is perhaps an evocation of France, the France of elegance, comfort, dress, perfume.

Others seem to have found the second part, "Rubies," representative of America. I did not have that in mind at all. It is simply Stravinsky's music, which I have always liked and which he and I agreed to use, arranged for a leading couple, a soloist, and a *corps de ballet* of girls and boys. The couple and the soloist alternate in leading the ensemble.

Stravinsky's *Capriccio for Piano and Orchestra* was first performed in 1929, with the composer as soloist. The work is in three movements, *Presto, Andante rapsodico*, and *Allegro capriccioso ma tempo giusto*. In naming this piano concerto *Capriccio*, Stravinsky relates in his *Chronicle* that he was thinking of definitions of a *capriccio* given by Praetorius: "he regarded it as a synonym of the *fantasia* which was a free form made up of *fugato* instrumental passages."

"Diamonds," the final part of the ballet, is danced to Tchaikovsky's *Symphony No. 3 in D major*, which has five movements. I did not use the first movement, which is not really suitable for dancing, and concentrated on the remaining four, which include two scherzos, a slow movement, and a superb polonaise. This ballet is arranged for a girl and her partner, a group of soloists, and a large *corps de ballet*. The movements are marked: 2. *Alla tedesca, Allegro moderato a semplice*; 3. *Andante elagiaco*; 4. *Scherzo, Allegro vivo*; and 5. Finale: *Allegro con fuoco (tempo de Polacca)*. The first is danced by twelve girls and two soloists, the second is a *pas de deux* for the two principals, the third an ensemble with variations for the two principals, and the finale a polonaise for the entire group of thirty-four dancers.

Dancers in our ballets are always changing and sometimes I change the dances, too. April 30, 1976, I made some new ones for the "Emeralds" part of *Jewels*. Violette Verdy and Jean-Pierre Bonnefous were the dancers.

JINX

Ballet in one act. Choreography by Lew Christensen. Music by Benjamin Britten (Variations on a Theme by Frank Bridge). *Scenery by James Stewart Morcom. Costumes by Felipe Fiocca. First presented by Dance Players at the National Theatre, New York, April 24, 1942, with Janet Reed, Lew Christensen, and Conrad Linden in principal roles. Revised and presented by the New York City Ballet at the City Center, New York, November 24, 1949, with Janet Reed, Francisco Moncion, and Herbert Bliss in leading roles.*

Jinx is a dramatic ballet about superstition, in particular a superstition that comes to dominate the lives of performers in a small circus troupe. The setting for the ballet is simple. Two white poles on either side of the stage reach up toward the center of an invisible tent. The back curtains are drawn aside slightly for an entrance to the circus ring. Gaily colored performing boxes stand in a pile on the left, and in the center of the stage, on top of one of these boxes, stands a young girl dressed in pink. Sitting at her feet is a young bareback rider who obviously admires her. He takes the girl's hands and turns her in arabesque slowly, as if they were performing before a quiet but attentive imaginary audience. He lifts her down, and the two change places. From above, he supports the girl as she continues her modest display. Then he pulls her up to him, and they embrace warmly but gently. They sit together for a moment, and the boy goes off.

A clown enters on the right and watches the girl. She does not notice his presence, but it is apparent that he, too, admires her. He dances for a moment, assuming attitudes that make him appear grimly sad, rather than pathetic. The girl gets up to leave, the clown approaches her, and she accidentally runs into him. He catches her before she can fall and holds her in his arms, but only for an instant, for the girl breaks away in terror at this intimacy and runs off. Two men, the ringmaster of the troupe and one of the wire walkers, have come in quietly and observed this scene with interest.

Three girls enter as these men turn and leave the ring. Two of the girls are bareback riders and they go through a rehearsal of their act. The grotesque clown joins the wire walker and the boy whom we saw first on the stage, and the three men turn cartwheels in a vigorous athletic routine. In the middle of one of their tricks, the clown bumps into the boy and he falls. The wire walker helps him up and looks long and suspiciously at the clown. From this point on, the clown is Jinx to the whole troupe.

The ringmaster runs in, and, at a flourish of his whip, the company goes into an ensemble dance. They all exit, and through the entrance to the ring walk three girls in long capes. Their backs are to the audience. One by one, they turn and perform brief specialty numbers. The first girl drops her cape, to be revealed as the Tattooed Lady; the second is the muscled Strong Lady; and the third girl, the Bearded Lady, conceals her face as long as possible with a large orange ostrich feather. They dance together briefly, put their capes back on as if they were great ladies, and walk off in a stately fashion.

Next the bareback riders put on their act. The ringmaster stands in the center, and around and around him the two girls and the boy ride their imaginary horses. They finish and bow. Now Jinx is rolled in on a wheelbarrow, where he sits smelling a bouquet of rotten flowers and vegetables. The wire walker presents parasols to his two female partners, and in a straight line across the stage each does a turn on an imaginary wire. The lovely young girl in pink displays her skill first. Jinx climbs up on the boxes to watch her performance more closely. The girl is nervous at his nearness, but finds reassurance in the presence of the boy she loves, who stands at the other end of the wire. Jinx cannot take his eyes off her; after each of the wire walkers has done a turn and the three have begun their finale, his attention grows intense. Suddenly the girl slips and begins to fall. She is caught in the nick of time, and Jinx rushes to comfort her. He touches her, and the frightened girl jerks away from him. The bareback rider takes up the ringmaster's whip and chases Jinx out of the ring.

Now the entire troupe is thrown into confusion and terror. Jinx runs in. The boy is cracking the whip close behind him. They run around the group at top speed until Jinx stumbles and falls. The boy brings his whip down on him, lashing the clown over and over again to rhythmic chords from the orchestra. The troupe steps back and turns away in horror as the clown curls up in agony, straightens out, and, with a final spasmodic tremble, dies. The Bearded Lady comes to him and grieves for him in a slow dance that reveals her pathetic attachment. The Tattooed Lady and the Strong Lady try to comfort her, but she is inconsolable. The boy brings in the wheelbarrow, and when Jinx is placed on it, the troupe forms a procession. They march slowly behind the body, bowing their heads rhythmically. When they have placed the body high up on the boxes, the Bearded Lady collapses and all bow their heads.

The music now becomes ghostly. The company senses that something is wrong and turns to look at the body. It is not there. They separate the boxes and take them down, but Jinx has disappeared. As they gesticulate in astonishment, Jinx enters from the other side of the stage, where they cannot see him. He walks stealthily to pick up the forgotten whip and cracks it at the feet of the boy. Everyone turns and steps back in fright. Jinx follows them and, cracking the whip in the center of the ring, forces them to dance around him. He urges them to dance faster and faster, and gradually the whole troupe collapses from exhaustion. Jinx then revives them with a beseeching gesture, and all leave the stage but the boy and the girl. The boy holds the girl up and lifts her high over his head, but she cannot stand by herself. She stands on point for a moment, but falls forward over his supporting arm in an attitude of complete and pathetic helplessness. The boy himself loses his strength and dies. Jinx takes the girl's hands to claim her, but at his touch she, too, expires, falling across her lover's body. The rest of the circus troupe has come in and looks on this scene with dread. The clown turns and stares at them intently without moving. A jinx is something you cannot kill, he seems to say, and the curtain falls slowly.

JIVE

Music by Morton Gould. Choreography by Eliot Feld. Costumes by Wilma Kim. Lighting by Jennifer Tipton. Conducted by Seymour Lipkin. Clarinet solo: David Weber. First presented by the Joffrey City Center Ballet at the City Center, New York, February 21, 1973.

The name of the ballet and its four parts—*Warm-up, Blues, Rag,* and *Ride-out* —says all that needs to be said in words about a new dance piece that mirrors not only its music—Morton Gould's *Derivations for Clarinet and Band*—but aspects of the world as young people are observed in it. The light is bright at the start as eight couples in brilliantly dyed shirts and tights/stockings warm up in tennis shoes. There is a kind of challenge in the air. Team against team. After a romantic blues piece for three couples in a cool, impassioned dance, the mood brightens to a syncopated *Rag* for three other couples. The finale, *Ride-out,* for the whole company, features mock heroics to the clarinet and knees set vibrating by the music. The dancers shout exultantly at the end.

NOTES Writing in *The Village Voice,* the critic Deborah Jowitt said that *Ride-out* "is the best moment in the ballet—a phrase with quaking knees, a rock to one side, a big scooping leg gesture that leads into a turn, and I forget what else. It looks wonderful, as if the dancers are trying to keep their balance, and their cool, on a slippery log."

After the premiere, Clive Barnes wrote in the New York *Times:*

"Mr. Feld's use of rhythm is subtle and humorous, and he has never been so happy with it as here. He takes Mr. Gould's lightly jazzy music, and rides it out with dances of remarkable fluency. It is almost like an improvisation, except that improvisations are rarely lucky enough to look like improvisations.

"Mr. Feld has not worked very much in the jazz-dance idiom before, but here he does show a new talent.

"The dancing was very hip and hep. Pamela Nearhoof, who is really becoming a most interesting dancer, had her best chance so far. And, dancing with Christian Holder, especially in the 'Blues' section, she had a lovely and flip elegance. She moves her hips beautifully, and has a lovely slow smile.

"In addition to these two—for Mr. Holder is also exuberantly effective— probably Rebecca Wright and Gregory Huffman were the most prominent, and they were both joyous and relaxed. But the whole company does this sneakers tribute to time past with a Saturday-night high school gymnasium fervor. The dancers pick up Mr. Feld's style and carry it."

JOB

Masque for dancing in eight scenes. Music by Ralph Vaughan Williams. Choreography by Ninette de Valois. Book by Geoffrey Keynes. Scenery and

costumes by Gwendolen Raverat. Wigs and masks by Hedley Briggs. First
presented by Camargo Society at the Cambridge Theatre, London, July 5,
1931, with Anton Dolin as Satan and Stanley Judson as Elihu. First pre-
sented in the United States by the Sadler's Wells Ballet at the Metropolitan
Opera House, New York, November 2, 1949, with scenery and costumes by
John Piper. Robert Helpmann was Satan and Alexis Rassine was Elihu.

The subtitle of this ballet, *Being Blake's Vision of the Book of Job,* tells us that
this "masque for dancing" is based on the *Illustrations to the Book of Job* that
William Blake published in 1825. The ballet's book is based directly on Blake's
twenty-one engravings, as is its music; and the choreography, in its groupings
and tableaux, aims at a projection of Blake's imagination into the theatre.

SCENE ONE   Before a decorative back cloth Job sits with his family in a
group on the right. With him are his wife, his seven sons, and three daughters.
Job is content, materially prosperous, with no complaint in the world. He and
his wife watch as his children—first the boys, then the girls, then all together—
perform a light pastoral dance which symbolizes in its ordered balance and
harmony the respect and love that bind the family together.

Night begins to fall. The family gathers about Job, and he gives thanks
on this day for his earthly blessings. His children pray with him. There is no
servility in their attitude toward their father. Prayer is natural to them as it is
to him. Job and his wife bid the children good night, and the parents are left
alone. They sleep.

Satan enters. His spirit hovers over Job and his wife, and their sleep is disturbed. Satan invokes evil dreams for this good man and his wife, appealing to
heaven that Job's faith be tested. As Satan makes his appeal, heaven is
depicted before us by a broad, high flight of steps at the top of which sits the
Godhead, Job's spiritual self. The children of God dance before the Godhead,
moving between him and Satan, who rests below. The Godhead gestures toward Satan, to include him in his family, but Satan will not be one of them.
He proposes to Job's spiritual self that Job's material self be tested by temptation. The Godhead consents, and Satan, satisfied, leaves the scene, which
darkens as the children of God pay homage to their king.

SCENE TWO   When the lights come up, the scene again is heaven. Satan is
alone, standing before the throne of the Godhead. Delighted with the opportunity to tempt the faithful Job, he commences a triumphant dance, demoniac in
its impudent power, frightening in its strength. His dance over, he leaps to the
throne. His leg coils beneath him and he looks out over the scene gloatingly.
We think of Milton's lines:

High on a Throne of Royal State, which far
Outshon the wealth of Ormus and of Ind,
Or where the gorgeous East with richest hand
Showrs on her Kings Barbaric Pearl and Gold,
Satan exalted sat . . .

The children of Job enter, observe Satan in his exaltation, and gather together in a group, anticipating the trouble to come.

SCENE THREE   We return to the first scene, but now we see Job's family as Satan would wish us to see it. Job's sons and their wives and his daughters are wining and dining in an evil bacchanal, yielding to temptations of the flesh. Satan descends from the throne he has usurped and kills the children of Job.

SCENE FOUR   Now we see enacted the terrible dreams that Satan causes Job and his wife to experience in their sleep. Visions of war, pestilence, and famine appear to torment the God-fearing pair.

SCENE FIVE   Satan's worst is yet to come. Three messengers come to Job and dance before him. They inform him of the death of his children and the loss of all his material goods. Satan enters briefly to warn Job of his end and disappears. Three Comforters, insidious creatures of Satan, replace their leader and attempt to insinuate themselves into Job's confidence. They pretend at first to be sympathetic, to grieve with him over his loss, then they rail at him. Job cannot contain his grief and cannot understand that these things can be visited upon him. He rebels, as if crying out, "Let the day perish wherein I was born." He appeals to heaven, but when heaven opens before him, he sees Satan on the throne. Dark angels are gathered about Satan.

SCENE SIX   A handsome young man, Elihu, pure and beautiful in his simple holiness, appears to Job and in a dance indicates to the old man his error in accusing God of injustice. Job comes to see that he has done wrong and comprehends his sin of complacent materialism. Elihu is kind to him. Again Job appeals to heaven, and this time he sees the Godhead on the throne, surrounded by angels.

SCENE SEVEN   Satan reappears before the throne of the Godhead, claiming that Job has failed the test and demanding the fruits of his victory over him. The Godhead orders Satan to come to him. As he draws near to the throne, Satan kneels and kisses his flowing robe. The Godhead will not endure this absurd flattery. He extends his arm, and Satan rises to fall back, full-length, down the great flight of steps tumbling into darkness.

SCENE EIGHT   Again, as in Scene One, Job and his family rest together, but this time—in realization of spiritual, rather than material, wealth—Job blesses his wife and his children with new meaning.

JOURNAL

Music by Burt Alcantara. Choreography by Louis Falco. Décor and costumes by William Katz. First presented by the Netherlands Dance Theatre at the Royal Theatre, The Hague, October 27, 1971. First presented in the

United States by the same ensemble at the Brooklyn Academy of Music,
New York, March 30, 1972.

Journal is a dance narrative with music and words, a collage with a new dimension. The words, like news headlines or quick entries in a diary, punctuate
the action, rising over and above the music and the action, sometimes reflecting the action, sometimes calling attention to a complementary feeling or situation; they do not literally describe it or cogitate it; like *Strange Interlude*, they
accompany the action. The action is about men and women and what they
seem to mean to each other and what they might really mean. The dance en-
deavors to expose, often comically, actual situations that are concealed from
the participants, sometimes by themselves.

NOTES   Deborah Jowitt in the *Village Voice* wrote of *Journal:* "The dancers
engage in monologues, dialogues, bouts of screaming. Some of the material is
autobiographical, and it's all angry. Much of the movement is casual, scram-
bling. Some of it more formal—non-specific but colored by the arguments and
flung by dancers at other dancers as if it were cursing. Many of the dialogues
have to do with male-female bickering, and in one extremely effective final
scene between one couple, other dancers stand for the possessions that she is
taking with her when she leaves. The dancers stumble off with her like good
little animals. The dance is scraps of human hostility jumbled together, spilling
out of the bright, bitter little games Falco has set them. Grownups on a playground, using the swings to bash each other. . . ."

THE JUDGMENT OF PARIS

Music by Kurt Weill. Choreography by Antony Tudor. Scenery and cos-
tumes by Hugh Laing. First presented by the London Ballet at the West-
minster Theatre, London, June 15, 1938, with Therese Langfield as Juno,
Agnes de Mille as Venus, Charlotte Bidmead as Minerva, Antony Tudor as
the Client, and Hugh Laing as the Waiter. First presented in the United
States by Ballet Theatre at the Center Theatre, New York, January 20, 1940.
Scenery and costumes by Lucinda Ballard. Viola Essen as Juno, Agnes de
Mille as Venus, Lucia Chase as Minerva, and Antony Tudor and Hugh
Laing.

This is a comic ballet on a classic theme. Using music from Kurt Weill's
Threepenny Opera, the choreographer has made a clip joint the scene of a
modern version of the judgment of Paris, on who was the most beautiful goddess, Juno, Venus, or Minerva. A besotted customer arrives at a sleazy bar.
Three ladies of the evening try to ensnare him, each doing her own dance. Although, like Paris, he prefers Venus in the end, he is too drunk to give her a
proper prize. The ladies and the waiter pounce upon his wallet as he passes
out.

  The Judgment of Paris has been in the active repertory of the Ballet Rambert for many years, and is regularly presented on its programs of Tudor ballets that also include *Lilac Garden, Dark Elegies,* and *Gala Performance,* other works originally created by the choreographer with this company.

KETTENTANZ

Music by Johann Strauss and Johann Simon Mayer. Choreography by Gerald Arpino. Costumes by Joe Eula. Lighting by Thomas R. Skelton. First presented by the City Center Joffrey Ballet at the City Center, New York, October 20, 1971.

Kettentanz (Chain Dance) is a ballet of six couples who begin the piece, hands joined, to a vigorous *galop* by Strauss. It is Strauss's music (and a finale by his contemporary Johann Mayer) that gives the ballet its character, although it is used here through no sentimental screen of Old Vienna. It is, rather, the zest and energy of the polkas, galops, and other dances that have been used, with gestures of the past, to show new dances of contemporary interest. There are nine dances in all, performed in an unbroken chain: Strauss's *Gitana Galop, Opus 108; Annen Polka, Opus 137; Erste Kettenbrucke Walzer, Opus 4; Eisele und Beisele Sprunge, Opus 202; Chineser Galop, Opus 21; Seuzer Galop, Opus 9; Hofball Tanze, Opus 51; Cachucha Galop, Opus 97;* and Mayer's *Schnofler Tanz.*

NOTES   Writing in *Dance Magazine,* the critic Doris Hering said that "superlatives are the province of second-rate movie critics, but I can't resist one in connection with Gerald Arpino's *Kettentanz.* It is his loveliest ballet. . . . Arpino has soared blithely above the music to create a suite of tender miniatures, all growing out of an opening chain formation and eventually returning to it with the gleaming casualness of a meadow stream filtering through cluster after cluster of brightly nodding flowers."

In the *Christian Science Monitor,* Nancy Goldner wrote of the dances in *Kettentanz:* "They are . . . purely virtuoso essays. As such they are immensely enjoyable . . . as in a pensive duet for Rebecca Wright and Dermot Burke; a bobbing, sprightly exercise in small and quick footwork for Scott Bernard and Glenn White; and a brilliant *Cachucha Galop* for Susan Magno and Miss Wright, a dance that Fanny Elssler made famous about a century ago. . . ."

Reviewing *Kettentanz* in the *Daily News,* Joseph Gale said that the ballet "is one of Arpino's half-dozen or so neoclassical masterpieces. It is folk—perhaps even countryside—Viennese. . . . It is all ravishing—gay, insouciant, tender, frothy, and as is characteristic of Arpino's works of this genre, bravura."

KONSERVATORIET (Conservatory)

Music by H. S. Paulli. Choreography by Auguste Bournonville. First presented by the Royal Danish Ballet at the Royal Theatre, Copenhagen, May 6, 1849. First presented in the United States by the Royal Danish Ballet at the New York State Theatre, 1965. Revived by the City Center Joffrey Ballet at the City Center, New York, February 20, 1969, in a staging by Hans Brenaa, with Barbara Remington, Pamela Johnson, and Paul Sutherland in principal roles. Scenery by William Pitkin.

Most students of ballet are familiar with the name of the great Danish ballet master, Auguste Bournonville, whose work has been familiar to audiences for 150 years. We know it in the dancing of great stars like Erik Bruhn, who was schooled at the academy set up by Bournonville and who has written a book about it. We know it in the repertory of Bournonville's own Royal Danish Ballet and we know it, too, in fortunate revivals like this one of *Konservatoriet* —which is simply the Danish word for what we mean by conservatory, or a place of study.

The place of study here is a school of ballet, where a ballet master is in charge of a group of brilliant pupils. The dance style of the ballet is what Bournonville learned in France from Auguste Vestris, the *premier danseur* of his time. In the setting of an old Paris ballet studio, with crystal chandelier, covered with cloth to protect it from dust, and to the accompaniment of a violinist (the violin, we realize, was the instrument for ballet classes in those days), we watch a ballet master put his students through their paces.

NOTES The fact that *Konservatoriet* is, in fact, the first act of a much longer ballet (called *A Proposal of Marriage Through a Newspaper*) need not divert us, for that ballet tells the story of two girls, Elisa and Victorine, who come to Paris for adventures, beginning with the study of ballet. The ballet master prompts them to show their best form and he, too, shows them what he means by form, by dancing a solo of his own.

Writing of *Konservatoriet* in *Ballet Review* in 1969, Henry Haslam described the work's importance for both history and the present: In this particular work, he said, "could be seen the quintessence of the French school. It was choreographed by Bournonville in 1849 from memories of his stay in Paris more than twenty years earlier as a student of the great Vestris, a brilliant dancer in the age of male supremacy in the ballet world. Bournonville taught the French school of Vestris in his classes in Denmark. One of his students, Christian Johannson, went to St. Petersburg, where his teaching combined with the influence of the Italian school, which was then reintroduced to Paris and western Europe in 1909 by the Diaghilev Ballet. This Russian school is the background of many of the great teachers in America today. But the branch of the French school remained in Denmark, cut off from the mainstream of the dance world until the early 1950s.

"Hans Beck, a pupil of Bournonville who succeeded him as director of the company, was responsible for the revival of *Konservatoriet*. Hans Brenaa, who was dancing under Beck, is one of the foremost authorities on Bournonville and staged *Konservatoriet* this year for the City Center Joffrey Ballet. The ballet was originally in two acts, titled *Konservatoriet or A Proposal by Advertisement*. It had a very complicated plot about dancers and their adventures and flirtations in Paris. It is regrettable that the second act did not survive, for in it was a *can-can*, which was probably one of the first times such a dance appeared on a ballet stage. Only the first act remains, in which the ballet master, Victorine, and Elisa are introduced—the leading roles which still use the names but have lost their distinct characterizations. The scene is a ballet studio, with the ballet master conducting a class that contains a series of *enchaînements* which are exacting both technically and stylistically.

"I was delighted that an American company had obtained *Konservatoriet* for its repertoire, and I applauded Robert Joffrey, artistic director of the City Center Joffrey Ballet, for his decision to have the ballet staged for his company by Brenaa, who is a fine teacher and coach. The dancers were privileged to be able to work with him in a style and technique not part of their background."

LADY FROM THE SEA

Music by Knudage Riisager. Choreography by Birgit Cullberg. Costumes and scenery by Kerstin Hedeby. Lighting by Jean Rosenthal. First presented by Ballet Theatre at the Metropolitan Opera House, New York, April 20, 1960, with Lupe Serrano, Royes Fernandez, and Glen Tetley in the leading roles.

Inspired by Ibsen's play of the same name, *Lady from the Sea* tells the story of Ellida, who loves a sailor. The sailor leaves her and returns to sea. After much soul-searching, Ellida marries a widower, father of two daughters, but feels miserable in her new home. She dreams that she rejoins her sailor-lover at the bottom of the sea. When the sailor actually returns, her husband offers Ellida her freedom, but she does not leave him. The truth is, the sailor, like the sea, represents for her a romantic yearning, an escape from reality.

LAMENT OF THE WAVES

Music by Gérard Masson. Choreography by Frederick Ashton. Costumes by Derek Rencher. Projection sphere by Bill Culbert. Lighting by William Bundy. First presented by the Royal Ballet at the Royal Opera House, Covent Garden, London, February 9, 1970, with Marilyn Trounson and Carl Myers.

The theme of this dramatic dance for a girl and a boy is stated by the choreographer, Frederick Ashton: "Two young lovers are drowned." What we see in the ballet is not only the act of drowning but the reliving in their last moments of the love that has bound the lovers together. Projections and other intricacies of modern stagecraft are used to give an undersea setting. The music is the *Dans le Deuil des vagues* of Gérard Masson.

The English critic Peter Williams wrote in *Dance and Dancers* magazine after the premiere: "As you drown your whole life passes before you. . . . There they are, two lovers gradually floating down to the seabed with their movements already following the undulations, and caught up in the eddies, of the swirling waters. In the flickering shafts of submarine light they recall their love for each other. When they first sink to the floor of the sea they are separated; gradually they reach for each other and then in a series of comings-together they re-enact their moments of tenderness, of passion and of occasional antagonism until they become conscious of a vast flickering sea anemone shape, sinisterly emerging from the glooms, which brings realization of their lack of infinity. They lie down and tremulous waters descend to cover them forever."

THE LEAVES ARE FADING

Music by Antonin Dvořák. Choreography by Antony Tudor. Scenery by Ming Cho Lee. Costumes by Patricia Zipprodt. Lighting by Jennifer Tipton. First presented by American Ballet Theatre at the New York State Theatre, Lincoln Center, New York, July 17, 1975, with Kim Highton, Marianna Tcherkassky, Amy Blaisdell, Nanette Glushak, Linda Kuchera, Kristine Elliott, Hilda Morales, Elizabeth Ashton, Christine O'Neill, Michael Owen, Raymonda Serrano, Charles Ward, Richard Schafer, Clark Tippet, Gelsey Kirkland, and Jonas Kage. Conducted by Akira Endo.

While *The Leaves Are Fading* appears to be a danced recollection of a time past, it soon becomes clear that it might become a future time, too; it is a dance ballet with a definitive program; its inventiveness permits alternative views on final meanings. The music of the piece consists of selections from little-known works by Dvořák: the *Cypresses*, or *Evening Songs;* and other chamber music for strings written in the 1880s, the *String Quartet*, Op. 77, the *String Quartet*, Op. 80, and part of his *Terzetto*.

The critic George Jackson has called this ballet an E. M. Forster novella. The frame of the action of the dance is far simpler than what follows. We are in a wood after summer but before the autumn, when the leaves begin to fade but before they fall. A branch overhead to the right bears leaves that are still dominantly green but give signs of changing with the season. The background of heavy green is also tinged with brown. A woman walks into this wood, a mature person in a long green summer dress. She looks about slowly; we know she is in familiar surroundings. She walks across the scene with a faint kind of recollective introspection and regret and seems to retreat into its shadows. The dancers who follow are perhaps shadows of her own past.

First girls come, eight of them, then four boys, and there is an ensemble of pastoral creatures under a fading sun. There are varying combinations, a young couple dancing in a state of real joy that quiets down a bit, later a brilliant dance by a boy, followed by another ensemble. All of the dancers appear to know each other; the world they inhabit seems to be familiar and the knowing smiles and gestures they make are friendly without being insistent or flirtatious. The girls and boys seem to have special commitments the others acknowledge.

A new girl enters now to dance with a boy to expansively lyric music. The two lovers are so content in their lively, mutual joy that the dance does not pause for sentimental gestures or declarations. Yet there is no rush. The dramatic lifts and large, expressive movements that follow often stop suddenly for thoughtfulness. The entire *pas de deux* appears to be inner-directed, an expression of rapturous feeling rather than a display of brilliantly executed lyricism. Other couples enter. The girl hesitates; she wants to touch the boy's face, but then she notices others are present.

After an ensemble another *pas de deux* follows. This third pair of lovers dance their own tender commitment, a dance brief but full, too, of effulgent happiness. At the close of their dance, the girl greets another girl who has just come in. She and her partner celebrate their love in a dance that seems to seize on every passing moment. The leaves are fading . . .

In the music for the ensuing ensemble there are certain hints of warning, yet tempered joy dominates. The light darkens. The lovers return, there is a kind of leave-taking, and the woman in green who began the piece comes back. She carries now a red nosegay, looks about the scene again, and, her memories refreshed, goes away.

After the premiere of *The Leaves Are Fading*, the English critic Alexander Bland wrote in *The Observer* that one of American Ballet Theatre's triumphs was "to mount a new Tudor ballet after many years, *The Leaves Are Fading*. Characteristically it was totally uncharacteristic—neither enigmatic nor dramatic but gently charming and lyrical in a wistful English way. To a tuneful Dvořák score young people meet and flirt and part, visions in the memory of an older woman. Deft and fluent, it opens up a fascinating and promising new Tudor vein."

LEGEND OF LOVE

Ballet in three acts. Music by Arif Melikoff. Libretto by Nazim Hikmet. Choreography by Yuri Grigorovich. Scenery and costumes by Simon Virsaladze. First presented at the Kirov State Theatre of Opera and Ballet, Leningrad, 1961.

ACT ONE, SCENE ONE: A ROOM IN THE PALACE OF QUEEN MEKHMENEH BAHNU The queen's youngest sister, Princess Shyrin, is mortally ill and the queen, her attendants, and the vizier are in despair. Warriors usher in a stranger who claims he can cure the princess. When the vizier offers him gold and the queen her crown if he will cure Shyrin, the stranger says no; he demands only that the queen shall sacrifice her beauty to save her sister. She consents and the stranger restores the princess to health. When she rises from the bed she does not recognize her sister the queen, whose face has become disfigured.

ACT ONE, SCENE TWO: THE GARDEN OF THE PALACE A group of artisans, among them a young painter in blue named Ferkhad, are decorating an arch in the garden when the queen, her face now veiled, and the princess enter at the end of a long procession. They are both attracted at once by Ferkhad, and the procession halts as he dances for them. But the vizier orders the work to proceed. The royal attendants dance an ensemble, Ferkhad then emerges alone and the princess calls to him. They are irresistibly drawn to each other and dance a *pas de deux* of mutual praise and joy in which the boy never touches the princess. For he has learned that he has given his heart to a princess and that it is hopeless for him, a humble artisan, to aspire to her hand. She leaves and he lies in the garden, yearning for her.

ACT TWO, SCENE ONE The people of the country, who stand around a spring which has run dry, lament the lack of water in the kingdom. A high mountain must be cut through to bring water to the valley from upland streams, but the task is beyond human effort. Water is brought from afar, but only for the palace, where the queen is tormented by her passion for Ferkhad.

ACT TWO, SCENE TWO The court jester tries to distract the queen, who sits alone. The veiled figure, her body splendid and beautiful, rises and dances in despair. Her face has been disfigured to secure her sister's life and she knows that her love will never be returned by Ferkhad.

ACT TWO, SCENE THREE: SHYRIN'S ROOM Ferkhad enters and he and the princess dance together passionately. The princess decides that she cannot leave her lover and resolves to leave the palace and follow him. Learning of the flight, the vizier informs the queen, who at once orders the lovers to be seized and brought back. Warriors overtake the couple. The princess begs her sister not to separate them but the queen is unrelenting. She holds out one hopeless possibility: that if Ferkhad will succeed in cutting an opening into the mountain so that water might come to the valley, then may Shyrin be his wife.

ACT THREE: THE MOUNTAINS Alone at night, Ferkhad, exhausted from work, imagines that he has succeeded in his task and that water gushes from the mountain. In the flowing water he fancies he sees his beloved. Back in her chamber at the palace, Mekhmeneh Bahnu has lost her peace of mind. In her fevered fantasy, she sees herself as lovely as she was only a short time ago and finds that Ferkhad loves her. But her sister runs into the room, shattering her dream. The princess implores the queen to go with her into the mountains to Ferkhad.

Hope has brought the people to the mountains. If Ferkhad accomplishes his task, their sufferings will end! The queen and Shyrin arrive. Ferkhad is joyous and he and the princess are happy for a brief time. They think that the queen will permit her to remain with him. But the queen is crafty and says that her sister can remain only if Ferkhad abandons the task she has set him. But Ferkhad knows that it is impossible for him to betray the hopes that the people have in him. Shyrin understands this, too. The two lovers dance a *pas de deux* of farewell and part forever.

THE LESSON (*see* THE PRIVATE LESSON)

LIEBESLIEDER WALZER

Music by Johannes Brahms. Choreography by George Balanchine. Scenery by David Hays. Costumes by Karinska. First presented by the New York City Ballet at the City Center, New York, November 22, 1960, with Diana Adams, Melissa Hayden, Jillana, Violette Verdy, Bill Carter, Conrad Ludlow, Nicholas Magallanes, and Jonathan Watts.

"Brahms and waltzes! The two words stare at each other in positive amazement on the elegant title page of the score. The earnest, silent Brahms, a true younger brother of Schumann, and just as north German, Protestant, and unworldly as he—writing waltzes!" So wrote the music critic Eduard Hanslick when Brahms published his first group of *Liebeslieder Walzer* in 1869. Brahms had written them during his first year in Vienna and they were so successful that five years later he wrote a new series. They have been popular ever since, in the concert hall and in the home but most of all at home, for this music for piano, four-hands, and a quartet of voices was perhaps designed for the pleasure of performers. All the *Liebeslieder Walzer* performed together last about an hour, which is a very long time to hold an audience's attention in the theater, especially if the music is all in three-quarter time. But I felt I had to do dances, set to this music. And the music would seem to me the best preparation one can have for watching the dances, unless one wants simply to be naturally surprised at what might happen. What happens on stage is dancing and gesture and music. The setting is a ballroom of an earlier time. There are small tables with candles at the side. A piano stands on the left, a man and a girl in evening dress sit down to play and four singers join them. Four couples in formal dress stand in this ballroom. As the music starts, they begin to dance. The music is a waltz in slow time, the words are about love. The waltz does not last long. Neither does the second, which is more vigorous. It is sung first by the baritone and is then taken up by the other singers. Two couples dance this one, as the others watch. And so it goes, one waltz after another, all different, for changing combinations of voices, for changing couples, for changing aspects of love.

Sometimes friends ask me why we do not print the words to all of these long songs in the program so that everyone will understand the original German. I always answer that the words really have nothing to do with the dances; to print them would suggest that the dances were illustrations and I never had that in mind.

After the eighteenth waltz and the end of Brahms's first group of *Liebeslieder*, the curtain comes down for a few minutes. When it rises again, there is a new setting, still a ballroom, but one without walls and illumined by the stars. The dancers are dressed differently, too, in costumes for ballet dancing. The atmosphere here is more theatrical, if you like, than the intimacy of the first part. So, I think, is the music.

At the end, after fourteen waltzes, the dancers leave the stage. The last song is to words by Goethe:

> Nun, ihr Musen, genug!
> Vergebens strebt ihr zu schildren
> Wie sich Jammer und Gluck
> Wechseln in liebender Brust

(Now, Muses, enough! You try in vain to portray how misery and happiness alternate in a loving heart.)

As these words are sung, the dancers come back and listen. That is all. The words ought to be listened to in silence.

LIEUTENANT KIJÉ

Music by Sergei Prokofiev. Choreography by Alexander Lapauri and Olga Tarasova. Libretto by Andrei Veitsler, Alexander Lapauri, Alexander Misharin, and Olga Tarasova. Scenery and costumes by Boris Messerrer. First presented by the Bolshoi Ballet at the Bolshoi Theatre, Moscow, February 10, 1963.

The ballet began as a historical anecdote about a nonexistent Lieutenant Kijé appearing in the army lists through the oversight of a court official and brought to life by a flourish of the Tsar Paul's·pen. As time went on, promotions and titles were showered on this fictitious character until he rose to the very top rank of the Russian Imperial Army. From this story, Yuri Tynianov, a Soviet writer, devised the plot for a satirical novel. A film of the same name was also produced, with music by Prokofiev, who later made a symphonic suite of his score. The suite and the film music are both used for the ballet.

It is interesting that Prokofiev's music was used by Fokine for his last completed ballet, *Russian Soldier*, presented by Ballet Theatre at the Metropolitan Opera House, New York, April 6, 1942, with Yurek Lazowski in the title role. The ballet was dedicated to the gallant Russian soldiers of World War II.

LILAC GARDEN

*Dramatic ballet in one act. Music by Ernest Chausson. Choreography by
Antony Tudor. Setting and costumes by Hugh Stevenson. First presented
by the Rambert Ballet Club at the Mercury Theatre, London, January 26,
1936. Maude Lloyd, Hugh Laing, Peggy van Praagh, and Antony Tudor
were the principals. First presented in the United States by Ballet Theatre
at the Center Theatre, New York, January 15, 1940, with Viola Essen, Hugh
Laing, Karen Conrad, and Antony Tudor in the principal roles.*

This ballet is a tragedy of manners. It portrays the problem of a young woman
who is about to marry a man she does not love. The time is the latter part of
the Victorian era. It does not occur to the girl that her marriage can be put
off: that she can escape from its "convenience." *Lilac Garden* depicts her mute
acceptance in the kind of world where confession of any difficulty would be
impossible. The drama of the ballet arises from a social situation that seems to
demand confession and release.

The name of the girl is Caroline. She is giving a party for all of her friends
and relations before the wedding. The scene is a lilac garden; the time is evening. The music is Chausson's *Poème*, for violin and orchestra.

When the curtain rises, Caroline and the man she must marry are standing
together in the center of the garden. Giant shrubs of lilac surround the small
open space. The light is misty. The girl wears a long white dress and white
flowers in her hair. Her fiancé wears a formal suit with a long, formal coat
reaching to his knees. There is a boutonnière in his buttonhole. They are a
handsome couple, but each is preoccupied; they seem to have nothing to say
to each other, no gestures to make. The man looks off to the left as if he were
searching for someone. On the right, Caroline's lover enters. As she sees the
man she really loves, the girl motions him away. The dark young man in uniform turns away. Caroline takes her fiancé's arm and they walk off, side by
side. She glances back over her shoulder as they disappear. Another guest arrives at the party, a woman in a slate-blue dress. This is the former mistress of
Caroline's husband-to-be. Other women come onto the scene. Caroline re-
enters. She greets the newcomer. She does not know that this woman loves her
fiancé. Now Caroline is alone. She moves backward toward the right. Her
lover emerges; she falls back against him. He slips his arms under hers, and
the two begin to dance. Their steps are so in harmony that it is apparent they
have danced together many times before. Now the occasion is different.
Caroline nervously looks to left and right whenever they pause in motion.

The woman in blue, her back turned, moves ominously across the back of
the garden. The boy kisses Caroline's hand. The girl draws her hand back
quickly; the woman in blue turns around. Caroline nervously introduces her
two guests. Her hand moves to her lips; perhaps she should have kept them
apart. The three dance forward together. As soon as she dares, Caroline draws

her lover aside, and they dance away. Two men leap onto the stage and exit with the woman in blue.

Caroline re-enters, alone. She dances plaintively to the threnody of the violin's romantic theme. She holds her hand to her forehead in a gesture of hopelessness. As a group of her guests disturb her solitude, the girl moves her hand slightly, pretending that she is smoothing her hair. The melody mounts in intensity. The guests leave as two of the girls are lifted high by their escorts. Caroline pirouettes desperately toward the other side of the garden. Her lover appears while she turns frantically, and he catches her in his arms. He lifts her high above him, then the two kneel together. Then Caroline is afraid, suddenly, and hurries off.

Three couples and a girl come into the garden. Caroline's lover takes the girl for a partner, and the couples separate and bow, preparatory to a formal dance. Caroline disturbs the pattern by entering swiftly and dancing down the line between the couples. She moves off to the right.

The woman in blue joins the couples. She is searching for Caroline's fiancé, her former lover. By common instinct, the other women turn away and leave the garden. The woman bows to Caroline's lover. He turns away and follows the other men off. One man is attracted to the woman and remains until it is apparent that she will not notice him.

Caroline's fiancé steps out into the garden. The woman in blue runs to him, though the man turns aside, afraid to acknowledge her. He catches her as she leaps toward him, and the woman is poised for an instant high over his shoulder, looking down on his head. She has been his mistress, he has loved her, perhaps still does. He wishes to see her, but not here. He releases the woman he has renounced for Caroline, and they move together, mutually fearful of the consequences. The guests rush across the garden, and their rendezvous is interrupted swiftly. In what is apparently a single movement, the woman is lifted high and carried by Caroline's lover as Caroline is caught up in mid-movement by her fiancé.

All the guests dance together in a wide circle, as if nothing had happened. All leave the stage but Caroline and her lover. Her arms are rigid as she falls back into his arms. They dance forward; the music builds to a climax. He lifts the girl up straight and catches her body at full length as he lets her fall. He dips her body gently toward the ground and releases the girl to kneel at her feet.

Two of the older married women at the party see the lovers together. The boy rushes off. One of the women whispers to her companion, revealing Caroline's secret. Now she bows to Caroline. She approaches her softly and takes her hand, and the two move back to the rear of the garden. The woman reassures Caroline by her sympathy for her situation: all women, she suggests, love the man they do not marry. Caroline buries her face in her hands for a frantic instant. This is the first sympathetic advice she has ever received about her lover; she understands, to her horror, the sympathy that she in turn may someday give to someone else. The girl pulls her hands away from her face before she can weep. Caroline walks off.

Her lover re-enters. He gestures after Caroline, his hands clasped before him, hoping. The woman who has befriended Caroline and two other women repeat his gesture, then stand aside with bowed heads as the man sees that he can do nothing. They try to comfort him, but Caroline returns. The women leave the lovers alone. Now the music of the violin piercingly responds to the unhappiness of their passion; their fear that it will be perceived increases. Their ecstasy in being close is destroyed as they turn away from each other curtly and cruelly, lest they be seen. They stand apart, holding hands, as Caroline's fiancé enters. Her lover releases her, and the engaged couple walk away together. Now that all seems to be known, the boy rushes off alone.

The fiancé's former love, the woman in blue, dances into the garden, her movements quick, unyielding, and desperate. She leaves as Caroline and her own lover approach with two other couples. The three couples dance with stilted, subdued steps. The woman in blue tries to approach her lover. Fiercely he motions his former mistress away with his hand. The other couples walk away. He is afraid that Caroline may see, but directly the woman approaches her fiancé, Caroline disappears. The man is desperate: he has lost them both. He follows after the woman in blue, his hand shaking in anxiety.

Caroline and her lover enter and dance frantically, oblivious to their surroundings, and go off together. The entire orchestra takes up the theme of the violin fully. As the music gathers volume, the fiancé enters. The woman in blue leaps to his arms. Caroline and her lover run across the back. When they enter the garden, Caroline's fiancé turns away from the woman in blue and catches Caroline about the waist to lift her high above him. Caroline's arm points straight up over her head; she will not touch him. He lets her down. The other guests have come in; the orchestra sounds the climax of the melody. Caroline's fiancé bends down to kiss her hand. The girl stands beside him in stiff resignation; all movement is frozen: the guests are caught, with the engaged couple, in a tense, frigid tableau.

Caroline is the first to break the spell. Her fiancé stands holding the hand of an imaginary girl as she moves out to her lover; the music subsides. The guests move, the woman in blue approaches the fiancé, and all four lovers move forward in a slow line—Caroline and her lover at either end, reaching out into space. The two couples dance, the rejected lovers moving in unison with Caroline and her husband-to-be. The dresses of the girls flow with their retarded movement.

Suddenly the fiancé walks away. The woman in blue opens her arms. Caroline's lover runs off and returns to present to her a bouquet of lilacs. He kneels and kisses her hand. Caroline holds the flowers listlessly in her hand. Her fiancé returns with her cloak. He places it about her shoulders. The girl in white steps toward her and places her head on Caroline's shoulder in farewell. Caroline gestures to all of her guests, bidding them good-by. The violin mirrors her movement. As she reaches out her hand to her lover, her fiancé draws her hand back to her side. Caroline takes his arm and walks away with the man she must marry. The other guests depart. Her lover remains in the garden, his back turned.

NOTES   *Lilac Garden* was one of the first ballets by the English choreographer and dancer Antony Tudor to be staged in the United States. It immediately became popular and has been so ever since. The New York City Ballet staged a new production of it on November 30, 1951, at the City Center, New York. This production provoked the following remarks from John Martin of the New York *Times:* "*Lilac Garden,* a modern classic, begins a new phase of its existence with the notable restudying it has received. Antony Tudor has given it back its choreographic substance . . . All its esthetic values have been deepened; so, too, have its emotional values. Nora Kaye, who has danced her role many times, has found new warmth, new womanliness, new quiet eloquence of movement and of spirit, and Tanaquil LeClercq, who has never danced the role of the other woman before, illumines it with electric tensions that are taut and tragic. As a crowning glory, Horace Armistead has provided a setting that actually participates in the drama by its subtly authoritative establishment of the mood and the mores of the action."

Alicia Markova, Nora Kaye, Diana Adams, and Alicia Alonso have all danced the part of Caroline. Maria Tallchief danced the part of the other woman in guest appearances with Ballet Theatre in 1949. Tanaquil LeClercq and Yvonne Mounsey danced it in the New York City Ballet revival. Hugh Laing and Antony Tudor resumed their customary roles in first performances of that revival; Tudor's role was danced later by Brooks Jackson.

Dame Marie Rambert, in whose ballet company *Jardin aux Lilas* (*Lilac Garden*) was created, has recalled its beginnings in her book *Quicksilver:* "Tudor wrote *Jardin aux Lilas* in 1936. The subject was suggested to him by Hugh Stevenson, who did a perfect, though obvious, setting of clumps of lilac bushes and beautiful costumes, very expressive of the various characters. Here is the synopsis as printed in the program: Caroline, on the eve of her marriage to the man she does not love, tries to say farewell to her lover at a garden reception, but is constantly interrupted by guests and in the end goes off on the arm of her betrothed with hopelessness in her eyes. The situation is complicated by the presence of her betrothed's former love.

"The interplay of feelings between these characters was revealed in beautiful dance movements and groupings, with subtle changes of expression, which made each situation clear without any recourse to mime or gesture. It could be called a '*ballet psychologique*' on the same ground as Stendhal's '*roman psychologique.*' It had one quite startling moment: at the height of the drama the movement froze and the music continued alone for several bars. It made you hold your breath. The whole ballet was perfect and has become a classic. Although it had been composed on the small stage of the Mercury, it bore transference to the Metropolitan Opera House in New York. In fact, as I have indicated, those of our Mercury ballets that were good became even better on big stages, because the dancers could take wing after the restricted space of our own stage—and the integrity of the work itself shone the brighter."

THE LITTLE HUMPBACKED HORSE

Ballet in three acts. Music by Cesare Pugni. Choreography by Arthur Saint-Léon. First presented at the Bolshoi Theatre, St. Petersburg, December 27, 1864. Revised and presented in a new version at the Bolshoi Theatre, Moscow, 1959. Music by Rodion Shchedrin. Libretto by Vasili Vainonen and Paval Malyarevsky. Choreography by Alexander Radunsky. Sets by Boris Volkiv. First presented in the United States by the Bolshoi Ballet at the Metropolitan Opera with Maya Plisetskaya and Vladimir Vasiliev in the leading roles.

In the Russian repertory for more than a hundred years, this is one of the first ballets to be based on a Russian theme. It has had two major revisions, the first at the turn of the century, by Gorsky, and a new one with an original score that is now in the Bolshoi repertory.

Vigorous chords begin the overture of rousing music. A piping of pastoral music signals the rise of the curtain.

ACT ONE, SCENE ONE: A HUT   Once upon a time there was a peasant who had three sons, Danila, a clever lad, Gavrila, not so bright, and Ivan, a fool. Ivan is lonely as his brothers play with friends. Alone, he plays on his pipe. His brothers ridicule him. The bearded father enters and though the brothers try to exclude Ivan from what he has to say to them—that they must keep watch for a thief who is stealing their corn—Ivan listens and cares.

ACT ONE, SCENE TWO: A FIELD AT NIGHT   Watching and waiting for the thief, the brothers drink and pass out. In the lovely lonely night Ivan enters. He finds his brothers, throws away their bottle, removes their boots and covers them up. He marvels at the stars. As the night draws on, a whirlwind is heard over the field and with it the neighing of a horse. A white horse with a red mane leaps across the sky. Ivan grabs her waving tail and leaps onto her back. She implores him to let her go free. Ivan agrees and in gratitude she gives him two gold-maned horses and a little one, barely six inches high, with two humps on its back and ears down to the ground. She tells Ivan that he can sell the two large horses but must never part with the humpbacked horse, who will be forever his friend. Suddenly, as firebirds fly overhead, one of them drops a feather, which the little horse warns Ivan not to pick up because of the possible trouble it will bring. Ivan ignores the warning and chases it. The two brothers now return to steal the two golden-maned horses and take them off to market. Ivan returns, cannot believe it. The humpbacked horse is sympathetic, gathers up Ivan's brothers' boots, and takes him off into the sky.

ACT ONE, SCENE THREE: A MARKET   A huge walled castle with church spires looks down upon the market place, where an old violinist plays for dancing. The two brothers enter with their horses. Trumpeters and a drummer herald the arrival of the Tsar, who enters on a dilapidated horse followed by an escort. The Tsar sneezes and descends from his horse, but gets tangled up in his cloak. He sees the horses then and is not so ridiculous after all when he admires them and makes an offer. But Ivan arrives at this point with his little humpbacked horse and explains that he is the owner and will take for them two bags of gold, thank you. He returns his brothers' boots and knocks their heads together. The Tsar shows his crown imperiously and, after he has purchased the two horses, makes Ivan chief of his stables. Obviously no one else can handle these curious horses. The Gentleman of the Bedchamber in the Tsar's entourage is angered by this and vows to avenge himself on Ivan.

ACT TWO, SCENE ONE: THE TSAR'S BEDCHAMBER   Trumpets and a drum roll herald the arrival of the Tsar. He eats and sleeps. A fly settles on his forehead and Ivan is the only one who dares to kill it. This naturally annoys the former head groom. One day a Gentleman of the Bedchamber, anxious to discover how Ivan is looking after the horses, goes to the stables and finds the firebird's feather. He steals it and reports Ivan to the Tsar for hiding such a treasure. The old Tsar is fascinated by the feather and, touching a painting of sea birds with the feather, is astonished that they should come alive. He is so delighted that he decides thus to touch the portrait of the maiden-Tsar. She, too, comes to life, but only long enough for the Tsar to fall in love with her. Then she vanishes. That old Gentleman of the Bedchamber, bent always on Ivan's downfall, swears that Ivan has boasted that he can bring her back. The Tsar summons Ivan and gives him an ultimatum to secure her return. Ivan weeps as the Tsar insists, but his little humpbacked horse consoles him.

ACT TWO, SCENE TWO: A SILVER MOUNTAIN BY THE SEASHORE   The little horse takes Ivan to the Silver Mountain, where at night the maiden-Tsar appears in a silver boat. She dances a long quiet variation. At last, with the help of the little horse, Ivan captures her in the midst of her flurried escort of maids. She tries to hide her face in her hands but Ivan takes them away. He is astonished at her beauty and plays his pipe for her. She dances to his music and then they dance together, but the little horse will not permit them to fall in love and interrupts their rendezvous. He lulls the maiden-Tsar to sleep and Ivan sets off with her on the journey to the palace.

ACT TWO, SCENE THREE: THE TSAR'S BEDCHAMBER   We see the Tsar sitting on a high throne, close to a portrait of the maiden, for whom he pines. An announcement is made, he prepares for the arrival of his beloved. The Tsar begs her to marry him but she won't unless a ring she lost in the ocean can be found in three days. Ivan is ordered to find it. Again it is clear that the maiden loves Ivan and is not moved by the Tsar in any way. When the Tsar at the end tries to snatch her hand, she pulls it away.

ACT THREE, SCENE ONE: THE UNDERWATER KINGDOM   The little horse leads Ivan into the kingdom with a silver moon the maiden has given him. Ivan offers the silver moon to the empress of the water sprites in exchange for the ring. She says that only the perch can find it for him but that he is away. While they look for him, the sea creatures amuse Ivan with dances that embody the liveliness of the water kingdom. Ivan is so pleased that he gets down from his sea shell and dances too. Finally the perch is found and brings up a chest with the ring.

ACT THREE, SCENE TWO: THE TSAR'S PALACE   Peasants carrying a suckling pig and other foods prepare for the Tsar's wedding. The Tsar plays hide-and-seek with the maiden, placing the crown at her feet. Ivan enters, greets her, and presents the Tsar with the ring. The Tsar puts the ring on her finger, but it is perfectly clear that she prefers Ivan. She tells the Tsar that she will not marry him unless he can become young and handsome. The Tsar threatens to cut off Ivan's head. The maiden informs the Tsar that he himself can become young and handsome if he will jump into a caldron of boiling milk. The Tsar says no, Ivan must go first. Ivan, emboldened by the promises of the little horse, says all right, takes off his shirt and jumps in. The Tsar is about to claim the maiden as his own forever when Ivan emerges from the caldron. He is handsomer than ever, the maiden adores him more than ever, and the Tsar is so furious that he jumps into the pot himself. He never comes out. The nobility anxiously peer into the caldron but nothing happens. The poor Tsar has been boiled alive.

ACT THREE, SCENE THREE: THE PALACE   Feted by the people, Ivan and the maiden rejoice in their happiness. They welcome the peasants who encircle them and dance in their midst, she in lyric and folk gestures and then he in a variation that ends at her feet. Now the little humpbacked horse enters and brings flowers to the couple as all hail them. He then flies away into the sky.

NOTES   Reviewing the first performance of this ballet in London in 1963, Andrew Porter wrote in the *Financial Times:* "It seems that Vladimir Vasiliev will conquer London on this Bolshoi visit as decisively as Soloviev did on the Kirov one. It is not just that he moves rapidly, jumps high, turns stunningly, lands precisely, has extension, energy, and control. Not just that he is a captivating actor, with a charming presence. It is that all these gifts are contained in a personality that projects itself, unforced, naturally, in a way that tells instantly of a great dancer."

A LITTLE MUSICAL (*see* DUMBARTON OAKS)

LE LOUP

Music by Henri Dutilleux. Choreography by Roland Petit. Book by Jean Anouilh and Georges Neveux. Decor and costumes by Jean Carzou. First presented by Les Ballets de Paris de Roland Petit at the Théâtre de l'Empire,

Paris, March 17, 1953, with Violette Verdy and Roland Petit in the principal roles. First presented in the United States by the same ensemble, January 19, 1954.

Le Loup, a dramatic ballet in several scenes, tells the remarkable story of a young bride who is enchanted by a wolf. This comes about after her husband leaves her for a Gypsy girl; the bride, distraught, imagines that her beloved has turned into a wolf. When she later finds out that she is deceived, she has become so devoted to the wolf that she will not leave him—despite the perils of the hunt, which now confront the wolf, and the opposition of the villagers. He and she are hunted down and killed.

MADRIGALESCO

Music by Vivaldi. Choreography by Benjamin Harkarvy. Costumes by Nicolaas Wijnberg. Lighting by Nicholas Cernovitch. First presented by the Netherlands Dance Theatre July 5, 1963, at Gravenhage. First presented in the United States by the Pennsylvania Ballet at the Walnut Street Theatre, Philadelphia, February 15, 1973, with Alba Calzada and Michael Lucci in leading roles.

A work for twelve dancers, Madrigalesco is named for the first of two concertos by Antonio Vivaldi that accompany the action: the Concerto in D Minor, Madrigalesco, and the Concerto in D Minor, Op. 3, No. 11. The ballet evokes a world of manners, attitudes, and sentiments suggested by various paintings of the Italian Renaissance. The dress of the dancers is formal, as is the way they present themselves, but the situations they suggest have the variety of the extraordinary art they imitate in action.

THE MAIDS

Music by Darius Milhaud. Choreography, based on the play by Jean Genet, by Herbert Ross. Designed by William Pitkin. First presented by Ballet Theatre Workshop at the Phoenix Theatre, New York, May 13, 1957.

Revived in 1969 and 1973 in New York and 1970 in London, The Maids tells a story that was regarded as too controversial for the general public in 1957, when it was first presented. A famous play by Jean Genet, the story involves the contrast between servants and master as a way of looking at a split in the world between the individual and society. The program note, by Jean-Paul Sartre, reads: "Genet suggested the maids be played by two boys, hoping by this device to confuse the audience, and thereby to force upon them that effect of ambiguity which terrorizes the maids. For Genet, theatrical procedure is demoniacal. Appearance, which is constantly on the point of passing itself off as reality, must constantly reveal its profound unreality."

The choreographer took Genet's advice; the two maids, Claire and Solange,

are played by boys. As they act out in effect two different aspects of one servant, the two portray the games of master and servant to which their lives
have become accustomed. In the end these games are intolerable and in what
Clive Barnes has called the "most terrifying death I have ever seen in dance,"
one maid smothers another with a pillow. The charade and self-destructive
slavery of the servant are seen to be, literally, impossible.

NOTES   *The Maids* was revived by Eliot Feld's American Ballet Company in
1969 and by American Ballet Theatre in 1973. It was staged by the Royal Ballet
at the Wimbledon Theatre, London, October 19, 1971. Reviewing a performance of the revival of *The Maids* by American Ballet Theatre (January 16, 1973,
at the City Center, New York), the critic Anna Kisselgoff wrote in the New York
Times: "A superlative performance, danced straight from the gut, was
offered by Daniel Levans and Gayle Young. Mr. Young and particularly Mr.
Levans as Claire consistently caught the fierce desperation and violence of the
Jean Genet play that inspired the ballet. Mr. Levans's characterization—both
his acting and his movements—was always sharp, and its aggressiveness was
appropriate. Mr. Young was properly conspiratorial, and . . . the result was
electrifying and dramatic tension."

MA MÈRE L'OYE (Mother Goose)

*Music and scenario by Maurice Ravel. First staged by Jacques Rouché at
the Théâtre des Arts, Paris, January 28, 1912. First presented in the United
States by the New York City Ballet at the Hommage à Ravel at the New
York State Theatre, Lincoln Center, May 22, 1975. Choreography by Je-
rome Robbins. Costumes by Stanley Simmons. Lighting by Ronald Bates.
Conducted by Robert Irving.*

Jerome Robbins subtitles his ballet "Fairy Tales for Dancers," giving us the
key to his own *Mother Goose.* While Ravel's subtitle to his music's scenario
might be "What the Sleeping Beauty Dreamed," Robbins extends the idea so
that we have "What the Sleeping Beauty as Dancer Dreamed on Stage at the
New York City Ballet." For what this new and fascinating version of Ravel's
script does, in fact, is to take Ravel's wonderful concept of imagining the
dreams of the Sleeping Beauty but to see the Sleeping Beauty *as a dancer* and
all the other characters, too, as dancers who know the old fairy stories so well,
having done them so abysmally often, that finally they have a chance to get
even and to portray the stories as *they* wish. We have not only a fairy story
within a fairy story but the performers' own variations. The dancers, in
Deborah Jowitt's phrase, "look like children who have ransacked the attic to
find costumes and props for a game of charades." The result is a remarkable
entertainment for those who know Ravel's intention, know ballets like *The
Sleeping Beauty* and *The Nutcracker,* etc., and know something of the New
York City Ballet's scenery and costumes. And our dancers, too! *Ma Mère l'Oye*
is an in-house joke for our faithful audiences.

Ravel originally composed his *Mother Goose* as five piano pieces. Later, in 1911, writing a scenario of his own, he added more pieces plus connective transitions. His script, charming and wittily detailed as the score itself, contains delightful invention. To the spellbound Sleeping Beauty (the Princess Florine, a character, of course, in a fairy tale by Perrault) he gives dreams of other fairy-tale characters (also by Perrault or his imitators).

Ravel's script might be summarized as follows:

PROLOGUE   Stories are told, then enacted.

ONE: DANCE OF THE SPINNING WHEEL   The Princess Florine is celebrating her birthday. During the festivities she accidentally pricks her finger on a spindle. According to the curse of the Bad Fairy she now must die. But through the intervention of the Good Fairy, her death is altered into a one-hundred-year sleep from which she will be awakened only by the kiss of someone who loves her. The court prepares her for bed and departs.

TWO   To entertain her during her long sleep, the Good Fairy decides to provide her with dreams, and she evokes for the Sleeping Princess a series of fairy tales:

BEAUTY AND THE BEAST   Beauty breaks the evil enchantment which has changed a prince into a Beast by accepting his love.

HOP O' MY THUMB   An impoverished woodcutter has purposely lost his seven little sons in the forest. Hop o' My Thumb, the youngest, seeks to avoid their fate by leaving a trail of crumbs to lead them back home.

LAIDERONNETTE, EMPRESS OF THE PAGODAS   Cursed by a demon, Laideronnette has been changed into the ugliest woman in the world. Similarly, her paramour, once a handsome young man, has been transformed into a Green Serpent. After bathing in waters whose magical powers they are unaware of, the two are restored to their former selves and all celebrate.

THE FAIRY-TALE GARDEN   The dreams of the Princess are interrupted by the arrival of Prince Charming led by Cupid, who breaks the Sleeping Beauty's spell, and the Prince is happily married to the Princess in the presence of the joyous court and attendant dream figures.

Jerome Robbins in his choreography follows Ravel's script closely but gives it special character within the New York City Ballet ambience. It is of interest that when Jerome Robbins first joined City Ballet, he made his debut in *Mother Goose Suite*, Todd Bolender's ballet, dancing Hop o' My Thumb.

Writing at length of the premiere in *The New Yorker*, Arlene Croce said that in the poetic style of *Ma Mère l'Oye*, Jerome Robbins "returns to those qualities which first defined him as a unique theatre artist."

MANIFESTATIONS

Music by Primous Fountain III. Choreography by Arthur Mitchell. Scenery and lighting by Gary Fails. Costumes by Zelda Wynn. First presented by the Dance Theatre of Harlem at the Auditorium Theatre, Chicago, February 25, 1976.

A modern parable on the Adam and Eve story, *Manifestations* is set in Eden before the Fall. The Serpent is the first to appear, somewhat dramatically as he dangles down from on high to interrupt the action of love below. Adam and Eve nevertheless persist in their impassioned devotion. The wit with which their situation is appreciated not only by themselves but by the Serpent gives character to what John Percival, in the *Times* of London, called a "highly entertaining . . . classical ballet cabaret."

MANON

Ballet in three acts. Music by Jules Massenet, orchestrated and arranged by Leighton Lucas with the collaboration of Hilda Gaunt. Produced by Kenneth MacMillan. Choreography by Kenneth MacMillan. Designs by Nicholas Georgiadis. First presented by the Royal Ballet at the Royal Opera House, Covent Garden, London, March 7, 1974, with Antoinette Sibley, Anthony Dowell, David Wall, and Derek Rencher in principal roles. First presented in the United States by the same ensemble, May 7, 1974, at the Metropolitan Opera House, New York.

Based on Abbé Prévost's great eighteenth-century romantic novel *Manon Lescaut* and not on the famous operas derived from that work, this ballet tells the story of a girl who has much charm but little character. She suffers accordingly, but not before she has brought down with her a lover who persists in finding in her charm a character no one else can see. The choreographer, Kenneth MacMillan, has said that what interested him from the start was Manon's amoral nature, which shifts from scene to scene, and within scenes.

ACT ONE, SCENE ONE takes place in the courtyard of an inn near Paris. The music that introduces it is not the familiar music by Massenet we might expect from that composer's opera to this story; indeed, all of Massenet's music used in the ballet comes from any work of his except his opera *Manon*. This particular inn is frequented by actresses, gentlemen, and the demimonde from Paris; it is artificially gay, a set-up and a snare for the unwary; it is not surprising to find a ratcatcher one of the principal personages in the courtyard. Coaches come and go, depositing pretentious ladies with large muffs who are escorted by gouty gentlemen. In the crowd we begin to distinguish a young man, Lescaut by name, who seems to know what everything is all about and has it all under control; he dances a vigorous solo. After an interlude featuring a bunch of ragpickers, we notice, too, a young divinity student who walks about in a broad-brimmed hat reading, preoccupied with his holy studies. This is Des Grieux, a handsome boy who seems to shun the world. The worldly persons who dominate the courtyard are Lescaut, who is there to meet his sister, Manon, on her way to join a convent, and Monsieur G.M., a wealthy Parisian. A coach arrives bringing Manon and an old gentleman who has been very much attracted to her. Manon is young, about sixteen she seems (as in Prévost), and much dazzled by the bustle of the courtyard. But it is clear that she has the old gentleman under control and shuns his advances. Des Grieux does not notice her, nor she him, at first; he sits reading. Monsieur G.M. does notice her and wants her as much as the old man does; he asks Lescaut to intercede on his behalf and secure Manon's favors for him. Lescaut is happy to oblige and all but auctions his sister off between Monsieur G.M. and the old man. In the midst of this undertaking, Manon is horrified to see a ratcatcher in the crowd. Des Grieux, watching a bit now, moves over to a table on the right, fanning his face with his hat and removing his jacket. He and Manon, both all innocence, watch as a courtesan dances for Lescaut and G.M. Then suddenly Des Grieux has forgotten his book and is staring at Manon. The old man kisses her hand. Des Grieux rises. The old man gives money to Lescaut. Manon is suddenly face to face with Des Grieux. The lights dim; they seem to be all alone; he dances for her, then kneels at her feet and kisses her hand. She is embarrassed, touched, and clearly attracted. To soft strings, he openly adores her. When she rises, he takes her in his arms and they begin to dance together of their growing passion. The dance is cool, detached from its environment.

Manon and Des Grieux, now much in love, decide to escape to Paris with the help of the money she has meanwhile taken from the old gentleman. Lescaut and the old gentleman, having made a bargain about Manon, emerge from the inn. To their dismay, Manon has gone: Des Grieux has mounted the driver's seat in the coach and taken her away. Monsieur G.M., always eager to join the crowd, at this point informs Lescaut that he, too, is interested in Manon. G.M.'s wealth is known to Lescaut, who promises to find his sister and persuade her to abandon Des Grieux and accept the rich G.M.

In SCENE TWO, Lescaut remarkably succeeds. The setting is Des Grieux's rooms in Paris, where he writes a letter, by candlelight, to his father asking him for money. Manon, languishing near the large bed at the left, does not like to be unattended and tries to interrupt her lover. They dance, reassuring each other of the depth of their love. Manon then helps Des Grieux into his overcoat and he goes off to mail the letter. In his absence, her brother, the perpetual fixer, arrives with Monsieur G.M. When the latter presents her with a fine gown and jewelry, it is as if she had never been a sweet sixteen-year-old on the way to any convent. She forgets Des Grieux, although she does hang on to the bed draperies a bit in fleeting recollection. There is a *pas de trois* in which her brother guides the girl and with G.M. swings Manon between them as if she were a toy. Lescaut swings her up to G.M.'s shoulder and, seeing the self-satisfaction that has matured between the two "lovers," asks for payment from G.M.

Manon says "adieu" to the bed and leaves with G.M. while Lescaut jiggles the purse he has received. Des Grieux returns and, sharing the purse with him, Lescaut tries to persuade him that they will all be rich if he, Des Grieux, will sanction the liaison between Manon and G.M. Lescaut is thoroughly in control of this situation and the impoverished Des Grieux consents.

In ACT TWO, the first scene is a gambling house and bordello, a "*hôtel particulier* of Madame.*"* This Madame bustles about in her hall of mirrors and shiftily clad young girls making matches with the men who turn up. It is all *ancien régime* and polite; the men put their swords away upon arrival and even with the raucous music there is an agreed on code of behavior that prevents the expression of true feeling.

Lescaut, drunk, brings in Des Grieux, who is horrified at it all. Lescaut dances brilliantly of his spirited exhilaration and the girls try to close in on Des Grieux. When Manon arrives on the scene with G.M. and finds Des Grieux there, she gradually is seen to be torn between the wealth of her present lover and her recollection of the impetuous youth who saved her from the convent. Wearing a black and gold dress of rich embroidery and brilliant jewelry, Manon dances with her assembled admirers at the party while Des Grieux watches. She is manipulated in the *sarabande* and passed from one man to another as G.M. watches. Finally, she is lifted to G.M. and placed at his feet.

Although Manon is increasingly shattered by Des Grieux's presence and tries to avoid him, he at length tries to persuade her to leave with him. She tells him that the time is not right and engineers an arrangement for Des Grieux to cheat at cards with G.M. Her older lover is highly suspicious, however, and in the midst of the card game catches Des Grieux cheating. Des Grieux and Manon rush away.

In SCENE TWO, back at Des Grieux's lodgings, he and Manon once again declare their love for one another. She touches the curtains of their bed. G.M. interrupts them, however, just as Des Grieux has succeeded in reminding Manon that if she is to stay with him, she must give up the jewelry G.M. has lavished on her. It is precisely the jewelry's return that G.M. in his vengeance seeks. Lescaut is brought in, in handcuffs, and G.M. is triumphant. In the ensuing struggle and her arrest as a prostitute, Manon's brother is killed. Manon and Des Grieux look on in horror. Monsieur, holding Manon's arm, is gleeful.

In ACT THREE, the scene shifts to New Orleans, then a penal colony for the French. In his office, the jailer of the penal colony has a rendezvous with his girl. Two soldiers enter to remind him of certain duties and he leaves for the port.

The port dominates the second scene, busy with the unloading of ships. Cargo and passengers descend onto the dock while the soldiers and natives watch. Many of the exiled prisoners are girls, prostitutes like Manon, who lament their lot in a dance. Yet the jailer flirts with them and, above all, with Manon, who enters with Des Grieux. The jailer's girl despairs of her lover and tries to deflect his attention from the new riffraff from France, but the man persists and she is dragged away by his soldiers. Manon is also taken away to his room. Here the jailer, strangely drawn to this pathetic emaciated creature who has seemingly lost all her charm, is completely captivated. He is a displaced G.M. all over again and can offer her much. The dance he compels her to perform is done passively on her part and she appears to despise the man. He does not notice, however, and places a bracelet on her wrist in gratification. Des Grieux enters and stabs him. Manon throws the bracelet on the jailer's body and flees with Des Grieux.

Trying to escape capture, the lovers hide in a swamp, where mists and menacing foliage envelop their passage. Exhausted from their flight, Manon and Des Grieux rest. In a kind of delirium, the girl recalls her past and sees it travel in the mist before her—the jailer, the Madame of the bordello, the ratcatcher, G.M. Roused by her delirium, Des Grieux tries to comfort her. The two perform an impassioned dance in which Manon seeks a comfort as yet unknown; in a turmoil of abandonment, she is flung high into the air and spins there hysterically, only to be caught again in her lover's arms. All her former notions of wealth and splendor have been renounced for her love for Des Grieux. As she gradually expires, the demented man tries to revive her and to prop her up, but he cannot succeed. She has given up the ghost and Des Grieux laments.

NOTES   The music for *Manon* by Massenet, arranged by Leighton Lucas and Hilda Gaunt, is taken from the operas *Le Cid, Griselda, Thérèse, Cinderella, Cléopâtre, Don Quixote, Eve, Thaïs, Bacchus, Ariane,* and *Le Roi de Lahore,* the orchestral works *Scènes alsaciennes, Scènes pittoresques, Scènes dramatiques, La navarraise, Valse très lente, Chanson de Capri,* and *Aubade de Chérubin.*

The music for the Prelude to the ballet is from *Le dernier sommeil de la Vierge* and the *Cantata de la Vierge.* The score for Act One, Scene One is derived from *Aubade de Chérubin, Scènes dramatique, Scènes pittoresques, Le Cid, Crépuscule, Pastorale* from *L'esclaramonde, First Orchestral Suite, Scènes dramatiques, Si tu le veux, mignonne*—a song, *Griselda, Thaïs, Ariane, Élégie, Menuet d'Amour* from *Thérèse.* Act One, Scene Two: *Cendrillon, Ouvre tes yeux bleus*—a song, *Cendrillon,* and a salon piece.

Act Two, Scene One: *Scènes dramatiques, Au Cabaret—Scènes alsaciennes, Ariane, Bacchus,* a salon piece, *Don Quixote, Cléopâtre, Le Roi de Lahore, Crépuscule, Air de ballet, La navarraise, Élégie, Il pluvait*—a song, *Griselda, Cléopâtre.* Scene Two: *Adam and Eve, Bacchus.*

Act Three, Scene One: *Cendrillon, Griselda, Don Quixote, Cendrillon, Don Quixote, Don Quixote, Crépuscule, Sappho,* and *Adam and Eve.* Scene Two: Symposium of hallucinations. Scene Three: *La vierge, La vierge.*

Interviewed in *The New Yorker* in 1974 about *Manon,* Kenneth MacMillan said: "The characters fascinate me. You have a sixteen-year-old heroine who is beautiful and absolutely amoral, and a hero who is corrupted by her and becomes a cheat, a liar, and a murderer. Not exactly our conventional ballet plot, is it? One of the intriguing things about Prévost's Manon is that there doesn't seem to be any logic in the way she thinks. One minute, she tells Des Grieux that she loves him, the next minute she's deceiving him with an elderly count. My clue to her behavior is her background of poverty. Manon is not so much afraid of being poor as *ashamed* of being poor. Which brings me to the other theme of the ballet—the contrast between great wealth and great poverty in eighteenth-century France. . . ."*

MARGUERITE AND ARMAND

Ballet in one act. Music by Franz Liszt, orchestrated by Humphrey Searle. Choreography by Frederick Ashton. Scenery and costumes by Cecil Beaton. Lighting by William Bundy. First presented by the Royal Ballet at the Royal Opera House, Covent Garden, March 12, 1963, with Margot Fonteyn, Rudolf Nureyev, Michael Somes, and Leslie Edwards in the principal roles. First presented in the United States by the Royal Ballet at the Metropolitan Opera House, New York, May 1, 1963, with the same principals. Present orchestration by Gordon Jacob.

This dramatic ballet in four scenes and a prologue is Frederick Ashton's version of *The Lady of the Camellias* by Dumas *fils*, the famous novel about a Parisian courtesan, beautiful but fatally consumptive, who renounces her lover to save his reputation. The dance narrative is so arranged that in the last stages of her fatal illness Marguerite relives some incidents of her tragic life. The music is an orchestration of Liszt's *Sonata in B minor*.

In the Prologue, as Marguerite lies dying, she looks back in her delirium on her life with Armand. Huge projections of the two lovers are thrown against the background to the scene, and we see in a series of flashbacks her recollections. Meanwhile, Armand enters and moves like a distracted mourning spirit before visions of his life with Marguerite. When she sees his face in her fever she reaches out frantically and tosses in agony on her couch. Then, in a moment, through a gauzy curtain their time together is recaptured realistically on stage: on the same couch Marguerite sits in a stunning red dress, camellias at her breast and in her hair, surrounded by a group of admirers. As the orchestra sounds fully a major theme of Liszt's sonata, Armand enters, handsome, excited, intense. Marguerite is interested in him at once. The duke, her present lover and protector, watches with the others as Armand kisses her hand. The two begin then to dance. It is a dance of gay abandon with an undertone of seriousness. She coughs suddenly but it is only a passing thing. They are alone briefly, the others returning just as she falls back into Armand's arms. The duke angrily breaks in, takes her away; as she leaves, Marguerite tosses a camellia to the floor near Armand. Another man starts to pick it up but sees Armand's interest. Armand takes it and dashes off.

In a flash it is spring; the two lovers are living an idyllic life in the country. They dance joyously. Armand then goes off riding and Marguerite sits alone in lovely profile, contemplating a happiness she had not thought possible. Just then his father enters. The music portends his stern moral character. He bears down on her insistingly, but Marguerite is so astonished that she does not at

* From "MacMillan's Manon" by Jane Boutwell in "The Talk of the Town." Reprinted by permission; © 1974 The New Yorker Magazine, Inc.

first understand what on earth he can be saying. Then in agony, she comprehends: she must give up Armand, free him for the life his father wants. She prays, beseeches the father not to make such a demand, but he is unrelenting. The music quiets, she sits exhausted on the couch, touches a pillow, tries to rise but falls fainting almost into the father's arms. She seems then to gather courage; her body, her forced posture, suggest that, but this crumbles in a moment and she pursues the father to relent. He exits. She takes to her bed and when Armand returns she hides her face from him. But they dance, this time with savage passion; he flings her body about him again and again and faster and faster. He sits on the couch and she is at his knee. He lies back and she joins him, but of a sudden she rises and rushes out in a flurry of movement. Blackout.

The lights are on again in a moment and we are in another room with candelabra. The duke escorts Marguerite into the room, she in diamonds and a black dress with a spray of camellias on velvet at her skirt. She goes quickly to the couch. She coughs and it is apparent that she is now seriously ill. Armand enters, shocked at finding her again in such a place and she shocked that he should see her so. He tears off her diamond necklace and flings it away. She tries to flee but he throws money in her face. He stands there, gesturing desperately, seemingly cleansing himself of her, and she cannot bear it. Armand's father enters. Marguerite quivers but rejects the father's help.

In the final scene a nurse and Armand's father are in Marguerite's apartment. He tries to comfort Marguerite. She begins in her fever to see only Armand, who runs in in a black cloak. He seizes his beloved in ecstasy. They kiss and she on hobbled point is lifted up, swimming in a kind of final hope as she dies. Armand places her on the floor. His father turns his back as his son in anguish lifts Marguerite's hand uncomprehendingly. It falls away from him to the floor.

NOTES   Reviewing *Marguerite and Armand* in the *Times* of London, Clive Barnes said that "the swiftness of the ballet gives it an hallucinatory quality and sense of flying passion, of a tragedy fitfully illuminated by flashes of Keats' 'spangly doom' . . . Here is the true Romantic agony distilled into a brief ballet, far more pungent in its effect than any *Giselle*." Writing in *Dance and Dancers*, Barnes said of the performances: "For Fonteyn, like Ashton, ever expanding and developing, this role is something new. It shows as never before Fonteyn the dance actress . . . The power she first tested out in *Ondine* and later in *Giselle* is here seen at full-stretch . . . Even to a greater extent than Fonteyn's Marguerite, Armand is derived from Nureyev . . . He has never been seen to such advantage in the West . . . He goes through *Marguerite and Armand* like a fiery arrow shot by destiny. The wild theatricality of Nureyev, the charge he can give the simplest pose or movement, the impact of his dancing, are used to telling effect."

The critic Dale Harris has written a long essay of great interest on Margot Fonteyn's career in *Ballet Review* (Vol. 4, No. 6). The essay, "Snowflake to Superstar," reviews the book *Fonteyn: The Making of a Legend* by Keith Money (London, 1973). Margot Fonteyn has since written her own book, *Au-*

tobiography (London and New York, 1976). Reviewing the volume in the New York *Times*, the critic Anna Kisselgoff said that "in the future it can be said that Dame Margot Fonteyn wrote the way she danced. Her autobiography has the same attention to form, interlaced with emotion, as her most memorable performances."

MEADOWLARK

Music by Franz Joseph Haydn. Choreography by Eliot Feld. First presented by the Royal Winnipeg Ballet, October 3, 1968, at the Manitoba Centennial Concert Hall, Winnipeg, Canada. First presented in the United States by the American Ballet Company at the Brooklyn Academy of Music, New York, October 23, 1969, with scenery by Robert Munford, costumes by Stanley Simmons, and lighting by Jules Fisher. The principal dancers were Elizabeth Lee and John Sowinski, Christine Sarry and Richard Munro, Olga Janke, Edward Verso, and Alfonso Figueroa. Conductor: Christopher Keene.

A dance ballet to music by Haydn (selections from the flute quartets arranged and orchestrated by Hershy Kay), *Meadowlark*, like its title, suggests a perpetual spring of good humor, competition, and love. The ballet is in seven parts, the first three a series of *pas de deux*. The backdrop, a huge watercolor of flowers, cliffs, and the sea in the distance, evokes the pastoral atmosphere of warmth and otherworldliness that the dances make specific in their different ways. Pledges are made, possibly serious betrayals seem imminent, consolations are promised, and there is gentle mockery of useless lamentation in other dances. The girls are courted, one of the boys is disappointed, and there are some humorous regrets. Civilized behavior sets everything in order and a varied, complex finale brings the ballet to a joyous finish for all concerned.

Meadowlark was produced by Festival Ballet at the Hippodrome, Bristol, England, December 9, 1968, and by the City Center Joffrey Ballet at the City Center, New York, in 1972.

Readers who wish to know more about the early work of Eliot Feld will wish to read the book *At the Vanishing Point*, by Marcia B. Siegel. She wrote: "He is important because he is the first choreographer of this generation to break with the idea that ballet is about another world—a universe peopled with invincible beautiful beings who are possessed of superhuman powers. Feld's ballet is about this world."

MEDEA

Music by Béla Bartók, orchestrated by Herbert Sandberg. Choreography by Birgit Cullberg. First presented by the Royal Swedish Ballet at the Princes Theatre, London, February 12, 1951. First presented in the United States by the New York City Ballet at the City Center, New York, November 26, 1958, with costumes by Lewis Brown, lighting by David Hays. Melissa Hay-

den (Medea), *Jacques d'Amboise* (Jason), *and Violette Verdy* (Creusa) *danced the principal roles.*

Based on the Euripides drama, *Medea* tells the classic story of the revenge of the beautiful Medea, skilled in magic, for her husband Jason's desertion. Medea murders the two children she has had by Jason and slays his new wife Creusa with a poisoned garment. The music is thirteen piano pieces by Bartók, arranged by Herbert Sandberg.

The ballet is in five scenes. In Scene I, Medea and Jason lie together with their two children. They play with the children. Before the happy family interlude is over, however, Jason is attracted by the beauty of Creusa, daughter of Creon, King of Corinth, and follows her. Jason woos Creusa in Scene II and their romance is approved by Creon. Medea in Scene III hears of Jason's faithlessness. He returns to ask her forgiveness but she rejects him. Jason returns to Creusa. In Scene IV he is married to Creusa in Creon's palace. Medea enters, feigning homage to the bride, and presents her with a crown of gold and a rich veil. Admiring these gifts, Creusa puts them on. She dies thus attired, for the gifts are poisoned, and Jason will not have a new bride. In the final scene, the grief-stricken Jason returns to his home and attempts to take his children. Medea drags them into the house and, while a crowd rages outside, kills them.

MEDITATION

Music by Peter Ilyich Tchaikovsky. Choreography by George Balanchine. Costumes by Karinska. First presented by the New York City Ballet at the New York State Theatre, December 10, 1963, with Suzanne Farrell and Jacques d'Amboise.

Meditation is a dance for two people, a dramatic *pas de deux* rather than a formal *divertissement*. The drama is the music, one of a set of three pieces for violin and piano, Opus 42, No. 1, by Tchaikovsky, orchestrated by Glazunov. I called the piece *Meditation* because it is contemplative. The Tchaikovsky music is thoughtful too. A friend of mine once called the dance very sad and very Russian. He said he thought there was a kind of pleasure in unhappiness in it, what he called a kind of Russian pleasure. I disagree, although there is of course pleasure and happiness in meditation.

MEDITATION FROM "THAÏS"

Music by Jules Massenet. Choreography by Frederick Ashton. First presented by the Royal Ballet at a gala performance at the Adelphi Theatre, London, March 21, 1971, with Antoinette Sibley and Anthony Dowell. Costumes by Anthony Dowell. First presented in the United States by the Royal Ballet with the same cast at the Metropolitan Opera House, New York, 1972.

A dramatic *pas de deux*. The *Meditation* is set to music used at one time by Anna Pavlova's company. It is a romantic work, typified by the unveiling of a quasi-Oriental figure by her admirer soon after their entry. He adores her, displays his love in splendid thrusts of his lady into the air, daringly, only to catch her with dashing courage. David Vaughan, in his biography of Frederick Ashton, says that no matter what her position, the heroine "had to be like a disembodied weightless spirit."

MENDELSSOHN SYMPHONY

Music by Felix Mendelssohn. Choreography by Dennis Nahat. Costumes and scenery by Peter Farmer. Costume supervision by David Guthrie. Lighting by Nananne Porcher. First presented by American Ballet Theatre at the New York State Theatre, Lincoln Center, July 19, 1973, with Martine van Hamel, Fernando Bujones, and Ian Horvath in leading roles.

This dance ballet was designed to the music of Mendelssohn's *Italian Symphony* (*No. 4 in A Major*, Op. 90), a popular work in the concert hall that serves equally well as a base for dancing. The scene is abstract—a colorful perspective that stretches into the distance—and the costumes are not suggestive of any time or place. These dances to this music are the subject.

The first movement, *Allegro vivace*, is performed by twelve girls, who develop the several lively themes and fantasia. Six of them remain at the end, to be supported by six boys in the *Andante*. In their midst, a girl emerges to lead the dance in this somewhat mournful and dejected sequence (the second movement of this symphony has been called the "Pilgrims' March"). She dances alone to the melancholy music, others return, and the dance ends as a boy in white enters to hold her in a final submissive pose.

The boy remains for the sweetly singing third movement, a minuet and trio (*Con moto moderato*). The lights dim and the temper is thoughtful, introspective, as the dancer explores his gifts of accent, rhythm, and line to the graceful flow of sound. The finale is a bright *saltarello*—a characteristic Roman dance, like the Neapolitan *tarantella*, in triple time, performed by another boy who leads the entire cast to a flourishing finale.

MESSE POUR LE TEMPS PRÉSENT

A ceremony in nine episodes. Percussion and sound effects under direction of Maurice Béjart, with special composition by Pierre Henry. Choreography by Maurice Béjart. First presented by the Ballet of the Twentieth Century at the Avignon Festival, August 3, 1967. First presented in the United States by the same ensemble at the Brooklyn Academy of Music, New York, January 27, 1971.

This *Mass for Today* has as its motto a quotation from Nietzsche: "I could only have faith in a God who knew how to dance." Its theme is love, militarism, alienation. Perhaps its most famous part, *The Jerk,* with rock music by Pierre Henry, energizes its dancers into a frenzy of display. The remainder of the ballet, which occupies the whole evening, recapitulates in dance terms "the history of the West in the past thirty years."

METAPHORS

Music by Daniel-Lesur. Choreography by Hans van Manen. Scenery and costumes by Jean-Paul Vroom. First presented by the Netherlands Dance Theatre at The Hague, Holland, December 6, 1965. First presented in the United States by the Dutch National Ballet at the Minskoff Theatre, New York, November 9, 1976.

A dance ballet set to the *Variations for Piano and Orchestra* of Daniel-Lesur, *Metaphors* had been popular in Europe for some years before it was first introduced to America. The ballet has a basic theme that we begin to discern as the dance progresses—everything is in twos, two groups, two soloists. No dancer stands alone and a preoccupation with duality and duplication emerges. Two couples dominate the piece, first two sets of a girl and a boy and then a dance for the two boys. They dance a *pas de deux* very much in the classic style of reliance and support, dependence and strength. This is followed by a duet for the girls and other combinations in which soloists and groups reflect each other. The music is bright and the accent sharp but occasionally lyrical. Everything is good-humored but we take seriously the suggestion in the dualities depicted that mutual help and respect are essential aspects of living as well as performing.

A MIDSUMMER NIGHT'S DREAM

Ballet in two acts and six scenes. Music by Felix Mendelssohn. Choreography by George Balanchine. Scenery and lighting by David Hays. Costumes by Karinska. First presented by the New York City Ballet at the City Center, New York, January 17, 1962, with Arthur Mitchell as Puck, Jillana as Helena, Edward Villella as Oberon, Melissa Hayden as Titania, Roland Vasquez as Bottom, Francisco Moncion as Theseus, Patricia McBride as Hermia, Nicholas Magallanes as Lysander, Bill Carter as Demetrius, Gloria Govrin as Hippolyta; Violette Verdy, Conrad Ludlow, and the entire company.*

Shakespeare's *A Midsummer Night's Dream* has always been a favorite of mine ever since I first saw it and appeared in the play as a child in Russia. I was an elf in a production at the Mikhailovsky Theatre in St. Petersburg when

* See also THE DREAM.

I was about eight years old. I suppose it was then that I came to know so many lines from the play; even now I can recite in Russian speeches like the famous one of Oberon's beginning:

I know a bank where the wild thyme blows,
Where oxlips and the nodding violet grows . . .

I worked on a production of the play at the Shakespeare Memorial Theatre in Stratford, Connecticut, in 1950, arranging some dances. But what has really interested me more than Shakespeare's words in recent years has been the music that Mendelssohn wrote to the play, and I think it can be said that the ballet was inspired by the score.

Mendelssohn did not, however, write music for the whole play. To fill out the danced action that developed as the ballet was being made, I selected other scores of Mendelssohn's that neatly fitted into the pattern we were making. (The pieces incorporated along with the incidental music in the first act are the overtures to *Athalie, The Fair Melusine, The First Walpurgis Night;* in the second act the *Symphony No.* 9 and the overture *Son and Stranger.*)

The story of the ballet, of course, concerns the adventures and misadventures of a group of mortals and immortals in their resolutions of the confusions and problems of loving and being loved. It is called a "dream" because of the unrealistic happenings that occur to the characters . . . real yet unreal events such as crossed loves, meaningless quarrels, forest chases, and magic spells woven by the infamous Puck. I think it is possible to see and enjoy the ballet without knowing the play. At least that was my hope in creating the piece.

The first act takes place in a forest near the duke's palace. Oberon, King of the Fairies, and Titania, his queen, quarrel. Oberon orders Puck to bring the flower pierced by Cupid's arrow (which causes anyone coming under its influence to fall in love with the first person the eyes behold), and while Titania is asleep and unknowing, he casts the flower's spell over her.

Meanwhile, Helena, wandering in the wood, meets Demetrius, whom she loves but who does not love her. Demetrius rejects her and goes his way. Oberon watches and tells Puck to use the flower on Demetrius that he may return Helena's affection.

Another couple, Hermia and Lysander, very much in love, are also wandering in the forest. They become separated. Puck, eager to carry out Oberon's orders, mistakenly anoints Lysander. Helena appears and Lysander, under the flower's spell, at once and to her amazement tells her how much he loves her.

Hermia now returns. She is astonished and then dismayed to see Lysander paying attention only to Helena. Puck manages to bring Demetrius, too, under the flower's spell, much to the delight of Helena, who doesn't care for Lysander at all.

Demetrius and Lysander, now both in love with Helena, begin to quarrel over her. Puck, at Oberon's order, has separated Bottom, a weaver, from his companions, transformed his head into that of an ass, and placed him at the sleeping Titania's feet. Awakening, Titania sees Bottom, thinks him fair, and pays him close and loving attention. At last Oberon, his anger over, has Bottom sent away and releases Titania from her spell.

Hermia now gets no attention, Helena too much. The men, completely at odds, quarrel seriously and begin to fight. Puck by his magic causes them to separate, lose one another and wander apart in the forest, until exhausted they fall asleep, with Puck arranging for Helena to fall asleep beside Demetrius and Lysander (his spell removed) by Hermia.

The duke and Hippolyta discover the lovers asleep in the forest, awaken them, find their differences are resolved and proclaim a triple wedding for themselves and the two couples.

The second act opens in the duke's palace with parades, dancing, and *divertissements* in honor of the newly married couples. When the celebrations are over and the mortals retire, we return to the demesne of Oberon and Titania, who are now reunited and at peace. And at last Puck having put order into disorder sweeps away the remnants of the night's doings. The fireflies twinkle in the night and reclaim the forest.

MISS JULIE

Ballet in four acts. Music by Ture Rangström, arranged and orchestrated by Hans Grossman. Choreography by Birgit Cullberg. Scenery and costumes by Allan Friderica. First presented by Riksteatern at Västerås, Sweden, March 1, 1950, with Elsa-Marianne von Rosen and Julius Mengarelli in the principal roles. First presented in the United States by the American Ballet Theatre at the Metropolitan Opera House, New York, September 18, 1958, with Violette Verdy and Erik Bruhn in the principal roles. Scenery and costumes by Sven Erixon.

Based on the play of the same name by the Swedish master August Strindberg, *Miss Julie* portrays the downfall of a young woman of noble birth who is bent on willful conquest. On Midsummer Night, Julie, the daughter of a count, rejects the suitor her father has chosen and joins the local villagers and the castle servants at a barn dance, where she captivates the head butler, Jean. In the next scene, in the castle kitchen, she seduces him. The next morning, finding that the servant has become the master, she contemplates flight with him. But portraits of her ancestors torment her with guilt. Suicide is offered as the only way out. The butler returns and assists her death.

NOTES   *Miss Julie* is also in the repertory of the Royal Danish Ballet. Clive Barnes, reviewing a performance by this company in New York in 1965, wrote: "Erik Bruhn as Jean is superlative. This is probably his finest role . . . His portrayal is not only breath-catchingly well danced, but his whole characterization is among the greatest pieces of ballet acting we have ever seen. Servile, common, attractive, brutish, arrogant, the whole spectrum of Strindberg's remarkable character finds a place in Mr. Bruhn's portrait. His stiff little bows from the waist with his arms stiffly curved at the side, his nervous pulling down of his jacket, his sly sexuality, his sudden shifts of manner, everything he does or looks makes a contribution to the whole."

MOMENTUM

Music by Peter Ilyich Tchaikovsky. Choreography by Dennis Nahat. Lighting design by Jean Rosenthal. First presented by American Ballet Theatre at the Walt Whitman Auditorium of Brooklyn College, New York, March 15, 1969.

A dance ballet to Tchaikovsky's *Souvenir de Florence*, and the first work by the dancer Dennis Nahat, *Momentum* is arranged in two parts, each for three girls and two boys. Writing in the New York *Times*, the critic Don McDonagh said that in the first movement Mimi Paul, with "her long, supple and dynamic style was an interesting contrast to that of the two couples who formed an undulating background to her solo. Eleanor d'Antuono led the group in the second movement with clean vigor."

MONOTONES 1 AND 2

Music by Erik Satie. Choreography and costumes by Frederick Ashton. Monotones 1, Trois Gnossiennes, orchestrated by John Lanchbery, first presented by the Royal Ballet at the Royal Opera House, Covent Garden, April 25, 1966, with Antoinette Sibley, Georgina Parkinson, and Brian Shaw. Monotones 2, Trois Gymnopédies, orchestrated by Claude Debussy and Roland Manuel, first presented by the Royal Ballet at the Royal Opera House, Covent Garden, March 24, 1965, with Vyvyan Lorrayne, Anthony Dowell, and Robert Mead. It was revived on April 25, 1966, with the same cast, and presented with Monotones 1. Monotones 1 and 2 first presented in the United States by the Royal Ballet at the new Metropolitan Opera House, May 3, 1967, with Michael Coleman replacing Brian Shaw.

This is a dance ballet for six people, three in each *Monotone. Monotones 2*, first given as a *pièce d'occasion* in 1965 for the Royal Ballet Benevolent Fund Gala, was so admired that it was supplemented the following year and introduced into the company's regular repertory.

There is no plot, no decor. The dancers perform against a black background. This major lyric dance, which must be seen to be properly appreciated, was staged by the City Center Joffrey Ballet in 1975. Writing about it in *Dance and Dancers*, the critic Patricia Barnes said: "A real coup for Joffrey was his acquisition of Ashton's exquisite *Monotones*. A small-scale masterpiece, the choreography makes visible the cool melodic line of Satie's music to perfection, flowing as it does from one exquisite pose to another. There is a simplicity here, an inevitability, that is seen only in the greatest art. The lambent purity of these lovingly arranged attitudes and arabesques with their always complementary ports de bras move one not just by the beauty of their design but also by the uncluttered freshness of Ashton's vision.

"The first pas de trois (the second of Ashton's creations) to the *Trois Gnossiennes* was just slightly less effective than the second trio to *Trois Gymnopédies*. By the season's end, however, Rebecca Wright, Starr Danias and Burton Taylor were already beginning to get to the work's still centre. Pamela Nearhoof, supported by Kevin McKenzie and Robert Thomas, could hardly have been better. Her serene assurance and long-legged elegance were just right."

A MONTH IN THE COUNTRY

Ballet in one act. Music by Frédéric Chopin, arranged by John Lanchbery. Choreography by Frederick Ashton. Scenery and costumes by Julia Trevelyan Oman. First presented by the Royal Ballet at the Royal Opera House, Covent Garden, London, February 12, 1976, with Lynn Seymour as Natalia Petrovna, Alexander Grant as Yslaev, Wayne Sleep as Kolia, Denise Nunn as Vera, Derek Rencher as Rakitin, Marguerite Porter as Katia, Anthony Conway as Matvei, and Anthony Dowell as Beliaev. First presented in the United States by the same ensemble at the Metropolitan Opera House, New York, April 27, 1976.

In a laconic note to his ballet, based on Turgenev's masterpiece, Frederick Ashton has written that "the action takes place at Yslaev's country house in 1850. Beliaev, a young student, engaged as a tutor for Kolia, disrupts the emotional stability of the household. Finally Rakitin, Natalia's admirer, insists that he and the tutor must both leave in order to restore a semblance of order to Yslaev's family life.

"The ballet is dedicated to the memory of Sophie Fedorovich and Bronislava Nijinska, Chopin's compatriots and my mentors."

Frederick Ashton first saw Ivan Turgenev's masterpiece of a play forty years and more before he was able to make a ballet to it, but he always wished to. Reading the play is of course the best preparation for the ballet, especially as Ashton's work might be called the distillation—in Ashton's words the "pill"—of the Russian master's drama. Those who wish to explore the life of Turgenev and the inspiration for the action of the play will be rewarded by a most moving story: the Russian writer is in fact the Rakitin of the drama, the man who says there that "all love, happy or unhappy, is a disaster when you give way to it."

The action of the ballet is all a giving way, posed against a responsive will to control and survive. The central figure, a young man of twenty-one, Beliaev, tutor to Yslaev's young son Kolya, is adored not only by the family's ward, the seventeen-year-old Vera, but by the lady of the house, Natalia Petrovna, twenty-nine. Natalia Petrovna in her turn has been for many years beloved by Rakitin, who has watched and still continues to observe her detachment from emotional life.

The ballet's compression of this drama takes place in a splendid drawing room in the Russian countryside. The family life, and the life of their perpetual house guests, appears to be an idyll of existence. The admirer of Natalia, Rakitin, knows his place, the limits beyond which he cannot go. In the midst of the summer, Natalia herself, challenged by her young ward's love for the tutor of her son, goes to an unspeakable limit and permits a declaration of love for the younger man. Observing the return of her passion, and Natalia Petrovna's possible doom, Rakitin rescues her by taking himself and the tutor away. In an ultimate expression of regret that their passion cannot be fulfilled, Beliaev kisses the ribbons of Natalia's dress.

The music for the ballet consists of Chopin's *Variations on "La ci darem la mano,"* the *Fantasy on Polish Airs,* and the *Andante Spianato and Grande Polonaise.*

MONUMENT FOR A DEAD BOY

Music by Jan Boerman. Choreography by Rudi van Dantzig. Scenery and costumes by Toer van Schayk. First presented by the Het National Ballet, 1966. First presented in the United States by the Harkness Ballet, November 3, 1967, with Lawrence Rhodes in the principal role.

This ballet traces the history of a young boy who, at his death, looks back. It is preceded by a quotation from Truman Capote: "Unafraid, not hesitating, he paused only at the garden's edge where, as though he'd forgotten something, he stopped and looked back at the bloomless, descending blue, at the boy he had left behind." Verbal themes for the eight parts of the narrative are derived from *The Inner Wallpaper* by Hans Lodeizen. The music is an electronic score by Jan Boerman.

Six huddled dark figures, perhaps the furies who haunt the boy's life, are seen in shadow as the ballet begins. The mature boy and his younger self, portrayed by a smaller dancer, enter and move together, identifying and differing in gesture and emphasis. ("I am playing with the sad rope of time.") Then suddenly the older boy is lifted away to watch the youth. ("Springtime makes doors, the wind is an open hand, we must yet begin to love.") His parents enter and soon, in an excess of affection, they all but tear the child in two in a tug-of-war. ("Soon we will all have died; What is memory? What is love?") The boy seeks refuge in the arms of his older self. Where can I go, he seems to ask, but to myself?

Two visions now haunt him, one a girl in blue ("As I am standing in the yellow night on the blue floorcloth of my heart"), the other a girl in white. ("In a block of buildings I live as a child, suspecting fingers everywhere, darkness and kisses.") Both attracted and repelled, the boy finds alternating comfort, understanding, and tenderness with another boy at school. (". . . happiness with you means the past.") Next, a painting of a playground, the back wall embellished with graffiti and five boys spaced in front of it, comes suddenly alive. The hero is attacked, hurt, humiliated. (". . . like jellyfish on a beach, they soil the horizon.") The Girl in Blue finds him. They dance together in sympathy and passion but it is too late. Back at home, the boy watches in horror the aggressive lust of his parents. At this point the older boy and his youth portray his despair, a hopelessness that finds release only in death. (". . . like a curtain I jerked open darkness, to see the night.") As the hero dies, his younger self grieves, hailing him, celebrating him forever, in a silent lament, and remembering.

NOTES   Revived by American Ballet Theatre at the City Center, New York, January 11, 1973, *Monument for a Dead Boy* starred Ivan Nagy as the Boy. Scenery and costumes were by Toer van Schayk. Lighting by George Bardyguine.

The critic Robb Baker of *FM Guide* wrote of this revival: *Monument for a Dead Boy* "is a powerful psychological dance drama depicting a teenaged boy looking back at his own homoerotic fantasies." Rudolf Nureyev and Helgi Tomasson have danced the principal role in this ballet. The English critic Oleg Kerensky has said in his book *The World of Ballet* that "it is a powerful theatrical work. . . . It grips its audience at least as much by its subject matter, its psychological interest, and its skillful staging as by its dance content."

MONUMENTUM PRO GESUALDO (*see* MOVEMENTS)

MOON REINDEER

Music by Knudager Riisager. Choreography by Birgit Cullberg. Scenery and costumes by Per Falk. First presented by the Royal Danish Ballet, Copenhagen, November 22, 1957, with Mona Vangsaae, Henning Kronstam, and Fredbjørn Bjørnsson in the leading roles. First presented in the United States by the American Ballet Theatre at the Fifty-fourth Street Theatre, New York, October 2, 1961, with Lupe Serrano, Royes Fernandez, and Felix Smith in the leading roles.

Based on an ancient Arctic legend, *Moon Reindeer* tells the story of a lovely young girl, Aili, who, rejected by the man she loves, seeks the aid of Naiden, the Witch Doctor. Naiden agrees to help her but in return she must provide him with a human sacrifice to appease the gods of the underworld. Aili thus assumes by the light of the moon the guise of a white reindeer who so enchants young men that they fall over a precipice and perish. When the Laplanders try to avenge these deaths, the Moon Reindeer is killed and Aili resumes her human form.

THE MOOR'S PAVANE

Music by Henry Purcell (arranged by Simon Sadoff). Choreography by Jose Limon. Costumes by Pauline Lawrence. First presented by Jose Limon and Company at the Connecticut College American Dance Festival, Palmer Auditorium, New London, Connecticut, August 17, 1949, with Jose Limon, Betty Jones, Lucas Hoving, and Pauline Kohner. First presented by American Ballet Theatre at the New York State Theatre, Lincoln Center, June 27, 1970, with Bruce Marks, Sallie Wilson, Royes Fernandez, and Toni Lander. Assistants to Mr. Limon: Daniel Lewis, Clive Morgan, and Jennifer Muller. Conducted by Akira Endo.

Long acknowledged as a masterwork of modern dance and performed in the United States and abroad by Jose Limon and his company, *The Moor's Pavane* is fortunately available to the public also in the repertories of American Ballet Theatre, the City Center Joffrey Ballet and other ensembles. Subtitled "Variations on a Theme of Othello," it is assumed that the spectator is familiar with Shakespeare's play. Here all subplots, or non-essentials of that story, are eliminated, and in a stately quadrille, the four principals—Othello, Desdemona, Iago, and Emilia, called here the Moor, his wife, the Friend, and his wife, dance a minuet of love, comradeship, jealousy inflamed, betrayal, death, and discovery.

NOTES   Reviewing this revival of *The Moor's Pavane* in the New York *Times*, Clive Barnes wrote: "*The Moor's Pavane* is a totally engrossing work and likely to remain among Mr. Limon's most enduring ballets. . . . What Mr. Limon has set out to do is to picture the corrosive force of jealousy and the destruction of good by evil, and to encapsulate this into the patterns of a ballroom dance.

"The dance starts simply enough, with bows and graces, and all manner of Elizabethan furbelows. But as it proceeds, the undercurrents of feeling beneath the courtly observances make themselves felt, the dance takes on a new urgency, moves into a new dimension. . . . Mr. Limon has been fortunate here in an ideal cast. I will never forget Mr. Limon himself and Lucas Hoving as the original Othello and Iago. They were fantastic—a bull and a matador come to judgment. Yet now Bruce Marks and Royes Fernandez are no less impressive. Mr. Marks, bearded, noble, anguished, and with all the passion and agony of the world on his broad shoulders, is brought low by a sinuously insinuating Mr. Fernandez, a very proper villain with the graceful movements of a snake.

"This admirable cast is completed by Sallie Wilson as the wicked Emilia (Mr. Limon is less charitable with her than is Shakespeare) and Toni Lander as the yielding and wronged Desdemona. It is a shrewd and subtle work that will be a credit to Ballet Theatre."

Writing in the Washington *Post* of Jose Limon's work after his death in

1972, Jean Battey Lewis said: "Perhaps his best-known work is *The Moor's Pavane*, his conception of the Shakespearean tragedy of Othello. He and his company danced the work at the White House before President and Mrs. Johnson in 1967 and the dance is in the repertoire of several ballet companies here and abroad. (It was danced at the Kennedy Center last season by American Ballet Theatre.)

"Eric Bentley once said that of all the works created on the American stage the one he would choose above all others to send abroad as a showcase of our art would be *The Moor's Pavane*.

"Describing himself as 'either the most atheistic of Catholics or the most Catholic of atheists,' Limon was often inspired by Biblical themes—*The Traitor*, based on the betrayal of Jesus; *There Is a Time*, and *The Exiles*, a dance about Adam and Eve, are among them. *A Choreographic Offering* to the music of Bach was his tribute to his mentor, Doris Humphey.

"A few years ago the dancer declared, 'I try to compose works that are involved with man's basic tragedy and the grandeur of his spirit. I want to dig beneath empty formalisms, displays of technical virtuosity, and the slick surface; to probe the human entity for the powerful, often crude beauty of the gesture that speaks of man's humanity.

"'I reach for demons, saints, martyrs, apostates, fools, and other impassioned visions. I go for inspiration and instruction to the artists who reveal the passion of man to me, who exemplify supreme artistic discipline and impeccable form: to Bach, Michelangelo, Shakespeare, Goya, Schonberg, Picasso, Orozco,' he continued.

"This wrestling with elemental themes is obviously not a currently fashionable approach in an art that in recent years has leaned toward abstraction, impersonality and a structure based on chance. Talking to Limon last year after a rehearsal at Juilliard School in New York it was clear that he had no use for fashion in the arts.

"He was working at the time on a new dance, *Dances for Isadora*, which he said he was composing in memory of his wife.

"*Dances for Isadora* is a study of Isadora Duncan, the first great revolutionary American dancer. Somewhat as a companion piece (*Isadora* was a dance for five women), Limon was completing *The Unsung*, a suite of male solos on eight American Indian chieftains—our unsung heroes.

"Of his choice themes, Limon said at the time, 'What are we here on earth for if not to illuminate our experience, for ourselves and others?'"

MOTHER GOOSE SUITE

Classic ballet in five scenes. Music by Maurice Ravel. Choreography by Todd Bolender. First presented by the American Concert Ballet at the Central High School of Needle Trades Auditorium, New York, October 1943, with a cast headed by Mary Jane Shea and Francisco Moncion. Revised and presented by the New York City Ballet at the City Center, New York, No-

vember 1, 1948, with Marie-Jeanne, Francisco Moncion, Todd Bolender, and Beatrice Tompkins in the principal roles.

This ballet is based on Ravel's score *Ma Mère l'Oye,* rather than on the "Mother Goose" fairy tales of Perrault that inspired Ravel to compose his well-known suite. The choreographer has devised a fantasy in which an older woman dreams of her adventures as a young girl. Her dreams are presented by groups of dancers, who portray in mime and movement certain flash backs of her youth, while the woman herself watches from the side lines. The parts of Ravel's suite are played in the following order: "Pavanne," "Enchanted Garden," "Hop o' My Thumb," "Enchanted Princess," "Beauty and the Beast."

The stage is dimly lighted as the curtain rises. A girl stands in a soft blue spotlight. She bows slowly, as if waking from some romantic reverie, and circles the stage on her points. Clouds drift by, enclosing the girl in her dream. The music is quiet and illusive. A strange woman enters in a stiff, long dress. Her face is veiled; she carries a fan. She does not see the girl at first, but turns to look at her lingeringly. The strange woman crosses over to the small theatre box at the side of the stage. She sits carefully under a small crystal chandelier. As she looks out to the stage, the clouds return to perpetuate the dream she watches.

The young girl, the spectator's second self, stands alone in the center of the stage. Four girls in red join her and support her as she poses in arabesque. The girls weave in and out under her extended arms. They bow to her, and she returns their greetings.

The music of the "Enchanted Garden" begins to build to a sumptuous, flowing climax. Four other girls enter, then four boys, who partner the girls alternately in a continuous dance in which they surround the young girl. She chases them, imitates the girls to attract the attention of the boys, and stands sad and helpless as the couples seem unaware of her existence. The girl goes over to the spectator and gestures questioningly: what is she to do? The spectator has no answer. Now desperate, the girl goes to each couple and asks to be recognized. The music pulsates. To its rhythms, the boys lift their partners high and carry them off over the girl's head. The girl stands with bent head. All is quiet again.

Hop o' My Thumb enters. This character is derived from the fairy-tale hero who dropped bread crumbs as he went away from home, imagining that they would lead him back. Here in the ballet, he is accompanied by the bird who ate his crumbs and caused him to lose his way. The bird-girl drapes her long blond hair over the boy's head, ensnaring him. The boy is undisturbed.

The young girl watches, astonished. The bird leaves the boy. He looks after her longingly, then begins to dance with the young girl. They kneel together and look at each other's hands, reading their fortunes. In the background, the bird can be seen crossing the stage in open flight. The boy and girl stare at each other, then rise to stand in front of the spectator. The girl stands motionless as the clouds flow in, envelop the boy, and carry him back to his true love. The girl leaves the stage.

Four girls in red, with long green gloves, enter with a Chinese prince who is dressed in brilliant gold. The orchestra plays a tinkling, Oriental tune, and the prince dances blithely. The young girl re-enters. Momentarily she is blinded by the strange, foreign spectacle. The prince approaches her deferentially and takes her hand, but she refuses to believe that a real prince has appeared to her. The prince takes her hands from her eyes, and now the girl dances with him gaily. He lifts her high, and the two dance before the group. Just as the girl has begun to enjoy herself thoroughly, the magical prince and his escort hop off into the wings.

A young man with the hideous and frightening head of a lion comes in. Before she knows what she is doing, the girl leaps to his shoulder; he lets her down softly. The beast looks into her eyes; the girl is terrified and backs away. The beast falls to the floor and, as the music moans and groans his agony, he mimes his misery and ugliness. Still frightened, the girl approaches the spectator. What can she do with the pathetic creature? The spectator presents her with a magic ring.

The girl runs about the stage rapidly, then puts her hand gently on the beast's shoulder. They dance. Clouds drift in and surround the beast. When they have passed by, he has become a handsome youth. He holds the beautiful girl softly and possessively. The spectator rises and leaves her box. The girl's fairy godmother intervenes and stands over the couple. The boy kneels, holding out his arms. The girl falls against him. He lifts her and carries her out. The spectator exits slowly, openly rejecting her own dream. The clouds drift by. The spell of the dream is still with her.

MOVEMENTS

Ballet in two parts. Music by Igor Stravinsky. Choreography by George Balanchine. Part I, Monumentum pro Gesualdo, first presented by the New York City Ballet at the City Center, New York, November 16, 1960, with Diana Adams and Conrad Ludlow in the leading roles. Decor by David Hays. Part II, Movements for Piano and Orchestra, first presented by the New York City Ballet, April 9, 1963, with Suzanne Farrell and Jacques d'Amboise in the leading roles. Scenery and lighting by David Hays and Peter Harvey.

The two ballets *Monumentum* and *Movements*, first presented separately, have been performed together since 1963. Both have music by Stravinsky, both are short works, and it has been convenient for our audiences, and for us in the New York City Ballet, to see them combined. Their music is also an interesting contrast. In the first, Stravinsky was inspired by the music of the Italian composer Don Carlo Gesualdo, 1560–1613, "Prince of Madrigalists." In *Movements for Piano and Orchestra*, one of Stravinsky's first complete works in serial style, we have the composer speaking directly, in terms of his own preoccupations.

Monumentum was composed in 1960, to commemorate the four-hundredth anniversary of Gesualdo's death. Stravinsky's self-discovery here in the work of another composer works to the same advantage as it has done on other occasions, as we recall from his working to the inspiration of Tchaikovsky in *Baiser de la Fée* and to Pergolesi's example in *Pulcinella*. Stravinsky and his collaborator Robert Craft have prepared a splendid recording of some of Gesualdo's music that concludes with the *Monumentum*.

The music consists of three madrigals for five voices "re-composed for instruments." Like the music, the short ballet is in three parts, arranged for a leading dancer, her partner, and six couples. Each of the three sections is very brief, lasting just over two minutes.

At the conclusion of *Monumentum*, there is a short pause and *Movements* begins. Stravinsky has said that my ballet might also have been called "Electric Currents." It is, as he says, a double concerto for male and female solo dancers, both identified with the piano solo. There is an accompanying *corps de ballet* of six girls. The ballet is in five parts, lasting eight and a half minutes. Each part begins with a short instrumental introduction. Two groups of three girls set the tone for each section and the lead couple takes up the music as the piano enters. I seriously think that the best preparation for seeing this ballet is to listen to Stravinsky's recording of it a number of times. Its complexity and compression are remarkable. Eric Walter White has said that the composition "has the specific gravity of a tonal work of three times that duration.* I myself had to see it, to make a ballet of it, to understand it. Nothing gave me greater pleasure afterwards than Stravinsky's saying the performance "was like a tour of a building for which I had drawn the plans but never explored the result."**

MOVES

A Ballet in Silence about Relationships. Choreography by Jerome Robbins. First presented by Jerome Robbins's Ballets: U.S.A. at the Festival of Two Worlds, Spoleto, Italy, July 3, 1959. First presented in the United States by Ballets: U.S.A. at the ANTA Theatre, New York, October 8, 1961.

Jerome Robbins has called his ballet without music or scenery a "ballet in silence about relationships." Without a score to fall back on, the eye is focused in a new way on stage action. As the choreographer explains, "the score supports, conditions, predicts, and establishes the dynamics, tempo, and mood not only for the dance but also for the audience. Music guides the spectators' emotional responses to the happenings on the stage and creates a persuasive atmosphere for reaction. *Moves* severs that guidance . . . I wanted the audience to concentrate on movement. I wanted to do two things: one, an exploration of movement that the audience can interpret only as movement . . . two, I

---

* *Stravinsky, the Composer and His Works*, by Eric Walter White, University of California press, Berkeley, Calif., 1966.

** *Themes and Episodes*, by Igor Stravinsky and Robert Craft, Alfred A. Knopf, New York, 1966.

wanted to do a ballet about relationships between people—man and woman, one and another, the individual and the group."

The dance narrative explores, without a story, relationships and disconnections between dancers. They first appear coming at the audience in single file from the back of the stage. Different things happen. A boy and a girl dance together and we understand what they are about. Five boys dance and while four of them are doing classical *entrechats* the fifth does the "frog sag." Three couples dance. With no music, the dancers establish their own personal rhythms; they seem moved by their own impulses. At the end, the company files off just as it entered.

NOTES Reviewing *Moves* in *The Dancing Times* in 1961 after its first London performances, Mary Clarke said: "A distinct and disturbing emotion of involvement in the whole human predicament is created by these silent movers, in their casual clothes on a bare stage. I don't think dancing has ever said so much, speaking alone and in its own language."

MOZART CONCERTO

Music by Wolfgang Amadeus Mozart. Choreography by John Cranko. Lighting by Gilbert V. Hemsley, Jr. First presented by the Stuttgart Ballet at the Württemberg State Theatre, Stuttgart, March 26, 1966. First presented in the United States by the same ensemble, June 20, 1969, at the Metropolitan Opera House, New York.

This dance ballet to Mozart's *Concerto for Flute and Harp in C Major* (K. 299) is arranged for four soloists—two girls and two boys—and a supporting group of ten boys. The soloists, the two girls, like the flute and harp in the score, lead the work but there is no one-to-one correspondence. The ballet is in three movements. The finale, a *Rondo*, the critic Abraham Veinus has said, "is furnished with enough melodies to fit out at least two ordinary concertos."

Writing of this ballet in the New York *Times*, Clive Barnes said, "The effect is most interesting. For one thing this new arrangement leads to a greater flexibility in the work's structuring, for the two ballerinas can not only be partnered by their cavaliers but also by the ensemble. It also places a new and rather more glamorous emphasis on the two girls, who instantly become objects of seemingly universal admiration."

MUTATIONS

Music by Karlheinz Stockhausen. Choreography by Glen Tetley. Cine-choreography by Hans van Manen. Film visualization by Jean-Paul Vroom. Production designs by Nadine Baylis. Costumes by Emmy van Leersum and Gijs Bakker. Lighting by John B. Read. First presented by the Netherlands Dance Theatre at the Circustheater, Scheveningen, Holland, July 3, 1970.

First presented in the United States by the same ensemble at the Brooklyn Academy of Music, New York, March 29, 1972.

With the presentation of *Mutations*, New York saw a nude ballet performed for the first time by a major company on a major stage. In addition to nudity, unusual aspects of the work include film episodes, shown on three screens at the back of the stage while live dancers perform in front of them, and action which extends from the stage along a ramp into the center aisle.

The first of the ballet's films is of naked Gérard Lemaitre and is in such slow motion that his body appears to float freely and effortlessly through space. The final scene is a nude *pas de deux* danced by Anja Licher and Lemaitre while all three films are shown behind them. The *pas de deux* repeats in part some of the filmed choreography as well as sections of the live choreography.

The ballet is not entirely nude, for it also concerns the emotional influences of costume. The clothed dancers have movements that are correspondingly rigid. Those half-undressed use their freedom for aggression and competition. And finally, the totally nude dancers explore the possibilities of fluid, unencumbered motion.

NOTES   Glen Tetley says, "You construct a game, you set your own restrictions, and then you challenge yourself to find your way through these restrictions."

Writing after the first performance of *Mutations* in London, in 1970, the critic Alexander Bland said in *The Observer:* ". . . It is sincere, shapely, rich in those plastic movements which Tetley excels in. . . . Nudity is used in this ballet as a stimulating but serious ingredient which completely justifies itself artistically. The scene is a kind of arena (by Nadine Baylis) into which white-clad figures gradually fight their way. Once arrived, the mood changes. A nude figure appears dancing on film, and this is followed by a nice trio for girls . . . and some all-in applications of red paint suggesting violence. A couple dance, clad and unclad on screen and stage, to gently variegated electronic sounds by Stockhausen; more join in and the film triplicates until some mysterious figures in transparent suits sweep the action off stage—naked and strangely vulnerable —alone as the lights fade."

NOTES   The choreographer Hans van Manen has described the evolution of *Mutations* in detail in an account by Glenn Loney published in *Dance Magazine*, February 1974. Asked to do a ballet to mark the twenty-fifth anniversary of the liberation of the Netherlands from the Nazis, he responded: "I thought it would be ridiculous to do a ballet symbolizing twenty-five years of freedom from the Germans. After twenty-five years? If the ballet has to be about freedom, then we should make the ballet completely *free*. That's the best symbol of freedom. We must be completely free in what we are doing." In the end, the ballet was worked out with Glen Tetley, then closely associated with the Netherlands Dance Theatre, Tetley creating the live part and van Manen the film.